Systems Factorial Technology

Systems Factorial Technology

A Theory Driven Methodology for the Identification of Perceptual and Cognitive Mechanisms

Edited by

Daniel R. Little

Nicholas Altieri

Mario Fifić

Cheng-Ta Yang

ELSEVIER

ACADEMIC PRESS

An imprint of Elsevier

Academic Press is an imprint of Elsevier
125 London Wall, London EC2Y 5AS, United Kingdom
525 B Street, Suite 1800, San Diego, CA 92101-4495, United States
50 Hampshire Street, 5th Floor, Cambridge, MA 02139, United States
The Boulevard, Langford Lane, Kidlington, Oxford OX5 1GB, United Kingdom

Library of Congress Cataloging-in-Publication Data
A catalog record for this book is available from the Library of Congress

British Library Cataloguing-in-Publication Data
A catalogue record for this book is available from the British Library

ISBN: 978-0-12-804315-8

For information on all Academic Press publications
visit our website at https://www.elsevier.com/books-and-journals

Publisher: Nikki Levy
Acquisition Editor: Emily Ekle
Editorial Project Manager: Timothy Bennett
Production Project Manager: Julie-Ann Stansfield
Designer: Matthew Limbert

Typeset by VTeX

Contents

List of Contributors

Daniel Algom
Tel-Aviv University, Tel-Aviv, Israel

Nicholas Altieri
Idaho State University, Pocatello, ID, United States

Leslie M. Blaha
Pacific Northwest National Laboratory, Richland, WA, United States

Anthea G. Blunden
The University of Melbourne, Melbourne, VIC, Australia

Devin M. Burns
Framingham University, Framingham, MA, United States

Xue-Jun Cheng
The University of Melbourne, Melbourne, VIC, Australia

Nicole Christie
The University of Melbourne, Melbourne, VIC, Australia

Denis Cousineau
University of Ottawa, Ottawa, ON, Canada

Maria Densmore
The University of Western Ontario, London, ON, Canada

Ami Eidels
The Newcastle University, Callaghan, NSW, Australia

Adam Ferguson
University of Melbourne, Melbourne, VIC, Australia

Mario Fifić
Grand Valley State University, Allendale, MI, United States

Daniel Fitousi
Ariel University, Ariel, Israel

Marc-André Goulet
University of Ottawa, Ottawa, ON, Canada

David W. Griffiths
The University of Melbourne, Melbourne, VIC, Australia

Bradley Harding
University of Ottawa, Ottawa, ON, Canada

Yuan He
Indiana University Bloomington, Bloomington, IN, United States

Amanda D. Hornbach
Indiana University Bloomington, Bloomington, IN, United States

Joseph W. Houpt
Wright State University, Dayton, OH, United States

Zachary L. Howard
University of Newcastle, Callaghan, NSW, Australia

Piers D.L. Howe
University of Melbourne, Melbourne, VIC, Australia

Glyn W. Humphreys
University of Oxford, Oxford, United Kingdom

Erin M. Ingvalson
Florida State University, Tallahassee, FL, United States

Vincent LeBlanc
University of Ottawa, Ottawa, ON, Canada

Jennifer J. Lentz
Indiana University Bloomington, Bloomington, IN, United States

Daniel R. Little
The University of Melbourne, Melbourne, VIC, Australia

Yanjun Liu
Indiana University Bloomington, Bloomington, IN, United States

Sarah Moneer
The University of Melbourne, Melbourne, VIC, Australia

Zargol Moradi
University of Oxford, Oxford, United Kingdom

Richard W.J. Neufeld
The University of Western Ontario, London, ON, Canada

Stephanie E. Rhoten
The University of Oklahoma, Norman, OK, United States

Pia Rotshtein
University of Birmingham, Birmingham, United Kingdom

Noah H. Silbert
University of Cincinnati, Cincinnati, OH, United States

Jie Sui
University of Oxford, Oxford, United Kingdom

Reggie Taylor
The University of Western Ontario, London, ON, Canada

Jean Théberge
The University of Western Ontario, London, ON, Canada

James T. Townsend
Indiana University Bloomington, Bloomington, IN, United States

Michael J. Wenger
The University of Oklahoma, Norman, OK, United States

Peter Williamson
The University of Western Ontario, London, ON, Canada

Cheng-Ta Yang
National Cheng Kung University, Tainan, Taiwan

Alla Yankouskaya
University of Oxford, Oxford, United Kingdom

Ru Zhang
Indiana University Bloomington, Bloomington, IN, United States

Foreword

Chapter 1, authored by the editors of this book, offers an overview of the historical backdrop to the branch of scientific psychology that foreshadowed the development of Systems Factorial Technology. In addition, model mimicking, that omnipresent and sometimes vexatious challenge to model building, theory building, and testing in psychology are outlined, and a rigorous but highly readable tutorial is presented there. Hence, my comments here should be read subsequently, or at least in concert with that material, by the non-expert.

Systems factorial technology is most appropriately interpreted as living within the broad approach known as the "information processing approach". This approach has been defined in many ways but the essence is captured by a view of human perception, cognition, and action as describable through a decomposition of the mechanisms associated with these into separate, but often interacting, processes. As such, though the roots in the embryonic 19th century experimental psychology, its modern re-birth and evolution were closely associated with the cognitive revolution roughly commencing in the late 1950s and early 1960s. And the decomposition, study of the properties and interactions, and testing through behavioral experimentation and neuroscience were intimately connected to progenitors in the form of Shannon's information theory, Wiener's theory of cybernetics, and von Neumann's, Turing's and other's theory of automata.

Almost simultaneously, the field of *mathematical psychology* was being founded primarily by two separate tributaries: (i) Mathematical learning theory through W.K. Estes' *stimulus sampling theory* (e.g., 1950) and R.R. Bush and F. Mosteller's *linear operator theory* (e.g., 1955), and (ii) Theory of signal detection through the efforts of W.P. Tanner, J. Swets and their colleagues at University of Michigan (e.g., 1954). Neither of these were directly related to what was to become the cognitive juggernaut but they set the stage for the inevitable application of mathematical modeling within the information processing approach and cognition in general. In fact, Estes himself as well as a number of mathematical psychologists in very short order began to explore this territory.

I was especially impressed by the theoretical issues and attendant experiments put forth by investigators like G. Sperling, S. Sternberg, D. Broadbent, H. Egeth, D. Green, J. Swets, W.P. Tanner, and my own teachers W.K. Estes, R.C. Atkinson, and P. Suppes.

It had never been easy to test two or more psychological theories against one another. Witness the long standing battle between E. Tolman, whose so-called neo-behavioristic theory granted even the lowly rat the benefits of a fairly high order of cognition, and C. Hull, whose mathematically specified theory was based on more truly behavioristic notions. Their struggle culminated in the 1940s and early 1950s but without resolution, melting away and providing an unavoidable message for scientific psychology that our field might possess challenges not faced by the harder sciences. This enigma has become known as the challenge of *model mimicking*.

The information processing approach, since it emphasized analytic theorizing and clear definitions, ironically made it easier to espy and investigate questions of model mimicking. Natural topics of study for the information processing approach included whether processing (e.g., comparisons of stimulus items with memory items) is serial or parallel, the so-called architecture issue; stopping rule (can rapid processing cease when sufficient information has been accumulated to make a correct response—self-terminating stopping vs. always finishing all items—exhaustive processing); work load capacity (how an increase of the number of things to do affects response times or accuracy), and stochastic independence or not, of the mechanisms involved in the ongoing information processing.

Seminal experiments wherein response times were recorded for a varying number of memory items (n), by Sternberg (1966), and shortly, many others, offered evidence that short term memory search was exhaustive and serial (though the conclusion that all these response time data were truly straight lines was occasionally questioned as in Swanson and Briggs, 1969). In any case, shortly out of graduate school at Stanford, I began mathematical analyses of these and similar issues and soon began to unearth problems of model mimicking.

In fact, the simple and elegant type of serial processing proposed by Sternberg and others, when given precise mathematical interpretation, turned out to be deeply mimicable by intuitively reasonable parallel models. That is, for every such serial model for varied-n memory search experiment, it was possible to find a parallel model that was mathematically equivalent to that serial model (Townsend, 1969, 1971, 1972, 1974, 1976a). It is extremely important to observe that the impossibility of strongly testing serial vs. parallel processing in a particular experimental paradigm such as that of Sternberg (1966) does not imply that there exist no experimental designs capable of this achievement.

Although impossibility (to test!) theorems certainly make a contribution to the field in order to avert weak or wrong conclusions, if we just stopped there, important questions such as the parallel vs. serial issue would go unsolved.

From the very beginning, however, my colleagues, students, and I devoted considerable effort to discovering more powerful methods (see, e.g., Townsend, 1972, 1976b; Snodgrass, 1980; Townsend & Ashby, 1983; Townsend & Wenger, 2004). Now, there exist a sizable number of experimental methodologies qualified to accomplish parallel–serial testability (and related issues). Most of these are presented in a number of reviews over the past decade or so, including some quite up to date accounts in the *Oxford Handbook of Computational and Mathematical Psychology* (Chapter 3, Algom, Eidels, Hawkins, Jefferson & Townsend, 2015) and in the upcoming *The Stevens' Handbook of Experimental Psychology and Cognitive Neuroscience*, Fourth Edition (Chapter by Townsend, Wenger & Houpt).

Interestingly, Sternberg himself invented a novel methodology which served as a predecessor of systems factorial technology. He referred to that approach as the *additive factors method* (1969). It included the assumption that distinct experimental factors could affect the speed of the mean of the sub-processes of a serial system. The predictions and tests were at the level of mean response times.

In the late 1970s, R. Schweickert constructed a factorial methodology for not only serial and parallel systems, but virtually any architecture describable as a forward flowing, connected graph (1978; again, we cannot be precise herein). The durations consumed by the processes were mostly treated as deterministic rather than stochastic, although he was able to proffer stochastic bounds in some instances. Later efforts laid a complete stochastic foundation under his approach, when the mean response time is the dependent (observable) variable (Townsend & Schweickert, 1989; Schweickert & Townsend, 1989).

Like many, if not most, intellectual territories in science in general, "systems factorial technology" is a topic with fuzzy, or at least graded, boundaries. Strictly speaking, it refers to the tight set of definitions, theorems, and proofs first appearing in Townsend and Nozawa (1995), along with the experimental design designated the *double factorial paradigm*. As will be seen in the Introduction offered by the editors and a number of the constituent chapters, a hallmark of that paradigm is that it permits direct assessment, employing the tenets of systems factorial technology, of the most fundamental characteristics mentioned above: 1. Architecture; 2. Stopping Rule; 3. Work load capacity. Only certain kinds of independence cannot be directly assayed with the double factorial paradigm, although sometimes indirect inference might be made. Also, another branch of research, which is associated with *general recognition theory* (Ashby & Townsend, 1986; Ashby, 1992; Maddox, 1992; Kadlec & Townsend, 1992), was developed precisely for the purpose of appraising various important types of dependence.

Moreover, the Townsend and Nozawa (1995) paper for the first time put forth theorems about how to distinguish models based on the ability of experimental factors to order response time cumulative distribution functions. The inspiration behind the present volume was to commemorate the anniversary of publication of that paper in Journal of Mathematical Psychology.

However, if one is willing to loosen the boundaries a bit, then it turns out that certain other methodologies might be viewed as lying close to, if not within, the confines of systems factorial technology. The theorem of Ashby and Townsend (1980) which states that $F_{\mathrm{hh}} * F_{\mathrm{ll}} = F_{\mathrm{hl}} * F_{\mathrm{lh}}$, where "$*$" is the convolution operation, h = "high factor settings", and l = "low factor setting", can surely be claimed to lie within even a narrowly defined province, because a strict factorial combination of factors intended to speed up (high) vs. slow down (low) processing speed is utilized. The *parallel–serial testing paradigm* (e.g., see Chapter 13 of Townsend & Ashby, 1983) is somewhat further away from the central precepts of systems factorial technology but might be let in the door, if one interprets the manipulation of matching vs. mis-matching comparison as a factorial manipulation and certain other facets are overlooked.

Furthermore, one might well wish to encompass the broader networks envisaged by Schweickert, especially those using the entire distributions rather than the means alone (e.g., Schweickert, 1978; Schweickert, Giorgini & Dzhafarov, 2000) within the fold of systems factorial technology.

Another core principle of systems factorial technology is the principle of *selective influence*, first formulated by Sternberg for the mean response times of serial systems and since expanded and made more precise in a number of papers and books (e.g., Townsend & Ashby, 1983; Townsend, 1984; Townsend & Schweickert 1989; Townsend & Thomas, 1994). In recent years, Dzhafarov and colleagues have provided further deep explorations, including new definitions and theorems regarding selective influence (e.g., a small selection but with references is given by Dzhafarov, 2003; Dzhafarov & Kujala, 2010, 2011). The profound underpinnings and scientific interrelationships entailed by selective influence are suggested by its intimate connections with the notions of *entanglement* and so-called *contextuality* in quantum physics.

Should these topics, principles, tributaries, and so on be included within systems factorial technology? It is doubtful that all the investigators who have contributed to the above and other accounts which may brush up again the latter would be enthusiastic about such apparent annexation. And that is eminently reasonable because that work was accomplished by them independently, in many cases, and in an important sense, is their intellectual property alone.

However, with regard to the scientific enterprise, the foremost aspect in our minds perhaps should be not so much in what belongs to whom or the names we give specific bodies of knowledge. Rather, that the overall corpus of research, alluded to above and whatever it be called, not only be made of use in the wide variety of areas and topics that appear in this book, and more, but also aid in succoring new theory driven methodologies and a legitimate fruitful and evolving psychological systems theory. Within this psychological systems theory we would hope and expect to see an increasing number of researches, both theoretical and empirical, at the exceptionally high level of rigor and creativity found within the covers of this book. The editors and authors as well deserve high praise indeed.

Dr. James T. Townsend

Acknowledgements

We are indebted to Distinguished Rudy Professor James (Jim) T. Townsend. It is clear throughout that Jim's work has inspired and motivated the extensions and applications of SFT that appear in this book. Beyond that, Jim's encouragement was a key motivation in ensuring the completion of this book.

The editors would like to thank all of the reviewers who contributed their time critiquing the content of this book. Many reviews were provided by contributing authors, but we would like to thank Dr. Andrei Teodorescu and Dr. Robert De Lisle.

We would also like to thank Dr. Ami Eidels for providing the initial suggestion that the 20th Anniversary of Townsend and Nozawa (1995) might be honored with a published volume on Systems Factorial Technology. That idea coalesced at the workshop on Theory and Methodology in Configural Perception held at the National Cheng Kung University in Tainan, Taiwan (ROC) and was further prompted by a Symposium on SFT at the 2015 Society for Mathematical Psychology Conference in Newport Beach, CA.

Finally, we would like to acknowledge the work of Glyn Humphreys, who passed away in January 2016. Glyn Humphreys was among the most prominent researchers in the psychology and neuropsychology of attention and cognition. His work was instrumental in applying SFT to the social domain. Glyn's and his students' contribution to this book appears as the closing chapter of this book.

Daniel R. Little
Nicholas Altieri
Mario Fifić
Cheng-Ta Yang

Part One

Introduction to Systems Factorial Technology

Historical Foundations and a Tutorial Introduction to Systems Factorial Technology

1

Nicholas Altieri, Mario Fifić[†], Daniel R. Little[‡], Cheng-Ta Yang[§]*
*Idaho State University, Pocatello, ID, United States, [†]Grand Valley State University, Allendale, MI, United States, [‡]The University of Melbourne, Melbourne, VIC, Australia, [§]National Cheng Kung University, Tainan, Taiwan

Not only is every sensation attended this by a corresponding change localized in the sense-organ, which demands a certain time, but also, between the stimulation of the organ and consciousness of the perception an interval of time must elapse, corresponding to the transmission of stimulus for some distance along the nerves.

Abu Rayhan al-Birnuni (c. 973–1048 AD)

Time reveals all things

Erasmus

Introduction

Conscious experience encompasses a wide variety of rich phenomena: some of which involve the processing of separate sources of information relegated to one sensory modality, and often times, the integration of auditory, visual, tactile, or even olfactory information across sensory modalities.[1] An age-old question in the cognitive and perceptual sciences therefore relates to how the brain processes and combines segregated streams of inputs and unifies them into a conscious experience. Even processes that seem rather mundane, such as visually recognizing a tree or a face, or identifying a spoken word, requires a complex cascade of sensory processes and the association of the various forms of information. (For practical purposes, this chapter defines *recognition* as the conscious categorization of an object, sound, or event.)

The great Persian scientist al-Birnuni was perhaps the first to notice the interrelationship between temporal and mental processes and task execution. Nonetheless, with the exception of Donders' subtraction method and Helmholtz' assays into muscle neurophysiology (i.e., "nerve and muscle physics"; Helmholtz, 1850) formulated in the 19th century, only since the middle of the 20th century have reaction times (RTs) been systematically examined to make inferences about psychological processes. This chapter will briefly summarize some of the major highlights of these fascinating historical developments before providing a tutorial on one of the more recent but seminal developments of RT methodology known as Systems Factorial Technology (SFT) formulated by Townsend and colleagues in the 1990s.[2]

Systems Factorial Technology, DOI: 10.1016/B978-0-12-804315-8.00002-1

Examples of Cognitive Processes in the Psychological Literature

Intra-modal visual and auditory recognition both require intact sensory systems that can process or detect incoming information. This detection and early-stage sensory accumulation process by itself is necessary for recognition, though it is hardly sufficient. To illustrate this point, consider examples of visual agnosia. Patients with visual or other forms of *agnosia*—which essentially translates to *not knowing*—subsequent to stroke or brain injury generally retain the ability to describe the visual or auditory features of a stimulus. What these patients lack is the ability to combine the features in such a way that allows them to understand what they are seeing or hearing. In prosopagnosia, which is a deficit in holistic or configural facial recognition, people lose the ability to identify a face based on information gleaned from seeing individual features such as the eyes, nose, and mouth (e.g., Bauer, 1986). Recognizing a familiar face requires the simultaneous accumulation of information about several different features; however, this is not enough. The information pertaining to the eyes, nose, mouth, and face shape must be somehow associated across feature dimensions or combined in such a way that allows a decision to be made about what face was perceived.

Beyond the scope of recognizing faces (e.g., Wenger & Townsend, 2001, 2006), the basic logic above applies to identifying letters or numbers in a visual display (e.g., Berryhill, Kveraga, Webb, & Hughes, 2007), recognizing simple stimulus items such as tones or dots (e.g., Miller, 1982, 1986; Miller & Ulrich, 2003; Townsend & Nozawa, 1995), written words (Townsend & Fifić, 2004; Houpt, Townsend, & Donkin, 2014), and even multimodal speech recognition (Altieri, Pisoni, & Townsend, 2011; Altieri & Townsend, 2011; Altieri & Wenger, 2013). An example of multimodal recognition is audiovisual speech perception, such as the McGurk effect; this occurs when listeners are presented with mismatched auditory and visual signals (such as an auditory sound of /ba/ paired with a lip-movement producing "ga"; refer to McGurk & MacDonald, 1976). Often times, the listener will report hearing a fused percept such as "da" or "tha", rather than the "ba" or "ga" that was actually present.

Several innovative methodologies have been utilized to empirically distinguish between different viable information processing strategies within individual observers. Importantly, these statistical strategies are applicable to various situations and questions in the psychophysical, language, memory, decision making, and vision sciences. These include, but are not limited to: detection of simple visual stimuli (Miller, 1982), change detection (Yang, 2011; Yang, Chang, & Wu, 2013), face recognition (Wenger & Townsend, 2001), multisensory recognition (e.g., Altieri, Stevenson, Wallace, & Wenger, 2015), and so on. This discussion will be accomplished by dissecting processing strategies that describe cognitive processes at a foundational level. We shall see, however, that despite the basic level of these questions, the processes for measurement and computation are highly complex and have undergone considerable theoretical revision over the past century.

The foundational questions that we speak of encompass both *mental architecture* and *workload capacity*. Mental architecture refers to the information processing strategy utilized to, for example, consciously categorize items in a display. Are items—

dots, letters, facial features, etc.—processed one at a time in a serial manner? Or are they instead processed at the same time in a parallel manner? A subsidiary issue that we shall explore is the decision strategy: this concerns whether all items in a display must be processed before recognition occurs (so-called *exhaustive processing*), or instead, whether one can stop and identify the stimulus before all the display items have been processed (*self-terminating processing*). *First-terminating* processing constitutes a special case of self-termination, occurring when processing can finish as soon as the first item in the display is correctly identified or otherwise reaches threshold. There are numerous factors which can work to determine the processing strategy; these include several factors which have formed the central research focus of perception and cognition including individual factors (e.g., in learning, Houpt & Blaha, 2016; cognitive ability, Yu, Chang, & Yang, 2014; personality trait, Chang & Yang, 2014), task specific factors (e.g., response biases; Blaha, 2017, this book), and stimulus-specific factors (e.g., separability and integrality; Griffiths, Blunden, & Little, 2017, of this book; relative saliency, Yang, 2011; Yang et al., 2013).

Next, *workload capacity* deals with whether information processing becomes more or less efficient as the number of items in a display is manipulated. As we shall see, architecture and capacity are logically independent: it is possible, for example, for efficiency or high workload capacity in a serial system, and on the other hand, limited capacity or efficiency in a parallel system. Indeed, quite plausible systems of the latter type have been evoked to explain visual attention processes (Yang, 2017, this book).

The following section provides details about how the methodology for assessing architecture and capacity has been refined over the past century. We shall see that the methods are complex in the sense that they do not solely rely on obtaining mean accuracy or mean RTs and averaging that data across participants, as is the norm in many experimental paradigms. Instead, the time course of processing is considered at the level of the entire RT distribution, typically by contrasting RTs collected for different experimental manipulations. In later sections, we shall demonstrate how the *Double Factorial Paradigm*, or DFP, makes important and strong assumptions, all while relying on RT distributions, to infer internal information processing strategies.

Historical Background

In spite of al-Birnuni's millennia old idea that temporal processes form an important barometer of cognitive and sensory processes, laboratory work using RTs to infer mental or neurophysiological processes was only commenced in the 19th century. Helmholtz reported physiological studies in the middle of the 19th century in which an electrical shock was administered to the skin, and participants were required to respond by moving their hand as soon as they perceived the shock (Helmholtz, 1850). Importantly, these ideas foreshadowed later developments that subdivided RTs into constituent components including stimulus encoding time, decision time, response selection time, and motor execution time (e.g., Luce, 1986).

Other experiments using RT methodology were carried out by Donders (1969), who devised what became known as the "subtraction method." The subtraction method is essentially a way to measure processes that occur in a serial fashion. For example, suppose we obtain mean response times from an experiment that requires participants to categorize an object (task A) and respond by choosing between one of two category options (task B), and then we obtain RTs when participants are just asked to respond with either category to some simple stimulation (task B alone). By subtracting the time it takes to complete task B from the total amount of time it takes to complete A and B, we can obtain the estimated time it takes to complete task A alone, the mental time taken for categorization. The assumption underlying the subtraction method is that completion times are strictly additive; however, this is not always true as tasks can interact with one another. In other words, the assumption of strict seriality of certain mental processes does not always hold and must be assessed empirically.

Wilhelm Wundt, the 19th century father of modern psychology, also made forays into the temporal processing domain. According to Wundt's psychological approach of introspection, complex psychological processes can be reduced to simpler components. Accordingly, and similar to Donders, Wundt's approach makes the assumption that RTs to complex stimuli should be slower than (i.e., the sum of) simpler stimuli (cf. Robinson, 2001). The goal of more recent statistical methodology in the psychological sciences has been developed to allow us to test the processing assumptions underlying mental processing derived from these forbearers.

One century later, Saul Sternberg's (1966, 1969) *additive factors method* was developed for the purpose of assessing whether short-term memory search was in fact serial, or alternatively, occurred in parallel; that is, do all stored items from a memory set become activated for recognition simultaneously? In Sternberg's classic paradigm, participants are given a list of digits to memorize and then shown a "probe" digit after a brief study period. The task for the participant is to answer as quickly and as accurately as possible, as to whether the probe digit was contained in the list of digits. Sternberg's paradigm included one crucial manipulation: testing what happens to mean RTs when the number of items in the list (i.e., the set size) increases. Hypothetically, as the list of items in short-term memory increases, the time it takes to determine whether the probe is contained in the list should also increase. In a significant development in RT research, Sternberg (1969) found evidence that mean RT does increase as the number of items stored in memory increases and that this increase occurred at the same rate (across set sizes) regardless of whether the probe was presented in the memory set or not. The former result was taken by Sternberg to imply that search occurred in a serial fashion; the latter result was taken to imply that the search did not terminate as soon as the probe was located in the list (i.e., which would result in a decreased rate of increase for target-present trials compared to target-absent trials) but scanned all of the items exhaustively. Together these findings were considered indicative of a serial exhaustive search mechanism.

Soon after the development of Sternberg's (1969) additive factors method, Townsend and colleagues further refined statistically-motivated RT methodology (SFT) to improve the identification of mental architecture. One key limitation of several approaches that use mean RTs, such as the additive factors method, is the problem of "model mimicry." Model mimicry refers to the myriad of cases in which parallel and serial models can produce identical mean RT signatures. For example, a parallel model with capacity limitations can yield a mean RT slope that increases linearly with set size such as that described by Sternberg (see, e.g., Townsend, 1972; Townsend & Ashby, 1983; Wenger & Townsend, 2000). Conversely, a serial model with very efficient processing (i.e., supercapacity) can yield the flat RT set-size function that was commonly believed to be associated with parallel architecture. To further complicate issues, parallel models and coactive models, which pool resources into one common accumulator, can also predict identical mean RT signatures.[3] We refer the interested reader to Townsend and Ashby (1983), Townsend (1990a), and Townsend and Wenger (2004b) for further mathematical and theoretical description of these issues.

To address this problem of model mimicry, Townsend and Nozawa (1995) developed a more fine-grained theory driven methodology for model testing known as SFT. SFT is a suite or toolbox of methods and statistical tools which improve upon and expand the ability to use RTs to discover important properties of the information processing system. For instance, within SFT, the DFP uses a combined analysis of interaction contrasts across factorial conditions, together with assessments of workload capacity that measure system-level efficiency as a function of workload. These ideas build on the extensive history of Donders, Sternberg, and many others whose work we have not covered here. We direct the reader to the excellent historical reviews by Townsend and Ashby (1983), Luce (1986), Jensen (2006), Schweickert, Fisher, and Sung (2012), and Algom et al. (2015). For the remainder of the chapter, we focus on explaining precisely what aspects of the processing system we seek to understand, discussing how to construct the DFP, and showing how to use the theoretical SFT tools.

Properties of Information Processing Systems

As illustrated by Sternberg's (1969) considerations, an important perspective in the cognitive sciences is that mental operations must occur in some sequence. While a wide variety of hypothetical cognitive and information processing systems can be devised to account for empirical data, this chapter will focus on three broad classes of models. First, as discussed in relation to Donders', general serial systems assume that object or feature identification occurs one at a time; importantly, processing on the second item cannot begin until the first item is identified. Another type of architecture is a parallel processing architecture. In a parallel system, items, features, letters, or objects can be processed simultaneously. A third type of architecture is termed a coactive processing architecture (cf. Diederich, 1995; Diederich & Colonius, 2004; Miller, 1982; Schwarz, 1989; Townsend & Nozawa, 1995; Townsend & Wenger, 2004a, 2004b). Coactive systems are similar to parallel systems in many ways. For example, they assume that information processing occurs simultaneously in different channels. Coactive systems differ inasmuch as they assume that the accrued information is pooled into a common processing channel, and hence, the decision is made on the combined information rather than on the individual channels. In each of these "basic" serial and parallel architectures, it is assumed that the processing of each channel proceeds independently. The processing architectures can be made vastly more complex by allowing interactions or cross-talk between the processing channels. Hence, an interactive parallel system might contain facilitatory or inhibitory interactions (Eidels, Houpt, Altieri, Pei, & Townsend, 2011; Houpt, Pei, Eidels, Altieri, Fifić, & Townsend, 2008; Mordkoff & Yantis, 1991). (Similarly, interactions might also occur across channels in serial mechanisms, although this may intuitively appear less plausible. See Townsend & Ashby, 1983.)

For serial and parallel systems, one must also consider the issue of the decisional stopping rule. As discussed in the context of Sternberg's (1969) results, one may intuit that if a system ceases processing as soon as a single item is completed, the RT signature will be different, regardless of the architecture, from cases where all items must be completed before a response is made. First-terminating systems can reach a decision and emit a response time as soon as the first channel accumulates sufficient information. Exhaustive systems, on the other hand, can only emit a response when processing has terminated in each of the channels. Crucially, both serial and parallel systems can be combined with first or self-terminating or exhaustive stopping rule; in other words, architecture is logically independent of decisional rule. Coactive systems differ from parallel and serial models because the exhaustive stopping rule is mandatory. This is due to that fact that coactive models emit a response time when the channel containing all of the combined information reaches its decision threshold. Fig. 1.1 shows a schematic diagram of serial, parallel, and coactive systems in the context of a prototypical detection paradigm with two targets (Townsend & Ashby, 1983; Townsend & Nozawa, 1995; see also Miller, 1982, for an early account of coactive processing using simple auditory and visual stimuli).

SFT also allows one to assess whether the decision is made exhaustively or in a self-terminating fashion. We will focus on the combination of serial and parallel models endowed with an exhaustive or self-terminating stopping rule and on the coactive processing model, for which the question of self-termination is moot. These five models, namely serial self-terminating, serial exhaustive, parallel self-terminating, parallel exhaustive, and the coactive model, form the "Big-5" models of SFT for which theoretical measures are fully developed. More recent work by Eidels et al. (2011) has focused on the characterization of the spectrum of interactive parallel models using the same methods.

A final aspect of information processing systems concerns how the efficiency of the processing system changes with its processing workload, termed *workload capacity* (or just *capacity*, for short). In general, we consider systems whose capacity can be thought of as limited, unlimited, or even better than unlimited (so-called *supercapacity*). Like the other properties, capacity is logically independent of considerations of architecture, stopping rule, and independence between channels. However, empirically, certain capacity signatures tend to co-occur with certain architectures: Serial systems are usually limited capacity whereas coactive systems are usually supercapacity. Reasonable parallel systems can be limited, unlimited, or supercapacity (see Eidels et al., 2011; Townsend and Wenger, 2004b).

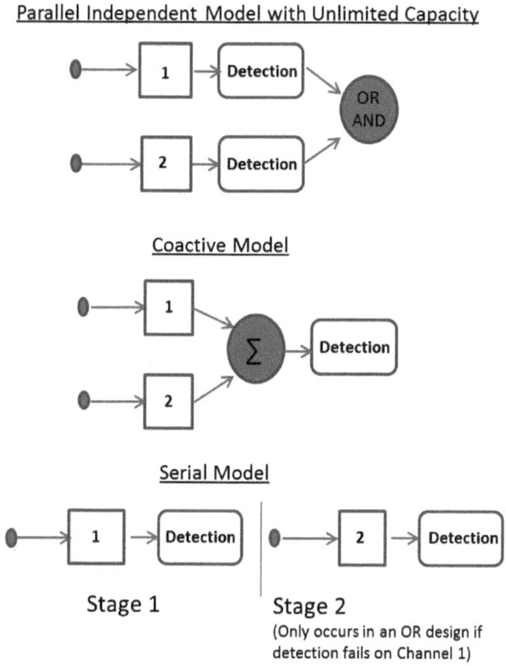

Figure 1.1 This is a schematic representation of a parallel independent model (top) with an OR as well as an AND gate; this is similar to the parallel model depicted in Townsend and Nozawa (1995). The coactive model assumes that each channel is pooled into a common accumulator where evidence is accumulated prior to making a decision. Lastly, the figure shows a serial OR model which assumes that processing does not begin on channel 2 until processing completes on channel 1. In an AND design, processing would always begin on channel 2 when processing terminates on channel 1, and detection waits for processing to complete on both channels.

The Double Factorial Paradigm

Stated briefly, the DFP involves the factorial manipulation of experimental conditions and the statistical analysis of RT distributions to make inferences about the aspects of mental processes reviewed above. Although other variations are possible, a prototypical double or "redundant-target" detection paradigm presents participants with one, two, or zero stimuli on each trial (see Fig. 1.2). Depending on the task instructions, the participant is required to make a speeded response of one type (e.g., a left button press) when either one or two targets are detected in the display and an alternative speeded response (e.g., a right button press) when no targets are detected in the display. This task is termed an OR-rule task because an affirmative response is made whenever any target is detected on redundant-target trials (e.g., in location 1 *or* location 2), which is when a system can terminate. We contrast this with an AND rule task in which one type of speeded response is made only when two targets are presented (e.g., in location 1 and location 2) and the other response is made when one or no targets are presented. This occurs when a system exhaustively analyzes all inputs.

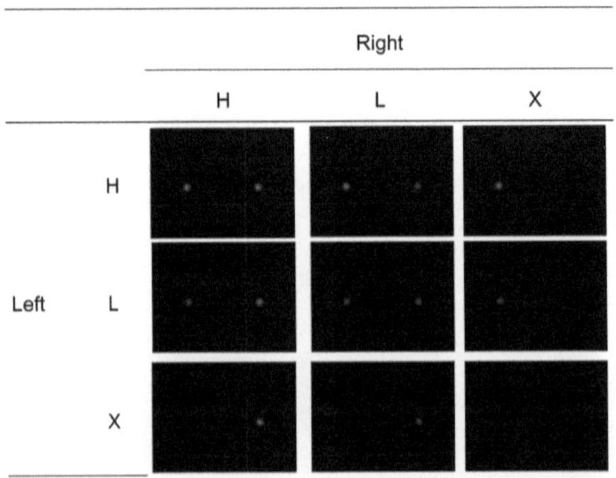

Figure 1.2 DFP design showing high- and low-detectability manipulations, along with the redundant-target and single-target trials.

In the DFP the saliency or strength of the targets is manipulated factorially on both the redundant and single-target trials. The goal of this manipulation is to speed up or slow down the RT in each channel. This property has been alternatively referred to stimulus salience (Townsend & Nozawa, 1995) or stimulus discriminability (Fifić, Little, & Nosofsky, 2010). In the context of redundant-target trials, for instance, we refer to stimuli in which a *high* detectability target appears in both locations (HH), a high detectability target appears in the first location but a low detectability target appears in the second location (HL), the converse of this situation (LH), and the case in which a low detectability target appears in both locations (LL). In addition, the salience manipulation (L and H) is applied to the conditions in which only one item is presented in either of the location (X) (Fig. 1.2). Hence, the DFP combines both a manipulation of workload by varying the number of possible targets that is useful for assessing information processing capacity, and a factorial manipulation of target detectability that is useful for assessing information processing architecture and stopping rule. We next provide a tutorial introduction to both of these applications starting with the latter assessment of architecture and stopping rule.

Assessing Processing Architecture and Decisional Stopping Rule

This section deals with how the DFP can be used to measure architecture. As we shall see, the DFP essentially involves inferring cognitive processes by computing RTs and quantifying potential interactions between experimental factors.

Selective Influence

The tools comprising the DFP make an important assumption of *selective influence* (e.g., Dzhafarov, 2003; Schweickert et al., 2012; Townsend and Schweickert, 1989).

Selective influence implies that there is a strict relationship between the experimental manipulation and the effects of the manipulation on the processes of interests such that an experimental manipulation affects only a single channel (sub-process) within a mental architecture. For example, in a brightness detection task, one has to detect a presence of a stimulus that varies in brightness. The standard finding is that increasing brightness of a stimulus shortens the detection time. The detection time is thought to be composed of several subcomponents (e.g., identification time, decision time, and motor execution time; Luce, 1986). Although it seems natural to believe that the brightness manipulation should only affect the dot detection time, there is no simple way to prove that this is true.

Let us consider another example in which the task is to detect the presence of any of the two spatially separated dots. In this case, we assume that the cognitive system has to process two channels: one for each dot. Each dot could be presented at either high (H) or low (L) brightness. When testing architecture, the mean RTs for the high level in a given channel should be faster than mean RTs for the low level in the same channel. The classical method used to test for selective influence in a double-dot task is to determine whether the individual survivor functions, defined as $1 - F(t)$, are properly ordered: $S_{LL}(t) > S_{LH}(t)$, $S_{HL}(t) \geq S_{HH}(t)$. The ordering of distributions is a necessary condition for architectural assays within the context of the DFP. Importantly, Townsend (1990b) proved that an ordering of survivor functions ($S(t)$) or cumulative distribution functions ($F(t)$) implies that the means of the distribution are ordered, although an ordering of means does not imply that the survivor functions are ordered.

It is also important to stress that the methodology does not depend on any specific probability distributions or parameters. The relevant data characteristics are predicted by the various classes of architectures (Sternberg, 1969; Schweickert, 1978; Townsend & Ashby, 1983) and are consequently non-parametric. An exception to this is the coactive model predictions, which have been proved for Poisson counting models (although even these predictions happen to be independent of particular parameter values; Townsend & Nozawa, 1995), Wiener diffusion models (Houpt & Townsend, 2011), and have been shown to hold for discrete random walk models (Fifić et al., 2010; Little, 2012).

Mean Interaction Contrast

One statistic that can be computed using the factorial manipulation is the mean interaction contrast or $MIC = [RT_{LL} - RT_{LH}] - [RT_{HL} - RT_{HH}]$ (see Sternberg, 1969; Townsend & Nozawa, 1995). In this formula, RT_{LL} is used to denote mean RT of the LL (low–low) detectability target, for example.

The absence of an interaction (i.e., $MIC = 0$) indicates that the effects of experimental factors are additive—a feature that strongly indicates serial processing regardless of the stopping rule. Subsequent theoretical effort led to extensions of *MIC* tests to parallel and more complex architectures (e.g., Schweickert, 1978; Townsend & Schweickert, 1989; Schweickert & Townsend, 1989; Townsend & Ashby, 1983).

While an interaction indicates a lack of evidence for serial architecture, parallel processing cannot be inferred based on a non-zero MIC alone: one notable shortcoming of the *MIC* mimicry of parallel self-terminating models and coactive models; both predict $MIC > 0$. Another shortcoming of the *MIC* is that it is a coarse measure only representing one point at each level of detectability (i.e., the mean of the distribution).

Survivor Interaction Contrast

Townsend and Nozawa (1995; also Townsend & Wenger, 2004a for further review) developed a more sensitive contrast that analyzes the functional form of curve of the entire distribution of RTs, namely, the *survivor interaction contrast* ($SIC(t)$). We may define the *SIC* mathematically as

$$SIC(t) = \left[S_{\mathrm{LL}}(t) - S_{\mathrm{LH}}(t)\right] - \left[S_{\mathrm{HL}}(t) - S_{\mathrm{HH}}(t)\right]. \tag{1.1}$$

Notice that the $SIC(t)$ uses the same sequence of terms as the *MIC*, only now survivor functions, $S(t)$, are used rather than the mean RTs. The survivor function $S(t)$, a statistical tool used in *survival analysis* (e.g., Elandt-Johnson & Johnson, 1999), is a function indicating the probability that a process has not completed at time t. $S(t)$ equals one minus the cumulative distribution function, $F(t)$, and contains more information than the mean value as it describes the process of interest over the time dimension. Thus, $S(t)$ possesses more statistical inferential power than the mean *RT* (Townsend, 1990b).

Fig. 1.3 shows a diagram of the step-by-step processes involved in computing SIC. First, we obtain vectors of *RT*s from the LL, LH, HL, and HH experimental conditions for an individual participant. While averaging data across participants is possible, there are both statistical and philosophical issues that can arise when averaging data (e.g., Ashby, Maddox, & Lee, 1994; Estes, 1956; see also Fifić, 2014, for the effect of averaging data on the *MIC* analysis): One particular drawback is that group averages can obscure important trends arising for an individual participant to such an extent that the average does not resemble any of the individuals. Generally, the number of responses should each contain a large number of trials (i.e., greater than $N = 100$ is a good rule of thumb). Next, from each of these vectors, we empirically calculate the normalized probability density function $f(t)$. Third, we obtain the cumulative sum of the $f(t)$ values, otherwise known as the empirical cumulative distribution function, which is a close estimate of real cumulative distribution function $F(t)$. A simple transformation, namely $1 - F(t)$, yields the survivor function. We refer the reader to Van Zandt (2000) and Van Zandt and Townsend (2012) for further details.

The survivor functions should be plotted on the same plot to ensure that they are ordered and that the assumption of selective influence holds. Houpt, Blaha, McIntire, Havig, & Townsend (2014; see also Heathcote, Brown, Wagenmakers, & Eidels, 2010; Houpt & Burns, 2017, this book) introduce various statistical methods for checking this assumption. If the stochastic ordering of the target stimuli survivor functions holds, then we can compute the interaction at each point of the function to give us

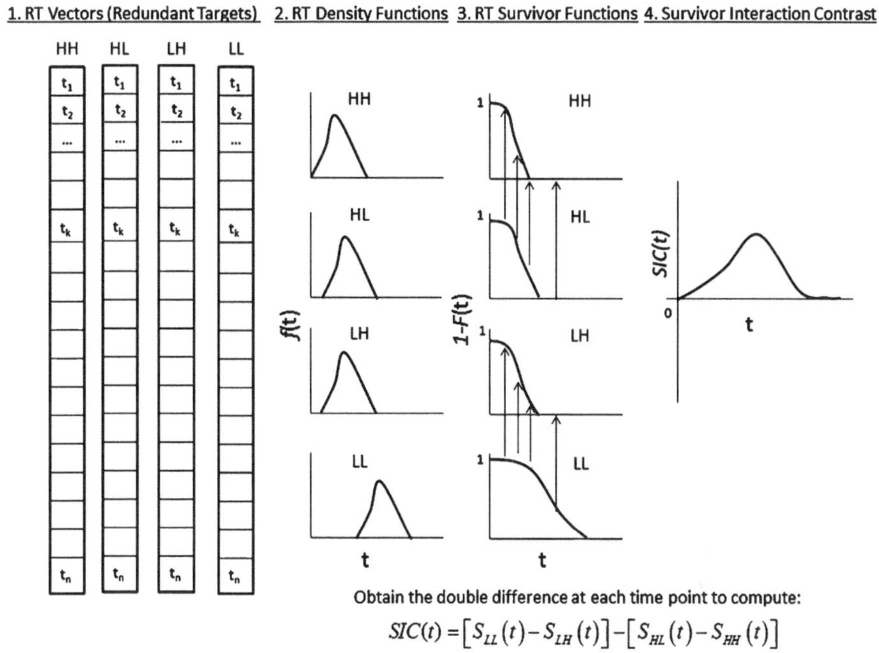

Figure 1.3 The steps involved in computing the survivor interaction contrast. In the case of the figure, we can surmise parallel processing with an OR decisional stopping rule because the function is over-additive at each point. Of course, the *MIC* would be greater than 0 as well; however, the $SIC(t)$ gives us more powerful and fine-grained information. The arrows refer to a specific point in time and are provided to aid the visual comparison across the different functions.

the continuous $SIC(t)$. The shape of the function can then be used to diagnose mental architecture.

$SIC(t)$ *Predictions*

We now turn to the $SIC(t)$ predictions for each of the standard mental architectures and decisional rules (the proofs of the related theorems are presented in Townsend & Nozawa, 1995). The $SIC(t)$ predictions for standard parallel, serial, and coactive models with self-terminating and exhaustive stopping rules are shown in Fig. 1.4.

For a parallel self-terminating processing model, the $SIC(t)$ function is entirely positive (i.e., revealing *RT* over-additivity; see Fig. 1.4). This model is appropriate to test when completion of any of the processing channels can correctly decide the response. The intuition for why a parallel self-terminating $SIC(t)$ is positive is because the $S_{\text{LL}}(t) - S_{\text{LH}}(t)$ term is always larger than the $S_{\text{HL}}(t) - S_{\text{HH}}(t)$ term in Eq. (1.1). This is because for a parallel self-terminating model, the *RT* for a redundant target is the minimum time to complete any of the target channels. Hence, the processing time for the LH, HL, and HH stimuli will be much faster than for the LL stimulus be-

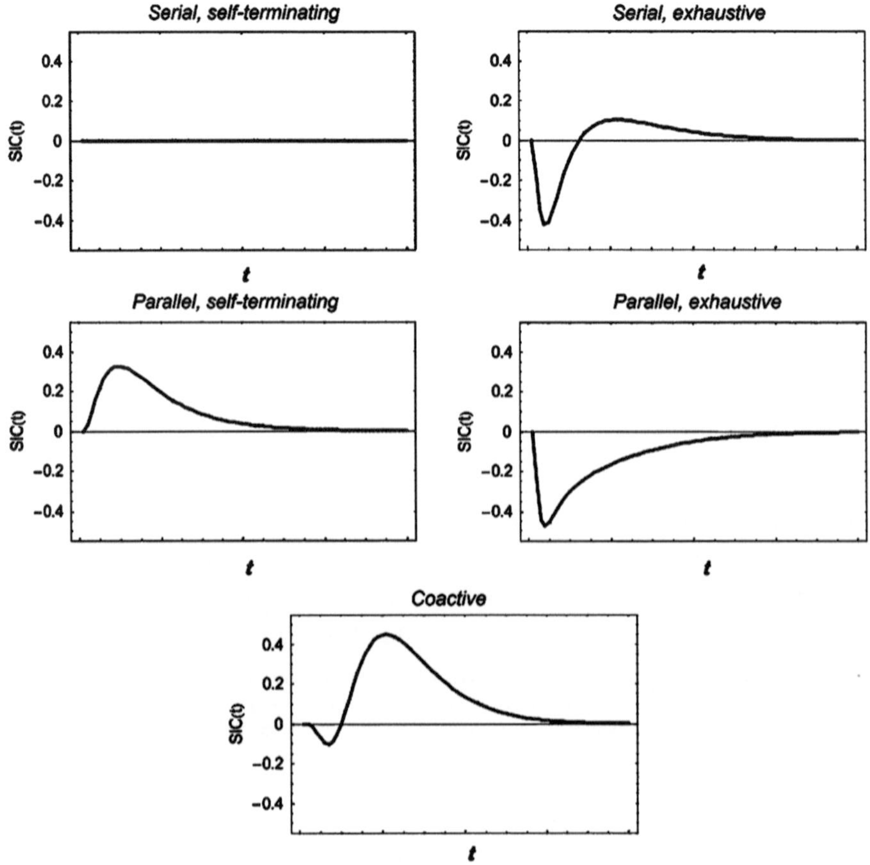

Figure 1.4 *SIC*(t) predictions for independent parallel, serial, and coactive models. The top panels display the predictions of the independent parallel self-terminating and exhaustive models respectively, while the middle panels display the predictions of the serial self-terminating and exhaustive models, respectively. The bottom panel displays the coactive predictions. Notice that the predictions of the coactive model appear similar to the serial exhaustive model, the difference being that the predicted size of the negative region in coactive models is smaller than the positive region.

cause the High detectability component will have a faster *RT* than a Low detectability component.

A parallel exhaustive model predicts an *SIC*(t) that is entirely negative (i.e., revealing *RT* under-additivity, see Fig. 1.4). This exhaustive stopping rule is required in cases where all channels must reach completion before it is certain that a correct response can be made. The intuition for why a parallel exhaustive model predicts a negative *SIC*(t) is because the $S_{\mathrm{LL}}(t) - S_{\mathrm{LH}}(t)$ term is always smaller than the $S_{\mathrm{HL}}(t) - S_{\mathrm{HH}}(t)$ term in Eq. (1.1), for all time points t. This is because, in a parallel exhaustive model, the *RT* for a redundant stimulus is the maximum time necessary to complete any of the target channels. Hence, the processing time for the LL, LH, and HL stimuli will be much slower than for the HH stimulus.

A serial self-terminating process predicts an *MIC* of 0 as does a serial exhaustive process. By contrast, the $SIC(t)$ functions for serial self-terminating and exhaustive processing take on very different shapes. When processing is serial and self-terminating, the $SIC(t)$ is flat and equal to 0 at every point of time (Townsend & Nozawa, 1995). When processing is serial and exhaustive, the $SIC(t)$ is an S-shaped curve with a negative region for early processing times and a positive region for later processing times. The negative and positive regions of the curve are equal to each other in the serial exhaustive model, and if we integrate over the curve, the total area is equal to the *MIC* and must equal zero. Hence, the *SIC* function delivers strikingly distinct signatures for the important architectures *and* their stopping rules.

Coactive models form a class of parallel models in which the information from each channel is pooled, typically by being added, together into a single channel. While the proofs for $SIC(t)$ functions in coactive models in Townsend and Nozawa (1995) rely on Poisson summation processes, other coactive models, such as those based on superimposed diffusion processes, have also been proposed (e.g., Diederich, 1995; Diederich & Colonius, 1991; Miller & Ulrich, 2003; Schwarz, 1989, 1994). Simulations of linear dynamic and Poisson models indicate that the results are general across at least Poisson counter models and Wiener diffusion models (Eidels et al., 2011).

The survivor interaction contrast function for the coactive model is negative at the beginning for the fast *RT*s and becomes positive at the later or slower *RT*s. This is similar in shape to the serial exhaustive $SIC(t)$, but note that the initial negative deflection is smaller than the later positive deflection in the coactive model. The *MIC* for coactive models is positive, similar to self-terminating parallel models. Due to the relation between the survivor function and mean *RT* (i.e., for *RT*s, $\int S(t)dt = E(RT)$ where $E(RT)$ is the mean *RT*, Townsend, 1990b), the integral of the $SIC(t)$ function equals the *MIC*.

In summary, this section has demonstrated how to use the *RT*s recorded from redundant targets in a double factorial experiment to construct a factorial contrast test that allows differentiation of different processing architectures and stopping rules. We focused on a detection task, but the double factorial paradigm can be generalized to a wide variety of different domains including recognition memory (Townsend & Fifić, 2004), categorization (see Griffiths et al., 2017; Cheng, Moneer, Christie, & Little, 2017, this book), cued attention (see Yang, 2017, this book), multimodal processing (Altieri, 2017a, 2017b, this book), and face recognition (Wenger & Townsend, 2001, 2006). In the next section we turn to the analysis of the remaining component of the DFP; namely, the manipulation of workload across single targets and redundant targets. We describe how information from this manipulation can be used to compute a measure of workload capacity termed the *capacity coefficient*.

Assessing Workload Capacity

Assessing a system's capacity helps answer the question as to whether there is a significant cost, benefit, or no change in processing efficiency as a function of workload. Processing efficiency is essentially determined by comparing processing when multiple processing channels are operating, relative to an unlimited-capacity system whose predictions are derived from single-target trials. Generally, if the processing rate on each channel is unaffected by increasing the number of channels, the system operates at unlimited capacity. If the system slows down on redundant-target trials relative to an unlimited-capacity system, then processing operates at limited capacity. Finally, if the system speeds-up upon the activation of more than one channel, relative to the predictions of an unlimited-capacity system, then the system operates at supercapacity.

As with the architecture tests, capacity predictions and measurements are invariant across specific distributions and parameter values. In addition to often being of interest in its own right, the capacity measure can help arbitrate matters when two distinct architectures and stopping rule combinations yield the same qualitative picture with the $SIC(t)$.

Measuring capacity requires examining the ratio of the integrated hazard functions. To compute this ratio, one could first compute the hazard function as $h(t) = \frac{f(t)}{1-F(t)}$. The hazard function, $h(t)$, indicates the probability that a process will terminate at the next moment in time $(t + \Delta t)$, conditioned on the fact that it has not yet terminated at time t. Because $f(t) = \frac{dF(t)}{dt}$,

$$h(t) = \frac{dF(t)/dt}{1 - F(t)} = -\frac{d}{dt} \ln\big[1 - F(t)\big]$$

(Luce, 1986, p. 14); hence, the integrated hazard function is $H(t) = -\ln[1 - F(t)] = -\ln[S(t)]$. In the classical case of particle arrival at a Geiger counter (Parzen, 1962), the hazard function captures the instantaneous and time-invariant likelihood of a particle's arrival at any point in time given non-arrival before that point. $H(t)$ is a slightly coarser measure of efficiency, or work completed by time t, since it integrates $h(t)$; importantly however, it still carries with it inferential statistical advantages over means (Townsend, 1990b). Further, in estimation from data, it has been our experience that it tends to smooth out irregularities and provide more robust estimates.

To empirically calculate the capacity coefficient at each time interval, the integrated hazard functions must be calculated for the conditions in which the participant is presented with redundant-target information and divided by the sum of the integrated hazard functions obtained from the single-target conditions. The subscripts "1" and "2" in the following equation denote the information presented in each of the two processing channels:

$$C(t) = \frac{H_{12}(t)}{H_1(t) + H_2(t)}. \tag{1.2}$$

Capacity assesses performance in a system when redundant targets are present versus when only a single target is present by using predictions derived from independent parallel models with unlimited capacity (UCIP). In an OR rule, the UCIP model, in addition to assuming unlimited capacity and stochastically independent processing times, also assumes a self-terminating stopping rule. The standard parallel model thus acts as a benchmark for measuring workload capacity and predicts $C(t) = 1$, for all $t > 0$. Note that alternative benchmark models could also be used (see, for instance, Houpt, Townsend et al., 2014); however, the parallel model is convenient due to its historical precedence in devising other tests of processing (e.g., the role of the race model inequality found in Miller, 1982).

Capacity outcomes can be divided broadly into three categories based on the assessment of its values into: *Unlimited capacity*, $C(t) = 1$, means that RTs obtained from redundant-target trials equal UCIP predictions; *Supercapacity*, $C(t) > 1$, occurs when a parallel model, of equal efficiency with a workload of n items to process, will have one or more of its channels speeding up when compared to cases with a workload of $n-1$ or smaller. In other words, it means that the amount of work done on, say, two units is smaller than the sum of the work done on each unit separately; Finally, *limited capacity*, $C(t) < 1$, indicates that processing is less efficient compared to baseline UCIP models.

An upper bound on performance for separate activation parallel models, also known as *independent race models* or UCIP models, was provided by Miller (1982). It stipulates that in such models, it must be the case that $F_{12}(t) \leq F_1(t) + F_2(t)$. In this equation, $F_{12}(t)$ represents the cumulative distribution function (CDF) for the redundant-target trials, and $F_1(t)$ and $F_2(t)$ are the corresponding distributions for the single-target trials (e.g., when only one visual stimulus is presented). If $C(t) > 1$ for even a small interval early in processing then the above inequality has to be violated. And conversely, if there are values of t where $F_{12}(t) > F_1(t) + F_2(t)$ then it must be the case that $C(t) > 1$ for any such values.

Coactive models possess a strong propensity to exhibit supercapacity: This tendency was one of the reasons for the advent of the concept, first primarily in an operational form. Models were classified as "faster than race models" if Miller's race inequality was violated. Quantitative interpretations began to appear (Colonius & Townsend, 1997; Diederich & Colonius, 1991; Miller, 1991; Schwarz, 1994; Townsend & Nozawa, 1995). The Townsend and Nozawa (1995) study proved that a wide variety of coactive models based on counting processes with arbitrary distributions (including, but not limited to, the Poisson distributions) imply not only $C(t) > 1$, but also that such models will at some point violate the race inequality. Subsequently, Houpt and Townsend (2011) demonstrated supercapacity for coactive Wiener processes.

Limited capacity occurs when $C(t) < 1$ (Neufeld, Townsend, & Jetté, 2007; Townsend & Nozawa, 1995; Wenger & Townsend, 2000). Limited capacity could easily result from the allocation of a limited capacity source to the various operational channels. A special case of interest occurs when the processing source, measured by the integrated hazard function, is fixed. The system is then said to operate at *fixed capacity* and the $H_{12}(t)$ will be the average of the two single-target integrated hazard functions $H_{12}(t) = pH_1(t) + (1-p)H_2(t)$ with p lying between 0 and 1 according to the axioms of probability theory. An intuitive example is found if we assume equal distribution parameters with $H_{12}(t) = H_1(t) = H_2(t)$; this implies that the system operates at so called *fixed capacity* when $C(t) = 1/2$.

In the same way that the race model inequality places an upper bound on the level of supercapacity achievable by a UCIP model, there is an analogous bound on limited capacity termed the "Grice bound" (Grice, Canham, & Gwynne, 1984). This bound assumes that the fastest of the two channels (or items) is slower than responses to the redundant-target condition; it is expressed as $\max\{F_1(t), F_2(t)\} \leq F_{12}(t)$. (We refer the interested reader to Townsend and Eidels, 2011 for translations of upper and lower bounds into capacity space). When redundant-target processing speed is lower than this bound, we say that capacity is "extremely limited." Furthermore, if $F_1(t) = F_2(t) = F(t)$ in a parallel model, then the system operates at "fixed capacity." Standard serial models also make the same prediction, which highlights the importance of distinguishing the concepts of "capacity" and "architecture.

The UCIP baseline model described above clearly provides a benchmark of performance when processing can self-terminate and still respond accurately. This would be true when the task responses were defined by an OR decision rule; consequently, the capacity coefficient defined in Eq. (1.2) is sometimes denoted by $C_{\mathrm{OR}}(t)$. By contrast, in an AND decision task, both target locations must be processed exhaustively to ensure accurate detection of the double target. Termination after processing only a single target would, on some trials, results in inaccurate responding. In this situation, capacity is measured relative to an alternative baseline: a parallel exhaustive model, which expects the double-target processing time to be consistent with the maximum time taken to process either of the targets (i.e., $F_{12}(t) = F_1(t) \times F_2(t)$). Hence, capacity for an AND task is computed as

$$C_{\mathrm{AND}}(t) = \frac{K_1(t) + K_2(t)}{K_{12}(t)} \tag{1.3}$$

where $K(t)$ is the integrated reverse hazard function, which is defined analogously to $H(t)$ as $K(t) = \log[F(t)]$. Defining capacity in this way and inverting the locations of the single and double targets in the numerator and denominator of the function (compare Eqs. (1.2) and (1.3)) has the effect of (a) measuring capacity relative to a UCIP model with an exhaustive stopping rule and (b) maintaining all of the expected relationships from the computation of $C_{\mathrm{OR}}(t)$ regarding limited capacity, $C_{\mathrm{AND}}(t) < 1$, and supercapacity, $C_{\mathrm{AND}}(t) > 1$.

Probabilistic Contingencies

Finally, another important component of DFP design concerns the avoidance of probabilistic contingencies. In order to prevent probabilistic information from facilitating or alternatively inhibiting redundant-target speed relative to the single-target trials, it must be impossible for the observer to predict the occurrence of a target in channel 1 given the presence of a target in channel 2, and *vice versa* (cf. Mordkoff & Yantis, 1991). Suppose, for instance, that the probability of a target appearing in channel 2 increases with a target appearing in channel 1; here, redundant-target processing speed will be faster than single-target trials. One straightforward way to avoid probabilistic contingencies within the context of a simple go/no-go visual detection paradigm is to equate the number of redundant-target, single-target, and target-absent trials. Such a scenario is shown in the example OR detection design shown in Fig. 1.5, which requires the observers to say "yes" when a dot appears either above or below a central fixation and withhold their response in the target absent condition.

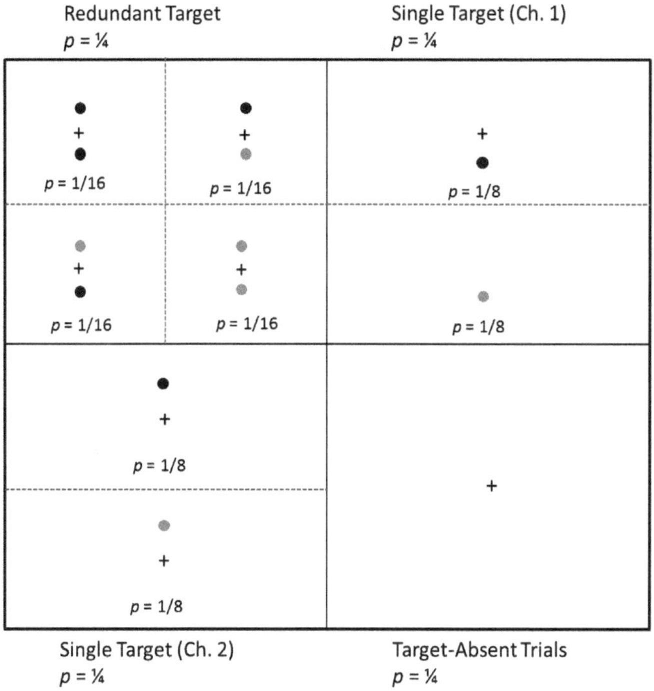

Figure 1.5 Trial types and probabilities for the redundant-target, single-target, and target-absent conditions in a DFP design in which contingencies are avoided. The black dot represents high-salience trials, whereas the lighted gray dots represent low-salience trials.

Conclusion

In this chapter, we introduced and reviewed two of the major theoretical contributions arising from Townsend and Nozawa's (1995) introduction of Systems Factorial Technology. This included an exploration of architecture and capacity measures, accompanied by a brief presentation of the prototypical experimental design. Numerous other extensions exist, and relevant adaptations continue to appear in the psychological literature: For example, a promising line of neuroimaging research has extended the concept of additive factors from the realm of RTs to neural-biological markers (Stevenson & James, 2009), as well as effects of cross-channel interactions on architecture and capacity (see Eidels et al., 2011; see also Townsend & Wenger, 2004b for effects on capacity).

Additionally, numerous theoretical developments, many of which were highlighted in this chapter, deal with extensions of theoretical issues (Townsend & Liu, 2017; Algom & Eidels, 2017, this book), the capacity function (Cheng et al., 2017), the double factorial paradigm for three or more channels (Yang, Fifić, & Townsend, 2014), statistical measures applicable to systems factorial technology and the survivor interaction contrast (e.g., Houpt & Townsend, 2010; Houpt & Burns, 2017, this book), applications in cognitive brain science, and quantitative relationships to other statistical measures will be discussed. The remainder of the book focuses on many of the important extensions to methodology and theory arising from this work along with the application of SFT.

First, the capacity measure described in this introductory chapter only is applicable to correct decisions and only to the case where the single targets are presented in isolation. Altieri's (2017a, 2017b) chapter on the capacity assessment function describes an extension of capacity to also account for accuracy and for *RT*s generated from error responses. In this book, Cheng et al.'s (2017) chapter describes an extension of capacity to account for the case where distractors are presented along with the single targets. Blaha's (2017) chapter describes how specific task demands might influence the observed capacity measure.

To facilitate the methodological growth of the SFT applications, a general approach for understanding methodological SFT manipulations is proposed in Fifić and Little's (2017) chapter in this book. The chapter provides an overview of different SFT applications across various psychological modalities and cognitive tasks, and shows how to integrate the seemingly different type of factorial process *RT* stretching manipulations into one framework.

In terms of new statistical developments, Houpt and Burns' (2017) chapter in this book proposes a number of statistical tests that can be utilized to determine whether the capacity coefficient, $C(t)$, is significantly greater or less than UCIP predictions, or whether two capacity coefficients differ significantly from each other.

Finally, the remaining chapters shall review specific applications of SFT beyond simple detection tasks. Some of these include applications in multisensory speech perception (Altieri, 2017b), categorization (Griffiths et al., 2017), auditory processing (He, Lentz, & Townsend's, 2017), selective responding (Algom & Eidels, 2017), attention (Yang, 2017), and configurality (Wenger, Ingvalson, & Rhoten, 2017). Appropriately, links between SFT and related paradigms such as the simultaneous–sequential paradigm (Howe & Ferguson, 2017), multidimensional scaling (Eidels & Howard, 2017), parametric modeling (Harding et al., 2017; Griffiths et al., 2017), and clinical neuroscience (Taylor, Theberge, Williamson, Densmore, & Neufeld, 2017) will also be addressed in this book.

References

Algom, D., & Eidels, A. (2017). Relation of SFT architectures to selective responding: Associations and dissociations. In D. R. Little, N. Altieri, M. Fifić, & C-T. Yang (Eds.), *Systems factorial technology: A theory driven methodology for the identification of perceptual and cognitive mechanisms*. Elsevier (in this book).

Algom, D., Eidels, A., Hawkins, R. X., Jefferson, B., & Townsend, J. T. (2015). *Features of response times: Identification of cognitive mechanisms through mathematical modeling. The Oxford handbook of computational and mathematical psychology* (p. 63).

Altieri, N. (2017a). Development and applications of the capacity-function that measures accuracy. In D. R. Little, N. Altieri, M. Fifić, & C-T. Yang (Eds.), *Systems factorial technology:*

A theory driven methodology for the identification of perceptual and cognitive mechanisms. Elsevier (in this book).

Altieri, N. (2017b). An introduction to the double factorial paradigm: How it can answer questions for multisensory researchers. In D. R. Little, N. Altieri, M. Fifić, & C-T. Yang (Eds.), *Systems factorial technology: A theory driven methodology for the identification of perceptual and cognitive mechanisms*. Elsevier (in this book).

Altieri, N., Pisoni, D. B., & Townsend, J. T. (2011). Behavioral, clinical, and neurobiological constraints on theories of audiovisual speech integration: A review and suggestions for new directions. *Seeing and Perceiving*, *24*, 513–539.

Altieri, N., Stevenson, R. A., Wallace, M. T., & Wenger, M. J. (2015). Learning to associate auditory and visual stimuli: Capacity and neural measures of efficiency. *Brain Topography*, *28*(3), 479–493.

Altieri, N., & Townsend, J. T. (2011). An assessment of behavioral dynamic information processing measures in audiovisual speech perception. *Frontiers in Psychology*, *2*(238), 1–15.

Altieri, N., & Wenger, M. (2013). Neural dynamics of audiovisual integration efficiency under variable listening conditions: an individual participant analysis. *Frontiers in Psychology*, *4*(615), 1–15.

Ashby, F. G., Maddox, W. T., & Lee, W. W. (1994). On the dangers of averaging across subjects when using multidimensional scaling or the similarity-choice model. *Psychological Science*, *5*(3), 144–151.

Bauer, R. M. (1986). The cognitive psychophysiology of prosopagnosia. In H. Ellis, M. Jeeves, F. Newcombe, & A. W. Young (Eds.), *Aspects of face processing* (pp. 253–267). Martinus Nijhoff.

Berryhill, M., Kveraga, K., Webb, L., & Hughes, H. C. (2007). Multimodal access to verbal name codes. *Perception & Psychophysics*, *69*(4), 628–640.

Blaha, L. (2017). An examination of task demands on the elicited processing capacity. In D. R. Little, N. Altieri, M. Fifić, & C-T. Yang (Eds.), *Systems factorial technology: A theory driven methodology for the identification of perceptual and cognitive mechanisms*. Elsevier (in this book).

Chang, T.-Y., & Yang, C.-T. (2014). Individual differences in Zhong–Yong tendency and processing capacity. *Frontiers in Psychology*, *5*.

Cheng, X. J., Moneer, S., Christie, N., & Little, D. R. (2017). An information processing perspective to understanding conflicting information. In D. R. Little, N. Altieri, M. Fifić, & C-T. Yang (Eds.), *Systems factorial technology: A theory driven methodology for the identification of perceptual and cognitive mechanisms*. Elsevier (in this book).

Colonius, H., & Townsend, J. T. (1997). Activation-state representation of models for the redundant-signals-effect. In A. A. J. Marley (Ed.), *Choice, decision and measurement*. Mahwah, NJ: Erlbaum Associates. Volume in honor of R. Duncan Luce.

Diederich, A. (1995). Intersensory facilitation of reaction time: Evaluation of counter and diffusion coactivation models. *Journal of Mathematical Psychology*, *39*(2), 197–215.

Diederich, A., & Colonius, H. (1991). A further test of the superposition model for redundant signals effect in bimodal detection. *Perception & Psychophysics*, *50*, 83–86.

Diederich, A., & Colonius, H. (2004). Bimodal and trimodal multisensory enhancement of reaction time: Effects of stimulus onset and intensity on reaction time. *Perception & Psychophysics*, *66*(8), 1388–1404.

Donders, F. C. (1969). Over de snelheid van psychische processes. Onderzoekingen gedann in het Physiologish Laboratorium der Utrechtsche Hoogeschool, 1868–1869, Tweede Reeks, II. In W. G. Koster (Ed.), *Attention and performance II* (pp. 92–120). Amsterdam: North-Holland. Reprinted from *Acta Psychologica*, *30* (1969) 412–431.

Dzhafarov, E. N. (2003). Selective influence through conditional independence. *Psychometrika, 68*, 7–26.

Eidels, A., Houpt, J., Altieri, N., Pei, L., & Townsend, J. T. (2011). Nice guys finish fast and bad guys finish last: A theory of interactive parallel processing. *Journal of Mathematical Psychology, 55*, 176–190.

Eidels, A., & Howard, Z. (2017). Relating systems factorial technology to other measures of human performance. In D. R. Little, N. Altieri, M. Fifić, & C-T. Yang (Eds.), *Systems factorial technology: A theory driven methodology for the identification of perceptual and cognitive mechanisms*. Elsevier (in this book).

Elandt-Johnson, R., & Johnson, N. (1999). *Survival models and data analysis*. New York: John Wiley & Sons.

Estes, W. K. (1956). The problem of inference from curves based on group data. *Psychological Bulletin, 53*(2), 134–140.

Fifić, M. (2014). Double jeopardy in inferring cognitive processes. *Frontiers in Psychology, 5*, 1130.

Fifić, M., & Little, D. R. (2017). Stretching mental processes: An overview of and guide for SFT applications. In D. R. Little, N. Altieri, M. Fifić, & C-T. Yang (Eds.), *Systems factorial technology: A theory driven methodology for the identification of perceptual and cognitive mechanisms*. Elsevier (in this book).

Fifić, M., Little, D. R., & Nosofsky, R. M. (2010). Logical-rule models of classification response times: A synthesis of mental-architecture, random-walk, and decision-bound approaches. *Psychological Review, 117*, 309–348.

Grice, G. R., Canham, L., & Gwynne, J. W. (1984). Absence of a redundant-signals effect in a reaction time task with divided attention. *Perception & Psychophysics, 36*, 565–570.

Griffiths, D. W., Blunden, A. G., & Little, D. R. (2017). Logical-rule based models of categorization: Using systems factorial technology to understand feature and dimensional processing. In D. R. Little, N. Altieri, M. Fifić, & C-T. Yang (Eds.), *Systems factorial technology: A theory driven methodology for the identification of perceptual and cognitive mechanisms*. Elsevier (in this book).

Harding, B., Goulet, M-A., LeBlanc, V., Trembley, C., & Cousineau, D. (2017). Applying systems factorial technology to discrete accumulators with varying thresholds. In D. R. Little, N. Altieri, M. Fifić, & C-T. Yang (Eds.), *Systems factorial technology: A theory driven methodology for the identification of perceptual and cognitive mechanisms*. Elsevier (in this book).

He, Y., Lentz, J. J., & Townsend, J. T. (2017). Are two ears always better than one? The capacity function says no. In D. R. Little, N. Altieri, M. Fifić, & C-T. Yang (Eds.), *Systems factorial technology: A theory driven methodology for the identification of perceptual and cognitive mechanisms*. Elsevier (in this book).

Heathcote, A., Brown, S., Wagenmakers, E. J., & Eidels, A. (2010). Distribution-free tests of stochastic dominance for small samples. *Journal of Mathematical Psychology, 54*(5), 454–463.

Helmholtz, H. (1850). Vorläufiger Bericht über die Fortpflanzungsgeschwindigkeit der Nerventhätigkeit. Archive of the Berlin Brandenburgische Akademie der Wissenschaften.

Houpt, J. W., & Blaha, L. M. (Eds.). (2016). *Mathematical models of perception and cognition: A Festschrift for James T. Townsend (Vols. 1, 2)*. Psychology Press.

Houpt, J. W., Blaha, L. M., McIntire, J. P., Havig, P. R., & Townsend, J. T. (2014). Systems factorial technology with R. *Behavior Research Methods, 46*(2), 307–330.

Houpt, J. W., & Burns, D. (2017). Statistical analyses for systems factorial technology. In D. R. Little, N. Altieri, M. Fifić, & C-T. Yang (Eds.), *Systems factorial technology: A theory driven methodology for the identification of perceptual and cognitive mechanisms*. Elsevier (in this book).

Houpt, J., Pei, L., Eidels, A., Altieri, N., Fifić, M., & Townsend, J.T. (2008). *An exploration of parallel-interactive information processing models*. Paper presented at the 41st Annual Meeting of the Society for Mathematical Psychology, Washington D.C.

Houpt, J. W., & Townsend, J. T. (2010). The statistical properties of the survivor interaction contrast. *Journal of Mathematical Psychology*, *54*, 446–453.

Houpt, J. W., & Townsend, J. T. (2011). An extension of SIC predictions to the Wiener coactive model. *Journal of Mathematical Psychology*, *55*(3), 267–270.

Houpt, J. W., Townsend, J. T., & Donkin, C. (2014). A new perspective on visual word processing efficiency. *Acta Psychologica*, *145*, 118–127.

Howe, P. D. L., & Ferguson, A. (2017). The identity-location binding problem. In D. R. Little, N. Altieri, M. Fifić, & C-T. Yang (Eds.), *Systems factorial technology: A theory driven methodology for the identification of perceptual and cognitive mechanisms*. Elsevier (in this book).

Jensen, A. R. (2006). *Clocking the mind: Mental chronometry and individual differences*. Elsevier.

Little, D. R. (2012). Numerical predictions for serial, parallel, and coactive logical rule-based models of categorization response time. *Behavior Research Methods*, *44*(4), 1148–1156.

Luce, R. D. (1986). *Response times: Their role in inferring elementary mental organization*. New York: Oxford University Press.

Marrot, G., Brochet, F., & Dubourdieu, D. (2001). The color of odors. *Brain and Language*, *79*, 309–320.

McGurk, H., & MacDonald, J. W. (1976). Hearing lips and seeing voices. *Nature*, *264*, 746–748.

Miller, J. (1982). Divided attention: Evidence for coactivation with redundant signals. *Cognitive Psychology*, *14*, 247–279.

Miller, J. (1986). Time course of coactivation in bimodal divided attention. *Perception & Psychophysics*, *40*(5), 331–343.

Miller, J. (1991). Channel interaction and the redundant-targets effect in bimodal divided attention. *Journal of Experimental Psychology: Human Perception and Performance*, *17*, 60–169.

Miller, J., & Ulrich, R. (2003). Simple reaction time and statistical facilitation: A parallel grains model. *Cognitive Psychology*, *46*, 101–151.

Mordkoff, J. T., & Yantis, S. (1991). An interactive race model of divided attention. *Journal of Experimental Psychology. Human Perception and Performance*, *17*(2), 520–538.

Neufeld, R. W. J., Townsend, J. T., & Jetté, J. (2007). Quantitative response time technology for measuring cognitive-processing capacity in clinical studies. In R. W. J. Neufeld (Ed.), *Advances in clinical cognitive science: Formal modeling and assessment of processes and symptoms*. Washington, D.C.: American Psychological Association.

Parzen, E. (1962). On estimation of a probability density function and models. *The Annals of Mathematical Statistics*, 1065–1076.

Robinson, D. K. (2001). Reaction time experiments in Wundt's institute and beyond. In R. W. Rieber, & D. K. Robinson (Eds.), *Wilhelm Wundt in history: The making of scientific psychology* (pp. 161–204). New York: Kluwer/Plenum.

Schwarz, W. (1989). A new model to explain the redundant-signals effect. *Perception & Psychophysics*, *46*, 498–500.

Schwarz, W. (1994). Diffusion, superposition, and the redundant targets effect. *Journal of Mathematical Psychology*, *38*, 504–520.

Schweickert, R. (1978). A critical path generalization of the additive factor method: Analysis of a Stroop task. *Journal of Mathematical Psychology*, *18*, 105–139.

Schweickert, R., Fisher, D. L., & Sung, K. (2012). *Discovering cognitive architecture by selectively influencing mental processes*, *Vol. 4*. World Scientific.

Schweickert, R., & Townsend, J. T. (1989). A trichotomy method: Interactions of factors prolonging sequential and concurrent mental processes in stochastic PERT networks. *Journal of Mathematical Psychology*, *33*, 328–347.

Sternberg, S. (1966). High speed scanning in human memory. *Science*, *153*, 652–654.

Sternberg, S. (1969). Memory-scanning: Mental processes revealed by reaction-time experiments. *American Scientist*, *57*, 421–457.

Stevenson, R. A., & James, T. W. (2009). Neuronal convergence and inverse effectiveness with audiovisual integration of speech and tools in human superior temporal sulcus: Evidence from BOLD fMRI. *NeuroImage*, *44*, 1210–1223.

Taylor, R., Theberge, J., Williamson, P., Densmore, M., & Neufeld, R. W. J. (2017). Using SFT to elucidate the “f” of clinical fMRS (functional magnetic resonance, spectroscopy). In D. R. Little, N. Altieri, M. Fifić, & C-T. Yang (Eds.), *Systems factorial technology: A theory driven methodology for the identification of perceptual and cognitive mechanisms*. Elsevier (in this book).

Townsend, J. T. (1972). Some results concerning the identifiability of parallel and serial processes. *British Journal of Mathematical and Statistical Psychology*, *25*(2), 168–199.

Townsend, J. T. (1990a). Serial vs. parallel processing: Sometimes they look like Tweedledum and Tweedledee but they can (and should) be distinguished. *Psychological Science*, *1*, 46–54.

Townsend, J. T. (1990b). Truth and consequences of ordinal differences in statistical distributions: Toward a theory of hierarchical inference. *Psychological Bulletin*, *108*(3), 551–567.

Townsend, J. T., & Ashby, F. G. (1983). *The stochastic modeling of elementary psychological processes*. Cambridge: Cambridge University Press.

Townsend, J. T., & Eidels, A. (2011). Workload capacity spaces: A unified methodology for response times. *Psychonomic Bulletin & Review*, *18*, 659–681.

Townsend, J. T., & Fifić, M. (2004). Parallel & serial processing and individual differences in high-speed scanning in human memory. *Perception & Psychophysics*, *66*, 953–962.

Townsend, J. T., & Liu, Y. (2017). Selective influence and categorical separability (perceptual separability) in perception and cognition: Similarities and distinctions. In D. R. Little, N. Altieri, M. Fifić, & C-T. Yang (Eds.), *Systems factorial technology: A theory driven methodology for the identification of perceptual and cognitive mechanisms*. Elsevier (in this book).

Townsend, J. T., & Nozawa, G. (1995). Spatio-temporal properties of elementary perception: An investigation of parallel, serial, and coactive theories. *Journal of Mathematical Psychology*, *39*(4), 321–359.

Townsend, J. T., & Schweickert, R. (1989). Toward the trichotomy method: Laying the foundation of stochastic mental networks. *Journal of Mathematical Psychology*, *33*, 309–327.

Townsend, J. T., & Wenger, M. J. (2004a). The serial-parallel dilemma: A case study in a linkage of theory and method. *Psychonomic Bulletin & Review*, *11*, 391–418.

Townsend, J. T., & Wenger, M. J. (2004b). A theory of interactive parallel processing: New capacity measures and predictions for a response time inequality series. *Psychological Review*, *111*(4), 1003–1035.

Van Zandt, T. (2000). How to fit a response time distribution. *Psychonomic Bulletin & Review*, *7*(3), 424–465.

Van Zandt, T., & Townsend, J. T. (2012). Designs for and analyses of response time experiments. In T. K. Little (Ed.), *The Oxford handbook of quantitative methods*. New York: Oxford University Press.

Wenger, M. J., Ingvalson, E. M., & Rhoten, S. E. (2017). The evolution of systems factorial theory and evolving conceptions of configurality. In D. R. Little, N. Altieri, M. Fifić, & C-T. Yang (Eds.), *Systems factorial technology: A theory driven methodology for the identification of perceptual and cognitive mechanisms*. Elsevier (in this book).

Wenger, M. J., & Townsend, J. T. (2000). Basic response time tools for studying general processing capacity in attention, perception, and cognition. *The Journal of General Psychology, 127*(1), 67–99.

Wenger, M. J., & Townsend, J. T. (2001). Faces as gestalt stimuli: Process characteristics. In M. J. Wenger, & J. T. Townsend (Eds.), *Computational, geometric and process perspectives on facial cognition: Contexts and challenges* (pp. 229–284). Mahwah, NJ: Lawrence Erlbaum Associates.

Wenger, M. J., & Townsend, J. T. (2006). On the costs and benefits of faces and words: Process characteristics of feature search in highly meaningful stimuli. *Journal of Experimental Psychology. Human Perception and Performance, 45*, 283–323.

Yang, C.-T. (2011). Relative saliency in change signals affects perceptual comparison and decision processes in change detection. *Journal of Experimental Psychology. Human Perception and Performance, 37*(6), 1708–1728.

Yang, C-T. (2017). Attention and perceptual decision making. In D. R. Little, N. Altieri, M. Fifić, & C-T. Yang (Eds.), *Systems factorial technology: A theory driven methodology for the identification of perceptual and cognitive mechanisms*. Elsevier (in this book).

Yang, C.-T., Chang, T.-Y., & Wu, C.-J. (2013). Relative change probability affects the decision process of detecting multiple feature changes. *Journal of Experimental Psychology. Human Perception and Performance, 39*(5), 1365–1385.

Yang, H., Fifić, M., & Townsend, J. T. (2014). Survivor interaction contrast wiggle predictions of parallel and serial models for an arbitrary number of processes. *Journal of Mathematical Psychology, 58*, 21–32.

Yu, J.-C., Chang, T.-Y., & Yang, C.-T. (2014). Individual differences in working memory capacity and workload capacity. *Frontiers in Psychology, 5*.

Endnotes

1. To use just one of many possible examples, tasting wine involves the integration of visual with olfactory cues. Interestingly, simply adding red food coloring to white wine has caused it to be described as a red wine by a panel of experts (Marrot, Brochet, & Dubourdieu, 2001).
2. For further information on historical precedents in this field, we refer the reader to excellent reviews by Algom, Eidels, Hawkins, Jefferson, and Townsend (2015).
3. In this chapter, we use the term *channel* to refer to a sensory, cognitive, or psychological process directed toward a specific stimulus element or goal.

Stretching Mental Processes: An Overview of and Guide for SFT Applications

2

Mario Fifić, Daniel R. Little*[†]
*Grand Valley State University, Allendale, MI, United States, [†]The University of Melbourne, Melbourne, VIC, Australia

Scientific work on decoding cognitive system operations is analogous to reverse engineering. Reverse engineering in software development and electrical circuits design is not strictly focused on learning the exact blueprint of the device, but rather the goal is to design a surrogate device that shows input–output behavior resembling the original. A famous example is the reverse engineering of the original IBM-PC BIOS code that resulted in creation of a completely different code but with operation identical to the original (e.g., Schwarz, 2001). By contrast, the main goal of modeling in cognitive psychology is to learn the exact blueprint of the cognitive system.

To learn a system's blueprint, both cognitive scientists and engineers resort to the analysis of the relationship between inputs and outputs of the system of interest. This procedure is based on probing the system with different input values and observing the system's responses. Unlike engineers, cognitive scientists face a complex problem: even when there is a fixed input to system, the output is stochastic. Thus, the analysis of cognitive activities requires unique tools that can deal with the output variability.

As discussed in the tutorial chapter (Altieri, Fifić, Little, & Yang, 2017), cognitive activities can be organized according to a *mental architecture*, a systematically organized set of mental operations, which entails the fundamental properties of: *processing order* (e.g., serial vs parallel), *stopping rule* (e.g., self-terminating vs exhaustive), *process interdependency* (e.g., independence vs dependence), and *processing capacity* (e.g., limited, unlimited, or super-capacity).

For example, to provide evidence about whether processing order is serial or parallel, one must probe the system with inputs such that only the processing order is affected. To ensure that the output will provide meaningful interpretation, two key elements are required: First, the assumption of selective influence, which states that varying the values of an external variable, X, should affect only one mental process in the mental architecture. There is no *a priori* way to test the selective influence assumption; however, it is possible to test the resulting output of the system for possible violations of the assumption. (See Townsend, Liu & Zhang, 2017 for more details on selective influence.) Second, the adoption of the factorial design ensures that specific input probes can be generated. Selective influence is important, but it is not sufficient to uncover the true blueprint of the system. To uncover underlying mental architectures consisting of the number of processes, n, it is necessary to use the n input probes, one for each of the processes of interest. The factorial design allows one to input all of the

Systems Factorial Technology, DOI: 10.1016/B978-0-12-804315-8.00003-3

probes at the same time and examine the output as a function of lengthening different combinations of processes.

In this chapter, we will present a general framework for understanding the methodological manipulations required for using SFT. We will then review four different SFT applications. These include: (i) visual detection (Townsend & Nozawa, 1995), (ii) the Stroop effect (Eidels, Townsend, & Algom, 2010), (iii) categorization (Fifić, Little, & Nosofsky, 2010; Little, Nosofsky, & Denton, 2011), and (iv) memory search (Townsend & Fifić, 2004). To provide better insights into creating an SFT factorial design, these four studies will be compared at the conceptual level of the fundamental organization of processes. Additionally, the tutorial provides basic instructions on applying SFT to an original study design.

Factorial Design: The Reverse Engineering Tool in Cognitive Psychology

A factorial design is obtained by cross-combining of all the factors' values. Fig. 2.1 displays a two-factorial design in which each factor is represented by a single dimension. The factors form a Cartesian coordinate system (i.e., all combinations of each level of each dimension). In Fig. 2.1, the first dimension is the variable that is assumed to affect the speed of processing of process one. The second dimension is the variable that is assumed to affect speed of processing of process two. Each factor in Fig. 2.1 has two values defined as an external manipulation that either slows down (value of Low) or speeds up (value of High) the processing of each stimulus.

How does the factorial research design aid the discovery of underlying mental structures?

The factorial design provides two tests:

1. *Main effects* or *existence test*. This test provides information as to whether or not a variable had an impact on the mental architecture under investigation. In the example in Fig. 2.1, the main effect of dimension one is achieved by marginalization of dimension two and the comparison of the resulting marginal values of processing speed. If a difference is found, then one can conclude that the manipulation of that dimension affected the process of interest. However, main effects have limited diagnostic power as their analysis cannot provide any interesting information about the fundamental properties (processing order, stopping rule, or interdependency).
2. *Interaction effect* or *coexistence test*. Whereas the main effect focuses on one variable at a time, the interaction test analyzes the relationship between both (or several) variables. When applied to the appropriate dependent variable (e.g., the estimated survivor function), the fundamental properties can be successfully diagnosed by the presence of different types of interactions.

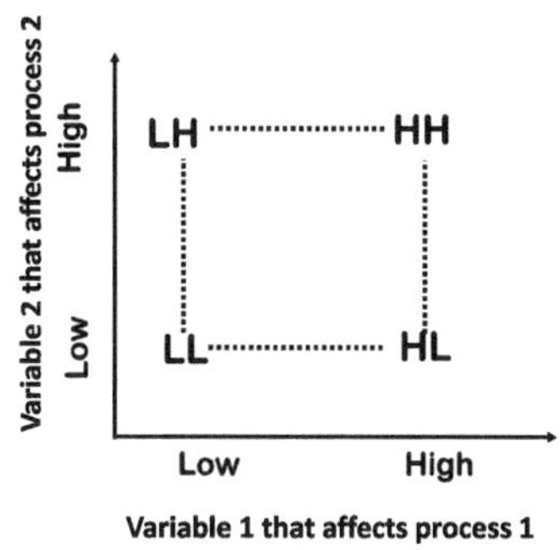

Figure 2.1 A 2 × 2 factorial design: Variable 1 (Low, High) × Variable 2 (Low, High). Variable values are orthogonally combined, resulting in the four experimental conditions. The letter position indicates variable (first and second), and the letter L = Low, H = High.

Probing the Processes: Stretching and Inserting

Manipulating each of the input factors serves to probe an unknown system in order to reverse engineer that system. Electrical engineers perform reverse engineering by sending a weak electrical current through the system and observing the response in the output circuit. Similarly, cognitive scientists present an input stimulus and observe the human response. For these stimulus inputs, the dimensions (and their levels) are selected to affect the duration of mental processing. We will denote the unknown process with a capital letter X. The experimental manipulation (probe) is denoted with small letter x. The effect of manipulation x on the process X is designed to selectively slow down or speed up the process X and is denoted as *stretching*. In practice, such an experimental factor could be, for example, the brightness or contrast of a target varied in two levels during a detection task. Lower levels of brightness will lead to a slower detection (i.e., in the context of a darker background) while higher levels of brightness will lead to faster detection.

The stretching effect is defined as the two-state output difference: probing a system with a low input value x_{low} and then with high input value x_{high} should lead to the output difference measured as response time (*RT*): $RTx_{low} - RTx_{high}$. The stretching effect is the difference in the *RT*s that a system takes to process the information at the Low versus High levels. To be able to deal with the inherent output variability, the stretching effect of process X is defined as a first-order difference Δ on expected processing time of the process X (see also Townsend and Thomas, 1994; Fifić, 2017)

$$\Delta E[t_X; x] = E[t_X; x_{low}] - E[t_X; x_{high}] > 0. \quad (2.1)$$

Selective influence operates at the level of mean *RT*s and is satisfied if the order of expected response time holds, $E[t_X; x_{low}] > E[t_X; x_{high}]$. The unbiased estimator of the true population's expected response times is a simple mean response time value. Thus the inequality could be rewritten in a simpler form as $RT_{low} > RT_{high}$.

Stretching of Two Factors and Additivity

Testing for factorial interactions employs the mean interaction contrast (*MIC*) which has its origins in the analysis of variance (ANOVA). To calculate the *MIC* for the two processes, the second-order difference Δ^2 is derived for two variables, (x, y), each belonging to distinct process X and Y, respectively, within an unknown mental network:

$$\begin{aligned}\Delta^2 E[t_X, t_Y; x, y] = &\big(E[t_X, t_Y; x_{low}, y_{low}] - E[t_X, t_Y; x_{low}, y_{high}]\big)\\ &- \big(E[t_X, t_Y; x_{high}, y_{low}] - E[t_X, t_Y; x_{high}, y_{high}]\big). \qquad (2.2)\end{aligned}$$

Each term in (2.2) represents the expected response time for two joint processes t_X and t_Y combined within the same mental architecture. The stretching manipulation for each process is manipulated at the low and high level so, for example, the notation (x_{low}, y_{high}) represents an experimental condition in which process X is stretched at the low level and process Y at the high level. The above equation could be written in the form of mean response times for each condition (Altieri et al., 2017, Chapter 1) as

$$\begin{aligned}MIC &= (RT_{\mathrm{LL}} - RT_{\mathrm{LH}}) - (RT_{\mathrm{HL}} - RT_{\mathrm{HH}})\\ &= RT_{\mathrm{LL}} - RT_{\mathrm{LH}} - RT_{\mathrm{HL}} + RT_{\mathrm{HH}}. \qquad (2.3)\end{aligned}$$

Factorial additivity is revealed when the second order difference is zero, overadditivity is indicted by the positive value, and underadditivity by the negative value. As discussed in the tutorial chapter (Altieri et al., 2017), in addition to this mean level contrast, SFT provides a stronger statistic using survivor functions. Both the *MIC* and *SIC* statistics provide sufficient information to explore the fundamental properties of the two mental process.

Implementing Systems Factorial Technology

For novices in using SFT technology, one of the main concerns is how to implement the methodology in an examined cognitive task. In the following, we describe three important steps to implementing SFT. These steps include:

1. Defining a processing model of interest with respect to its fundamental properties: processing order, stopping rule, and process interdependency, and identifying the processes within the model that will be explored.[1]
2. Stretching the durations of the processes by using new external variables that selectively affect the processes of interest.
3. Collecting multiple trials *RT* data, analyzing the corresponding response distributions, and interpreting the results using the inference tools provided from SFT, and then using the inferences either to falsify or to validate the candidate models.

Step 1. Modeling and identification of mental processes

In the first step, we will review the process of identification of mental processes within proposed cognitive models and identify the fundamental components of the competing cognitive models that could be validated by SFT. To facilitate this overview, we will briefly summarize some of the applications which are reviewed in this volume but at a broad general level.

Stimulus Detection and Redundant Target Task

As discussed in the tutorial chapter (Altieri et al., 2017), SFT was initially applied to the question of stimulus detection (see also Townsend & Nozawa, 1995). In the task either one or two dots are displayed in either the left or right visual field. The task is to detect any dot and make a decision by pressing a response button.

Research Design

The original study had three factors, showed in white boxes in Fig. 2.2A. The factor of target presence indicates whether a target dot was presented or not in a display (Yes or No). The target absent conditions are indicated by the empty box; the factor of number of targets indicates how many target stimuli were presented in the display (1, 2, or none-empty box); The factor of target position indicates whether a target was presented in the left (L) or right (R) visual field, and in the two-target conditions both positions were used (two boxes joined by a frame). Conceptually, what SFT adds to the original study is represented in Fig. 2.2A using the shaded boxes. The factor of target brightness was manipulated at the low (L) and high (H) brightness levels. The magnitude of the targets brightness is carefully selected so that its manipulation either slows down or speeds up the rate of processing of each processing unit (i.e., the left or right dot). The diagnostic SFT conditions, HH, HL, LH, and LL, are displayed at the very bottom of the factorial tree (numbered as 5, 6, 7, and 8). These conditions are all target-present conditions with two dots. Each dot is manipulated at the high and low level of brightness and factorially combined with the brightness level of the other simultaneously presented dot. The four conditions are also displayed in Fig. 2.2B, which is another view of the factorial tree in Fig. 2.2A, obtained by renaming some of the variables from the panel A. Panel B shows the two orthogonal dimension variables, the brightness of a target dot in the left and right locations. The two dimensions in panels B and C combine information about the target dot position, target dot brightness, and the number of target dots within the full factorial design. Panel C shows the actual study trials, defined in the panel B.

It is important to note that although the stimulus conditions (1, 2, 3, and 4) are factorially combined with the target brightness level, they do not permit the SFT analysis, since only one target dot is presented in a display. Nonetheless, these conditions can be used to conduct the additional contrast test that could be used to validate the SFT analyses, as will be described later (e.g., Fifić et al., 2010).

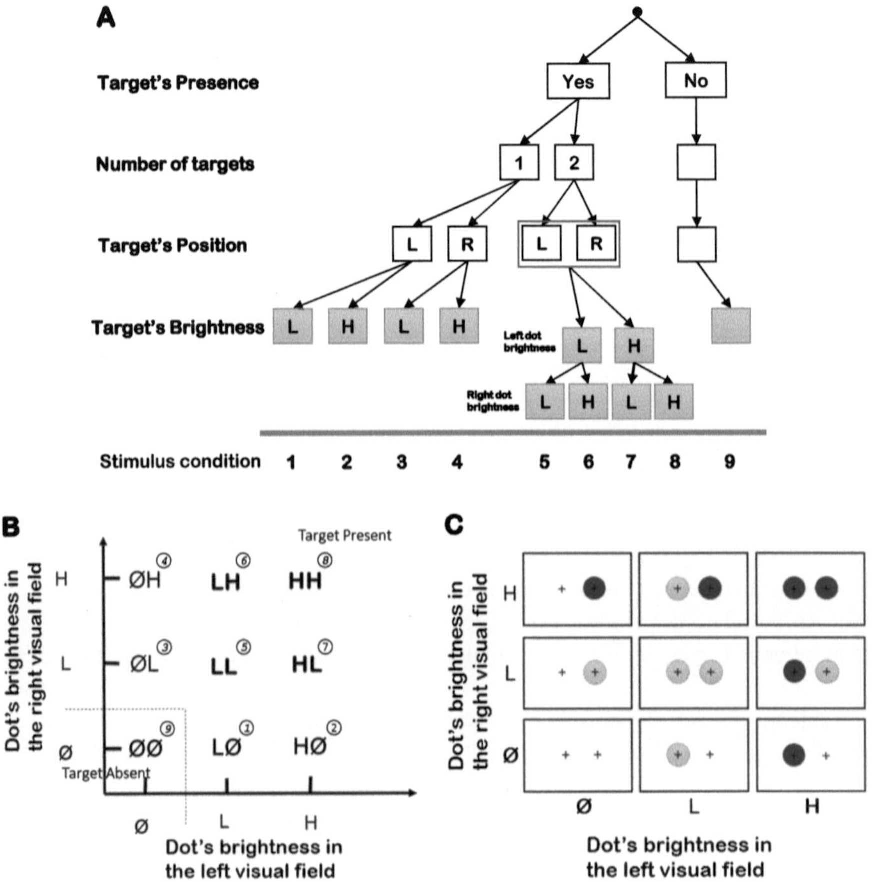

Figure 2.2 Stimulus detection in the redundant target task. (A) The factorial tree represents the factors on left and the factor levels in boxes on right. The white boxes indicate the original study factorial design prior to the SFT modification. The shaded boxes indicate the added conditions after SFT process stretching has been applied. The double-factorial conditions are shown at the tree's bottom, in the form of another two-branch factorial tree made of two factors (left and right dot brightness). (B) The corresponding stimulus configuration space is defined by the two continuous dimensions: brightness of a target at either left or right stimulus fields. Empty set symbol ∅ indicates the absence of the stimulus intensity. The double-factorial design is presented in the upper right corner (HH, HL, LH, and LL). The piecewise linear function separates the two response mapping regions: target present – which uses a disjoint rule (OR) to classify stimuli, and target absent – which uses a conjoint stimulus classification rule (AND). The encircled numbers indicate the stimulus conditions denoted in the factorial tree panel A, bottom line. (C) Actual stimulus condition realizations of the configuration presented in panel B.

Defining a Model

The typical finding in this task is that detection time decreases as the number of targets increases. Using a parallel processing model, several alternative explanations have been offered for this result. According to the first, *RT* decreases due to so-called statistical facilitation (Todd, 1912; Grice, Canham, & Boroughs, 1984;

Diederich & Colonius, 1987). As the number of possible target increases, the response time decreases as the probability to detect any target item increases. This is a statistical effect for systems characterized as parallel self-terminating mental architectures. The alternative explanation is based on the idea that detection of a single target depends on detection of other targets. According to this approach, there is facilitatory effect between target detectors within a parallel architecture. One version of that model is the coactive model (Miller, 1982; Townsend & Nozawa, 1995; Colonius, 1990). This particular coactive architecture is probably best described as a parallel facilitatory system, meaning that the stopping rule is not terminating, but rather the system "pools" the evidence coming from separate channels into one channel.

The most important distinction between the two approaches is focused on the role of the fundamental properties of process interdependence. The coactive model assumes that the processes of interest are interdependent while the statistical summation model assumes that the processes are independent. The statistical facilitation model which assumes a parallel race has a strictly positive *SIC* function. The coactive model assumes parallel interdependent processes and has an S-shaped *SIC* function (with a smaller negative part then positive part). The use of this task in the study of attention is discussed by Yang (2017; this book).

The Stroop Task

The Stroop effect demonstrates the inability of humans to selectively attend to one source of information, while trying to ignore a second source of information (Stroop, 1935; also reviewed in more detail in this chapter Algom, Fitousi, & Eidels, 2017). A focused attention task is used to demonstrate the Stroop effect: subjects were asked to respond as to whether a word stimulus is displayed in, e.g., red and to ignore other sources of information such as word meaning or the presence of other colors than red. The Stroop effect is operationalized as a performance decrement for an incongruent condition ("Green" word in red color) compared to a congruent condition ("Red" word in red color). In a dividend attention version of the Stroop task (Eidels et al. 2010) a word is displayed, and the subject is asked to detect whether the word contains any information about a target color either in the word or the color of the font. The question in both tasks is how the information, from each source, word and color, is combined to make a decision?

Research Design

The study used in Eidels et al. (2010) had three factors represented in the white boxes of Fig. 2.3A. The factor of target presence indicates whether the red information was presented or not (Red or No Red). There are two targets of different modality: red as a color or red as a word. The target-absent conditions in which no red information is present are indicated by the empty box. The factor of number of targets indicates how many target stimuli were presented in the display (color red and/or word "Red"). The target modality indicates whether the target was color Red or a word "Red", while in the two-target conditions both modalities were used (two boxes joined by a frame).

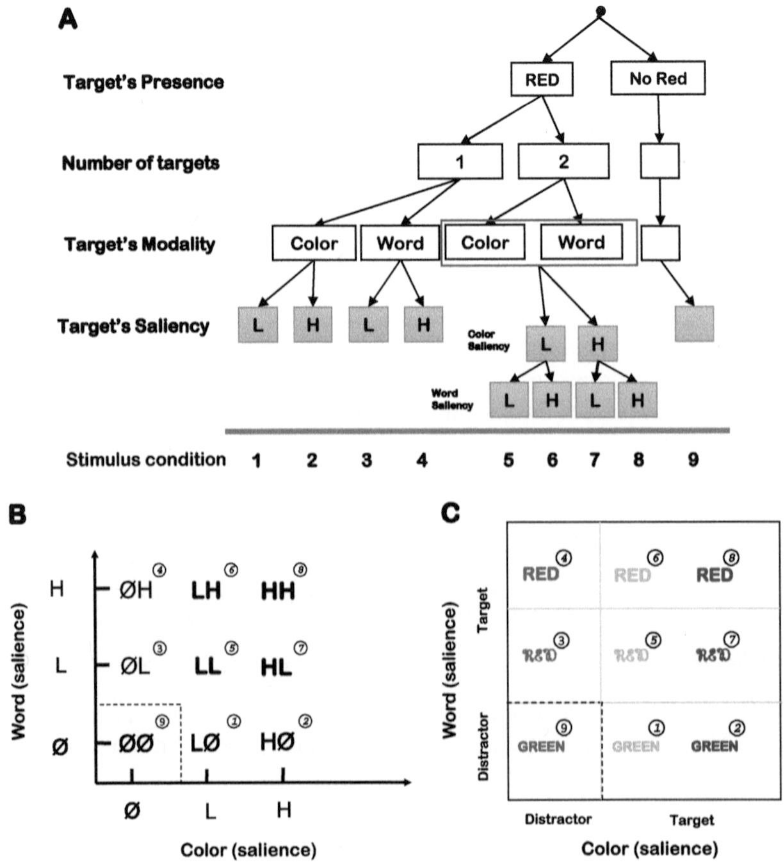

Figure 2.3 The Stroop task. (A) The factorial tree represents the factors on left and the factor levels in boxes on right. The white boxes indicate the original study factorial design prior to the SFT modification. The shaded boxes indicate the added conditions after SFT process stretching has been applied. The double-factorial conditions are shown at the tree's bottom as a two-branch factorial tree made of two factors (Color and Word saliency). (B) The corresponding stimulus configuration space is defined by the two continuous dimensions: Color saliency and Word saliency. The symbol ∅ indicates the absence of the saliency magnitude. The "∅∅" condition has the zero value of redness and the zero value of alphanumeric "Red" to indicate meaning of red. The double-factorial design is presented in the upper left corner (HH, HL, LH, and LL). The piecewise linear function separates the two response mapping regions: target present – which uses a disjoint rule (OR) to classify stimuli, and target absent – which uses a conjoint stimulus classification rule (AND). The OR region is defined by presence of any of the targets indicating "Red", while the AND region is defined by the absence of all targets indicating "Red" (a word "Green" displayed in green color). The encircled numbers indicate the stimulus conditions denoted in the factorial tree panel A, bottom line. (C) Actual stimulus condition realizations of the configuration presented in panel B.

The SFT addition to the original study is showed in Fig. 2.3A, as the shaded boxes. The factor of target saliency was factorially manipulated and defined as either low (L) and high (H) saliency depending on the level of the manipulation. The magnitude of the saliency manipulation (the stretching effect) is carefully selected so that it either slows down or speeds up the rate of processing of each target modality: either the readability of the words' letters or the magnitude of the red color saturation. Readability was manipulated by using fonts which allowed for either faster or slower word recognition. Color identification was achieved by manipulating the amount of color saturation. The double factorial conditions (HH, HL, LH, and LL) are displayed at the very bottom of the factorial tree – these are achieved by factorial combination of the word and color saliency – and are numbered as the 5, 6, 7, and 8 conditions. The four conditions are also displayed in Fig. 2.3B, which is obtained by collapsing and combining of some factors from the factorial tree in panel A. Panel B uses the two continuous orthogonal dimension variables, the color and word saliency that combine information about target presence, number of targets, target modality, and target's saliency, within a fully factorial design. The experimental condition values (1–9) shown in panel A, are also displayed in panel B. The panel C shows the actual trials, defined in the panel B.

Defining a Model

There is shared agreement between many researchers that the Stroop effect is due to some form of antagonistic competition between processes analyzing the color and word information (e.g., Cohen, Dunbar, & McClelland, 1990; Logan, 1980; MacLeod & Dunbar, 1988; Phaf, Van der Heijden, & Hudson, 1990; Roelofs, 2003; Virzi & Egeth, 1985; Zhang, Zhang, & Kornblum, 1999). An overview of the literature reveals a general consensus that the organization of mental processes underlying the Stroop effect conforms to an interactive parallel architecture.

One alternative approach proposes that the parallel minimum time race model architecture can account for the Stroop effect (Algom, Dekel, & Pansky, 1996; Dishon-Berkovits & Algom, 2000; Melara & Algom, 2003; Melara & Mounts, 1993; Sabri, Melara, & Algom, 2001; Eidels et al., 2010). In contrast to the class of models adopted by the first approach, the proposal is that the processes analyzing sources of information (color and words) are independent.

Without belaboring the details, it is clear that the most important distinction between the two approaches is focused on the role of the fundamental properties of process interdependence. Both approaches assume that the color and word meaning are organized in parallel. The difference is that the first approach assumes that the two processes inhibit each other while the second approach assumes that the two processes are independent. When both models are tested at the level of the mean *RT*, the analysis is inconclusive since both models predict slower mean *RT*s for the incongruent condition then for the congruent condition.

The two models can be distinguished at the *RT*-distribution level using the *SIC*. The parallel interactive model predicts an S-shaped *SIC* function with smaller negative part then positive part; by contrast, the parallel race model predicts a strictly positive *SIC* function (Townsend & Nozawa, 1995). Further contrasting evidence can be found by measuring the capacity coefficient (see Eidels, Houpt, Altieri, Pei, & Townsend, 2011). Further details about this task are discussed in Algom et al. (2017; this book).

Categorization – Rule Based vs Exemplar Based Processing

According to the exemplar-based models (Hintzman, 1986; Medin & Schaffer, 1978; Nosofsky, 1986), people form categories by storing individual exemplars in memory, while a decision process is based on similarity comparisons between target-items and stored exemplars. For example, an exemplar-based model represents categories *elephant* and *mouse* by storing all previously acquired exemplars that belong to these categories along with a category label. When a new animal is presented, it is compared to all exemplars belonging to the elephant category and mouse category. Finally, a decision whether the displayed animal is an elephant or a mouse is made based on the overall summed similarity of the displayed animal to each category.

An alternative to the similarity-based exemplar model is the idea that people use rules in order to classify objects. One rule-based approach assumes that people use decision boundaries for dividing a multidimensional psychological space into category-response regions (see, e.g., Ashby & Gott, 1988; Ashby & Lee, 1991; Ashby & Maddox, 1990; Ashby & Perrin, 1988). An observer can make independent decisions regarding a stimulus's value along each of its multiple dimensions and then combine these separate decisions to reach the final classification response. Take, for example, classification between mice and elephants based on two rules: an animal could be categorized as a mouse if its weight is less than 1 pound and its whiskers are longer than one inch; or it could be categorized as an elephant if its weight is greater than 1 pound and whiskers are shorter than one inch.

Research Design

Fifić et al. (2010) examined rule-based processing using a stimulus set which varied on three factors now instantiated using cartoon lamps rather than mice and elephants (see the white boxes, Fig. 2.4A). The factor of stimulus category indicates the stimulus category membership (category A or B) determined by the two properties: the width of the lamp base and the curvature of the lamp top. The factor of target type indicates the lamp features that could be used to correctly classify a lamp into category B. These features are termed the target features and can be used to uniquely identify the category B membership. For instance, to classify B category lamps, one can specify a criterion for each target feature against which each observed target features can be compared. The category B lamps have at least one target feature with a value lower than the criterion value for that feature. For example, in Fig. 2.4C the three leftmost vertical lamps all have the least curved top element (x_1) of all the lamps ($x_1 < x_2 < x_3$). All three leftmost lamps could be easily classified as B by using a simple disjoint classification rule: compare x value to the criterion value (represented as a vertical dotted line), and if it less than the criterion, classify the lamp as B.

Depending on the type of the target feature, the three conditions are possible in which the top, base, or both features can be used for successful classification of a B member. The distractor features cannot be used to correctly categorize a B category lamp. These features are shared between A and B category members. In the category A, both lamp features are denoted as distractors so they can't be use to classify the category B membership when considered in isolation. If both features present in

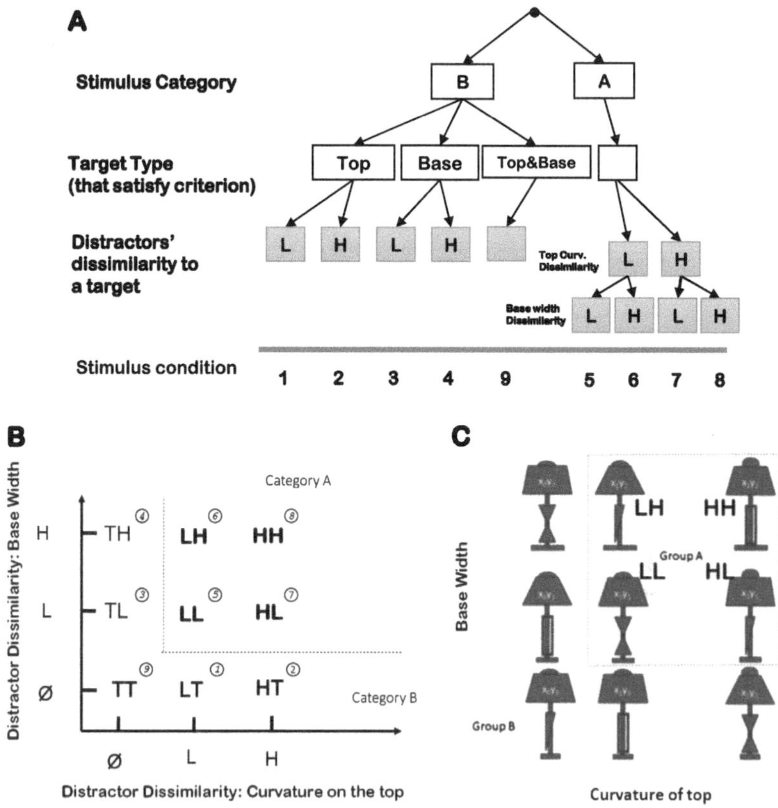

Figure 2.4 The categorization task – rule based vs exemplar based processing. (A) The factorial tree represents the factors on left and the factor levels in boxes on right. The white boxes indicate the original study factorial design prior to the SFT modification. The shaded boxes indicate the added conditions after SFT process stretching has been applied. The double-factorial conditions are shown at the tree's bottom as another two-branch factorial tree made of two factors (distractor dissimilarity of the curvature on the top, and distractor dissimilarity of the base width). (B) The corresponding stimulus configuration space is defined by the two continuous dimensions: distractor dissimilarity of the curvature on the top, and distractor dissimilarity of the base width. The "TT" condition is the so-called stimulus redundant condition in which each of the both distinctive features available could be used to make B category classification. The distractor features are denoted as L and H as they are stretched across both dimensions. If a distractor feature is close to the linear decision bound (or an opposing category group member) this is defined as Low stretching effect. If a distractor feature is more distant, then this is defined as the High stretching effect. The double-factorial design is presented in the upper right corner (HH, HL, LH, and LL). The piecewise linear function separates the two response mapping regions: target present – which uses a disjoint rule (OR) to classify stimuli, and target absent – which uses a conjoint stimulus classification rule (AND). The encircled numbers indicate the stimulus conditions denoted in the factorial tree panel A, bottom line. (C) Actual stimulus condition realizations of the configuration presented in panel B.

the lamp are distractors, then the lamp must be a member of A category (empty white box), which could be described as the conjoint rule that must be satisfied to make a correct classification of A lamp: check the values of each lamps feature and if both values are larger than their respective criteria values, then classify the lamp as A.

The third factor is related to the properties of the distractor feature. The factor of distractor dissimilarity indicates to what extent the distractor feature is similar to the nearest opposing category stimulus. The factor of distractor dissimilarity was manipulated at the low (L) and high (H) levels, depending on the stretching level for each process. The SFT addition to the original study is shown in Fig. 2.4A, gray boxes. The diagnostic SFT conditions, displayed at the very bottom of the factorial tree, factorially combine the base width dissimilarity and the top curvature dissimilarity. The four conditions (HH, HL, LH, and LL) are also displayed in Fig. 2.4B providing another view of the factorial tree in Fig. 2.4A obtained by renaming and combining the factors from the panel A. It is interesting to note that the two psychological dimensions of base and top dissimilarity correspond to the two continuous physical dimensions of base width and top curvature, respectively. The experimental condition values (1–9) shown in panel A are also displayed in panel B. The panel C shows the actual trials, defined in the panel B.

Defining a Model

For multidimensional stimuli, an important consideration is how the individual features of objects are processed in order make a categorization decision. For example, in the exemplar-based approach, all of the stimulus features are weighted and summed into an overall similarity-strength measure. By contrast, one can also examine which feature source was processed first or second, whether processing of separate sources of information was conducted serially or in parallel, and whether the perceptual sources of information were treated independently. Fifić et al. (2010) introduced a class of rule-based models that can be used to assess different information-processing decision strategies employed by humans (see Griffiths, Blunden, & Little, 2017, this book).

In the categorization task shown in Fig. 2.4, subjects are presented with one of the lamp stimuli at the time and have to make decisions whether the lamp is a member of Category A or Category B.

The similarity-based exemplar model and the logical-rule based models make two distinct *SIC* predictions. The exemplar model predicts an S-shaped *SIC* function, with smaller negative part and then a positive part consistent with coactivity. The logical-rule models, however, also allow for parallel or serial processing (Fifić et al., 2010; Little et al., 2011; Little, Nosofsky, Donkin, & Denton, 2013), which predict differently-shaped *SIC*s. More information about these models is discussed in Griffiths et al. (2017; this book) and Cheng, Moneer, Christie, and Little (2017, this book).

Short Term Memory (STM) Search

Short term memory (STM) is operationalized as a temporary storage for mental representations used for immediate cognitive operations. One of the important questions about the organization of STM regards the assumption about the processing order when searching stored representations.

In one STM task, subjects have to memorize a set of items and subsequently make decisions concerning whether or not a target item was member of that memorized set (e.g., Sternberg, 1966, 1969). An example of such a task using only two memorized items is presented in Fig. 2.5C (Townsend & Fifić, 2004). The memorized sets consist of two three-letter words, in the consonant–vocal–consonant CVC form. Subjects would first learn the items in the memorized set and then, after a brief period, a target item was presented. If each memorized item word represents one source of information, one can ask how are these sources combined, and what is the processing when these items during STM search?

Research Design

Townsend and Fifić's (2004) study had two factors, shown in the white boxes, Fig. 2.5A. The factor of target's presence indicates whether a target item was presented in a memorized set or not (Yes or No). The factor of target position indicates the target position in the list of memorized items. (1 = first place in the set, 2 = second place in the set). The empty white box indicates that the target-absent condition in which both items must be searched to make a correct response. The items that are not identical to the target item are distractors.

The SFT addition to the original study is shown in the gray boxes, Fig. 2.5A. The added factor of interest was the distractors' phonemic item-to-target dissimilarity. The factor of distractor's phonemic item-to-target dissimilarity was binary manipulated at the two values, low (L) and high (H), depending on the stretching level for each distractor item. This is achieved by manipulating phonemic dissimilarity of all the items used in the task. All three-letter word items were grouped into a two phonemic categories: stimuli having nasal phonemes (L, M, N) and having fricative phonemes (F, S, V). For simplicity, the low item-to-target dissimilarity level was defined as the within-category relation. That is, both the memorized item and the target were selected from the same category (say LAM to NAM or FAV to VAS). In contrast, the high item-to-target dissimilarity was defined as the between-category relation. That is, both the memorized item and the target item were selected from the different categories (say LAM to FAV or NAM to VAS). The dissimilarity conditions of the distractors factorially combined with their position in the memorized set is shown in Fig. 2.5C.

The diagnostic SFT conditions are displayed at the very bottom of the factorial tree in Fig. 2.5A. These conditions are obtained by factorial combination of the phonemic dissimilarity of the first item in a memorized list, at the high and low levels, with the phonemic dissimilarity of the second item in a memorized list, at the high and low levels, but only for the target-absent responses. Fig. 2.5B provides useful information of how the distractor item-to-target dissimilarity manipulation works. The two dimensions are defined on the continuous dimension scale of the item-to-target dissimilarity. All of the 8 experimental conditions from Fig. 2.5A can be mapped onto such a space. The target-absent conditions are positioned in the upper right corner and separated from the target-present conditions by a piecewise linear decision bound. The vertical bound requires analysis of the first item in the memorized set, comparison to the target, and a decision about whether this item is a target based on its dissimilarity level. If the dissimilarity level is zero (a match) or smaller than the critical decision value, then the item is identified as a target; otherwise, it is identified as a distractor. The same process also occurs (if necessary) for the second list item. The stretching effect is determined by the relative position of the stimulus condition relative to the imagined

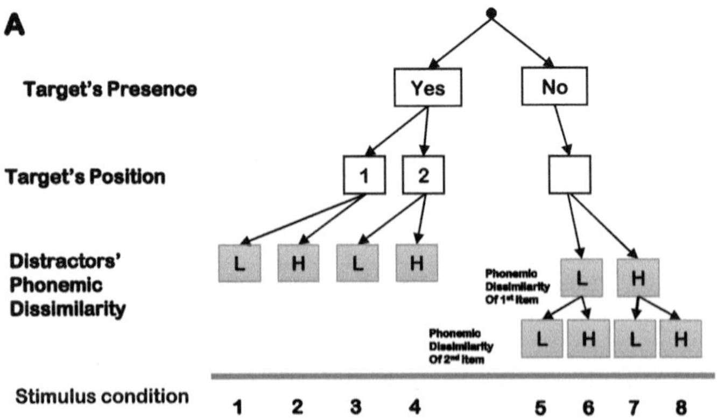

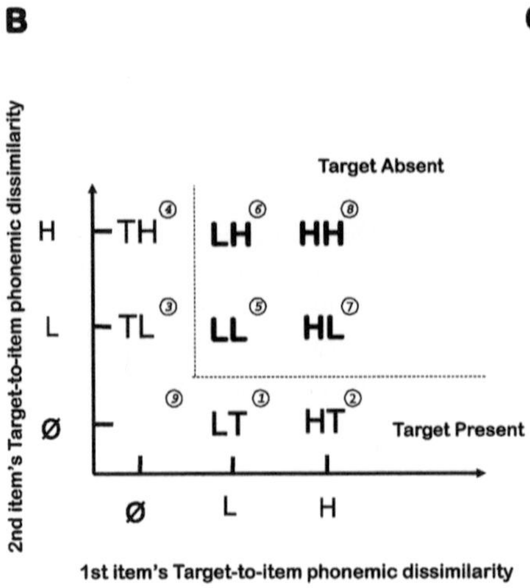

C

Stimulus conditions		Memorized Items	Target
5	LL	MAL, NAM FAS, SAV	NAL VAF
7	HL	NAM, SAV FAS, NAM	VAS LAM
6	LH	NAL, FAS VAS, MAL	NAM FAV
8	HH	VAS, FAV MAN, NAL	NAL FAS
4	TL	**MAL**, NAM **FAS**, SAV	MAL **FAS**
3	TH	**NAM**, SAV **FAS**, NAM	NAM FAS
1	HT	NAL, **FAS** VAS, **MAL**	FAS MAL
2	LT	VAS, **FAV** MAN, **NAL**	FAV NAL

Figure 2.5 The short-term memory task. (A) The factorial tree represents the factors on left and the factor levels in boxes on right. The white boxes indicate the original study factorial design prior to the SFT modification. The shaded boxes indicate the added conditions after SFT process stretching has been applied. The double-factorial conditions are shown at the tree's bottom as another two-branch factorial tree made of two factors (distractor's phonemic dissimilarity of a distractor at the list position one, and the list position two). (B) The corresponding stimulus configuration space is defined by the two continuous dimensions: distractor phonemic dissimilarity of the distractor at the first list position, and at the second list position. The distractor features are denoted as L and H as they are stretched across both dimensions. The piecewise linear function separates the two response mapping regions: target present – which uses a disjoint rule (OR) to classify stimuli, and target absent – which uses a conjoint stimulus classification rule (AND). The double-factorial design is presented in the upper right corner (HH, HL, LH, and LL). The encircled numbers indicate the stimulus conditions denoted in the factorial tree panel A, bottom line. (C) Actual stimulus condition realizations of the configuration presented in panel B. The second column indicates the type of factorial conditions, as shown in panel B. The third column shows some examples of two memorized items, each consisting of three letters. The target item is show in the fourth column. By reading these three-letter pseudo-words, one can get a feeling of the phonemic dissimilarity effects, shown in the second column.

piecewise linear decision bound that separates the two response types. If a distractor item is close to the linear decision bound, then in practice this item phonemically sounds more like the target item. If a distractor item is distant from the linear decision bound, then in practice this item sounds more distinct from the target item. Conceptually, an exemplar-based approach could replace the linear decision bounds by the similarity-based functions between the items (Fifić, Nosofsky, & Townsend, 2008; Fifić, Townsend, & Eidels, 2008; Nosofsky, Little, Donkin, & Fifić, 2011).

Defining a Model

In his seminal studies, Sternberg (1966; 1969) found that, in both the target-present and target-absent conditions, the mean *RT* increased linearly with the size of the memorized list and inferred that STM is scanned in a serial exhaustive fashion. One alternative approach proposed a parallel processing STM model in which all stored representations are analyzed simultaneously (Ratcliff, 1978). A third approach assumed that comparison of a recognition probe to all of the list items is pooled into a single, global memory strength variable (and is consequently commensurate with a coactive decision model; Nosofsky et al., 2011).

It is well-known that serial and parallel models of STM search cannot be distinguished at mean *RT* level due to model mimicry (e.g., Townsend, 1969, 1971, 1972; Townsend and Ashby, 1983, Chapter 14). Further attempts to differentiate processing using memorized set size functions have been unable to find conclusive evidence as to the underlying scanning architecture (Donkin & Nosofsky, 2012). SFT allows one to clearly delineate the predictions of each of the models at the *RT* distribution level (Townsend & Nozawa, 1995). The serial exhaustive, parallel exhaustive, and coactive models make distinct *SIC* signature predictions: serial exhaustive predicts the S-shaped *SIC* function, with equal positive and negative parts; the parallel exhaustive model predicts a strictly negative *SIC* function; and the coactive model predicts an S-shaped *SIC* function with a smaller initial negative component (Townsend & Fifić, 2004; see also Altieri et al., 2017; Chapter 1, Fig. 1.3).

Integrative Workspace

Figs. 2.2–2.5A show the standard factorial research design for four example tasks (displayed in the white boxes). Each tasks' factorial design is represented as a schematic factorial tree that branches across each factors' values. An immediate concern is to notice that all the original factorial designs cannot be characterized as full-factorial designs. When these designs are viewed as a factorial tree, one can see that the two main branches (left and right from the main bifurcation point) are not symmetric (Figs. 2.2–2.5A, white boxes). In other words, the research design does not permit factorial combination of the all of the factors' values. They are defined as fractional factorial research design (FFD; e.g., Anderson & Whitcomb, 2015). Although helpful, FFDs do not allow for conducting the complete full factorial interaction test and certainly limit the number of applications. Nevertheless, researchers can conduct the set of simple factorial analysis by selecting the branches that make full factorial designs. In practice, this is achieved by conditioning the analysis on a certain fixed values (see Fifić, 2017, for more details).

Step 2. SFT design implementation (stretching)

Once the model(s) underlying the specific task is(are) specified, one has to make a decision concerning how to proceed with the model testing using SFT. This step requires considering which processes within the model will be tested for their fundamental mental properties (processing order, stopping rule, and process interdependency). Probing targeted processes within the model is achieved by stretching the duration of these processes through the manipulation of external factors. A researcher must establish a one-to-one relationship between the external factor and the underlying process, such that only one process is selectively affected by the single external factor. Furthermore, such an external manipulation should only affect the duration of the mental process of interest and should not incur speed accuracy trade-off or overall drop in accuracy.

The stretching effect has also been denoted as factor *saliency* or *discriminability* (Fifić, Nosofsky et al., 2008; Fifić & Townsend, 2010; Eidels, Townsend, & Algom, 2010; Eidels, Houpt, Altieri, Pei, & Townsend, 2011). A highly salient feature or processing unit (thus process) stands out among other processes and is associated with faster processing in the perceptual and cognitive literature (e.g., Treisman and Gelade, 1980).

The kinds of variables that could be used for process stretching depend on the type of research design and the task per se. In general, SFT-related research has brought out two types of stretching: The first type is (i) *external stretching*, which affects the processing speed of a target process due to manipulation of external stimulus' intensity. In the case of external stretching, the experimental variable directly affects the process of interest. There are different types of visual obstructions, such as stimulus masking, brightness (the redundant target task), size reduction, stimulus intensity (the Stroop task), and stimulus blurring, each of which could lead to slowing down or speeding up the processing rate of the process of interest. In Fig. 2.2C, each of the two stimulus dimensions (left and right dot) is defined on a continuous scale. The values of L and H are arbitrary satisfying the condition that the L value is associated with the lower brightness and the H value with the higher brightness. In Fig. 2.3C, the color salience dimension is also stretched through the direct stretching method: as we go along the horizontal dimension the amount of redness is decreased.

The second stretching type is (ii) *internal stretching*, which affects processing speed of the target process by affecting its cognitive properties. To internally stretch a process, one can use a similarity function between item representations within the system. The concept of the item-similarity function can be instantiated as the distance in a Euclidian psychological space (Ashby & Maddox, 1994; Ashby, 2000; Nosofsky & Stanton, 2005; Fifić, Little, & Nosofsky, 2010). For example, if a target item is closer in the similarity space to the non-target item(s) then discrimination of the target item should be slower. An alternative is to assume that it is the distance between an item and a decision boundary which determines the speed of processing (Ashby & Maddox, 1994; Nosofsky & Stanton, 2005). In these examples, the manipulation by internal stretching does not directly affect the processing rate but rather it specifies the distance of the item in a space to other used items, which in turn affects processing rate.

For example, in the lamp classification task (Fig. 2.4C), the position of the target item is specified by two continuously-valued dimensions: the curvature of the top and the base width. The location of the target item specifies its relative position to the non-target items: the closer the distance, the more processing time is needed to classify the target item as a member of the target group. Thus, placing one item closer to the bound on one dimension should lead to creating a Low salience factor for that dimension. Placing an item farther away from the bound on one dimension should lead to creating a High salience factor for that dimension. In that manner, one can easily generate the four factorial conditions (HH, HL, LH, and LL).

In each of the task figures, the dotted lines are used to divide the regions of the stimulus space into two regions: one that contains the factorial manipulated targets and another that contains non-targets. The decision bound is presented in the form of the piecewise linear function, with each component parallel with one of the axes. To correctly categorize a stimulus, for any member of the target A category lamp stimuli in Fig. 2.4B, one has to check two stimulus properties and compare them to two decision values.

It is important to note that the psychological decision bounds could be nonlinear, or linear but also not orthogonal to the stimulus dimension axes. In such cases, the factorial placements of stimuli in the stimulus space would not necessarily lead to the desired level of stretching. Such a situation is defined as a violation of decisional separability (Ashby & Townsend, 1986). The test for a violation of selective influence could be used to indicate such violations and the inferences about the fundamental properties from such cases would be most likely invalid.

Although there is no trivial solution for detecting possible violations of decisional separability, several actions are possible: parametric models could be fitted to the *RT* (Fifić et al., 2010; Little et al., 2011, 2013) to disentangle possible variants of the violations and verify the fundamental properties. Another less computer-intensive approach is to make the qualitative predictions about the diagnostic patterns not only limited to the double-factorial conditions (LL, LH, HL, and HH) but also to other stimulus conditions (the contrast category, see Fifić et al., 2010). The violation of the decisional separability and other concepts such as stimulus separability and independence (Ashby & Townsend, 1986; Maddox & Ashby, 1996; Kadlec & Townsend, 1992; Silbert & Thomas, 2013) can be included within the SFT parametric approach (e.g., Blunden, Wang, Griffiths, & Little, 2014; Little, Nosofsky, Donkin, & Denton, 2013). These approaches are discussed in Griffiths, Blunden, and Little (2017, this book).

Step 3. SFT data collection and diagnosing mental architectures

The SFT approach uses *RT*s in each experimental condition collected over repeated trials. Selection of stretching effect for the experimental factor should permit error free performance of the subjects, although some moderate amount of error is permissible (see Fifić, Nosofsky et al., 2008, Appendix A). The *MIC* statistic uses mean *RT*s, while the *SIC* statistics uses distribution properties of *RT*s in the form of estimated survivor functions. It is important to check the possibility of violation of selective influence assumption before we proceed to the final diagnostic test.

The quickest test for the failure of the selective influence is to check the mean *RT* orderings, i.e.,

$$RT_{\mathrm{LL}} > (RT_{\mathrm{LH}}, RT_{\mathrm{HL}}) > RT_{\mathrm{HH}}, \tag{2.4}$$

where each of the four terms represents the mean reaction time for one critical factorial condition. If the test fails and any of the inequalities is violated then the results cannot be interpreted straightforwardly, and one has to approach the result with the caution or provide a good explanation of why and how selective influence might fail in such situations.

Even more confidence in selective influence can be achieved by showing that Eq. (2.4) inequality holds when using survivor functions instead of using mean *RT*s. This can be achieved first by visual inspection:

$$S_{\mathrm{LL}}(t) \geq \left[S_{\mathrm{LH}}(t), S_{\mathrm{HL}}(t)\right] \geq S_{\mathrm{HH}}(t), \quad \text{for all } t. \tag{2.5}$$

Statistical tests of the ordering can also be applied (Houpt & Townsend, 2010; Heathcote, Brown, Wagenmakers, & Eidels, 2010; Houpt, Blaha, McIntire, Havig, & Townsend, 2014; Yang, Little, & Hsu, 2014; Yang, Fifić, & Townsend, 2014). The appropriate tests are the Kolmogorov–Smirnov test or other nonparametric test (e.g., the cosphericity test, Kujala and Dzhafarov, 2008).

Statistical Tests

The *MIC* values can be tested by using a corresponding ANOVA design. In addition to testing for the main effects to determine whether the stretching manipulation on each factor was effective,[2] it is possible to test the hypothesis on whether or not an observed *MIC* value significantly departs from zero value.

There is a close relation between the results obtained using the *MIC* and *SIC* tests. This is because the *MIC* value is the integral of the *SIC* for all values of t (Townsend, 1990). This relationship can serve to provide a basic statistical hypothesis test for the visually observed *SIC* results, by using ANOVA on the *MIC* results (e.g., Fifić & Townsend, 2010; Fifić, Nosofsky et al., 2008; Fifić, Townsend et al., 2008). Such inference could hold only if the selective influence assumptions also hold: the order of the stretching effects (L $>$ H) and the ordering of the mean *RT*s and survivor functions are satisfied. The limitation of the *MIC* ANOVA test is that when attempting to distinguish between the parallel self-terminating and coactive models. Note that the *MIC* > 0 for both models so an *MIC* ANOVA test would fail to distinguish between the two *SIC* signatures[3] (see Houpt et al., 2014). For this comparison, one needs to examine the *SIC*.

The second nonparametric test involves using bootstrapping (see Van Zandt, 2002, for details) to construct confidence intervals on the observed *MIC* values. Bootstrapping can also be used to generate the confidence regions around *SIC* function. The inference logic is similar to that of the *MIC* bootstrapping test: one has to check whether the function sufficiently departs from x-axis (zero value) such that for some times neither the *SIC* function nor the confidence interval around the *SIC* function captures zero value (see, e.g., Yang, Little, & Hsu, 2014; Yang, Chang, & Wu, 2013).

The third non-parametric approach, specifically created to fit the SFT tools, was designed to test the maximal and minimal deviations in the *SIC* function shape using the mathematical properties of Brownian bridge. The test is a generalization of the two-sample Kolmogorov–Smirnov test, and is available as an R-software package (Houpt et al., 2014). See the chapter by Houpt and Burns (2017, this book) for details.

Simple Double-Factorial Design

The design is termed the double-factorial design (2 × 2: HH, HL, LH, and LL) when analyzing only two processes within a mental architecture. However, as we can see in Figs. 2.2–2.5B, the double-factorial design is only a subset of the full-factorial design (depicted here as 3 × 3). A worthwhile question is whether all factorial conditions can be used to make even stronger conclusions in diagnostic fundamental properties?

First, one can apply further stretching manipulations to the factors, providing that one can find appropriate factor manipulations. Hence, one can produce both L, H, and an in-between value, M, such that the stretching effect are ordered: $S_L(t) \geq S_M(t) \geq S_H(t)$. Using these values, one can create a 3 (H, M, L) × 3 (H, M, L) design. Out of the 3 × 3 design, it is possible to construct several simple double-factorial designs, for example, (H, M) × (H, M), (M, L) × (M, L), (H, M) × (H, L), etc. Note that all conditions for the SFT analysis should be met in the simple tests as well. In addition, the simples tests must be conducted on the experimental conditions that are located on only one side of the imaginary decision bound, that separates the two different response regions (Figs. 2.2–2.5, panel B). The first rationale is that stimulus conditions on the same side of the decision bound are usually (but not necessarily) fixed with respect to using only one stopping rule. So, combining the experimental conditions across the decision bound for the double factorial test could combine response trials with different stopping rules used. This is comparable to testing a probabilistic mixtures model of fundamental properties within one cognitive system and introducing the new mixture parameters of relative proportions of terminating and exhaustive stopping rules. The second rationale is that the stretching effect is monotonically related to the distance from a stimulus condition to the decision bound, and combining response trials across different sides of the decision bound could lead to combining different stretching effects that may not satisfy the conditional stretching effect order at the marginal level ($RT_{low} > RT_{high}$).

Once the factorial conditions are collected (on one side of the decision bound) then the interpretation of the simple SFT tests are straightforward. Providing that the system doesn't change its underlying architecture across stretching levels, all of the simple double-factorial designs should predict the same outcome. For example, all the simple double-factorial tests should indicate the same type of *MIC* or *SIC* signatures. If different SFT results are found for different factorial combinations then this would indicate that the mental architectures changed for different levels of stimulus saliency. Such a result could be a strong indicator that there are some other properties used in the study that are not controlled by the researcher.

Summary

In the past decades, cognitive psychologists have laboriously tested models of cognitive operations. The models have varied in their scope with domain general models on the one hand and domain specific models on the other hand. The veridicality of the models has usually been judged by whether or not the model can fit some pattern of data, typically using likelihood measures. The most advanced approaches utilize Bayesian inference to find the most probable model given the observed data among several candidate models. A disadvantage of the Bayesian approach is that it requires adopting (sometimes numerous) assumptions about the distribution of parameters and the distribution of the data. Similar, but not identical, approaches in model selection are based on maximizing likelihood functions of the observed data given the candidate models. This approach depends on intensive data simulation and parameter value search. In contrast, SFT is a parameter-free approach which uses the double-factorial design seeking data patterns which could rule out entire model classes. These model classes are defined by the fundamental properties of processing order, stopping rule, process interdependency, and processing capacity.

The qualitative forms of the *SIC* and *MIC* signatures are invariant across cognitive domains. Assuming the same organization of mental processes, the same *SIC* signature should be observed in the domain of visual search or in categorization. Likewise, *SIC* and *MIC* are invariant with regard to the distribution of stochastic variables. The same *SIC* signature should hold for two, e.g., serial exhaustive processing systems, assuming different distributions of the random variable completion times (e.g., exponential, gamma; but see the chapter by Harding, LeBlanc, Goulet, & Cousineau, 2017, this book).

SFT cannot be seen as a substitute for the model selection methods such as Bayesian inference. Rather than comparing and selecting full processing models, SFT can be used to test the proposed components of the models of interest and to verify whether or not the components are valid. For example, consider a scenario in which a complex cognitive model has been tested using SFT. If the cognitive model fails on the SFT test for the proposed processing order, then the model is immediately falsified. As a consequence, it is not reasonable to include this model in the set of plausible models. Consider another hypothetical example in which one compares three cognitive models using Bayesian model selection. Assume that in truth all three of the models are incorrect with respect to one of the assumed fundamental properties such that the compared models would be falsified by the SFT tests. Although this failure would reduce the likelihood of the model, one could still erroneously conclude that one of the three models was the correct model. While it is true that all models are false, some models can be immediately falsified as not possessing the critical processing component, by using SFT.

Over the course of the last decades, the number of publications utilizing SFT has steadily soared. To the initiate the requirements of using, SFT may seem somewhat daunting at first glance. The current tutorial, as well as this book, aims at providing the integral overview of how to master the mental process stretching within SFT and how to apply the SFT to different cognitive tasks and models.

References

Algom, D., Dekel, A., & Pansky, A. (1996). The perception of number from the separability of the stimulus: The Stroop effect revisited. *Memory and Cognition*, *24*(5), 557–572. http://dx.doi.org/10.3758/BF03201083.

Algom, D., Fitousi, D., & Eidels, A. (2017). Bridge-building: SFT interrogation of major cognitive phenomena. In D. R. Little, N. Altieri, M. Fifić, & C-T. Yang (Eds.), *Systems factorial technology: A theory driven methodology for the identification of perceptual and cognitive mechanisms*. Elsevier (in this book).

Altieri, N., Fifić, M., Little, D. R., & Yang, C-T. (2017). Historical foundations and a tutorial introduction to systems factorial technology. In D. R. Little, N. Altieri, M. Fifić, & C.-T. Yang (Eds.), *Systems factorial technology: A theory driven methodology for the identification of perceptual and cognitive mechanisms*. Elsevier (in this book).

Anderson, M. J., & Whitcomb, P. J. (2015). *DOE simplified: Practical tools for effective experimentation* (3rd ed.). Boca Raton, FL: CRC Press.

Ashby, F. G. (2000). A stochastic version of general recognition theory. *Journal of Mathematical Psychology*, *44*, 310–329.

Ashby, F. G., & Gott, R. E. (1988). Decision rules in the perception and categorization of multidimensional stimuli. *Journal of Experimental Psychology: Learning, Memory, and Cognition*, *14*, 33–53.

Ashby, F. G., & Lee, W. W. (1991). Predicting similarity and categorization from identification. *Journal of Experimental Psychology: General*, *120*(2), 150–172.

Ashby, F. G., & Maddox, W. T. (1990). Integrating information from separable psychological dimensions. *Journal of Experimental Psychology: Human Perception and Performance*, *16*, 598–612.

Ashby, F. G., & Maddox, W. T. (1994). A response time theory of separability and integrality in speeded classification. *Journal of Mathematical Psychology*, *38*, 423–466.

Ashby, F. G., & Perrin, N. A. (1988). Toward a unified theory of similarity and recognition. *Psychological Review*, *95*(1), 124–150.

Ashby, F. G., & Townsend, J. T. (1986). Varieties of perceptual independence. *Psychological Review*, *93*(2), 154–179.

Blunden, A. G., Wang, T., Griffiths, D. W., & Little, D. R. (2014). Logical-rules and the classification of integral dimensions: Individual differences in the processing of arbitrary dimensions. *Frontiers in Psychology*, *5*, 1531.

Cheng, X. J., Moneer, S., Christie, N., & Little, D. R. (2017). An information processing perspective to understanding conflicting information. In D. R. Little, N. Altieri, M. Fifić, &

C-T. Yang (Eds.), *Systems factorial technology: A theory driven methodology for the identification of perceptual and cognitive mechanisms*. Elsevier (in this book).

Cohen, J. D., Dunbar, K., & McClelland, J. L. (1990). On the control of automatic processes: A parallel distributed processing account of the Stroop effect. *Psychological Review*, *97*, 332–361.

Colonius, H. (1990). Possibly dependent probability summation of reaction time. *Journal of Mathematical Psychology*, *34*(3), 253–275.

Diederich, A., & Colonius, H. (1987). Intersensory facilitation in the motor component? *Psychological Research*, *49*, 23–29.

Dishon-Berkovits, M., & Algom, D. (2000). The Stroop effect: It is not the robust phenomenon that you have thought it to be. *Memory and Cognition*, *28*(8), 1437–1449.

Donkin, C., & Nosofsky, R. M. (2012). The structure of short-term memory scanning: An investigation using response time distribution models. *Psychonomic Bulletin & Review*, *19*(3), 363–394.

Eidels, A., Houpt, J. W., Altieri, N., Pei, L., & Townsend, J. T. (2011). Nice guys finish fast and bad guys finish last: Facilitatory vs. inhibitory interaction in parallel systems. *Journal of Mathematical Psychology*, *55*(2), 176–190.

Eidels, A., Townsend, J. T., & Algom, D. (2010). Comparing perception of Stroop stimuli in focused versus divided attention paradigms: Evidence for dramatic processing differences. *Cognition*, *114*, 129–150.

Fifić, M. (2017). Simple factorial tweezers for detecting delicate serial and parallel processes. In J. W. Houpt, & L. M. Blaha (Eds.), *Mathematical models of perception and cognition: Essays in honor of James T. Townsend*. New York: Psychology Press.

Fifić, M., Little, D. R., & Nosofsky, R. M. (2010). Logical-rule models of classification response times: A synthesis of mental-architecture, random-walk, and decision-bound approaches. *Psychological Review*, *117*, 309–348.

Fifić, M., Nosofsky, R. M., & Townsend, J. T. (2008). Information-processing architectures in multidimensional classification: A validation test of the systems factorial technology. *Journal of Experimental Psychology. Human Perception and Performance*, *34*(2), 356–375.

Fifić, M., & Townsend, J. T. (2010). Information-processing alternatives to holistic perception: Identifying the mechanisms of secondary-level holism within a categorization paradigm. *Journal of Experimental Psychology. Learning, Memory, and Cognition*, *36*, 1290–1313.

Fifić, M., Townsend, J. T., & Eidels, A. (2008). Studying visual search using systems factorial methodology with target—distractor similarity as the factor. *Perception and Psychophysics*, *70*(4), 583–603.

Grice, G. R., Canham, L., & Boroughs, J. M. (1984). Combination rule for redundant information in reaction time tasks with divided attention. *Perception and Psychophysics*, *35*, 451–463.

Griffiths, D. W., Blunden, A. G., & Little, D. R. (2017). Logical-rule based models of categorization: Using systems factorial technology to understand feature and dimensional processing. In D. R. Little, N. Altieri, M. Fifić, & C-T. Yang (Eds.), *Systems factorial technology: A theory driven methodology for the identification of perceptual and cognitive mechanisms*. Elsevier (in this book).

Harding, B., LeBlanc, V., Goulet, M.-A., & Cousineau, D. (2017). Applying systems factorial technology to accumulators with varying thresholds. In D. R. Little, N. Altieri, M. Fifić, & C-T. Yang (Eds.), *Systems factorial technology: A theory driven methodology for the identification of perceptual and cognitive mechanisms*. Elsevier (in this book).

Heathcote, A., Brown, S., Wagenmakers, E. J., & Eidels, A. (2010). Distribution-free tests of stochastic dominance for small samples. *Journal of Mathematical Psychology*, *54*(5), 454–463.

Hintzman, D. L. (1986). "Schema abstraction" in a multiple-trace memory model. *Psychological Review*, *93*(4), 411–428.

Houpt, J. W., Blaha, L. M., McIntire, J. P., Havig, P. R., & Townsend, J. T. (2014). Systems factorial technology with R. *Behavior Research Methods*, *46*, 307–330.

Houpt, J. W., & Burns, D. (2017). Statistical analyses for system factorial technology. In D. R. Little, N. Altieri, M. Fifić, & C-T. Yang (Eds.), *Systems factorial technology: A theory driven methodology for the identification of perceptual and cognitive mechanisms*. Elsevier (in this book).

Houpt, J. W., & Townsend, J. T. (2010). The statistical properties of the survivor interaction contrast. *Journal of Mathematical Psychology*, *54*, 446–453.

Kadlec, H., & Townsend, J. T. (1992). Implications of marginal and conditional detection parameters for the separabilities and independence of perceptual dimensions. *Journal of Mathematical Psychology*, *36*(3), 325–374.

Kujala, J. V., & Dzhafarov, E. N. (2008). Testing for selectivity in the dependence of random variables on external factors. *Journal of Mathematical Psychology*, *52*(2), 128–144.

Little, D. R., Nosofsky, R. M., & Denton, S. (2011). Response time tests of logical rule-based models of categorization. *Journal of Experimental Psychology. Learning, Memory, and Cognition*, *37*, 1–27.

Little, D. R., Nosofsky, R. M., Donkin, C., & Denton, S. E. (2013). Logical-rules and the classification of integral dimensioned stimuli. *Journal of Experimental Psychology. Learning, Memory, and Cognition*, *39*, 801–820.

Logan, G. D. (1980). Attention and automaticity in Stroop and priming tasks: Theory and data. *Cognitive Psychology*, *12*, 523–553.

MacLeod, C. M., & Dunbar, K. (1988). Training and Stroop-like interference: Evidence for a continuum of automaticity. *Journal of Experimental Psychology: Learning, Memory, and Cognition*, *14*(1), 126–135.

Maddox, W. T., & Ashby, F. G. (1996). Perceptual separability, decisional separability, and the identification-speeded classification relationship. *Journal of Experimental Psychology. Human Perception and Performance*, *22*(4), 795–817.

Maxwell, S. E., & Delaney, H. D. (1999). *Designing experiments and analyzing data: A model comparison perspective*. Mahwah, NJ: Lawrence Erlbaum Associates, Inc.

Melara, R. D., & Algom, D. (2003). Driven by information: A tectonic theory of Stroop effects. *Psychological Review*, *110*(3), 422–471.

Melara, R. D., & Mounts, J. R. W. (1993). Selective attention to Stroop dimensions: Effects of baseline discriminability, response mode, and practice. *Memory and Cognition*, *21*(5), 627.

Medin, D. L., & Schaffer, M. M. (1978). Context theory of classification learning. *Psychological Review*, *85*(3), 207–238.

Miller, J. O. (1982). Divided attention: Evidence for coactivation with redundant signals. *Cognitive Psychology*, *14*, 247–279.

Nosofsky, R. M. (1986). Attention, similarity, and the identification–categorization relationship. *Journal of Experimental Psychology: General*, *115*(1), 39–57.

Nosofsky, R. M., Little, D. R., Donkin, C., & Fifić, M. (2011). Short-term memory scanning viewed as exemplar-based categorization. *Psychological Review*, *118*(2).

Nosofsky, R. M., & Stanton, R. D. (2005). Speeded classification in a probabilistic category structure: Contrasting exemplar-retrieval, decision-boundary, and prototype models. *Journal of Experimental Psychology. Human Perception and Performance*, *31*(3), 608–629.

Phaf, R. H., Van der Heijden, A. H. C., & Hudson, P. T. W. (1990). SLAM: A connectionist model for attention in visual selection tasks. *Cognitive Psychology*, *22*(3), 273.

Ratcliff, R. (1978). A theory of memory retrieval. *Psychological Review*, *85*(2), 59–108.

Roelofs, A. (2003). Goal-referenced selection of verbal action: Modeling attentional control in the Stroop task. *Psychological Review*, *110*(1), 88–125. http://dx.doi.org/10.1037/0033-295X.110.1.88.

Sabri, M., Melara, R. D., & Algom, D. (2001). A confluence of contexts: Asymmetric versus global failures of selective attention to Stroop dimensions. *Journal of Experimental Psychology. Human Perception and Performance*, *27*(3), 515–537.

Schwartz, M. (2001). How to reverse-engineering. Computer world Retrieved from http://www.computerworld.com/article/2585652/app-development/reverse-engineering.html.

Silbert, N., & Thomas, R. D. (2013). Decisional separability, model identification, and statistical inference in the general recognition theory framework. *Psychonomic Bulletin and Review*, *20*(1), 1–20.

Sternberg, S. (1966). High-speed scanning in human memory. *Science*, *153*, 652–654.

Sternberg, S. (1969). Memory scanning: Mental processes revealed by reaction time experiments. *American Scientist*, *4*, 421–457.

Stroop, J. R. (1935). Studies of interference in serial verbal reaction. *Journal of Experimental Psychology*, *18*, 643–662.

Todd, J. W. (1912). *Reaction to multiple stimuli*. New York, NY: The Science Press.

Townsend, J.T. (1969). *Stochastic representations of serial and parallel processes*. Paper presented at Midwest mathematical psychology meetings, Indiana University.

Townsend, J. T. (1971). A note on the identifiability of parallel and serial processes. *Perception and Psychophysics*, *10*, 161–163.

Townsend, J. T. (1972). Some results concerning the identifiability of parallel and serial processes. *British Journal of Mathematical and Statistical Psychology*, *25*, 168–199.

Townsend, J. T. (1990). The truth and consequences of ordinal differences in statistical distributions: Toward a theory of hierarchical inference. *Psychological Bulletin*, *108*(3), 551–567.

Townsend, J. T., & Ashby, F. G. (1983). *Stochastic modeling of elementary psychological processes*. Cambridge, UK: Cambridge University Press.

Townsend, J. T., & Fifić, M. (2004). Parallel versus serial processing and individual differences in high-speed search in human memory. *Perception and Psychophysics*, *66*(6), 953–962.

Townsend, J. T., Liu, Y. J., & Zhang, R. (2017). Selective influence and classificatory separability (perceptual separability) in perception and cognition: Similarities, distinctions, and synthesis. In D. R. Little, N. Altieri, M. Fifić, & C-T. Yang (Eds.), *Systems factorial technology: A theory driven methodology for the identification of perceptual and cognitive mechanisms*. Elsevier (in this book).

Townsend, J. T., & Nozawa, G. (1995). On the spatio-temporal properties of elementary perception: An investigation of parallel, serial, and coactive theories. *Journal of Mathematical Psychology*, *39*, 321–359.

Townsend, J. T., & Thomas, R. (1994). Stochastic dependencies in parallel and serial models: Effects on systems factorial interactions. *Journal of Mathematical Psychology*, *38*, 1–34.

Treisman, A. M., & Gelade, G. (1980). A feature-integration theory of attention. *Cognitive Psychology*, *12*(1), 97–136.

Van Zandt, T. (2002). Analysis of response time distributions. In J. T. Wixted, & H. Pashler (Eds.), *Methodology in experimental psychology: Vol. 4* (3rd ed.). *Stevens' handbook of experimental psychology* (pp. 461–516). New York: Wiley Press.

Virzi, R. A., & Egeth, H. E. (1985). Toward a translation model of Stroop interference. *Memory and Cognition, 13*, 304–319.

Yang, C-T. (2017). Attention and perceptual decision making. In D. R. Little, N. Altieri, M. Fifić, & C-T. Yang (Eds.), *Systems factorial technology: A theory driven methodology for the identification of perceptual and cognitive mechanisms*. Elsevier (in this book).

Yang, C.-T., Chang, T.-Y., & Wu, C.-J. (2013). Relative change probability affects the decision process of detecting multiple feature changes. *Journal of Experimental Psychology. Human Perception and Performance, 39*(5), 1365–1385.

Yang, C.-T., Little, D. R., & Hsu, C.-C. (2014). The influence of cueing on attentional focus in perceptual decision making. *Attention, Perception, and Psychophysics, 76*(8), 2256–2275.

Yang, H., Fifić, M., & Townsend, J. T. (2014). Survivor interaction contrast wiggle predictions of parallel and serial models for an arbitrary number of processes. *Journal of Mathematical Psychology, 58*, 21–32.

Zhang, H., Zhang, J., & Kornblum, S. (1999). A parallel distributed processing model of stimulus–stimulus and stimulus–response compatibility. *Cognitive Psychology, 38*(3), 386–432.

Endnotes

1. Only the case of a mental architecture with two processes has been considered in this chapter. The analyses of larger mental architectures ($n > 2$) are described in the recent publication (Yang, Fifić, & Townsend, 2014).
2. Note that in ANOVA it is generally accepted that the interpretation of the main effect should always precede the analysis of an interaction term (e.g., Maxwell & Delaney, 1999). One can employ the same logic here and propose that the main effect (the effect of stretching) can only be unambiguously interpreted after the analysis of the interaction test (a *MIC* value).
3. To distinguish between parallel self-terminating and coactive models, one could augment this analysis with the capacity coefficient analysis (Townsend & Nozawa, 1995; see also the tutorial chapter by Altieri et al. 2017). An independent parallel self-terminating model predicts unlimited capacity; by contrast, the coactive model predicts supercapacity (e.g., Eidels et al., 2011).

Part Two

Recent Advances in Systems Factorial Technology

Statistical Analyses for Systems Factorial Technology

3

Joseph W. Houpt, Devin M. Burns*[†]
*Wright State University, Dayton, OH, United States, [†]Framingham University, Framingham, MA, United States

Introduction

Systems Factorial Technology (SFT; Townsend & Nozawa, 1995) is a well defined approach based on rigorously mathematical definitions of constructs and derivations of measures. Inferences about cognitive processing based on the Survivor Interaction Contrast (SIC) and capacity coefficients (Ct) are broad, allowing the rejection of entire classes of models (e.g., all serial processes) because the approach relies on so few parametric assumptions. Although this generality is a strength of the framework, one drawback is that it complicates data analysis. Models based on specific parametric assumptions, such as Linear Ballistic Accumulator models (Brown & Heathcote, 2008), can be evaluated based on the likelihood of the observed data precisely because they make such strong assumptions. Hence, the challenge in analyzing data within the SFT framework is to develop statistical analyses that do not compromise the generality of the core theory.

In this chapter we review the current inferential and exploratory statistical methods associated with SFT. We begin with survey of the non-parametric, null-hypothesis-significance tests for the SIC and Ct. Next, we cover recently developed semiparametric and nonparametric Bayesian tests. We then conclude with a section on exploratory analysis of Ct across individuals and/or conditions using of functional principal components analysis (fPCA).

Nonparametric Null Hypothesis Tests

Our general approach in this section will be to introduce estimators for the components of SIC and Ct functions, i.e., survivor functions and cumulative (reverse) hazard functions. We will then demonstrate that those estimators are unbiased and consistent and we will state their limit distributions. Finally, we will show how the estimators of the component can be combined to estimate the relevant SFT measures and that those estimators are again unbiased, consistent and have similar limit distributions.

The Survivor Interaction Contrast

The first step in estimating the SIC is to obtain a reasonable estimate of the survivor functions associated with each of the factorial conditions. The NHST tests are based

Systems Factorial Technology, DOI: 10.1016/B978-0-12-804315-8.00005-7

on estimators that are considered to have both good small-sample properties (e.g., unbiasedness) and large-sample properties (e.g., consistency). From those estimates, test statistics are derived for which the limit distribution is known (often Gaussian) and form the basis of the p-value that is then used to reject (or fail to reject) the null hypothesis.

The most commonly used estimator for the distribution function (at least when there is no censoring involved) is the empirical cumulative distribution function (ECDF). Recall that the cumulative distribution (CDF; $F(\cdot)$) function gives the probability that the associated random variable is less than or equal to a particular value, i.e.,

$$F(t) = \Pr\{X \leq t\}.$$

The ECDF simply takes the count of all the observed samples from X that were less than t divided by the total number of samples as the estimate of $F(t)$. With $\mathcal{I}$ representing the indicator function which equals 1 whenever its argument is true and 0 otherwise, and $\{x_1, x_2, \ldots, x_n\}$ the set of samples,

$$\tilde{F}^{(n)}(t) = \frac{1}{n}\sum_{i=1}^{n} \mathcal{I}(x_i \leq t).$$

That the ECDF is unbiased is relatively straightforward to demonstrate. For example, if we consider a random sample $\{X_1, X_2, \ldots, X_n\}$, for each point t, the expected value of $\tilde{F}^{(n)}(t)$ is the expected number of samples that are less than t. Whether or not a sample X_i is less than t is a binary random variable, so its expected value is its probability,

$$\mathrm{E}\big[\mathcal{I}(X_i \leq t)\big] = \Pr\{X_i \leq t\} = F(t).$$

Assuming each sample is independent, the expected value of the sum of the indicators is the sum of the expected value of the indicators. Hence the expected value of $\tilde{F}^{(n)}(t)$ is given by

$$\frac{1}{n}\sum_{i=1}^{n} \mathrm{E}\big[\mathcal{I}(X_i \leq t)\big] = \frac{1}{n}\sum_{i=1}^{n} F(t) = F(t).$$

The ECDF is also consistent, i.e., the probability that the ECDF at a given time is within any $\epsilon > 0$ of the true cumulative distribution function at that time is 1 for n large enough. In fact, a much stronger property holds: the ECDF converges uniformly to the true cumulative distribution function almost surely (with probability 1), as $n \to \infty$,

$$\sup_t \big|\tilde{F}^{(n)}(t) - F(t)\big| \overset{\text{a.s.}}{\to} 0.$$

This is known as the Glivenko–Cantelli Lemma. We do not include the proof as it is a bit longer and more complex than the proof of unbiasedness, but is available in many texts on probability theory (e.g., Billingsley, 1995).

Next, we consider the limit distribution of the ECDF. Recall that for each point in its domain $\tilde{F}^{(n)}(t)$ is given by the number of samples that are less than or equal to t. In other words, the value at t is a random variable representing the number of successes out of n samples where the probability of success is $F(t)$, i.e., $\tilde{F}^{(n)}(t)$ has a binomial distribution. It is well known (and included in many introductory probability and statistics textbooks) that in the limit of n, random variables with a binomial distribution with parameters n and p converge in distribution to a Gaussian (with mean $p = F(t)$). This indicates that the distribution of $\tilde{F}^{(n)}(t) - F(t)$ converges to a Gaussian process with $\mu(t) = 0$.[1] Establishing the covariance function is less trivial, and in fact we skirt the general question to focus specifically on a test statistic of interest, the supremum of the differences (positive, negative or both) between the ECDF and the true CDF,

$$
\begin{aligned}
D &= \sup_t \left|\tilde{F}^{(n)} - F(t)\right|, \\
D^+ &= \sup_t \left(\tilde{F}^{(n)} - F(t), 0\right), \\
D^- &= \sup_t \left(F(t) - \tilde{F}^{(n)}, 0\right).
\end{aligned}
$$

Each of these statistics converge in distribution to analogous statistics of the Brownian bridge, $\mathcal{B}(\cdot)$, a Gaussian process defined on the range [0, 1] with mean 0 and covariance function $s(1-s)$, $s \in [0, 1]$. In particular, the distribution of the largest deviation of the Brownian bridge from zero, $K = \sup_s |\mathcal{B}|$, is the same as the largest deviation of the estimated SIC from the true SIC (when scaled by $\sqrt{n}$).[2] This distribution is given by

$$
\Pr\{K \leq x\} = 1 - 2\sum_{j=1}^{\infty}(-1)^{j-1}e^{-2j^2x^2}.
$$

The distribution of the maximum positive (and negative) deviation of a Brownian bridge from zero and of $\sqrt{n}D^+$ ($\sqrt{n}D^-$) is given by

$$
\Pr\left\{K^+ \leq x\right\} = \Pr\left\{K^- \leq -x\right\} = e^{-2x^2}.
$$

This result is the foundation of the Kolmogorov–Smirnov Test (Kolmogorov, 1933). A concise proof is given in Billingsley (1999).

These same basic results can be generalized to more than one sample, e.g., for comparing two or more distributions. The expected value of any linear combination of random variables is that linear combination of their expectation. Hence, the sum (difference) of ECDFs is an unbiased estimate of the sum (difference) of the true CDFs.

If both $\tilde{F}_1^{(n)}(t)$ and $\tilde{F}_2^{(m)}(t)$ converge uniformly to the true distribution as $n \to \infty$ and $m \to \infty$, so too does their sum. One way to summarize both n and m increasing to infinity is that $1/(1/n+1/m)$ increases to infinity (e.g., if n is small, then even if m increases to infinity, $N \to 1/(1/n) = n$). Likewise, if each term in an interaction contrast converges uniformly to the true distribution, then the interaction contrast will converge uniformly to the true distribution as long as the number of samples for each term (n_i) are all increasing (or if $N = (\sum_i 1/n_i)^{-1}$ goes to infinity).

Table 3.1 Expected pattern of significance of the generalized Kolmogorov–Smirnov test and MIC test for SIC shape. Note that if a test is not significant, models that predict that test to be significant cannot be ruled out. A model can only be ruled out if a test is significant and a model predicts that it should not be

Model	$\hat{D}^{+}$	$\hat{D}^{-}$	MIC
Parallel OR	✓	N.S.	✓
Parallel AND	N.S.	✓	✓
Serial OR	N.S.	N.S.	N.S.
Serial AND	✓	✓	N.S.
Coactive	✓	✓	✓

To obtain a result for the limit distribution of the difference between the estimated SIC, $\tilde{SIC}^{(k,l,m,n)}(t)$ and the true SIC, we first examine the limit distribution of the estimated difference between two CDFs (i.e., the difference between two ECDFs) relative to the difference between the corresponding true CDFs. Essentially, because the limit distribution of the difference between one ECDF and its true CDF, $\hat{F}_1^k(t) - F_1(t)$, is a Gaussian process, the difference of two ECDFs compared the difference of the true CDFs, $\hat{F}_1^k(t) - F_1(t) - [\hat{F}_2^l(t) - F_2(t)]$, is a Gaussian process. Just as with univariate Gaussian distributions, the mean of the sum is the sum of the means and the covariance of the sum is the sum of the covariances. This results in a limit distribution for the difference that shares many properties with a Brownian bridge process (with the covariance scaled by the sum of the covariances of each individual process). More concretely, if D is the maximum of $|\tilde{F}_1^{(n)} - \tilde{F}_2^{(m)}|$, then D converges in distribution to the supremum of the absolute value of $\sqrt{1/(1/n+1/m)}$ times a standard Brownian bridge. Building on this, we can now examine interaction contrasts of CDFs: the limit distribution behaves similarly, but is now scaled by $N = 1/\sum_i n_i$.

Therefore we can apply the same KS test to interaction contrasts of survivor functions. For example, a selectively-influenced Parallel–First-Terminating model predicts the SIC is positive but never negative. Hence, if the observed maximum negative value of an SIC (D^-) is statistically significant, then that model may be rejected. To test the MIC for distinguishing between Coactive and Serial-AND processes, any test for an interaction can be applied (e.g., two-way ANOVA, adjusted-rank-transform, etc.). The predicted pattern of significance predicted by model type is summarized in Table 3.1.

The Capacity Coefficients

Much like our discussion of statistical analyses for the SIC, our discussion of the capacity statistics begins with the estimator. Recall that the OR capacity coefficient is defined by a comparison of cumulative hazard functions. As we have already seen, the survivor function can be estimated by one minus the ECDF and hence a common way to estimate the cumulative hazard function is with the negative logarithm of one minus the ECDF. Alternatively, it can be directly estimated with the empirical cumulative hazard function (ECHF),

$$\hat{H}(t) = \sum_{i:T_i \le t} \frac{1}{\text{\# of RTs longer than } T_i}.$$

The basic motivation for this estimator is that the density is estimated by 1 over the total number of RTs at any time there is an observed RT and 0 otherwise, while the survivor function is estimated by the number of RTs that have not occurred by t divided by the total number of RTs. Hence, the hazard $(f(t)/S(t))$ is estimated by 1 over the number of RTs that have not occurred by t any time there is an observed RT and zero otherwise. Because there are only a discrete number of response times and the hazard function estimate is zero at all other times, the integral of the estimated hazard simplifies to a sum over observed response times.

For the AND capacity coefficient, an estimate of the cumulative reverse hazard function is needed. Like the cumulative hazard function, the cumulative reverse hazard function can be estimated with either the logarithm of the ECDF or directly with a modified version of ECHF. The only difference between the hazard function and reverse hazard function is the denominator, $S(t)$ for the hazard function and $F(t)$ for the reverse hazard function. Thus, the empirical cumulative reverse hazard function (ECRHF) can be defined as

$$\hat{K}(t) = -\sum_{i:T_i \le t} \frac{1}{\text{\# of RTs less than or equal to } T_i}.$$

One advantage of these estimates of the cumulative hazard and cumulative reverse hazard is that they are easily adjusted for censored RTs. In this case, the only change is that all samples are included in the denominator (e.g., the count includes trials that timed out), although the censored RTs are not included in the index set of the sum. In this case, the estimator is known as the Nelson–Aalen estimator (NAH/NAK, Aalen, Borgan, & Gjessing, 2008). Houpt and Townsend (2010) suggested treating incorrect response times as random censoring events for estimating the correct response time cumulative hazard and cumulative reverse hazard functions.

If the incorrect response times are independent censoring events (as in an independent correct/incorrect race model but not in an accumulator model with response determined by first exit time), NAH and NAK are unbiased estimators of the true cumulative hazard function and cumulative reverse hazard functions, respectively (Andersen, Borgan, & Keiding, 1993; Aalen et al., 2008; Houpt & Townsend, 2010), i.e.,

$$\mathrm{E}\big[\hat{H}(t)\big] = H(t),$$
$$\mathrm{E}\big[\hat{K}(t)\big] = K(t).$$

Furthermore, both estimators converges uniformly to the true functions (Andersen et al., 1993; Houpt & Townsend, 2010).

A commonly used estimate of the variance of the NAH is

$$\widehat{\mathrm{Var}}\big[\hat{H}(t)\big] = \sum_{i:T_i \le t} \frac{1}{(\text{\# of RTs longer than } T_i)^2}.$$

Houpt and Townsend (2010) suggested an analogous estimator for the variance of the NAK,

$$\widehat{\mathrm{Var}}\big[\hat{K}(t)\big] = \sum_{i:T_i \le t} \frac{1}{(\text{\# of RTs less than or equal to} T_i)^2}.$$

Similar to the limit distribution of the ECDF, the limit distribution of the NAH and NAK estimators are Gaussian processes, although cumulative hazard function does not have a determined limit as $t \to \infty$ (similarly for cumulative reverse hazard functions as $t \to 0^+$) as does the CDF, so the limit process is not a Brownian bridge. Nonetheless, the limit distribution properties can be used for null hypothesis testing, including comparing between cumulative hazard functions. Because the limit distributions are Gaussian processes, they are univariate normally-distributed for any fixed t; hence, the difference between two NAHs or NAKs is univariate normally-distributed in the limit as well. This suggests a z-test for the null hypothesis that two cumulative (reverse) hazard functions estimated with their respective NA estimators are the same,

$$\mathrm{H}_0\text{:} \quad \frac{\hat{H}_1(t) - \hat{H}_2(t)}{\mathrm{Var}(\hat{H}(t)) + \mathrm{Var}(\hat{H}(t))} \sim \mathcal{N}(0, 1),$$

$$\mathrm{H}_0\text{:} \quad \frac{\hat{K}_1(t) - \hat{K}_2(t)}{\mathrm{Var}(\hat{K}(t)) + \mathrm{Var}(\hat{K}(t))} \sim \mathcal{N}(0, 1).$$

Although we do not go in to details here, the same z-test approach can be used if a function is used to differentially weight differences in the hazard function across time (for details, see Aalen et al., 2008; Houpt & Townsend, 2010).

To estimate the capacity coefficient, simply combine the estimated cumulative hazard or cumulative reverse hazard functions appropriately,

$$\hat{C}_{\mathrm{OR}}(t) = \frac{\hat{H}_{\mathrm{redundant}}(t)}{\sum_i \hat{H}_i(t)},$$

$$\hat{C}_{\mathrm{AND}}(t) = \frac{\sum_i \hat{K}_i(t)}{\hat{K}_{\mathrm{redundant}}(t)}.$$

For hypothesis testing, the difference between the predicted model baseline and the observed performance (rather than ratio) is more convenient,

$$\hat{C}_{\mathrm{OR}}(t) = \hat{H}_{\mathrm{redundant}}(t) - \sum_i \hat{H}_i(t),$$

$$\hat{C}_{\mathrm{AND}}(t) = \sum_i \hat{K}_i(t) - \hat{K}_{\mathrm{redundant}}(t).$$

This difference form allows us to again take advantage of the fact that linear combinations of Gaussian processes are again Gaussian processes. Analogous to the comparison between two hazard functions, we can test if the difference form of the capacity coefficients are significantly different from zero,

$$\text{H}_0\colon \frac{\hat{H}_{\text{redundant}}(t) - \sum_i \hat{H}_i(t)}{\text{Var}(\hat{H}(t)) + \text{Var}(\hat{H}(t))} \sim \mathcal{N}(0, 1),$$

$$\text{H}_0\colon \frac{\hat{K}_1(t) - \hat{K}_2(t)}{\text{Var}(\hat{K}(t)) + \text{Var}(\hat{K}(t))} \sim \mathcal{N}(0, 1).$$

If the true underlying process is a UCIP process, then the distribution of the test statistic will have a standard normal distribution for any t. In principle, one could test the hypothesis at many different time points although this will lead to α inflation. Following Aalen et al. (2008), Houpt and Townsend (2012) recommend a single test at some t larger than the longest response time. This allows the statistic to include all of the observed response times, and hence the test is based on all of the available, relevant data.

Bayesian Analyses for SFT

While null-hypothesis testing still underlies the majority of inference in psychology, Bayesian alternatives have continued to increase in popularity. In many cases, these Bayesian approaches offer benefits over traditional null-hypothesis significance testing.

One of the strengths of the SFT is the lack of strong assumptions about the distributional form of the response time variables. As we mentioned in the introduction, this comes at the cost of making it more complicated to define an appropriate likelihood function for observed response times and estimated SICs and capacity functions. Much like our approach to nonparametric frequentist statistics, the goal of this section is to build inferential tools using the least amount of a priori structure possible. A lack of structure usually comes with a concomitant lack of inferential power, so in the next two sections we explore both nonparametric and semiparametric Bayesian statistics for inferences within SFT.

Nonparametric Bayesian Tests

Nonparametric Bayesian analysis can be achieved using a prior that assigns probability to any possible distribution function of the response times. Samples from that prior then serve as the likelihood for the observed response times. Following a standard approach in nonparametric Bayesian data analysis, Houpt, Heathcote, and Eidels (in press) proposed the Dirichlet process prior (Ferguson, 1973) as the prior over distributions for analyzing SICs. Although samples from the Dirichlet process prior are discrete distributions almost surely (i.e., with probability one), the approach is quite flexible. Practically speaking, one can consider it a distribution over all possible histogram shapes for a set of bins. For a given sample, the likelihood of the data is taken directly from that histogram.

SIC

To obtain samples from the posterior over the SIC, Houpt et al. (in press) independently sampled from the posterior of each response time distribution in the contrast, then calculated the interaction contrast. Hence, the Monte Carlo approximation for the posterior for each RT distribution can be translated into a Monte Carlo approximation for the SIC. In turn, this posterior can be used to quantify the uncertainty of the SIC estimate.

For more direct conclusions about which SIC shape is most likely to have produced the RT distributions (and hence the observed RTs), Houpt et al. (in press) use the encompassing Bayes Factor approach (Klugkist, Kato, & Hoijtink, 2005). After obtaining samples from both prior and the posterior, these samples are collapsed to categorical posteriors over SIC shapes, namely those shapes predicted by the models of interest. Because the prior includes all of the SIC shapes (i.e., is an encompassing prior), the Bayes factor for each SIC shape can be approximated by using the number of posterior samples divided by the number of prior samples that have that SIC shape. These Bayes factors can then be directly compared across models.

One caveat of this approach is that the better the approximation to continuous the Dirichlet process prior, the less likely a zero MIC or SIC is. Indeed, if the distribution were continuous, zero SIC and MIC would have zero probability in the prior (and hence the posterior). To alleviate this potential bias against serial SIC shapes, Houpt et al. (in press) suggested using a region of practical equivalence (ROPE; cf. Kruschke, 2011; Klugkist et al., 2005) for the SIC and MIC. This means that as long as long as the SIC (MIC) is within a criterion range of zero it is treated as zero for both the prior and the posterior. These parameters can be used to some degree to shift the bias of the analysis, although because the criterion applies to both the MIC and the SIC, and hence changes both the estimate of the numerator and the denominator, its effects are not necessarily straightforward. Based on a series of simulations, Houpt et al. (in press) indicated that 0.3 worked well for both the SIC and MIC criteria.

Capacity Coefficient

The same principle can be applied to the capacity coefficient. The Dirichlet process prior with multinomial likelihood serves as the structure for the estimation of the cumulative distribution for each condition in the capacity coefficient. Samples from the posterior estimates of the distribution can be converted to the estimates of the cumulative (reverse) hazard function using the appropriate transformation, $H(t) = \log[1 - F(t)]$ ($K(t) = \log[F(t)]$), then combined to obtain a Monte Carlo estimate of the posterior distribution over the capacity coefficient.

Because each of the distributions in the prior is treated separately, the prior allows for the capacity coefficient to be above 1 (supercapacity), below 1 (limited capacity), within a predefined ROPE around 1 (unlimited capacity), or one of many other shapes, such as first below 1, then later above 1. Hence, the encompassing prior approach can be used to estimate Bayes Factors for each class of capacity coefficient. In turn, the Bayes Factors can be used as quantifications of the evidence for supercapacity, unlimited capacity or limited capacity.

Semiparametric Bayesian Tests

Although the nonparametric Bayesian approach is ideal as it imposes the weakest structure on the data, there is potential advantage in building prior knowledge about RT distributions into the structure of the analysis. In this section, we consider the semiparametric approach proposed by Houpt, MacEachern, Peruggia, Townsend, and van Zandt (2016) as a compromise between the goals of nonparametrics and taking advantage of the knowledge we have about RT distributions. In this approach, a hierarchical prior structure is developed for the hazard function of each distribution. The hazard function is then used to estimate the likelihood of each response time in the MCMC algorithm using the relation

$$l(t|\Theta) = h(t|\Theta)\exp\left[\int_{s=0}^{t} h(s)\,ds\right].$$

Houpt et al. (2016) follow Ibrahim, Chen, and Sinha (2005) by using a piecewise constant function to approximate the hazard function. Because a constant hazard function corresponds to an exponential distribution, the distribution is referred to as a piecewise exponential distribution.

Similar to the bins in the nonparametric Bayesian approach above, the set of points at which the hazard function changes levels must be chosen, $\{s_0, s_1, \dots, s_J\}$ where s_0 is lower than the shortest response time and s_J is higher than the longest response time. The hazard function is given by the collection of magnitudes within each of those bins, $\{h_1, \dots, h_J\}$. In this case, if t falls in the ith bin, the likelihood can be rewritten as

$$l(t|\Theta) = h_i \exp\left[(t - s_{i-1})h_i + \sum_{j=0}^{i-1}(s_j - s_{j-1})h_j\right].$$

This likelihood can then be used to obtain posterior samples using MCMC (e.g., using STAN; Stan Development Team, 2014). The posterior samples are in terms of the hazard level in each bin, so to obtain posterior samples for the SIC, it is necessary to translate the hazard levels of each sample to a survivor function. This is done using the relationship

$$S(t) = \exp\left\{-\int_{0}^{t} h(s)\,ds\right\},$$

or, specifically for the piecewise exponential model when t is between s_{i-1} and s_i,

$$S(t) = \exp\left\{-(t - s_{i-1})h_i \sum_{j=1}^{i-1}(s_j - s_{j-1})h_j\right\}.$$

Combining a posterior sample for each survivor function with the interaction contrast then gives a posterior sample for the SIC. By using the samples, one can estimate various properties of the SIC, such as the pointwise posterior uncertainty of the shape and the probability that the function is negative and/or positive for any time range.

In the same manner, posterior estimates of the properties of the capacity coefficients can be obtained. Furthermore, Because this analysis is defined on hazard functions, it is straightforward to constrain the model to follow the UCIP assumptions, i.e., the (reverse) hazard function of the multiple information source should be equal to the sum of the (reverse) hazard functions of the single source conditions. This approach allows for an additional method for testing against a UCIP model using the various likelihood based metrics. Houpt et al. (2016) used the Watanabe–Akaike Information Criterion (WAIC Watanabe, 2010) following the suggestion of Vehtari, Gelman, and Gabry (2016). Although Houpt et al. (2016) simulations indicate the WAIC was biased against the UCIP model, further exploration is warranted due to the potential benefits of the WAIC.

Exploratory Analysis with Functional Principal Component Analysis

Workload capacity is often thought of as a unitary concept, where participants are characterized as performing either above or below some baseline expectation. Although implementations of the capacity coefficient often revert back to this limited, qualitative comparison, the measure itself contains a wealth of quantitative information with the potential to disambiguate models or compare between subjects and conditions within an experiment. The capacity coefficient, $C(t)$, is a function of processing efficiency across reaction time, meaning that the very same subject could perform more efficiently than baseline for early responses and yet less efficiently for slow responses. Rather than just reporting if the function is greater or less than one (which denotes UCIP processing), analyses could report the quantitative height of the function, its slope, changes in concavity, and much more.

A potential explanation for the relatively cursory examination of capacity functions seen in the literature is simply that functions are difficult to talk about. Our typical language for comparisons falls short with functional data, where quite often one function will be greater than another not in an absolute sense, but for only a subset of timepoints. The language and tools of functional data analysis (Ramsay & Silverman, 2005) can aid us in making fuller use of this rich measure.

Burns, Houpt, Townsend, and Endres (2013) show how functional principal component analysis (fPCA) can be used to quantitatively and succinctly compare capacity coefficient functions across participants and conditions. Much like standard principal component analysis, this technique computes a mean capacity function for the full data set and then finds component functions to maximally distinguish between the various pieces of data (participants and/or conditions). The first component is specified as $f_{i1} = \int \beta_1(s)x_i(s)\,ds$, where $x_i(s)$ are the data functions, and $\beta_1(s)$ is a weighting function chosen to maximize the following equation, which is a continuous analog to the mean square in the standard analysis:

$$\frac{1}{N}\sum_i f_{i1}^2 = \frac{1}{N}\sum_i\left(\int \beta_1 x_i\right)^2. \tag{3.1}$$

We must use the further constraint that $\int \beta_1(s)^2\,ds = 1$. Additional components can then be found by again maximizing the variance explained while ensuring new components are orthogonal to all previous components:

$$\int \beta_k(s)\beta_m(s)\,ds = 0. \tag{3.2}$$

Each $C(t)$ function can now be described by a sequence of scalar *score* values, which denote how much of each component function needs to be added to the mean to approximate their data. These components can often be made more interpretable through a rotation of the bases. The total amount of variance explained by a set of functions will remain constant through rotation, but methods such as *varimax* will concentrate the effects of each function. Often a set of only two or three component functions is needed to account for 95% of the variance in the data, yielding a much more tractable set of scores for comparing participants and conditions.

Although the principal component functions will be fully determined by the particular data set being used, it is usually the case that the first component will in some degree correspond to the overall height of the functions. Scores for this component will then support quantitative comparisons showing which participants or conditions were more efficient overall. The second component, guaranteed to be orthogonal to the first, will often capture differences in slope: one participant's function may be relatively constant across reaction times, while another participant may be efficient for fast responses and less so for slower responses. This second order information already moves us beyond the current theoretical literature in this area: we do not yet know what import it may have for information processing systems to know how values of the capacity coefficient change with response times. Burns et al. (2013) show that such differences are apparent between participants and conditions, making this a promising area for future development of the capacity coefficient. It is quite possible that models which are capable of making identical predictions for the overall level of capacity are more greatly constrained, and could therefore be more readily distinguished, at the level of change in capacity across reaction times.

Conclusions

The greatest strength of SFT is that its core constructs are rigorously defined based on the minimum assumptions necessary to delineate them. The two main measures within SFT, the SIC and Ct, are built on the same principle: they are rigorously defined based on minimal assumptions, and yet make strong predictions about the possible values that could be produced by various classes of cognitive systems. Despite this rigor, the nonparametric nature of the approach hindered the development of inferential statistics. It is testament to the value of SFT that it had been widely applied despite the lack of a well-defined hypothesis testing framework. With the development of the many statistical tests presented within this chapter, there is even more opportunity for the application of SFT.

References

Aalen, O. O., Borgan, Ø., & Gjessing, H. K. (2008). *Survival and event history analysis: A process point of view*. New York: Springer.

Andersen, P. K., Borgan, Ø., & Keiding, N. (1993). *Statistical models based on counting processes*. New York: Springer.

Billingsley, P. (1995). *Probability and measure* (third edition). New York: Wiley.

Billingsley, P. (1999). *Convergence of probability measures* (second edition). New York: Wiley.

Brown, S. D., & Heathcote, A. (2008). The simplest complete model of choice response time: Linear ballistic accumulation. *Cognitive Psychology*, *57*(3), 153–178.

Burns, D. M., Houpt, J. W., Townsend, J. T., & Endres, M. J. (2013). Functional principal components analysis of workload capacity functions. *Behavior Research Methods*, *45*, 1048–1057.

Ferguson, T. S. (1973). A Bayesian anlaysis of some nonparametric problems. *The Annals of Statistics*, *1*, 209–230.

Houpt, J.W., Heathcote, A., & Eidels, A. (in press). Bayesian analyses of cognitive architecture. http://dx.doi.org/10.1037/met0000117.

Houpt, J. W., MacEachern, S. N., Peruggia, M., Townsend, J. T., & van Zandt, T. (2016). Semiparametric Bayesian approaches to systems factorial technology. *Journal of Mathematical Psychology*, *75*, 68–85.

Houpt, J. W., & Townsend, J. T. (2010). The statistical properties of the survivor interaction contrast. *Journal of Mathematical Psychology*, *54*, 446–453.

Houpt, J. W., & Townsend, J. T. (2012). Statistical measures for workload capacity analysis. *Journal of Mathematical Psychology*, *56*, 341–355.

Ibrahim, J. G., Chen, M.-H., & Sinha, D. (2005). *Bayesian survival analysis*. Wiley Online Library.

Klugkist, I., Kato, B., & Hoijtink, H. (2005). Bayesian model selection using encompassing priors. *Statistica Neerlandica*, *59*, 57–69.

Kolmogorov, A. (1933). Sulla determinazione empirica di une legge di distribuzione. *Giornale dell' Instituto Italiano degli Attuari*, *4*, 83–91.

Kruschke, J. K. (2011). Bayesian assessment of null values via parameter estimation and model comparison. *Perspectives on Psychological Science*, *6*, 299–312.

Ramsay, J. O., & Silverman, B. W. (2005). *Functional data analysis* (2nd edition). *Springer series in statistics*. New York: Springer.

Stan Development Team (2014). *Stan: A C++ library for probability and sampling, version 2.5.0*.

Townsend, J. T., & Nozawa, G. (1995). Spatio-temporal properties of elementary perception: An investigation of parallel, serial, and coactive theories. *Journal of Mathematical Psychology*, *39*(4), 321–359.

Vehtari, A., Gelman, A., & Gabry, J. (2016). Practical Bayesian model evaluation using leave-one-out cross-validation and WAIC. *Statistics and Computing*, *59*, 1–20. http://dx.doi.org/10.1007/s11222-016-9696-4.

Watanabe, S. (2010). Asymptotic equivalence of Bayes cross validation and widely applicable information criterion in singular learning theory. *Journal of Machine Learning Research*, *11*, 3571–3594.

Endnotes

1. A Gaussian process is a stochastic process for which any finite set on its domain has a multivariate Gaussian distribution. This heuristic argument is technically incomplete for convergence across the entire function; the formal proof that the limit distribution is a Gaussian process is known as the functional central limit theorem (or Donsker's theorem); see Billingsley (1999).
2. The additional scaling term comes from the fact that the variance of the estimator decreases as a function of $\sqrt{n}$. When multiplying D by $\sqrt{n}$, the variance (in the limit) matches the variance of the standard Brownian bridge.

Development and Applications of the Capacity Function that also Measures Accuracy

4

Nicholas Altieri
Idaho State University, Pocatello, ID, United States

> *The secret of happiness, you see, is not found in seeking more, but in developing the capacity to enjoy less.*
>
> ***Socrates***

Introduction

A fundamental endeavor in the psychological sciences consists of examining the efficiency of a cognitive system (see, e.g., Hick, 1952; Jastrow & Cairnes, 1891; Neisser, 1967; Pachella, 1974). The importance of assessing efficiency encompasses many subdomains of the psychological sciences, including attention in audition and vision (Kahneman, 1967, 1973; Schneider & Shiffrin, 1977), and even in clinical settings with studies investigating cognitive impairment and schizophrenia (Bundesen & Habekost, 2008; Neufeld, Carter, Boksman, Jette, & Vollick, 2002). Several important reviews and discussions involving varying degrees of breadth and depth have been published over the years, especially those that relate capacity to attention (Kahneman, 1973; Gopher & Navon, 1980; Neufeld, Townsend, & Jette, 2007; Norman & Bobrow, 1975; Palmer, Verghese, & Pavel, 2000; Schweickert & Boggs, 1984; Townsend & Altieri, 2012; Townsend & Ashby, 1978).

We may begin by conceptualizing efficiency in a psychological context as mental capability often times referred to as simply "capacity." Speaking intuitively, capacity and efficiency are intimately related; systems with higher capacity process, utilize, or hold information more efficiently as a function of workload, while lower capacity connotes a system with lower efficiency. Somewhat more formally, *capacity* refers to the extent to which an observer can retain and mentally manipulate sensory cues or internal representations as a function of cues present in a display.

Still, in many respects, our notion of "mental capacity" relates to intuitive notions of capacity in everyday situations. We commonly hear of such notions as the capacity to perform work, an elevator's capacity to hold weight, or the capacity of a vessel to hold liquid. While these metaphors may be beneficial for purposes of discussion—much like Aristotle's idea of human memory being akin to a wax tablet—they are often just that: metaphors. One difference of critical importance between capacity in the context of human information processing, and the more generalized notion of capacity pertaining to static physical systems, concerns the dynamic nature of perception. By this, I mean that "mental capacity" often changes as a function of time, task

Systems Factorial Technology, DOI: 10.1016/B978-0-12-804315-8.00006-9

demands, and even the nature of the stimuli in a given experiment; this happens to be rather unlike the capacity of the static physical systems we regularly encounter such as bridges, elevators, and coffee cups—which change on a time scale so long as to be perceived as having constant capacity. I can empty and refill a coffee cup any number of times, but the amount of coffee that can fit in the cup remains constant.

Finally, this discussion brings to bear an important distinction in our definition of capacity: *item* versus *system*-level capacity (see Townsend, 1974). Item level capacity refers to the extent to which processing changes as a function of the number of items needing to be processed. For example, does processing time change on each item as more items are added to the display? On the other hand, we may speak of capacity at the level of the system. Here, we speak of how processing times change at the level of the system as a function of the number of items needing to be processed; this may become relevant when we cannot observe processing at the level of the item.

Theoretical Foundations for Measuring Capacity

Determining how to measure capacity is not necessarily straightforward, and consequently, many alternative approaches have been proposed. When assuming that a system is static, one may assign a single numerical value to represent the total capacity. Miller's number of 7 ± 2 for short-term memory capacity comes to mind (Miller, 1956). In these cases, we may rely on descriptive statistics to compare capacity between systems or conditions. For purposes of assessment, we may compare the mean response-time or mean accuracy in two experimental conditions: One condition may involve identifying a target letter in a display consisting of *five* distractor items, while the other condition may include a greater number of distractors, say *ten*.

An alternative approach that speaks to the dynamic nature of information processing, and one expounded upon in this chapter, involves the use of statistical procedures connected to the properties of mathematically defined models. The basic idea is to compare the data of interest to some sort of benchmark; one prominent example consists of comparing information processing to the predictions of unlimited capacity independent parallel (UCIP) models (Townsend & Nozawa, 1995; also refer to Miller, 1982, 1986; Raab, 1962). In this framework, simultaneously presented sensory inputs accrue evidence and race toward a threshold. As more inputs are added, say two versus one, such recognition occurs more quickly due to statistical reasons; as more horses enter a race, the average completion time decreases even if the processes—or horses running on a race track in our metaphor—are not influencing one another. As I shall demonstrate later in the capacity derivations, the UCIP assumptions allow us to measure item-level capacity. Of course, other benchmarks, such as serial models with inherent capacity limitations, could be theoretically viable in some cases.

Regardless, the important point is that the data obtained in a condition in which two or more targets are present should be compared to a mathematically tractable model whose predictions are derived from conditions in which only one stimulus is presented (*single target conditions*; Townsend & Nozawa, 1995). This notion of assessing efficiency as a function of change in workload is fundamental to the notion of capacity. We may operationally define *workload* as the number of *entities* that require attention or consideration on the part of a perceiver in a display. In controlled experimental settings, the investigator controls and determines the quantity of the entities, which can include objects, facial features, angles, or even auditory and visual cues. Assume that the experimenter adds increasingly more entities to a trial, hence requiring more work on the part of the subject. If the subject fails to show observable benefit in terms of accuracy or processing time, then we may say the system performs inefficiently. Conversely, if adding more processes contributes to a large enough increase in accuracy or processing time relative to our benchmark, we may refer to processing as efficient. Socrates' metaphor of happiness used as an epigraph to this chapter elegantly captures this concept. Socrates appears to proclaim the idea that efficiency does not necessarily denote more, but rather the ability to achieve some benefit using less effort.

The following example should help clarify to the conceptualization of efficiency, and also the dynamic adaptability in human information processing. This logic will be relevant to the subsequent descriptions of RT-only capacity, $C(t)$, and the accuracy adjusted capacity measure, $A(t)$. Suppose a hypothetical experiment requires a perceiver to identify two types of objects—A and B—each of which comprises multiple parts. These could be faces, cars, etc. Further, assume that object B, although containing an identical number of parts as object B, is more complex and therefore more difficult to identify. The following scenarios can arise to affect the efficiency or capacity of the participant: (i) The observer may alter the speed at which she identifies the individual components of the object, (ii) accuracy may increase or decrease as a function of speed, and (iii) the factors of speed or accuracy may change as a function of stimuli; in this case, whether A or B (e.g., a face or a car) is being identified. The relevant point here is that the interaction of these factors can contribute to the overall capacity of the system. To see exactly how, consider a scenario where the experimental participant is tasked with identifying object A. The perceiver may adjust his or her processing speed and integrate the individual parts faster—without sacrificing accuracy—and thus more efficiently. Conversely, since object B is more difficult to identify, increasing speed may come at the expense of sacrificing accuracy. This latter scenario points to a speed–accuracy tradeoff in capacity where the benefits of speed may in fact be outweighed by the simultaneous decrement in accuracy.

A Response-Time Measure of Capacity Using Integrated Hazard Functions

This section will introduce parallel independent race (UCIP) models, integrated hazard functions, and the original reaction-time (RT) only measure of capacity, $C(t)$, developed over two decades ago by Townsend and colleagues (Townsend & Nozawa, 1995). The RT-only capacity equation described in this section is ideal in detection situation where RT is the dependent variable, and accuracy is near ceiling in each of the experimental conditions. From there, this chapter will show how the more complete capacity measure that also incorporates accuracy can be derived for both OR (disjunctive) and AND (conjunctive) decision rules (Townsend & Altieri, 2012). I shall conclude by exploring applications of the accuracy-adjusted capacity function, $A(t)$, using examples from tasks that present listeners with incongruent auditory-visual speech cues (McGurk & MacDonald, 1976).

Generically speaking, capacity computes "efficiency as a function of change in workload" using some dependent variable such as RT; this is typically done when two targets are presented relative to UCIP predictions derived from conditions where only one stimulus, or target, is present. Parallel independent race model predictions are derived from the single target trials, as shown in Fig. 4.1 which reveals an example of an experimental paradigm where either only one target (e.g., a dot) is presented above or below the fixation (single-target trials), two dots are presented (redundant-target), or no information is presented (catch trials). The task in this type of paradigm is to respond by pressing a button labeled "YES" as quickly and as accurately as possible if at least one target is present (OR decision rule), or responding "YES" only if two targets are present (AND decision rule). (Fig. 4.1 shows the OR rule explicitly.)

Without loss of generality, when the processing rate on each single channel is unaffected by increasing the number of channels, the system operates at "unlimited capacity". Conversely, if it slows down relative to parallel independent model predictions, then the system operates at limited capacity and exhibits low efficiency. Finally, suppose there is a benefit in processing rate in the redundant target condition relative to independent parallel race model or UCIP predictions, then the system is said to operate at "supercapacity" or otherwise exhibit high efficiency. One benefit of capacity measures devised by Townsend and colleagues (e.g., Townsend & Nozawa, 1995) is that these measures do not depend on any specific parameter or distribution. Therefore, capacity is nonparametric and distribution free. For example, the inferences do not depend on assuming that the variable of interest follows a normal distribution, for instance. Capacity assessments using RT distributions are carried out using integrated hazard functions instead of comparing means.

The capacity coefficient can be computed by using integrated hazard functions, which we may write as $H(t)$. These functions describe the probability that a process, such as the recognition of one of the dots in Fig. 4.1, terminates in the next instant $(t+\Delta t)$ given that recognition has not yet occurred. We refer readers interested in other details regarding hazard functions to the tutorial chapter in this book. Using integrated hazard functions is helpful for deriving the predictions of independent parallel model predictions (Townsend & Nozawa, 1995). Let $F_1(t)$ represent the CDF when only the bottom stimulus is present, and $F_2(t)$ when only the top is present.

Under basic UCIP assumptions, we can derive predictions for the redundant target condition CDF, $F_{12}(t)$. By the assumption of independence between channels, we get $F_{12}(t) = F_1(t)+F_2(t)-F_1(t)\times F_2(t)$. This quantity describes the probability of being correct on channel 1 OR 2, while subtracting out the joint probability, $F_1(t) \times F_2(t)$. Importantly, the assumption of independence between channels allows us to write the joint probability as multiplication. By subtracting each side of the equation from 1, we arrive at

- $1 - F_{12}(t) = 1 - [F_1(t) + F_2(t) - F_1(t) \times F_2(t)]$,

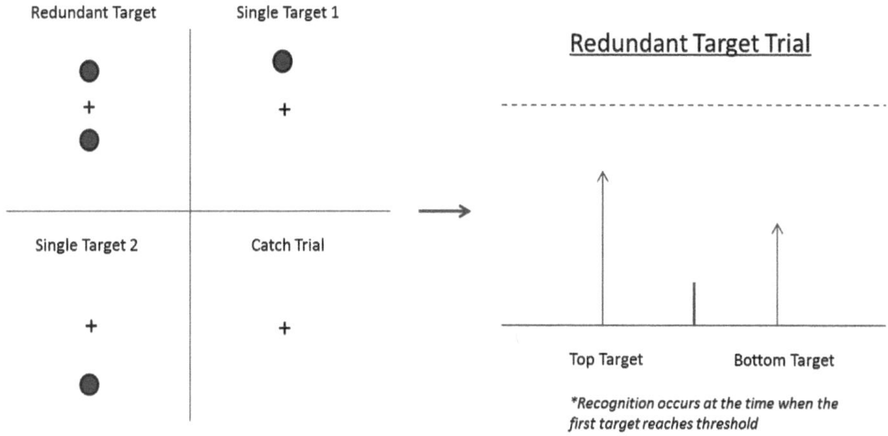

Figure 4.1 An example of four trial types in a visual detection study. The parallel independent race in the redundant target condition between top and bottom sensory information is shown in the right panel.

- which simplifies to $1 - F_{12}(t) = 1 - F_1(t) - F_2(t) + F_1(t) \times F_2(t)$.
- Factoring this result gives $1 - F_{12}(t) = [1 - F_1(t)] \times [1 - F_2(t)]$.
- Further simplification is possible using survivor functions $(1 - F(t) = S(t))$. By writing this in terms of survivor functions, we get $S_{12}(t) = S_1(t) \times S_2(t)$.
- We can then obtain the negative logarithm of each side of the equation to yield $-\log(S_{12}(t)) = [-\log(S_1(t))] + [-\log(S_2(t))]$. This is significant, since the integrated hazard function $H(t)$ can be written as $-\log(S(t))$.
- Therefore, we arrive at the rather simple quantity, $H_{12}(t) = H_1(t) + H_2(t)$, where the sum on the right indicates the predictions of UCIP.

The suggested method for calculating capacity, or $C(t)$, using an OR decision rule involves dividing the redundant target data, $H_{12}(t)$, by the sum of the integrated hazard functions, i.e., the independent model predictions. Capacity, $C(t)$, is given as

$$C(t) = \frac{H_{12}}{H_1(t) + H_2(t)}. \tag{4.1}$$

Capacity calculations assume unlimited capacity on each channel, stochastically independent processing times. Therefore, this standard model acts as a benchmark for measuring capacity as a function of perceptual workload, and predicts $C(t) = 1$ as a null hypothesis for all response times.

Suppose instead that there is a benefit over and above the advantage from taking the minimum processing time in RTs as a result of the information provided by the additional channel, in such a way that $C(t) > 1$ for some processing time t; here, we would say that the system operates at *supercapacity* at that time. Semi-parametric statistical methods have been recently developed by Houpt and Townsend (2012) using methods that directly estimate hazard and integrated hazard functions. These methods allow us to determine whether UCIP assumptions have been violated. Nonetheless, deciding whether violations of UCIP predictions have occurred has traditionally relied on examining whether $C(t)$ exceeds theoretical bounds encompassing the upper and lower bounds of UCIP performance. One such upper bound on performance for UCIP models was initially suggested by Miller (1982). It was derived from independence assumptions reflecting the fact that $F_{12}(t) = F_1(t) + F_2(t) - F_1(t) \times F_2(t) \leq F_1(t) + F_2(t)$.

Townsend and Eidels showed how this bound can be plotted in the same space as the capacity function Townsend and Eidels (2011). By substituting the survivor function $1 - S_1(t)$ for $F_1(t)$, and then flipping the inequality, we arrive at

- $1 - S_{12}(t) = [1 - S_1(t)] + [1 - S_2(t)] - ([1 - S_1(t)] \times [1 - S_2(t)]) \leq [1 - S_1(t)] + [1 - S_2(t)]$.
- $1 - S_{12}(t) = 2 - S_1(t) - S_2(t) - [1 - S_1(t) - S_2(t) + S_1(t) \times S_2(t)] \leq 2 - S_1(t) - S_2(t)$
- which yields $1 - S_1(t) \times S_2(t) \leq 2 - S_1(t) - S_2(t)$.
- $-S_1(t) \times S_2(t) \leq 1 - S_1(t) - S_2(t)$.
- Multiplying each side by -1 simplifies to $S_1(t) \times S_2(t) \geq S_1(t) + S_2(t) - 1$.
- By obtaining the logarithm of each side, we get $H_1(t) + H_2(t) \geq \log\{S_1(t) + S_2(t) - 1\}$.

$$\therefore C(t) \geq \frac{\log[S_1(t) + S_2(t) - 1]}{H_1(t) + H_2(t)}.$$

Once again, the UCIP predictions are shown in the denominator. If $C(t) > 1$ for some time interval, then the inequality has been violated. Logically, if $C(t) < 1$, then the inequality cannot have been violated. The question becomes, what type of processing systems can violate UCIP model predictions? Coactive models typically exhibit supercapacity. As a result, quantitative interpretations of these models began to appear in the literature (Colonius & Townsend, 1997; Diederich & Colonius, 1991; Miller & Ulrich, 2003; Schwarz, 1994; Townsend & Nozawa, 1995). The Townsend and Nozawa (1995) study proved that a wide variety of coactive models based on counting processes with arbitrary distributions have this property. These distributions include Poisson distributions but are not limited to them. Such models will at some point in time violate the race model inequality.

Besides supercapacity, other violations of UCIP predictions may occur. Limited capacity occurs when $C(t)$ is substantially less than 1 (Neufeld et al., 2007; Townsend & Nozawa, 1995; Wenger & Townsend, 2000). Limited capacity could be caused by inhibition across channels or the allocation of limited resources to the individual channels. The lower bound of interest for limited capacity is known as the Grice bound. It is represented by $F_{12}(t) = F_1(t) + F_2(t) - F_1(t) \times F_2(t) \geq \max\{F_1(t) \times F_2(t)\}$ (see Grice, Canham, & Gwynne, 1984). The Grice bound in capacity space, also derived by Townsend and Eidels (2011), is $C(t) < \frac{\max\{H_1(t), H_2(t)\}}{H_1(t)+H_2(t)}$. What types of systems are associated with limited capacity? Often times, violations of the Grice bound can be produced by serial models (Townsend & Nozawa, 1995) or by models with inhibition across channels (Eidels, Houpt, Altieri, Pei, & Townsend, 2011). We refer the interested reader to Townsend and Eidels (2011) for further information regarding the derivations of upper and lower bounds on parallel systems in capacity space.

These RT based measures of capacity were developed to assess the UCIP model, or to use another term, "horse race" model, assuming an OR stopping rule. What about

AND predictions? In other words, how might we assess redundant target processing relative to parallel independent model predictions in a task requiring participants to make a "YES" response if and only if both targets are present (see Fig. 4.1)? Townsend and Wenger (2004) derived predictions for these models using a capacity function similar to Eq. (4.1) with logarithmic transformed distribution functions of RTs. Instead of $H(t)$ functions, the authors developed "$K(t)$" functions; both consist of logarithmic transformed cumulative sums of RTs. The $K(t)$ functions, however, utilize the cumulative distribution function, $F(t)$, rather than the survivor function, $1 - F(t)$. Deriving parallel independent model predictions for an AND design is straightforward, since a "YES" response requires detection in channels 1 and 2 (or top and bottom components, respectively), $F_{12}(t) = F_1(t) \times F_2(t)$. We can then obtain the negative logarithmic transformation to give us $\log[F_{12}(t)] = \log[F_1(t)] \times \log[F_2(t)]$, yielding $\log[F_{12}(t)] = \log[F_1(t)] + \log[F_2(t)]$, and so

$$\therefore C(t) = \frac{K_1(t) + K_2(t)}{K_{12}(t)}. \tag{4.2}$$

Similar to the OR case, derivations of upper and lower bounds were additionally provided by Townsend and Eidels (2011). The derivation for the upper and lower bounds for the AND decision rule is shown in part 1 of Appendix.

A Capacity Measure Incorporating Accuracy

The capacity equations described in the preceding rely entirely on RTs; this can somewhat be unfortunate because often accuracy represents a vital dependent measure in information processing tasks. Furthermore, speed and accuracy can trade-off with each other in instances where participants speed up at the expense of accuracy, or slow down, thereby increasing accuracy (Link & Heath, 1975; Pachella, 1974; Vickers, 1979). Crucially, in the former case, capacity might cross the threshold into the realm of supercapacity; however, would we really want to say that processing is efficient relative to UCIP predictions if accuracy decreases substantially? In that vein, the question becomes "how much of a decrement in accuracy can we tolerate before processing becomes inefficient?" Relatedly, in the latter case, we might ask ourselves "to what extent can we tolerate a decrement in speed in an effort to create accuracy?" Addressing these questions concerning speed accuracy trade-offs requires a unified capacity function that also incorporates accuracy predictions. This is crucial because real-word applications, as we shall see in the final section of the chapter, may involve speed–accuracy trade-offs. We can use the unified $A(t)$ function first to assess the extent to which processing is "superior" or "inferior" compared to UCIP predictions. Then, we can subsequently analyze $C(t)$ and accuracy predictions separately to determine the locus of an individual participant's performance. Hence, we can use these tools to inquire whether deviations from independent model predictions are due to alterations in speed, accuracy, or both.

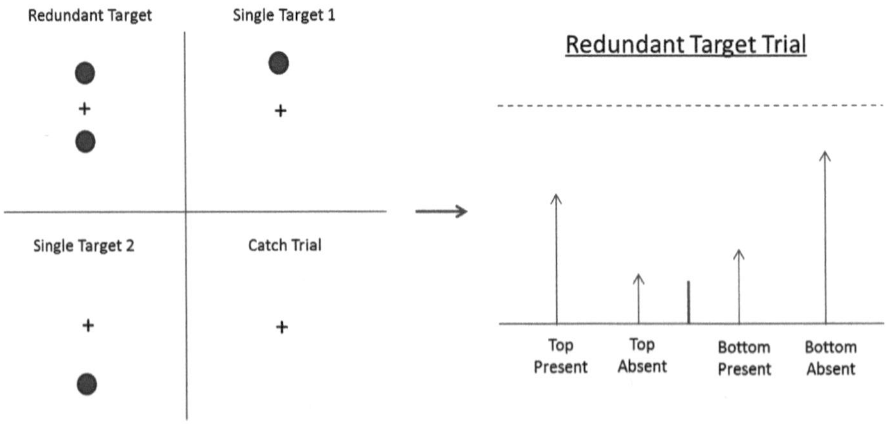

Figure 4.2 The same four trial types in a visual detection study shown in Fig. 4.1. The race in the right hand panel shows competition between target present and absent information for the top and bottom stimuli.

This section will provide a summary of the development of such a capacity function developed by Townsend and Altieri for the OR and AND rules (2012; see also Altieri, Townsend, & Wenger, 2014). The derivations for the incorrect and fast, and correct and slow $A(t)$ equations described by Townsend and Altieri (2012) can be found in part 2 of Appendix. I shall begin by reintroducing Fig. 4.1 which shows a parallel race occurring in the redundant target condition, with a modification allowing for errors during the identification of each stimulus. The experimental set-up and redundant target trial informational accrual are displayed in Fig. 4.2. In this hypothetical case, both a bottom and top target are displayed; importantly, stimulus and "absence of stimulus" information race toward a threshold. The addition of an "absent" accumulator allows for the fact that errors (i.e., misses) might be committed.

Equation for the OR Decision Rule

Townsend and Altieri (2012; see also Altieri et al., 2014) proved that the likelihood function for deriving UCIP predictions for the accuracy adjusted capacity coefficient using the OR decision rule is given by a more complex set of relations that the derivation for $C(t)$. The logic for UCIP predictions for how a participant can correctly identify a target in channel 1 OR 2 by a certain time is given by the following. First, one may correctly identify the target in channel 1 by a certain time and also be incorrect on the target in channel 2 (i.e., a "miss" on target 2). OR they may correctly identify the target in channel 2 by a certain time while also being incorrect on the target in channel 1 (i.e., "miss" target 1). OR the participant can correctly identify the target in channel 1 by a certain time (without correct recognition occurring *yet* in channel 2), OR they may correctly identify the target in channel 2 by a certain time (without correct recognition occurring *yet* for target 1). Finally, we add the likelihood that both targets in channels 1 and 2 reach threshold by a certain time. These UCIP predictions, the probability being correct in the redundant target condition in the context of an OR decision rule by a certain time, can be expressed mathematically by the following quantity:

$$\begin{aligned}
&\int_0^t P_{12}(T_{12C} = t' < T_{12I})\,dt' \\
&\quad = \int_0^t P_1(T_{1C} = t' < T_{1I})\,dt' \times P_2(I) + \int_0^t P_2(T_{2C} = t' < T_{2I})\,dt' \times P_1(I) \\
&\quad + \int_0^t P_1(T_{1C} = t' < T_{1I})\,dt' \times \int_{t'=t}^{\infty} P_2(T_{2C} = t' < T_{2I})\,dt' \\
&\quad + \int_0^t P_2(T_{2C} = t' < T_{2I})\,dt' \times \int_{t'=t}^{\infty} P_1(T_{1C} = t' < T_{1I})\,dt' \\
&\quad + \int_0^t P_1(T_{1C} = t' < T_{1I})\,dt' \times \int_0^t P_2(T_{2C} = t' < T_{2I})\,dt'.
\end{aligned}$$

Notice how each term in the likelihood function is directly related to the $F(t)$ and $S(t)$ (i.e., $1 - F(t)$) functions described previously; the difference now is that they are weighted by probability correct or incorrect, and henceforth termed "defective" CDF or survivor functions. They are called "defective" because they do not integrate or sum to 1. Consider, for instance, the following term $\int_0^t P_1(T_{1C} = t' < T_{1I})\,dt'$. This equals the empirical CDF from top-only trials where the participant responds correctly (i.e., since a correct response, denoted by subscript 'C', is made before an incorrect one, denoted by subscript 'I'), weighted by the probability correct on those trials. It is similar to a cumulative distribution function, but instead of summing to 1, it integrates to the probability correct on those trials. Consider another term, this one being an analogue of the survivor functions $\int_{t'=t}^{\infty} P_2(T_{2C} = t' < T_{2I})\,dt'$. This is equal to the probability that one will correctly identify the bottom-only stimulus, weighted by the probability correct on those trials; however, a correct response has not yet been made by time t. Hence, this term is similar to the survivor functions, except that it begins at the probability correct instead of 1.

Similar to the RT-only capacity coefficient, $C(t)$, in Eq. (4.1), we may derive the accuracy adjusted capacity coefficient, $A(t)$, by obtaining the – log, and then dividing:

$$A^{OR}(t) = \frac{\log\left[\begin{array}{l}
\int_0^t P_1(T_{1C} = t' < T_{1I})\,dt' \times P_2(I) \\
\quad + \int_0^t P_2(T_{2C} = t' < T_{2I})\,dt' \times P_1(I) \\
\quad + \int_0^t P_1(T_{1C} = t' < T_{1I})\,dt' \times \int_{t'=t}^{\infty} P_2(T_{2C} = t' < T_{VI})\,dt' \\
\quad + \int_0^t P_2(T_{2C} = t' < T_{2I})\,dt' \times \int_{t'=t}^{\infty} P_1(T_{1C} = t' < T_{1I})\,dt' \\
\quad + \int_0^t P_1(T_{1C} = t' < T_{1I})\,dt' \times \int_0^t P_2(T_{2C} = t' < T_{2I})\,dt'
\end{array}\right]}{\log[\int_0^t P_{12}(T_{12C} = t' < T_{12I})\,dt']}.$$

Additionally, there are numerous possible cases in which adjusting capacity for accuracy may be useful besides simple detection designs. Suppose, for example, a case where listener attempts to understand a conversation partner in a noisy listening environment, such as a party. It may be possible for that listener to attempt to recognize the talker quickly using a combination of auditory and lip-reading information, but at the expense of understanding him or her incorrectly. Here, $C(t)$ might be high (indicating efficiency), even though accuracy can be low. Conversely, it is possible for a listener to take his/her time when responding to audiovisual stimuli but in doing so, increase the overall accuracy (e.g., Altieri & Hudock, 2014a; Altieri et al., 2014). Other applications include face recognition or word recognition (e.g., Wenger & Townsend, 2001, 2006); the latter of which this chapter will demonstrate in an example. Before moving to applications, the $A(t)$ equation for the AND decision rule will be described.

Equation for the AND Decision Rule

Luckily, the derivation of the UCIP predictions for the AND decision rule is considerably simpler compared to the OR rule. The logic for the likelihood function, specifically, states that correct recognition occurs in the redundant target condition by a certain time if and only if the target in channels 1 AND 2 are both detected by that time. (Being an AND decision rule, the system terminates when the slower of the two processes is completed.) This likelihood can be expressed mathematically using our defective CDF functions $\int_0^t P_{12}(T_{12C} = t' < T_{12I})\,dt' = \int_0^t P_1(T_{1C} = t' < T_{1I})\,dt' \times \int_0^t P_2(T_{2C} = t' < T_{2I})\,dt'$.

Again, we can derive the $A(t)$ function for the AND rule by obtaining the logarithm of each side of the function and then dividing, which yields

$$A^{AND}(t) = \frac{\log[\int_0^t P_1(T_{1C} = t' < T_{1I})\,dt'] + \log[\int_0^t P_2(T_{2C} = t' < T_{2I})\,dt']}{\log[\int_0^t P_{12}(T_{12C} = t' < T_{12I})\,dt']}.$$

These accuracy adjusted $A(t)$ functions are conceptually similar to the RT-only $C(t)$ in the sense that each measures performance in the redundant target condition relative to parallel independent models of unlimited capacity. The difference with the $A(t)$ functions is that capacity increases when speed, accuracy, or a combination thereof improves relative UCIP predictions. $C(t)$, as we recall, increases *only* when speed improves relative to UCIP predictions for correct and fast equations.

Lastly, one may also assess efficiency using an accuracy-only capacity-like equation within the context of OR and AND decision rules. Such equations can prove useful for decomposition purposes; that is, they can be used to separately determine whether speed and/or accuracy drives $A(t)$ values (see Townsend & Altieri, 2012). In either case, the obtained probability correct on redundant target trials can be compared to the predicted probability correct stipulated by UCIP. For the OR decision rule, the probability of being correct in the redundant target condition when we assume independence between channels 1 and 2 is given by $pc(1, 2) = pc(1) + pc(2) - pc(1) \times pc(2)$. In this equation, $pc(1)$, for instance, denotes the overall probability of being correct when a stimulus was presented in channel 1. Next, the predicted accuracy for the AND rule slightly differs: the probability of being correct on redundant target trials is given by the probability of identifying the target in channel 1 *and* channel 2, or $pc(1, 2) = pc(1) \times pc(2)$.

Experimental Application

This section presents direct applications illustrating the importance of using the unified capacity function introduced in the last section to assess efficiency as a function of change in workload. Potential applications abound in the psychological and cognitive sciences; this is perhaps especially true for procedures involving speech, language, and object recognition where multiple sources of information converge to define the event to be identified (Altieri et al., 2014; Altieri, Stevenson, Wallace, & Wenger, 2015; Altieri & Wenger, 2013). The example used in this chapter is auditory-visual speech perception. A large body of literature, beginning with Sumby and Pollack's (1954) pioneering study, suggests that the information gleaned by seeing a talker's face in noisy listening conditions actually helps improve auditory recognition capabilities. For approximately 20 years after their publication, little work had been carried out on audiovisual speech integration. In fact, it was not until McGurk and MacDonald's (1976) investigation of responses to mismatched auditory visual signals that significant progress in the field was made. The authors observed that when listeners were presented with mismatched auditory-visual stimuli—such as an auditory articulated /b/ dubbed over a visually articulated "g"—they often perceived a fusion of the audiovisual components (i.e., "d"). These percepts are referred to as fusions because the consonant heard by the listener differs from the auditory and visual consonants actually presented.

A deluge of research on the McGurk Effect has contributed to a vast array of findings. Model-based research has sought to predict confusion matrices and susceptibility to the McGurk Effect and mismatched audiovisual signals (e.g., Mallick, Magnotti, & Beauchamp, 2015; Massaro, 2004; Nath & Beauchamp, 2011), while clinical research endeavors to discover what populations are more likely to be influenced by the visual signal (Dodd, McIntosh, Erdener, & Burnham, 2008; Dupont, Aubin, & Menard, 2005). In spite of these applications, however, a more basic theoretical question remains unanswered as of yet: To what extent does a mismatched visual signal (e.g., auditory /b/ + visual "g") contribute to (in)efficient auditory recognition? Notice we can simply reformulate this question using the framework of capacity and parallel independent race model predictions. Hence, we may assess the efficiency of recognizing auditory /b/ in conjunction with visual "g", versus independent race model predictions derived from uni-sensory auditory /b/ and visual "g" stimuli. Measuring capacity or "integration" efficiency will allow us to take into account RTs—which have been absent in studies of the McGurk effect—and accuracy; both $C(t)$ and $A(t)$ shall be computed.

As we shall see in the methods outlined next, we must clarify some specific assumptions about the tasks. In doing so, OR and AND stopping rules shall be employed. Within the context of audiovisual speech integration, the OR stopping rule makes sense in an experiment requiring the listener to identify an audiovisual stimulus using either auditory or visual speech cues. Most ecologically valid experimental set-ups would likely use an OR stopping rule, such as those that require a decision as to what phoneme was heard. To that end, the $A(t)$ function was adapted to account for congruent audiovisual speech recognition by using an OR version of the function renamed as

$C_I(t)$. AND stopping rules are useful in multidimensional detection paradigms, such as full factorial identification studies requiring both the auditory and visual stimuli to be identified. The example AND design, for example, presents listeners with a four alternative forced-choice experiment presented listeners with auditory /b/ + visual "b", auditory /b/ + visual "g", auditory /g/ + visual "b", and auditory /g/ + visual "g" trials, along with auditory and visual-only trials. Consequently, correct identification on audiovisual trials necessitates correct identification of both the auditory and visual components (e.g., Lentz, Altieri, & Townsend, 2014).

Methods

The following studies will assess a listener's performance using audiovisual McGurk stimuli; specifically, the contributions of speed and accuracy toward integration efficiency will separately using both the $C(t)$ and $A(t)$ measures for the OR and subsequently AND stopping rule.

Experiment 1: OR Design

This experiment was originally reported by Altieri (Altieri, Lentz, Townsend, & Wenger, 2016); further details can be obtained from that reference. Five right-handed listeners recruited from the Indiana University, Bloomington campus were presented with randomized audiovisual, auditory, and visual-only trials. One participant was selected for analysis in this study. The stimuli used in this study consisted of movie clips of a female talker speaking the consonants /b/ and /g/. Participants were instructed to make a "yes" response, via right mouse button press, "as quickly and as accurately as possible" when either an auditory OR visual "b" was present in the stimuli. On target absent trials, when only auditory or visual "g" was presented, listeners were instructed to make a "no" response via left mouse button press. The response mappings are shown in Table 4.1.

Experiment 2: AND Design

For this study, data were obtained from a different group of five participants (2 female and 3 male) recruited from the Idaho State University, Pocatello campus. Data from two different listeners who exhibited diverging data patterns were selected for analysis.

The visual portion of the stimulus consisted digitized videos of two female talkers speaking the monosyllables /b/ ("ba") and /g/ ("ga"). Point light displays consist of green fluorescent dots arranged on the talker's articulators including the teeth, jaw, and facial muscles. The point light stimuli appeared as a configuration of moving glow in the dark points on a black screen (Rosenblum, Johnson, & Saldaña, 1996). The auditory component of the files was processed as *sine wave speech* (SWS). SWS

Table 4.1 **This table shows the "Yes" versus "No" response mappings for the different stimulus categories in Experiments 1 and 2**

Auditory	Visual	Percept	Experiment 1	Experiment 2
/b/	b	/b/	Yes	1 ("AbVb")
/b/	g	/d/ or /th/	Yes	2 ("AbVg")
/g/	b	/b/ and /g/	Yes	3 ("AgVb")
/g/	g	/g/	No	4 ("AgVg")
Unisensory				
/b/	NA	/b/	Yes	1 "b"
/g/	NA	/g/	No	2 "g"
NA	/b/	/b/	Yes	1 "b"
NA	/g/	/g/	No	2 "g"

comprises sinusoids approximating the amplitude and frequency of natural speech, but with many of the acoustic characteristics found in normal speech removed (Remez, Rubin, Pisoni, & Carrell, 1981). This was done in order to avoid ceiling effects, and establish bi-stability in a speech versus non-speech perception in another study (Lentz et al., 2014).

Each of the four combinations of auditory/visual "b" and "g" (2×2; bb, bg, gb, and gg) was presented in the experiment. The numbers 1 through 4 on the keyboard corresponded to the following labels: "1" → A/b/Vb, 2 → A/b/Vg, 3 → A/g/Vb, and 4 → A/g/Vg. Practice trials included 100 presentations of each of the four categories. The experiment included 100 trials of each audiovisual stimulus type. Feedback was provided immediately after every practice and experimental trial; the words "correct" or "incorrect" appeared in the center of the computer monitor. The trials in the auditory and visual-only blocks required participants to make a simple categorization judgment. Each trial presented the listener with either an auditory stimulus of the talker saying /b/ or /g/ or articulating "b" or "g". Participants were instructed that the content corresponding to button 1 on the keyboard was the consonant "b", while button 2 was labeled as the consonant "g". To promote learning of the response mappings, participants received 80 practice trials with feedback. These included 40 auditory and 40 visual-only trials (20 = "g" and 20 = "g" each). The experimental phase consisted of 200 auditory and 200 visual only trials (100 = "b" and 100 = "g"). The response mappings for Experiment 2 are shown in Table 4.1 as well.

Results

The purpose of discussing these example data is to illustrate how speed and accuracy individually contribute—in this specific case—to audiovisual speech processing. The data analysis for the AND rule, for instance, demonstrates how increasing processing speed is not necessarily beneficial, as one may readily observe from the unified capacity function $A(t)$; that is, processing speed on audiovisual trials may come at

Table 4.2 Mean accuracy (probability correct) and mean RT, shown in the last three rows for the audiovisual, as well as auditory and visual-only conditions. The table displays the predicted accuracy as well for the sample participants in Experiments 1 and 2

	Experiment 1	Experiment 2	Experiment 2
Decision Rule	OR	AND	AND
AV Accuracy	0.99	0.79	0.30
AV Accuracy (Predicted)	0.99	0.64	0.52
A Accuracy	0.97	0.79	0.96
V Accuracy	0.93	0.81	0.54
Mean AV_RT	971 ms	1432 ms	1241 ms
Mean A_RT	1181 ms	882 ms	930 ms
Mean V_RT	1027 ms	890 ms	1036 ms

a cost of accuracy. This, and related phenomena, can be detected by deconstructing the $A(t)$ function into two components: the RT only capacity of $C(t)$, and accuracy predictions using the *predicted_AV* equations described in the following paragraph. Together, these pieces of the puzzle can separately shed light on how efficient processing is relative to race model predictions in the RT and accuracy domains.

The descriptive statistics for Experiment 1 displayed in Table 4.2. Predicted accuracy for the OR rule within the context of this study is $predicted\_AV = \mathrm{A} + \mathrm{V} - \mathrm{A} \times \mathrm{V}$ (see Altieri & Hudock, 2014a, 2014b). The terms "AV", "A", and "V" denote mean audiovisual, auditory, and visual-only accuracy, respectively. Second, the equation for predicted accuracy levels in the AND decision rule is $predicted\_AV = \mathrm{A} \times \mathrm{V}$, which was used for Experiment 2.

OR Decision Rule (Experiment 1)

Next, for the capacity function results, the left panel of Fig. 4.3 shows results from the sample listener obtained from the OR experimental paradigm (Experiment 1) designed to explore how efficiently listeners identify consonant when the McGurk effect is present. Both the RT-only $C(t)$ function results along with the accuracy-adjusted capacity coefficient $A(t)$ were plotted using dotted and solid lines, respectively. The right panel in Fig. 4.3 shows results for two separate participants because the pattern of results was different: one participant's results are shown for the lighted lines, and the other, for the darker set of lines. For both experiments, capacity was calculated using the AbVg trials compared to the Ab and Vb (uni-sensory) trials because all of these trials required a "yes" response: in other words, they all contained one consonant "b". The difference being that audiovisual trials had an accompanying "g" phoneme in the visual modality. In this way, we can use capacity to determine the extent to which seeing conflicting information from the talker's face affects processing speed relative to independent race model predictions.

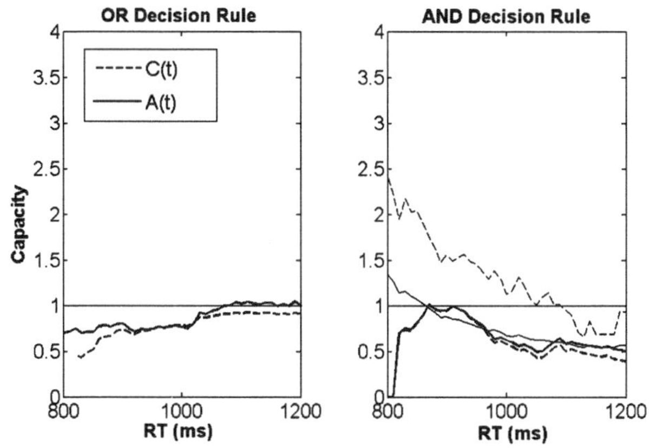

Figure 4.3 Capacity results from Experiments 1 (OR; left panel) and 2 (AND; right panel). Both $C(t)$ and $A(t)$ (dotted and solid lines, respectively) were plotted for comparison purposes.

Results show evidence for slightly limited capacity in the response time domain (see the $C(t)$ function) – at least for response times faster than approximately 1000 ms. Qualitatively, this reveals that listeners failed to show evidence for the statistical advantage associated with parallel race models when presented with visual speech cues; in this case, this is because the visual viseme "g" conflicts with the auditory phoneme "b". The resulting percept of "d", which most listeners reported, masked the target phoneme "b" and thus slowed responses. Importantly, this pattern of results holds true for both the RT only and $A(t)$ capacity measures. This makes sense given the results in Table 4.1; the obtained and predicted accuracy levels are identical and both near ceiling. Hence, there is not any room for improvement in terms of accuracy. The slightly limited capacity afforded by the *RT* results could not be overcome, so to speak, by an improvement in accuracy relative to parallel independent model predictions.

AND Decision Rule (Experiment 2)

This time, $C(t)$ and $A(t)$ were calculated using the AND decision rule. These results also suggested slight capacity limitations for listener 1—indicated using the bold lines—in the right panel of Fig. 4.3. From approximately 900 to 1200 ms, capacity continued to decrease until it reached the level of about $1/2$: this often indicates a phenomenon known as "fixed capacity" in which resources are divided across channels (Townsend & Ashby, 1983). Similar to the results from Experiment 1, the $C(t)$ and $A(t)$ functions did not substantially differ, nor showed a different qualitative pattern of results. In terms of audiovisual accuracy, a small benefit was observed in terms of the difference between obtained and predicted accuracy scores (see Table 4.1). This can also be observed in Fig. 4.3 where $A(t)$ was marginally higher than $C(t)$. Similar to the OR results, these data reveal how McGurk stimuli, by virtue of the perceived fusion, can lead to slower responses compared to race model predictions. For this participant at least, slower responses coincided with a modest benefit in the accuracy domain. This type of trade-off would have been unobservable if we only viewed the $C(t)$ function.

Next, consider the data for the second listener shown using the other (non-bold) set of lines. These data were plotted to demonstrate how a speed-accuracy tradeoff could occur in an audiovisual speech processing experiment. First, let's analyze the accuracy data in Table 4.1. These results show a considerable decrement in obtained versus predicted accuracy: 30% versus 52% correct. On the other hand, the $C(t)$ function shows significantly faster audiovisual responses compared to UCIP predictions, with capacity values hovering around 1.5 or greater for response times faster than 1000 ms. While this listener's responses to audiovisual stimuli were "fast" compared to UCIP, it came at the cost of accuracy. The unified capacity function, $A(t)$, takes into account both speed and accuracy information; in this case, it shows a profile consistent with limited capacity similar to the other listener in Experiment 2. In each case, we can see the importance and contribution of the $A(t)$ function. This is because mean accuracy, or RT alone proved incapable of capturing a listener's true potential to respond to multiple sources of stimulation.

General Discussion

The methods in this chapter go beyond assessments of audiovisual speech integration ability: They represent a culmination of years of research exploring how we can measure cognitive efficiency as a function of workload using the most advanced dependent measures at our disposal. Our metaphorical understanding of capacity has changed over the years in an analogous way as our metaphors for memory; Aristotle viewed memory as an indelible imprint on a tablet, whereas nowadays, our metaphors are shaped by more up to date technology such as computational devices. Hence, the emphasis on parallel distributed processing systems or other computationally driven models in the learning and memory literature.

In a similar vein, our metaphors for a system's capacity have undergone modification. Miller's 7 ± 2 makes one think of capacity as something with little flexibility, perhaps like a receptacle or container. The key aspect of this metaphor is that capacity, or memory described in this manner, is the inherent limitation in such a system. A container, after all, has only so much space to fill. Capacity limitations may, nonetheless, represent an appropriate description in certain cognitive domains. Working memory comes to mind, as does some tasks such as recalling a list of digits backwards, or recalling phrases or sentences (Cowan, 2010). As we have witnessed, capacity measures are applicable to elementary and holistic perception just as much as they are to the domains of learning and memory.

Yet unlike working memory, memory does not "fill up" so to speak; hence, a person's capacity to learn new information and convert it to long-term memory is not limited in the same sense as a storage device. When discussing learning and perception then, it probably makes more sense to think of capacity as something inherently time variable. In this way, one can assess efficiency as a function of both time and work completed in the double target condition relative to UCIP predictions. Capacity need not be limited to three or four chunks of information (e.g., Cowan, 2010), but instead, can vary across perceptual configuration (e.g., faces vs other objects, Cornes, Donnelly, Godwin, & Wenger, 2011), task complexity, and even across individuals. This notion of capacity, measured as a function of workload relative to UCIP predictions (Townsend, & Ashby, 1983; Townsend & Nozawa, 1995) has provided us with statistical methodology that makes comparatively few assumptions (see Colonius, 1990, for further discussion of *context invariance* and *stochastic independence*).

The benefits provided by the capacity coefficient are exceedingly multifaceted. The measure can be implemented across variable experimental designs using different decision rules, namely OR and AND logic gates, while also allowing efficiency to change as a function of fast or slower responses. Moreover, capacity functions using RT distributions alone can be of great assistance in diagnosing the cognitive architecture: the major architecture subtypes examined at length by Townsend and colleagues include serial, parallel, and coactive (Townsend & Nozawa, 1995). Capacity (e.g., limited, unlimited, and super) is logically independent of architecture since different capacity signatures can theoretically co-occur with different architecture subtypes; nonetheless, certain capacity values are empirically associated with certain architectures. For example, parallel models with independent channel predicts capacity equal to 1 for both OR as well as AND stopping rules. On the other hand, limited capacity has traditionally been associated with serial systems, while supercapacity has been associated with coactive systems (Miller, 1982). Hence, the capacity approach relies on procedures that capture processing efficiency, at a given point in time, to a basic model that assumes stochastic independence whose performance is driven by the statistical properties of a "horse race" (Raab, 1962; Townsend & Nozawa, 1995).

More recent developments and applications of parallel linear dynamic models to RT data have allowed us to further revise our notions of capacity as it relates to processing architecture. Both Townsend and Wenger (2004) and more recently Eidels et al. (2011) demonstrated that parallel models with inhibition across channels can produce capacity limitations; conversely, facilitation across channels can produce supercapacity. Crucially, this holds true for both the OR and AND decision rules. In a similar vein, research using neuroimaging techniques such as EEG has indicated that the capacity to associate novel stimuli (Altieri et al., 2015) and benefit from visual signals in noise (Altieri & Wenger, 2013) appear to be driven by facilitation across distinct brain regions. As such, developments such as these in neuroscience help confirm our understanding of capacity that is, first of all, something inherently dynamic, and also something that can change across tasks and conditions. Finally, the capacity data obtained in psychophysical and perceptual tasks is likely produced by a combination of facilitatory or inhibitory interactions across parallel channels.

One shortcoming of the original RT-only capacity coefficient is that it did not incorporate accuracy. It turns out that ignoring accuracy has negligible impact on capacity under high accuracy settings, which commonly arise in supra-threshold detection experiments. Experiments that typically yield near ceiling accuracy levels mainly consist of psychophysical auditory or visual detection studies (e.g., Townsend & Nozawa,

1995; Townsend & Wenger, 2004), although high-accuracy is also achievable in language and face perception studies when the signal-to-noise ratio is high. Nonetheless, ecologically valid perceptual explorations do not always give us the luxury of high accuracy: understanding words in noise, faces at different angles, and even dimly presented flashes of light can have detrimental influences on accuracy levels. In light of this, a complete account of a system's capacity must also make use of accuracy. To that end, the development of the capacity coefficient for OR and AND tasks by Townsend and Altieri (2012) aimed to adjust the capacity coefficient for changes in accuracy. As we witnessed in previous sections, the accuracy adjusted capacity coefficient is vital in cases of speed–accuracy trade-offs; faster redundant target processing speed compared to independent model predictions is not necessarily efficient, especially when accuracy takes a substantial hit. Viewed in an alternative framework then, slow responses may not always be inherently inefficient when accompanied by high accuracy. In an important recent development, modeling work on speed–accuracy trade-offs has indicated that capacity is often less limited in redundant target detection tasks (under certain circumstances) than expected, especially when observers are forced to respond quickly (i.e., lower their threshold) and accuracy suffers. This finding is in contrast to cases where observers are encouraged slow-down (i.e., increase their threshold) in order to improve accuracy (Donkin, Little, & Houpt, 2014). The upshot is that these findings lead to novel predictions arguing that certain manipulation of decision threshold may have a more negligible effect on efficiency than previously assumed.

In summary, the $A(t)$ functions for the OR and AND decision rules has proven quite effective for assessing responses relative to UCIP. In particular, the $A(t)$ function has proven exceptionally useful for more complex cognitive tasks, such as audiovisual speech integration and likely face recognition as well.

Conclusion

While the original capacity coefficient has been aptly used across many domains as well as assessments comparing control versus clinical populations, future applications of the $A(t)$ function should similarly prove fruitful. Already, the $A(t)$ function has been modified to assess audiovisual speech integration skills assuming an OR experimental design (Altieri et al., 2014); applications have shown differences in efficiency in hearing-impaired versus normal-hearing listeners (Altieri & Hudock, 2014a, 2014b). Ideally, these measures will find applications in face perception, word recognition, and the perception and integration of speech and non-speech stimuli. Finally, statistical measures developed by Houpt and colleagues for comparing two capacity coefficients, or simply comparing the capacity coefficient to race model predictions should be extended to the accuracy adjusted capacity coefficient.

Acknowledgements

The research was supported by an internal University Research Office Grant awarded to the author at Idaho State University, the INBRE Program, NIH Grant Nos. P20 RR016454 (National Center for Research Resources) and P20 GM103408 (National Institute of General Medical Sciences).

Appendix

Part 1: Derivation of AND Capacity Bounds

The derivations for the upper and lower bounds in the context of the AND design were provided by Colonius and Vorberg (1994). The derivations for the transformation into capacity space were furnished by Townsend and Eidels (2011) and are provided below for convenience.

We already know that $F_{12}(t) = F_1(t) + F_2(t) - F_1(t) \times F_2(t)$, so $F_{12}(t) \le F_1(t) + F_2(t)$. On the other hand, $F_1(t) + F_2(t) - 1 \le F_{12}(t) \le \min\{F_1(t), F_2(t)\}$.

From Eq. (4.2) in the main text, we know that $C(t) = \frac{\log[F_1(t)] + \log[F_2(t)]}{\log[F_{12}(t)]}$.

Therefore, the upper and lower bounds are:

$$\frac{\log[F_1(t)] + \log[F_2(t)]}{\log[F_1(t) + F_2(t)] - 1} \le C^{AND}(t) = \frac{\log[F_1(t)] + \log[F_2(t)]}{\log[F_{12}(t)]} \le \frac{\log[F_1(t)] + \log[F_2(t)]}{\log[\min\{F_1(t), F_2(t)\}]}.$$

Part 2: Capacity Derivations

OR Decision Rule

Correct and Slow (CS)

This scenario occurs when a participant ends up correctly identifying the stimulus in channel 1 or 2; however, the equation stipulates correct identification, given that the process has not yet terminated. This is evidenced by the defective survivor functions in the equation, rather than defective CDFs (which were used in the $A(t)$ "correct and fast" equation shown in the main text):

$$A^{CS}(t) = \frac{\log\left[\begin{array}{l}\int_{t'=t}^{\infty} P_1(T_{1C} = t' < T_{1I})\,dt' \times P_2(I) \\ \quad + \int_{t'=t}^{\infty} P_2(T_{2C} = t' < T_{2I})\,dt' \times P_1(I) \\ \quad + \int_{t'=t}^{\infty} P_1(T_{1C} = t' < T_{1I})\,dt' \times \int_{t'=t}^{\infty} P_2(T_{2C} = t' < T_{2I})\,dt'\end{array}\right]}{\log[\int_{t'=t}^{\infty} P_{12}(T_{12C} = t' < T_{12I})\,dt']}.$$

Incorrect and Slow (IS)

This equation functions similar to the CS case, the difference being that the participant will end up identifying the incorrect stimulus first in either channel:

$$A^{IS}(t) = \frac{\log\left[\begin{array}{l}\int_{t'=t}^{\infty} P_1(T_{1I} = t' < T_{1C})\,dt' + \int_{t'=t}^{\infty} P_2(T_{2I} = t' < T_{2C})\,dt' \\ \quad - \int_{t'=t}^{\infty} P_1(T_{1I} = t' < T_{1C})\,dt' \times \int_{t'=t}^{\infty} P_2(T_{2I} = t' < T_{2C})\,dt'\end{array}\right]}{\log[\int_{t'=t}^{\infty} P_{12}(T_{12I} = t' < T_{12C})\,dt']}.$$

Incorrect and Fast (IF)

In order to be both incorrect and fast (i.e., incorrect on an OR trial by time t), the participant must be incorrect on channel 1 and channel 2 by a certain time. This is spelled out in the following $A(t)$ equation:

$$A^{IF}(t) = \frac{\log[\int_0^t P_1(T_{1I} = t' < T_{1C})\,dt'] + \log[\int_0^t P_2(T_{2I} = t' < T_{2C})\,dt']}{\log[\int_0^t P_{12}(T_{12I} = t' < T_{12C})\,dt']}.$$

AND Decision Rule

Correct and Slow (CS)

Being correct but slow on an AND trial requires the participant to correct identify stimulus components 1 and 2; however, processing has not yet terminated by time t:

$$A^{CS}(t) = \frac{\log\left[\begin{array}{l}\int_{t'=t}^{\infty} P_1(T_{1C} = t' < T_{1I})\,dt' + \int_{t'=t}^{\infty} P_2(T_{2C} = t' < T_{2I})\,dt' \\ \quad - \int_{t'=t}^{\infty} P_1(T_{1C} = t' < T_{1I})\,dt' \times \int_{t'=t}^{\infty} P_2(T_{2C} = t' < T_{2I})\,dt'\end{array}\right]}{\log[\int_{t'=t}^{\infty} P_{12}(T_{12C} = t' < T_{12I})\,dt']}.$$

Incorrect and Slow (IS)

In order to be incorrect on an AND trial, the participant must "recognize" the incorrect stimulus in channel 1 or 2. The derivation given by Townsend and Altieri (2012) is

$$A^{CS}(t) = \frac{\log\left[\begin{array}{l}\int_{t'=t}^{\infty} P_1(T_{1I} = t' < T_{1C})\,dt' \times P_2(C) \\ \quad + \int_{t'=t}^{\infty} P_2(T_{2I} = t' < T_{2C})\,dt' \times P_1(C) \\ \quad + \int_{t'=t}^{\infty} P_1(T_{1I} = t' < T_{1C})\,dt' \times \int_{t'=t}^{\infty} P_2(T_{2I} = t' < T_{2C})\,dt'\end{array}\right]}{\log[\int_{t'=t}^{\infty} P_{12}(T_{12I} = t' < T_{12C})\,dt']}.$$

Incorrect and Fast (IF)

Finally, the incorrect and fast case for the AND rule is given below. Notice that it follows the same functional format as the OR correct and fast case. In this scenario, one is incorrect and fast when they are incorrect on channel 1, channel 2, or both channels 1 and 2 so that

$$A^{OR}(t) = \frac{\log \left[\begin{array}{l} \int_0^t P_1(T_{1I} = t' < T_{1I})\, dt' \times P_2(C) \\ \quad + \int_0^t P_2(T_{2I} = t' < T_{2C})\, dt' \times P_1(C) \\ \quad + \int_0^t P_1(T_{1I} = t' < T_{1C})\, dt' \times \int_{t'=t}^{\infty} P_2(T_{2I} = t' < T_{VC})\, dt' \\ \quad + \int_0^t P_2(T_{2I} = t' < T_{2C})\, dt' \times \int_{t'=t}^{\infty} P_1(T_{1I} = t' < T_{1C})\, dt' \\ \quad + \int_0^t P_1(T_{1I} = t' < T_{1C})\, dt' \times \int_0^t P_2(T_{2I} = t' < T_{2C})\, dt' \end{array} \right]}{\log[\int_0^t P_{12}(T_{12I} = t' < T_{12C})\, dt']}.$$

References

Altieri, N., & Hudock, D. (2014a). Hearing impairment and audiovisual speech integration ability: A case study report. *Frontiers in Psychology*, *5*(678), 1–10.

Altieri, N., & Hudock, D. (2014b). Variability in audiovisual speech integration skills assessed by combined capacity and accuracy measures. *International Journal of Audiology*, *53*, 710–718.

Altieri, N., Lentz, J., Townsend, J. T., & Wenger, M. J. (2016). The McGurk effect: An investigation of attentional capacity employing response times. *Attention, Perception, & Psychophysics*, *78*, 1712–1727.

Altieri, N., Stevenson, R. A., Wallace, M. T., & Wenger, M. J. (2015). Learning to associate auditory and visual stimuli: Capacity and neural measures of efficiency. *Brain Topography*, *28*(3), 479–493.

Altieri, N., Townsend, J. T., & Wenger, M. J. (2014). A measure for assessing the effects of audiovisual speech integration. *Behavior Research Methods*, *46*, 406–415.

Altieri, N., & Wenger, M. (2013). Neural dynamics of audiovisual integration efficiency under variable listening conditions: An individual participant analysis. *Frontiers in Psychology*, *4*(615), 1–15.

Bundesen, C., & Habekost, T. (2008). *Principles of visual attention*. Oxford, England: Oxford University Press.

Colonius, H. (1990). Possibly dependent probability summation of reaction time. *Journal of Mathematical Psychology*, *34*, 253–275.

Colonius, H., & Townsend, J. T. (1997). Activation-state representation of models for the redundant signals effect. In A. A. J. Marley (Ed.), *Choice, decision, and measurement: Essays in honor of R. Duncan Luce* (pp. 245–254). Mahwah, NJ: Erlbaum.

Colonius, H., & Vorberg, D. (1994). Distribution inequalities for parallel models with unlimited capacity. *Journal of Mathematical Psychology*, *38*(1), 35–58.

Cornes, K., Donnelly, N., Godwin, H., & Wenger, M. J. (2011). Perceptual and decisional factors influencing the discrimination of inversion in the Thatcher illusion. *Journal of Experimental Psychology: Human Perception and Performance*, *37*, 645–668.

Cowan, N. (2010). The magical mystery four: How is working memory capacity limited, and why? *Current Directions in Psychological Science*, *19*(1), 51–57.

Diederich, A., & Colonius, H. (1991). A further test of the superposition model for the redundant-signals effect in bimodal detection. *Perception & Psychophysics*, *50*, 83–86.

Dodd, B., McIntosh, B., Erdener, D., & Burnham, D. (2008). Perception of the auditory-visual illusion in speech perception by children with phonological disorders. *Clinical Linguistics and Phonetics*, *22*(1), 69–82.

Donkin, C., Little, D. R., & Houpt, J. W. (2014). Assessing the speed–accuracy trade-off effect on the capacity of information processing. *Journal of Experimental Psychology: Human Perception and Performance*, *40*, 1183–1202.

Dupont, S., Aubin, J., & Menard, L. (2005). A study of the McGurk effect in 4 and 5-year-old French Canadian children. *ZAS Papers in Linguistics*, *40*, 1–17.

Eidels, A., Houpt, J., Altieri, N., Pei, L., & Townsend, J. T. (2011). Nice guys finish fast and bad guys finish last: A theory of interactive parallel processing. *Journal of Mathematical Psychology*, *55*(2), 176–190.

Gopher, D., & Navon, D. (1980). How is performance limited: Testing the notion of central capacity. *Acta Psychologica*, *46*(3), 161–180.

Grice, G. R., Canham, L., & Gwynne, J. W. (1984). Absence of a redundant-signals effect in a reaction time task with divided attention. *Perception & Psychophysics*, *36*, 565–570.

Hick, W. E. (1952). On the rate of gain of information. *Quarterly Journal of Experimental Psychology*, *4*, 11–26.

Houpt, J. W., & Townsend, J. T. (2012). Statistical measures for workload capacity analysis. *Journal of Mathematical Psychology*, *56*, 341–355.

Jastrow, J., & Cairnes, W. B. (1891). The interference of mental processes–a preliminary survey. *The American Journal of Psychology*, *4*, 219–223.

Kahneman, D. (1967). An onset–onset law for one case of apparent motion and metacontrast. *Perception & Psychophysics*, *2*, 577–584.

Kahneman, D. (1973). *Attention and effort*. Englewood Cliffs, NJ: Prentice-Hall.

Lentz, J., Altieri, N., & Townsend, J. T. (2014). Differences in the integration of speech versus non-speech stimuli. In G. R. Patching, M. Johnson, E. Borg, & A. Hellström (Eds.), *Fechner day 2014: 30th annual meeting of the international society for psychophysics*. Lund, Sweden.

Link, S. W., & Heath, R. A. (1975). A sequential theory of psychophysical discrimination. *Psychometrika*, *40*, 77–105.

Mallick, D. B., Magnotti, J. F., & Beauchamp, M. S. (2015). The noisy encoding of disparity model of the McGurk effect. *Psychonomic Bulletin & Review*. http://dx.doi.org/10.3758/s13423-015-0817-4. Online First Edition.

Massaro, D. W. (2004). From multisensory integration to talking heads and language learning. In G. A. Calvert, C. Spence, & B. E. Stein (Eds.), *The handbook of multisensory processes* (pp. 153–176). Cambridge, MA: The MIT Press.

McGurk, H., & MacDonald, J. W. (1976). Hearing lips and seeing voices. *Nature*, *264*, 746–748.

Miller, G. A. (1956). The magical number seven, plus or minus two: Some limits on our capacity for processing information. *Psychological Review*, *63*, 81–97.

Miller, J. O. (1982). Divided attention: Evidence for coactivation with redundant signals. *Cognitive Psychology*, *14*, 247–279.

Miller, J. (1986). Time course of coactivation in bimodal divided attention. *Perception & Psychophysics*, *40*, 331–343.

Miller, J., & Ulrich, R. (2003). Simple reaction time and statistical facilitation: A parallel grains model. *Cognitive Psychology*, *46*, 101–151.

Nath, A. R., & Beauchamp, M. S. (2011). A neural basis for inter-individual differences in the McGurk effect, a multisensory speech illusion. *NeuroImage*. July 20 (e-Pub).

Neisser, U. (1967). *Cognitive psychology*. East Norwalk, CT: Appleton-Century-Crofts.

Neufeld, R. W. J., Carter, J. R., Boksman, K., Jette, J., & Vollick, D. (2002). Application of stochastic modeling to group and individual differences in cognitive functioning. *Psychological Assessment, 14*, 279–298.

Neufeld, R. W. J., Townsend, J. T., & Jette, J. (2007). Quantitative response time technology for measuring cognitive-processing capacity in clinical studies. In R. W. J. Neufeld (Ed.), *Advances in clinical cognitive science: Formal modeling and assessment of processes and symptoms* (pp. 207–238). Washington, DC: American Psychological Association.

Norman, D. A., & Bobrow, D. J. (1975). On data-limited and resource limited processes. *Cognitive Psychology, 7*, 44–64.

Pachella, R. G. (1974). The interpretation of reaction time in information processing research. In B. Kantowitz (Ed.), *Human information processing* (pp. 41–82). Potomac, MD: Erlbaum.

Palmer, J., Verghese, P., & Pavel, M. (2000). The psychophysics of visual search. *Vision Research, 40*, 1227–1268.

Raab, D. H. (1962). Statistical facilitation of simple reaction times. *Transactions of the New York Academy of Sciences, 24*, 574–590.

Remez, R. E., Rubin, P. E., Pisoni, D. B., & Carrell, T. D. (1981). Speech perception without traditional speech cues. *Science, 212*, 947–950.

Rosenblum, L. D., Johnson, J. A., & Saldaña, H. M. (1996). Visual kinematic information for embellishing speech in noise. *Journal of Speech and Hearing Research, 39*, 1159–1170.

Schneider, W., & Shiffrin, R. M. (1977). Controlled and automatic human information processing: I. Detection, search, and attention. *Psychological Review, 84*, 127–190.

Schwarz, W. (1994). Diffusion, superposition, and the redundant-targets effect. *Journal of Mathematical Psychology, 38*, 504–520.

Schweickert, R., & Boggs, G. J. (1984). Models of central capacity and concurrency. *Journal of Mathematical Psychology, 28*, 223–281.

Sumby, W. H., & Pollack, I. (1954). Visual contribution to speech intelligibility in noise. *The Journal of the Acoustical Society of America, 26*, 12–15.

Townsend, J. T. (1974). Issues and models concerning the processing of a finite number of inputs. In B. H. Kantowitz (Ed.), *Human information processing: Tutorials in performance and cognition* (pp. 133–168). Hillsdale, NJ: Erlbaum Press.

Townsend, J. T., & Altieri, N. (2012). An accuracy-response time capacity assessment function that measures performance against standard parallel predictions. *Psychological Review, 119*(3), 500–516.

Townsend, J. T., & Ashby, F. G. (1978). Methods of modeling capacity in simple processing systems. In J. Castellan, & F. Restle (Eds.), *Cognitive Theory, Vol. III* (pp. 200–239). Hillsdale, NJ: Erlbaum Associates.

Townsend, J. T., & Ashby, F. G. (1983). *The stochastic modeling of elementary psychological processes.* Cambridge, England: Cambridge University Press.

Townsend, J. T., & Eidels, A. (2011). Workload capacity spaces: A unified methodology for response time measures of efficiency as workload is varied. *Psychonomic Bulletin & Review, 18*, 659–681.

Townsend, J. T., & Nozawa, G. (1995). Spatio-temporal properties of elementary perception: An investigation of parallel, serial, and coactive theories. *Journal of Mathematical Psychology, 39*, 321–359.

Townsend, J. T., & Wenger, M. J. (2004). A theory of interactive parallel processing: New capacity measures and predictions for a response time inequality series. *Psychological Review, 111*, 1003–1035.

Vickers, D. (1979). *Decision processes in visual perception.* New York, NY: Academic Press.

Wenger, M. J., & Townsend, J. T. (2000). Basic response time tools for studying general processing capacity in attention, perception, and cognition. *The Journal of General Psychology*, *127*, 67–99.

Wenger, M. J., & Townsend, J. T. (2001). Faces as gestalt stimuli: Process characteristics. In M. J. Wenger, & J. T. Townsend (Eds.), *Computational, geometric, and process perspectives on facial cognition* (pp. 229–284). Mahwah, NJ: Erlbaum.

Wenger, M. J., & Townsend, J. T. (2006). On the costs and benefits of faces and words: Process characteristics of feature search in highly meaningful stimuli. *Journal of Experimental Psychology: Human Perception and Performance*, *32*, 755–779.

Selective Influence and Classificatory Separability (Perceptual Separability) in Perception and Cognition: Similarities, Distinctions, and Synthesis

5

James T. Townsend, Yanjun Liu, Ru Zhang
Indiana University Bloomington, Bloomington, IN, United States

In our opinion, psychology and its close cousin (and partial offspring), cognitive science, are properly viewed as black-box sciences where for the most part, the inner workings must be divined from the orderliness of input–output relationships. Even today, physiology can offer, at best, relatively modest resources to this end, though we hope for massive improvements in the marriage of physiological recordings and behavioral technologies as the future unfolds.

One fundamental theme in psychology concerns whether a change in one entity causes an alteration in another entity or not. Unsurprisingly, the issue of invariance vs. change is fundamental in psychological science and plays out in many forms. Of course, orderly dependence is the obverse of independence or invariance. We earlier have defined the very general *principle of correspondent change* as the correlative structure and function in a theory with concomitant change, or invariances, in nature,[1] such as parameter invariance across certain variations of experimental circumstance (Townsend & Ashby, 1983, Chapter 15, p. 481). Absent this precept, mathematical applications to science are little more than descriptive exercises at best, or useless, scientifically vacant meanderings at worst. The present concepts are special cases of this foundational notion.

Of course, where the element of chance is ubiquitous, as within psychology, dependence and independence have to be interpreted in a probabilistic framework. This aspect, by itself, forms no serious challenge since dependence, or no, has long been a hallmark of probability theory.[2,3]

Two types of functional dependence that have played a central role in our own theories and methodologies are *selective influence* and *perceptual separability*. There have been hundreds of papers utilizing these concepts.[4] It would be especially agreeable if the investigator were able to directly observe samples of the random variables themselves. With regard to selective influence, the operative observable random variable has usually been response time (*RT*) and with separability, usually confusion frequencies. For instance, if we could observe the actual processing times of the processes in a serial system, we would probably not require the more removed, but as it turns

Systems Factorial Technology, DOI: 10.1016/B978-0-12-804315-8.00007-0

out, essential, statistics on response times. Similarly, in general recognition theory, we can typically only observe probabilities of recognition and confusion rather than the underlying percepts themselves.

More rigorous and deeper characterizations will be offered subsequently, although we strive for communicability at the possible expense of a stark logico-deductive approach. To initiate the discussion, selective influence lies at the heart of the popular *additive factors method* (Sternberg, 1969), a methodology which can support or disconfirm serial processing. It also underpins the subsequent *systems factorial technology* (SFT), which permits testing of parallel and more exotic mental architectures (e.g., Townsend & Nozawa, 1995; Townsend & Wenger, 2004; see Algom, Eidels, Hawkins, Jefferson, & Townsend, 2015, for history and general discussion; of course, this volume contains a treasure trove of this theory, methodology, and applications), stopping rules, capacity, and independence. Its power derives from its mathematical rigor but also that it provides tests that are nonparametric as well as distribution free. These characteristics are almost unique in the annals of the study of perceptual, cognitive, and action systems. Informally, selective influence of an experimental factor means that exactly one of the two or more psychological processes are affected by that factor. Selective influence is essential to uncovering the architecture and stopping-rule of the attendant cognitive processes.

Now let us dig deeper into the concept of selective influence with an experimental example. This study by Wenger and Townsend (2001) used the *double factorial paradigm*, invented by Townsend and Nozawa (1995; the present volume celebrates the 20th anniversary of that publication). One factor is simply the presence vs. absence of each target (typically two) whereas the other factor is really a set of two factors meant to speed up or slow down processing of one or the other, or both, targets.

The Wenger and Townsend double factorial paradigm investigated detection of presence vs. absence of two target features, eyes and mouth, either in standard position in a normal face stimulus or as location-disorganized features. For our example, we now consider the normal face. The experimental factors consisted of the degree of visual clarity of the separate features.

Taking combinations of different levels of the clarity factors on trials when both targets were present, they created a double-factorial design of 4 stimuli: high-clarity eyes^high-clarity mouth (hh), high-clarity eyes^low-clarity mouth (hl), low-clarity eyes^high-clarity mouth (lh), low-clarity eyes^low-clarity mouth (ll). It was expected, and confirmed, that a higher level of salience of either feature should lead to faster perception of that feature.

The early usage of selective influence was only concerned with demonstrating influence at the mean *RT* level. Townsend and colleagues (Townsend, 1984, 1990a; Townsend & Schweickert, 1989) demonstrated that in order to empirically distinguish parallel from serial systems, it was necessary for the selective influence operate at a more fundamental level. Recall that the *cumulative distribution function* for *RT*s yields the probability, for an arbitrary time t, that the response was made faster than that duration. Likewise, the so-called *survivor function* is just 1 minus the cumulative distribution function and gives the likelihood that the response took longer than any given t. The "survivor" part of the term comes from its use in actuarial statistics in

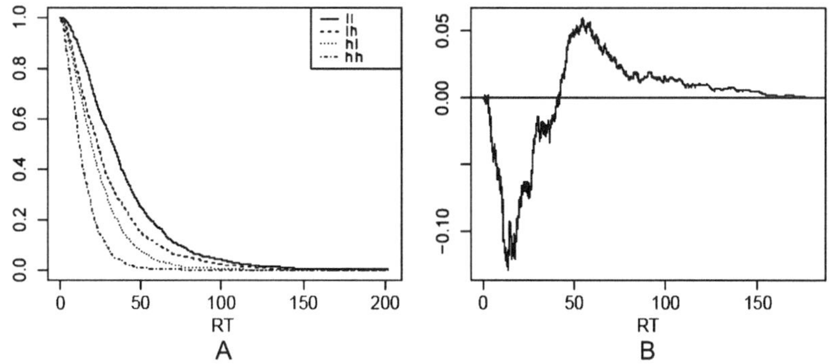

Figure 5.1 (A) Distributional ordering holds for survival functions of simulated response time of ll, lh, hl, and hh. This indicates the fulfillment of selective influence. (B) Estimated SIC function from the simulated data. The SIC pattern indicates the two processes are arranged in a serial exhaustive manner.

calculating the probability that a person, machine, etc., survives beyond any certain point of time, t. Then, a sufficiently strong level of influence, even at the level of mean *RT*s, is that the factors order the *RT* cumulative distribution functions, or equivalently, the survivor functions (e.g., Townsend, 1990a). Significantly, when selective influence fails, then at least at the level of mean *RT*s, virtually any pattern of interactions can occur (Townsend & Thomas, 1994).

Ensuing developments showed that the same level of selective influence as that testing mean *RT*s, made much more distinctive predictions for the distribution functions themselves (Townsend & Nozawa, 1995). Thus, once the selective influence holds at the level of distribution ordering, SFT would predict unique patterns of *survival interaction contrast* (SIC) that corresponds to a certain combination of architecture (serial, parallel, or coactive) and stopping rule (self-termination or exhaustive). Figs. 5.1A and 5.1B are examples of the fulfillment of selective influence at the distributional ordering of survival functions and the estimated SIC from simulated data.

These unique patterns therefore help to unveil the human's cognitive systems and their dynamics (e.g., as an impressive application, see Wenger & Ingvalson, 2003). More technical details and discussion of selective influence will unfold later on in the chapter.

Perceptual separability has been more confined to perception per se at least in literature that employs precisely that name and has not received quite as much theoretical analysis as selective influence. It is nevertheless an exceedingly important topic in human information processing and its identifiability in data continues to be investigated (Garner & Morton, 1969; Ashby & Townsend, 1986; Kadlec & Townsend, 1992; Maddox, 1992; Ashby & Soto, 2015). Again informally, its defining characteristic is that, given two dimensions or features, the percept of one psychological dimension is invariant across stimulus changes in the other (see also Silbert & Thomas, 2013; Soto, Vucovich, Musgrave, & Ashby, 2015).

For a starting example, consider the perceptual dimensions of loudness and pitch. Then, perceptual separability stipulates that the probability of perceiving one level of a dimension is constant across different levels of the other dimension. Similarly,

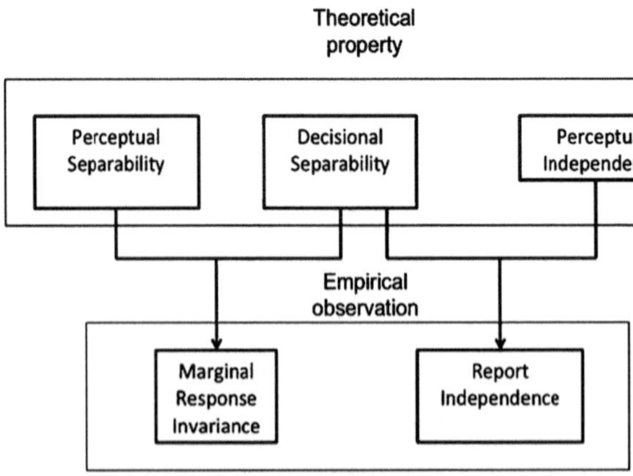

Figure 5.2 Theoretical structure of General Recognition Theory.

in the example from above of selective influence on the facial features of mouth and eyes, perceptual separability demands that the perception of eyes, say, be invariant across the presence or absence of the other. If two distinct sets of eyes or mouths were employed as stimuli then again, the ability to say, perceive which mouth was present, would not be a function of the level of the eyes.

Although observing the process of perception is impossible, *general recognition theory* (GRT, Ashby & Townsend, 1986; Ashby & Soto, 2015) provides us with a mathematical approach that could induce the perceptual separability and other underlying cognitive processes from empirical observations of response frequencies. The theoretical structure of GRT is summarized in Fig. 5.2 and the detailed description of the theory can be found in Ashby and Townsend (1986), Kadlec and Townsend (1992) and Soto et al. (2015).

GRT predicts that if we observe *marginal response invariance* such that the distribution of response to one level of dimension is invariant across different levels of the alternative dimensions, then we could induct the fulfillment of perceptual separability. Thus, if pitch and loudness perception are perceptually separable, then manipulations of either stimulus pitch or loudness should only affect the respective perceptual dimension. It is obvious that this concept of invariance readily extends beyond perception per se.

Interestingly, in addition to the fact that both these vital concepts have something to do with cognitive invariances, it turns out that they share certain profound characteristics. Selective influence and perceptual separability are similar concepts to each other in the sense that both depict the relation that the percept of one dimension is invariant across manipulation of the orthogonal dimensions. Selective influence was originally response time-oriented; whereas perceptual separability was originally response classification.

We will later come to see that although selective influence has received more theoretical analysis, some of the same questions and characteristics also pertain to questions about separability. In addition, we will subsequently contemplate whether either classificatory separability or selective influence could be enlisted in the other's goals.

To our knowledge, there has never been an investigation aimed at explicating their similarities and, if there are any except for linguistics, substantive differences. In the present enquiry, we think it is important to include not only what appear to be deep-seated mathematical or semantic distinctions or resemblances, but also the purpose and intent of the users. Typical conventions will also be grist for discussion.

As pointed out above, the term "selective influence" implies manipulation of something with psychological relevance in order to produce evidence from an observable variable that is intended to reveal some type of psychological structure or function. Perceptual separability, on the other hand, refers to a dimensional or featural percept remaining invariant with a stimulus change on a distinct dimension or feature.

However, the epistemological implications of this part of the discussion go far beyond perception as will become more apparent below. We thereby coin the new term *classificatory separability* to substitute for "perceptual separability." In fact, the following characterizations intend to be inclusive of earlier usage, but attempt to expand their generality and potential scope of applicability. This tack is especially helpful when discussing the scientific purpose of the concepts. References will be given to literature which makes available the mathematical underpinnings.

Selective Influence

The basics tenets of selective influence are:

I. The purpose of selective influence. The experimenter manipulates one or more variables (typically at least two) with the design of separately affecting distinct psychological processes.

II. The selective influence variable may be external or internal to the observer: (A) It is external if applied to an external sense organ, for instance, the eyes, ears, skin, etc.; (B) It is internal if applied to an internal organ, sensory or not. For instance, an ingested pharmaceutical might induce a migraine headache (sensory) vs. causing slowed gastric motility without sensation (non-sensory).

III. The selective influence variable may be qualitative or quantitative, though the quantitative instances, if not universal, were the first employed and still appear to form the most potent in reaching the aims of the researcher.

IV. If quantitative, the variables could be unidimensional or multidimensional and the dimensionality may or may not be expressly defined. Expressly defined dimensionality could be features of an object such as brightness, shape; whereas the implicitly dimension could be psychological dimensions.

V. The experimenter specifies not only the putative selective influence variable but also one or more dependent variables, which have been shown to respond differentially to the stipulated selective influence variables.

VI. The selective influence variable may be part of the stimulus with which the observer is presented, or not.

VII. If part of the stimulus, the selective influence variable may be an aspect or dimension which directly relates to the observer's task or it might be unrelated to the task.

Most of the foregoing may be immediately evident but (VI) and (VII) might be unpacked a bit. An example of a case when the selective influence variable is not part of the stimulus is the following: Suppose it has been hypothesized that the motor system of the observer will act more slowly when the ambient temperature is turned up higher than normal but that this operation does not affect early perceptual processing times. This manipulation is not an inherent part of the observer's task. A case of a selective influence variable which is an integral part of the stimulus would be the brightness of a visual stimulus which the observer must perceive.

With regard to (VII), suppose now that light intensity as a selective influence variable is used where the actual task of the observer is to identify an English letter from the usual 26 letter alphabet. The light intensity itself is not part of the task. However, if the similarity of the stimulus letters is manipulated, this facet may be considered to be an intimate particulate of the basic task. A reviewer points out that the aforementioned ambient temperature and stimulus brightness might be assessed with regard to the architecture of their processing.

The prior discussion holds whether interpreted probabilistically or deterministically. Now assume, as in most psychological milieus, we are dealing with probabilities.

Definition 1. A *Psychological System* is a collection of connected entities called *processes*.

Every process is usually taken to interact with at least one other process to avoid triviality.

Definition 2. A *Set of Experimental Factors* is a collection of entities that can affect one or more of the subprocesses under study.

Definition 3. *Process* is a proper part of a psychological system, which performs a psychological function. It is assumed to have some set of inputs and a set of outputs and usually is expected to expend time to do its job.

Definition 4. *Influence* by an experimental factor on a process implies that the probability distribution on some dependent variable affected by that process is altered under change of the factor values.

If an experimental factor affects a single process, its influence is said to be *selective*.[5] The original definition from Sternberg (1969) did not make entirely clear what might or might not satisfy selective influence, and the emphasis was on mean *RT* and thus the means of the pertinent random times. Suppose that processing times T_x and T_y are bivariate normally distributed, there are three properties to characterize T_x (T_y): the mean of T_x (T_y), the variance of T_x (T_y), and the covariance between T_x and T_y. If the distribution of T_x is affected by a variable X while the distribution of T_y is affected by a distinct variable Y and T_x and T_y were stochastically independent, then

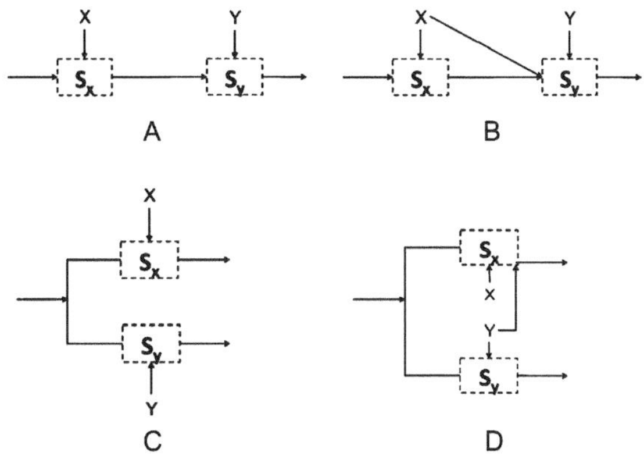

Figure 5.3 (A) Selective influence fulfilled in a serial system with experimental factors: X, Y. (B) A direct non-selective influence in a serial system with experimental factors X and Y. (C) Selective influence fulfilled in a parallel system with experimental factors X and Y. (D) A direct non-selective influence in a parallel system with experimental factors X and Y.

selective influence could be claimed on the distributional level. If T_x and T_y are interdependent, one cannot claim selective influences without inquiring the cause of the interdependence. Having the mean of T_x depend on X and the mean of T_y depend on Y, the independence between the means and the stochastic dependence of T_x and T_y implies that the stochastic dependence of T_x and T_y depends on some variable that is independent of X and Y. Hence manipulating $Y(X)$ influences neither the mean of $T_x(T_y)$ nor the covariance between T_x and T_y. Then selective influences at the level of mean RTs can be claimed. Attempts were made subsequently to deepen the definition as in the following.

Definition 5. (E.g., Townsend, 1984; Townsend & Schweickert, 1989.) Consider two processes S_x and S_y with processing times T_x and T_y. Selective influence holds if and only if there exist two experimental variables, X and Y, such that T_x is affected only by X and T_y is affected only by Y.

This definition does move the emphasis on means to that of the underlying random time variables, but it leaves fuzzy just what role stochastic dependencies might play. This important aspect will be further developed below.

Townsend and colleagues (Ashby & Townsend, 1980; Townsend, 1990b; Townsend & Ashby, 1978; Townsend & Schweickert, 1989) have shown that how, and to what depth, an experimental factor affects the observable statistic is strongly linked to how much of an operating system can be identified from that statistic. Figs. 5.3A through 5.3D exhibit the fundamental serial and parallel architectures, which either satisfy, or not satisfy, selective influence. *Direct non-selective influence* is said to occur if an experimental factor has a direct impact on the "wrong" process, for example, factor X affects T_y. A more subtle type of failure will be discussed later.

The way in which a factor effect operates probabilistically can simply be defined through a deformation of a probability distribution, which leads to the next pivotal definition.

Definition 6. An experimental factor influences a processing time distribution at the level of *stochastic dominance*, if it orders the distribution so that $F(t; X_2) = P(T \leq t; X_2) > F(t; X_1) = P(T \leq t; X_1)$ if and only if the experimental factor satisfies $X_2 > X_1$.

Stochastic dominance is a fairly weak type of dominance in a hierarchy of potential echelons of influence (Townsend, 1990a; Townsend & Ashby, 1978). However, influence only at the even more coarse level of mean processing times, an example of an 'ineffective' influence in most studies of response times, is too weak to prove the important theorems pertaining to testing various architectures and stopping rules (e.g., Townsend, 1984; Townsend & Ashby, 1983).

For instance, if the researcher is attempting to assess whether visual identification of separate letters takes place in serial or parallel, then one may manipulate brightness and determine whether or not the response time cumulative distribution function on an individual letter is always larger at any arbitrary time for the brighter stimulus. When Schweickert (1978) began to expand the kinds of architecture that could be identified by factorial manipulations, he assumed that psychological process durations were affected by adding a time increment (or decrement) to each process time. The main results at that time were confined to deterministic systems, that is, systems for which the constituent process durations were constant, although Schweickert presented certain RT bounds for stochastic situations (e.g., Schweickert, 1982).

Taking this concept to fully stochastic systems, it had long been known that if a positive and independent increment is added to a random variable, stochastic dominance occurs. However, this situation is a special case of the latter. Townsend and Schweickert (1989) showed that if one gives up the idea of independence of the increment, then stochastic dominance and adding a positive random increment to the random variable are mathematically equivalent.[6,7]

It is important before proceeding to re-emphasize that the simple satisfaction of selective influence will not automatically lead to, for instance, identification of parallel vs. serial processing. In fact, even if T_x is affected only by X and T_y is affected only by Y with attendant stochastic independence, tests of parallel vs. serial processing at the level of mean *RT*s will not be feasible (e.g., Townsend & Ashby, 1983; Townsend, 1984). As an apt example, suppose that the variance of T_x is affected by X but the mean of T_y is influenced by Y. It is not clear how to even necessarily detect these effects, much less how to use them to determine aspects such as architecture.

As another example, consider that the prediction by a parallel system with a minimum time stopping rule is that the means, as functions of the experimental factors, should exhibit a certain interaction (in fact, positive in this case as opposed to zero in the serial model). If the experimental factors order only the means of the individual channels, then this interaction could be anything.

Figs. 5.4 and 5.5 illustrate these concepts. First, Fig. 5.4A shows dominance at the mean level. Since, it appears that one distribution is simply a shift of the other, one expects dominance at the distributional level to hold as well (Townsend, 1990a), which is illustrated in Fig. 5.4B. Fig. 5.4C then indicates a valid SIC signature for parallel processing with an exhaustive stopping rule, when dominance at the level of Fig. 5.4B is true.

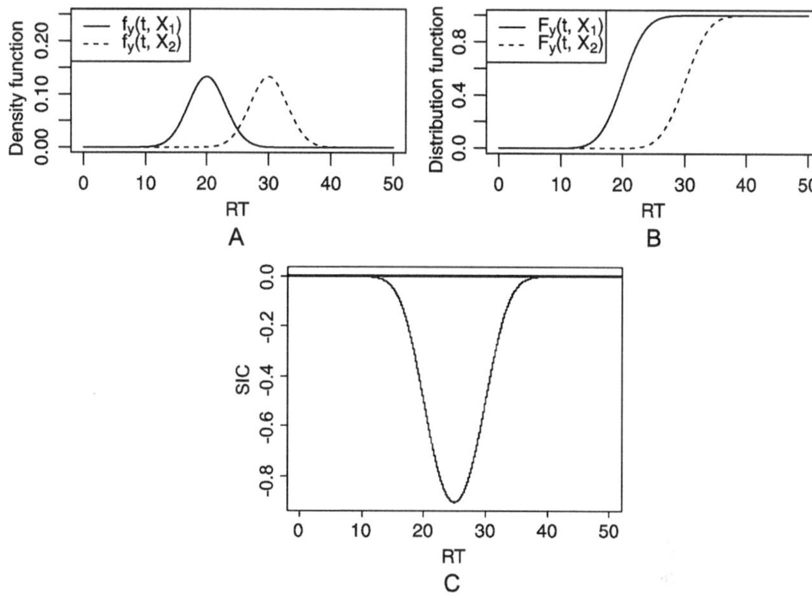

Figure 5.4 (A) Stochastic dominance holds at the mean level. (B) Stochastic dominance holds at the distributional level. (C) Survival interaction contrast of parallel exhaustive processing with stochastic dominance holding at the distributional level.

On the other hand, Figs. 5.5A, 5.5B, and 5.5C reveal what can go wrong if mean dominance occurs but distributional dominance fails. Observe in Fig. 5.5C that an invalid SIC signature results.

Dzhafarov and colleagues (e.g., Dzhafarov & Kujala, 2012; see also, footnote 5) have performed a series of mathematical analyses on selective influence at the distributional level. The most important specification from this sector, for present purposes, was that the germane process random variables could be probabilistically dependent on a third random variable which was itself totally independent of the experimental factors (e.g., Dzhafarov, 2003). A simplified special case of his definition, but which will suffice for our purposes, follows.

Definition 7. (Dzhafarov, 2003.) Selective influence holds for random times T_x and T_y if and only if T_x is a function of X and C whereas T_y is a function of Y and C. X and Y are distinct experimental variables while C is a random variable independent of X and Y.

It can be readily shown that if $C = c$ a particular value, T_x and T_y are conditionally independent (as shown in Fig. 5.6). Furthermore and more importantly, all the theorems of Townsend and Nozawa (1995) that permit identification of process characteristics such as architecture and stopping rule then go through immediately (e.g., Dzhafarov, 2003). This issue will be revisited below.

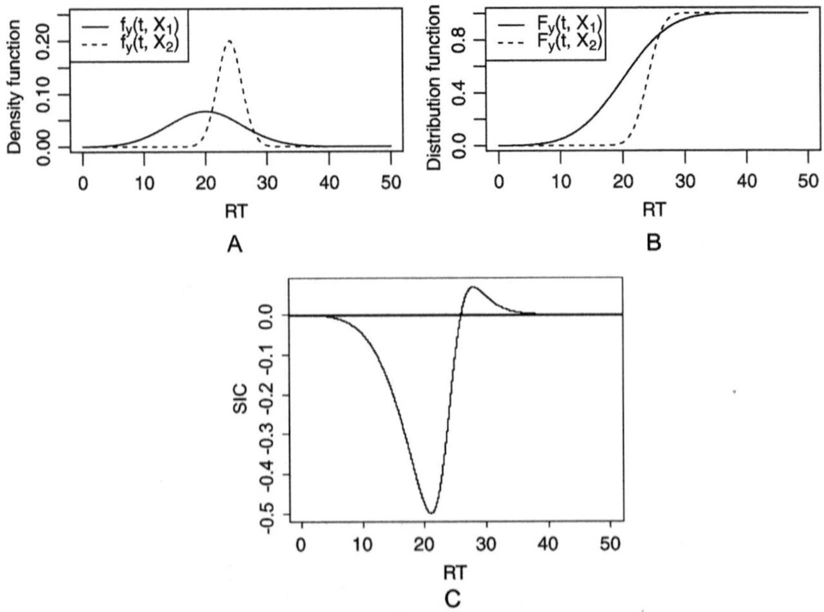

Figure 5.5 (A) Stochastic dominance holds at mean-level. (B) Stochastic dominance fails at the distributional level. (C) SIC with absence of stochastic dominance at the distributional level. The shape of this SIC function does not follow any typical four SIC functions defined in Townsend and Nozawa (1995). But it is similar to the characteristic SIC pattern of serial exhaustive processing.

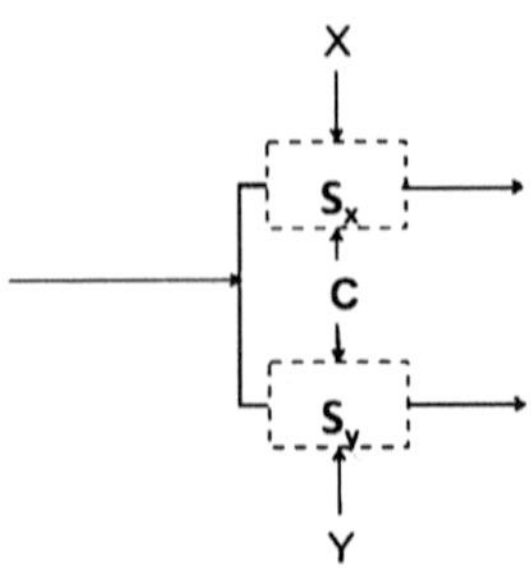

Figure 5.6 A parallel system with experimental factors: X and Y. X, Y, and C are independent of each other. For this case, conditional independence (conditioning on C) holds.

Classificatory Separability

To make sense of our generalization of perceptual separability, we need the concept of a collection of entities that belong to a psychological family of some sort, some type of resemblance as it were. This kind of invariance or not, as observed earlier, has been of interest in psychology back to its philosophical roots. In psychophysics, it has been of concern whether, for example, the perception of pitch changes when loudness is changed through manipulation of the sound intensity and vice versa. It has long been known that neither is invariant as the other dimension of the stimulus is altered.

A full panoply of types of independence, when response frequencies are analyzed, is presented in Ashby and Townsend (1986). Related early statements can be found in Kadlec and Townsend (1992) and Maddox (1992).

Psychological dimensions such as expression and age of a face form another example. For instance, an informal observation suggests that a middle aged face appears older in wearing a dour expression and younger with a happy expression. This particular example is probably asymmetric since it seems less likely that the degree of, say, happiness or sadness might be perceived as more extreme in old vs. young faces. In a deterministic environment, where, for example, faces are completely visible, without noise, the invariance of expression with age or its failure, are obvious (e.g., Townsend & Spencer-Smith, 2004). But what about viewing a face through fog or in a bad photograph? We require interpretations in terms of probability distributions again.

Then, we define classificatory separability as the invariance of a particular member of that class when experienced consciously when another class is changed. Thus, in more rigorous terms:

The basic tenets of classificatory separability are:

I. Psychological class A is classificatory separable from B if the identity of a value from A is unaffected by a change in class B.

II. Classificatory separability or its failure can occur: (i) due to manipulations by an experimenter, or (ii) can occur autonomously.

III. If II(1), the experimenter stipulates one or more dependent variables which refer to the processing of A and B and that will reflect in some way whether or not invariance eventuates.

Let A_i represent the levels of class A, and B_j those of class B with $i, j = 1, 2$ within the context of a so-called *complete identification paradigm*, that is, one where all four combinations of class values appear across the trials of the experiment. Also, let $g_{ij}(a, b)$ be the joint distribution of psychological values a and b, where a is associated with A and b with B, for stimulus compound $A_i B_j$.

The original definition of perceptual separability in Ashby and Townsend (1986) was as follows, with that term replaced by "classificatory separable". It is also sketched in Fig. 5.7.

Definition 8. Psychological class A is classificatory separable across levels of B for a given level A_i if and only if

$$g_{i1}(a, b) = g_{i2}(a, b).$$

Similarly, psychological class B is classificatory separable across levels of A for a given level B_j if and only if

$$g_{1j}(a, b) = g_{2j}(a, b).$$

Observe that separability could hold for one level of a class but not the other and/or for one class but not the other. As noted above, such a situation might obtain in that perceived age might be a function of expression but not vice versa. The marginal

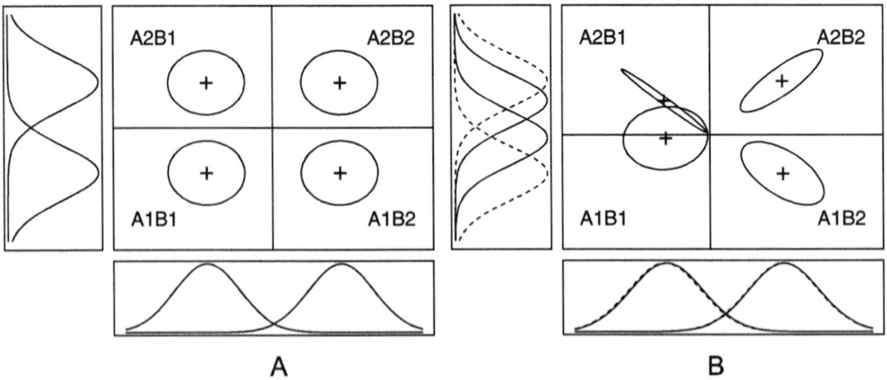

Figure 5.7 (A) The four ellipses are the contours of the joint distributions of responses to the two dimensions. The marginal distributions are plotted on the bottom and on the left. Perceptual separability holds for both dimensions: the marginal distributions of each dimension are invariant across the change of the other stimulus dimension. (B) Perceptual separability fails for dimension A as marginal distributions at each level of dimension A is different across the change of dimension B. However, the separability still holds for dimension B.

distribution on perceived age of an individual would be shifted higher when paired with the dour expression as opposed to that paired with a happy expression.

Finally, it is important to grasp that those interactions among percepts or other categories could occur, just as in selective influence any one of a hierarchy of relations might obtain (Townsend, 1990a). With that fact in mind, we next delve into an essential quantitative correlate of both our major concepts. That notion is the marginal distribution of the central joint distributions, processing times in the case of selective influence and perceptual or cognitive observation random variables in the case of separability.

The Pivotal Notion and Role of Marginal Selective Influence

Marginal Selective Influence in RT Studies

Since selective influence has received more theoretical analysis than separability, over the past two or three decades, we first take up selective influence with respect to *marginal selective influence*.

Townsend and colleagues (e.g., Townsend & Ashby, 1983; Townsend, 1984; Townsend & Thomas, 1993) allowed for probabilistic interactions of the processes as long as the marginal distributions remained unaffected by the "wrong" experimental factors. For instance, in the serial case, processes might be *across-stage independent*, or *dependent* meaning that the second process in a serial chain could depend stochastically (e.g., be on average faster or slower) on the first, depending on how long the first

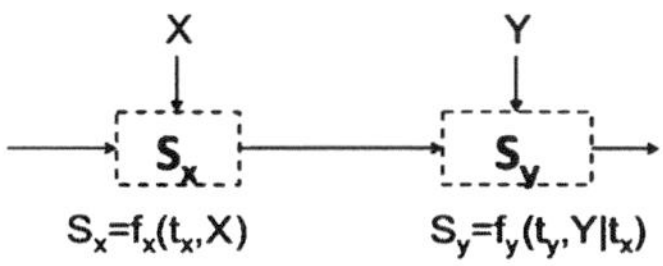

Figure 5.8 A serial system with the potential for indirect non-selective influence due to the dependency of density function of the second stage on the time taken by the first stage.

process took to complete. Let T_x be the random time associated with the first stage in a serial system and T_y that for the second stage. Let t_x and t_y be the specific values for T_x and T_y, respectively. X and Y are experimental variables, which the experimenter hopes would separately affect the first and second stages, respectively.

Definition 9. I. Across-stage independence occurs if the density functions satisfy $f_Y(t_y, Y|t_x) = f_Y(t_y, Y)$. II. Across-stage dependence occurs if and only there exist values of t_x such that $f_Y(t_y, Y|t_x) \neq f_Y(t_y, Y)$.

Suppose the two stages were across stage independent, then $f_Y(t_y, Y|t_x) = f_Y(t_y, Y)$. And assume there is no direct non-selective influence so that $f_Y(t_y, Y, X|t_x) = f_Y(t_y, Y|t_x)$. Then as a direct consequence of across stage independence $f_Y(t_y, Y|t_x) = f_Y(t_y, Y)$, selective influence follows perforce.

Next, what about when across stage independence fails, that is, $f_Y(t_y, Y|t_x) \neq f_Y(t_y, Y)$, and the left hand side is a non-trivial function of the previous stage time, t_x? We can consider the density on T_y, written as a random function, depending on the first stage time t_x, $f(T_y, Y|T_x = t_x)$. When across stage dependence occurs, as indicated, then the (random) distribution of $f(t_y, Y)$, conditioned on $T_x = t_x$ will be a non-trivial function of t_x: $E_{ty}[f(T_y, Y|T_x = t_x)] = f(t_y, Y|T_x = t_x)$ is clearly a function of t_x and not, ordinarily, equal to its marginal distribution. In fact, the latter will usually be a function of the wrong experimental variable X. We may find it by taking the expectation of $f(T_y, Y|T_x = t_x, X)$ over $T_x = t_x$:

$$E_{tx}\{E_{ty}[f(T_y, Y|T_x, X)]\} = \int E_{ty}[f(T_y, Y|t_x, X)]f(t_x, X)dt_x = f(t_y, Y, X).$$

The integral, of course, is taken over $0 < t_x < \infty$. Observe that the final marginal density for t_y is a non-trivial function of the "wrong" factor X!

Definition 10. *Potential indirect non-selective influence* occurs when there is across stage dependence.

Fig. 5.8 indicates the incidence of indirect non-selective influence in a serial system. Nonetheless, if somehow the dependence on X disappears on marginalization, then selective influence still is in force. This will not ordinarily occur for arbitrary conditional distributions $f(T_y, Y|T_x = t_x)$, but can under certain circumstances. In that event we have an instance of Definition 11.

Definition 11. *Marginal selective influence* holds if and only if $E_{tx}\{E_{ty}[[f_Y(T_y, Y|T_x)]] = f_Y(t_y, Y)$.

Just to firmly instantiate this last principle, suppose $f_Y(t_y, Y|t_x) \neq f_Y(t_y, Y)$, that is, across stage independence does not hold and potential indirect non-selective influence (Definition 10) does. Then, it could then be, and probably will be, that the marginal distribution on T_y, after integrating over T_x, will, indirectly, be a function of X as detailed just before Definition 10. It is an instance of indirect non-selective influence. We formalize this concept in Definition 12.

Definition 12. If X does not directly affect T_y yet $E_{tx}[f_{ty}(T_y, Y)|T_x = t_x, X] = f_Y(t_y, Y, X) \neq f_Y(t_y, Y)$, then marginal selective influence fails and indirect non-selective influence is said to occur.

At the time (e.g., Townsend & Nozawa, 1995; Townsend & Schweickert, 1989) it was not investigated as to whether, when and how the "marginalizing out" might occur, when potential indirect non-selective influence was present, due to dependence across stages. But, note that if Dzhafarov's definition of selective influence is satisfied (e.g., Dzhafarov, 2003; see Definition 7 above) then marginal selective influence will indeed be satisfied. Thus, even with the dependence of two random variables say T_x and T_y on a third random variable, C in addition to selective factors, respectively X and Y, marginal selectivity could, in principle, hold and, further including the assumption of distribution ordering mentioned above, permits the proofs of architecture identification to go through unimpeded. However, if marginal selectivity does not hold, then havoc even in mean *RT* predictions erupts (Townsend & Thomas, 1994).

Further, as Dzhafarov and Kujala (2010) demonstrate, even a stronger version of marginal selectivity does not imply Dzhafarov's definition of selective influence in the presence of certain kinds of stochastic dependencies. They have produced a straightforward counter example, based on discrete probability distributions, in which the variables do satisfy even a somewhat more stringent version of marginal selectivity, yet fail to actually fulfill the condition of selective influence (Kujala & Dzhafarov, 2010). This counter-example may be thought of as an instance of indirect non-selective influence. Thus, at least within the class of discrete distributions, marginal selectivity is a necessary but not sufficient condition for the Dzhafarov (2003) definition of selective influence. Nonetheless, it is not at all clear whether marginal selectivity might be sufficient when in the presence of, say, continuous probability density functions that are continuous in their experimental variables. Moreover, we suspect that a supplementation of such densities with the strong condition of distribution ordering by the factors may be enough to force sufficiency. We are presently exploring this branch of the field.

At this point in time, there exists a test that is a necessary and sufficient condition for selective influences on finite discrete variables (Dzhafarov & Kujala, 2010). This is a test that can be performed without having to assume the distribution ordering. It is called the *Linear Feasibility Test*. In a complete identification paradigm if the test is passed, or in other words, selective influence on discrete variables is established, if one can find four jointly distributed variables $(H_{X1}, H_{X2}, H_{Y1}, H_{Y2})$, each corresponding to a level of a factor, satisfy the following constraints:

$$\sum_{ln} \Pr(H_{X1} = k \wedge H_{X2} = l \wedge H_{Y1} = m \wedge H_{Y2} = n)$$
$$= \Pr(T_{X1} = k \wedge T_{Y1} = m \mid X_1Y_1),$$
$$\sum_{lm} \Pr(H_{X1} = k \wedge H_{X2} = l \wedge H_{Y1} = m \wedge H_{Y2} = n)$$
$$= \Pr(T_{X1} = k \wedge T_{Y2} = m \mid X_1Y_2),$$
$$\sum_{kn} \Pr(H_{X1} = k \wedge H_{X2} = l \wedge H_{Y1} = m \wedge H_{Y2} = n)$$
$$= \Pr(T_{X2} = k \wedge T_{Y1} = m \mid X_2Y_1),$$
$$\sum_{km} \Pr(H_{X1} = k \wedge H_{X2} = l \wedge H_{Y1} = m \wedge H_{Y2} = n)$$
$$= \Pr(T_{X2} = k \wedge T_{Y2} = m \mid X_2Y_2),$$

and

$$1 \geq \Pr(H_{X1} = k \wedge H_{X2} = l \wedge H_{Y1} = m \wedge H_{Y2} = n) \geq 0,$$

where k, l, m, n are values of $T_{X1}, T_{X2}, T_{Y1}, T_{Y2}$.

There are some necessary conditions for selective influences. One is called the *distance test* (Kujala & Dzhafarov, 2008). An alternative test that can be used when one has access to covariance matrices is the *cosphericity test* (Kujala & Dzhafarov, 2008). We observe that if the distributions are multivariate Gaussian, then the following condition holds under transformations to standard form, that is, with means equal to 0 and variances equal to 1. Then, letting $r(i, j)$ be the covariances (= correlations here) for each pair of bivariate distributed variables, we have

Definition 13. (Kujala & Dzhafarov, 2008.) Correlations $r(i, j)$, $i, j = 1, 2$ satisfy *cosphericity* if and only if

$$\left|r(1,1)\cdot r(2,1) - r(1,2)\cdot r(2,2)\right| \leq \left[\left(1-r(1,1)^2\right)\cdot\left(1-r(2,1)^2\right)\right]^{1/2} + \left[\left(1-r(1,2)^2\right)\cdot\left(1-r(2,2)^2\right)\right]^{1/2}.$$

Moreover, if the researcher is willing to relinquish some generality, then by assumption of bivariate Gaussian distributions, the relevant condition above becomes necessary as well as sufficient. If, in addition, the pertinent random variables are directly observable, Kujala and Dzhafarov (2008) have adduced another test. Since it is virtually never true that the pertinent random variables are directly observable in either typical *RT* or accuracy paradigms, we do not consider it here.

As intimated earlier, a taxonomy of distributional correlations is lacking, for example, based on across-stage dependencies in serial processes that yet permit marginal selectivity. Nonetheless, it is quite important to appreciate that marginal selectivity at the level of distribution ordering suffices for a proof of the fundamental theorems of

Townsend and Nozawa (1995) on the identification of mental architectures and stopping rules. These and related predictions also appear in a number of chapters in this volume.

Marginal Selective Influence in Response Frequency Designs

Strikingly, we can immediately espy from Definition 8 that classificatory separability is equivalent to marginal selectivity in the distribution on A or B, as in Definition 11: When an experimenter changes the value of a stimulus dimension, say auditory frequency and thereby alters the perceived pitch, if the sense of loudness were unaffected at the level of the marginal distribution, then loudness would be perceptually separable from that of pitch. Since under noisy or low-energy conditions, pitch will be stochastic, the thinking was (e.g., Ashby & Townsend, 1986) that we can only ask that its distribution be unaffected.

A number of considerations long embedded in discussions of architecture and its related topics in the theoretical response time literature have been absent from those associated with accuracy and general recognition theory simply because they didn't arise naturally. Thus, on the one hand, notions such as the conditional dependencies within Definition 12 could exist, but were not treated because they failed to arise within some context analogous to, say, serial vs. parallel processing. And, the static form of the original general recognition theory and the traditional concepts associated within psychometrics, signal detection theory and multidimensional scaling, undoubtedly encouraged researchers to disassociate correlation structures from the values of the distributional means. Conversely, the milieu within the field of response time studies was and is, immediately dynamic and thus promotes such conceptions as "state of processing or activation" as intimately related to the "states of processing" of other psychological systems or stages.

The next step forward is to provide a formulation within which the concepts of selective influence and classificatory separability are special cases. But, this generality is, in fact, inherent in the definition provided by Dzhafarov (2003), recalled in our Definition 7.

A Synthesis of Classificatory Separability and Selective Influence

Both Selective Influence and Classificatory Separability Involve Psychological Processes

Earlier parts of this study have emphasized that classificatory separability and selective influence differ in their genesis, purpose, and usage. Nonetheless, the reader may well have already detected, particularly from the abstract definitions of selective influence offered above, given in terms of random entities, such as random variables, that they can be brought together in a tidy fashion.

Suppose the psychological value of a class on a trial, for instance, a percept of a psychological dimension, say A, is associated with a *process* as defined in Definition 3. And, a change in its value is associated with a value-changing *factor*, say X and similarly for dimension B and factor Y. Then, all the aspects of selective influence can be applied to perceptual separability and an extension to arbitrary classification issues is evident.

Within this new setting, we can also discern that just as selective influence can occur in different ways (e.g., simply any change to a distribution vs. some ordering associated with the distribution), so could the degree of invariance in classificatory separability. So, an alteration on dimension A could affect any aspect of the distribution such as the mean or it might order the cumulative distribution functions, hazard functions or some other statistic. For instance, with dimensions such as pitch, we won't expect a change to necessarily order the cumulative distribution functions.

Less frequently considered, even in the selective influence literature, is the possibility of failure of invariance at distinct levels. For instance, if for the distribution functions, $F_y(t_y, Y|t_{x2})\ F_y(t_y, Y|t_{x1})$ when $t_{x2} > t_{x1}$ and $F_x(t_x, X_2) > F_x(t_x, X_1)$ if $X_2 > X_1$ then perforce $E_{Tx}\{E_{Ty}[f_y(T_y, Y|T_x, X)]\} \neq f_y(t_y|Y)$ and even more intriguingly, $E_{Tx}\{E_{Ty}[f_y(T_y, Y|T_x, X)]\}$ will be indirectly and non-selectively ordered in X! In the context of our synthesis, exactly the same kind of thing could happen in success and failures of classificatory separability.

Next, we entertain a general class of models within which both selective influence and separability can be theoretically lodged.

Accrual Halting Models

We have been making strides in recent years in building bridges between our strategies which have emphasized invariances associated with separability and independence and those constructed to identify mental architecture, workload capacity, and decisional stopping rules. The first, of course, belongs to the material above on classificatory behavior expressed in response probabilities whereas the latter is primarily associated with *RT*s, although there are subdivisions where this coupling does not hold.

Although the global mission is far from accomplished, we can point to several recent advances. Accordingly, we have generalized our nonparametric measure of workload capacity, $C(t)$, t = time, which gauges performance with more than one process in operation against a prediction from one-process trials, based on an independent, unlimited capacity, parallel model. The new measure, $A(t)$, and called the assessment function, also rests on predictions from an independent, unlimited capacity, parallel model, but one which now allows errors to occur and, in fact, evaluates accuracy as well as response time in producing that measure (Townsend & Altieri, 2012).

More germane to our present situation, we have extended our general recognition theory of classification from response probabilities only to response probabilities and response times. With response times comes the question of architecture, so a particular class of architectures must be assumed in further developments. Our first theoretical efforts were founded on parallel processes. The individual processes were termed *accrual halting models*. All these models assume that activation (e.g., information) is being accrued in the relevant channels with a decision occurring when the first one reaches its own threshold. The definitions and theorems encompass all of the constituent models, which include most of the extant stochastic models of perception, action and decision making (see Townsend, Houpt, & Silbert, 2012 for details and more related studies and theories). The reader can find related developments along a somewhat different path, in Griffiths and colleagues' stochastic differential equations approach to a subclass of accrual models (Griffiths, Blunden, & Little, 2017).

This class of models seems to present an ideal environment for the bringing together of selective influence and classificatory separability and related notions. A sticking point would seem to be that up to now, almost all theorems and predictions relating to selective influence have been dedicated to response times and not accuracy (but see Schweickert et al., 2012 for exceptions). We are currently in the midst of theoretical developments intended to expand tests of architecture and stopping rule, founded on selective influence, to include both response probabilities as well as *RT*s (see dissertation of Yang, 2016).

How would these emerging tools be employed within parallel or serially arranged accrual halting models? If two physical values on two dimensions order distributions conditioned on, say, being correct, then tests of architecture and stopping rule could be straightaway applied. Needless to say, the assays of various types of independence and separability would also be available for implementation with the same set of data (Townsend et al., 2012).

In theory, other experimental factors, for instance, related to speed of processing of the dimensions, could be varied with selective influence in mind, besides the traditional values on the dimensions themselves.

And naturally, the general scope of such principles as classificatory separability and selective influence are relevant to any set of processes within a temporary or permanent processing system.

References

Algom, D., Eidels, A., Hawkins, R. X. D., Jefferson, B., & Townsend, J. T. (2015). *Features of response times: Identification of cognitive mechanisms through mathematical modeling. The Oxford handbook of computational and mathematical psychology*. New York, NY: Oxford University Press (pp. 63–98). Retrieved from http://ezproxy.lib.indiana.edu/login?. http://search.proquest.com/docview/1680462905?accountid=11620.

Ashby, F. G. (2014). Is state-trace analysis an appropriate tool for assessing the number of cognitive systems? *Psychonomic Bulletin & Review*, *21*(4), 935–946. http://dx.doi.org/10.3758/s13423-013-0578-x.

Ashby, F. G., & Soto, F. A. (2015). *Multidimensional signal detection theory. The Oxford handbook of computational and mathematical psychology, Vol. 13*.

Ashby, F. G., & Townsend, J. T. (1980). Decomposing the reaction time distribution: Pure insertion and selective influence revisited. *Journal of Mathematical Psychology*, *21*(2), 93–123. http://dx.doi.org/10.1016/0022-2496(80)90001-2.

Ashby, F. G., & Townsend, J. T. (1986). Varieties of perceptual independence. *Psychological Review*, *93*, 154–179. http://dx.doi.org/10.1037/0033-295X.93.2.154.

Devaney, R. (1986). *An introduction to chaotic dynamical systems*. New York: Addison Wesley.

Dzhafarov, E. N. (2003). Selective influence through conditional independence. *Psychometrika*, *68*(1), 7–25. http://dx.doi.org/10.1007/BF02296650.

Dzhafarov, E. N., & Kujala, J. V. (2010). The joint distribution criterion and the distance tests for selective probabilistic causality. *Frontiers in Psychology: Quantitative Psychology and Measurement*, *1*, 151. http://dx.doi.org/10.3389/fpsyg.2010.00151.

Dzhafarov, E. N., & Kujala, J. V. (2012). Selectivity in probabilistic causality: Where psychology runs into quantum physics. *Journal of Mathematical Psychology*, *56*(1), 54–63. http://dx.doi.org/10.1016/j.jmp.2011.12.003.

Garner, W. R., & Morton, J. (1969). Perceptual independence: Definitions, models, and experimental paradigms. *Psychological Bulletin*, *72*(4), 233–259. http://dx.doi.org/10.1037/h0028024.

Griffiths, D. W., Blunden, A. G., & Little, D. R. (2017). Logical-rule based models of categorization: Using systems factorial technology to understand feature and dimensional processing. In D. R. Little, N. Altieri, M. Fifić, & C.-T. Yang (Eds.), *Systems factorial technology: A theory driven methodology for the identification of perceptual and cognitive mechanisms*. Elsevier (in this book).

Kadlec, H., & Townsend, J. T. (1992). Implications of marginal and conditional detection parameters for the separabilities and independence of perceptual dimensions. *Journal of Mathematical Psychology*, *36*(3), 325–374. http://dx.doi.org/10.1016/0022-2496(92)90027-5.

Kujala, J. V., & Dzhafarov, E. N. (2008). Testing for selectivity in the dependence of random variables on external factors. *Journal of Mathematical Psychology*, *52*(2), 128–144. http://dx.doi.org/10.1016/j.jmp.2008.01.008.

Kujala, J. V., & Dzhafarov, E. N. (2010). Erratum to "Testing for selectivity in the dependence of random variables on external factors". *Journal of Mathematical Psychology*, *54*(4), 400. http://dx.doi.org/10.1016/j.jmp.2010.05.001.

Maddox, W. T. (1992). Perceptual and decisional separability. In F. G. Ashby (Ed.), *Multidimensional models of perception and cognition* (pp. 147–180). Hillsdale, NJ: Lawrence Erlbaum Associates, Inc. Chapter xiii, 523 pages. Retrieved from http://ezproxy.lib.indiana.edu/login?. http://search.proquest.com/docview/618227072?accountid=11620.

Schweickert, R. (1978). A critical path generalization of the additive factor method: Analysis of a Stroop task. *Journal of Mathematical Psychology*, *18*(2), 105–139. http://dx.doi.org/10.1016/0022-2496(78)90059-7.

Schweickert, R. (1982). The bias of an estimate of coupled slack in stochastic PERT networks. *Journal of Mathematical Psychology*, *26*, 1–12.

Schweickert, R., Fisher, D. L., & Sung, K. (2012). *Discovering cognitive architecture by electively influencing mental processes*. Singapore: World Scientific.

Silbert, N. H., & Thomas, R. D. (2013). Decisional separability, model identification, and statistical inference in the general recognition theory framework. *Psychonomic Bulletin & Review*, *20*(1), 1–20. http://dx.doi.org/10.3758/s13423-012-0329-4.

Soto, F. A., Vucovich, L., Musgrave, R., & Ashby, F. G. (2015). General recognition theory with individual differences: A new method for examining perceptual and decisional interactions with an application to face perception. *Psychonomic Bulletin & Review*, *22*(1), 88–111.

Sternberg, S. (1969). The discovery of processing stages: Extensions of Donders' method. *Acta Psychologica*, *30*, 276–315. http://dx.doi.org/10.1016/0001-6918(69)90055-9.

Townsend, J. T. (1984). Uncovering mental processes with factorial experiments. *Journal of Mathematical Psychology*, *28*(4), 363–400. http://dx.doi.org/10.1016/0022-2496(84)90007-5.

Townsend, J. T. (1990a). Truth and consequences of ordinal differences in statistical distributions: Toward a theory of hierarchical inference. *Psychological Bulletin*, *108*(3), 551–567. http://dx.doi.org/10.1037/0033-2909.108.3.551.

Townsend, J. T. (1990b). Serial vs. parallel processing: Sometimes they look like Tweedledum and Tweedledee but they can (and should) be distinguished. *Psychological Science*, *1*(1), 46–54. http://dx.doi.org/10.1111/j.1467-9280.1990.tb00067.x.

Townsend, J. T. (1992). Chaos theory: A brief tutorial and discussion. In *From learning processes to cognitive processes: Vol. 2. Essays in honor of William K. Estes, Vol. 1: From learning theory to connectionist theory* (pp. 65–96). Hillsdale, NJ: Lawrence Erlbaum Associates, Inc. Retrieved from http://ezproxy.lib.indiana.edu/login?. http://search.proquest.com/docview/618222203?accountid=11620.

Townsend, J. T., & Altieri, N. (2012). An accuracy-response time capacity assessment function that measures performance against standard parallel predictions. *Psychological Review*, *199*(3), 500–516.

Townsend, J. T., & Ashby, F. G. (1978). Methods of modeling capacity in simple processing systems. In J. Castellan, & F. Restle (Eds.), In *Cognitive theory: Vol. III* (pp. 200–239). Hillsdale, NJ: Erlbaum Associates. Retrieved from http://www.indiana.edu/~psymodel/papers/towash78.pdf.

Townsend, J. T., & Ashby, F. G. (1983). A general discussion of equivalent and nonequivalent properties of serial and parallel systems and their models. In *The stochastic modeling of elementary psychological processes* (p. 481). Cambridge: Cambridge University Press. Chapter 15. Retrieved from http://www.indiana.edu/~psymodel/papers/Townsend_and_Ashby_Part3.pdf.

Townsend, J. T., Houpt, J. W., & Silbert, N. H. (2012). General recognition theory extended to include response times: Predictions for a class of parallel systems. *Journal of Mathematical Psychology*, *56*(6), 476–494. http://dx.doi.org/10.1016/j.jmp.2012.09.001.

Townsend, J. T., & Nozawa, G. (1995). Spatio-temporal properties of elementary perception: An investigation of parallel, serial, and coactive theories. *Journal of Mathematical Psychology*, *39*(4), 321–359. http://dx.doi.org/10.1006/jmps.1995.1033.

Townsend, J. T., & Schweickert, R. (1985). Interactive effects of factors prolonging processes in latent mental networks. In G. d'Ydewalle (Ed.), In *XXIII international congress of psychology: Vol. 3. Cognition, information processing, and motivation* (pp. 255–276). Amsterdam: North Holland.

Townsend, J. T., & Schweickert, R. (1989). Toward the trichotomy method of reaction times: Laying the foundation of stochastic mental networks. *Journal of Mathematical Psychology*, *33*(3), 309–327. http://dx.doi.org/10.1016/0022-2496(89)90012-6.

Townsend, J. T., & Spencer-Smith, J. B. (2004). Two kinds of global perceptual separability and curvature. In C. Kaernbach, E. Schröger, & H. Müller (Eds.), *Psychophysics beyond sensation: Laws and invariants of human cognition*. Mahwah, NJ: Erlbaum.

Townsend, J. T., & Thomas, R. D. (1993). On the need for a general quantitative theory of pattern similarity. In *Foundations of perceptual theory* (pp. 297–368). Amsterdam: North-Holland/Elsevier Science Publishers.

Townsend, J. T., & Thomas, R. (1994). Stochastic dependencies in parallel and serial models: Effects on systems factorial interactions. *Journal of Mathematical Psychology*, *38*, 1–34.

Townsend, J. T., & Wenger, M. J. (2004). The serial-parallel dilemma: A case study in a linkage of theory and method. *Psychonomic Bulletin & Review*, *11*(3), 391–418. http://dx.doi.org/10.3758/BF03196588.

Wenger, M. J., & Ingvalson, E. M. (2003). Preserving informational separability and violating decisional separability in facial perception and recognition. *Journal of Experimental Psychology: Learning, Memory, and Cognition*, *29*(6), 1106.

Wenger, M. J., & Townsend, J. T. (2001). Faces as gestalt stimuli: Process characteristics. In M. J. Wenger, & J. T. Townsend (Eds.), *Face perception and cognition*. Erlbaum Press.

Yang, H. (2016). *Survivor interaction contrast extended to include response accuracy* (Unpublished doctoral dissertation). Bloomington, IN: Indiana University.

Endnotes

1. The ways in which theory manifests change vs. invariance takes on highly recondite and powerful forms in 20th century physics. The prime example must be Emmy Noether's stupendous theorem which, with simplified language, demonstrated that for every symmetry in nature such as invariance under rotation, some type of physical quantities will be preserved in action over a path (see "Invariante Variations Probleme" [Invariant Variation Problems], *Nachr. D. König. Gesellsch. D. Wiss* (in German) (Göttingen: Math-phys. Klasse) 1918: 235–257. English translation by M.A. Tavel (1918); the interested reader will also delight in "Emmy Noether's Wonderful Theorem", charming and immensely informative, D.E. Neuenschwander, 2011).
2. There are curious features related to dependencies that can arise in nonlinear dynamics (such as chaos theory, Townsend, 1992; Devaney, 1986) but these lie outside our present concerns.
3. The question of probabilistic dependence arises in many guises, even in our own work, which must be sidestepped here. Starting references on those within our approaches are (a) Townsend and Ashby (1983) and (b) Ashby and Townsend (1986).
4. For instance, the main foundations of perceptual separability lie in General Recognition Theory (Ashby & Townsend, 1986) which itself has been cited in hundreds of papers (Ashby, 2014, personal communication). It undoubtedly figures in hundreds more in diverse studies of independence of perceptual dimensions (e.g., Garner & Morton, 1969). The notion of selective influence, lying as it does at the feet of the *additive factors method* (e.g., Sternberg, 1969) and its generalization, *systems factorial technology* (Townsend & Nozawa, 1995), has also been highly popular in experimental and methodological literature.
5. The concept of selective influence as stated here can be generalized to include more factors affect more processes and it is possible to differentiate between, say, random vectors, random variables and most generally, random entities (see, e.g., Dzhafarov & Kujala, 2010) but this simpler version will suffice for our purposes. And, since 1978 (Journal of Mathematical Psychology), Schweickert and colleagues have been investigating architectures which are more complex than the canonical serial vs. parallel arrangements (Schweickert, 1978; Townsend & Schweickert, 1985; see comprehensive review in Schweickert, Fisher, & Sung, 2012).

6. Similar statements apply to the notion of separability.
7. This curious recurrence of the same notion in palpably distinct settings, suggests that it may refer to a reasonably profound concept. That it has relevance to rather weighty conceptions is bolstered by Dzhafarov and colleagues' discovery of the relationship of marginal selectivity to logic associated with long-standing issues in quantum mechanics, including the famous Einstein–Podalsky–Rosen experiment and the linked Bell's inequality. However, this avenue lies outside our present concerns.

Bridge-Building: SFT Interrogation of Major Cognitive Phenomena

6

Daniel Algom, Daniel Fitousi†, Ami Eidels‡*
*Tel-Aviv University, Tel-Aviv, Israel, †Ariel University, Ariel, Israel, ‡The Newcastle University, Callaghan, NSW, Australia

The SFT has a long past, but a short history. In this volume we celebrate the latter, marked by the publication of the seminal article by Townsend and Nozawa in 1995. However, all of the main ingredients of the SFT, conceptual and technical, appeared virtually *ex nihilo* already in 1974 much like goddess Athena springing fully adult from Zeus's head at birth (Townsend, 1974; Townsend & Nozawa, 1995; see also Townsend, 1971, 1972). It is a tribute to the perseverance of Jim Townsend, but mainly to the brilliance of his ideas, that the foundations laid down in 1974 remained virtually unchanged over the course of the ensuing half of a century. Great ideas take on a life of their own.

For the most part, early applications of the SFT have considered simple detection and search tasks, whether visual or memory-based. More recently, the purview has been broadened to inform performance in tasks of classification. Throughout these applications, the stimuli were simple visual signals: dots, circles, triangles, or letters of the alphabet. Using simple stimuli in the formative years of the SFT is understandable: Investigators were preoccupied with theorems, proofs, and resolution of sundry methodological issues. The downside, of course, has been the attenuation of the potential impact of the SFT on mainstream cognitive psychology. This chapter represents an attempt to rectify this situation by establishing a cross-talk between SFT and basic phenomena of cognitive science (cf. Algom, Eidels, Hawkins, Jefferson, & Townsend, 2015).

We discuss four domains in which the SFT has led to important theoretical advances. We devote separate sections to discussing SFT-based interrogations of the effects of *Stroop*, *Garner*, *Size-Congruity*, and *Redundant Targets*. Application of the SFT in each case has contributed to the reformulation of old problems by way of suggesting new and profitable lines of investigation. Within each domain, we consider important subordinate or satellite phenomena as well. Concerning the Stroop effect (Stroop, 1935; MacLeod, 1991, 1992; Melara & Algom, 2003), applying insights based on SFT leads to a radical new perception of this benchmark measure of the selectivity of attention. Concerning Garner effects (Garner, 1970, 1974, 1976, see also, Algom & Fitousi, 2016), the SFT analysis poses intriguing challenges to the integrality–separability distinction, a pillar of current cognitive science. The SFT analysis of the size-congruity effect within numerical cognition (Fitousi & Algom, 2006) similarly challenges traditional theories in the field. Finally, an SFT examination of the redundant target effect reveals the role of shared names over and above that of physical identity in governing the size of redundancy gains (Ben-David & Algom, 2009).

Systems Factorial Technology, DOI: 10.1016/B978-0-12-804315-8.00008-2

An SFT Analysis of the Stroop Effect: Potential for a Radical New Theory

The Stroop effect (Stroop, 1935) is a prime example of the human failure to attend selectively to a single attribute of the stimulus (for reviews, see MacLeod, 1991; Melara & Algom, 2003). When naming the ink-color in which color words are printed, people are unable to overcome their tendency to read the words even when doing so can hurt color performance. Reading the words, in turn, compromises fully selective attention to the target colors. To gauge the extent of the breakdown of selectivity, the Stroop effect is defined as the difference in color-naming performance between congruent (the word naming its color such as RED in red, with the former indicating the word and the latter the color) and incongruent (GREEN in red) stimuli. The effect thus registers the impact of the task-irrelevant words: Had people attended exclusively to the target color, there would not have been a word-dependent difference in performance (i.e., the Stroop effect). Formally,

$$\text{Stroop effect} = \text{MRT(incongruent)} - \text{MRT(congruent)} \tag{6.1a}$$

where MRT the is mean reaction time to name the ink color. An analogous formula exists for error. In terms of response probability, P, the effect can be written as

$$\text{Stroop effect}(t) = P(RT \leq t|\text{congruent}) - P(RT \leq t|\text{incongruent}). \tag{6.1b}$$

More than 80 years after its discovery, the Stroop effect continues to fascinate researchers for both theoretical and pragmatic reasons. For theory, the robustness of the Stroop pattern and its potential utility for understanding central aspects of human attention and automatic action rendered the effect the single most popular phenomenon in current cognitive science (cf. Eidels, Townsend, & Algom, 2010). Indeed, MacLeod (1992, p. 12) called the Stroop effect "the gold standard" of all attention measures. In everyday life, selective attention is needed for performing the simplest of tasks. In its absence, one cannot read the newspaper in a cafeteria or negotiate the traffic while walking or driving. By definition, each activity of everyday life requires some ability to attend selectively to certain features in the environment, excluding other irrelevant or distracting features. Facility in isolating targeted experiences is indispensable for human adaptation and survival.

Theoretical Approaches

Despite its popularity, the Stroop effect has proven surprisingly resilient to a final theoretical resolution. Color–word interaction (often in the form of interference) is the basic processing assumption of virtually all major theories of the Stroop effect (MacLeod, 1991). Given the conflict residing in the (incongruent) stimulus and its impact on behavior (the Stroop effect), the inference that a processing conflict enfolds on the psychological theater of action seems eminently reasonable. The typical assumption is that the interaction of word and color is governed by the automatic dominance of word over color when the two clash within the semantic conflict engendered by the specific makeup of the Stroop (incongruent) stimulus. The principal difference among mainstream Stroop theories concerns the way that the interaction is instantiated in processing. Word and color could interact at several loci along their separate processing channels and a number of possibilities have been offered in the literature. The reader may wish to consult Eidels et al. (2010) or MacLeod and MacDonald (2000) for brief overviews of major Stroop theories and MacLeod (1991) for an extensive examination. Our main point is that all theories entail (a) automatic word reading and (b) an interaction between word and color as main ingredients.

A notable exception to traditional Stroop theorizing is the scheme developed by Melara and Algom (2003), which minimizes the role of automatic activation and semantic conflict in generating the Stroop effect (see also Lindsay & Jacoby, 1994, for an early proposal of independent processing of word and color). Melara, Algom, and their associates have shown that the Stroop effect is malleable by a wealth of stimulus factors. By judiciously manipulating these factors, one is able to fix the direction, the magnitude, and, in fact, the very appearance of the Stroop effect (Algom, Dekel, & Pansky, 1996; Dishon-Berkovits & Algom, 2000; Eidels, Ryan, Williams, & Algom, 2014; Fitousi, 2014; Fitousi & Algom, 2006; Melara & Algom, 2003; Melara & Mounts, 1993; Pansky & Algom, 1999, 2002; Sabri, Melara, & Algom, 2001). Such plastic, contextual determination of the Stroop effect is inharmonious with strong automaticity.

In the Melara and Algom (2003) theory, the advantage of congruent over incongruent stimuli (i.e., the Stroop effect) is explained by the trivial fact that with the former both of the attributes that are presented for view (e.g., RED in red) count for the correct response, whereas with the latter only the color does (GREEN in red). The role of semantic clash or agreement thus is minimized to the number of elements in each display counting for or counting against the correct response (with the processing of each element remaining the same in congruent and incongruent preparations).

In view of the limited role of automaticity and semantic factors in generating the Stroop effect (in the approach advanced by Melara and Algom, at the least), it seems only appropriate to ask: Can some form of *independent parallel processing* of word and color (i.e., processing without a color–word interaction) predict the Stroop effect? Consider the two types of *parallel* processing of color words and their ink colors presented in Fig. 6.1. Both models depict parallel processing because neither the word channel nor the color channel waits for the other channel to finish before it starts to process its own input. In the race model depicted in Fig. 6.1A, the processing is entirely separate: The response is determined completely by whichever channel that wins the race. In the coactivation model depicted in Fig. 6.1B, by contrast, information from the two channels is combined before a decision is made. The two sources of information coalesce downstream to satisfy the criterion for responding. This is an extreme form of parallel channel interaction. How does one decide between the two alternatives, indeed between two completely disparate classes of Stroop theories?

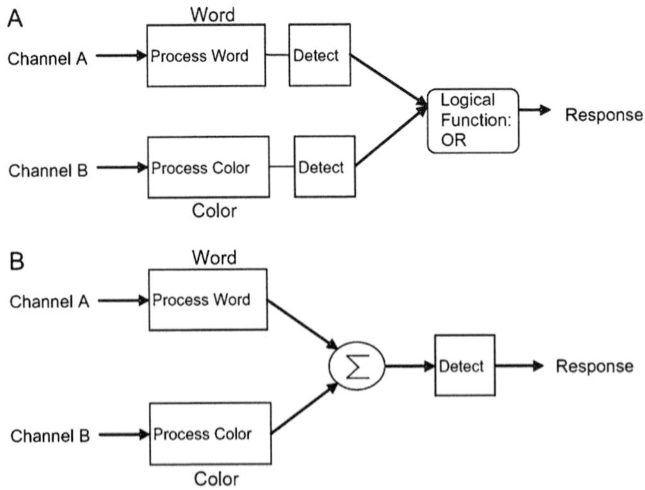

Figure 6.1 Schematic illustration independent parallel processing (A) and coactive processing (B). An architecture consistent with that in panel A is suggested by the SFT analysis below (and one that is invited by the Melara & Algom model). The architecture depicted in panel B represents major Stroop theories that entail color–word interaction in processing (from Eidels et al., 2010).

SFT-Based Adjudication of Theories

It is at this juncture that SFT plays an extremely valuable role. The full machinery of the SFT can be profitably deployed to inform the effort at model diagnosis. Note, however, that harnessing the SFT to examine Stroop color–word stimuli mandates departure from the standard Stroop task of *selective attention* (to the color). The paradigmatic target detection task of the SFT is that of *divided attention* (across color *and* word). Therefore, the focused attention task used with Stroop stimuli should be complemented by the SFT's target detection task applied to the same stimuli. For illustration, consider a small stimulus ensemble that includes all four combinations of the words, RED and GREEN, and the ink colors, red and green. In the Stroop task, the participants are instructed to respond to the ink colors while ignoring the carrier words. In the SFT task, by contrast, the participants are instructed to respond to "redness" in the Stroop stimulus, regardless of whether the "redness" comes in the word (RED), the color (red), or both (RED in red). Observe that, from an operational angle, the Stroop task and the detection task differ merely in the way that the four stimuli map onto two response options (Fig. 6.2).

According to accepted Stroop models, the divided attention task invites color–word interaction *more* than does the traditional Stroop task. In the standard Stroop task, the participants are directed to focus on a single channel (color) and to ignore information in another channel (word). The task itself does not invite interaction. In the detection task, by contrast, the participants are directed to attend to information in *both* channels. Therefore, the detection task actually invites interaction or coactivation, and it does so with force given targets as strongly related semantically as are color words and ink colors.

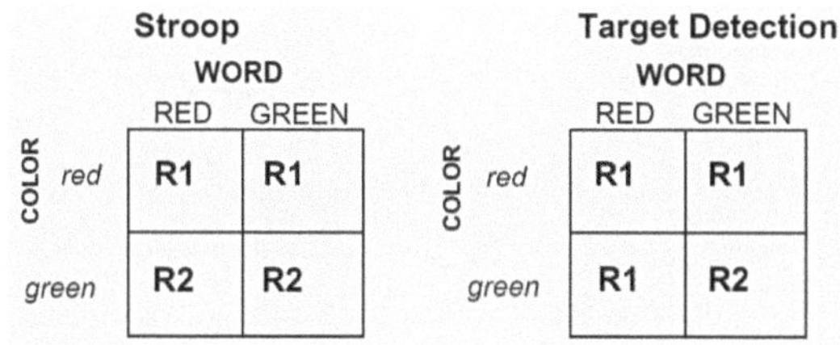

Figure 6.2 Different allocation of the same color–word stimuli into two response options (R1, R2) in the Stroop and the Target-Detection tasks (from Eidels et al., 2010).

These predictions were tested in a series of experiments by Eidels et al. (2010), applying SFT's *double factorial paradigm* to the color–word stimuli. To implement the double factorial paradigm, the words RED and GREEN appeared in highly legible and in less highly legible (yet still fully legible) font and the ink colors red and green were presented in good and bad quality (by manipulating their saturation). This manipulation of saliency enabled the creation of the second factorial design based on the subset of double-target trials with the Target Word (salient, less salient) and Target Color (salient, less salient) as the main factors.

The SFT Analysis

All SFT measures converged on the conclusion that the system is of unlimited capacity. Recall that, within the SFT, the capacity of the observer's system is captured formally by the capacity coefficient, $C(t)$,

$$C(t) = \log\big[S_{cw}(t)\big] / \log\big[S_c(t) + \log S_w\big], \tag{6.2}$$

where S is the survivor function, and the subscripts c and w denote the color and the word targets. The survivor function is defined with respect to the random variable T such that $S(t) = P(T > t)$. Note that $S(t) = 1 - F(t)$, with $F(t)$ denoting the distribution function for the same process, i.e., $F(t) = P(T \leq t)$. When $C(t) < 1$, the system is of limited capacity meaning that the processing of a target attribute (word or color) is impaired when both targets are present. When $C(t) = 1$, the system is of unlimited capacity, which means that a target is processed as efficiently (or inefficiently) when presented alone as when presented along with the other target. Finally, when $C(t) > 1$, the system is of supercapacity meaning that the processing of a target is actually improved when another target is also present, which attests to unlimited capacity.

Clearly, unlimited capacity in processing of Stroop stimuli is a striking result. After all, supercapacity is the expected mode of processing for attributes as strongly bonded semantically as RED and red. Yet supercapacity was *absent* from the data of all experiments. Despite the presence of Gestalt-like semantic congruity, the components of RED in red (double targets) were processed as efficiently, not more efficiently, and apparently in a parallel mode, as they were when appearing (singly) in the incongruent

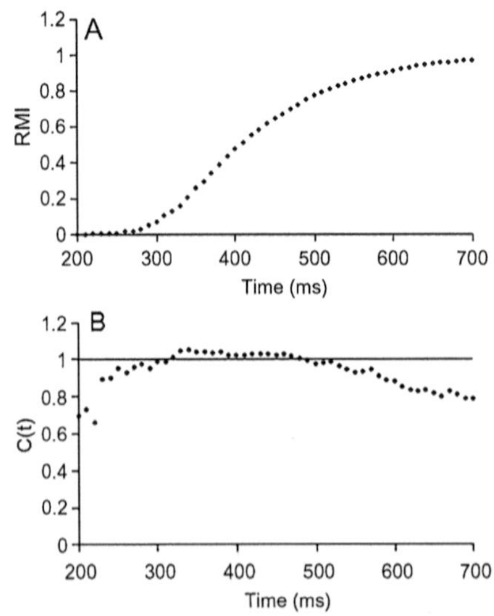

Figure 6.3 (A) depicts the survivor function test of the race model inequality. All the data are positive, hence the inequality is satisfied at all times t. (B) shows the results with respect to Townsend's capacity coefficient, $C(t)$. Virtually all the data points hover at around unity or a bit lower, meaning unlimited or slightly limited capacity. Supercapacity is definitely ruled out (from Eidels et al., 2010).

combinations. The results suggested a minimum time horse race along separate channels for the processing of Stroop color–word stimuli. This structure is inconsistent with coactivation or other interactive-channels models.

Inspection of the data unequivocally mandated these conclusions. Fig. 6.3A, presents the outcome of testing the Miller inequality (Miller, 1978, 1982), also known as the race model inequality (RMI). The inequality relates the probability of responding within time t to single- versus double-targets as follows:

$$F_{cw}(t) \leq F_c(t) + F_w(t), \tag{6.3}$$

where $F(t)$ is, again, the distribution function for the color-target only (c), the word-target only (w) and the double-target (cw) presentations inequality. In the survivor function test of the race model inequality used in the Eidels et al. (2010) study, positive values of the expression, $S_{cw}(t) - S_c(t) - S_w(t) + 1$, satisfy the inequality, whereas negative values violate it. Fig. 6.3B presents the outcome with respect to SFT's capacity coefficient calculations.

Observe that both separate channels theory (race architecture) and interaction or coactivation theory predict a redundant target effect, favoring responses to double- over single-target presentations. According to former theory, the responses to RED in red (double-targets) are speedy because they are determined by the faster process on any particular trial. According to the latter theory, the responses to RED in red are especially fast because information from the word and color targets combines to swiftly satisfy a single decision criterion. In terms of capacity, the separate channels model is

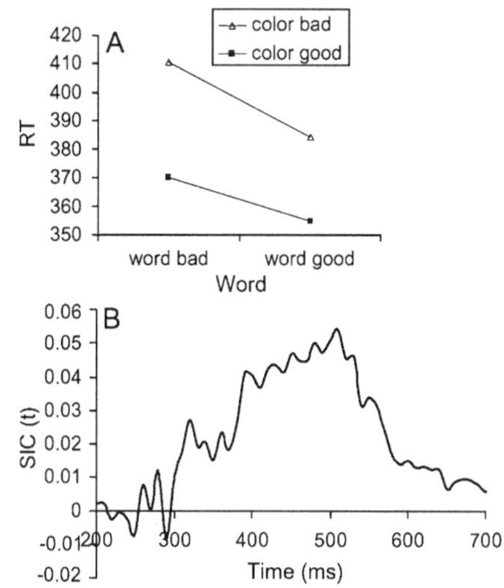

Figure 6.4 (A) Plot of the mean interaction contrast with word and color targets in salient and less salient presentations. The over-additive pattern observed supports minimum-time parallel processing of either race or coactivation. (B) The survivor interaction contrast function (SIC) for the same stimuli. Virtually all data points are positive, an outcome supporting a race architecture (from Eidels et al., 2010).

consistent with unlimited capacity, meaning that the quality of processing a target in any one channel is not impaired, limited, or enhanced by other ongoing processing. Therefore, this model is consistent with satisfying the race model inequality. In contrast, the coactivation model is consistent with supercapacity, meaning that the quality of processing a target in a given channel improves when other ongoing processing intensifies. The race model inequality is always violated under coactivation.

Concerning the race model inequality (top panel), the massive concentration of positive values in the survivor form of the test argues against supercapacity. The inequality is *not* violated at any value of t. The results show that an RTE occurs for double targets (i.e., of RED in red), but that this gain does not derive from the integration of the target attributes or from a particularly efficient processing of these redundant attributes. The results with respect to the $C(t)$ measure of capacity (bottom panel) support unlimited capacity (and reject supercapacity) because the data points are very close to 1 for all values of t. When presenting RED in red for view, the individual processing capacity in the word channel and in the color channel is exactly as good as it is when these respective targets are presented singly for view (i.e., in RED in green, or GREEN in red). In other words, adding a harmonious (redundant) target attribute did not affect the processing of the word RED or of the color red (i.e., when RED in red was presented).

In order to cross-validate the conclusion of a parallel race, it is useful to examine the subset of data from the redundant targets trials – the second leg of the double factorial design. In the factorial plot of target attribute (RED, red) by salience (good, bad) at the top panel of Fig. 6.4, the mean interaction contrast (MIC) is positive, indicating an over-additive interaction. An over-additive pattern supports (minimum time) parallel processing, but it does not distinguish between race and coactivation. To decide between the two models, the pertinent survivor interaction contrast, SIC(t), was calculated and is presented in the bottom panel of Fig. 6.4. Recall the different predictions derived in Townsend and Nozawa's seminal SFT paper: coactivation, SIC(t) < 0 for small t but SIC(t) > 0 for larger values of t; parallel race, SIC(t) > 0 at all times, t. The survivor interaction contrasts are overwhelmingly positive, a pattern consistent with processing along separate channels. The evidence for a parallel race is strong as is the counterevidence against coactivation.

Consider a final piece of evidence, which is related to the definition of targets. In the experiments discussed so far, the double-target stimulus, RED in red, was also a Stroop-congruent stimulus. Despite the congruity, the observed performance was neither supercapacity nor coactive. Notably, Eidels et al. (2010) have also employed other targets, including RED and green – a *Stroop-incongruent* combination. Consequently, RED in red and GREEN in green (i.e., *Stroop-congruent* combinations) formed the single-target stimuli. The results showed that, in the face a wholesale reversal of roles, the underlying model remained invariant. The Stroop-status of the attributes, congruent or incongruent, mattered little to mode of processing. Note that this reshuffle provides a strong test for the role of semantic relations in processing. They play a major role in the interactive model, but do not play a role in a race model, which assumes separate (parallel) processing of word and color. The remarkable outcome of model invariance validates the race architecture, one that does not afford a role to semantic relations.

At this point, a note on methodology is in order considering the original setup with RED in red as double targets and RED in green and GREEN in red as single targets. When calculating capacity in this set (i.e., the comparing double- and single-targets), load and semantic compatibility are always confounded. The reshuffle of targets just mentioned was meant to address this problem. However, one can envisage another way of addressing the issue. Think of a within-experiment design, entailing the presentation of "pure" (or neutral) single targets such as a color word in black or the row, "xxxxx", in color. Recall that, in the Eidels et al. (2010) experiments, a single target always came with a distractor, whereas the new method does not include distractors. Quite naturally, the new method also invites testing with congruent and incongruent double-targets. An intriguing question relates then to a difference in capacity. If Eidels et al. (2010) is any guide, then no such a difference is expected (these authors found no role for semantic factors). Be that as it may, performing this and further SFT tests of the Stroop phenomenon is a prudent direction for future research.

In sum, the outcome of the current SFT analysis is surprising. Separate processing of the word and the color of the Stroop stimulus is a counterintuitive finding given that the components are not simple meaningless visual marks, but rather words and colors bearing logical relations of conflict and agreement. The task instructions, too, invite interactive processing, yet none was found. These results cast doubt on the validity of the motif underlying major Stroop theories, namely, that the behavioral Stroop effect results from an actual processing conflict between the color and word. From a *logical* point of view, the presence of conflict inhering in Stroop stimuli, on the one hand, and of the Stroop effect, on the other hand, does not mandate a processing conflict. The

Stroop effect can ensue from completely unrelated psychological processes that do not entail a conflict mirroring inherent in the stimulus (cf. Garner, 1974). Hence, the mental structure can be different from the stimulus structure. Uttal (2001) underscored this same point: A system's macroscopic behavior might not be that of the real component processes at the microscopic level. One is not compelled to assume a processing conflict to support the putative conflict at the behavioral level. Given the independent race found, the Stroop color horse does not "know" the position, speed, indeed, the very existence of the Stroop word horse.

A New Separate Channels Theory of the Stroop Effect?

The overall results of the SFT analysis virtually invite the following intriguing question: Can a Stroop effect arise when the word and its color are processed along separate channels? Assuming a common architecture across tasks, Eidels (2012, Eidels et al., 2010) answered this question in the positive, offering a new Stroop theory that radically departs from existing theories. The idea was first suggested by Eidels et al. (2010), but was further developed by Eidels (2012). Eidels' point of departure is that the Stroop effect comprises a special case of the redundant target effect: Responses to a congruent Stroop stimulus (RED in red) are fast simply because it comprises a double- or redundant-target display, whereas an incongruent stimulus (e.g., GREEN in red) is a single target display. The critical point is that the redundant target effect can ensue from a strictly parallel and independent system where the different sources of information (word and color) need not interact. This core idea is augmented by the assumption that all channels, those for presented information as well as those for merely remembered information, are activated on all trials (with the former enjoying an advantage in processing). Eidels (2012) formalized the process as a counter model (Townsend & Ashby, 1983), with four parallel and independent counters. There are four rate parameters, one for each of the channels (presented word, presented color, non-presented word, non-presented color), and there are four corresponding criterion values. The prototypical schemata for this parallel, four-channel Stroop model, is shown in Fig. 6.5.

Eidels (2012) showed, by fitting empirical data and by numerical simulations, that the model *can* produce a Stroop effect, at least for a subset of parameter values. Eidels thus provided an existence proof for separate channels theory, and a challenge to many existing theories. The theoretical implications are nothing less than startling. Given the results, the Stroop effect cannot be exclusively viewed as the inevitable outcome of word–color conflict. In many occasions, it may simply be an instance of the redundant target effect by which the congruent (i.e., double-target) stimulus enjoys the benefit of redundancy over the incongruent (single-target) stimulus. Faster responses to the former merely reflect the activation gained from processing two presented targets as opposed to processing just one.

Although Separate Channels Theory has nontrivial support from several experiments, there remain unresolved issues. One apparent problem is the often claimed finding that interference (from incongruent stimuli) is greater than facilitation (produced by congruent stimuli). We do not think that this is a major drawback, however,

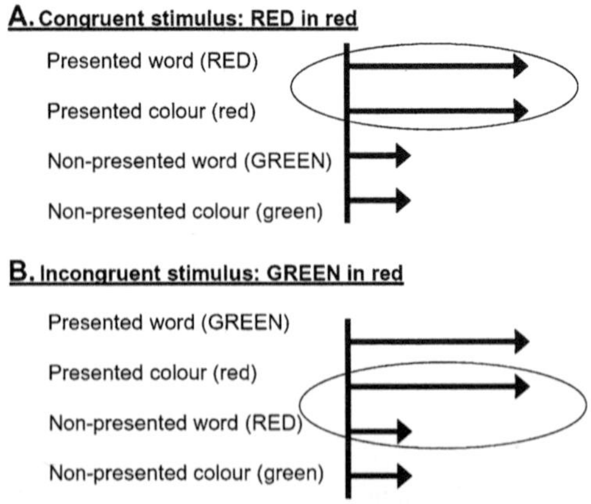

Figure 6.5 Illustration of a separate-channel model of the Stroop effect. In this simple example of a 2 (word: RED, GREEN) × 2 (color: red, green) design, each stimulus presentation activates four channels, one for each attribute. The response is determined by the winner of this four-headed race. The channels that lead to the correct response in the congruent and in the incongruent case are encircled. There are two such channels with both stimuli, yet the two channels are perceptual with congruent stimuli, but only one channel is perceptual (the other is memory-based) with incongruent stimuli (from Eidels, 2012).

because the composition of the Stroop effect (i.e., larger interference) is a conjectural result, contingent on the particular (often biased) design used (e.g., Algom et al., 1996; Melara & Algom, 2003; Pansky & Algom, 1999, 2002; Pomerantz, 1983; Sabri et al., 2001). Note also that the decomposition depends on the neutral stimulus used, yet there is no consensus on what constitutes a neutral stimulus or even if a neutral stimulus belongs in the Stroop environment in the first place. One gets vastly different results with different "neutral" stimuli (e.g., the word TABLE in color versus XXXXX in color; e.g., Brown, 2011). Other problems concern generalizability to Stroop-like stimuli. Work on producing a general and fully satisfactory analytic proof for a separate channels Stroop theory continues.

SFT-Based Examination of Garner Effects: Challenges to the Integrality–Separability Contrast

Inspection of Eq. (6.1) shows that the Stroop effect is calculable only for stimuli that can be characterized as congruent or incongruent (i.e., Stroop stimuli). However, all multidimensional stimuli are not also Stroop stimuli. A red triangle is a multidimensional stimulus, but it is neither more nor less congruent (or incongruent) than, say, a blue circle. The quality of congruity does not apply to stimuli composed of a shape and color. However, the question of selectivity is present with equal force with respect to non-Stroop stimuli, too. Can people attend selectively to color and ignore the shape of the stimulus (Cohen, 1997)? Can a pilot focus on azimuth and momentarily ignore altitude? The Stroop effect is no longer serviceable to answer these consequential questions. Another measure is needed to assess selectivity, one that is applicable to Stroop and non-Stroop stimuli alike: This measure is Garner interference.

In Garner's speeded classification paradigm (Garner, 1970, 1974, 1976; Fitousi, 2015; Melara & Algom, 2003, see Algom & Fitousi, 2016, for review), the same target dimension varies in a random fashion within different blocks of trials. The observer's task is to respond to the momentary value of this target dimension in all blocks. The various blocks differ by what happens to the task-irrelevant dimension. In the *Baseline* block, the irrelevant dimension is held at a constant value throughout all trials. In the *Filtering* block, the irrelevant dimension varies from trial-to-trial in an orthogonal fashion. Comparable performance in Filtering and Baseline indicates perfect selective attention to the target dimension. The parity shows that irrelevant variation in Filtering did not take a toll on performance. In contrast, worse Filtering performance indicates that fully selective attention to the target dimension has failed. The detriment shows that irrelevant variation did take a toll on selective performance. The difference in performance between Baseline and Filtering favoring the former is known as Garner Interference:

$$\text{Garner Interference} = \text{MRT(filtering)} - \text{MRT(baseline)} \tag{6.4a}$$

where MRT the is mean reaction time to classify the value of the relevant dimension. Another formula exists for error. In terms of response probability, P, the effect can be written as

$$\text{Garner Interference } (t) = P(RT \leq t|\text{baseline}) - P(RT \leq t|\text{filtering}). \tag{6.4b}$$

The size of Garner Interference, like the size of the Stroop effect, reflects on the extent of the breakdown of selective attention: The larger the interference, the greater the failure of exclusive attention to the target attribute. Two points are important to keep in mind. First, the Garner measure is a consistent property of a given pair of dimensions (it need not be symmetric: one dimension can suffer interference from the other, but not vice versa). Second, any observed instance of Garner Interference is typically supported by converging evidence on the failure of selectivity obtained by other methods. Therefore, Garner Interference is a *theoretical* result, not merely a particular experimental result. The most important theoretical notion to emerge from this branch of Garner's work is the distinction between *integral* and *separable* dimensions. Gestalt objects are composed of integral dimensions that interact in processing, hence suffer Garner Interference, whereas non-Gestalt objects are composed of separable dimensions that do not interact in processing and hence do not suffer Garner Interference. This partition has evolved into a pillar of contemporary cognitive science (Fig. 6.6).

The results of the SFT analysis of Stroop effects, and, in particular, Eidels' revolutionary theory (2012) of the Stroop phenomenon, pose a challenge to the integrality–separability distinction. In standard Garner theory, integral dimensions interact in processing (hence, they are often called "interactive dimensions"). Because color and word are integral dimensions (exhibiting Garner interference along with further defining properties), they, too, are assumed to interact in processing. However,

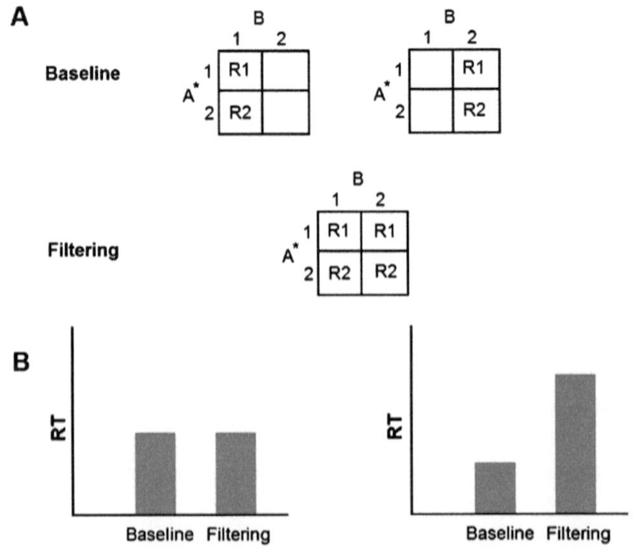

Figure 6.6 (A) The Baseline condition (once with irrelevant dimension B kept constant at B1 and once at B2) and the Filtering condition of the Garner design. R1 and R2 denote the correct responses to the values, A1 and A2 of the relevant dimension A (signified by the asterisk). (B) Two prototypical results: separable dimensions (left-hand graph) and integral dimensions (right-hand graph). The difference in performance depicted at the right is Garner interference.

Eidels (2012) demonstrated that Stroop dimensions need not interact and still produce what seems to be an integral outcome (i.e., the Stroop effect). If integral dimensions do not (necessarily) interact, then what distinguishes them from separable dimensions? Is separate processing always limited to separable dimensions? If not, one must search for further subtle differences to sustain the separability–integrality distinction.

Categorization

At first glance, the SFT is ill suited to inform categorization. The basic SFT experiment requires the factorial combination of the binary values of a pair of dimensions. Specifically, this design creates *four* stimulus combinations presented for the target detection task. In contrast, in the majority of categorization tasks the stimulus ensemble is partitioned into only *two* groups (defined by critical values on the two reference dimensions). Presented with a stimulus, the participant decides the category in which the stimulus was most likely a member. How can the SFT be applied to analyze categorization?

An ingenious solution was offered by Fifić, Nosofsky, and Townsend (2008; see also, Fifić & Townsend, 2010, and, in particular, Fifić, 2006, for pioneering this kind of research). In standard categorization experiments, the stimuli within each category do not form any particular configuration. In a clever feat, Fifić et al. (2008) modified this feature by imposing a factorial design on the stimuli within the category of in-

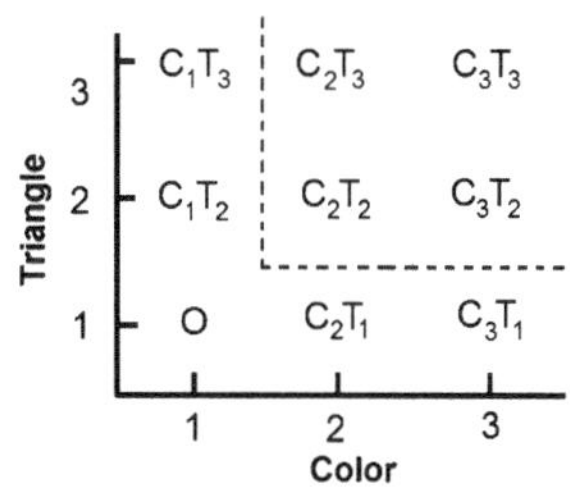

Figure 6.7 The categorization structure used by Fifić et al. (2008). Notice the 2 × 2 factorial design created in the target category.

terest. This arrangement enabled the application of SFT to the speeded categorization responses. Suppose that the stimuli are colored triangles. The color (C) can be dim (C1), medium (C2), or bright (C3), and the triangle (T) can be small (T1), intermediate (T2), or large (T3). Color and triangle size are combined in a factorial fashion to yield 9 colored triangle combinations. These are presented singly for view for speeded categorization. The rule for creating the two categories is as follows. The stimulus belongs to Category A, the target category, if it has a sufficiently bright color, $C \geq C2$, AND if the triangle is of a sufficiently large size, $T \geq T2$. Otherwise, the triangle belongs to Category B, the contrast category (Fig. 6.7).

Fifić et al. (2008) measured speeded-categorization in this design for stimuli composed of separable dimensions and for stimuli composed of integral dimensions. The results revealed different architectures. For separable stimuli, the dimensions were processed in a serial fashion – the processing of a dimension awaited completion of the processing of the other dimension – and the response was given only after all information was accrued (this exhaustive strategy is actually mandated by the AND rule defining the target category). For integral stimuli, by contrast, the processing was parallel coactive. Building on the foundations of the Fifić et al. (2008) study, the goal of subsequent, logical-rule-based models, was to provide a processing account for the observed differences between separable and integral stimuli (Fifić, Little, & Nosofsky, 2010; Little, Nosofsky, & Denton, 2011; Little, Nosofsky, Donkin, & Denton, 2013; see also, Fifić, 2014; Nosofsky, Little, Donkin, & Fifić, 2011). Notably, Fifić et al. (2010) extended the model to include predictions with respect to the contrast category (governed by an OR rule). For further examination of the assumptions of logical-rule models, see the chapter by Griffith, Blunden, and Little (2017) in this book (see also, Blunden, Wang, Griffiths, & Little, 2014).

The collective results of the studies based on the Fifić et al. (2008) paradigm pose a theoretical dilemma. They document a separability–integrality contrast that differs from the original Garnerian definition. According to Garner's definition (Eq. (6.2)), separability exists when the observer successfully ignores (variation along) the task-irrelevant dimension. Note that separability in this sense is already compromised in these categorization studies by virtue of the fact that the task requires attention to both dimensions. There is no relevant (or irrelevant) dimension in categorization: All of the dimensions are relevant. How does one reconcile the two sets of definitions and findings? Are there two types of separability (and integrality)? Is there a top-down separability (in speeded categorization) and a data-driven separability (in speeded classification)? This challenge to the original definition of the integrality–separability distinction awaits an in-depth exploration in future studies (see Little et al., 2013, for a recent discussion).

An SFT Analysis of the Size Congruity Effect

The Size Congruity effect is the bedrock of modern numerical cognition science (Besner & Coltheart, 1979; Dehaene, 1997; Fitousi, 2010; Fitousi & Algom, 2006; Fitousi, Shaki, & Algom, 2009; Henik & Tzelgov, 1982; Pinhas & Tzelgov, 2012; Pansky & Algom, 1999, 2002; Pinhas, Tzelgov, & Guata-Yaakobi, 2010; Tzelgov, Ganor-Stern, & Maymon-Schreiber, 2009). When people decide the *physically* larger member of a pair of numerals, their judgments are affected by the task-irrelevant numerical values. People select the physically larger stimulus in the congruent pair (8 2) faster than in the incongruent pair (8 2). The dimensional values of physical size and numerical magnitude match in the first pair, but mismatch in the second pair. The difference in performance favoring the former pair defines the size congruity effect. One does not need to present pairs of numerals in order to observe the size congruity effect. With a single numeral in view, it takes people longer to decide that the physical format is small when the numeral is 9 than when the numeral is 2 (Algom et al., 1996; Choplin & Logan, 2005; Fitousi, 2014).

According to the accepted view, the presence of the size congruity effect supports the automatic activation of numerical magnitude. In this respect, we note that the size congruity effect is related to the Stroop effect, but the two are not the same. Stroop stimuli are defined in an absolute sense: One does not need information on the particular experimental design or results to know that RED in red is a congruent stimulus. In contrast, the stimuli in the size congruity effect are relative and context bound: There does not exist a pre-experimental physical size that singularly matches the number 3 to create a congruent stimulus under all circumstances. Nevertheless, the theoretical interpretations seem similar: Numerical magnitude is activated in an automatic fashion just whenever a numeral is presented for view for any purpose. As a result, numerical value intrudes ineluctably on judgments of physical size, thereby generating the size congruity effect. The size congruity effect has been serving as a popular marker of the automatic processing of numerical magnitude.

However, Algom and his associates (e.g., Algom, Dekel, & Pansky, 1996; Fitousi, 2014; Fitousi & Algom, 2006; Fitousi et al., 2009; Pansky & Algom, 1999, 2002; see also, Melara & Algom, 2003; Sabri et al., 2001) have challenged the mandatory nature of the size congruity effect. These authors identified systematic biases in the pertinent studies that could, by themselves, produce the size congruity effect. For example, the majority of published studies used a greater number of values for numerical magnitude (typically, all the numbers between 1 and 9) than for physical size (typically, small and large); an asymmetry that already explains the dominance of the former over the latter. For another context, the numbers presented were more discriminable from one another than were the values of physical size presented from one another. A large literature (Algom et al., 1996; Garner & Felfoldy, 1970; Melara & Mounts, 1993; Melara & Algom, 2003; Sabri et al., 2001) documents the fact that the more discriminable dimension intrudes on the less discriminable dimension more than vice versa. By judiciously manipulating these and other contextual factors, Algom and colleagues were able to fabricate a size congruity effect, to eliminate the effect, or to reverse it (so that physical size intruded on number more than vice versa; the reverse size congruity effect, Fitousi & Algom, 2006). These developments invite conclusions inconsistent with the accepted view: The size congruity effect might be malleable rather than mandatory and automatic.

Fitousi and Algom (under review) subjected the size congruity effect to an SFT analysis within the framework of an ongoing comprehensive research. The goal was to gain information on the architecture and further properties of the cognitive system underlying the size congruity effect. According to the traditional view, numerical magnitude and physical size are *integral dimensions*, with physical size being the relevant dimension for responding. This view is consistent with a *parallel interactive* architecture: It is the interaction of numerical value and physical size, dominated by the former, which generates the size congruity effect. The developments by Algom and his associates, by contrast, are consistent with *separate and independent* processing of numerical value and physical size, whether parallel or serial. On this account, numerical value and physical size are *separable dimensions*. The size congruity effect is the result of biasing contexts that can affect an otherwise separate processing. The SFT is a singularly suitable toolkit to decide between the alternatives.

To apply the SFT, Fitousi and Algom (under review) changed the task to that of target detection. The binary values of numerical magnitude (large, small) and physical size (large, small) were combined to form the four stimuli of the factorial design. The target was defined as a large stimulus on either dimension or on both. To apply the double-factorial paradigm, the former basic factorial design was complemented by another one referring to the subset of double-target stimuli. This design was created by manipulating the salience of the number and size targets (number salience: low, high; size salience: low, high). The number target was salient (noticeably larger than the criterial number) or less salient (closer to the boundary number yet still larger) and the size target was salient (noticeably larger than the criterial size) or less salient (closer to the boundary, yet still larger).

The results of the SFT analysis were intriguing. It was found that, presented with a number at a given physical size, the observer processed the two dimensions in a *serial* fashion. The factorial plot for the trials with redundant targets exhibited parallel lines so that the mean interaction contrast [MIC] was zero. The survivor interaction contrast [SIC] functions hovered at around zero at all times t, with an exhaustive stopping rule with some of the observers, but a minimum time stopping rule with others. These features of the data are the signature of serial processing of number and physical size. Assuming invariance of the architecture across tasks, these results invite a wholesale revision of the accepted automatic interaction theory of the size congruity effect. These data imply that processing is neither interactive nor automatic. To a first approximation, the outcome of the SFT analyses is consistent with Algom's account of the effect. More work is needed to settle the sundry facets of the size congruity effect.

An SFT Interrogation of the Redundant Target: The Role of Names

Virtually every behavior is prompted by multiple signals when each signal alone suffices to produce the behavior. The presence of multiple, hence redundant, signals often facilitates the behavior. Reaching for the brakes in your car can be engendered by the red lights in the intersection, by the police officer signaling to stop, or by the little girl crossing the road. Again, each of these signals alone is sufficient for triggering your braking response, but together they increase the speed of responding. The red lights *and* the officer usually produce a faster braking response than each of them alone. This difference in performance between single and double or redundant-targets defines the redundant target effect. The basic SFT factorial design is eminently suitable for testing the effect. Suppose that the stimuli include the letters A and D with A defined as the target. With two letters presented on each trial, AA is the redundant target display, AD and DA are single-target displays, and DD is a no-target display. In this setup, faster detection of target A in AA than in AD or in DA documents the redundant target effect.

It is at this point that we issue an important caveat with respect to the typical redundant stimulus display. A pair of letters (the popular stimuli used in studies of SFT and of the redundant target effect) can be the same, hence redundant, in (at least) three ways: by physical identity (AA), by shared names (Aa, nominal identity), or by shared category membership or meaning (Ae entails vowels, semantic identity). Each of these species of sameness can affect performance in a different manner (Posner, 1978; Posner & Mitchell, 1967). Note that the physically identical signals that usually serve as redundant targets always go by the same name and always mean the same thing, whereas nominally or semantically identical signals are not necessarily so congruent. Consequently, it is possible that physically identical targets are detected very speedily due to the trivial fact that such targets are congruent at all conceivable levels of analysis.

Recognizing the multiple meanings of the core concept of sameness, and hence of the concept of redundant targets, Ben-David and Algom (2009) conducted a series of investigations into the effect of common names across targets and distractors on visual target detection. When the target and the distractor go by the same name, detection is impeded. The reason is the diminished discriminability of the stimuli wrought by the common name. A shared name renders the target less salient, hence more difficult to notice. This effect emulates that of physical similarity: Both act to camouflage the target (Bjork & Murray, 1977).

Consider again the factorial design with the letters A and D as target and distractor, respectively. Consider next a similar design with the letters A and a as target and distractor. The former stimuli, A and D, are different physically and nominally, a common characteristic of redundant target studies. The latter stimuli, A and a, are also different physically, but are the same nominally. Does this make a difference with respect to detecting the common target A? The results show that it does. Name sharing between the target and the distractor slowed down detection. The almost single source of the slowdown was the single-target displays: It took noticeably longer to detect target A in the pair Aa than in the pair AD. Associated with this difference was a parallel difference in the respective magnitudes of the redundant target effect – AA versus AD or DA, on the one hand, and AA versus aA or Aa, on the other hand. The redundant target effect in the second condition was almost three times its value in the first. The advantage accrued by exposure to replicas of a given signal is larger in an environment in which everything goes by the same name.

In SFT, the redundant target effect is often cast as a statement about capacity. Does name sharing across a target and a distractor affect the capacity of the system? Ben-David and Algom (2009) found that it does. Commensurate with the difference in the redundant target effect, the race model inequality was satisfied in the data with the letters A and D, but was sometimes violated in the data with the letters A and a. The Grice inequality – a lower bound on performance marking limited capacity (e.g., Townsend & Eidels, 2011) – was sometimes violated with the letters A and D, tapping regions of severe capacity imitations, but was satisfied at all time t when using the letters A and a. Capacity itself was well below unity with the letters A and D, approaching fixed capacity through large windows of time, but it was only slightly limited with the letters A and a – with the system sometimes evincing supercapacity. All of the analyses converged on tapping a system that was somewhat less limited capacity when performing with A and a than when performing with A and D.

The collective results mandate the following conclusions. First, names are noticed and processed in tasks of visual target detection. They are extracted along with physical features upon the presentation of a stimulus. Second, name sharing imped detection. If the signal and the distractor go by the same name, it takes the observer longer to respond to the signal. Third, in situations in which the to-be-detected signal and the to-be-ignored distractor go by the same name, responses to displays with two signals, i.e., displays without distractors, are relatively very fast. Consequently, a large redundancy gain is reaped in these situations. This speedup with double targets results from the absence of namesake distractors in the display, not necessarily from coactive processing of the two targets. Fourth, the existence of distractors bearing the name of the signals (even when absent from the particular display) engenders changes in the processing of the signals.

Summary: The Role of Nominal Factors

This SFT investigation of the redundant target effect highlights the role of names. Humans are probably the only species whose detection of signals in the environment is affected by the names or symbols attached to those signals. Critical delay in detection can occur when the to-be-detected target goes by the same name as to-be-ignored distractor. Simultaneously, the processing of the targets is relatively more efficient under such conditions. A natural explanation for the effect of target-distractor name sharing is that it is a form of camouflage (Bjork & Murray, 1977).

Language cannot afford a separate name to the virtually endless variation of states of nature. The net result is that different signals often go by the same name. This situation takes a toll on the speed of detection despite the fact that physical features define the target. The gain in detection when only targets are present (in particular, replicas of a given signal) is relatively large. The quality of processing a target is not strained by the presence and processing of another concurrent target. This means that the capacity of processing of the same signals is affected by the identity of the distractors despite the fact that the distractors do not play any direct role in signal processing (as examined recently by Little, Eidels, Fifić, & Wang, 2015). The hypothesis that the redundant target effect is partly or fully accounted by the (trivial) fact that target-only presentations do not include distractors (that can inhibit action) has been entertained in the past (Grice, Canham, & Gwynne, 1984; Eriksen, Goettl, James, & Fournier, 1989; Fournier & Eriksen, 1990). Ben-David and Algom's (2009) results show that the composition of the distractors (beyond their mere presence or absence) affects signal processing in systematic ways. When the distractor goes by the signal's name, the processing of double signals is more efficient.

Concluding Remarks

We have looked at four major cognitive phenomena aided by the results of dedicated SFT analyses. In each case, the SFT analysis provided new insights on the domain of interest.

1. The SFT analysis of the Stroop effect entailed the startling discovery about the feasibility of an independent-race architecture in processing color–word Stroop stimuli. This discovery is conductive, in turn, to a novel theory that radically departs from existing interactive theories of the Stroop effect.
2. The SFT results with respect to the Stroop phenomenon challenge accepted conceptions of the separability–integrality divide suggested by Garner. The color and word of the Stroop stimulus form integral dimensions. If the components of this integral stimulus are processed in a separable fashion, then the Garnerian distinction should be subjected to new scrutiny. The results obtained with tasks of categorization add another puzzle to be solved with respect to the separability–integrality contrast.
3. The SFT examination of the size congruity effect in numerical cognition resulted in the need for a wholesale revision of accepted models of numerical perception. Our analyses show that numerical magnitude is not processed in an automatic fashion and that number and size need not even interact in processing.
4. Finally, our SFT interrogation of the redundant-target effect showed that this effect, as well as the associated race model inequality and capacity coefficient, is modulated by the names that human attach to the stimuli. Shared names across tar-

gets and distractors impede target detection but, simultaneously, augment effects of redundancy and capacity.

Acknowledgement

The preparation of this chapter was supported by an Israel Science Foundation grant (ISF-274-15) to Daniel Algom.

References

Algom, D., Dekel, A., & Pansky, A. (1996). The perception of number from the separability of the stimulus: The Stroop effect revisited. *Memory & Cognition*, *50*, 557–572.

Algom, D., Eidels, A., Hawkins, R. X. D., Jefferson, B., & Townsend, J. T. (2015). Features of response times: Identification of cognitive mechanism through mathematical modeling. In J. R. Busemeyer, Z. Wang, J. T. Townsend, & A. Eidels (Eds.), *The Oxford handbook of computational and mathematical psychology* (pp. 63–98). New York: Oxford University Press.

Algom, D., & Fitousi, D. (2016). Half a century of research on Garner interference and the separability–integrality distinction. *Psychological Bulletin*, *142*, 1352–1383.

Ben-David, B. M., & Algom, D. (2009). Species of redundancy in visual target detection. *Journal of Experimental Psychology: Human Perception and Performance*, *35*(4), 958–976.

Besner, D., & Coltheart, M. (1979). Ideographic and alphabetic processing in skilled reading of English. *Neuropsychologia*, *17*, 467–472.

Bjork, E. L., & Murray, J. T. (1977). On the nature of input channels in visual processing. *Psychological Review*, *84*, 472–484.

Blunden, A. G., Wang, T., Griffiths, D., & Little, D. R. (2014). Logical-rules and the classification of integral dimensions: Individual differences in the processing of arbitrary dimensions. *Frontiers in Psychology*, *5*, 1531.

Brown, T. L. (2011). The relationship between Stroop interference and facilitation effects: Statistical artifacts, baselines, and a reassessment. *Journal of Experimental Psychology: Human Perception and Performance*, *37*, 85–99.

Choplin, J. M., & Logan, G. D. (2005). A memory-based account of automatic numerosity processing. *Memory & Cognition*, *33*(1), 17–28.

Cohen, D. J. (1997). Visual detection and perceptual independence: Assessing color and form. *Perception & Psychophysics*, *59*(4), 623–635.

Dehaene, S. (1997). *The number sense: How the mind creates mathematics*. New York, NY: Oxford University Press.

Dishon-Berkovits, M., & Algom, D. (2000). The Stroop effect: It is not the robust phenomenon that you have thought it to be. *Memory & Cognition*, *28*, 1437–1449.

Eidels, A. (2012). Independent race of color and word can predict the Stroop effect. *Australian Journal of Psychology*, *64*, 189–198.

Eidels, A., Ryan, K., Williams, P., & Algom, D. (2014). Depth of processing in the Stroop task: Evidence from a novel forced-reading condition. *Experimental Psychology*, *61*, 385–393.

Eidels, A., Townsend, J. T., & Algom, D. (2010). Comparing perception of Stroop stimuli in focused versus divided attention paradigms: Evidence for dramatic processing differences. *Cognition*, *114*, 129–150.

Eriksen, C. W., Goettl, B., James, J. D. S., & Fournier, L. R. (1989). Processing redundant signals: Coactivation, divided attention, or what? *Perception & Psychophysics*, *45*, 356–370.

Fifić, M. (2006). *Emerging holistic properties at face value: Assessing characteristics of face perception* (Unpublished Ph.D. dissertation). Indiana University.

Fifić, M. (2014). Double jeopardy in inferring cognitive processes. *Frontiers in Psychology*, *5*, 1–14.

Fifić, M., Little, D. R., & Nosofsky, R. M. (2010). Logical-rule models of classification response times: A synthesis of mental-architecture, random walk, and decision-bound approaches. *Psychological Review*, *117*, 309–348.

Fifić, M., Nosofsky, R. M., & Townsend, J. T. (2008). Information-processing architectures in multidimensional classification: A validation test of the systems factorial technology. *Journal of Experimental Psychology: Human Perception and Performance*, *34*, 356–375.

Fific, M., & Townsend, J. T. (2010). Information-processing alternatives to holistic perception: Identifying the mechanisms of secondary-level holism within a categorization paradigm. *Journal of Experimental Psychology: Learning, Memory, and Cognition*, *36*(5), 1290–1313.

Fitousi, D. (2010). Dissociating between cardinal and ordinal and between the value and size magnitudes of coins. *Psychonomic Bulletin & Review*, *17*, 889–894.

Fitousi, D. (2014). On the internal representation of numerical magnitude and physical size. *Experimental Psychology*, *61*, 149–163.

Fitousi, D. (2015). Composite faces are not processed holistically: Evidence from the Garner and redundant target paradigms. *Attention, Perception, & Psychophysics*, *77*, 2037–2060.

Fitousi, D., & Algom, D. (2006). Size congruity effects with two-digit numbers: Expanding the number line? *Memory & Cognition*, *34*, 445–457.

Fitousi, D., & Algom, D. (under review). A system factorial technology exploration of the size congruity effect.

Fitousi, D., Shaki, S., & Algom, D. (2009). The role of parity, physical size and magnitude in numerical cognition: The SNARC effect revisited. *Attention, Perception, & Psychophysics*, *71*, 143–155.

Fournier, L. R., & Eriksen, C. W. (1990). Coactivation in the perception of redundant targets. *Journal of Experimental Psychology: Human Perception and Performance*, *16*(3), 538–550.

Garner, W. R. (1970). The stimulus in information processing. *The American Psychologist*, *25*, 350–358.

Garner, W. R. (1974). *The processing of information and structure*. Potomac, MD: Erlbaum.

Garner, W. R. (1976). Interaction of stimulus dimensions in concept and choice processes. *Cognitive Psychology*, *8*, 98–123.

Garner, W. R., & Felfoldy, G. L. (1970). Integrality of stimulus dimensions in various types of information processing. *Cognitive Psychology*, *1*, 225–241.

Grice, G. R., Canham, L., & Gwynne, J. W. (1984). Absence of a redundant-signals effect in a reaction time task with divided attention. *Perception & Psychophysics*, *36*, 565–570.

Griffiths, D. W., Blunden, A. G., & Little, D. R. (2017). Logical-rule based models of categorization: Using systems factorial technology to understand feature and dimensional processing. In D. Little, N. Altieri, M. Fific, & C.-T. Yang (Eds.), *Systems factorial technology: A theory driven methodology for the identification of perceptual and cognitive mechanisms*. Elsevier (in this book).

Henik, A., & Tzelgov, J. (1982). Is three greater than five: The relation between physical and semantic size in comparative tasks. *Memory & Cognition, 10*, 389–395.

Lindsay, D. S., & Jacoby, L. L. (1994). Stroop process dissociations: The relationship between facilitation and interference. *Journal of Experimental Psychology: Human Perception and Performance, 20*, 219–234.

Little, R. D., Eidels, A., Fifić, M., & Wang, T. (2015). Understanding the influence of distractors on workload capacity. *Journal of Mathematical Psychology, 68–69*, 25–36.

Little, D. R., Nosofsky, R. M., & Denton, S. E. (2011). Response-time tests of logical-rule models of categorization. *Journal of Experimental Psychology: Learning, Memory, and Cognition, 37*, 1–27.

Little, D. R., Nosofsky, R. M., Donkin, C., & Denton, S. E. (2013). Logical rules and the classification of integral-dimension stimuli. *Journal of Experimental Psychology: Learning, Memory, and Cognition, 39*, 801–820.

MacLeod, C. M. (1991). Half a century of research on the Stroop effect: An integrative review. *Psychological Bulletin, 109*, 163–203.

MacLeod, C. M. (1992). The Stroop task: The "gold standard" of attentional measures. *Journal of Experimental Psychology: General, 12*, 1–12.

MacLeod, C. M., & MacDonald, P. A. (2000). Interdimensional interference in the Stroop effect: Uncovering the cognitive and neural anatomy of attention. *Trends in Cognitive Sciences, 4*, 383–391.

Melara, R. D., & Algom, D. (2003). Driven by information: A tectonic theory of Stroop effects. *Psychological Review, 110*, 422–471.

Melara, R. D., & Mounts, J. R. (1993). Selective attention to Stroop dimensions: Effects of baseline discriminability, response mode, and practice. *Memory & Cognition, 21*, 627–645.

Miller, J. (1978). Multidimensional same–different judgments: Evidence against independent comparisons of dimensions. *Journal of Experimental Psychology: Human Perception and Performance, 4*, 411–422.

Miller, J. (1982). Divided attention: Evidence for coactivation with redundant signals. *Cognitive Psychology, 14*, 247–279.

Nosofsky, R. M., Little, D. R., Donkin, C., & Fifić, M. (2011). Short-term memory scanning viewed as exemplar-based categorization. *Psychological Review, 118*, 280–315.

Pansky, A., & Algom, D. (1999). Stroop and Garner effects in comparative judgment of numerals: The role of attention. *Journal of Experimental Psychology: Human Perception and Performance, 25*, 39–59.

Pansky, A., & Algom, D. (2002). Comparative judgment of numerosity and numerical magnitude: Attention preempts automaticity. *Journal of Experimental Psychology: Learning, Memory & Cognition, 28*, 259–274.

Pinhas, M., & Tzelgov, J. (2012). Expanding on the mental number line: Zero is perceived as the "smallest". *Journal of Experimental Psychology: Learning, Memory, and Cognition, 39*, 972–976.

Pinhas, M., Tzelgov, J., & Guata-Yaakobi, I. (2010). Exploring the mental number line via the size congruity effect. *Canadian Journal of Experimental Psychology, 64*, 221–225.

Pomerantz, J. R. (1983). Global and local precedence: Selective attention in form and motion perception. *Journal of Experimental Psychology: General, 112*, 516–540.

Posner, M. I. (1978). *Chronometric explorations of mind*. Hillsdale, NJ: Erlbaum.

Posner, M. I., & Mitchell, R. F. (1967). Chronometric analysis of classification. *Psychological Review, 74*, 392–409.

Sabri, M., Melara, R. D., & Algom, D. (2001). A confluence of contexts: Asymmetric versus global failures of selective attention to Stroop dimensions. *Journal of Experimental Psychology: Human Perception and Performance*, *27*, 515–537.

Stroop, J. R. (1935). Studies of interference in serial verbal reactions. *Journal of Experimental Psychology*, *18*, 643–662.

Townsend, J. T. (1971). A note on the identifiability of parallel and serial processes. *Perception & Psychophysics*, *10*, 161–163.

Townsend, J. T. (1972). Some results concerning the identifiability of parallel and serial processes. *British Journal of Mathematical and Statistical Psychology*, *25*, 168–199.

Townsend, J. T. (1974). Issues and models concerning the processing of a finite number of inputs. In B. H. Kantowitz (Ed.), *Human information processing: Tutorials in performance and cognition* (pp. 133–168). Hillsdale, NJ: Erlbaum.

Townsend, J. T., & Ashby, F. G. (1983). *Stochastic modeling of elementary psychological processes*. Cambridge, UK: Cambridge University Press.

Townsend, J. T., & Eidels, A. (2011). Workload capacity spaces: A unified methodology for response time measures of efficiency as workload is varied. *Psychological Bulletin & Review*, *18*, 659–681.

Townsend, J. T., & Nozawa, G. (1995). Spatio-temporal properties of elementary perception: An investigation of parallel, serial, and coactive theories. *Journal of Mathematical Psychology*, *39*, 321–359.

Tzelgov, J., Ganor-Stern, D., & Maymon-Schreiber, K. (2009). The representation of negative numbers: Exploring the effects of mode of processing and notation. *The Quarterly Journal of Experimental Psychology*, *62*, 605–624.

Uttal, W. R. (2001). *The new phrenology: The limits of localizing cognitive processes in the brain*. Cambridge, MA: The MIT Press.

An Examination of Task Demands on the Elicited Processing Capacity

7

Leslie M. Blaha
Pacific Northwest National Laboratory, Richland, WA, United States

Introduction

The term supercapacity evokes images of highly effective experimental designs accompanied by efficient—fast and accurate—decisions. It's the superhero of performance, cape and all. And as with most superheroes, the sightings of supercapacity performance amongst the experimental literature seem elusive.

Although the formal concept of information processing capacity was introduced in the early 1970s (Townsend, 1972, 1974), it has only been since the introduction of Systems Factorial Technology (SFT) and its theory-driven methodology, the double-factorial paradigm (DFP), that in-depth assessments of capacity have been tractable. Consequently, capacity analyses are increasing in many areas of perception and cognition, including visual and auditory perception, multisensory integration, visual and memory search, and memory recall. As more tools for capacity analysis are developed, new experimental paradigms are developed to leverage them. This is of great benefit to the impact that SFT and the study of capacity can have on cognitive psychology. But this also raises questions about whether each design variation is capable of eliciting capacity in an unbiased fashion. Of interest to this chapter is the question: across the uses of capacity measures, can we find principles or guidelines about when or how we might observe supercapacity processing?

Capacity, from the information processing perspective, is defined as the amount of information processed by the system in a given amount of time. In this way, capacity can be conceptualized as information throughput or processing bandwidth, in contrast to other uses of the term as amount of space (e.g., working memory capacity; Baddeley, 1986) or availability of cognitive resources (e.g., Navon & Gopher, 1979; Wickens, 1980). There are three classes of possible information processing capacity levels, which are defined relative to the number of processes that must be completed in a given cognitive task. "Processes" can refer to numbers of features in a stimulus to be processed or the number of individual decisions that must be made within a task. When discussed alongside processing architectures, these processes are often termed stages (in serial architectures), channels (in parallel architectures), branches (in processing trees), or subprocesses. But regardless of the term, we assume that as we change the number of components within a task, we influence the numbers of processes that must be completed.[1] Unlimited capacity is the term used to describe processing wherein increasing the number of processes has no effect on information processing speeds; speed does not increase or decrease, so any number of processes can be completed at a consistent rate. Should an increase in the number of processes slow down the re-

Systems Factorial Technology, DOI: 10.1016/B978-0-12-804315-8.00009-4

sponses, then limited capacity is inferred. Or if increasing the number of processes results in an improvement in processing, defined as a speed-up of responses, then we infer supercapacity processing.

Note that processing capacity can be assessed at multiple levels of a processing system. Overall response times for a task give an indication of the capacity for the whole system response. Visual search slopes, determined with mean response time as a function of the number of items in a search array, are an example of analysis at this level (Townsend & Ashby, 1983). Zero-slope search functions, in which mean response time is flat or constant as a function of search array size, reflect unlimited capacity at the whole system level. Positive search slopes or increasing response time functions reflect limited capacity of the whole system response. Negative slopes would indicate supercapacity of the system because response speed is decreasing as a function of search array size (see Duncan & Humphreys, 1989, for evidence for all types of slopes).

Capacity can also be assessed at the level of individual processing channels. To do this, we must leverage experimental conditions or models that seek to isolate the effect of each channel on the response times. This assessment is often executed with the capacity coefficient function. Alternatively, appropriate functions that combine analyses of the responses of individual processes compared with multiple cognitive processes, including the individual process of interest, can be used. Inference in this space can be more difficult, because it can be tricky to isolate the individual processes. SFT revolutionized the approach to isolating individual processes. It does this by manipulating the speed of the individual processes when present and manipulating the number of processes at the same time. SFT leverages benchmark processing models in order to ground capacity interpretations. The most common benchmark, utilized in all the capacity coefficient functions, is an unlimited capacity independent parallel (UCIP) processing model. In this model, channels are operating simultaneously, without any stochastic interactions (no correlated inputs, no crosstalk), and in an unlimited capacity manner at the individual channel level. This means that if additional processes are added to the task, the processing speed of each individual channel remains unchanged even if the overall response time for the system increases. Assessment of task performance relative to this baseline model enables inferences about individual channel processing capacity. This is arguably the most popular capacity assessment approach within SFT applications, because this underlies the capacity coefficient assessment tools (Blaha & Houpt, 2015; Houpt & Townsend, 2012; Little, Eidels, Fific, & Wang 2015; Townsend & Altieri, 2012; Townsend & Eidels, 2011; Townsend & Nozawa, 1995; Townsend & Wenger, 2004).

In the first application of the capacity coefficient to visual detection in Townsend and Nozawa (1995), the results elicited both limited and supercapacity performance. Two experiments in the paper both entailed simple visual detection decisions. In Experiment 1, dots of light were presented tachistoscopically to the observer. One light was presented to the each of the right and left visual fields, with separate channels of the tachistoscope ensuring dichoptic stimulation. In Experiment 2, light diodes were placed on an optical bench in front of the viewer with one to the left of a fixation diode and the other to the right of fixation. A polarized filter was used to ensure dichoptic stimulation of the observer. Both experiments utilized the double-factorial paradigm for redundant signals in which either of the two dots could be present or absent; when present, the luminance (brightness) was either low or high. Participants were asked to respond "yes" if they detected any lights; this decision rule is the well-known standard OR stopping rule (see the tutorial chapter in this volume for more details). Speed and accuracy of light diode detection were measured, with the analysis emphasizing high accuracy response times.

The data for Townsend and Nozawa's Experiment 1 exhibited consistent limited capacity processing, with multiple violations of the Grice inequality lower bound on standard parallel processing (Grice, Canham, & Gwynne, 1984). Experiment 2, on the other hand, found overwhelming supercapacity performance, paired with violations of the race model inequality upper bound on standard parallel processing (Miller, 1982). This indicates strong supercapacity performance. In such similar tasks, what was the reason for the difference in results? Why was supercapacity from the redundant signals not found in both cases? Townsend and Nozawa proposed that the difference might have resulted from binocular (not dichoptic) stimulation that was possible in Experiment 2, or the possible infringement of base time in the computations, biasing the results in Experiment 1. At present, to my knowledge, this debate is unresolved. Regardless of the reason, there is one thing clearly suggested by these data: small experimental manipulations can result in striking differences in processing capacity.

The purpose of this chapter is to review a variety of applications of processing capacity analyses, focusing on hazard function and capacity coefficient approaches, in order to address two questions: (i) is supercapacity a rare finding, and (ii) are supercapacity findings dependent on the choice of experimental methods? In particular, to address the latter question, I will look for consistent trends in the methodological choices between studies that do and do not elicit supercapacity information processing behaviors. Many studies of cognitive capacity employ the double factorial paradigm (DFP) developed by Townsend and Nozawa (1995). And there is an increasing trend, especially since about 2010, in expanding the types of paradigms employing manipulations for capacity alone or modifying paradigms to at least enable hazard function analysis or proportional hazard modeling. As the number of paradigms enabling capacity assessment expand, I expect that the numbers of researchers and experiment incorporating the analyses will expand. But as a research community, we will likely continue to ask: what does it take to produce supercapacity processing?

The discussion herein will be limited to assessments of capacity leveraging hazard functions of response times. This nonparametric transformation of the response time distribution was suggested by Townsend and Ashby (1978) as a fundamental measure of cognitive work. Given that there are multiple tutorial papers on the measures of capacity (Harding et al., 2016; Houpt, Blaha, McIntire, Havig, & Townsend 2014; Wenger & Townsend, 2000, see also the tutorial chapter in this book), I will not reiterate all the variations of hazard function analysis, which include orderings and ratios of integrated hazard functions, the Cox proportional hazard function model (Wenger & Gibson, 2004), and the capacity coefficient functions (Blaha & Houpt, 2015; Little et al., 2015; Townsend & Nozawa, 1995; Townsend & Wenger, 2004).

Capacity and Gestalt Processing

Gestalt object perception should exhibit supercapacity, according to the processing characteristics proposed by Wenger and Townsend (2001). One hallmark of Gestalt perception is that object features configure into holistic percepts. This is the idea captured in Koffka's famous phrase (usually translated as), "The whole is other than the sum of its parts" (Koffka, 1935). Using face perception as their exemplar, Wenger and Townsend argued that performance on Gestalts would benefit from having more of their features available. Such a benefit is commensurate with supercapacity processing.

Gestalt perception sometimes manifests as superiority effects, where whole objects exhibit a speed or accuracy gain over parts of the same object or less meaningful configurations of those features. For example, word superiority effects occur when words or letters within real words are recognized or discriminated more quickly and accurately than individual letters alone or letters in non-word letter strings (Cattell, 1886; McClelland & Johnston, 1977; Reicher, 1969). Houpt and colleagues approached the study of word superiority effects with capacity analyses in order to determine if word superiority resulted from a perceptual advantage that would manifest in higher processing bandwidth for words (Houpt & Townsend, 2010; Houpt, Townsend, & Donkin 2014). They utilized a categorization task designed to elicit whole word/string processing for a correct "category one" response, similar to the task in Goldstone (2000). In this task, a string of four letters was placed into one category (e.g., CARE). The second category contained a very specific set of four distractor letter strings; each distractor contained one letter varying from the word/string in the first category (e.g., BARE, CURE, CAVE, CARD). The UCIP prediction was estimated from classification of the individual letters that comprised the letter strings. The full experiment included five types of letter strings: words, pseudowords (pronounceable non-words), non-word letter strings, non-word letter strings turned upside down, and Japanese Katakana character strings (no participants could read or speak Japanese). Capacity coefficient results generally indicated supercapacity processing for word and pseudoword conditions and limited capacity processing for non-word letter strings, upside-down letter strings, and Katakana character strings. No conditions elicited unlimited capacity processing from any participants, with the exception of one participant in the non-word string condition in Experiment 2 of Houpt, Townsend et al. (2014). The only difference between the two experiments was the use of explicit instructions reminding participants of the stimulus-response mappings on every trial, to eliminate any need for memory in the task. These findings confirm supercapacity for word superiority conditions, as well as for pseudowords, consistent with the capacity hypothesis about Gestalt perception.

Configural or object superiority effect is the term given to more general shape perception where the whole object perception was superior to the isolated features or collections of features that did not conform to Gestalt principles (continuity, closure, etc.; Pomerantz, Sager, & Stoever, 1977). Like the literature on word superiority effects, the measurement of configural superiority effects are typically made as gains in average response speed or accuracy. Eidels, Townsend, and Pomerantz (2008) tackled a first study applying SFT to configural superiority effects leveraging a redundant targets paradigm; results at a first glance showed a mix of limited and supercapacity. However, these results were very much dependent on both the configuration of the redundant targets as well as the configuration of the redundant distractors (the target absent stimuli). In Experiment 1, both the redundant target stimulus and the redundant distractor stimulus configured into Gestalt triangles; no superiority effects were observed and capacity, as measured by the capacity coefficient, was extremely limited. When no stimuli configured into triangles (Experiment 2) or only the redundant distractors stimulus configured into a triangle (Experiment 4), redundancy gains were observed but processing was still limited capacity. Supercapacity performance was observed when only the redundant targets configured into a triangle (Experiment 3). Additional observations of supercapacity performance were made in Experiment 5 when a variety of shape combinations were mixed together, but then these data were averaged across all the stimulus types and so the effect of "triangle-ness" was harder to isolate. Some of these results seem to contradict the Wenger and Townsend (2001) hypothesis of supercapacity for Gestalt processing.

Eidels and colleagues interpreted their findings from an object topology perspective: objects with a similar topology can produce some object confusability and more time is needed to tease out the exact properties when certain shapes are classified as target and others are not. From the present perspective, perhaps supercapacity Gestalt processing can only occur in experimental conditions that allow the observer to take full advantage of the Gestalt mechanisms; that is, when all configured objects map to the same response, then that response only requires the Gestalt recognition response. Any conditions that require observers to look beyond the Gestalt to distinguish differences among the component features undermine the natural Gestalt perception tendencies and produce slower, limited capacity processing. A similar explanation might be part of the results in Houpt, Townsend et al. (2014). The word and pseudoword conditions, which exhibited supercapacity, take advantage of human tendency to read words, so the classification task can be performed in part by the mental "sound" of the word. The other conditions, exhibiting limited capacity, required a more detailed search of the letters within the strings and could not take advantage of a secondary cognitive tendency that might make processing faster. We might conclude that supercapacity Gestalt processing will be observable only when we set up experiments to take advantage of Gestalt processing.

Although they did not pose this as a question, Wenger and Townsend (2006) actually tested some aspects of this idea in both face and word stimuli. The goal of their work was to utilize the SFT approach to tease apart the role of meaning and organization in configural objects, faces and words, that are often used in superiority studies. Meaning was defined as belonging to a pre-specified target set (i.e., features mean "target"), and organization was defined as proper configuration of the meaningful features (i.e., natural, Gestalt objects). In their experiment, the features (two eyes, nose, mouth) within a face could be scrambled between their natural positions, and the letters within words could be rearranged to form words, pseudowords, and letter strings. Two faces (words) were used, with one's features (letters) designated the target set and the other's designated the distractor set. Participants were instructed to indicate if at least one feature was from the target set (OR condition) or if all features were from the target set (AND condition). On each trial, the stimulus shown could have been a non-Gestalt object (scrambled face features or non-word strings), a source-inconsistent Gestalt (faces/words containing a mix of target and distractor features in their proper, interpretable locations), or source-consistent Gestalts (target items in their proper, interpretable locations). Analyses were conducted by proportional hazard modeling comparing the latter conditions to the non-Gestalt object, in order to determine if organization alone or organization and target membership would improve performance. For the face stimuli, source-consistent Gestalt objects reliably produced supercapacity performance, while source-inconsistent Gestalts actually slowed processing, resulting in limited capacity. For the word stimuli, the data showed no improvement in capacity for the source-consistent Gestalts and a decrease in processing capacity for the source-inconsistent Gestalts, relative to the non-Gestalt strings. From a task perspective, then, Gestalts are different from non-Gestalt images, but the presence of the Gestalt organization may have slowed the recognition of targets amongst distractors (source-inconsistent stimuli) because participants had to break apart that Gestalt mentally to isolate the meanings of the individual features.

Faces as Gestalt Percepts

Faces are considered by some to be the consummate Gestalts (see Wenger & Townsend, 2001, for a detailed argument on this point). Consequently, supercapacity is expected for face perception tasks. As we have seen in Wenger and Townsend (2006), supercapacity can occur but appears to be dependent on experimental/stimulus constraints. We can probe this further by considering the many applications of capacity to face perception tasks.

In the face processing literature, Gestalt (also called holistic, configural) face processing is often juxtaposed against so-called featural processing, which is often circularly defined as processing that is not holistic (Bartlett & Searcy, 1993; Maurer, Le Grand, & Mondloch 2002). It has often been argued that upright, natural faces can take advantage of configural processing mechanisms but that upside-down or otherwise manipulated faces can only take advantage of featural processing. If this is the case, any featural processing should not exhibit supercapacity but holistic face processing should. Ingvalson and Wenger (2005) offered an SFT-based test of this dual-model face processing hypothesis. Two types of stimuli were used: images of a female face and schematic faces created by oval and rectangle shapes in a face-like (two eye, nose, mouth) layout within an oval (head) surround. Manipulations were changes in the coloring of the features (lips and eye colors) or a change of mouth position (normal position or tilted counterclockwise). The task was to determine if a test face contained a different image from a similar study image shown on the trial. This could be considered a same-different judgment or a change detection task. The results showed supercapacity processing for all participants, for both upright and inverted images and for both face photos and schematic face drawings. Regardless of the mode of processing potentially enabled by the stimuli, change/difference detection between faces appears to enable supercapacity processing.

Perry, Blaha, and Townsend (2008), on the other hand, did not find compelling evidence for supercapacity processing of faces in a same-different paradigm. They engaged a same–different paradigm combined with SFT manipulations to assess face processing architectures. The stimuli were face illustrations consisting of eyes, nose, and mouth features within a common head surround (no ears, no hair, no additional features). The set of face features used in this task were created by first selecting a set of possible features, and then morphing them together to produce sets of high dissimilarity (unmorphed) and low dissimilarity (morphed) features. Faces were created by selecting combinations of high and low dissimilarity, consistent with DFP designs (see Houpt, Blaha et al. 2014, for a tutorial on DFP). Then two faces were presented such that they were either the same or the differences between the features matched the needed high/low DFP conditions. Thus, different decisions required close inspection, particularly in the low dissimilarity conditions, in order to render a correct response. Judgments on faces with only a single feature present were used to form the UCIP benchmark, and then multi-feature same–different judgments were assessed with the capacity coefficient. Performance consistently reflected limited capacity processing for both two- and three-feature faces, with some evidence for supercapacity at fast response times in the two-feature conditions.

Did Ingvalson and Wenger (2005) do a better job of allowing participants to take advantage of Gestalt mechanisms than Perry et al. (2008)? Or are color and position differences just easier to detect than potentially more subtle feature morphing differences? Additional research is needed to directly compare these types of manipulations. However, it is clear that the morphing manipulations used by Perry et al. (2008) would have required participants to mentally disrupt the face configurations to find the subtle differences between the features, particularly when two features were very similar (low dissimilarity morphs). Alternatively, perhaps color and position changes are faster to nab the attention of the observer than feature shape (not position) changes as the observer searches for possible differences in the images.

Consider the capacity data from a study of the Thatcher illusion by Donnelly, Cornes, and Menneer (2012). A Thatcherized face is produced when both the eyes and mouth are isolated and flipped upside-down within a face. The illusion is that when the face is upright, the face appears grotesque to observers, but when the image is turned upside-down, the inversion of the features is harder to detect and the face is rated much less grotesque (Thompson, 1980). Donnelly and colleagues hypothesized that because the Thatcher illusion was supposed to be processed configurally, then upright Thatcherized faces should exhibit supercapacity processing. They utilized both a categorization task and a same–different judgment task to assess Thatcherized face capacity, with analyses both by capacity coefficient and proportional hazards modeling. Experiment 1 utilized upright Thatcherized faces and required participants to classify faces, presented one at a time, as "odd" or "normal." A minority of participants exhibited supercapacity processing for fast response times; all later times and all other participants exhibited limited capacity processing, despite the presence of mean-level redundancy gains. Experiment 2 required same–different judgments on Thatcherized faces comprising either eye, mouth, or both differences. Proportional hazards modeling showed no evidence for supercapacity and some evidence for unlimited or limited processing as the number of differences increased, with no redundancy gains in response speed (only gains in accuracy).

There appears to be a growing amount of evidence that face processing is not typically supercapacity when the tasks require distinctions to be made between the individual features themselves. In many cases, it would seem that the experiments are not leveraging the face Gestalts to help produce supercapacity; participants in all the above reviewed tasks must examine the features themselves, not the whole faces, to make their decisions.[2] Yet only in Ingvalson and Wenger (2005) was supercapacity consistently observed. It does not appear that this difference is between the number of possible differences to be detected; all studies leveraged combinations of eye and mouth manipulations. But Ingvalson and Wenger (2005) was the only study, so far, to use manipulations that were not changes in the shapes of the features (keeping those features in their natural positions). It would seem that capacity of face processing might be very sensitive to the nature of the manipulations utilized.

The above studies all entailed manipulations of the inner face features. Fitousi (2015) examined the processing capacity for faces using composite face manipulations. Composite faces are created by manipulating the identity and position of top and bottom face halves. In some conditions, they are aligned properly to appear like a natural face, but the top and bottom identities are manipulated to be either halves from same or different original faces. Similar top and bottom identity manipulations are used in the misaligned conditions, but the halves are offset so that they do not configure into a natural face. It is hypothesized that the misaligned condition produces featural processing wherein the individual top and bottom identities are easier to recognize. The aligned faces should be processed as holistic faces, and the individual top and bottom identities are harder to recognize (Young, Hellawell, & Hay, 1987). Fitousi (2015) hypothesized that in a redundant targets task, if they were exhibiting holistic processing, participants would exhibit supercapacity for aligned faces and unlimited capacity for misaligned faces. This pattern was observed in only three of eight participants. Remaining participants exhibited other combinations of limited and unlimited processing. In another experiment, Fitousi instructed participants to make a same–different judgment between the composite faces and a target original face. Again, only three of eight participants exhibited the predicted supercapacity for aligned faces and unlimited capacity for misaligned faces.

Given the limited findings of supercapacity face processing in other studies, it is not surprising that Fitousi (2015) also found limited evidence for supercapacity processing. Fitousi did not manipulate the features within any of the faces, in so far as the horizontal division into top and bottom faces did not change the features. However, his tasks required participants to decompose the aligned faces into the component halves for mental comparison to pre-defined target faces. Perhaps like the feature manipulations in Ingvalson and Wenger (2005), Perry et al. (2008), and Donnelly et al. (2012), composite faces also undermine people's ability to leverage face Gestalts. This would particularly be the case, for example, if a person adopts a task strategy of confirming there are no differences (always closely examining both face halves) rather than affirming the same halves are present. Those participants exhibiting non-supercapacity processing in aligned composite faces were may not have been using the Gestalts because of the other task conditions. Note that it was not the case that the misaligned faces performed better than the aligned faces. In the same–different task, capacity on misaligned stimuli was usually lower than for the aligned faces. In the redundant targets task, results were split between better or worse capacity on misaligned than aligned faces. This gives some evidence that the alignment helps some participants, but does not overcome the manipulations that disrupt the Gestalt perceptions. Indeed, Fitousi argued that composite face perception likely involved sources of response conflict that were unrelated to Gestalt perception. This may be related to our general findings that manipulating the features within a face seem to disrupt Gestalt perceptual processes and prevent good, supercapacity information processing.

Considering a second facet of Wenger and Townsend's (2001) Gestalt processing characteristics, they also hypothesized that Gestalt processing would entail a mandatory exhaustive stopping rule. Clearly, Gestalt stimuli like words and faces can be utilized in tasks that do not require exhaustive processing; all the different decisions within a same–different task, for example, require the detection of only a single difference for a response to be made. But are we likely to observe supercapacity more often when exhaustive processing is required? Although this does not explain the supercapacity in Ingvalson and Wenger (2005), there is evidence supporting this in that both Houpt, Townsend et al. (2014) and Wenger and Townsend (2006) observed supercapacity in Gestalt stimuli with exhaustive stopping rules. But this might bear further scrutiny through experiments designed to directly assess capacity differences based on stopping rule.

An example of such a direct comparison is found in Fitousi and Wenger (2013), in which minimum time and exhaustive stopping rules were tested with the same stimuli. In Experiment 3, Fitousi and Wenger factorially combined familiar (female celebrity) and unfamiliar (female research assistants) faces with happy or neutral emotions to create a set of faces. Eyes or mouths were sometimes blocked from view (sunglasses or scarf, respectively) to obtain capacity manipulations. Within both OR and AND conditions, participants were asked to identify either the identity or emotion of the faces. While they observed a mixture of limited and unlimited capacity in the OR condition, participants consistently produced supercapacity in the exhaustive response conditions. This provides confirmatory evidence that exhaustive rules for face stimuli (maybe other Gestalt stimulus classes) encourages supercapacity processing.

Perceptual Decision Making

Moving away from faces and Gestalts, the use of capacity analysis has expanded in many areas of visual and multimodal sensory perceptual decision making. While many of these stimuli or tasks have similarities to some of the face studies, particularly in the use of redundant target and DFP designs, there is not necessarily a common hypothesis that suggests the presence or absence of supercapacity across them all. However, as we have observed with the Gestalt results above, data tend to either show supercapacity or limited capacity processing, depending on the task.

Consider the hierarchical form (global–local) perception tasks in Blaha, Johnson, and Townsend (2007) and Johnson, Blaha, Houpt, and Townsend (2010). In typical hierarchical form studies, congruent information at both the global and local stimulus levels produces faster and more accurate responses than incongruent information, which is thought to compete across levels (Kimchi, 1992; Navon, 1977). This suggests global–local perception, like Gestalts, is supercapacity. In Blaha et al. (2007) and Johnson et al. (2010), participants (including adults and adolescents with and without an autism spectrum disorder) were asked to make OR decisions in a DFP version of a global–local perception task. Stimuli were compound arrows, where small (local) arrows were arranged into large (global) arrows. Targets were right-pointing arrows; distractors or target-absent place holders were dashes that did not point left or right. Participants were asked to determine if any right-pointing arrows were present at the local, global, or both levels. Though redundancy gains were observed in this task, consistent with typical global–local perception tasks, capacity was limited, with some evidence for supercapacity for early response times in some participants. In fact, the results are quite consistent with the findings of Eidels et al. (2008) in that redundant targets produced some processing gains, but they did not simply equate to supercapacity processing. It is possible in this case, though, that redundant target decisions were made just as quickly as global decisions, and the potential gain from redundant local information provided no capacity boost. Comparisons are needed to conditions where the global and local information might compete more for attentional resources in the decision process to help tease this apart.

Altieri and Townsend (2011) predicted redundancy gains and supercapacity in audio-visual discrimination decisions. In their experiments, two words were used, one as target and one as distractor. Stimuli were either the auditory track spoken words alone, video clips of the a female speaking the words alone, or the combined audio-visual recording. The hypothesis was that the combined audio-visual information would have a multisensory integration advantage in processing, reflected in supercapacity response times. The signal-to-noise ratio was also manipulated, to test if the integration would produce a greater capacity gain in less-than-ideal listening conditions. Results indicated that redundant audio-visual information produced supercapacity when listening conditions were degraded the most (lowest signal-to-noise ratio), and capacity decreased to extremely limited as listening conditions improved.

Experimentally, does this, taken together with the results of Johnson et al. (2010), suggest that for tasks where performance can reliably be achieved on a single dimension, despite the redundant information provided, observed capacity will always be limited? Or inversely, should we only expect supercapacity when we degrade performance on at least one dimension so that the additional dimensions provide a much-needed information boost? Important to note that in both these studies, information was either congruent or absent on the two dimensions; competing information was not presented.

Let us consider the study of the Stroop effect (Stroop, 1935), one of the most compelling examples of stimulus competition for attentional resources. Eidels, Townsend, and Algom (2010) conducted a series of experiments to examine the information processing mechanisms supporting Stroop task performance. The emphasis of this study was on the processing architecture, assessing if Stroop performance could be supported by parallel processing. In this way, capacity was used as secondary, converging evidence. But for our purposes in this chapter, I will emphasize just the capacity results. In the Stroop task, congruent stimuli (color words printed in the same color as the word) should show less between-dimension competition or even facilitation, compared to incongruent color–word combinations. The latter should produce limited capacity due to the cross-dimensional competition, while the former may exhibit supercapacity. Across their four experiments, Eidels and colleagues found unlimited capacity at best, but results were predominantly mildly limited capacity, for both Stroop congruent and incongruent target stimuli. Interestingly, capacity was never limited enough to suggest inhibitory competition between the dimensions, nor was capacity super, suggesting facilitation between the dimensions. Thus, the Stroop stimuli did not behave like Gestalt percepts either (but in this book, also see Algom, Fitousi, & Eidels, 2017; Taylor, Theberge, Williamson, Densmore, & Neufeld, 2017, for new Stroop-related findings).

We might infer from these perceptual studies that only presenting redundant target information is not enough to produce supercapacity. Nor is supercapacity driven by stimulus congruency or incongruency. But they do support the observation that when Gestalt perception is not at play, redundancy results in supercapacity when stimulus information is degraded. That is, when some task relevant information is not clear enough to support a fast decision, the addition of more information will result in a boost to information processing throughput. At least one implication for experimental designs is clear: when you want to observe supercapacity, start with a harder task or degraded stimuli.

Perceptual Learning

Supercapacity emerges over the course of perceptual learning. Perceptual learning is the well-observed phenomenon wherein practice improves perceptual task performance (Dosher & Lu, 1999; Gold, Sekuler, & Bennett, 2004). There are multiple mechanisms proposed to capture the ways in which perceptual learning tunes the perceptual processing mechanisms, including improvements in thresholds and ideal observer-based efficiency. From the information processing perspective, practice can serve to improve both the processing of the individual task components as well as task performance on the combinations in redundant or multi-target situations. When those improvements are reflected in fast response times, we expect to observe changes in processing capacity. When the performance on the redundant targets improves above and beyond individual channels, then supercapacity results.

One of the first studies to leverage hazard function analysis and the capacity coefficient in perceptual learning was conducted by Blaha and Townsend (Blaha, 2010; Blaha, Busey, & Townsend, 2009). This study focused on perceptual unitization or configural learning, wherein participants are required to learn a set of features that belong together (for further definitions, see Goldstone, 1998). Over the course of training, features are "chunked" together, or unitized, into holistic object percepts; that is, the features configure into a whole object that people recognize as fast as they can discriminate the individual features. Goldstone (2000) demonstrated that perceptual unitization in a categorization task improved response times, at both the mean and cumulative distribution ordering levels. Blaha (2010) replicated Goldstone's task, applying capacity coefficient analysis in order to assess not just improvement in speed but also changes to the underlying information processing mechanisms. The categorization task utilized in these studies engaged a very specific combination of object characteristics. First, an object was created for one category consisting of five randomly chosen features. Then, the second category was created by systematically swapping a single feature from the original object with a novel feature. Each of the five objects in the second category, then, contained only one swapped feature and four features identical to the first category's object. Because of this construction, participants were required to attend to all object features in order to make a correct "category one" assignment; that is, mandatory exhaustive processing was required. Early in training, while participants learned to distinguish the individual features, "category two" responses were faster than "category one" responses, but efficiency was extremely limited. Over training, as features were unitized into perceptual wholes, the "category one" responses shifted to be faster than "category two" responses and as fast as individual feature discrimination times. Capacity shifted from extremely limited to super, sometimes extremely super, capacity levels. Perceptual unitization produced highly efficient, supercapacity perceptual configural object responses.

Capacity has also been observed to improve with training of audio-visual cue associations Altieri, Stevenson, Wallace, and Wenger (2015). In their audio-visual integration task, visual stimuli consisted of foveally presented Gabor patches oriented at 45 degrees and varying in spatial frequency (six steps from 4 to 25 Hz). The auditory stimuli were pure tones at a constant 68 dB SPL varying in frequency (six steps, 400 to 2500 Hz). All factorial pairings were used in the experiment; a single pair was presented simultaneously for 100 ms on each trial. Participants were trained for 7 days each, with every session consisting of 120 visual-only, 120 audio-only, and 360 audio-visual pairing trials. Participants gave a "yes" response if an audio-visual pair matched and a "no" response to all mismatches and single-modality trials. Participants used feedback on every trial to learn the correct associations, which were the corresponding steps in the frequency ranges. Results showed an increase in processing capacity, measured by proportional hazard modeling, for correct audio-visual association over training. This was captured by increasing hazard functions for each training day. Accuracy and sensitivity also increased with training.

To date, studies in perceptual learning from the capacity perspective have focused predominantly on tasks that emphasized learned groupings or associations of data. Thus it is clear that learning to group (chunk, unify) perceptual features together results in improvements in processing. We might consider that learned associations can be thought of has having the effective impact of reducing the number of individual features to which an observer must allocate attention. This is similar to Gestalt perceptions, where the whole is attended to rather than the parts and supercapacity is the hypothesized efficiency. By effectively reducing the number of features in the task, capacity will improve. Indeed, if the result of perceptual learning facilitates the use of Gestalt-like configurations, then we can take advantage of the superiority such percepts enable, as discussed earlier in this chapter. But is supercapacity always the result of perceptual learning? Or does it only result from learning groupings or associations? Additional work in other perceptual learning paradigms, like perceptual differentiation, is needed to determine if supercapacity results from any perceptual learning or practice, or if it is only the outcome under certain learning conditions.

Memory

Stepping away from perceptual decision making tasks, capacity analysis has seen recent applications in the study of memory. This is an important shift in the thinking about memory, which is typically considered in terms of working memory capacity meaning the number of items that can be stored in working memory at a given time. The general thinking is that this is some number between four and seven (Luck & Vogel, 1997; Miller, 1956), and that the span of one's working memory might indicate things about general levels of executive function and cognition. Less attention has been given to the bandwidth of memory information processing. With capacity analyses, though, we can ask questions about how much information, which may equate to items in short term memory, can be processed through the memory system during task performance. Given the generally accepted limits of short term memory space capacity, is memory throughput capacity also limited?

Endres, Houpt, Donkin, and Finn (2015) examined working memory capacity through a redundant signals memory task. Leveraging a DFP design, the study stimuli were colored letters, which could be probed in terms of single features (color or letter) or with redundant color–letter combinations. Memory lists varied in length, using either two-, four-, or six-item study lists. Contrary to limitations on memory space, Endres et al. found that redundant probes improved memory recall, with observers exhibiting supercapacity on redundant probes relative to individual feature recall. Endres and colleagues confirmed this improvement in efficiency by utilizing the linear ballistic accumulator model to capture increases in evidence accumulation rates under the redundant memory probe conditions, relative to the single probe conditions assuming fixed memory capacity. Limited capacity was observed in mixed target–distractor conditions and redundant distractor responses, so this boost was a product of the redundancy in the task. There are ways in which we can draw some parallels between the color–letter task demands in Endres et al. (2015) and the Stroop perception tasks of Eidels et al. (2010) (ignoring the difference between non-word letter strings and words). Recall that in both consistent and inconsistent color–word combinations, redundancy did not give perceptual identification a strong capacity boost. But color–letter redundancy does improve memory bandwidth. This suggests that the results might not be about color–letter combinations, but about the task using the redundant information.

Recently, in order to better align working memory concepts of capacity, Heathcote and colleagues (Heathcote et al., 2014, 2015) introduced the Gatekeeper task. This task combines n-back working memory recall (2-back, specifically) with audio-visual association. Stimuli on a given trial are a visual image of three doors, one of which is colored red, and an audio "password" letter (one of three possible). If the same door–letter combination was presented $n = 2$ trials back, then the observer is to respond with a "block" response; otherwise they give an "allow" response. Capacity is assessed by comparing performance on this complex audio-visual n-back task with performance on single target (audio or visual alone) n-back trials. By design, the Gatekeeper task should elicit proactive interference between tasks, so Heathcote et al. (2015) predicted limited to unlimited capacity performance levels. Capacity assessment utilized the capacity coefficient, as well as related statistics and accuracy capacity. There was overwhelming evidence for severely limited capacity across all measures.

It is hard to draw strong conclusions about the bandwidth capacity of memory on only two studies. But the difference in the experimental designs did produce drastically different capacity results. Thus, like perceptual decision making domains, memory is an area where experimental demands will shape the types of capacity observed. And tracking these results early and often will help us make sense out of the working memory space.[3]

An Aside on Methods, Mechanisms, and Interpretation

One of the key new facets working its way into information processing capacity analyses is the search for meaningful connections between capacity as bandwidth or efficiency and other metrics of cognitive performance popular in many applied domains. The studies by Heathcote et al. (2015) and Endres et al. (2015) are exemplars of this new trend, in that they both sought to relate response time capacity with metrics for working memory span (see also Yu, Chang, & Yang, 2014a, 2014b). Heathcote and colleagues found weak correlations between the complex operation-span (OSPAN) measure of working memory capacity and the multiple processing capacity metrics in the Gatekeeper n-back task. Similarly, Endres and colleagues also found only weak correlations between working memory span and capacity in the redundant memory probe task. Although both these suggested only weak correlations between the capacity coefficient and OSPAN, from our present experimental design perspective, they strongly illustrate how we can make smart methodological choices to bring together hazard function-based throughout capacity assessment with other notions of capacity in order to map potential relationships between notions of capacity.

But this really reflects a larger point at the heart of the SFT approach: capacity cannot be fully studied or understood in isolation from other system characteristics. The argument that no information processing mechanism should be studied without the others is pervasive in Townsend's work related to SFT (Townsend, 1972, 1974; Townsend & Ashby, 1978, 1983; Townsend & Nozawa, 1995; Townsend & Wenger, 2004; Wenger & Townsend, 2000). Capacity is one of the fundamental characteristics of human information processing system, together with architecture, stopping rule, and process (in)dependence. If all constructs can be assessed together, then we have the theoretically grounded context in which we can understand why supercapacity (or any level of capacity, really) has or has not been observed. In this author's opinion, the interest in further connecting information processing constructs to other metrics of cognitive behavior, such as complex span or executive function, as well as other psychological constructs (e.g., personality, clinical constructs), is likely to only increase in the future. And more work in these areas will provide a thorough theoretical foundation to ground our understanding of the relationship between available mental resources and the ways in which they are leveraged for different cognitive processes.

Elusive Supercapacity?

Across the 16 published studies of information processing capacity considered in this chapter, the results have generally been a mix of supercapacity and limited capacity processing. Indeed, 10 of the 16 studies reliably observed supercapacity processing in at least one experiment or condition. Others had evidence for supercapacity at some fast response times. So to answer the first question posed in the introduction: supercapacity may not be as rare as we have thought it to be. What does appear to be rare from the present survey is unlimited capacity processing. Only 4 of the 16 studies reported findings of unlimited capacity, with 2 (Donnelly et al., 2012; Wenger & Townsend, 2006) providing statistical support for unlimited processing. This raises the question of whether information processing capacity is more dichotomous than previously thought. That is, are we likely to only regularly observe supercapacity or limited capacity processing, with an absence of the occurrence of unlimited capacity?

If it is the case that supercapacity is actually hiding in plain sight, are there principled experimental guidelines for eliciting supercapacity? Given the flexible and stochastic nature of human performance, I suspect there are not unchangeable rules. Indeed, the fact that perceptual learning changes processing capacity suggests that improvements in performance due to practice may be sufficient to influence the observed capacity in just about any task (of course, this is a testable hypothesis, too). Leveraging the DFP does seem to encourage some consistency in the experimental designs employing capacity analyses, but the results are not equally consistent. Johnson et al. (2010) and Endres et al. (2015), for example, both employed DFP design but had opposite findings of limited capacity and supercapacity, respectively. In some cases, we should probably consider if forcing a DFP design changes the nature of the task in ways that disrupt the task of interest, or that task's predisposition to engage supercapacity processing. Eidels et al. (2008) is a case where trying to adapt the odd-man-out paradigm, which easily highlights configural superiority effects, to match the DFP constraints drastically changed the nature of the task. Stimuli that would have exhibited equally strong configural superiority pop-out effects now are confusable and produce the slowest overall processing when they have to be directly compared. Careful attention to the ways in which adapting a task for DFP should be paid so that the results can be understood, at least in part, by those methodological changes.

A potentially strong factor in supercapacity sightings might be the decision rule or choice of task. Indeed, as Wenger and Townsend (2001) hypothesized, mandatory exhaustive stopping rules may elicit more supercapacity processing when combined with well-configured or Gestalt stimuli. This is evidenced by the supercapacity in Blaha (2010), Fitousi and Wenger (2013), Houpt, Townsend et al. (2014), and Wenger and Townsend (2006). Another decision design choice that seems to help encourage some supercapacity is whether the decision entails direct comparison between stimuli or comparison of a stimulus to a rule or previously studied target set. This was definitely the case in the memory probe task compared to the Gatekeeper task for working memory applications. In perceptual decision making, only the same–different or change detection tasks entailed direct comparisons between stimuli; all other tasks provided a pre-specified target set. Many of the latter exhibited limited capacity processing, which raises a question of the role that memory might be playing in those tasks. But the results are mixed on the same–different tasks, with Ingvalson and Wenger (2005) showing supercapacity, Perry et al. (2008) finding limited capacity, and Fitousi (2015) (Experiment 3) finding a mixture of supercapacity and unlimited capacity for aligned faces and unlimited/limited capacity for misaligned faces. As is discussed above, perhaps this result is more attributable to stimulus difficulty than decision rule. Or there may be a more complex interaction at play between stimulus manipulations and decision rule. Note that in the present review I have not delved into the stimulus presentation ordering. Behavior may be variably influenced if different stimulus conditions/manipulations were presented interleaved within experimental blocks or separated between blocks. This experimental factor may be one useful tool for teasing out the interactions of decision rules and stimulus manipulations on the processing capacity elicited from participants.

Considering stimulus structure, the applications to Gestalt perception suggest that we should try to employ tasks that harness natural stimulus structures in order to encourage supercapacity processing in perceptual tasks. The perceptual learning studies together with the Endres et al. (2015) results further suggest that providing redundancy and reinforcement (natural or learned associations) about the target sets can boost performance. And instances of this seem to be strongest when the task either entails Gestalt perception (where the features are somewhat redundant with the perceptual whole) or in tasks where performance on individual dimensions is hard (e.g., degraded features). That is, when the additional workload is going to serve to help the baseline workload, rather than just to be additional information present but not helping, then supercapacity is likely to be seen.

Acknowledgements

I wish to thank Jim Townsend and participants in the 20 Years of Systems Factorial Technology Symposium at the 2015 Society for Mathematical Psychology Annual Meeting for the discussions that inspired this chapter. The views expressed in this chapter are those of the author and do not reflect the official policy or position of the US Government, Department of Defense, or Department of Energy.

References

Algom, D., Fitousi, D., & Eidels, A. (2017). Bridge-building: SFT interrogation of major cognitive phenomena. In D. R. Little, N. Altieri, M. Fifić, & C.-T. Yang (Eds.), *Systems factorial technology: A theory driven methodology for the identification of perceptual and cognitive mechanisms*. Elsevier (in this book).

Altieri, N., Stevenson, R. A., Wallace, M. T., & Wenger, M. J. (2015). Learning to associate auditory and visual stimuli: Behavioral and neural mechanisms. *Brain Topography*, *28*(3), 479–493.

Altieri, N., & Townsend, J. T. (2011). An assessment of behavioral dynamic information processing measures in audiovisual speech perception. *Frontiers in Psychology*, *2*(238), 10–3389.

Baddeley, A. D. (1986). *Working memory*. Oxford: Oxford University Press.

Bartlett, J. C., & Searcy, J. (1993). Inversion and configuration of faces. *Cognitive Psychology*, *25*, 281–316.

Blaha, L. M. (2010). *A dynamic Hebbian-style model of configural learning* (Ph.D. thesis). Bloomington, Indiana: Indiana University.

Blaha, L. M., Busey, T., & Townsend, J. T. (2009). An LDA approach to the neural correlates of configural learning. In *Proceedings of the 31st annual conference of the Cognitive Science Society*. Austin, TX: Cognitive Science Society.

Blaha, L. M., & Houpt, J. W. (2015). An extension of workload capacity space for systems with more than two channels. *Journal of Mathematical Psychology*, *66*, 1–5.

Blaha, L. M., Johnson, S. A., & Townsend, J. T. (2007). An information processing investigation of hierarchical form perception: Evidence for parallel processing. *Visual Cognition*, *15*, 73–77.

Cattell, J. M. (1886). The time it takes to see and name objects. *Mind*, *11*(41), 63–65.

Donnelly, N., Cornes, K., & Menneer, T. (2012). An examination of the processing capacity of features in the Thatcher illusion. *Attention, Perception, & Psychophysics*, *74*(7), 1475–1487.

Dosher, B. A., & Lu, Z.-L. (1999). Mechanisms of perceptual learning. *Vision Research*, *39*(19), 3197–3221.

Duncan, J., & Humphreys, G. W. (1989). Visual search and stimulus similarity. *Psychological Review*, *96*(3), 433–458.

Eidels, A., Townsend, J. T., & Algom, D. (2010). Comparing perception of Stroop stimuli in focused versus divided attention paradigms: Evidence for dramatic processing differences. *Cognition*, *114*(2), 129–150.

Eidels, A., Townsend, J. T., & Pomerantz, J. R. (2008). Where similarity beats redundancy: The importance of context, higher order similarity, and response assignment. *Journal of Experimental Psychology: Human Perception and Performance*, *34*(6), 1441–1463.

Endres, M. J., Houpt, J. W., Donkin, C., & Finn, P. R. (2015). Working memory capacity and redundant information processing efficiency. *Frontiers in Psychology*, *6*.

Fitousi, D. (2015). Composite faces are not processed holistically: evidence from the Garner and redundant target paradigms. *Attention, Perception, & Psychophysics*, *77*(6), 2037–2060.

Fitousi, D., & Wenger, M. J. (2013). Variants of independence in the perception of facial identity and expression. *Journal of Experimental Psychology: Human Perception and Performance*, *39*(1), 133–155.

Gold, J. M., Sekuler, A. B., & Bennett, P. J. (2004). Characterizing perceptual learning with external noise. *Cognitive Science*, *28*(2), 167–207.

Goldstone, R. L. (1998). Perceptual learning. *Annual Review of Psychology*, *49*(1), 585–612.

Goldstone, R. L. (2000). Unitization during category learning. *Journal of Experimental Psychology: Human Perception and Performance*, *26*, 86–112.

Grice, G. R., Canham, L., & Gwynne, J. W. (1984). Absence of a redundant-signals effect in a reaction time task with divided attention. *Perception & Psychophysics*, *36*, 565–570.

Harding, B., Goulet, M.-A., Jolin, S., Tremblay, C., Villeneuve, S.-P., & Durand, G. (2016). Systems factorial technology explained to humans. *The Quantitative Methods for Psychology*, *12*(1), 39–56.

Heathcote, A., Coleman, J. R., Eidels, A., Watson, J. M., Houpt, J., & Strayer, D. L. (2015). Working memory's workload capacity. *Memory & Cognition*, *43*(7), 973–989.

Heathcote, A., Eidels, A., Houpt, J., Colman, J., Watson, J., & Strayer, D. (2014). Multi-tasking in working memory. In *Proceedings of the 32nd annual conference of the cognitive science society*. Austin, TX (pp. 601–606).

Houpt, J. W., Blaha, L. M., McIntire, J. P., Havig, P. R., & Townsend, J. T. (2014). Systems factorial technology with R. *Behavior Research Methods*, *46*, 307–330.

Houpt, J. W., & Townsend, J. T. (2010). A new perspective on visual word processing efficiency. In S. Olhsson, & R. Catrambone (Eds.), *Proceedings of the 32nd annual conference of the cognitive science society* (pp. 1148–1153). Austin, TX: Cognitive Science Society.

Houpt, J. W., & Townsend, J. T. (2012). Statistical measures for workload capacity analysis. *Journal of Mathematical Psychology*, *56*, 341–355.

Houpt, J. W., Townsend, J. T., & Donkin, C. (2014). A new perspective on visual word processing efficiency. *Acta Psychologica*, *145*, 118–127.

Ingvalson, E. M., & Wenger, M. J. (2005). A strong test of the dual-mode hypothesis. *Perception & Psychophysics*, *67*(1), 14–35.

Johnson, S. A., Blaha, L. M., Houpt, J. W., & Townsend, J. T. (2010). Systems factorial technology provides new insights on global–local information processing in autism spectrum disorders. *Journal of Mathematical Psychology*, *54*, 53–72.

Kimchi, R. (1992). Primacy of wholistic processing and global/local paradigm: A critical review. *Psychological Bulletin*, *112*(1), 24–38.

Koffka, K. (1935). *Principles of gestalt psychology*. Routledge.

Little, D. R., Eidels, A., Fifić, M., & Wang, T. (2015). Understanding the influence of distractors on workload capacity. *Journal of Mathematical Psychology*, *68*, 25–36.

Luck, S. J., & Vogel, E. K. (1997). The capacity of visual working memory for features and conjunctions. *Nature*, *390*(6657), 279–281.

Maurer, D., Le Grand, R., & Mondloch, C. J. (2002). The many faces of configural processing. *TRENDS in Cognitive Sciences*, *6*, 255–260.

McClelland, J. L., & Johnston, J. C. (1977). The role of familiar units in perception of words and nonwords. *Perception & Psychophysics*, *22*(3), 249–261.

Miller, G. A. (1956). The magical number seven, plus or minus two: Some limits on our capacity for processing information. *Psychological Review*, *63*(2), 81–97.

Miller, J. (1982). Divided attention: Evidence for coactivation with redundant signals. *Cognitive Psychology*, *14*, 247–279.

Navon, D. (1977). Forest before trees: The precedence of global features in visual perception. *Cognitive Psychology*, *9*(3), 353–383.

Navon, D., & Gopher, D. (1979). On the economy of the human-processing system. *Psychological Review*, *86*(3), 214–255.

Perry, L., Blaha, L., & Townsend, J. (2008). Reassessing the architecture of same–different face judgments. *Journal of Vision*, *8*(6), 889.

Pomerantz, J. R., Sager, L. C., & Stoever, R. J. (1977). Perception of wholes and of their component parts: Some configural superiority effects. *Journal of Experimental Psychology: Human Perception and Performance*, *3*(3), 422–435.

Reicher, G. M. (1969). Perceptual recognition as a function of meaningfulness of stimulus material. *Journal of Experimental Psychology*, *81*(2), 275–280.

Stroop, J. R. (1935). Studies of interference in serial verbal reaction. *Journal of Experimental Psychology*, *18*, 643–662.

Taylor, R., Theberge, J., Williamson, P., Densmore, M., & Neufeld, R. W. J. (2017). Systems-factorial-technology-disclosed stochastic dynamics of Stroop processing, in the cognitive neuroscience of schizophrenia. In D. R. Little, N. Altieri, M. Fifić, & C.-T. Yang (Eds.), *Systems factorial technology: A theory driven methodology for the identification of perceptual and cognitive mechanisms*. Elsevier (in this book).

Thompson, P. (1980). Margaret Thatcher: A new illusion. *Perception*, *9*, 483–484.

Townsend, J. T. (1972). Some results concerning the identifiability of parallel and serial processes. *British Journal of Mathematical and Statistical Psychology*, *25*, 168–199.

Townsend, J. T. (1974). Issues and models concerning the processing of a finite number of inputs. In B. H. Kantowitz (Ed.), *Human information processing: tutorials in performance and Cognition* (pp. 133–168). Hillsdale, NJ: Erlbaum Press.

Townsend, J. T., & Altieri, N. (2012). An accuracy–response time capacity assessment function that measures performance against standard parallel predictions. *Psychological Review*, *119*(3), 500–516.

Townsend, J. T., & Ashby, F. G. (1978). Methods of modeling capacity in simple processing systems. In J. N. Castellan, & F. Restle (Eds.), *Cognitive theory* (pp. 199–239). Hillsdale, NJ: Lawrence Erlbaum Associates.

Townsend, J. T., & Ashby, F. G. (1983). *The stochastic modeling of elementary psychological processes*. Cambridge, UK: Cambridge University Press.

Townsend, J. T., & Eidels, A. (2011). Workload capacity spaces: A unified methodology for response time measures of efficiency as workload is varied. *Psychonomic Bulletin & Review*, *18*, 659–681.

Townsend, J. T., & Fifić, M. (2004). Parallel versus serial processing and individual differences in high-speed search in human memory. *Perception & Psychophysics*, *66*(6), 953–962.

Townsend, J. T., & Nozawa, G. (1995). Spatio-temporal properties of elementary perception: An investigation of parallel, serial and coactive theories. *Journal of Mathematical Psychology*, *39*, 321–360.

Townsend, J. T., & Wenger, M. J. (2004). A theory of interactive parallel processing: New capacity measures and predictions for a response time inequality series. *Psychological Review*, *111*, 1003–1035.

Wenger, M. J., & Gibson, B. S. (2004). Using hazard functions to assess changes in processing capacity in an attentional cuing paradigm. *Journal of Experimental Psychology: Human Perception and Performance*, *30*(4), 708–719.

Wenger, M. J., & Townsend, J. T. (2000). Basic tools for attention and general processing capacity in perception and cognition. *Journal of General Psychology: Visual Attention*, *127*, 67–99.

Wenger, M. J., & Townsend, J. T. (2001). Faces as gestalt stimuli: Process characteristics. In M. J. Wenger, & J. T. Townsend (Eds.), *Scientific psychology series. Computational, geometric and process issues in facial cognition: Progress and challenges* (pp. 229–284). Lawrence Erlbaum Associates.

Wenger, M. J., & Townsend, J. T. (2006). On the costs and benefits of faces and words: Process characteristics of feature search in highly meaningful stimuli. *Journal of Experimental Psychology: Human Perception and Performance*, *32*(3), 755–779.

Wickens, C. D. (1980). The structure of attentional resources. *Attention and Performance*, *VIII*, 8.

Young, A., Hellawell, D., & Hay, D. (1987). Configurational information in face perception. *Perception*, *16*, 747–759.

Yu, J.-C., Chang, T.-Y., & Yang, C.-T. (2014a). Individual differences in working memory capacity and workload capacity. *Frontiers in Psychology*, *5*, 1465.

Yu, J.-C., Chang, T.-Y., & Yang, C.-T. (2014b). Working memory capacity predicts workload capacity. *Visual Cognition*, *22*(8), 1046–1049.

Endnotes

1. Additional terms that come into play are workload, cognitive load, or task load. But in the present discussion, I will avoid these terms in order to not sidetrack the present chapter by discussion of the myriad other meanings and measures of those terms as well.
2. This is also the case in Wenger and Townsend (2001), which tested the capacity of face feature detection in upright, inverted, feature-isolated, and scrambled faces. They found limited capacity in all conditions. However, although it is clear in that chapter that an OR feature detection task was used, no information is provided about the non-target or distractor conditions to fully understand the experimental manipulations within the main discussion of this present chapter.
3. In addition to the studies summarized here, Fifić and colleagues have presented DFP designs for memory search tasks (e.g., Townsend & Fifić, 2004); however, their analyses have been limited to questions of architecture, so the capacity of memory search remains poorly defined.

Categorization, Capacity, and Resilience

8

Xue-Jun Cheng, Sarah Moneer, Nicole Christie, Daniel R. Little
The University of Melbourne, Melbourne, VIC, Australia

Decisions often require the accumulation and combination of information from multiple sources. For instance, buying a car requires consideration of attributes such as price, reliability, and performance. Perceptual decisions, such as determining whether a piece of modern art is Surreal or Dada (i.e., categorization), also require the integration of multiple attributes (e.g., the artist, medium, use of color and design, the presence of melting clocks or futuristic lobster suits). Attributes vary in importance, the extent to which they can be processed independently of one another, the order in which they are processed, and processing difficulty. As described in Altieri, Fifić, Little, and Yang (2017; this book), these attributes can be assessed through the analysis of response times (RTs) using Systems Factorial Technology (SFT; Townsend & Nozawa, 1995; Townsend & Wenger, 2004).

SFT offers measures that allow inferences about the architecture or organization of information processing (e.g., whether sources of information are processed in serial or in parallel; Kantowitz, 1974; Schweickert, 1992; Sternberg, 1969; Townsend, 1984), decisional stopping rules (e.g., whether processing is exhaustive or self-terminating), the independence of processing channels (e.g., whether there is any "cross-talk" between processing channels), and the efficiency of processing (workload capacity, or simply, capacity). Measures of capacity assess the effect of varying workload (i.e., the amount of information that has to be processed) on processing efficiency (Snodgrass & Townsend, 1980; Townsend, 1972, 1974; Townsend & Ashby, 1978, 1983). In SFT, capacity is measured by comparing processing rates on double target trials (or trials with even more than two targets) with that of the single targets on their own. The current chapter examines a recent extension to this method which measures capacity when the two single targets are not presented on their own but in the presence of distracting or conflicting information.

Capacity with Distractors

Capacity in the Redundant Target Detection Task

As discussed in Altieri et al. (2017), capacity can be measured through the redundant target detection paradigm (e.g., Snodgrass & Townsend, 1980; Townsend & Nozawa, 1995). To illustrate this paradigm, let us assume that there are two locations (left or right) in which targets (e.g., colored dots) may potentially appear. These targets may appear in one, both, or neither of the locations. In the OR design of this task (see

Systems Factorial Technology, DOI: 10.1016/B978-0-12-804315-8.00010-0

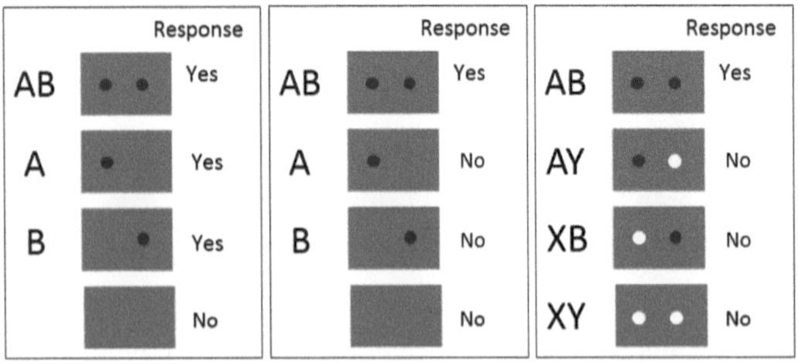

Figure 8.1 An illustration of the OR (left) and the AND (middle) designs of the redundant target detection paradigm. In the OR design, participants respond "Yes" when one or both dots appear, otherwise they respond "No." In the AND design, participants respond "Yes" only if both targets are present. The right hand panel shows a redundant target detection task in which the single target trials contain distractor information. We term these trials single target + distractor trials.

Fig. 8.1, left panel), participants respond "Yes" if a target is detected in either the left OR the right locations. If there is no target present, participants respond "No." In contrast, in the AND design of this experiment (see Fig. 8.1, middle panel), participants respond "Yes" only if a target is present on the left AND on the right; otherwise, they should respond "No." By design, a correct "Yes" response in the AND task is exhaustive as both locations must be processed before the response can be made accurately. In both the OR and AND designs, the pattern of RTs across the double- and single-target trials is used to calculate capacity (Altieri et al., 2017).

Linking the Categorization and Detection Designs

Fifić, Nosofsky, and Townsend (2008) introduced a categorization task in which the goal was not the detection of a target, but the decision about whether the values of specified stimulus dimensions satisfied certain rules (e.g., a conjunction rule; Griffiths, Blunden, & Little, 2017, this book; see also, Blunden, Wang, Griffiths, & Little, 2015; Fifić, Little, & Nosofsky, 2010; Little, 2012; Little, Nosofsky, & Denton, 2011; Little, Nosofsky, Donkin, & Denton, 2013). The category space used in these experiments is shown in Fig. 8.2.

As detailed in Griffiths et al. (2017), this category space has been used successfully to uncover detailed information about the architecture underlying the processing of different types of stimulus dimensions. For instance, Little et al. (2013) contrasted integral and separable dimensions showing that the former were processed coactively but the latter were processed in an independent manner, either in serial or in parallel. A natural question then is whether one might also be able to examine the capacity of the processing system using the same category space.

Consider that, analogous to the OR detection task shown in Fig. 8.1, stimuli to the left of *or* below the dotted category bounds shown in Fig. 8.2 belong to what we will term the OR category. The OR category contains stimuli which satisfy both of the disjunctive category decision rules (e.g., x_1y_1, where the subscripted values indicate

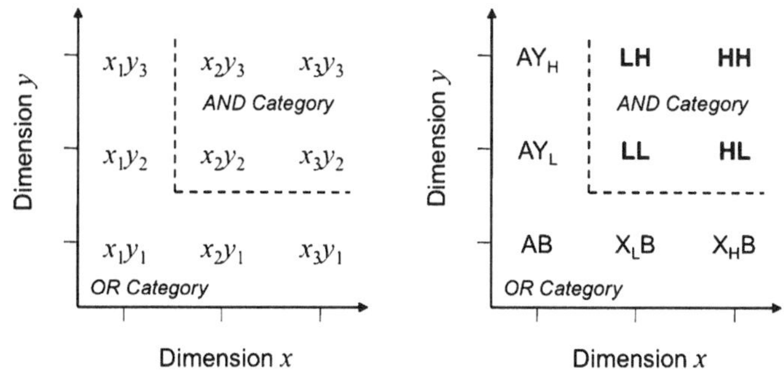

Figure 8.2 (Left panel) Category structure used in the categorization experiments. For the present discussion, we term the stimuli in the upper right quadrant of the space as belonging to the AND category (for which members need to satisfy a conjunction rule), whereas the remaining stimuli are members of the OR category (for which members need to satisfy a disjunctive rule). We use the lowercase x and y to refer to the values of dimensions for individual stimuli. By contrast in the right panel, the uppercase X and Y are reserved for distractor channel information. Likewise, the uppercase A and B will be used to represent target channel information. (Right panel) For the AND category, H and L refer to the high- and low-discriminability dimension values, respectively. In order to relate the categorization task to the redundant target detection task, we adopt a nomenclature which highlights that the OR category stimuli combine evidence for the OR category (indicated by an A or a B) *and* evidence for the AND category (indicated by an X or a Y). The OR stimulus that satisfies both disjunctive OR rules is denoted as the redundant (AB) stimulus. The remaining OR stimuli are indexed as a combination of one dimension value which satisfies one of the OR rules (either A for dimension x or B for dimension y) and a dimension value which provides evidence for the AND category (X for the x dimension or Y for the y dimension). The subscripts H and L for the OR category stimuli reflect whether the conflicting information provides evidence for the AND category of high or low salience, respectively. For example, the OR stimulus AY_L provides only weak evidence for the AND category on dimension x (i.e., because this dimension is close to the horizontal boundary on dimension x but falls on the AND category side of that boundary).

the level of each of the dimensions with regard to Fig. 8.2, left panel) and stimuli which satisfy only one of the disjunctive category decision rules (e.g., x_2y_1 satisfies the horizontal boundary rule for the OR category but does not satisfy the vertical boundary rule for the OR category).[1] These stimuli can be thought of as single targets in the sense that only one of the disjunctive rule boundaries is satisfied. Likewise, there are also stimuli which satisfy the conjunction rule for the other category (e.g., x_2y_2); we term this category the AND category, again in comparison to the detection task shown in Fig. 8.1. Hence, the category space contains information analogous to the detection tasks, and the RTs from the categorization task can be used to compute the capacity coefficient in a manner analogous to the use of the capacity coefficient in detection.

Although outlined in the tutorial chapter (Altieri et al., 2017), we review some of the concepts for capacity here that will be useful for the following discussion. The capacity coefficient in the OR task is defined as the ratio of the integrated hazard functions for the double-target, $H_{AB}(t)$, over the sum of the integrated hazard functions for the two single-targets, $H_A(t)$ and $H_B(t)$, namely

$$C_{OR}(t) = \frac{H_{AB}(t)}{H_A(t) + H_B(t)}. \tag{8.1}$$

The capacity coefficient uses the unlimited capacity parallel model as the standard of comparison. This standard parallel processing model predicts that the rate of processing will be unaffected by the workload and therefore will satisfy the equality

$$H_{AB}(t) = H_A(t) + H_B(t) \tag{8.2}$$

where the term on the left is the integrated hazard function for the double target, AB, and the term on the right is the expected minimum processing time (i.e., under independent parallel self-termination) derived by summing the integrated hazard functions of the two single targets.

A system with unlimited capacity will therefore produce a capacity coefficient equal to one across the entire time course of processing, $C_{OR}(t) = 1$. A system with limited capacity, such as a standard serial architecture, will produce a capacity coefficient less than one, $C_{OR}(t) < 1$, and a coactive system with supercapacity will produce a capacity coefficient greater than one, $C_{OR}(t) > 1$ (Townsend & Ashby, 1983; Townsend, Fifić, & Neufeld, 2007; Townsend & Nozawa, 1995; Wenger & Townsend, 2000).[2]

As the AND design requires exhaustive processing for the "Yes" response, a different measure is required in order to maintain the same interpretation of performance relative to the standard parallel model. Consequently, capacity for the AND design, $C_{AND}(t)$, requires use of the reverse integrated hazard function, $K(t)$ (Townsend & Wenger, 2004). $C_{AND}(t)$ is hence defined as the ratio of the sum of the reverse integrated hazard functions for the single targets, $K_A(t)$ and $K_B(t)$, divided by the reverse integrated hazard function for the double target, $K_{AB}(t)$, namely

$$C_{AND}(t) = \frac{K_A(t) + K_B(t)}{K_{AB}(t)}. \tag{8.3}$$

$C_{AND}(t)$ can be interpreted in the same manner as $C_{OR}(t)$. That is, $C_{AND}(t) = 1$ indicates unlimited capacity, $C_{AND}(t) < 1$ indicates limited capacity, and $C_{AND}(t) > 1$ indicates supercapacity.

Certain standard information processing architectures make reliable predictions about capacity. For example, the standard independent parallel model predicts unlimited capacity whereas a standard serial processing model predicts limited capacity and a coactive model predicts supercapacity. We note that capacity and architecture are logically distinct; for instance, a limited capacity parallel model is a highly plausible candidate model of visual attention processing and memory scanning (e.g., Thornton & Gilden, 2007; Townsend, 1972; van der Heijden, 1975). Nevertheless, under the assumptions of selective influence and context invariance (i.e., the assumption that a manipulation only affects the process of interest and the assumption that a component process – such as processing the left location – is unaffected by any other process, present or absent; see Altieri et al., 2017), calculating capacity should allow us to make some inferences about the system's processing architecture and vice versa. In the following section, we apply the capacity coefficient to data from two experiments which utilized the categorization design shown in Fig. 8.2 (see also the chapter by Griffiths et al., 2017), demonstrating that a key difference between the categorization design and the redundant target design, namely the presence of distractor information, breaks this coupling between architecture and capacity.

Capacity in Categorization

A fundamental distinction in the study of perception and cognition is the difference between separable dimensions and integral dimensions. For separable dimensions (such as the size and shape of an object or changes in two separate parts of an object), attention can be efficiently allocated and each dimension is processed in a seemingly independent manner (Garner, 1974). By contrast, integral dimensions (such as the brightness and saturation of a color) are processed as relatively undifferentiated wholes. A large number of converging empirical findings confirm this distinction (see Griffiths et al., 2017). In the present chapter, we use the categorization of these dimensions to examine the implications for capacity.

Separable Dimensions

Little et al. (2011; Experiment 1) tested categorization using a set of lamp stimuli which varied in the width of the base (dimension x) and the curvature of the finial (top piece; dimension y) to implement the category space shown in Fig. 8.2. Fig. 8.3 shows the results of a set of analyses applied to the RT data from this experiment. As reported in Little et al. (2011), the SIC functions computed from the AND category were consistent with serial processing. Examination of the $C_{OR}(t)$ functions revealed that capacity is less than 1 in three of the four cases; however, for the observer shown in the top row, the $C_{OR}(t)$ function has a value approximately equal to 1 for a substantial portion of time, indicating some early unlimited capacity for this observer.

By contrast, the $C_{AND}(t)$ functions are highly variable across observers, and the wide confidence bands mean that we cannot easily dismiss the possibility that capacity is unlimited.[3] Observers 1 and 4 show some evidence of limited capacity at short RTs, but observers 2 and 3 show evidence of supercapacity at short RTs. In some cases, the estimate of $C_{AND}(t)$ may be greater than 1. Contrary to what one might expect given the SIC, the categorization capacity results seem to provide only a weak link between limited capacity and serial processing architecture.

Integral Dimensions

In contrast to the separable dimensions, for the integral dimensions studied in Little et al. (2013; Experiment 1), the SIC functions were consistently coactive in agreement (see Fig. 8.4). Given the observed coactivity, if context invariance is preserved then we ought to find $C_{OR}(t)$ and$C_{AND}(t)$ functions greater than 1, indicating supercapacity (see Townsend & Wenger, 2004). However, as shown in Fig. 8.4, despite the overadditivity in the SIC indicating coactivity, capacity is consistently less than 1, in-

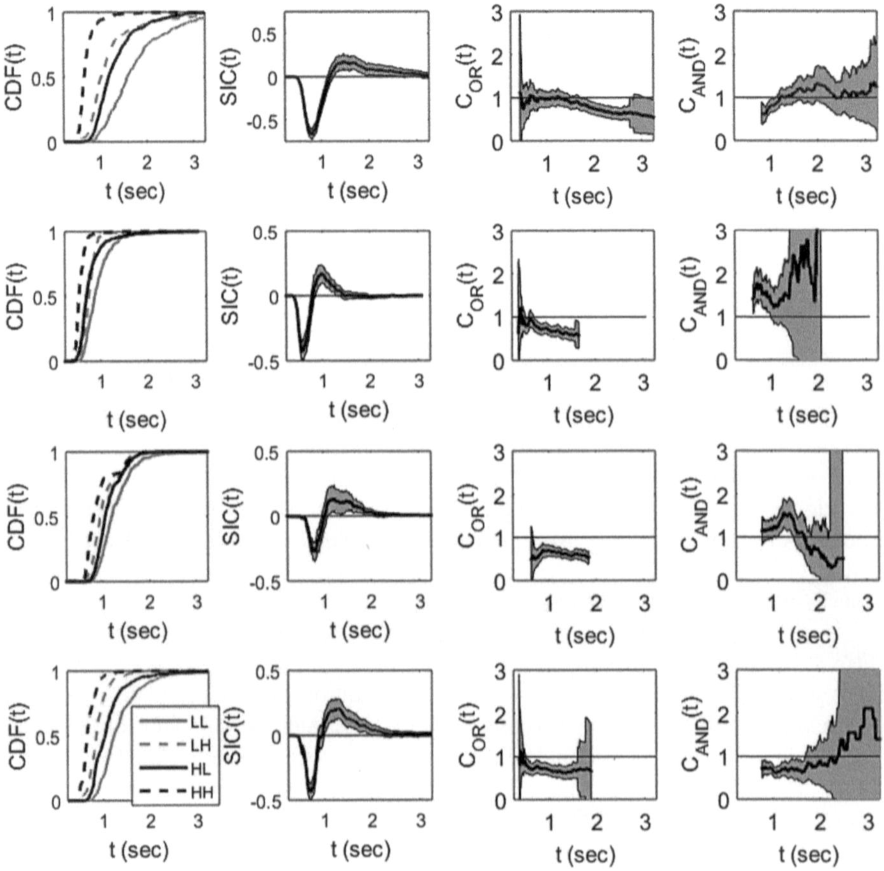

Figure 8.3 Separable dimension stimulus categorization data for four observers (shown in each row) from Little et al. (2011, Experiment 1). (First column) Cumulative distribution functions ($CDF(t)$) for the target category stimuli. (Second column) *SIC* functions. (Third column) $C_{OR}(t)$ functions. (Fourth column) $C_{AND}(t)$ functions. Shaded area shows 95% bootstrapped confidence intervals.

dicating limited capacity in both the $C_{OR}(t)$ and $C_{AND}(t)$case for all subjects. That is, the observed coactivity found in the data reported by Little et al. was not accompanied by supercapacity. Similar results were shown by Wenger and Townsend (2001) using schematic face stimuli in a redundant target detection task. Could these deviations from the expected predictions be explained by violation of context invariance?

Since discriminability is determined by a stimulus's location with respect to the category boundary, and since the observed response time depends on the discriminability of the stimulus (Ashby, Boynton, & Lee, 1994), context invariance can be violated when the discriminability of one of the hypothetical single targets is changed (e.g., A presented alone) without a co-occurring change in the discriminability of that component in the double target (A in AB). A violation of context invariance should reveal itself as a shift in single target stimuli relative to the double target stimuli (i.e., due

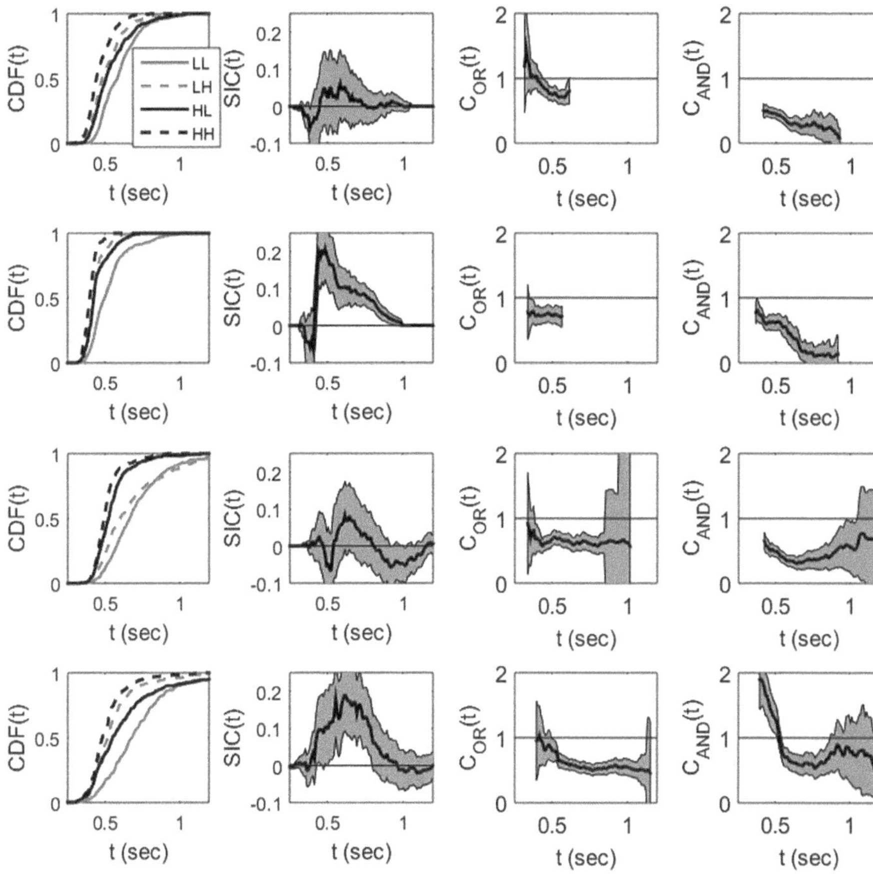

Figure 8.4 Integral dimension stimulus categorization data for four observers (shown in each row) from Little et al. (2013, Experiment 1). (First column) Cumulative distribution functions ($CDF(t)$) for the target category stimuli. (Second column) *SIC* functions. (Third column) $C_{OR}(t)$ functions. (Fourth column) $C_{AND}(t)$ functions. Shaded area shows 95% bootstrapped confidence intervals.

to a shift in the mean location of the perceived perceptual distribution of the stimulus termed mean shift integrality; see Ashby & Townsend, 1986; Griffiths et al., 2017). Fig. 8.5 shows the effect of altering the perceived location of a single target stimulus relative to the boundary on $C_{OR}(t)$. The top panels show the scenario when the hypothetical single target A is processed at the same rate when it was processed alone as when it was processed in the context of the double target, AB_{OR}. The middle panels show the scenario when the single target A is processed faster than the A component of the AB_{OR} double target because it is further from the category boundary. The bottom panel shows the scenario when the single target A is processed slower than the A component of the AB_{OR} double target because it is closer to the decision boundary (see Fig. 8.2). Both the middle and bottom cases represent a violation of context invariance. The middle panels of Fig. 8.5 demonstrate the effects of different perceived

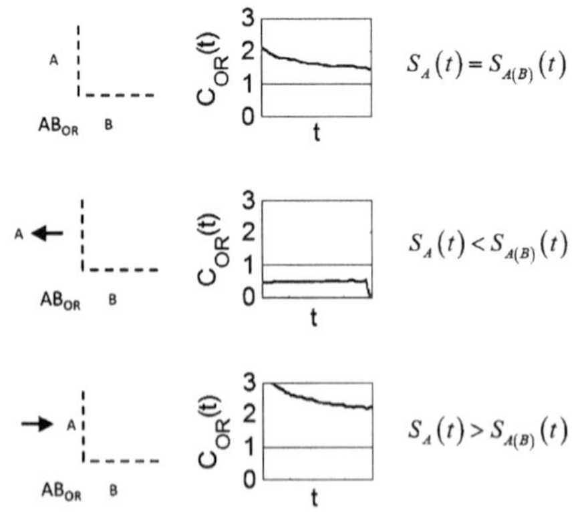

Figure 8.5 (Top) The top row shows the scenario in which context invariance holds because the single targets, A and B, are the same distance from the decision boundaries in both the single target cases and in the double target, AB_{OR}, case. Consequently, the coactive model predicts super capacity. (Middle) The middle row shows how context invariance can be violated by a shift in the perceived location of the stimulus. The arrow indicates that the single target, A, is perceived to be further away from the vertical decision boundary when presented alone than when presented as part of the double target, AB_{OR}. Hence, the single target is faster than the double target. In this scenario, the coactive model predicts limited capacity. (Bottom) The bottom panel shows the effect of mean shift integrality in which the single target, A, is perceived as closer to the boundary when presented alone than when presented as part of the double target, AB_{OR}. The arrow indicates that the single target A is shifted closer to the boundary and is, thus, harder to discriminate. Hence, the single target is slower than the double target. In this scenario, the coactive model predicts even larger super capacity than when context invariance holds.

shifts in stimulus location on the capacity predictions of the coactive model. Note that as the single targets become faster to process alone than in the context of the double target, capacity may be limited for a coactive model (middle right-hand panel). On the other hand, if the single targets are slower to process alone than in the context of the double target then capacity may be even more super than expected when the assumption of context invariance holds (bottom right-hand panel).

It appears that a violation of context invariance could provide a reasonable explanation for the limited capacity results found with the integral dimension data from Little et al. (2013). However, we have a good reason to believe that context invariance is preserved in this case, at least at the mean level (likewise in the case of the separable dimension stimuli above). Namely, multidimensional scaling analyses of the brightness and saturation stimuli revealed that the stimuli closely matched the ideal categorization space shown in Fig. 8.2 (Fifić et al., 2008).

Summary

The analyses of capacity across two categorization experiments involving different stimulus dimensions but using the same underlying category space and paradigm reveals no clear link between the cognitive architecture which best captures processing and the capacity of the information processing system. This is perhaps unsurprising since architecture and capacity are logically distinct aspects of information processing. Nonetheless, under reasonable assumptions, it has been demonstrated that serial processing predicts limited capacity, standard independent channel parallel processing predicts unlimited capacity, and coactive processing predicts supercapacity. So how can we account for the discrepancy between the predictions and the data in the present case?

A plausible explanation lies in the fact that the "single target" items in the categorization task are not directly analogous to the single targets in the detection task. For instance, compare the left-hand and right-hand panels of Fig. 8.1. The right-hand figure in analogous the categorization task in that the single targets (i.e., AY and XB) contain information which provides evidence for the incorrect response. For example, the single target AY_L contains not only the dimension which satisfies one of the disjunctive rules for the OR category but also dimension Y_L which provides positive evidence for the incorrect AND category. We term these items target + distractor items.

In the following sections, we review recent work by Little et al. (2015) that extends the concept of capacity to cases like the categorization design in which the single targets also contain conflicting information. The upshot of this analysis is that superior performance for the double target stimuli could reflect either greater efficiency of processing (i.e., increased capacity) or could rather be a consequence of slower performance due to the presence of unhelpful (and potentially harmful) conflicting information. This extension allows one to take into consideration the role of distractor information in the standard designs of many psychological tasks such as categorization (Fifić et al., 2010; Little et al., 2011, 2013), recognition memory (Nosofsky, Little, Donkin, & Fifić, 2011; Townsend & Fifić, 2004) detection (Feintuch & Cohen, 2002; Mordkoff & Yantis, 1993), discrimination (Donkin, Little, & Houpt, 2014), and visual search (Fifić et al., 2008; Thornton & Gilden, 2007).

Capacity and the Influence of Distractors

Little et al. (2015) showed that the inclusion of distractors will change the predictions of the capacity coefficient such that the serial self-terminating, serial exhaustive, parallel exhaustive, and coactive models no longer make the same predictions for the single targets (i.e., when no distractors are present). By contrast, independent parallel self-terminating models are unaffected by the presence of distractors since the inclusion of distractors does not change the finishing time of the relevant information. The implication of including distractor information, as shown in the previous capacity analyses, is that the capacity coefficient no longer provides an assessment of workload. Little et al. (2015) argued that the capacity coefficient instead reflects the relative rate of processing of the target information (i.e., the information channel which points to the correct decision) and the distractor information (i.e., the information which points to the incorrect decision). To demarcate this difference, Little et al. (2015) introduced the *resilience* function which takes the same form as the capacity function, but highlights the role that the distractors play in forming the denominator of the function

$$R(t) = \frac{H_{AB}(t)}{H_{AY}(t) + H_{XB}(t)} \tag{8.4}$$

where AB refers to the redundant or double target, and AY and XB refer to the target + distractor items (see Fig. 8.2).[4]

To illustrate this point, consider categorizing item x_2y_1 (i.e., X_LB). This item satisfies the rule boundary on dimension y (i.e., has a value lower than the value indicated by the boundary) which means that the item belongs to the OR category (see Fig. 8.2). On the other hand, the value of this stimulus on dimension x satisfies the vertical boundary for the AND category, hence, providing evidence (on that dimension) that the item could belong to the AND category. Consider the implications of this distracting information on a serial process: Without distractor information, a serial self-terminating process would just process the target information (i.e., because only the target information would be presented on a single target trial). For a serial model, the implication is that the time taken to categorize y_1 will be roughly the same as when y_1 is presented alone and when y_1 is presented in the redundant target (x_1y_1). Assume the same is true of the single target x_1. Since the processing time of x_1y_1 is equivalent to y_1 (when dimension y is processed first) and equivalent to x_1 (when dimension x is processed first), the processing time of x_1y_1 will be slower than the minimum time derived from x_1 and y_1 (i.e., expressed as the sum of the integrated hazard functions for the single targets where $H(t) = -\log[S(t)]$, $H_{x_1y_1}(t) < [H_{x_1}(t) + H_{y_1}(t)]$. Hence, capacity will be limited.

By contrast, when distractor information is present, the distractor channel can slow down the overall processing time of the single targets. For instance, if a serial, self-terminating system processes dimension x of stimulus x_2y_1 first and determines that this dimension provides evidence for category A, then, in order to correctly classify the stimulus, the system would need to then switch to processing dimension y. By contrast, the same system could terminate after processing either dimension of stimulus x_1y_1. Hence, the redundant target can, in fact, be processed faster than the minimum time derived from x_2y_1 and x_1y_2 (i.e., the two target + distractor stimuli needed to compute $R(t)$). The implication is that a serial system need not have *resilience* which is less than 1. In fact, $R(t)$ might equal 1 or be greater than 1 depending on the processing rate of the distractors.

Now consider the same comparison but applied to a parallel, self-terminating model. In this case, without distractors, the redundant target processing time will equal the minimum time derived from the single targets. This is because processing of both x_1 and y_1 proceeds simultaneously and because the process can terminate as soon as either dimension finishes (i.e., the minimum processing time). Hence, $H_{x_1y_1}(t) = [H_{x_1}(t) + H_{y_1}(t)]$, implying $R(t) = 1$ (i.e., unlimited resilience and, hence, unlimited capacity).

In contrast to the serial system, a parallel, self-terminating system will not be affected by the presence of distractors. For instance, when processing a target + distractor stimulus x_2y_1, both channels will still be processed simultaneously. However, a correct decision cannot be made until dimension y_1 completes processing. If dimensions x and y proceed independently (as is assumed by the baseline parallel model in the capacity coefficient; see Altieri et al., 2017) then only the processing time of dimension y will matter for determining the processing time of x_2y_1[5] (this is also true

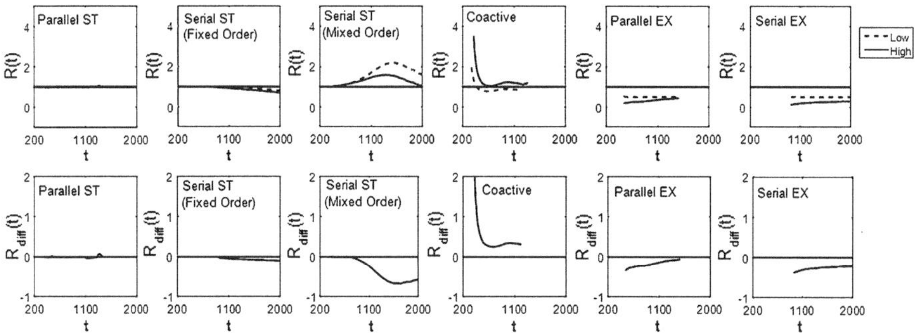

Figure 8.6 (Top row) $R(t)$ for each of the models computed from the low discriminability distractors (e.g., $X_L B$ and AY_L) and the high discriminability distractors (e.g., $X_H B$ and AY_H). (Bottom row) $R_{diff}(t)$ for each of the models. ST = self-terminating. EX = exhaustive. Fixed-order serial processing refers to the case when one dimension is always processed before another dimension. Mixed-order serial processing refers to the case when the order of the serial processing may change from trial to trial.

for, e.g., stimulus $x_1 y_2$). Hence, with distractors, $H_{x_1 y_1}(t) = [H_{x_1 y_2}(t) + H_{x_2 y_1}(t)]$ and $R(t) = 1$.

For the coactive and exhaustive models (both serial and parallel), whether the redundant target will be faster or slower than the expected minimum time depends on the relative processing rates of the target and distractor channels (see Fig. 8.6, top row; see also Little et al., 2015, for a full description of the predictions of each of these models).

Summary

When distractors are present, the parallel self-terminating system remains unperturbed. With a parallel self-terminating system, $R(t) = C(t) = 1$. By contrast, all of the remaining models are affected by how the distractor information influences the derived minimum processing time. This could be used to explain why, in the previous categorization example (see Figs. 8.3 and 8.4), very clear evidence of serial and coactive processing was not accompanied by limited and supercapacity, respectively. The presence of distractors complicates inference because it eliminates the tight linkage between capacity and architecture, at least for the standard class of models (i.e., excluding, for instance, the class of parallel models which allow for between-channel interactions; Eidels et al., 2011).

Resilience Difference Function $R_{diff}(t)$

Little et al. (2015) showed that for each of the standard models, the resilience function changed systematically as a function of discriminability of the distracting information (i.e., how easily the distracting information can be rejected). For instance, although a serial self-terminating model might no longer predict $R(t) < 1$ when distractors are presented along with the single targets, the value of the $R(t)$ will be larger if the distractors are of low discriminability rather than high discriminability. The reason for this difference is because the serial self-terminating model can dismiss the high discriminability distractor faster than the low discriminability distractor. The benefit of this change is that the minimum time derived from the single targets plus distractors, which forms the denominator of Eq. (8.4), will be larger in the low discriminability distractor case than in the high discriminability distractor case. Hence, resilience will be greater in the low discriminability case than in the high discriminability case. Consequently, one can construct a contrast between resilience computed with the low discriminability distractors and resilience computed with the high discriminability distractors. Little et al. (2015) termed this contrast the Resilience Difference function, $R_{diff}(t)$, and defined it as

$$\begin{aligned} R_{diff}(t) &= R_H(t) - R_L(t) \\ &= \frac{H_{AB}(t)}{H_{AY_H}(t) + H_{X_H B}(t)} - \frac{H_{AB}(t)}{H_{AY_L}(t) + H_{X_L B}(t)}. \end{aligned} \tag{8.5}$$

Fig. 8.6 shows the R_{diff} predictions for each of the standard models. Note that the $R(t)$ predictions (and, hence, the $C(t)$ predictions) may be greater than or less than 1 depending on the distractor discriminability for each of the models except the parallel self-terminating model. However, the $R_{diff}(t)$ predictions recover diagnostic information restoring the link between the architecture and (a form of) capacity. That is, the parallel self-terminating model predicts $R_{diff}(t) = 0$ and can be consequently used as a baseline measure for comparison to the other model $R_{diff}(t)$ predictions. The serial self-terminating, serial exhaustive, and parallel exhaustive models predict that $R_{diff}(t) < 0$, reflecting the fact that in each of these models the low discriminability distractors slow the derived minimum time more than the high discriminability distractors resulting in $R_L(t) > R_H(t)$. By contrast, this pattern is reversed for the coactive model, which predicts that the high discriminability distractors, when pooled together with the target information, will slow the RT more than the low discriminability distractors. This will result in the derived minimum time being faster when the distractors are of low rather than high discriminability. Consequently, $R_H(t) > R_L(t)$, resulting in $R_{diff}(t) > 0$.

Fig. 8.7 (left column) shows the resilience difference analysis applied to the categorization data shown in Fig. 8.3 (separable dimension stimuli) and Fig. 8.4 (integral dimension stimuli). Recall that the separable dimension data were most commensurate with the assumption of a serial model. The resilience difference analysis reveals that where computing capacity alone resulted in somewhat equivocal results (i.e., supporting either $C(t) < 1$ or $C(t) = 1$), the resilience difference function is less than one for all t in line with the inferences based on the SIC (see Fig. 8.3).

For the integral dimension data, the best explanation was given by the coactive model; however, as shown in Fig. 8.4, the capacity analysis did not match the predictions of the coactive model. Instead, $C(t)$ was consistently less than 1, implicating a limited capacity process. However, the resilience difference function shown in Fig. 8.7 (right column) is consistently greater than 1, supporting the inference of coactivity.

In summary, when distractors are presented along with the single targets, the capacity coefficient no longer provides diagnostic information about the underlying

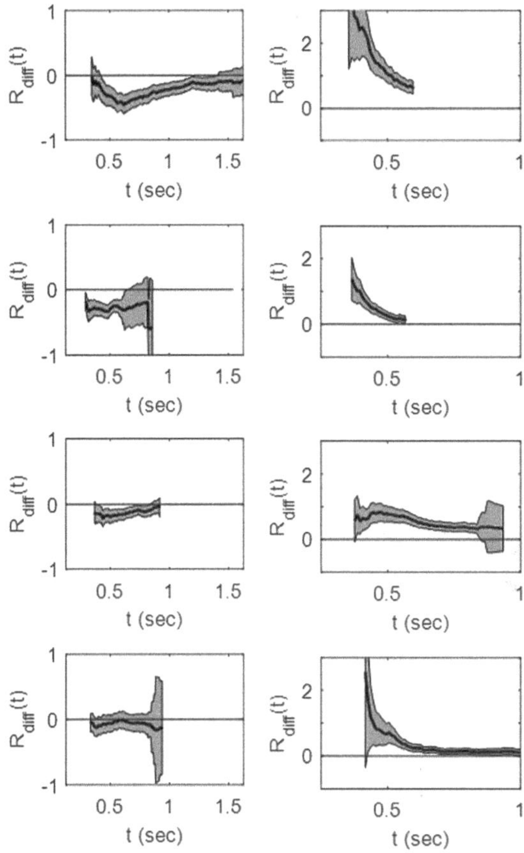

Figure 8.7 (Left column) Resilience difference analysis for the separable dimensions data (Little et al., 2011; Experiment 1). (Right column) Resilience difference analysis for the integral dimensions data (Little et al., 2013; Experiment 1). See Fig. 8.4. Shaded area shows 95% bootstrapped confidence interval.

processing architecture. In a nutshell, the reason for this loss of diagnosticity is because under circumstances in which the same number of channels are utilized across both the double target and the single target + distractor trials, capacity no longer measures changes in workload. Instead, the capacity coefficient function, which we term resilience, measures the relative effect of the distractors on the minimum time which is derived from the single target + distractor trials. By examining how resilience changes as a function of distractor strength (i.e., discriminability), we are able to reinstate the diagnosticity that is lost by the inclusion of distractor information. We have demonstrated this using categorization results, which were found to involve the use of a serial self-terminating strategy for separable dimensions and a coactive strategy for integral dimensions. We highlight here that Houpt and Little (2016) have developed statistical analyses that allow for testing whether the value of the resilience function and resilience difference function differs from 0. In the following sections, we examine some related developments regarding resilience that might prove useful in related experimental designs.

Using the Resilience Difference Function Without a Double Target

Because the relationship between the derived minimum times for the high and low discriminability distractors holds even without the double target, it is possible to simplify the resilience difference function but maintain the same diagnosticity. For instance, we can rearrange Eq. (8.5) as follows:

$$\frac{R_{diff}(t)}{H_{AB}(t)} = \frac{1}{H_{AY_H}(t) + H_{X_H B}(t)} - \frac{1}{H_{AY_L}(t) + H_{X_L B}(t)}. \tag{8.6}$$

Since the derived minimum time for a parallel model does not depend on the discriminability of the distractors, then

$$\frac{R_{diff}(t)}{H_{AB}(t)} = 0. \tag{8.7}$$

Similarly, since the minimum time derived from the single target + distractor stimuli is faster with high discriminability distractors than with low discriminability distractors for a serial self-terminating model (or a serial exhaustive or parallel exhaustive model), then

$$\frac{R_{diff}(t)}{H_{AB}(t)} = \frac{1}{H_{AY_H}(t) + H_{X_H B}(t)} - \frac{1}{H_{AY_L}(t) + H_{X_L B}(t)} \leq 0. \tag{8.8}$$

By contrast, since the derived minimum time is slower when high discriminability distractor information sources than when low discriminability information sources are included in the single targets, and hence, the negative log of the derived minimum time is smaller for high discriminability conflict items for a coactive model, then

$$\frac{R_{diff}(t)}{H_{AB}(t)} = \frac{1}{H_{AY_H}(t) + H_{X_H B}(t)} - \frac{1}{H_{AY_L}(t) + H_{X_L B}(t)} > 0. \tag{8.9}$$

Hence, we can plot $\frac{1}{H_{AY_H}(t)+H_{X_H B}(t)} - \frac{1}{H_{AY_L}(t)+H_{X_L B}(t)}$ and compare that to zero in the same manner as $R_{diff}(t)$ (i.e., to make inferences about architecture now via $\frac{R_{diff}(t)}{H_{AB}(t)}$).

Little, Eidels, Fifić, and Wang (2017) derived an alternative measure of information processing called the *conflict contrast function* ($CCF(t)$), which also eliminates the necessity of the double target stimulus, as

$$CCF(t) = \left[\log\left(S_{AY_H}(t)\right) - \log\left(S_{AY_L}(t)\right)\right] + \left[\log\left(S_{X_H B}(t)\right) - \log\left(S_{X_L B}(t)\right)\right] \tag{8.10}$$

where $S(t)$ is the survivor function (the subscript indicates the particular stimulus condition). The $CCF(t)$ has the same properties as $R_{diff}(t)$ but may be easier to use in some situations (i.e., like $\frac{R_{diff}(t)}{H_{AB}(t)}$ when no double target is present). In both cases, one simply uses these functions in the same manner as the $R_{diff}(t)$ function, and both are interpreted in the same way.

Conclusion

The capacity coefficient is a powerful tool for diagnosing information about the efficiency of a processing system. When distracting information is introduced, each of the standard processing architectures deals with the distracting information in a different manner. This leads to a breakdown in the diagnosticity of the capacity coefficient. Key work by Little et al. (2015) has shown that to restore the usefulness of the capacity framework when distractors are present, one should expand the analysis by considering variations in the difficulty of rejecting the distracting information. In a way, this analysis (i.e., the $R_{diff}(t)$ function in particular) combines aspects from both the workload capacity analysis and the SIC (see Altieri et al., 2017) to provide a new diagnostic measure. Hence, the methodological reach of SFT is extended to a new set of research designs.

References

Altieri, N. (2017). Development and applications of the capacity-function that measures accuracy. In D. R. Little, N. Altieri, M. Fifić, & C.-T. Yang (Eds.), *Systems factorial technology: A theory driven methodology for the identification of perceptual and cognitive mechanisms*. Elsevier (in this book).

Altieri, N., Fifić, M., Little, D. R., & Yang, C.-T. (2017). A tutorial introduction and historical background to systems factorial technology. In D. R. Little, N. Altieri, M. Fifić, & C.-T. Yang (Eds.), *Systems factorial technology: A theory driven methodology for the identification of perceptual and cognitive mechanisms*. Elsevier (in this book).

Ashby, F. G., Boynton, G., & Lee, W. W. (1994). Categorization response times with multidimensional stimuli. *Perception and Psychophysics*, *55*, 11–27.

Ashby, F. G., & Townsend, J. T. (1986). Varieties of perceptual independence. *Psychological Review*, *93*(2), 154–179.

Blunden, A., Wang, T., Griffiths, D., & Little, D. (2015). Logical-rules and the classification of integral dimensions: Individual differences in the processing of arbitrary dimensions. *Frontiers in Psychology*, *5*. Retrieved from http://dx.doi.org/10.3389/fpsyg.2014.01531.

Donkin, C., Little, D. R., & Houpt, J. W. (2014). Assessing the speed-accuracy trade-off effect on the capacity of information processing. *Journal of Experimental Psychology: Human Perception and Performance*, *40*, 1183–1202.

Donkin, C., Nosofsky, R. M., Gold, J. M., & Shiffrin, R. M. (2013). Discrete-slots models of visual working-memory response times. *Psychological Review*, *120*, 873–902.

Eidels, A., Houpt, J. W., Altieri, N., Pei, L., & Townsend, J. T. (2011). Nice guys finish fast and bad guys finish last: Facilitatory vs. inhibitory interaction in parallel systems. *Journal of Mathematical Psychology*, *55*, 176–190.

Feintuch, U., & Cohen, A. (2002). Visual attention and coactivation of response decisions for features from different dimensions. *Psychological Science*, *13*, 361–369.

Fifić, M., Little, D. R., & Nosofsky, R. (2010). Logical-rule models of classification response times: A synthesis of mental-architecture, random-walk, and decision-bound approaches. *Psychological Review*, *117*, 309–348.

Fifić, M., Nosofsky, R. M., & Townsend, J. (2008). Information-processing architectures in multidimensional classification: A validation of test of the systems factorial technology. *Journal of Experimental Psychology: Human Perception and Performance*, *34*, 356–375.

Garner, W. R. (1974). *The processing of information and structure*. Psychology Press.

Griffiths, D. W., Blunden, A. G., & Little, D. R. (2017). Logical-rule based models of categorization: Using systems factorial technology to understand feature and dimensional processing. In D. R. Little, N. Altieri, M. Fifić, & C.-T. Yang (Eds.), *Systems factorial technology: A theory driven methodology for the identification of perceptual and cognitive mechanisms*. Elsevier (in this book).

Houpt, J. W., & Little, D. R. (2016). Statistical analysis of the resilience function. *Behavior Research Methods* [accepted 12 Jul. 2016].

Kantowitz, B. H. (1974). *Human information processing: Tutorials in performance and cognition*. Lawrence Erlbaum.

Little, D. R. (2012). Numerical predictions for serial, parallel and coactive logical rule-based models of categorization response times. *Behavior Research Methods*, *44*, 1148–1156.

Little, D. R., Eidels, A., Fifić, M., & Wang, T. (2015). Understanding the influence of distractors on workload capacity. *Journal of Mathematical Psychology*, *69*, 25–36.

Little, D. R., Eidels, A., Fifić, M., & Wang, T. (2017). How do information processing systems deal with conflicting information? Differential predictions for serial, parallel, and coactive processing models. Manuscript submitted for publication. The University of Melbourne.

Little, D. R., Nosofsky, R., & Denton, S. E. (2011). Response time tests of logical rule-based models of categorization. *Journal of Experimental Psychology: Learning, Memory and Cognition*, *37*, 1–27.

Little, D. R., Nosofsky, R. M., Donkin, C., & Denton, S. E. (2013). Logical-rules and the classification of integral dimensioned stimuli. *Journal of Experimental Psychology: Learning, Memory and Cognition*, *39*, 801–820.

Mordkoff, J. T., & Yantis, S. (1993). Dividing attention between color and shape: Evidence of coactivation. *Perception and Psychophysics*, *53*, 357–366.

Nosofsky, R. M., Little, D. R., Donkin, C., & Fifić, M. (2011). Short-term memory scanning viewed as exemplar-based categorization. *Psychological Review*, *118*, 280–315.

Schweickert, R. (1992). Attention and performance. In *Synergies in experimental psychology, artificial intelligence, and cognitive neuroscience – a silver jubilee, Vol. 14* (pp. 535–566). MIT Press.

Snodgrass, J. G., & Townsend, J. T. (1980). Comparing parallel and serial models: Theory and implementation. *Journal of Experimental Psychology: Human Perception and Performance*, *6*, 330–354.

Sternberg, S. (1969). Memory scanning: Memory processes revealed by reaction-time experiments. *American Scientist*, *4*, 421–457.

Thornton, T. L., & Gilden, D. L. (2007). Parallel and serial processes in visual search. *Psychological Review*, *114*, 71–103.

Townsend, J. T. (1972). Some results concerning the identifiability of parallel and serial processes. *British Journal of Mathematical and Statistical Psychology*, *25*, 168–199.

Townsend, J. T. (1974). Issues and models concerning the processing of a finite number of inputs. In B. H. Kantowitz (Ed.), *Human information processing: Tutorials in performance and cognition* (pp. 133–185). Hillsdale, NJ: Lawrence Erlbaum Associates.

Townsend, J. T. (1984). Uncovering mental processes with factorial experiments. *Journal of Mathematical Psychology*, *28*, 363–400.

Townsend, J. T., & Altieri, N. (2012). An accuracy–response time capacity assessment function that measures performance against standard parallel predictions. *Psychological Review*, *119*, 500–516.

Townsend, J. T., & Ashby, F. G. (1978). Methods of modeling capacity in simple processing systems. In J. Castellan, & F. Restle (Eds.), *Cognitive theory, Vol. III* (pp. 200–239). Hillsdale, NJ: Lawrence Erlbaum Associates.

Townsend, J. T., & Ashby, F. G. (1983). *The stochastic modeling of elementary psychological processes*. Cambridge: Cambridge University Press.

Townsend, J. T., & Fifić, M. (2004). Parallel and serial processing and individual differences in high-speed scanning in human memory. *Perception and Psychophysics*, *66*, 953–962.

Townsend, J. T., Fifić, M., & Neufeld, R. W. (2007). Assessment of mental architecture in clinical/cognitive research. In T. A. Treat, R. R. Bootzin, & T. B. Baker (Eds.), *Psychological clinical science: Papers in honour of Richard M. McFall* (pp. 223–258). Mahwah, NJ: Lawrence Erlbaum Associates.

Townsend, J. T., & Nozawa, G. (1995). Spatio-temporal properties of elementary perception: An investigation of parallel, serial and coactive theories. *Journal of Mathematical Psychology*, *39*, 321–340.

Townsend, J. T., & Wenger, M. J. (2004). A theory of interactive parallel processing: New capacity measures and predictions for a response time inequality series. *Psychological Review*, *111*, 1003–1035.

van der Heijden, A. H. C. (1975). Some evidence for a limited capacity parallel self-terminating process in simple visual search tasks. *Acta Psychologica*, *39*, 21–41.

Wenger, M. J., & Townsend, J. T. (2000). Basic response time tools for studying general processing capacity in attention, perception, and cognition. *The Journal of General Psychology*, *127*, 67–99.

Wenger, M. J., & Townsend, J. T. (2001). Faces as gestalt stimuli: Process characteristics. In M. J. Wenger, & J. T. Townsend (Eds.), *Computational, geometric, and process perspectives on facial cognition*. Elsevier.

Endnotes

1. We use the lowercase x and y to refer to the values of dimensions for individual stimuli. By contrast, the uppercase X and Y are reserved for distractor channel information. Likewise, the uppercase A and B will be used to represent target channel information. See Fig. 8.2.
2. In this chapter, we focus on the predictions of a set of processing architectures which we demarcate as representing the *standard* model architectures of these types. These standard models include an unlimited capacity independent channel parallel self-terminating model, an independent channel serial self-terminating model, an independent channel serial-exhaustive model, an independent channel parallel-exhaustive model, and a coactive model. This analysis then necessarily precludes the important class of parallel models which al-

low for interactions, or "cross-talk", between processing channels (Eidels, Houpt, Altieri, Pei, & Townsend, 2011) or capacity sharing or reallocation between channels (Townsend & Ashby, 1983). Also excluded are serial models which allow interactions between channels (Townsend & Ashby, 1983) and mixture models (see, e.g., Little et al., 2011).

3. Note that to compute the $C_{AND}(t)$ function, the stimulus $X_L Y_L$ was used as the double target; AY_L and $X_L B$ were used as single targets. See Fig. 8.2.
4. The X and Y represent the distractor information in the target + distractor items. As $X_L B$ and $X_H B$ have the same value on dimension y as AB, they provide the same evidence for the OR category. However, as denoted by the H, the distractor X in $X_H B$ provides us with more evidence for the AND category than in $X_L B$.
5. Note that we are focusing only on the case where the categorization decision is correct. Adding distracting information could act to increase the error rate, but in the categorization task, accuracy tends to be quite high and the effect of the distracting information is on the RTs (Fifić et al., 2008, 2010; Little et al., 2011, 2013). An important extension to this analysis would be to generalize resilience to the also predict the relevant error RT distributions (i.e., as has been done for capacity; Altieri, 2017; Donkin, Nosofsky, Gold, & Shiffrin, 2013; Townsend & Altieri, 2012).

Part Three

Applications of Systems Factorial Technology

Applying the Double Factorial Paradigm to Detection and Categorization Tasks: An Example Using Audiovisual Speech Perception

9

Nicholas Altieri
Idaho State University, Pocatello, ID, United States

Introduction

A thriving topic in the perceptual sciences concerns how sources of sensory information interact to form a unified perception of an object or event. One may readily think of several real-world examples, all of which are at least tangentially relevant to the application explored here in this paper: the ability to recognize the face of a famous person by using holistic or so-called gestalt strategies (e.g., Wenger & Townsend, 2000, 2001, and 2006; Thompson, 1980), localizing an object in the environment when it makes a sound, or recognizing the words of a speaker when looking at their lips.

While this paper focuses on using statistical models to explore the implications of the latter issue of "multisensory speech integration", other instances of complex perception shall be relevant in at least a couple of ways. First, the strategies inspired by Systems Factorial Technology and the Double Factorial Paradigm (DFP) employed in this chapter are amendable to a variety of experimental settings. I particularly have in mind categorization tasks that require one to identify an object in a set with other competing items. This construction applies to spoken word, facial recognition, or even studies requiring the recognition of shapes (Griffiths, Blunden, & Little, 2016). Second, and perhaps more apt to future applications across disciplines, this chapter will demonstrate how the DFP uses reaction-time (*RT*) methodology to open B.F. Skinner's "black box", so to speak, in order to answer questions related to temporally driven constraints on cognitive operations.

Tasks commonly referred to as "higher-order cognitive tasks", such as speech or facial recognition, normally require a speeded judgment to be made in the real world. As Townsend and Nozawa (1995) showed in their initial exposition of the DFP, *RT* distributions can be used to infer a variety of properties: *mental architecture*, efficiency as a function of workload, or *capacity*, and finally *decision rule*. The tutorial chapter in this book provides historical background as well as basic mathematical and statistical approaches for computing the DFP measures (Altieri, Fifić, Little, & Yang, 2016). The following section defines the main terms and relates their importance to long-standing

Systems Factorial Technology, DOI: 10.1016/B978-0-12-804315-8.00012-4

issues in *auditory plus visual* ("audiovisual" from now on) speech perception that were hitherto unanswered prior to applications of the DFP.

Architecture and Audiovisual Speech Integration

Because hearing is the dominant speech-recognition modality in normal-hearing people, many of us are unaware that speech perception is a multimodal perceptual phenomenon that engages auditory, visual, and even tactile perceptual processes (e.g., Blamey, Cowan, Alcantra, Whitford, & Clark, 1989; Fowler & Dekle, 1991; McGurk & MacDonald, 1976; Sumby & Pollack, 1954). Incidentally, the field of audiovisual speech perception has essentially sought to address two long standing questions pertinent to DFP theory: one of the primary issues relates to efforts to quantify the extent to which being able to see a talker's face aids auditory perception. Then there is the related concern of identifying the listening conditions which afford the greatest benefit to the talker. The first study to do so was Sumby and Pollack's (1954) research on audiovisual benefit; the authors observed that being able to see a talker's face while that person is talking provided the equivalent of a 15 dB (SPL) benefit to the listener (i.e., it helped the listener understand what the talker was saying) when the auditory signal-to-noise ratio was low. Research on audiovisual benefit and the factors contributing to such a benefit has continued throughout the decades (e.g., Altieri and Hudock, 2014a, 2014b; Erber, 1969, 2003; Grant, Walden, & Seitz, 1998; Grant, 2002).

Another area of study has examined how the visual speech signal can sometimes warp or otherwise influence the auditory percept; one common way researchers have approached this is to observe how listeners perceive mismatched auditory and visual signals. This line of research began with McGurk and Macdonald's use of mismatched auditory and visual signals back in the 1970s. The authors presented listeners with the sound of a speaker saying the syllable /ba/ that was dubbed over a video of a face making the syllable /ga/. In a fascinating development in McGurk and Macdonald's seminal study, the authors found that adult listeners typically report hearing a consonant that is not contained in either the auditory or visual signal: most commonly, the consonant was /d/. Other researchers have measured susceptibility to the McGurk effect—or the influence of the visual signal on auditory processing—as a metric of integration ability (e.g., Setti, Burke, Kenny, & Newell, 2013). Additionally, clinical researchers have explored the differential effects that visual speech has on auditory perception in people with schizophrenia (e.g., Neufeld, Townsend, & Jetté, 2007), hearing impaired listeners, and in children with language impairment (e.g., Dupont, Aubin & Menard, 2005).

Models of Audiovisual Speech Integration

Emerging from discussion on audiovisual enhancement and the McGurk effect is a debate to which the DFP can add considerable clarity. The debate is whether auditory and visual speech cues are normally processed separately before final determination of the linguistic content—which we may refer to as "parallel processing"—or instead, combined early into some sort of unified code (we refer the interested reader to Bernstein, 2005; Massaro, 2004; Rosenblum, 2005; Fowler & Rosenblum, 1991, for discussion). This latter type of processing is referred to as "coactivation" in much of the mathematical psychology literature (e.g., Miller, 1982; Raab, 1962; Townsend & Nozawa, 1995). This debate on audiovisual speech perception architecture constitutes just one of many possible examples of a critical question that has been largely unanswered, but nonetheless surfaces in the literature. (I also refer the reader to Jesse & Massaro, 2010; Massaro, 1987, 1998; Massaro & Cohen, 2000.)

In fact, I argue that the issue of whether auditory and visual information is processed in separate independent information bearing channels prior to the final determination of the linguistic content, or instead, coalesced early on into a unified code, is one of the most basic and fundamental questions regarding cognitive operations on speech inputs. It is also somewhat intriguing that rigorous tests have not been put forth to determine if auditory and visual speech information acquisition actually takes place in parallel instead of a serial manner with distinct processing stages.

Combined Survivor Interaction Contrast and Capacity Information

Fig. 9.1A shows three models of audiovisual integration; Fig. 9.1B shows *survivor interaction contrast* ($S_{IC}(t)$) and workload capacity ($C(t)$) predictions for the models (we refer the reader to introductory chapters in this book, and also to Townsend & Nozawa, 1995 for more in depth tutorials on the DFP measures). This is presented in such a way because model identification often requires combined $S_{IC}(t)$ and capacity data, which will later become apparent.

The first diagram is a parallel model in which auditory and visual speech information is processed "separately and simultaneously", to use the words of Bernstein (2005). Decisions regarding the content of the utterance are made separately on each channel; if a horse race model is assumed with an OR logic gate, processing terminates as soon as recognition occurs on either the auditory or visual modality. This type of model predicts a positive or overadditive survivor interaction contrast function, and negative if an AND decision rule is present; another important prediction is that it predicts unlimited capacity (i.e., $C(t) = 1$). That is why these models are frequently referred to as Unlimited Capacity Independent Parallel model, or UCIP (Miller, 1982).

Next, we have a parallel interaction model shown below (Eidels, Houpt, Altieri, Pei, & Townsend, 2011). This version of a parallel model allows for visual speech related cues—such as place of articulation—to fill in or otherwise alter auditory processing; alternatively, it is possible for auditory information to compensate for degraded visual information. Survivor interaction contrast predictions differ depending on decision rule (OR vs. AND) and also whether the interactions are facilitatory or inhibitory. For brevity, this chapter shall focus only on the OR stopping rule; although the presence of an OR decision rule is ultimately an empirical question, it makes sense for the tasks described in the method section. Similar to UCIP, the parallel interactive facilitatory model also predicts a positive survivor interaction contrast function with an OR decision rule when selective influence is present (refer to Townsend & Nozawa, 1995,

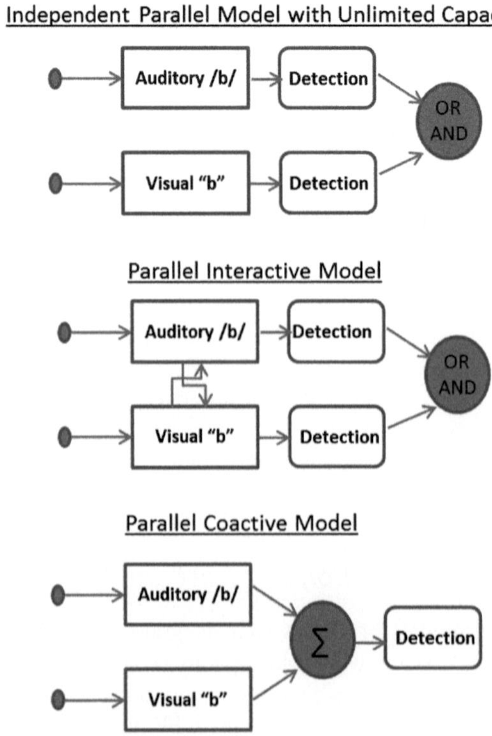

Figure 9.1A Diagrams showing the flow of auditory and visual speech information in parallel independent, parallel interactive models, and coactive models.

for discussion on selective influence). The difference is that a small negative region precedes the positive portion of the interaction contrast (Eidels et al., 2011). The predictions for the inhibitory model differ slightly inasmuch as the negative region is considerably larger and approaches the size of the positive region as inhibition increases.

An important test that can be used to differentiate UCIP from parallel interactive processing is capacity: for UCIP, capacity should be unlimited ($C(t) = 1$) whereas parallel interactive models predict supercapacity when cross-modal facilitation is present and limited capacity when cross-modal inhibition is present. The third model represents coactivation. Here, the auditory and visual cues initially undergo separate sensory processing; however, prior to conscious recognition, the cues are fused in such a way that the phonemic information is summed together. This means that recognition occurs on combined rather than in separate channels as expected under parallel processing.

Model Comparison

How may we distinguish coactive from parallel models? First, we have at our disposal the survivor interaction contrast. Similar to parallel OR processing with cross-modal

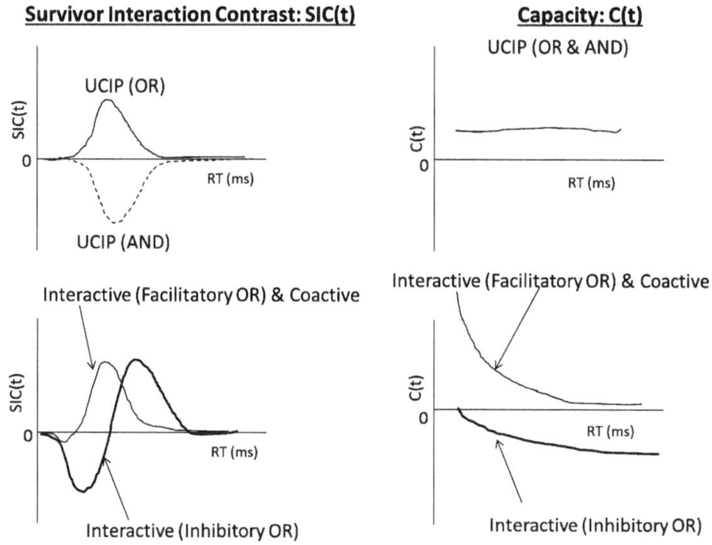

Figure 9.1B Survivor interaction contrast ($S_{IC}(t)$) and capacity function predictions for parallel independent, parallel interactive, and coactive models.

facilitation, the interaction contrast should be positive albeit with the exception of a small negativity for early response times (refer to Townsend and Nozawa, 1995, for mathematical proofs). Besides the survivor interaction contrast, processing capacity can be used to diagnose architecture. The predicted capacity signature, again similar to facilitatory OR processing, should be significantly greater than 1. Previous research has nonetheless indicated that coactive processing can perhaps be distinguished from parallel interactive OR because coactivation predicts supercapacity magnitudes higher than 1 (Eidels et al., 2011; Townsend and Wenger, 2004).

Evidence for Parallel and Coactive Audiovisual Speech Integration

Speech recognition unfolds in real-time as vowels and consonants are decoded in the auditory and visual modalities. How do these processes work, and what type of tractable model can be used to describe the flow of information? First, Rosenblum (2005) argued, in an indirect way, that auditory and visual speech information merge in coactive manner. In support of this position, he argued that the cognitive machinery involved in speech processing extracts modality neutral or rather *amodal* information from the auditory and visual sensory inputs. These types of theories of perception often make the assumption that the linguistic representations extracted from the signal are movements of the vocal tract rather than discrete units such as time invariant symbolic phonemes. Rosenblum argued that "sensory modality is largely invisible to the speech perception function and the relevant information for phonetic resolution is modality-neutral" (Rosenblum, 2005, p. 51). He concluded that much support for this idea comes from evidence showing that the auditory and visual speech cues converge prior to conscious recognition of words, consonants, or phonemes: The hypothesis is that the auditory and visual cues can be combined prior to speech recognition precisely because they both are stored in a similar modality neutral code. Much like the coactive models described by Townsend and colleagues then, the relevant information is summed together before a decision is made on the content of the utterance.

What existing empirical evidence points to this early merging of information? As one example, Green and Miller (1985) showed that visual information about place of articulation affects the perception of voice onset time (VOT). Place of articulation is defined as the point of contact in the vocal tract, or the place where the obstruction occurs, to create a consonant sound. Next, VOT denotes the time period between the release of a consonant and the beginning of vibrations in the vocal fold. In Green and Miller's experiment, listeners were shown audiovisual clips of a talker saying a syllable that varied auditorially on a continuum from /bi/ – /pi/ (pronounced like the words "bee" and "pea"). This was done by varying the VOT, where smaller VOTs are more likely to produce a percept of /bi/ rather than /pi/; hence, faster VOT increases the probability that one perceives the voiced consonant /b/ versus /p/, or /g/ versus /k/. The other independent variable was the speed at which the visual speech cues were presented: fast or slow. Results indicated that rapidly articulated visual syllables increased the probability that participants perceived /bi/ rather than /pi/. This suggests that visual speech affects auditory phoneme perception by influencing variable properties of the auditory signal. While lacking the rigor of the DFP, these results nonetheless point to a decision process that has access to both auditory and visual information and combines the two sources of information in the early stages of multisensory perception. However, as we shall find out, auditory and visual cross-modal information sharing can also potentially explain these results, which is another reason why the model comparison tools provided by the DFP are relevant.

On the other hand, Bernstein (2005) discussed studies showing that audiovisual integration might occur in parallel: in this framework, consonant recognition in audiovisual speech perception can happen separately on the auditory and visual modalities rather than on the combined information. If this is indeed the case, auditory and visual sensory processing occurs in separate channels in a manner akin to the *parallel* information systems described mathematically by Townsend and Nozawa (1995). In support of this "parallel processing" position, Bernstein described a study showing that the introduction of large stimulus onset asynchronies (SOAs) between the auditory and visual modalities often fails to abolish the McGurk effect (cf. Massaro, Cohen, & Smeele, 1996). This can be accomplished by moving the auditory and visual modalities "out of temporal synchrony" with each other in such a way that lip movement occur abnormally long before the sound, or vice versa. (The canonical case of the McGurk effect occurs when listeners are presented with an auditory /ba/ combined with an incongruently articulated visual "ga"; this combination often leads to the perception of the fused consonant /da/.). Additionally, there is evidence showing that the McGurk effect varies in strength across cultures (Sekiyama & Tohkura, 1993) and also occurs at a higher rate for familiar versus unfamiliar talkers (Mallik, Magnotti, & Beauchamp, 2015; Walker, Bruce, & O'Malley, 1995). To summarize,

Bernstein's argued that auditory and visual phonetic processing occur separately, in parallel channels, during audiovisual perception.

In spite of the information for coactive or parallel processing advanced by Rosenblum (2005) and by Bernstein (2005), rigorous testing of the information processing architectures in Fig. 9.1 requires statistical tests using reaction times. One of the advantages to using the DFP, then, is that previous modeling endeavors almost exclusively used only accuracy data (e.g., Braida, 1991; Grant et al., 1998; Grant, 2002; Massaro, 2004). While these approaches have been beneficial for certain purposes such as identifying consonant confusion probabilities, the dynamic nature of speech recognition lends itself to *RT* approaches. Therefore, the foundational question unanswered by conventional accuracy-based methods is: what are the underlying neuro-cognitive mechanisms responsible for speech recognition? In fact, the perception of multisensory speech serves as one of many interesting possible scenarios where we may wish to explore issues related to architecture, decision rule, and capacity.

In this chapter, I use audiovisual speech perception as an appropriate tutorial application of the DFP. As we can see, the problem is interesting to psychologists, yet the example is simple enough for the novice reader to understand how the DFP measures are calculated and truly appreciate the novelty of an application that goes above and beyond the simple detection paradigm that the DFP was originally designed for by Townsend and colleagues. The approach discussed next is designed to illustrate how *RT* distributions offer a vital set of tools that are helpful in parsing out the architecture, decision rule, and capacity in a complex task, as they have in the more general psychophysics literature that relies on simple detection procedures (e.g., Luce, 1986; Ratcliff & Smith, 2004; Townsend & Ashby, 1983; Van Zandt, 2000; Vickers, 1980; Welford, 1980). The purpose of this first study was to help establish architectural and capacity predictions for multisensory speech perception; in this phase, the intent was to investigate these issues for congruent or matched signals when accuracy was high, that is, for accuracy greater than 90%. It is conceivable, of course, that capacity and architectural configurations may change as a function of listening environment; changes in capacity across S/N ratio, for instance, were reported in an EEG study carried out by Altieri and Wenger (2013). This experiment constitutes an important step in assaying processing issues related to "early" versus "late" integration; or to use SFT and DFP language, "coactive" versus "parallel" processing. A second, follow-up study will explore these issues for incongruent audiovisual speech signals which evoke "McGurk fusions" in most normal-hearing adult listeners (see McGurk & MacDonald, 1976).

Methods

Experiment 1

Participants

Five participants, one male and four females, with normal or corrected 20/20 vision were paid $10.00 per hour. All participants were recruited from the Indiana University

Campus (Bloomington, IN). I present the data from one participant (4) for exemplary purposes in this chapter. This experiment was reported by Altieri and Townsend (2011).

Materials

The stimulus materials included two audiovisual movie clips of a female talker from the Hoosier Multi-talker Database saying the words "base" and "face". The two words in this set are minimal pairs and are intended to be moderately confusable, with only the onset phoneme (/b/ versus /f/) differing between them. A total of eight different stimuli were created from each video clip: two audio files at two levels of saliency, two video files at two levels of saliency, and four audiovisual clips at each factorial combination of high–high, high–low, low–high, and low–low levels of saliency. The audio, visual, and audiovisual files were created using Final Cut Pro HD version 4.5. The audio files were sampled at a rate of 48 kHz using 16-bit encoding. Pink noise was mixed with each audio file using Adobe Audition to create two different signal-to-noise ratios and two different levels of saliency. The two signal-to-noise ratios for both stimuli were 25 dB for the high salience condition and 0 dB SPL for the low saliency condition.

The level of brightness on the videos was manipulated to create two different levels of saliency in the visual modality. On the low saliency video files, the brightness was reduced 90 steps using the brightness video filter in Final Cut Pro HD. This had the effect of dimming the quality of the video and making the talker's articulators more difficult to perceive. The auditory and videos lasted approximately 1600 milliseconds for *Base*, and 1650 milliseconds for *Face*. The beginning of each audio and video file was edited in Final Cut Pro in order to create identical onset times for the spoken stimuli.

Design and Procedure

Listeners were seated in front of a Macintosh computer equipped with Beyer Dynamic-100 headphones. Trials consisted of auditory-only, visual-only, or audiovisual words. Each trial began with a fixation cross (+) appearing in the center of the computer monitor for 500 ms, followed immediately by the presentation of one of the eight stimuli. The timer began at the stimulus onset after the fixation cross, appearing for 500 ms. Participants were instructed to respond as quickly and accurately as possible by pressing the button on a button box labeled *Base* if they either heard the word "base", saw a video of the talker saying "base", or simultaneously saw and heard the speaker saying the word. Similarly, participants were instructed to press the button labeled *Face* if they heard the word "face", saw a video of the talker saying "face", or both. There was an intertrial interval of 1000 ms.

Participants were also presented with 3360 total trials: 1120 auditory-only trials (560 *Base* + 560 *Face* of h and l trial types), 1120 visual-only trials, (560 *Base* + 560 *Face*), and 1120 audiovisual trials (560 *Base* + 560 *Face*). There were 280 trials for each audiovisual condition (hh, hl, lh, ll) pooled across the two words. Listeners participated in 28 blocks that included 120 trials each with a break between each block. Trial types were intermixed in blocks. The experiment required one week to complete with no more than 48 hours between days. Finally, participants received sixteen practice trials at the onset of each experimental session that were not included in the subsequent data analysis.

Experiment 2

Participants

Five different listeners were recruited from Indiana University, Bloomington. Once again, each listener reported normal or corrected vision were paid ten dollars per session for their participation. Similar to Experiment 1, data will be reported for one example listener.

Materials

The stimulus materials included audiovisual recordings of the syllables /b/ and /g/ spoken by a female talker. The stimuli were obtained from the Hoosier Multi-talker Database. The stimuli were factorially combined using the audiovisual editor in Final Cut Pro HD (4.5) to create congruent and incongruent stimuli. The stimuli consisted of auditory /b/ and visual "b", auditory /b/ and visual "g", auditory /g/ and visual "b" and auditory /g/ and visual "g". Participants reported perceiving the congruent stimuli as "b" and "g", respectively, in most cases, while reporting perceptual fusions when presented with incongruent stimuli. Specifically, participants perceived "d" or "h" when presented with auditory /b/ and visual "g".

A total of eight different stimulus items were created from each category: two audio files at two levels of saliency, two video files at two levels of saliency, and four audiovisual clips at each factorial combination of high–high, high–low, low–high, and low–low levels of saliency. The auditory clips were sampled at a rate of 48 kHz using 16-bit encoding. White noise was mixed with each audio file using Adobe Audition to create two different signal-to-noise ratios. The two signal-to-noise ratios were "clear" in the high-saliency condition and −10 dB in the low-saliency condition. For the visual channel, brightness on the videos was adjusted to create two different saliency levels. On the low-saliency files, brightness was reduced by 90 steps via the brightness video filter in Final Cut Pro HD.

Design and Procedure

Similar to Experiment 1, listeners were seated in front of a Macintosh computer equipped with Beyer Dynamic-100 headphones. Each trial began with a plus sign (+) appearing for 500 ms in the center of the computer screen followed by one of the stimuli. There was an intertrial interval of 1000 ms. Experimental trials consisted of auditory-only, visual-only, or audiovisual stimuli. The timer began at the stimulus onset after the fixation sign disappeared from the screen. Participants were instructed to respond as "quickly and accurately as possible" by pressing the button labeled *YES* if they heard the consonant /b/ in the stimulus, saw the talker articulate a "b", or both.

Participants were instructed to press the button labeled *NO* if a "b" failed to appear in either the auditory or visual signals. These "No" trials occurred when the audiovisual /g/ or a target absent catch trial was presented.

Listeners were presented with 4320 trials: these consisted of 960 auditory-only trials which included (480 /b/ + 480 /g/ of high and low trial types), 960 visual-only trials: 480 "b" + 480 "g" of high and low trial types, and finally 960 audiovisual trials (480 /b/ + "g" consisting of *hh*, *hl*, *lh*, and *ll* trial types). There were also 960 trials comprised of single targets combined with auditory or visual distractors (480 auditory /b/ + visual /g/ and 480 auditory /g/ with visual /b/ consisting of *hh*, *hl*, *lh*, and *ll* trials). Each listener participated in 12 blocks with 320 trials. Target absent trials ($N = 480$), in which neither target ("b") nor distractor "g" appeared in either modality. [The number of trials was chosen in this way to avoid probabilistic contingencies (refer to Mordkoff & Yantis, 1991).] Each listener received practice trials that were not included in the subsequent data analysis.

Results: Experiment 1

For exemplary purposes, data from only one participant will be reported. To briefly summarize overall performance, the mean error rate across participants was less than 8%. The mean accuracy and *RT* values for the example participant showing strongest evidence of selective influence were: $M_{\text{HH}} = 97\%$ (1198 ms), $M_{\text{HL}} = 96\%$ (1320 ms), $M_{\text{LH}} = 95\%$ (1411 ms), $M_{\text{LL}} = 95\%$ (1532 ms). Townsend and Wenger (2004) found that variable error rates in either channel have minimal effect on workload capacity.

Step 1: Assessing Selective Influence

First, we shall discuss the survivor function data to assess *selective influence* before continuing on to analyze the $S_{\text{IC}}(t)$s. The left hand panel of Fig. 9.2 shows that the survivor functions were predictably ordered; this provided important initial support from visual inspection for the validity of selective influence. As one can observe, the predicted orderings in the survivor functions (i.e., $ll > lh, hl > hh$) were present for large enough time intervals in each of the participants to carry out the interaction contrasts on the survivor functions. As a statistical test on the $S(t)$'s, one-sided Kolmogorov–Smirnov tests were carried out on the *lh* and *hl* versus *ll* and again for the lh/hl versus *hh* cumulative distribution functions, and it was consistent with the presence of selective influence, or at least that both dimensions had an influence. Results were statistically significant in both cases ($p < 0.01$).

Step 2: Assessing the Shape of the $S_{\text{IC}}(t)$

The second and more important analysis consists of a qualitative examination of the $S_{\text{IC}}(t)$ function. The listener's $S_{\text{IC}}(t)$ in Fig. 9.2 was overadditive with the exception of a region showing early negativity. Additionally, this participant's M_{IC} was positive; together, these features indicate negative interactions between the auditory and visual

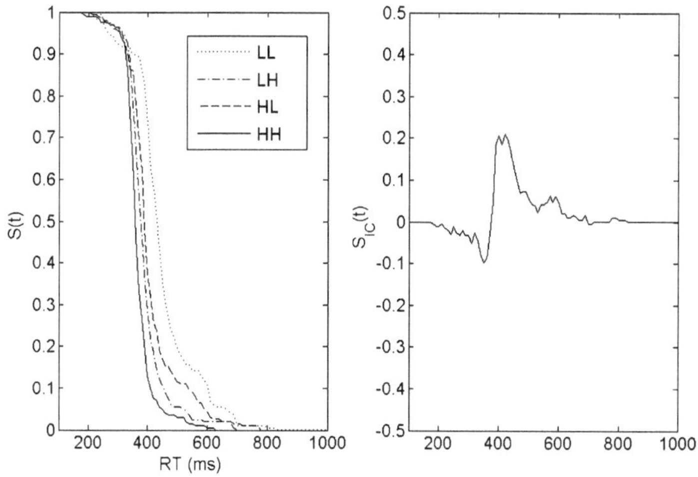

Figure 9.2 The individual survivor functions plotted on the left hand panel, and the $S_{IC}(t)$ on the right.

channels. The positive $S_{IC}(t)$ and M_{IC} are associated with the parallel model with an OR decision rule, and hence, late integration.

Statistical tests for significance of the $S_{IC}(t)$ curves have not been at our disposal until quite recently (Houpt & Townsend, 2010). Ideally, we would like to assess, using some nonparametric test, whether the positive or negative portion of the empirical $S_{IC}(t)$ represents a true deviation from zero. To that end, nonparametric statistical tests were recently developed by Houpt and Townsend for the purpose of assaying the validity of observed negative and positive departures from zero in the $S_{IC}(t)$. Houpt and Townsend (2010) developed the D statistic, which is related to the distribution over the maximum value and minimum value of a *Brownian Bridge*. This result was motivated by Kolmogorov's (1933) results showing the distribution over the maximum difference between two CDFs. For the D statistic, D^+ denotes the largest positive value of a Brownian Bridge and D^- denotes the magnitude of the smallest value. The distributions were described as follows:

$$S_{D^+}(x) = p\{D^+ \geq x\} = e^{-2x^2},$$
$$S_{D^-}(x) = p\{D^- \geq x\} = e^{-2x^2}.$$

These results can be readily extended for null hypothesis testing; the null hypothesis being that the maximum positive or negative deviation from 0 in the empirical $S_{IC}(t)$ is not greater than would be predicted by chance. Houpt and Townsend (2011) mathematically proved that the above equations lead to the p-values for hypothesis testing of the empirically measured D^+ and D^- where $p^- = \exp[-2N(D^+)^2]$ and $p^+ = \exp[-2N(D^-)^2]$. In each case, N indicates the number of trials in each redundant target condition. The results for both the D statistics and M_{IC} are shown in Table 9.1 which happens to confirm parallel first-terminating (OR) processing. This information should be considered supplementary to the $S_{IC}(t)$ and M_{IC} because it can

Table 9.1 The M_{IC} and values for the D^+ and D^- statistics. This listener showed evidence for significant positive deviations from 0, and a significant negative deviation from 0 as well

M_{IC}	D^+	p^+	D^-	p^-
33	**0.41**	<0.001	0.10	<0.01

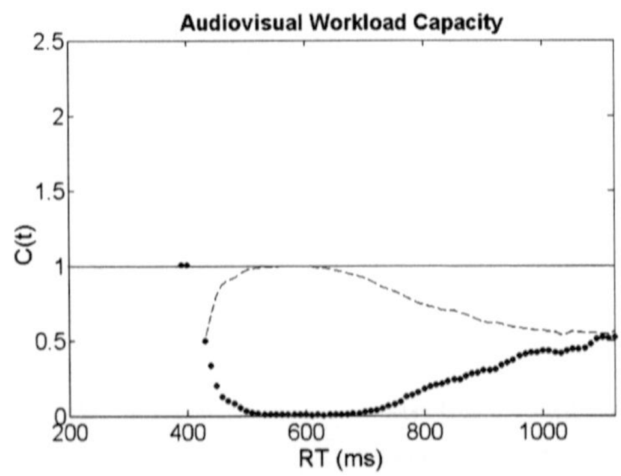

Figure 9.3 $C(t)$ plot for the example participant. The dots denote $C(t)$, while the dashed line denotes the Grice bound. $C(t)$ was limited capacity for all processing times.

help aid in the identification of architecture and stopping rule. If the $S_{IC}(t)$ is overadditive for most time points, the D^+ statistic should assist in confirming this observation, although an overadditive M_{IC} or significant D statistic by itself is only weak evidence for parallel first-terminating (or exhaustive processing if the M_{IC} is negative) processing.

Step 3: Measuring Workload Capacity

Fig. 9.3 displays the capacity $C(t)$ plot for this participant. Recall that limited capacity is observed in both serial models ($C(t)$ around $1/2$) and parallel models with negative dependencies, but is not a signature of standard coactive models. Only parallel models possessing a convergent flow like coactive models but with extraordinary channel inhibition could predict this highly limited $C(t)$ result. The capacity functions in Fig. 9.3 were consistent in showing that capacity, at all points in time, was very limited; this observation that fails to support a wide range of coactive models and instead lends support to parallel inhibitory processing. As expected, the Grice bound for extremely limited capacity was violated for each participant at nearly every point in time, while the bound for supercapacity was found to not be surpassed at any point in time. This shows convincingly that processing capacity was extremely limited, and that the limitations were too severe to be predicted by an independent parallel race model.

Results: Experiment 2

The error rate averaged across all participants in the redundant target condition was less than 5%. Mean accuracy and *RT*s for the congruent condition were: HH = 96% (986 ms); HL = 95% (1249 ms); LH = 100% (980 ms); LL = 84% (1302 ms). Next, for the incongruent condition, mean accuracy and *RT*s for the example participant were: HH = 92% (1154 ms); HL = 93% (1233 ms); LH = 91% (1233 ms); LL = 83% (1387 ms).

Architecture for Congruent Trials

The results from Experiment 1 showed an $S_{IC}(t)$ shape consistent with parallel inhibitory processing together with a capacity function also consistent with that type of processing architecture. The question now becomes: will this pattern of results remain consistent with the design and stimuli used in Experiment 2?

Step 1: Assessing Selective Influence

The survivor functions for this participant are shown in the left panel of Fig. 9.4. The predicted survivor function ordering – $S_{LL}(t) > S_{LH}(t)/S_{HL}(t) > S_{HH}(t)$ – held until approximately 500 ms when the LH and LL reversed order. I argue that this was probably caused by inhibitory cross-channel interactions from the visual to the auditory channel; that is, the salient visual cue might have somehow interfered with the low or degraded auditory signal. The assumption of selective influence might therefore not be in effect for this participant for certain time points. Still, the shape of the survivor interaction contrast shall be assessed and results compared with the architecture and decision rule findings described in Experiment 1. The specific question is: will we once again obtain evidence consistent with inhibitory OR parallel processing in spite of the differing demands imposed by the detection task?

Step 2: Assessing the Shape of the $S_{IC}(t)$

The aim of this study was once again to examine the functional form of the $S_{IC}(t)$ to make inferences about architecture; this was done for both congruent audiovisual trials when both the auditory and visual modalities contained the phoneme "b", and also for the "McGurk" trials, which contained a visual "g" paired with auditory "b".

The $S_{IC}(t)$ for the congruent trials is shown in the right panel of Fig. 9.4; similar to the forced choice task of Experiment 1, we see evidence for an early region of negativity followed by a positive region. Qualitatively speaking, this shape is consistent with parallel inhibitory processing thereby replicating previous results. The *D* statistics and M_{IC} are shown below in Table 9.2. These statistics show that overall, the M_{IC} was positive, and that the negative and positive regions were statistically different from 0. These results help statistically confirm that the $S_{IC}(t)$ was consistent with inhibitory parallel processing. Finally, workload capacity was extremely limited and once again consistent with parallel inhibitory processing. Capacity for Experiment 2 is not shown in order to save space, and because results were identical to Experiment 1.

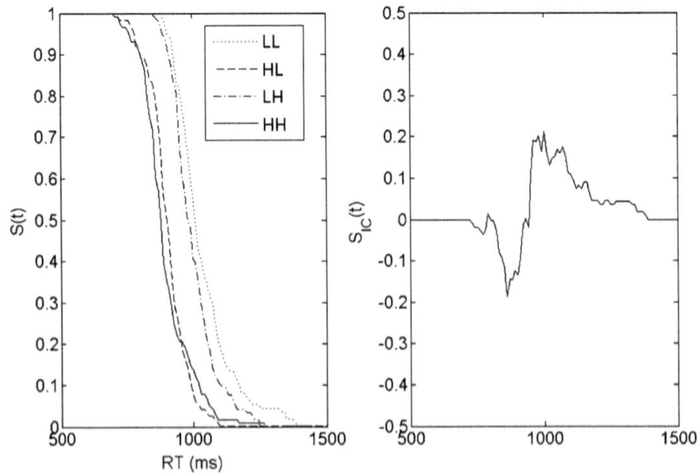

Figure 9.4 The survivor functions (left panel) and $S_{IC}(t)$ for one example participant in Experiment 2. This figure shows responses to congruent audiovisual stimuli.

Table 9.2 The Mean Interaction Contrasts (M_{IC}) and D^+ and D^- statistics. Corresponding p-values are also displayed

M_{IC}	D^+	p^+	D^-	p^-
66	**0.20**	<0.001	**0.18**	<0.001

Architecture for Incongruent (McGurk) Trials

This portion of the data analysis examines the responses of a participant to "McGurk" or incongruent audiovisual trials: auditory "b" plus visual "g". This analysis will explore whether incongruent audiovisual speech leads to changes in the $S_{IC}(t)$. In other words, when presented with McGurk fusions, will listeners process the modalities in a parallel facilitatory or coactive manner instead of inhibitory parallel? Common sense appears to dictate that audiovisual fusions occur coactively rather than parallel (e.g., Fowler & Dekle, 1991; Rosenblum, 2005; Rosenblum, Miller, & Sanchez, 2007). To effectively explore this issue, we present the following data analysis from one out of the five participants who showed evidence for selective influence.

Step 1: Assessing Selective Influence

Fig. 9.5 (left panel) shows the individual survivor functions from the example participant in the incongruent audiovisual condition. Overall, the survivor functions appear well-ordered for this participant in the time range from 1000–2000 ms: $S_{LL}(t) > S_{LH}(t)/S_{HL}(t) > S_{HH}(t)$.

Step 2: Assessing the Shape of the $S_{IC}(t)$

The panel on the right portion of Fig. 9.5 shows the $S_{IC}(t)$ function for this listener; interestingly, the form of the contrast function was consistent with the data set

Table 9.3 The Mean Interaction Contrasts (M_{IC}) plus the D^+ and D^- statistics

M_{IC}	D^+	p^+	D^-	p^-
75	**0.13**	0.02	**0.13**	0.02

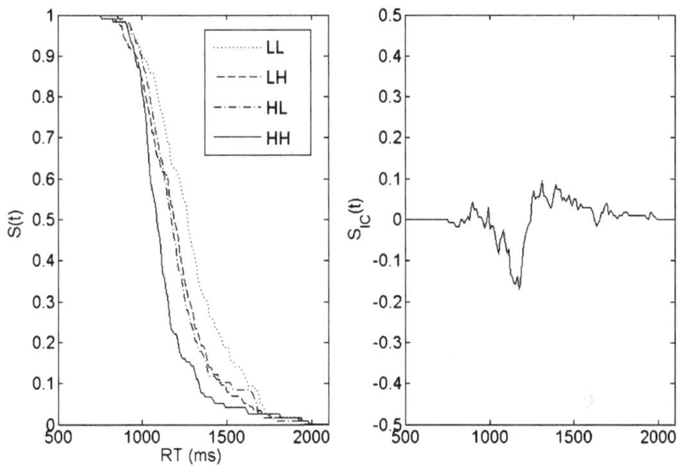

Figure 9.5 (Left panel) Survivor functions for the example participant in Experiment 2. Here, I display the results from the auditory "b" and visual "g" McGurk trials. (Right panel) The survivor interaction contrast for the same participant.

was consistent with the previous 2: both when the listener had to differentiate between congruent audiovisual "base" versus "face", and also when they were required to detect the phoneme "b" in the auditory OR visual modality. Qualitatively, the $S_{IC}(t)$ shows a rather large negative region followed by a positive curve that appears larger at first glance. The M_{IC} was measured empirically, and the statistical significance of the negative and positive regions of the curve was tested statistically using Houpt's D statistics as done previously. These results are displayed in Table 9.3. We may see that in each case, the statistic is positive.

Taken together, the shape of the curve and statistical results from Table 9.3 revealed an architectural form consistent with either parallel inhibitory and coactive processing. Previously, in Experiment 1, as well as Experiment 2 for the congruent audiovisual stimuli, workload capacity was employed to disambiguate competing processing architecture. This is due to the fact that even with the $S_{IC}(t)$, certain architectures can mimic one another as shown by Eidels, et al. (2011). As one example, we know that coactive architecture predicts extreme supercapacity, while inhibitory parallel architecture predicts limited capacity (see Townsend & Wenger, 2004). A complication, however, arises when attempting to calculate capacity for auditory "b" and visual "g" trials; this is because there were technically not any "Yes" visual-only "g" trials, which of course makes a calculation of the traditional capacity coefficient provided by Townsend and Nozawa (1995) impossible.

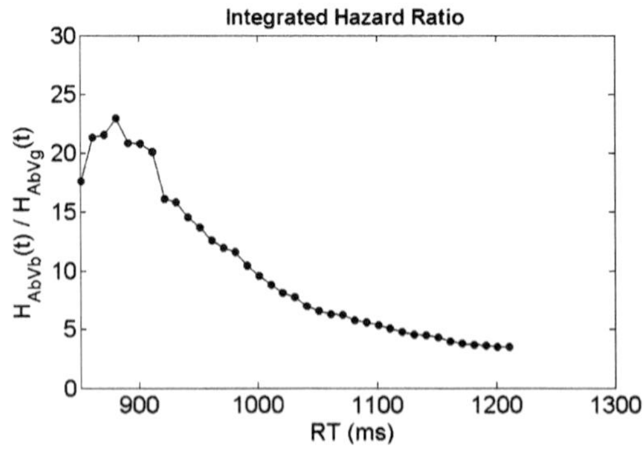

Figure 9.6 The line and dots show the integrated hazard ratio for the congruent divided by the incongruent condition.

I am therefore suggesting an alternative way to assess efficiency in situations such as these when traditional capacity calculations become impossible. Instead of capacity, one can assess efficiency by computing a hazard function ratio: In this case, the aim is to divide the hazard function obtained from the congruent trials by the hazard function obtained from the incongruent trials. This would tell us the following: If the ratio equals 1 or greater, we may argue that integration efficiency is similar across conditions, or in the case it is greater than 1, more efficient for congruent trials. This would provide evidence consistent with the hypothesis that the true capacity is limited for the incongruent trials, and therefore, that architecture is parallel inhibitory. On the other hand, supposing the ratio is less than 1, it would mean that McGurk trials yield higher efficiency than congruent trials, it could mean that processing is coactive or parallel facilitatory.

Results for the integrated hazard ratio—given by the quantity $\frac{H_{AbVb}(t)}{H_{AbVg}(t)}$—for this listener are shown in Fig. 9.6. The data pattern reveals a ratio greater than 1 for most *RT*s. Considering that capacity was limited for the congruent trials this pattern of results suggests that integration efficiency is even lower for McGurk trials (which participants typically reported hearing as the consonant "d"). I propose that the cause of this inefficiency is the presence of the visually articulated "g" inhibiting the identification of auditory "b": hence the reason why auditory "b" is identified less efficiently on average in the presence of a visual "g" compared to a visually articulated "b". This interpretation of results, together with the finding of limited capacity for congruent trials in conjunction with the $S_{IC}(t)$, leaves us with the interpretation of inhibitory parallel processing when the "McGurk" effect occurs.

General Discussion and Conclusion

These studies were designed to show how the DFP can be applied to language perception tasks and categorization tasks more generally in an effort to identify viable mental architectures that cannot be uniquely identified using mean *RT* or accuracy-based measures. The primary aim of this experiment was to provide a tutorial and introduction and show how architecture, decision rule, and capacity can be calculated using a detection paradigm that deviates from the prototypical "detection" studies associated with the psychophysics literature (Townsend & Nozawa, 1995).

In the discrimination tasks used in Experiment 1, the $S_{IC}(t)$ signature was analyzed to investigate the form of processing architecture that emerged: a similar approach was employed in the phoneme detection study in Experiment 2. These example data consistently showed evidence for parallel inhibitory or perhaps coactive processing. In addition to investigating the shape of the $S_{IC}(t)$, the capacity coefficient $C(t)$ was also computed to determine whether individual channel processing efficiency increased, decreased, or remained the same when two modalities were present relative to the case of an independent parallel race model. For this listener, limited capacity was observed, which happens to be a signature consistent with parallel inhibitory rather than coactive processing (ref. Eidels et al., 2011). Importantly, coactive models predict supercapacity ($C(t) \gg 1$) (Eidels et al., 2011; Townsend & Wenger, 2004), and thus constitute a first-order representation of early bimodal merging of information as described by Rosenblum (2005). These processes can produce the manner of facilitation and superadditivity reported in classic studies such as Erber's (2003) and Sumby and Pollack's (1954).

Regular parallel models with detections made first on the separate channels parsimoniously capture the theoretical notion of late modality integration. If the individual channels are unaffected by either limitations in a capacity source or by channel inhibition they normally produce $C(t)$ equal to 1. Extreme capacity limitations occurring as a result of cross-channel inhibition can lead to $C(t) \leq 1/2$. On the other hand, mutual facilitation can evoke supercapacity in such models while standard serial models predict $C(t)$ equal to $1/2$ (Townsend & Wenger, 2004).

Curiously, the survivor interaction function of the DFP per ipsum, as we saw in Experiments 1 and 2, is deficient for architectural identification when cross-channel interactions are present. In this study, the $S_{IC}(t)$ function which is used to identify architecture showed a region of negativity followed by a positive region. This functional form is characteristically associated with coactive processing, but importantly, Eidels, et al. (2011) showed that parallel processing with cross-modal inhibition can likewise furnish this "negative to positive" architectural form. The source of such inhibition is intuitively identifiable in the McGurk trial because it likely originates from the incompatible visual "g" which inhibits the correct identification of the auditory phoneme. However, inhibition in the discrimination tasks ("Base" vs. "Face") and congruent audiovisual detection tasks (detect the phoneme "b" in either the auditory OR visual modality) was also apparent for some reason. As such, when given an opportunity to be as fast as ordinary parallel processing models predict, the language perceiver is thus incapable of profiting from the redundant signal information regardless of the level of ecologically valid afforded by the visual speech cues. This is at least the case when accuracy is high (Altieri & Townsend, 2011).

Therefore, to summarize the overall findings in the context of a theoretical framework of audiovisual perception, the absence of supercapacity almost certainly rules out coactive processing models and first-terminating parallel models with facilitatory cross-modal interactions. Hence, the substantial limitations in capacity provided substantial evidence against these models. The combined results, for this individual listener at least, contributed support for parallel first-terminating processing with inhibitory channel interaction contributing to capacity limitations. Cross talk, or information sharing between the auditory and visual channels, is a distinct possibility given the capacity limitations and observed negativity in the $S_{IC}(t)$ signatures. Finally, the positive M_{IC} interactions also rule out serial processing, although this type of architecture is not historically considered for audiovisual speech integration frameworks. The results reported here hence require a theoretical framework that can capture both the observed negative region in the $S_{IC}(t)$ function and limited capacity. Townsend and Wenger (2004) demonstrated that inhibition between channels in parallel processing systems can induce heavy capacity penalties when workload is increased. Until now, no one had yet investigated the possible joint appearance of a positive-to-negative-shaped $S_{IC}(t)$ functions with an early negative area combined with moderate-to-extreme capacity limitations. However, we know that this is a strong possibility in light of theoretical and simulation research carried out by Eidels, et al. (2011).

One critical difference between most studies of audiovisual speech perception is that auditory accuracy is usually lower than the studies reported here; therefore, the cues furnished by the visual signal have greater opportunity to improve accuracy. By contrast, accuracy was generally high in the two experiments reported here in this chapter. Would architecture and capacity change as a function of listening conditions? Perhaps: Altieri and Townsend (2011) and Altieri and Wenger (2013) found evidence for supercapacity and hence facilitatory parallel interactions under degraded listening conditions when auditory accuracy decreased. Likewise, Altieri and Hudock (2014a) showed evidence for supercapacity when the accuracy adjusted capacity coefficient (refer to Altieri, Townsend, & Wenger, 2014; Townsend & Altieri, 2012) was fit to the data of some hearing-impaired participants.

Another broader purpose of this chapter, as stated previously in the introduction, is that research on audiovisual speech perception has generally failed to focus on dynamic models or RT predictions. This paradigm allowed for new evidence to be obtained in order to sufficiently investigate how cognitive processes integrate speech cues from the auditory and visual channels, and secondly, how efficiency vis-à-vis capacity was altered through the addition of the visual channel under high accuracy conditions with RT as the dependent variable (Altieri & Townsend, 2011). Under low signal-to-noise ratios where accuracy is measured, the auditory and visual channels can aid one another under challenging perceptual conditions.

Other Considerations and Future Directions

To summarize, this DFP application was theoretically interesting for multiple reasons: The failure of ecologically valid information from the auditory and visual realms to produce super- or even unlimited capacity is reminiscent of some findings in the context of studies on realistic face perception. Again, these implications—in face, object, or speech recognition—would not have been able to be uncovered using statistics that are more conventional in the psychology literature. This picture represents an intriguing theoretical enigma that we should continue exploring using combined accuracy and capacity methods, as well as dynamic neuroimaging tools such as EEG or MEG.

The next question that arises is how do these findings relate to other categorization studies in the literature? Wenger and Townsend (2001), for instance, showed that in high accuracy conditions natural visual features such as the eyes and nose are processed in parallel using an OR decision stopping rule; this conclusion comes in light of the positive M_{IC}s. Further, the authors reported evidence for similar $S_{\mathrm{IC}}(t)$ signatures to the contrasts for audiovisual speech recognition—a negative region followed by a positive curve—when observers were presented with both normal and inverted faces. While Houpt's D statistics were not employed as they were in the experiments in this chapter, the form of the curve implies either coactive or parallel inhibitory processing. Similar to our results, capacity was notably less than what ordinary unlimited capacity parallel race models predict. Together with the $S_{\mathrm{IC}}(t)$ then, we have more information that the discrimination of complex stimuli involving multiple features can lead to parallel inhibitory processing architecture.

Capacity limitations similar to this study have likewise been observed in speeded discrimination designs involving the detection of speech stimuli, namely printed numbers, paired with visually displayed numerals (Berryhill, Kveraga, Webb, & Hughes, 2007). Berryhill et al. (2007) presented participants with congruent audiovisual stimuli (i.e., the numerals "1" or "2") in the visual modality and auditory sounds of a speaker saying "one" or "two". Workload capacity was very limited when the auditory and visual signals were presented with a stimulus onset asynchrony (SOA) of 0 ("0" means at the same time); SOA indicates the number of milliseconds the visual tract leads the audio tract. When the SOA increased, capacity became less limited for reasons still unknown. At SOAs of 150 and 225 ms supercapacity; a redundancy gain consistent with parallel interactive or perhaps coactive processing, was observed in their study. Therefore, in certain types of stimuli at least, synchrony manipulations might affect the processing efficiency of the auditory and visual channels. Nonetheless, the original hypothesis was that visual speech cues combined with spoken words as employed in experiments 1 and 2 here would mutually facilitate one another in a more ecologically natural and powerful way than with letters combined with the speech sound.

References

Altieri, N., & Hudock, D. (2014a). Variability in audiovisual speech integration skills assessed by combined capacity and accuracy measures. *International Journal of Audiology*, *53*, 710–718.

Altieri, N., & Hudock, D. (2014b). Hearing impairment and audiovisual speech integration ability: A case study report. *Frontiers in Psychology*, *5*(678), 1–10.

Altieri, N., Fifić, M., Little, D., & Yang, C. (2016). Historical backgrounds and a tutorial introduction to systems factorial technology. In D. R. Little, N. Altieri, M. Fifić, & C.-T. Yang

(Eds.), *Systems factorial technology: A theory driven methodology for the identification of perceptual and cognitive mechanisms*. Elsevier (in this book).

Altieri, N., & Townsend, J. T. (2011). An assessment of behavioral dynamic information processing measures in audiovisual speech perception. *Frontiers in Psychology*, *2*(238), 1–15.

Altieri, N., Townsend, J. T., & Wenger, M. J. (2014). A measure for assessing the effects of audiovisual speech integration. *Behavior Research Methods*, *46*, 406–415.

Altieri, N., & Wenger, M. (2013). Neural dynamics of audiovisual integration efficiency under variable listening conditions: An individual participant analysis. *Frontiers in Psychology*, *4*(615), 1–15.

Bernstein, L. E. (2005). Phonetic perception by the speech perceiving brain. In D. B. Pisoni, & R. E. Remez (Eds.), *The handbook of speech perception* (pp. 79–98). Malden, MA: Blackwell Publishing.

Berryhill, M., Kveraga, K., Webb, L., & Hughes, H. C. (2007). Multimodal access to verbal name codes. *Perception & Psychophysics*, *69*(4), 628–640.

Blamey, P. J., Cowan, R. S. C., Alcantra, J. I., Whitford, L. A., & Clark, G. M. (1989). Speech perception using combinations of auditory, visual, and tactile information. *Journal of Rehabilitation Research and Development*, *26*, 15–24.

Braida, L. D. (1991). Crossmodal integration in the identification of consonant segments. *Quarterly Journal of Experimental Psychology*, *43*(3), 647–677.

Dupont, S., Aubin, J., & Menard, L. (2005). A study of the McGurk effect in 4 and 5-year-old French Canadian children. *ZAS Papers in Linguistics*, *40*, 1–17.

Eidels, A., Houpt, J., Altieri, N., Pei, L., & Townsend, J. T. (2011). Nice guys finish fast and bad guys finish last: A theory of interactive parallel processing. *Journal of Mathematical Psychology*, *55*, 176–190.

Erber, N. P. (1969). Interaction of audition and vision in the recognition of oral speech stimuli. *Journal of Speech and Hearing Research*, *12*, 423–425.

Erber, N. P. (2003). Use of hearing aids by older people: influence of non-auditory factors (vision, manual dexterity). *International Journal of Audiology*, *42*, 2S21–2S25.

Fowler, C. A., & Dekle, D. J. (1991). Listening with the eye and hand: Cross modal contributions to speech perception. *Journal of Experimental Psychology: Human Perception and Performance*, *17*, 816–828.

Fowler, C. A., & Rosenblum, L. D. (1991). Perception of the phonetic gesture. In I. G. Mattingly, & M. Studdert-Kennedy (Eds.), *Modularity and the motor theory of speech perception* (pp. 33–59). Hillsdale, NJ: Lawrence Erlbaum.

Grant, K. W. (2002). Measures of auditory-visual integration for speech understanding: A theoretical perspective (L). *Journal of the Acoustical Society of America*, *112*(1), 30–33.

Grant, K. W., Walden, B. E., & Seitz, P. F. (1998). Auditory-visual speech recognition by hearing impaired subjects: Consonant recognition, sentence recognition, and auditory-visual integration. *Journal of the Acoustical Society of America*, *103*(5), 2677–2690.

Green, K. P., & Miller, J. L. (1985). On the role of visual rate information in phonetic perception. *Perception & Psychophysics*, *38*, 269–276.

Griffiths, D., Blunden, A. G., & Little, D. (2016). Logical-rule based models of categorization: Using systems factorial technology to understand feature and dimensional processing. In D. R. Little, N. Altieri, M. Fifić, & C.-T. Yang (Eds.), *Systems factorial technology: A theory driven methodology for the identification of perceptual and cognitive mechanisms*. Elsevier (in this book).

Houpt, J. W., & Townsend, J. T. (2010). The statistical properties of the survivor interaction contrast. *Journal of Mathematical Psychology*, *54*, 446–453.

Houpt, J. W., & Townsend, J. T. (2011). An extension of SIC predictions to the Wiener coactive model. *Journal of Mathematical Psychology*, *55*, 267–270.

Jesse, A., & Massaro, D. W. (2010). The temporal distribution of information in audiovisual spoken-word identification. *Attention, Perception, & Psychophysics*, *72*(1), 209–225.

Kolmogorov, A. (1933). Sulla determinazione empirica di una legge di distribuzione. *Giornale dell'Istituto Italiano degli Attuari*, *4*, 1–11.

Luce, R. D. (1986). *Response times: Their role in inferring elementary mental organization*. New York: Oxford University Press.

Mallick, D., Magnotti, J. F., & Beauchamp, M. S. (2015). Variability and stability in the McGurk effect: contributions of participants, stimuli, time, and response type. *Psychonomic Bulletin & Review*, *22*, 1299–1307.

Massaro, D. W. (1987). Speech perception by ear and eye. In B. Dodd, & R. Campbell (Eds.), *Hearing by eye: The psychology of lip-reading* (pp. 53–83). Hillsdale, NJ: Lawrence Erlbaum.

Massaro, D. W. (1998). *Perceiving talking faces: From speech perception to a behavioral principle*. Cambridge, MA: MIT Press.

Massaro, D. W. (2004). From multisensory integration to talking heads and language learning. In G. A. Calvert, C. Spence, & B. E. Stein (Eds.), *The handbook of multisensory processes* (pp. 153–176). Cambridge, MA: The MIT Press.

Massaro, D. W., & Cohen, M. M. (2000). Tests of auditory-visual integration efficiency within the framework of the fuzzy logical model of perception. *Journal of the Acoustical Society of America*, *108*(2), 784–789.

Massaro, D. W., Cohen, M. M., & Smeele, P. M. (1996). Perception of asynchronous and conflicting visual and auditory speech. *Journal of the Acoustical Society of America*, *100*, 1777–1786.

McGurk, H., & MacDonald, J. W. (1976). Hearing lips and seeing voices. *Nature*, *264*, 746–748.

Miller, J. (1982). Divided attention: Evidence for coactivation with redundant signals. *Cognitive Psychology*, *14*, 247–279.

Mordkoff, J. T., & Yantis, S. (1991). An interactive race model of divided attention. *Journal of Experimental Psychology: Human Perception and Performance*, *17*(2), 520–538.

Neufeld, R. W. J., Townsend, J. T., & Jetté, J. (2007). Quantitative response time technology for measuring cognitive-processing capacity in clinical studies. In R. W. J. Neufeld (Ed.), *Advances in clinical cognitive science: Formal modeling and assessment of processes and symptoms*. Washington, D.C.: American Psychological Association.

Raab, D. H. (1962). Statistical facilitation of simple reaction times. *Transactions of the New York Academy of Sciences*, *24*, 574–590.

Ratcliff, R., & Smith, P. L. (2004). A comparison of sequential sampling models for two-choice reaction time. *Psychological Review*, *111*(2), 333–367.

Rosenblum, L. D. (2005). Primacy of multimodal speech perception. In D. B. Pisoni, & R. E. Remez (Eds.), *The handbook of speech perception* (pp. 51–78). Malden, MA: Blackwell Publishing.

Rosenblum, L. D., Miller, R. M., & Sanchez, K. (2007). Lip-read me now, hear me better later: Cross-modal transfer of talker-familiarity effects. *Psychological Science*, *18*(5), 392–395.

Sekiyama, K., & Tohkura, Y. (1993). Inter-language differences in the influence of visual cues in speech perception. *Journal of Phonetics*, *21*, 427–444.

Setti, A., Burke, K. E., Kenny, R., & Newell, F. N. (2013). Susceptibility to a multisensory speech illusion in older persons is driven by perceptual processes. *Frontiers in Psychology*, *4*, 575. http://dx.doi.org/10.3389/fpsyg.2013.00575.

Sumby, W. H., & Pollack, I. (1954). Visual contribution to speech intelligibility in noise. *Journal of the Acoustical Society of America*, *26*(2), 12–15.

Thompson, P. (1980). Margaret Thatcher: A new illusion. *Perception*, *9*(4), 483–484.

Townsend, J. T., & Altieri, N. (2012). An accuracy-response time capacity assessment function that measures performance against standard parallel predictions. *Psychological Review*, *119*(3), 500–516.

Townsend, J. T., & Ashby, F. G. (1983). *The stochastic modeling of elementary psychological processes*. Cambridge: Cambridge University Press.

Townsend, J. T., & Nozawa, G. (1995). Spatio-temporal properties of elementary perception: An investigation of parallel, serial, and coactive theories. *Journal of Mathematical Psychology*, *39*(4), 321–359.

Townsend, J. T., & Wenger, M. J. (2004). A theory of interactive parallel processing: New capacity measures and predictions for a response time inequality series. *Psychological Review*, *111*(4), 1003–1035.

Van Zandt, T. (2000). How to fit a response time distribution. *Psychonomic Bulletin & Review*, *7*(3), 424–465.

Vickers, D. (1980). Discrimination. In A. T. Welford (Ed.), *Reaction times* (pp. 25–72). New York: Academic Press.

Walker, S., Bruce, V., & O'Malley, C. (1995). Facial identity and facial speech processing: Familiar faces and voices in the McGurk effect. *Perception and Psychophysics*, *57*, 1124–1133.

Welford, A. T. (1980). Choice reaction time: Basic concepts. In A. T. Welford (Ed.), *Reaction times* (pp. 73–128). New York: Academic Press.

Wenger, M. J., & Townsend, J. T. (2000). Basic response time tools for studying general processing capacity in attention, perception, and cognition. *The Journal of General Psychology*, *127*(1), 67–99.

Wenger, M. J., & Townsend (2001). Faces as gestalt stimuli: Process characteristics. In M. J. Wenger, & J. T. Townsend (Eds.), *On face perception and cognition*. Erlbaum Press.

Wenger, M. J., & Townsend, J. T. (2006). On the costs and benefits of faces and words: Process characteristics of feature search in highly meaningful stimuli. *Journal of Experimental Psychology: Human Perception and Performance*, *45*, 283–323.

Attention and Perceptual Decision Making

10

Cheng-Ta Yang
National Cheng Kung University, Tainan, Taiwan

Attention and Perceptual Decision Making

Human information processing is limited in capacity (Baddeley, 1981; Broadbent, 1965). Selective attention plays an important role in reducing information overload by prioritizing relevant information for further processing. Information is assumed to be selected according to the behavioral goals and inhibited when it is irrelevant (Desimone & Duncan, 1995; Johnston & Dark, 1986; Yantis, 2008). Yet, task-irrelevant stimulus salience also attracts attention (Schreij, Owens, & Theeuwes, 2008). In visual search, studies have shown that a stimulus that matches a top-down attentional set captures attention (Folk, Remington, & Johnston, 1992); for example, a stimulus that matches the contents of working memory is located faster in a selection task (Downing, 2000; Olivers, Meijer, & Theeuwes, 2006; Woodman & Luck, 2007). By contrast, other studies (Theeuwes, 2004, 2010) illustrate automatic attentional capture by task-irrelevant salient distractors (e.g., abrupt onset, color singleton). Both top-down goals and bottom-up salience, and their interaction, bias attention to select information at perceptual processing level (i.e., biasing attention to a specific visual dimension for further processing; Bisley & Goldberg, 2010; Desimone & Duncan, 1995; Egeth & Yantis, 1997; Fecteau & Munoz, 2006).

The interaction between top-down and bottom-up factors during perception should affect subsequent decision-making because information accumulation is thought to involve sampling evidence from the percept to drive a decision process. However, few studies have systematically examined how top-down factors such as the task set and bottom-up factors such as stimulus saliency interactively affect the detection decision. In this chapter, I first introduce the redundant-target detection task that will be used as a standard framework from which to study the perceptual decision-making process (Townsend & Nozawa, 1995). Second, I review decision-theoretic models that may be extended to explain how attention biases and facilitates decisions about the sensory stimuli and the subsequent decision-making process. Third, I review our recent work including published studies and unpublished data in which we propose that attention can affect how multiple signals are processed by altering the architecture of the decision-making process. Finally, I discuss the relationship between the concept of processing capacity in the literature of perceptual decision-making and the concept of attentional capacity in the literature of attention.

Systems Factorial Technology, DOI: 10.1016/B978-0-12-804315-8.00013-6

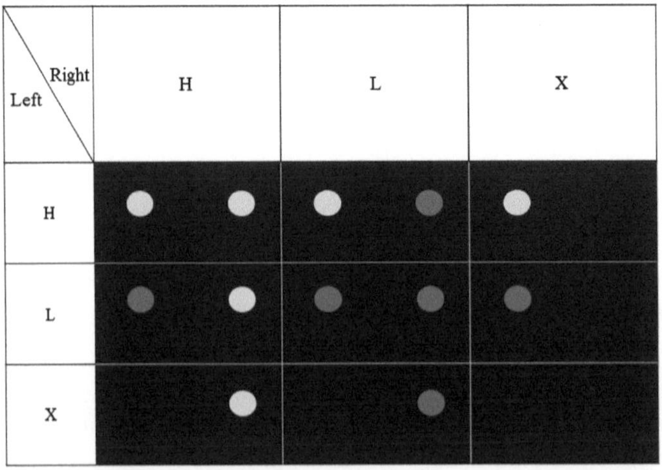

Figure 10.1 An illustration of the nine possible trials used in the redundant-target detection task. H represents high salience; L represents low salience; X represents no dot.

Redundant-Target Detection Task

The redundant-target detection task has been widely used to study the perceptual decision-making process (Chang & Yang, 2014; Eidels, Townsend, & Algom, 2010; Gondan, Lange, Rösler, & Röder, 2004; Grice, Canham, & Gwynne, 1984; Miller, 1982; Mordkoff & Yantis, 1991, 1993; Townsend & Nozawa, 1995; Yang, Little, & Hsu, 2014; Yu, Chang, & Yang, 2014). Townsend and Nozawa's (1995) classic paper introduced the conceptual framework known as systems factorial technology (SFT) to study information processing. In their version of the redundant-target task, participants are required to detect the appearance of a luminance stimulus or dot presented at one, both, or neither of two locations (left and right apart from the center fixation). The position of the dot (left/right) and the brightness level of the dot (high-/low-brightness) are factorially combined (see Fig. 10.1 for an illustration of the stimuli and design). As explained in the tutorial chapter (Altieri, Fifić, Little, & Yang, 2017), one can use several interaction contrasts to infer the processing architecture and the stopping rule, and one can infer the processing capacity by contrasting the reaction time distribution of the redundant-target trials to the single-target trials.

The processing characteristics of redundant-target detection with two luminance targets (i.e., in terms of SFT) are well-known (Eidels, Donkin, Brown, & Heathcote, 2010; Eidels, Houpt, Altieri, Pei, & Townsend, 2011; Townsend & Nozawa, 1995). Townsend and Nozawa (1995, Experiment 1) found that detection was consistent with a parallel self-terminating process that had limited capacity when there was no interstimulus contingency, suggesting that information from two locations is processed simultaneously and in parallel. When one of the processes is completed and the accumulated information reaches the detection threshold, a target-present response is made and the process is terminated. That is, the decision follows a minimum-time rule. Limited-capacity processing can be caused by inhibition across processes, or the allocation of limited resources to an individual process.

The question we seek to answer concerns the effect of spatial attention on the detection of redundant targets. If attention is oriented to one of the locations, does processing remain parallel and self-terminating? Or does attention alter the processing characteristics of detection? This is an important issue because different decision-theoretic models would make different predictions. The next section shows how the results of manipulating spatial attention in redundant-target detection challenge the basic assumptions of several decision models. A new perspective (termed the *relative saliency hypothesis*, Yang, 2011; Yang, Chang, & Wu, 2013; Yang, Hsu, Huang, & Yeh, 2011; Yang et al., 2014), is then introduced to characterize the impact of attention on decision process in target detection.

Decision-Theoretic Models

In the literature, researchers have proposed models to explain the processes underlying target detection (i.e., Bjork & Estes, 1971; Green & Swets, 1966; Kinchla, 1974; McLaughlin, Masterson, & Herrmann, 1972; Miller, 1982; Mordkoff & Yantis, 1991; Ratcliff & Smith, 2004; Wolford, Wessel, & Estes, 1968). Here, two of the most well-known models are reviewed to help elucidate how classic theoretical frameworks may predict the effect of attention on the process of detecting redundant targets.

The first model is the multidimensional signal detection model (SDT, Green & Swets, 1966); termed general recognition theory (GRT; Ashby, 2000; Townsend, Houpt, & Silbert, 2012). GRT generalizes the unidimensional Thurstonian-style SDT model to the case where the signals are multidimensional. This model conceptualizes the impact of attention on redundant-target detection in the following manner. Multiple signals from different locations are assumed to be processed simultaneously and in parallel. Evidence from different locations is weighted and pooled together. When the sum of the activation exceeds the decision criterion, participants will make a "yes" response; otherwise, they will respond that no target is detected. Attention can affect the weighting process prior to decision-making. When attention is oriented to one location, that location is given a higher weight than the other location, but it is still the sum of the information that drives the decision. That is, attention does not influence the architecture of multiple-signal processing in the redundant-target detection task.

Second, the diffusion decision model (DDM, Ratcliff, 1978), an example of a sequential sampling model (e.g., the runs model, Audley & Pike, 1965; recruitment models, LaBerge, 1962; accumulator models, Smith & Vickers, 1988), allows one to predict both accuracy and reaction time. The DDM is a continuous analog of a random walk model (Bogacz, Brown, Moehlis, Holmes, & Cohen, 2006). The DDM assumes that decisions are never reached instantaneously and that they are error prone. The DDM furthers the understanding of how a decision process evolves over time to reach correct and incorrect decisions. This model has been adapted to model simple reaction time data (e.g., Smith, 1995) and decision-making (e.g., Busemeyer & Townsend, 1993).

The DDM assumes that information from multiple locations is accumulated into a single evidence accumulation process that drives a decision. The accumulation of information begins from a starting point (z) and continues until the total amount of accumulated information reaches either a positive response boundary (a) (i.e., a target is detected) or a negative response boundary (0) (i.e., no target is detected). A starting point of $a/2$ ensures that the participants are not biased toward any response. The response time of a decision is the time required to reach a decision boundary (decision time) plus the time for encoding and the response execution time (*Ter*), also known as non-decision time or base time. The rate at which a process approaches a boundary, that is, the mean amount of information accumulated per unit of time, is called the drift rate (v). In the DDM view, attending to a location could increase the rate of information accumulation for the target at the attended location. Yet, biasing attention to a particular location should not change the architecture of multiple signal processing.

To summarize, both the SDT (Green & Swets, 1966) and DDM (Ratcliff, 1978) assume that information from multiple locations is pooled together into a single decision process. Attentional orienting to one of the locations would not change how multiple processes are conducted prior to decision making. Attention only affects the weighting process or the rate of information accumulation (the *weighted sum principle*). Recently, other attention models, including models by Bundesen (1990) and Smith and Ratcliff (2009) also assume that attention does not change the information processing architecture. Smith and Sewell (2013) generalized the integrated system model of Smith and Ratcliff (2009) to obtain a competitive interaction theory of attentional selection and decision making in brief, multi-element display. In this model, different tasks (e.g., detection, visual search) lead to different types of inhibition that can affect the strength of the evidence from each target that enters the decision process. The decision is conceptualized as a diffusion model with a rate that changes as perceptual and memory processes (e.g., serial search, lateral inhibition) change the rate of processing for the YES/NO decision. The success of this model then leads directly to the question about how architecture changes in detection – and prompts an investigation using SFT. In the following section, I will discuss the alternative processing models that can explain the decision-making process in redundant-target detection.

Alternative Processing Models

The order of multiple signal processing, emphasized in the previous section, is one of the properties of decision making (i.e., when the processing is coactive). According to SFT (Townsend & Nozawa, 1995), the decision-making process can be characterized by four important properties, including processing architecture (Egeth, 1966; Fifić, Nosofsky, & Townsend, 2008; Townsend, 1990; Townsend & Ashby, 1983; Townsend & Fifić, 2004; Townsend & Wenger, 2004a), stopping rule (Townsend, 2001; Townsend & Colonius, 1997; Townsend & Nozawa, 1995), processing dependency (Blaha, Johnson, & Townsend, 2007; Eidels et al., 2011; Mordkoff & Yantis, 1991, 1993), and processing capacity (Eidels et al., 2011; Fitousi & Wenger, 2011; Houpt & Townsend, 2012; Houpt, Townsend, & Donkin, 2014; Neufeld, Townsend,

& Jette, 2007; Townsend & Ashby, 1978; Townsend & Eidels, 2011; Townsend & Nozawa, 1995; Townsend & Nozawa, 1997; Townsend & Wenger, 2004b; Wenger & Gibson, 2004; Wenger & Townsend, 2000). These properties and their inferences are introduced in the tutorial chapter (Altieri et al., 2017).

SDT and DDM accounts can be thought of as being coactive, regardless of whether the evidence accumulation occurs as a random-walk process (Fifić, Little & Nosofsky, 2010) or as a diffusion process (Houpt & Townsend, 2011). Serial self-terminating model, serial exhaustive model, parallel self-terminating model, and parallel exhaustive model can be considered alternatives to the coactive processing architecture assumed by SDT and DDM. For example, in a parallel model, signals at different locations are processed in parallel and simultaneously and information is accumulated into different accumulators. In a serial model, multiple signals are processed in sequence, without any overlap between the processing times. In addition, whether a decision follows a winner-takes-all rule is dependent on the logical operation (i.e., OR vs AND) adopted in a task.

Relative Saliency Hypothesis

In contrast to the SDT (Green & Swets, 1966) and the DDM (Ratcliff, 1978) which assume a coactive processing architecture for detecting redundant targets, we (Yang et al., 2014) have proposed the relative saliency hypothesis, which assumes that decision making is flexible and can vary according to manipulations of attention. When information from two locations is equally salient and important for decision-making, participants should adopt a parallel processing strategy. By contrast, when the information at one location is more salient or more important than the information at the other location, participants may adopt a serial processing strategy. In this context, participants would first process the location that is more likely to contain a target dot and then process the location that is less likely to contain a target dot.

The relative saliency hypothesis challenges the basic assumption of coactive processing adopted in the SDT and DDM accounts. In these two accounts, the *process-invariance view* is the core assumption. From this assumption, one would expect the processing architecture to be invariant to any manipulation of attention in the context of redundant-target detection. That is, regardless of whether attention is biased or equally distributed, a coactive processing strategy is assumed. By contrast, the relative saliency hypothesis allows the flexibility of a shift between serial processing and parallel processing during decision making when participants' attention changes from an equal-distribution mode to a biased mode.

To examine this hypothesis, we have conducted a series of studies with manipulations that attempt to bias attention toward one of the locations, including spatial cueing, probability information, attentional instructions, and payoff.

Table 10.1 Summary of the experimental manipulations in our studies which combined the redundant-target detection task and the Posner's spatial cueing manipulations

	Cue type	Logical rule	Cue validity
Yang et al. (2014)	Exogenous	OR-rule	Uninformative cue/ informative cue
Yang and Chang (2014)	Exogenous	AND-rule	
Chang et al. (2015)	Endogenous	OR-rule	
Not yet studied	Endogenous	AND-rule	

Spatial Cueing

Attention can be oriented to a location via spatial cueing. In Posner's classic spatial cueing task, spatial attention can be cued in two ways (Posner, 1980; Posner, Snyder, & Davidson, 1980). An exogenous cue (e.g., abrupt onset) can direct attention to a cued location in a bottom-up manner, involuntarily, and automatically (referred to as *exogenous* or reflexive attention). On the other hand, an endogenous cue (e.g., a central arrow) can also direct attention to a cued location in a top-down manner, voluntarily, and consciously (referred to as *endogenous* control). Exogenous attention is drawn to a cued location due to the physical salience of the cue, whereas endogenous attention is directed toward a cued location by interpreting a cue guiding attention to a particular location.

As previous studies have shown, attentional orienting can boost the processing of a cued location to improve the accuracy of detecting a target and decrease the response time for the cued location (Posner, 1980; Posner et al., 1980). However, it is still unclear whether and how the decision-making process is affected by attentional orienting. We (Chang, Yu, Little, & Yang, 2015; Yang & Chang, 2014; Yang et al., 2014), therefore, conducted a series of studies integrating Posner's cueing method in the redundant-target detection paradigm. After a fixation point, a cue display (an abrupt onset or a central arrow) was presented to the participants. The participants were told to ignore the cue. Afterwards, a test display which contained two, one, or zero dots was presented. Participants were required to detect the target and make a decision according to the logical rule. The type of a cue (exogenous vs. endogenous cue), the validity of a cue (uninformative vs. informative), and the logical rule of decision-making (OR-rule vs. AND-rule) were manipulated in different experiments. See Table 10.1 for a summary of the experimental manipulations adopted in these studies.

Two important questions are raised: (i) *Does the type of attentional control and cue validity interactively affect the processing architecture?* If participants involuntarily and mandatorily follow an exogenous cue to bias attention to the cued location for target detection decision, serial processing may be expected regardless of its validity. When attention is controlled in a top-down manner by an uninformative endogenous cue, participants could ignore the cue and maintain a parallel processing strategy for target detection. Participants may adopt a serial processing strategy when the endogenous cue can predict the target location. That is, cue type and cue validity should interactively affect the processing architecture. (ii) *Does the processing architecture change according to the logical rule of decision-making?* In an OR-rule task, a correct decision can be made based on partial information from a cued location. As a result, both parallel processing for both locations (i.e., parallel self-terminating) and serially focusing on only the cued location (i.e., serial self-terminating) may be regarded as optimal strategies resulting in reduced effort and high accuracy. By contrast, in an AND-rule task, a correct decision requires the participants to mandatorily process both locations because a "yes" response is defined by the detection of the presence of two dots at both locations. Consequently, the benefits of parallel processing may outweigh any benefits of spatial cueing. Participants may adopt parallel exhaustive processing regardless of cue validity.

In Yang et al. (2014), an exogenous cue was used to cue the target location; the cue was either of 100% (informative cue) or 50% (uninformative cue) validity. The results indicated that the validity of an exogenous cue affected the processing architecture and processing capacity. When a cue was 50% valid, all of the participants demonstrated a positive MIC and positive SIC for all times t, suggesting that they adopted a parallel self-terminating processing strategy. In addition, processing capacity ranged from unlimited to moderately limited capacity, as $C(t)$ was equal to 1 or less than 1 for all times t. These results are consistent with Townsend and Nozawa's (1995, Experiment 1) initial redundant-target detection results.

By contrast, when a cue was 100% valid, all of the participants (each of whom showed parallel self-terminating processing in the 50% validity condition) switched to a serial self-terminating processing strategy, with a zero MIC and zero SIC for all times t. That is, participants first processed the cued location, and if the information was sufficient for decision making, a positive response was made (i.e., a target is detected). Otherwise, processing switched to the uncued location. Generally, capacity became much more limited in the informative-cue condition than in the uninformative-cue condition, as $C(t)$ was less than 1 for all times t, reflecting the switch to serial processing.

These findings are interesting and meaningful for several reasons. First, the authors did not find any evidence for coactive processing, which challenges the basic assumption held by the process-invariance view. The observation of a shift between parallel and serial processing was also against the prediction from this class of models. Second, although attention is known to be automatically and involuntarily drawn to a cued location through exogenous cueing, serial processing is not mandatory. Participants can exert effective top-down attentional control to utilize the knowledge of the cue validity to adjust their decision strategy. Specifically, when a cue cannot predict the target location, participants process the locations in parallel; one plausible explanation is that participants widen their attentional window to encompass both of the possible target locations. This diffuse attentional window results in parallel processing for both the cued and uncued locations. By contrast, when a cue is likely to predict the target location, participants strategically narrow their attentional window to process the cued location first. The focused attentional window is reflected by the fixed-order, serial first-terminating processing strategy. Top-down knowledge of cue validity overrides the mandatory capture induced by exogenous cueing.

We (Yang & Chang, 2014) tested whether the requirement of AND rule in decision making could alter the processing architecture. The AND task requires participants to exhaustively process both of the possible target locations; this may favor parallel processing. However, the results showed that the processing architecture varied according to the cue validity. The AND rule only affected the decisional stopping rule: participants followed an exhaustive rule to make a decision. Of course, this makes sense since terminating early with an AND stopping rule would lead to a decrease in accuracy. Specifically, most participants (5 of 6) adopted a parallel exhaustive processing strategy with negative MIC and negative SIC for all times t in the uninformative-cue condition and a serial exhaustive processing strategy with zero MIC and S-shape SIC in the informative-cue condition. One participant adopted a serial exhaustive processing strategy throughout the entire experiment.

We (Chang et al., 2015) further examined whether endogenous attentional cueing would replicate our previous results (Yang et al., 2014). This results is not necessarily a given since endogenous and exogenous attention appear to be two distinct mechanisms (Rohenkohl, Coull, & Nobre, 2011) with separate neural systems (Corbetta & Shulman, 2002). In addition, we also investigated whether decision-making strategies are affected by the test order of the cue conditions. Given that the selection history affects attentional processing (Awh, Belopolsky, & Theeuwes, 2012; Yeh, Lee, Chen, & Chen, 2014), it is possible that the decision-making strategies would be affected by the previously adopted strategies. Using a central arrow as a cue, we found a parallel-to-serial processing shift as cue validity varied, and more interestingly, the changes of the processing architecture depend on the test order. Specifically, we asked three participants to perform the uninformative-cue condition before the informative-cue condition and vice versa for the other three participants. Results showed that the participants who first performed the uninformative-cue condition started with a parallel self-terminating strategy with positive MIC and positive SIC for all times t. When they switched to the informative-cue condition, these participants changed to a serial self-terminating strategy with zero MIC and zero SIC for all times t. On the other hand, participants who first performed the informative-cue condition adopted a serial self-terminating strategy (zero MIC and zero SIC for all times t) throughout the entire experiment regardless of the cue validity. For all the participants, the processing capacity was of unlimited capacity to limited capacity in the uninformative-cue condition as $C(t)$ was equal to or less than 1 for all times t and capacity was of moderately limited capacity in the informative-cue condition as $C(t)$ were less than 1 for all times t. The more limited processing capacity in the informative-cue condition reflects a focused attentional mode by serially focusing one location then the other.

Similar to our previous findings (Yang et al., 2014), these results were inconsistent with the predictions based on the process-invariance view as the processing architecture varied as the cue validity changed. Most importantly, the test order effect was observed when an endogenous cue was adopted in the experiment whereas this effect was not observed when an exogenous cue was used. Individual differences manifested when top-down control was influenced by an endogenous cue and cue validity.

Participants who began the task with an uninformative endogenous cue showed the same pattern of results as participants who processed an exogenous cue. For these participants, they altered the processing strategy once the knowledge of 100% cue validity became evident. By contrast, participants who began the task with an informative endogenous cue did not alter the processing strategy even when the cue became uninformative. This asymmetry has been observed in another experimental context (a dual-task context; Fischer, Gottschalk, & Dreisbach, 2014), showing that participants shifted their control mode when a previous trial demanded weak conflict control and the current trial demanded strong conflict control, whereas they did not relax their control mode when a previous trial demanded strong conflict control and the current trial demanded weak conflict control.

In sum, we found that both exogenous and endogenous attentional cueing can affect the decision-making process of detecting redundant targets. The type of attentional control and test order of cue condition interactively affected the processing architecture. The processing capacity was affected by the cue validity. The manipulation of the decision rule affected the decisional stopping rule. The relative saliency hypothesis allows the flexibility of parallel-serial processing shift depending on whether attention is biased toward a location via spatial cueing.

Probability Information

In addition to the attentional bias induced by spatial cueing, people are sensitive to the spatial and temporal probabilities that govern target location and presentation (Geng & Behrmann, 2002, 2005; Jones & Kaschak, 2012). The *target location probability* denotes the likelihood that a target appearing at one location. This probability is regarded as an attentional cue that biases spatial attention; however, the bias cannot be explained in the exogenous/endogenous framework (Geng & Behrmann, 2002, 2005; Zhao, Al-Aidroos, & Turk-Browne, 2013). Chang, Little, and Yang (2016) tested whether the target location probability influences the decision-making process of redundant-target detection as spatial cueing does (Chang et al., 2015; Yang & Chang, 2014; Yang et al., 2014).

In Chang et al. (2016), four participants were required to perform a redundant-target detection task where the target location probability (i.e., the relative frequency of a target appearing at one location to the other location) and attentional instruction (i.e., participants were explicitly told to pay attention to a location with high target probability) were manipulated. Results showed individual differences. When a target appeared at two locations with equal frequency (Experiment 1), two participants adopted parallel self-terminating processing with unlimited capacity to limited capacity [positive MIC, positive SIC for all times t, $C(t)$ were equal to 1 or less than 1] whereas the other two participants adopted coactive processing with supercapacity [positive MIC, S-shape SIC, $C(t)$ were greater than 1]. When a target appeared at one location (e.g., left position) more frequently than at the other location (e.g., right position) without explicit attentional instruction (Experiment 2), results showed that all four participants adopted parallel self-terminating processing with limited capacity [positive MIC, positive SIC, $C(t)$ were less than 1].

After the participants completed the two experiments, we asked them to report whether or not they noticed any differences across the experiments and estimate the probability of a target presenting at each location. The postexperimental interviews revealed that the participants were not consciously aware of the relative target location probability. Implicit learning for the target location probability resulted in less efficient processing fort the redundant targets although it was not sufficient to cause a parallel-to-serial processing shift (see the results of Experiments 1 and 2). The more limited-capacity processing may have occurred because attention was biased toward the high-probability location and processing for the low-probability location may thereby interfere the processing for the high-probability location, leading to less efficient processing. In addition, a lack of the change from parallel to serial processing highlights the crucial role of controlled attention in strategy selection.

Finally, when participants were explicitly instructed to attend to the high-probability location (Experiment 3), the participants who had unlimited to limited capacity in Experiment 1 altered their strategies and were found to behave in accord with a serial self-terminating processing strategy with limited capacity. By contrast, the participants who had supercapacity in Experiment 1 maintained a parallel self-terminating processing strategy with limited capacity. The individual differences implied that processing capacity may constrain the adoption of a decision strategy to optimize the detection performance. That is, a certain type of processing strategies (i.e., coactive-parallel processing) might be available if a person has higher capacity in the unbiased condition. However, this is different from how we normally consider the link between processing architecture and capacity; we normally assume that a certain architecture has a certain capacity (e.g., serial models which assume independence between the serially-arrayed processes have limited capacity; however, that does not imply that capacity-sharing serial models are not possible). To break the circularity of this argument, future research is encouraged to investigate the individual differences in the processing capacity and the processing architecture.

Altogether, our results (Chang et al., 2016) supported the idea that attention is biased toward the high-probability location, which in turns affects the processing architecture and the processing capacity. Two participants showed coactivity in Experiment 1; however, the process-invariance view would not predict the extinction of coactivity when a target appeared at one location more frequently than at the other location. The results were consistent with our previous findings (Chang et al., 2015; Yang & Chang, 2014; Yang et al., 2014): an attentional manipulation can cause a shift from parallel to serial processing but this parallel-to-serial processing shift was modulated by the participants processing capacities.

Payoffs

Monetary rewards and incidental visual statistical learning of probabilities and regularities can also drive visual attention (Anderson, Laurent, & Yantis, 2011; Chelazzi, Perlato, Santandrea, & Della Libera, 2013; Chun & Jiang, 1998; Raymond & O'Brien, 2009). When the participants were told upfront about the payoff matrix indicating that a correct detection of a target at one location would receive more rewards than the detection of a target at the other location, their attention was drawn to the location with higher reward. This is known as the value-driven attentional capture. On the other hand, payoffs may affect the response criterion (i.e., the detection threshold of the high-reward location is lower) (Link & Heath, 1975) or the information accumulation rate (i.e., the drift rate of the high-reward location increases) (Ashby, 1983; Ratcliff, 1981). We (Yang & Hu, 2012) therefore examined whether the manipulation of payoffs can also result in a change of processing architecture while detecting redundant targets.

In that study (Yang & Hu, 2012), participants were first shown a payoff matrix and were told that their reward would be in proportion to their final scores. In Experiment 1 (unbiased payoffs), after a correct/incorrect detection of a left target, the participants would receive a $+1/-1$ point. Results showed that 10 of 12 participants adopted a parallel self-terminating processing strategy with unlimited capacity to limited capacity [all had positive MIC, positive SIC for all times t, $C(t)$ were equal to or less than 1]; the other two participants adopted coactive processing with supercapacity [both had positive MIC, S-shape SIC, $C(t)$ were greater than 1]. The observation of individual differences in the processing strategy was similar to what we (Chang et al., 2016) found with equal target probability at two locations.

In Experiment 2 (biased payoffs), after a correct/incorrect detection of a left target, the participants would receive a $+5/-5$ point; after a correct/incorrect detection of a right target, the participants would receive a $+1/-1$ point. Results showed that only one of the participants who adopted a parallel self-terminating processing strategy in the unbiased condition altered his decision strategy to a serial self-terminating processing strategy with extremely limited capacity [zero MIC, zero SIC for all times t, $C(t)$ were around 0.5]. The serial processing strategy occurred because this participant was extremely biased toward the high-reward location at the cost of being inaccurate in detecting a target at the low-reward location. Most participants (8 of 10, including one participant who adopted coactive processing in Experiment 1, and two participants who adopted parallel self-terminating processing in Experiment 1 dropped out) adopted a parallel self-terminating processing strategy with unlimited capacity to limited capacity [positive MIC, positive SIC for all times t, $C(t)$ were equal to or less than 1]. One of the participants who adopted coactive processing in the unbiased condition maintained coactive processing with supercapacity [positive MIC, S-shape SIC, $C(t)$ were greater than 1].

According to the results, we speculated that parallel processing persisted for most participants because the low-reward location was still rewarded with a greater than 0 payoff. In Experiment 3, after a correct or incorrect detection of a left target, the participants received $+10$ or -10 points, respectively. After a correct or incorrect detection of a right target, participants received no reward. In this experiment, four participants (4 of 5; the other five participants including one participant who adopted serial self-terminating processing and four participants who adopted parallel self-terminating processing in Experiment 2 dropped out) persisted with a parallel self-terminating processing strategy with unlimited capacity to limited capacity [positive MIC, positive SIC for all times t, $C(t)$ were equal to or less than 1]. The one participant who adopted coactive processing in Experiments 1 and 2 still adopted coactive processing with supercapacity [positive MIC, S-shape SIC, $C(t)$ were greater than 1].

The results are intriguing for several reasons. First, we found individual differences in redundant-target detection decision strategies (i.e., coactive processing and parallel self-terminating processing) when attention is equally distributed to the two locations in the unbiased condition. Second, only one participant altered his decision strategy from parallel self-terminating processing to serial self-terminating processing with biased reward contingency. Most participants maintained their processing strategies even when no reward was given after the correct detection at the null-reward location. Hence, unlike endogenous and exogenous cues, the reward manipulation did not cause a change in processing architecture. This is not due to ineffectiveness of the reward as we found that for all of the participants the response time of detecting a target at the high-reward location was faster than that at the low-reward location. Hence, the reward manipulation was effective, but possibly did not result in a change in the processing architecture.

Taken together with the cuing results, it is suggested that the mechanism of value-based attentional orienting is different from the mechanisms of the other types of attentional orienting. Future research is encouraged to study how different types of attentional orienting alter the adoption of decision-making strategies.

Attentional Capacity and Processing Capacity

The relationship between attentional capacity and processing capacity is intriguing. It is well-known that the attentional mechanism is limited in capacity (Kahneman, 1973); why is it possible to observe supercapacity or unlimited-capacity during decision-making? One possibility is that the attentional capacity describes the limitation of the amount of information to be selected into the decision-making process and the processing capacity describes the information processing efficiency during decision making such that the two capacities measure the limitation at different processing stages and are independent from one another. Fig. 10.2 shows how the attentional mechanism and the decision-making mechanism operate. Attention can be regarded as a filter to select relevant information for further processing based on the behavioral goal (Broadbent, 1965; Deutsch & Deutsch, 1963; Treisman, 1969) and the information that is irrelevant to the task or not salient enough is filtered out or attenuated.

Take an unlimited-capacity independent parallel model for an example (Parallel 1, Townsend & Ashby, 1983, pp. 83–84).[1] Assuming that the total available information is M, a limited amount of information (i.e., attentional capacity, $K = M/m$) can be selected into further processing by m individual channel. So, what remains available for the decision-making process is the K information that was filtered through attention. Let $C(n)$ refer to the processing capacity allocated to each individual channel. Then, a *Parallel 1* model assumes that every operating channel receives K capacity, so $C(n) = K$. Limited-capacity processing is defined by $C(n) < K$, unlimited-capacity

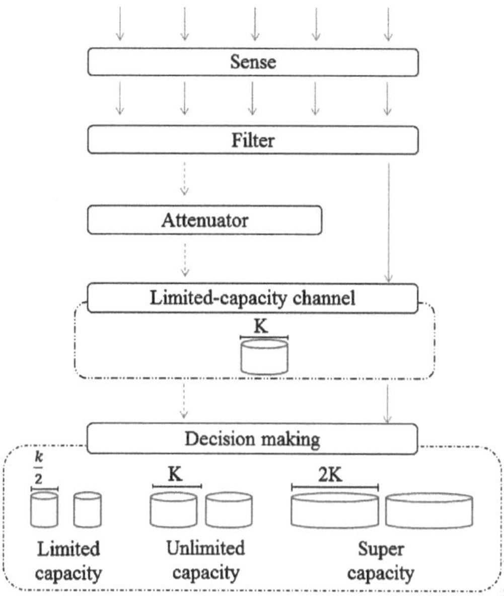

Figure 10.2 A schematic diagram shows how the attentional mechanism and the decision-making mechanism operate until a decision is made. Limited amount of information (K) is selected into the decision making process through attentional selection. During decision making, the processing capacity allocated to individual channel can be $K/2$ (limited-capacity processing), K (unlimited-capacity processing), or $2K$ (supercapacity processing).

processing by $C(n) = K$, and supercapacity processing by $C(n) > K$. Therefore, the first processing stage of attentional selection selects information at perception with limited capacity; but the second-stage of decision-making may possess a wide range of capacity (limited-capacity to supercapacity) depending on the processing architecture and the stopping rule.

Although attentional capacity appears to be independent from the processing capacity, the capacity of executive attention may relate the processing capacity in decision making. Our recent study (Yu et al., 2014) found that the processing capacity in a visual-auditory detection task was positively correlated to the operation span, which is a measure of working memory capacity (Conway et al., 2005); however, the processing capacities of double-dot detection and color-shape detection were unrelated to the operation span. Working memory capacity represents a limitation of executive attention in monitoring and integrating information from different hypothesized slave systems (Baddeley, 1992; Baddeley & Hitch, 1974; Engle, 2010). It is for future research to clarify how different measures of capacity relate to each other as independent or overlapping constructs (i.e., attentional capacity represents the selection limit whereas both working memory capacity and processing capacity may represent different aspects of capacity of information processing).

Concluding Remarks

The relative saliency hypothesis highlights the flexibility of the perceptual decision mechanism and the role of top-down attentional control and conscious awareness in selecting a decision strategy to optimize redundant-target detection decision. In considering the relationship between attentional capacity and processing capacity, it seems that attentional processing which is limited in capacity acts at an earlier perceptual processing stage. On the other hand, the decision-making stage of processing might be observed to be of limited, unlimited, or supercapacity even if it relies on processing a limited amount of information filtered through attention.

Acknowledgement

I thank Dr. Y.-Y. Yeh for providing helpful suggestions and comments.

References

Altieri, N., Fifić, M., Little, D. R., & Yang, C.-T. (2017). Historical foundations and a tutorial introduction to systems factorial technology. In D. R. Little, N. Altieri, M. Fifić, & C.-T. Yang (Eds.), *Systems factorial technology: A theory driven methodology for the identification of perceptual and cognitive mechanisms*. Elsevier (in this book).

Anderson, B. A., Laurent, P. A., & Yantis, S. (2011). Value-driven attentional capture. *Proceedings of the National Academy of Sciences*, *108*(25), 10367–10371.

Ashby, F. G. (1983). A biased random-walk model for two choice reaction times. *Journal of Mathematical Psychology*, *27*, 277–297.

Ashby, F. G. (2000). A stochastic version of general recognition theory. *Journal of Mathematical Psychology*, *44*(2), 310–329.

Audley, R. J., & Pike, A. R. (1965). Some alternative stochastic models of choice 1. *British Journal of Mathematical and Statistical Psychology*, *18*(2), 207–225.

Awh, E., Belopolsky, A. V., & Theeuwes, J. (2012). Top-down versus bottom-up attentional control: a failed theoretical dichotomy. *Trends in Cognitive Sciences*, *16*(8), 437–443.

Baddeley, A. (1981). The concept of working memory: A view of its current state and probable future development. *Cognition*, *10*(1–3), 17–23.

Baddeley, A. (1992). Working memory. *Science*, *255*(5044), 556–559.

Baddeley, A., & Hitch, G. J. (1974). Working memory. In G. H. Bower (Ed.), *Advances in research and theory*. In *Psychology of learning and motivation: Vol. VIII* (pp. 47–90). New York: Academic Press.

Bisley, J. W., & Goldberg, M. E. (2010). Attention, intention, and priority in the parietal lobe. *Annual Review of Neuroscience*, *33*(1), 1–21.

Bjork, E. L., & Estes, W. K. (1971). Detection and placement of redundant signal elements in tachistoscopic displays of letters. *Perception & Psychophysics*, *9*(5), 439–442.

Blaha, L. M., Johnson, S. A., & Townsend, J. T. (2007). An information processing investigation of hierarchical form perception: Evidence for parallel processing. *Visual Cognition*, *15*(1), 73–77.

Bogacz, R., Brown, E., Moehlis, J., Holmes, P., & Cohen, J. D. (2006). The physics of optimal decision making: A formal analysis of models of performance in two-alternative forced-choice tasks. *Psychological Review, 113*(4), 700–765.

Broadbent, D. E. (1965). Information processing in the nervous system. *Science, 150*(695), 457–462.

Bundesen, C. (1990). A theory of visual attention. *Psychological Review, 97*(4), 523–547.

Busemeyer, J. R., & Townsend, J. T. (1993). Decision field theory: A dynamic-cognitive approach to decision making in an uncertain environment. *Psychological Review, 100*(3), 432–459.

Chang, T.-Y., Little, D. R., & Yang, C.-T. (2016). Selective attention modulates the effect of target location probability on redundant signal processing. *Attention, Perception & Psychophysics, 78*(6), 1603–1624.

Chang, T.-Y., & Yang, C.-T. (2014). Individual differences in Zhong–Yong tendency and processing capacity. *Frontiers in Psychology, 5*.

Chang, T.-Y., Yu, J.-C., Little, D.R., & Yang, C.-T. (2015). *Exogenous and endogenous cues differentially influence the processing architecture during perceptual decision making*. Paper presented at the 48th annual meeting of the society for mathematical psychology, Newport Beach, California.

Chelazzi, L., Perlato, A., Santandrea, E., & Della Libera, C. (2013). Rewards teach visual selective attention. *Vision Research, 85*, 58–72.

Chun, M. M., & Jiang, Y. (1998). Contextual cueing: Implicit learning and memory of visual context guides spatial attention. *Cognitive Psychology, 36*(1), 28–71.

Conway, A. A., Kane, M., Bunting, M., Hambrick, D. Z., Wilhelm, O., & Engle, R. (2005). Working memory span tasks: A methodological review and user's guide. *Psychonomic Bulletin & Review, 12*(5), 769–786.

Corbetta, M., & Shulman, G. L. (2002). Control of goal-directed and stimulus-driven attention in the brain. *Nature Reviews. Neuroscience, 3*(3), 201–215.

Desimone, R., & Duncan, J. (1995). Neural mechanisms of selective visual attention. *Annual Review of Neuroscience, 18*, 193–222.

Deutsch, J. A., & Deutsch, D. (1963). Attention: Some theoretical considerations. *Psychological Review, 70*(1), 80–90.

Downing, P. E. (2000). Interactions between visual working memory and selective attention. *Psychological Science, 11*(6), 467–473.

Egeth, H. E. (1966). Parallel versus serial processes in multidimensional stimulus discrimination. *Attention, Perception, & Psychophysics, 1*(4), 245–252.

Egeth, H. E., & Yantis, S. (1997). Visual attention: Control, representation, and time course. *Annual Review of Psychology, 48*, 269–297.

Eidels, A., Donkin, C., Brown, S., & Heathcote, A. (2010). Converging measures of workload capacity. *Psychonomic Bulletin & Review, 17*(6), 763–771.

Eidels, A., Houpt, J. W., Altieri, N., Pei, L., & Townsend, J. T. (2011). Nice guys finish fast and bad guys finish last: Facilitatory vs. inhibitory interaction in parallel systems. *Journal of Mathematical Psychology, 55*(2), 176–190.

Eidels, A., Townsend, J. T., & Algom, D. (2010). Comparing perception of Stroop stimuli in focused versus divided attention paradigms: evidence for dramatic processing differences. *Cognition, 114*(2), 129–150.

Engle, R. (2010). Role of working-memory capacity in cognitive control. *Current Anthropology, 51*(S1).

Fecteau, J. H., & Munoz, D. P. (2006). Salience, relevance, and firing: a priority map for target selection. *Trends in Cognitive Sciences, 10*(8), 382–390.

Fifić, M., Little, D. R., & Nosofsky, R. M. (2010). Logical-rule models of classification response times: A synthesis of mental-architecture, random-walk, and decision-bound approaches. *Psychological Review*, *117*(2), 309–348.

Fifić, M., Nosofsky, R. M., & Townsend, J. T. (2008). Information-processing architectures in multidimensional classification: A validation test of the systems factorial technology. *Journal of Experimental Psychology: Human Perception and Performance*, *34*(2), 356–375.

Fischer, R., Gottschalk, C., & Dreisbach, G. (2014). Context-sensitive adjustment of cognitive control in dual-task performance. *Journal of Experimental Psychology: Learning, Memory, and Cognition*, *40*(2), 399–416.

Fitousi, D., & Wenger, M. J. (2011). Processing capacity under perceptual and cognitive load: A closer look at load theory. *Journal of Experimental Psychology: Human Perception and Performance*, *37*(3), 781–798.

Folk, C. L., Remington, R. W., & Johnston, J. C. (1992). Involuntary covert orienting is contingent on attentional control settings. *Journal of Experimental Psychology: Human Perception and Performance*, *18*(4), 1030–1044.

Geng, J. J., & Behrmann, M. (2002). Probability cuing of target location facilitates visual search implicitly in normal participants and patients with hemispatial neglect. *Psychological Science*, *13*(6), 520–525.

Geng, J. J., & Behrmann, M. (2005). Spatial probability as an attentional cue in visual search. *Perception & Psychophysics*, *67*(7), 1252–1268.

Gondan, M., Lange, K., Rösler, F., & Röder, B. (2004). The redundant target effect is affected by modality switch costs. *Psychonomic Bulletin & Review*, *11*(2), 307–313.

Green, D. M., & Swets, J. A. (1966). *Signal detection theory and psychophysics*. Oxford, England: John Wiley.

Grice, G., Canham, L., & Gwynne, J. W. (1984). Absence of a redundant-signals effect in a reaction time task with divided attention. *Perception & Psychophysics*, *36*(6), 565–570.

Houpt, J. W., & Townsend, J. T. (2011). An extension of SIC predictions to the Wiener coactive model. *Journal of Mathematical Psychology*, *55*(3), 267–270.

Houpt, J. W., & Townsend, J. T. (2012). Statistical measures for workload capacity analysis. *Journal of Mathematical Psychology*, *56*(5), 341–355.

Houpt, J. W., Townsend, J. T., & Donkin, C. (2014). A new perspective on visual word processing efficiency. *Acta Psychologica*, *145*, 118–127.

Johnston, W. A., & Dark, V. J. (1986). Selective attention. *Annual Review of Psychology*, *37*(1), 43–75.

Jones, J. L., & Kaschak, M. P. (2012). Global statistical learning in a visual search task. *Journal of Experimental Psychology: Human Perception & Performance*, *38*(1), 152–160.

Kahneman, D. (1973). *Attention and effort*. Englewood Cliffs, NJ: Prentice-Hall.

Kinchla, R. (1974). Detecting target elements in multielement arrays: A comfusability model. *Perception & Psychophysics*, *15*(1), 149–158.

LaBerge, D. (1962). A recruitment theory of simple behavior. *Psychometrika*, *27*(4), 375–396.

Link, S., & Heath, R. (1975). A sequential theory of psychological discrimination. *Psychometrika*, *40*(1), 77–105.

McLaughlin, J. P., Masterson, F. A., & Herrmann, D. J. (1972). Pattern redundancy and detection in very short-term memory. *Perception & Psychophysics*, *12*(2-B), 205–208.

Miller, J. (1982). Divided attention: Evidence for coactivation with redundant signals. *Cognitive Psychology*, *14*(2), 247–279.

Mordkoff, J. T., & Yantis, S. (1991). An interactive race model of divided attention. *Journal of Experimental Psychology: Human Perception and Performance*, *17*(2), 520–538.

Mordkoff, J. T., & Yantis, S. (1993). Dividing attention between color and shape: Evidence of coactivation. *Perception & Psychophysics, 53*(4), 357–366.

Neufeld, R. W. J., Townsend, J. T., & Jette, J. (Eds.). (2007). *Quantitative response time technology for measuring cognitive-processing capacity in clinical studies*. Washington, DC: American Psychological Association.

Olivers, C. N., Meijer, F., & Theeuwes, J. (2006). Feature-based memory-driven attentional capture: Visual working memory content affects visual attention. *Journal of Experimental Psychology: Human Perception and Performance, 32*(5), 1243–1265.

Posner, M. I. (1980). Orienting of attention. *The Quarterly Journal of Experimental Psychology, 32*(1), 3–25.

Posner, M. I., Snyder, C. R., & Davidson, B. J. (1980). Attention and the detection of signals. *Journal of Experimental Psychology. General, 109*(2), 160–174.

Ratcliff, R. (1978). A theory of memory retrieval. *Psychological Review, 85*(2), 59–108.

Ratcliff, R. (1981). A theory of order relations in perceptual matching. *Psychological Review, 88*(6), 552–572.

Ratcliff, R., & Smith, P. L. (2004). A comparison of sequential sampling models for two-choice reaction time. *Psychological Review, 111*(2), 333–367.

Raymond, J. E., & O'Brien, J. L. (2009). Selective visual attention and motivation: The consequences of value learning in an attentional blink task. *Psychological Science, 20*(8), 981–988.

Rohenkohl, G., Coull, J. T., & Nobre, A. C. (2011). Behavioural dissociation between exogenous and endogenous temporal orienting of attention. *PLoS ONE, 6*(1), e14620.

Schreij, D., Owens, C., & Theeuwes, J. (2008). Abrupt onsets capture attention independent of top-down control settings. *Perception & Psychophysics, 70*, 208–218.

Smith, P. L. (1995). Psychophysically principled models of visual simple reaction time. *Psychological Review, 102*(3), 567–593.

Smith, P. L., & Ratcliff, R. (2009). An integrated theory of attention and decision making in visual signal detection. *Psychological Review, 116*, 283–317.

Smith, P. L., & Sewell, D. K. (2013). A competitive interaction theory of attentional selection and decision making in brief, multielement displays. *Psychological Review, 120*(3), 589–627.

Smith, P. L., & Vickers, D. (1988). The accumulator model of two-choice discrimination. *Journal of Mathematical Psychology, 32*(2), 135–168.

Theeuwes, J. (2004). Top-down search strategies cannot override attentional capture. *Psychonomic Bulletin & Review, 11*(1), 65–70.

Theeuwes, J. (2010). Top-down and bottom-up control of visual selection. *Acta Psychologica, 135*(2), 77–99.

Townsend, J. T. (1990). Serial vs. parallel processing: Sometimes they look like Tweedledum and Tweedledee but they can (and should) be distinguished. *Psychological Science, 1*(1), 46–54.

Townsend, J. T. (2001). A clarification of self-terminating versus exhaustive variances in serial and parallel models. *Perception & Psychophysics, 63*(6), 1101–1106.

Townsend, J. T., & Ashby, F. G. (1978). Methods of modeling capacity in simple processing systems. In J. Castellan, & F. Restle (Eds.), *Cognitive theory, Vol. 3* (pp. 200–239). Hillsdale, NJ: Erlbaum.

Townsend, J. T., & Ashby, F. G. (1983). *The stochastic modeling of elementary psychological processes*. New York: Cambridge University Press.

Townsend, J. T., & Colonius, H. (1997). Parallel processing response times and experimental determination of the stopping rule. *Journal of Mathematical Psychology, 41*(4), 392–397.

Townsend, J. T., & Eidels, A. (2011). Workload capacity spaces: A unified methodology for response time measures of efficiency as workload is varied. *Psychonomic Bulletin & Review, 18*(4), 659–681.

Townsend, J. T., & Fifić, M. (2004). Parallel versus serial processing and individual differences in high-speed search in human memory. *Perception & Psychophysics, 66*(6), 953–962.

Townsend, J. T., Houpt, J. W., & Silbert, N. H. (2012). General recognition theory extended to include response times: Predictions for a class of parallel systems. *Journal of Mathematical Psychology, 56*(6), 476–494.

Townsend, J. T., & Nozawa, G. (1995). Spatio-temporal properties of elementary perception: An investigation of parallel, serial, and coactive theories. *Journal of Mathematical Psychology, 39*(4), 321–359.

Townsend, J. T., & Nozawa, G. (1997). Serial exhaustive models can violate the race model inequality: implications for architecture and capacity. *Psychological Review, 104*(3), 595–602.

Townsend, J. T., & Wenger, M. J. (2004a). The serial-parallel dilemma: A case study in a linkage of theory and method. *Psychonomic Bulletin & Review, 11*(3), 391–418.

Townsend, J. T., & Wenger, M. J. (2004b). A theory of interactive parallel processing: New capacity measures and predictions for a response time inequality series. *Psychological Review, 111*(4), 1003–1035.

Treisman, A. (1969). Strategies and models of selective attention. *Psychological Review, 76*(3), 282–299.

Wenger, M. J., & Gibson, B. S. (2004). Using hazard functions to assess changes in processing capacity in an attentional cuing Paradigm. *Journal of Experimental Psychology: Human Perception and Performance, 30*(4), 708–719.

Wenger, M. J., & Townsend, J. T. (2000). Basic response time tools for studying general processing capacity in attention, perception, and cognition. *Journal of General Psychology, 127*(1), 67–99.

Wolford, G. L., Wessel, D. L., & Estes, W. K. (1968). Further evidence concerning scanning and sampling assumptions of visual detection models. *Perception & Psychophysics, 3*(6), 439–444.

Woodman, G. F., & Luck, S. J. (2007). Do the contents of visual working memory automatically influence attentional selection during visual search? *Journal of Experimental Psychology: Human Perception and Performance, 33*(2), 363–377.

Yang, C.-T. (2011). Relative saliency in change signals affects perceptual comparison and decision processes in change detection. *Journal of Experimental Psychology: Human Perception & Performance, 37*(6), 1708–1728.

Yang, C.-T., & Chang, T.-Y. (2014). *The dynamic changes of the processing architecture in cued detection.* Paper presented at the 47th annual meeting of the society for mathematical psychology, Quebec, Canada.

Yang, C.-T., Chang, T.-Y., & Wu, C.-J. (2013). Relative change probability affects the decision process of detecting multiple feature changes. *Journal of Experimental Psychology: Human Perception & Performance, 39*(5), 1365–1385.

Yang, C.-T., Hsu, Y.-F., Huang, H.-Y., & Yeh, Y.-Y. (2011). Relative salience affects the process of detecting changes in orientation and luminance. *Acta Psychologica, 138*(3), 377–389.

Yang, C.-T., & Hu, Y. (2012). *Examining the effect of payoffs on stimulus detection in a redundant-target detection task.* Paper presented at the 45th annual meeting of the society for mathematical psychology, Columbus, Ohio.

Yang, C.-T., Little, D. R., & Hsu, C.-C. (2014). The influence of cueing on attentional focus in perceptual decision making. *Attention, Perception, & Psychophysics, 76*(8), 2256–2275.

Yantis, S. (2008). The neural basis of selective attention: Cortical sources and targets of attentional modulation. *Current Directions in Psychological Science*, *17*(2), 86–90.

Yeh, Y.-Y., Lee, S.-M., Chen, Y.-H., & Chen, Z. (2014). Selection history modulates the effects of dual mechanisms on flanker interference. *Journal of Experimental Psychology: Human Perception and Performance*, *40*(5), 2038–2055.

Yu, J.-C., Chang, T.-Y., & Yang, C.-T. (2014). Individual differences in working memory capacity and workload capacity. *Frontiers in Psychology*, *5*.

Zhao, J., Al-Aidroos, N., & Turk-Browne, N. B. (2013). Attention is spontaneously biased toward regularities. *Psychological Science*, *24*(5), 667–677.

Endnotes

1. I thank James T. Townsend and Daniel R. Little for providing helpful comments and suggestions.

Are Two Ears Always Better than One? The Capacity Function Says No

11

Jennifer J. Lentz, Yuan He, Amanda D. Hornbach
Indiana University Bloomington, Bloomington, IN, United States

Introduction

The work presented in this chapter is an outcropping from a collaborative effort between that of James Townsend, Jennifer Lentz, and Noah Silbert. While he was a PhD student, Noah Silbert began to apply the principles of General Recognition Theory (developed by James Townsend and Gregory Ashby) to complex sound perception under the mentorship of Jim (see Silbert, Townsend, & Lentz, 2009). This was perhaps the first time in which tools developed by Jim were applied to the auditory modality. Due to the success of that work, we pursued this collaboration by applying Jim's Systems Factorial Technology (SFT) framework by first testing the common assumption that frequencies are represented in parallel by the auditory system. Work in the auditory field is well-ensconced in this assumption, but the tools typically used to test the parallel assumption neither have the mathematical rigor nor the robust immunity from model mimicking like those rooted with reaction time (*RT*) and distributional levels of analysis as its measure.

We now are beginning an exciting new line of research in which we are applying these tools as a means to assess both healthy auditory processing as well as auditory disorders. As these tools have almost exclusively been applied to the visual modality (though see the work by Nicholas Altieri on auditory–visual integration, some of which is presented in this book), there is a wide playground within which to target these tools in the auditory domain: from the assessment of central auditory disorders, to better understanding the deficits experienced by listeners with sensorineural hearing loss, to the development of more advanced hearing aid algorithms. We present here some of our initial studies evaluating the processing characteristics of monaural (single ear) and binaural (two ear) hearing. This work is a great step toward building a foundation within which we can address more complex and applied questions. It is a testament to the breadth of Jim's work that his tools can be applied in many different fields, including hearing science. We are excited to continue this collaboration, and thank Jim for all of his helpful discussions, analysis, and insights into this new application of his work.

Applying SFT to the ear is a natural extension of the theory, as the ear functions on a multi-channel basis both within a single ear and between the ears. For monaural perception, one of the most fundamental characteristics of the auditory system is that of frequency analysis: At the level of the cochlea, the basilar membrane can be likened

Systems Factorial Technology, DOI: 10.1016/B978-0-12-804315-8.00014-8

to a bank of filters that separates the various frequencies of complex sounds akin to Fourier analysis. In this distributed system, high frequency sounds are represented at one end of the cochlea (the base, near the stapes) whereas low-frequency sounds are represented at the apical end. This tonotopic organization is maintained throughout all levels of the auditory system in which different neural populations are tuned to different frequencies. Further, we have two ears, separated in space, each processing somewhat different stimuli depending on the location of sound with respect to the head. Both binaural and monaural information is combined to yield the perception of single sound sources in the environment. Consequently, one of the fundamental research endeavors in psychoacoustics is elucidating the mechanisms that are responsible for combining information across frequency within a single ear (*monaural spectral integration*) and across ears (*binaural spectral integration*) to form unified perceptions associated with single sound sources.

Psychoacoustic Studies

There are many different approaches one may take to study spectral integration, and psychophysical experiments have evaluated both monaural and binaural spectral integration. Early psychophysical experiments testing monaural spectral integration measured performance for the detection of tones embedded in noise. The accuracy of detecting a single pure tone was compared to performance in which multiple tones were embedded in the noise (Schafer & Gales, 1949; Marill, 1956; Green, 1958). Today, it is generally accepted that the detection of long-duration tones (well-spaced in frequency to activate independent processing channels), follows Green's energy model (Green, 1958; Green, McKey, & Licklider, 1959; Buus, Schorer, & Zwicker, 1986; Van den Brink & Houtgast, 1990a, 1990b; Hicks & Buus, 2000). This model posits that the detection of two or more tones is based on a linear combination of the detectability of the individual tones. Detection is predicted to improve with increasing number of tones following $d' = \sqrt{\sum_N d_N'^2}$, where N equals the number of tones. Essentially such a model is equivalent to statistical summation of independent random variables generated by each tone (e.g., Tanner, 1956). In sum, it is observed that by using threshold and accuracy based measures, the monaural auditory system integrates spectral information akin to a linear combination of independent random variables.

Broadbent (1955) was one of the first to measure binaural spectral integration for both non-speech and speech stimuli. In his experiments, the low-frequency components were presented to one ear and the high-frequency components to the other. Subjects reported fused percepts and an inability to assess which ear was stimulated by which frequencies. Rand (1974) expanded upon Broadbent's finding for synthetic speech stimuli in which he presented the low-frequency formant of a consonant-vowel stimulus to one ear and the high-frequency formants to the opposing ear. Rand found that listeners could easily identify the stimuli with the formats presented across ears. However, attenuating the high-frequency formants degraded performance more for the binaural stimuli than the monaural stimuli, suggesting subtle differences in the way monaural and binaural information is combined. Cutting (1976) dubbed the binaural integration in which the ears are presented with unique frequencies as "binaural spectral fusion." Here, we use the term "binaural spectral integration"; terminology which allows for gradations in the amount of integration.

Reaction-time experiments also support the idea of binaural spectral integration: Schröter, Ulrich, and Miller (2007) argued that two tones of different frequencies presented to opposing ears were fused into a single percept. They argued that the lack of a redundancy gain (i.e., faster reaction times to two tones vs. one) implied binaural spectral integration, but this study did not compare binaural integration to monaural. Taken together, these studies demonstrated a strong ability of the binaural system to integrate frequencies presented to opposing ears. Notably, though, none of the studies demonstrated substantial advantages of binaural spectral integration over monaural spectral integration.

In contrast, other psychoacoustic studies have demonstrated that the binaural system possesses inferior integration abilities when compared to monaural spectral integration. In one experiment, Green and Kidd (1983) tested the abilities of listeners to discriminate between two sounds with different spectral shapes (i.e., the only reliable acoustic cue was the spectral profile). For example, listeners discriminated between a stimulus with a 'flat' spectral shape (where all components had the same amplitude), and a stimulus in which one component was incremented, so the spectral profile had a 'bump' in the middle. In the monaural condition, all stimulus frequencies were presented to the same ear. But in the binaural condition, the stimulus component with the increment was presented to the opposite ear. In this experiment and others with more complex spectral changes, Green and Kidd reported that listeners failed to integrate partial information from single ears into a full spectral profile, as they achieved higher spectral-shape discrimination performance in monaural compared to binaural tasks. Akeroyd and Summerfield (2000) further showed that although listeners could fuse vowel formants presented across the two ears, they experienced great difficulty when compared with monaural spectral fusion. Given the opposing results, it is clear that further study is necessary to establish the differences in mechanism between the monaural and binaural auditory systems.

An important feature of the aforementioned psychoacoustic studies is that they evaluated detection or discrimination at near-threshold levels (i.e., accuracy was well-below 100%; note that Schröter et al. was conducted at high accuracy as *RT* was the dependent variable). Although accuracy can be varied, it is generally restricted to a performance range between chance and 100% correct. For many psychophysical experiments, the overall accuracy level is thought to be of little consequence: the mechanisms for detection or discrimination are generally treated as being similar whether measurements are made around 60% correct or 90% correct (e.g., note that Green's model operates under the same assumptions and parameters whether d' is low or high). However, there is an emerging body of work indicating that the patterns of integration may be distinctly different depending on the accuracy level. For example, Altieri, Townsend, and Wenger (2014) demonstrated similar effects for auditory–visual integration, whereas Stevenson and James (2009) demonstrated physiological evidence using fMRI for efficient integration at lower SNR than higher SNR in speech perception. In a tone-in-noise detection task with *RT* as its measure, Lentz, He, and Townsend (2014) showed much more efficient integration at lower signal-to-noise ratios than at higher. We then propose a possible gain-controlled mechanism that encourages integration across channels when the sensory input is degraded but tends to shut down such facilitation and integration when signal strength is elevated (Lentz, He, Houpt, Delong, & Townsend, 2016).

We must continue to address the issue of performance level, as the ear functions in a variety of signal-to-noise ratios. Many environments encountered have favorable conditions for the listener, and it is rather difficult for psychophysical studies to assess these situations, as a feature of those studies is that errors are needed for model and theory testing.

Reaction Time Studies

Thus, we consider the *redundant signals approach*, which allows the investigator to assess integration of multiple signals and primarily uses reaction time (*RT*) for its dependent variable. The strong tools within that approach can assist an investigator in unveiling the dynamics of the underlying perceptual system and can provide additional tests to evaluate the detection of one vs. two signals. We suggest that the two basic measures, accuracy and *RT*, can together go a long way in answering fundamental questions within the auditory domain.

Reaction-time techniques can allow an elucidation of the architectural network for spectral integration and can assess the benefit in reaction time given by the simultaneous presentation of two signals over the presentation of one. Combined with the large foundation of accuracy data, this complementary approach may greatly refine and improve the models that exist for detection of complex sounds by the auditory system.

Very few studies have applied *RT* measurements to assess monaural spectral integration. In what may perhaps be the first study to evaluate spectral integration using reaction times, Wagner, Florentine, Buus, and McCormack (2004) demonstrated that broadband noise elicited a faster *RT* than narrowband noise when measured at the same sound pressure level within a single ear. Because Wagner et al.'s primary goal was to establish whether *RT* was determined by loudness rather than sound pressure level, it is ultimately difficult to make a quantitative assessment of the rate of monaural spectral integration. However, the decrease in *RT* with increasing bandwidth implies some degree of spectral integration for monaural stimuli. Lentz et al. (2016) was able to quantify the amount of spectral integration and found very inefficient spectral integration. The amount of integration (captured by the capacity function described in the next section) illustrated that participants received some benefit from having multiple signals presented to them, although the amount of benefit was considerably less than statistical summation would have predicted.

A seminal *RT* based study within the domain of redundant signals literature in which *RT* distributions were evaluated, was undertaken by Schröter et al. (2007) for detection of a 300-ms, 60 dB SPL (Sound Pressure Level, a logarithmic measure of the sound pressure relative to a reference value of 2×10^{-5} Pa) pure tone presented to the left ear, the right ear, or both ears. Importantly, Schröter et al.'s study was critical in that it evaluated *RT distributions* rather than mean *RT*s, which yields a more complete diagnostic test of integration. Further, Schröter et al.'s study evaluated binaural spectral integration, and notably, there was little evidence for a redundant-signal benefit. That is, although *RT*s were slightly faster for detecting two tones vs. one tone, the increase in *RT* was less than would be expected under probability summation. Their interpretation was that the absence of a redundant-signal benefit implied that spectral integration occurred, although their study did not allow for a quantification of how much integration was present. Whether the size of this effect is similar or different for monaural stimulation will be tested in this study.

The suite of tools from the theory-driven *RT* methodology, "systems factorial technology" (subsequently SFT) originated by Townsend and colleagues (e.g., Schweickert, 1978; Schweickert & Townsend, 1989; Townsend & Nozawa, 1995; Townsend & Wenger, 2004) allows a thorough assessment of monaural vs. binaural system architecture. This methodology permits the simultaneous assessment of a number of critical information processing mechanisms within the same experimental paradigm. Two notable architectures are serial and parallel processing architectures, which are sometimes indistinguishable using either accuracy or mean *RT*s. With respect to the auditory system, a parallel structure is almost always assumed (e.g., Durlach, Braida, & Ito, 1986), but such an assumption cannot be easily tested using accuracy-based tools. Although it seems implausible that the auditory system would process simultaneously presented tones serially, we can directly test such an assumption using the tools of SFT.

As mentioned earlier, *RT*s can be measured under conditions of high accuracy, tapping into different locations on the psychometric function. *RT* measures can provide a complement to accuracy-based measures in our attempt at converging on a unified understanding of the mechanisms responsible for perception. The reader is referred to Altieri, Fifić, Little, and Yang (2017) in this book for a review of the tools available in SFT, and we provide only a cursory review of these tools here.

SFT Principles

One of the major contributions of SFT is its ability to rigorously determine the form, or the architecture, used by a system. We are interested in evaluating the possibility of three distinct architectures: *serial processing*, processing sounds one at a time; *parallel processing*, processing all sounds simultaneously, and *parallel coactive processing*, in which the channels are summed together before a decision is made (Townsend & Nozawa, 1995; Houpt & Townsend, 2011). Although we expect both the monaural and binaural systems to follow a parallel or coactive architecture for the detection of two simultaneous tones, it is theoretically possible that other architectures (such as serial) are adopted.

No predictions can be made about architecture without a rule for when processing stops. The OR stopping rule allows a system to stop upon completion of any one of

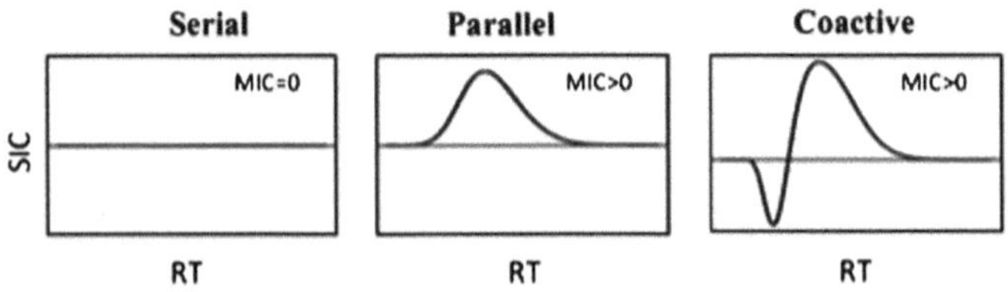

Figure 11.1 Patterns of *SIC* functions for an OR task for serial, parallel, and coactive system.

the inputs (e.g., Egeth, 1966; Townsend & Nozawa, 1995). The AND stopping rule requires completion of both processing channels (e.g., Sternberg, 1966; Townsend & Nozawa, 1995). To some extent, the stopping rule is determined by the experimental design – participants can be asked to respond to either input a or input b (an OR task) or to both input a and input b (an AND task).

Under certain constraints, the *RT* distributions to different stimuli can provide powerful evidence in distinguishing between various architectures (e.g., Townsend & Ashby, 1983; Townsend, 1984, 1990; Townsend & Schweickert, 1989). Using the double-factorial design, the two experimental variables (sounds a and b) are presented at two different levels (1 and 2). As long as the levels manipulate *RT*s (e.g., level 2 is associated with a faster *RT* than level 1), the system architecture can be derived from the *Survivor Interaction Contrast* [$SIC(t) = S_{11}(t) + S_{22}(t) - S_{12}(t) - S_{21}(t)$; where the subscripts denote the respective levels of variables a and b] and can be evaluated for all *RT*s. Note that the full distributions are characterized as survivor functions, which are determined from the cumulative distribution functions $(1 - F(t))$.

The distinct patterns of *SIC* functions that are indicative of different architecture types are illustrated in Fig. 11.1. Only those specific to an OR task are presened here, although it is possible that exhaustive (AND) processing be required of a system. Predictions for the interaction contrast based on the means (*MIC*) are also shown in the individual panels. As the *MIC* cannot separate coactive from parallel architectures (both are greater than zero), the importance of assessing architecture using distributions is stressed.

SFT, however, also offers additional analysis types that can address the issue of architecture, albeit indirectly. Parallel and serial systems also demonstrate properties related to workload capacity (defined below). Although we can only make indirect inferences using capacity metrics about the architecture, we can easily compare the benefit of two tones compared to one.

The term *workload capacity* [$C(t)$] refers to the effects on efficiency as the workload is increased (e.g., processing 2 tones vs. processing 1). Informally, our benchmark is the notion of *unlimited capacity*, which refers to the situation when the finishing time of a channel is identical to that of a standard parallel system in which the average finishing times of each channel do not depend on the others. Two alternative cases are worth considering: capacity values that are below 1.0 (limited capacity – processing speeds are slower than the benchmark) and those above 1.0 (supercapacity – processing speeds are faster than the benchmark, also suggestive of coactive architectures).

The purpose of this paper is to apply these techniques, with a focus on evaluating the architecture for the detection of one vs. two tones and the allocation of resources. To most closely follow the experiments set forth by Green (1958) and subsequent replications, we adopted an OR task here, which required a participant to push a button when a sound was heard. Thus, a participant would select 'yes' if sound a, sound b, or sound $a + b$ was presented. We are interested in addressing these fundamental questions: (i) Can we confirm a parallel architecture for monaural and binaural spectral integration? (ii) How efficient is the spectral integration for the monaural and binaural systems? The tools of SFT will allow assessment of both of these questions: *SIC* functions to assess architecture (if there is support for selective influence) and capacity functions can quantify the degree of efficiency.

Methods

Listeners

Four listeners (1 male, 3 female) aged from 19 to 44 participated in the experiment. All subjects had hearing thresholds of 15 dB HL (Hearing Level, dB relative to normative data) or better at the octave frequencies ranging from 250–8000 Hz. Observer 4 is the first author.

Stimuli

Stimuli were 350-ms 500 and 3020-Hz pure tones having 25-ms cosine-squared onset and offset ramps. These target tones were presented at two stimulus levels: 38 and 80 dB SPL. The levels were selected to better observe the potential distributional ordering in single targets; that is, the higher-level stimulus would be detected more quickly than the lower-level stimulus. We expected around a 50-ms difference in *RT* for the two different levels used here (Kohfeld, 1971).

Procedure

The experiment follows a two by two (double) factorial design, in which tones could be presented in isolation, together, or not at all. Overall, 75% of the trials were stimulus-present trials ("Yes" trials). Of these trials, 25% of total trials contained only the 500-Hz tone, 25% contained only the 3020-Hz tone, and 25% contained both 500 and 3020-Hz tones. The remaining 25% of trials were no-stimulus (NS) or "No" trials.

For the single targets, two different levels were presented in equal proportions: 12.5% contained the high level tones (H500 or H3020) and 12.5% contained the low level tones (L500 or L3020). For dual targets (the two tones are presented together), there are four equally probable types of stimuli: High–High (HH), both tones at the High level; Low–Low (LL), both tones at the low levels; High–Low (HL) the 500-Hz tone at the High level and the 3020-Hz tone at the Low Level; and Low–High (LH);

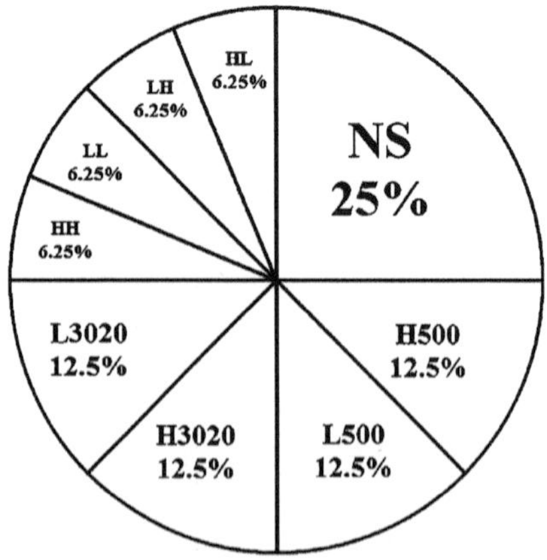

Figure 11.2 Illustration of the double-factorial design with tones at two levels (High and Low). NS represents no-stimulus trials.

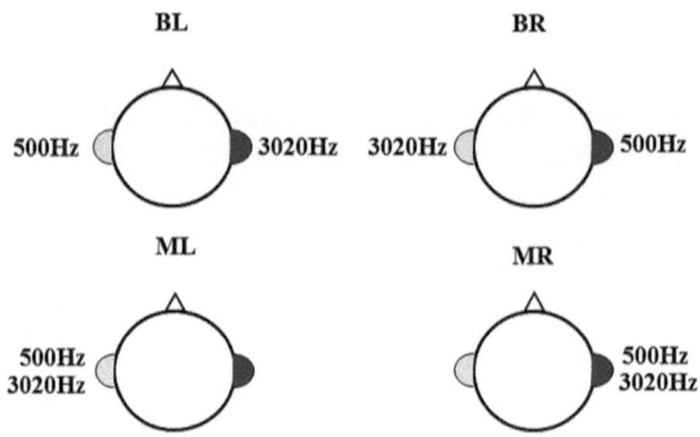

Figure 11.3 Illustration of the four conditions. All conditions are referenced to the monaural/binaural configuration (B or M) and the location of the 500-Hz tone [(L)eft or (R)ight].

the 500-Hz tone at the low level and the 3020-Hz tone at the High level. Fig. 11.2 illustrates the various percentages for each of the trial types.

Four different contexts were tested. Two of these were monaural presentations, in which both tones were presented to the same ear. Two of these were binaural presentations, in which one tone was presented to the left ear and one was presented to the right ear. The contexts (also referred to as conditions) are referenced to which ear contained the low-frequency (500-Hz tone). The two monaural contexts contained presentations to either the left ear or the right ear: Monaural Left (ML) and Monaural Right (MR). In the Binaural Left condition (BL), the 500-Hz tone was presented to the left ear and the 3020-Hz tone presented to the right. In Binaural Right (BR), the frequencies are reversed: the 500-Hz tone was presented to the right ear, and the 3020-Hz tone presented to the left. Fig. 11.3 illustrates the four conditions so that the reader can return here for reference if need be. Data from the monaural conditions are also reported in Lentz et al. (2016).

A visual warning of "listen" was presented on a computer monitor for 400 ms before each trial to notify the observers the coming target sound. Following the removal of the warning message, a random-duration, uniformly distributed, silent period ranging between 0 and 400 ms was inserted between the visual warning and the trial to minimize anticipation effects. Observers were instructed to respond as quickly and as accurately to the signal tone as possible by pressing the "yes" button if a sound was detected or pressing the "no" button if no sound was present. Consequently, the detection task used in this study is an "OR" design.

The reaction time was measured from the onset of the tone stimulus. In order to help observers to maintain attention and provide correct responses, visual feedback indicating correct or incorrect responses was presented after the reaction box was pressed. In addition, percent correct was monitored in order to ensure that subjects achieved high levels of performance for all conditions.

Stimuli were presented to the observers at a 24,414 kHz sampling rate using a 24-bit Tucker Davis Technologies (TDT) RP2.1 real-time processor. The two tones were summed at appropriate relative levels digitally prior to being played though a single channel of the RP2.1. Signals were then passed through a calibrated PA5 programmable attenuator and an HB6 headphone buffer. They were presented to observers through a Sennheiser HD280 Pro headphone set. Reaction times were measured using a button box interfaced to the computer through the TDT hardware.

This study was conducted over three to five sessions. Four listeners participated in the sessions lasting about 1 hour. One single session consisted of approximately 6–9 blocks of 128 trials. A randomized block design was used and the ordering of conditions was selected randomly without replacement. Three blocks for each condition were tested before a new condition was selected. Once three blocks from all four conditions were tested, the process was repeated until a total of 12 blocks in each condition were completed. The first two blocks were treated as practice, yielding a total of 80 trials for each dual target (HH, LL, HL, and LH) and 160 trials for the single targets (H500, H3020, L500, and L3020) to be analyzed. *RT*s slower than 800 milliseconds or faster than 80 milliseconds were treated as outliers and thus were also excluded. All subjects showed high accuracy (>97%) in the detection tasks. Both correct and incorrect responses were included in the later analyses.

Results

RT Distributions

Single Targets

We first report *RT*s of the single targets to illustrate the effects of the stimulus parameters on the size of the reaction time for the different conditions (see Fig. 11.4). The data set is of considerable size, therefore, we show the mean *RT*s collapsed across subjects, with data analysis conducted at the group level (mean analysis) and the individual level (distributional analysis, which provides a much stronger test). Note that

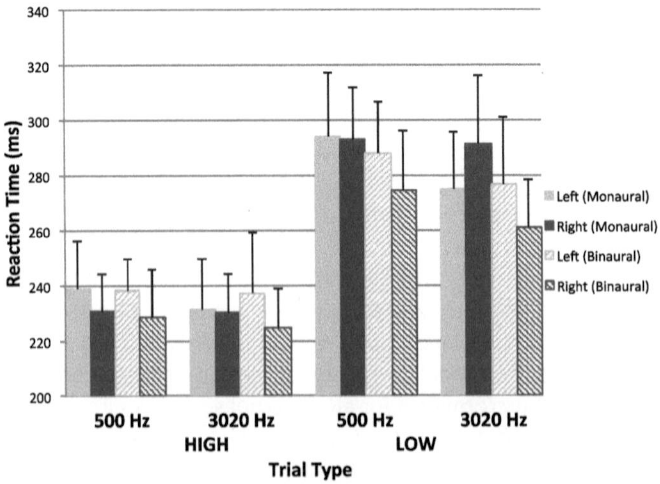

Figure 11.4 Mean (geometric) *RT*s ($N = 4$) for single targets plotted for the ear of presentation. "Left" indicates *RT*s when the single tones were presented in the left ear, and "Right" indicates *RT*s when the single tones were presented in the right ear. Error bars represent standard errors of the mean.

even though we are reporting the means, we stress that inferences at the distributional level provide a much stronger test of the various concepts than inferences made from means.

For the single target trials, we have three parameters of interest: the intensity of the tone, the frequency of the tone, and the context (or condition) in which that tone was presented. Intensity is the variable that we have manipulated in attempts to achieve selective influence, and therefore we expect large *RT* differences between the low and the high stimulus level. On the other hand, we expect either a small or no effect of frequency: The tone levels and frequencies were selected in the hopes of achieving similar reaction times for the two frequencies. Finally, we have the stimulus context (ear and monaural/binaural presentation). Numerous studies have demonstrated that there is little effect of ear of presentation for *RT*s to pure tones, and when there is an effect, faster *RT*s for the right ear are more likely related to the position of the "yes" button on a response box [which is frequently on the right side of the response box; see Schlittenlacher, Ellermeier, and Arseneau (2014) for a discussion of this result]. However, no study has evaluated whether a binaural or monaural context makes a difference for the *RT*s of single tones, and we can test this hypothesis here. In principle, one would not expect much effect of the monaural vs. binaural contexts on the *RT*s for the single targets, as the single target stimuli are the same regardless of the condition tested. Yet, there could be an effect of distributing one's attention across the ears (as in the binaural conditions) compared to having to only attend to a single ear (as in the monaural conditions).

To illustrate our findings, Fig. 11.4 plots the geometric mean reaction times for the two intensity levels, two frequencies, and four different contexts tested. Note that the single-target reaction time values in Lentz et al. (2016) Table 7.3 are incorrect; the corrected values are reported here. Error bars represent standard errors of the mean across the four subjects. Note that rather than referring to the condition in which the tone was presented in, these data are plotted with respect to the ear of stimulation. Here, the data are plotted with respect to the *presentation ear* for the various frequencies.

As Fig. 11.4 illustrates, mean *RT*s for the single targets range from slightly below 230 ms to about 290 ms. The largest observable effect in Fig. 11.4 is that *RT*s are much slower for the low stimulus level than for the high stimulus level (bars on the left side of the panel are shorter than on the right side of the panel; mean difference = 49 ms). There was small influence of frequency, as one can observe that the 3020-Hz tone led to *RT*s that were slightly faster than the 500-Hz tone (approximately 7 ms faster). Finally, condition appears to have small effect: This effect is most noticeable by the *RT*s associated with the tone presented in the right ear in a binaural context (red hatched bars) being faster than the *RT*s for all of the other conditions.

Results are supported by a 3-way repeated-measures ANOVA, with Greenhouse–Geisser correction for sphericity violations, which found significant main effects of intensity [$F(1,3) = 31.0$; $p < 0.015$], frequency [$F(1,3) = 13.0$; $p < 0.05$], and condition [$F(3,9) = 12.7$; $p < 0.015$]. Post-hoc t-tests for condition indicated support the observation of Fig. 11.4: *RT*s were 13 ms faster when in the binaural context when the tone was presented in the right ear. As intimated earlier, we suspect this result arises from the location of the "yes" button on the response box.

These conclusions are also supported by Kolmogorov–Smirnov (KS) tests on the *RT* distributions for individual subjects: For stimulus level, all conditions tested were significantly faster for the higher intensity than for the lower intensity ($p < 0.0005$) for each subject. Frequency and condition were less robust across subjects, but also indicated significant patterns. When a criterion of $p < 0.005$ was adopted, 17 of a possible 32 conditions revealed significantly different *RT*s for 500 and 3020 Hz. Fifteen of those 17 comparisons indicated a significantly faster *RT* for the 3020-Hz tone compared to the 500-Hz tone. Thus, we have some evidence that the 3020-Hz tone was associated with either a faster, or a similar, reaction time to the 500-Hz tone, though such effects are not robust across conditions and subjects. The KS tests revealed no patterns of significance that were consistent across subjects, although roughly 25% of the KS tests reached significance, suggesting that for the single targets, there is little difference in *RT* depending on the contextual format of the stimulus presentation at the distributional level.

Dual Targets

Fig. 11.5 plots the mean reaction times for the dual-target data in order to illustrate the general trends in the group. Evaluation of Fig. 11.5 suggests that stimulus level has a strong influence, with LL associated with slower *RT*s than any of the other levels. Condition does not appear to have much of an effect, as *RT*s are similar across the conditions for the different salience levels or the differences in *RT* across the conditions are not systematic. *MIC* values calculated for individual subjects in all four conditions (reported on Fig. 11.8) are positive, suggesting overadditivity and therefore a parallel structure. *MIC* values were not statistically different between monaural and binaural conditions.

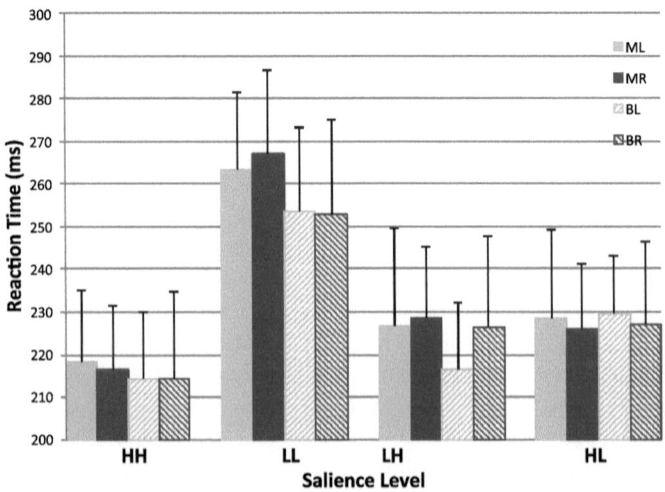

Figure 11.5 Mean (Geometric) *RT*s ($N = 4$) for the different dual targets are plotted for each condition. Error bars represent standard errors of the mean.

Results are supported by a 2-way repeated-measures ANOVA, with the Greenhouse–Geisser correction for sphericity violations, which found only a significant main effect of intensity [$F(3, 9) = 27.0$; $p < 0.001$]. Post-hoc paired t-tests suggest that this effect is driven by significant differences in mean between all levels tested, except between LH and HL. *RT*s for HH are significantly faster than for LL, LH, and HL, and *RT*s for LL are significantly slower than *RT*s for LH and HL ($p < 0.05$). Thus, at the mean and the group level, we have some evidence that selective influence holds. However, as will be discussed below, these effects do not hold for all subjects at the distributional level. There was no significant main effect of condition or interaction involving condition.

Monaural vs. Binaural Effects

As the primary interest of this study was to evaluate whether monaural and binaural spectral integration is similar, we first present the dual target distributional data organized to illustrate the effects of monaural vs. binaural listening. Note that the absence of an effect of condition based on mean reaction time analysis also suggests that any effects of condition will not be present at the individual levels, at least in a manner that is systematic across subjects.

Here, we first show the survivor functions obtained for each of the conditions (ML, MR, BL, and BR). Because there were little systematic differences in the survivor functions across subjects, we have plotted the data of Obs. 1, whose data shows the range of patterns observed within the group. To illustrate the primary differences between the monaural and binaural conditions, the different panels indicate the four salience levels tested: HH, LL, LH, and HL.

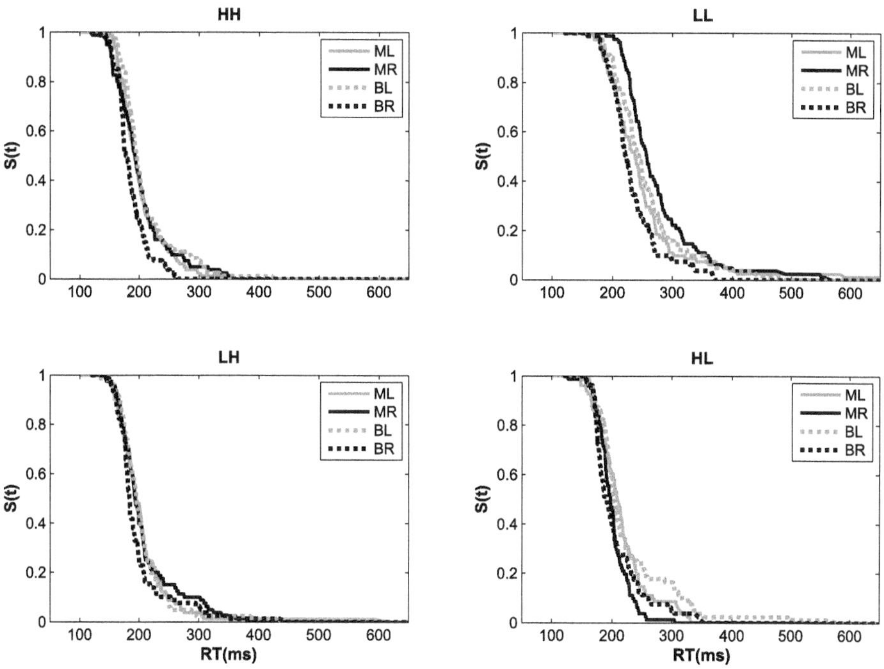

Figure 11.6 Survivor functions for the dual target data shown for Obs 1. Binaural conditions are shown with dashed lines and monaural conditions having solid. The different salience levels are shown in the four panels.

As Fig. 11.6 illustrates, any differences between the monaural and binaural presentation modes are relatively small, and differences between these two contexts are not manifest consistently across the different salience levels. For example, for LH, this subject shows very similar data across all four of the conditions tested (evident in the overlap of all survivor functions). On the other hand, the survivor functions are ordered for the LL salience level, with BR associated with the fastest reaction times and MR with the slowest.

A number of KS tests (48 per subject) were conducted to evaluate whether monaural the different conditions were faster or slower than the other conditions. If using the Bonferroni-corrected p-value, Obs. 1 was the only subject to demonstrate any significant orderings ($N = 2$) with BR being faster than BL and MR. However, if we adopt a less strict criterion of $p < 0.05$, we see that for Obs. 1 the BR condition was faster for all salience levels than in any other condition. Obs. 2 showed no systematic significance patterns. For Obs. 3, most of the BL trials were faster than for MR, and Obs. 4 tended to respond fastest in BL, though not consistently at all salience levels. Note that these differences are idiosyncratic, and so consequently we suggest there are no significant effects of condition either across or within subjects.

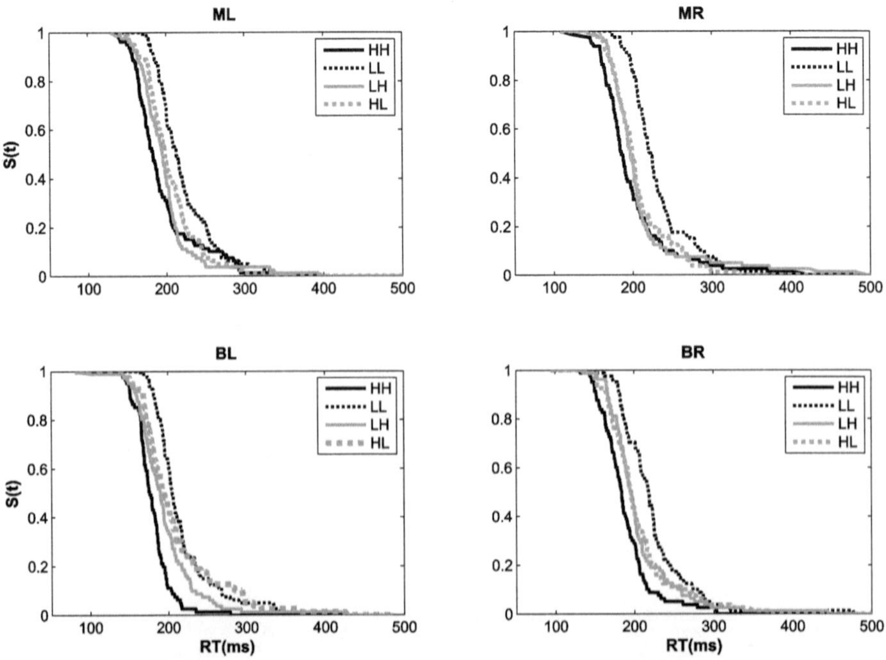

Figure 11.7 Survivor functions for the dual target data shown for Obs 3. Different salience levels are indicated by the different line types, and different conditions are shown in the four panels.

Intensity Effects

On the other hand, we expected there to be demonstrable effects of intensity variation as this was the parameter varied to obtain distributional ordering. The analysis based on the mean reaction times implies that selective influence is present within the group, but without assessment at the distributional level, our inferences are not strong. To illustrate the results across salience levels, we plot the estimated survivor functions from a single subject (Obs. 3, who showed the strongest support for distributional ordering) in Fig. 11.7. Overall, one can observe that *RT*s are the fastest for the HH conditions and slowest for the LL conditions. Support for distributional ordering would be present if the *RT* distributions are ordered as HH < LH and HL and LL > HL and LH. As one can see, the distributional ordering is evident in both BR and BL conditions, with HH being toward the left of the panels and LL being toward the right, with HL and LH in between. The ML and MR conditions do not demonstrate as strong support for distributional ordering upon observation, but even those conditions appear to have little overlap in the *RT* distributions.

Tests of distributional ordering were conducted for the monaural and binaural conditions separately for each subject. We conducted KS tests of distributional ordering for the following comparisons: HH vs. LL, LH, and HL and LL vs. LH and HL for a total of 5 tests. If a strict interpretation of the KS tests were taken, a significant result for distribution ordering would be supported if *all* comparisons were statistically different and ordered in which HH $<$ LH and HL and also LL $>$ HL and LH. Results from KS tests on dual targets revealed only one of the subjects (Obs. 3) demonstrated statistically significant distributional ordering in all four conditions ($p < 0.02$). This pattern is evident in Fig. 11.7 with survivor functions for HH being toward the left of the panels and LL being toward the right, with HL and LH in between.

Observer 1 showed significant distributional ordering for BR ($p < 0.005$) but at least one KS test was not significant in the other three conditions ($p > 0.05$). Strong distributional ordering was also not present in observers 2 and 4. For Obs. 2 and Obs. 4, one or two KS tests were not significant for each condition tested. As was discussed in Lentz et al. (2016), we think that some, but not all of these statistical tests failed because of a small difference in *RT* between HH, HL, and LH and insufficient trials to test for small differences in the means of the distributions.

To further support this idea, we also evaluated whether selective influence was present at the PDF level. For this analysis, we calculated empirical PDFs (ePDFs) from histograms based on the empirical cumulative distribution functions (CDF) and we also fit a Poisson distribution with the parameter (λ) to the *RT* distributions. Examination of the ePDFs suggested that distributional ordering was present for more subjects than those identified by KS tests. Similar to the KS tests, Obs. 1 demonstrated ordering for BR. However, Obs. 2 demonstrated ordering for BL, BR, and MR, and Obs. 4 demonstrated ordering for BL and BR. The Poisson estimates tended to support a similar pattern of ordering, though not as strongly as the tests on the actual *RT* distributions.

Although one may consider the lack of statistical significance to temper our results on architecture (shown in the next section), we believe that selective influence is in operation for most subjects and conditions. We present the architectural *SIC* functions so that the reader can make his/her own conclusions.

Architecture

In order to evaluate the architecture, Fig. 11.8 plots the *SIC* functions for all subjects. Recall that specific shapes of the *SIC* functions are expected depending on the processing architecture (as shown in Fig. 11.1). Parallel and coactive architectures all have *SIC* values greater than zero for the majority of the function, with coactive architectures having an early portion of the *SIC* function being negative. Serial architectures would be expected to yield $SIC = 0$ for all *RT*s. For the reader's reference, the predicted *SIC* functions for different architectures are shown in the left-most panels of Fig. 11.8.

Observation of Fig. 11.8 suggests that most subjects have a parallel architecture in the majority of conditions tested. Using the statistical tests of Houpt and Townsend (2012), we assessed whether the *SIC* functions are significantly different from what a typical serial structure suggests ($SIC = 0$). Statistical tests revealed 11 of 16 *SIC* functions were significantly different from serial OR processing ($p < 0.07$; only 10 *SIC* functions for $p < 0.05$). In these cases, the *SIC* statistic was also significantly positive and never significantly negative, suggesting a parallel and not coactive architecture.

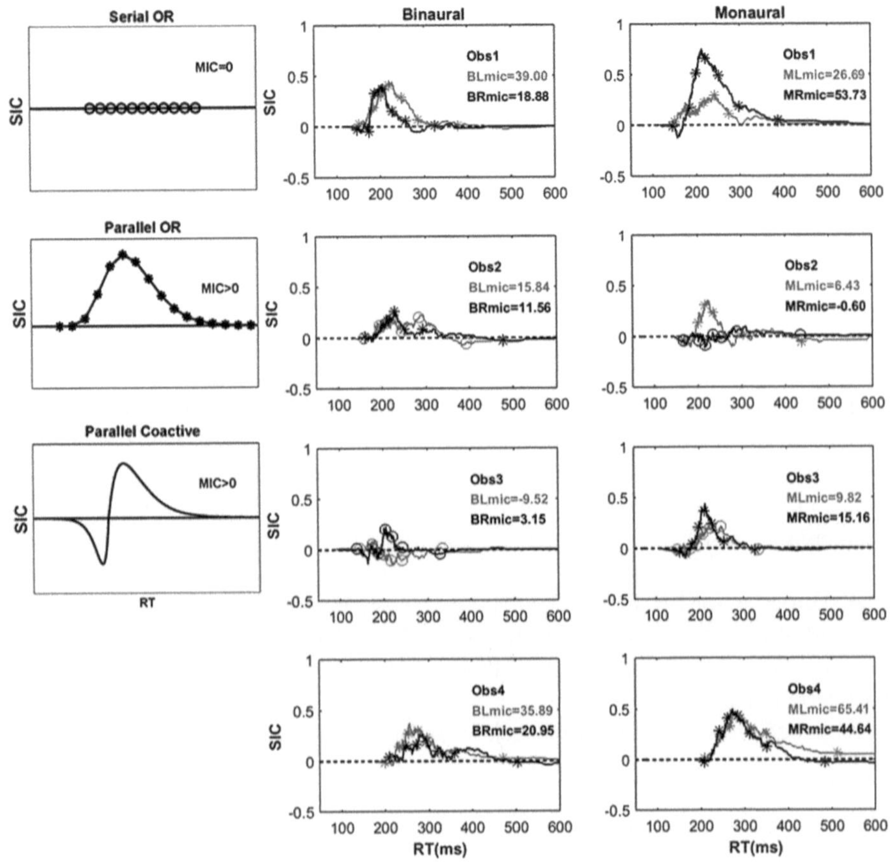

Figure 11.8 *SIC* functions for all subjects and all conditions. *MIC* values are reported in milliseconds in each panel. The leftmost two panels are the legend of markers. Statistically significant parallel structures are marked by asterisks. Statistically significant serial structures are marked by circles.

The other 5 *SIC* functions were not significantly different from zero. One possibility is that these architectures are serial or that they are parallel with limited statistical significance. Within the figure, significant parallel architectures are indicated by the asterisks.

Observers 1 and 4 demonstrated parallel processing in all four conditions. Observer 2 showed parallel processing in conditions ML and BR. Interestingly, Obs. 3, who had the strongest evidence for selective influence only demonstrated significantly parallel processing in MR. Thus, we cannot strongly reject the notion of serial processing for this subject. However, of the conditions that were not significantly parallel, only two of the functions look exceedingly serial (MR for Obs. 2 and BL for Obs. 3). The capacity data (discussed in the next section) support our thoughts that architecture is parallel for the conditions tested.

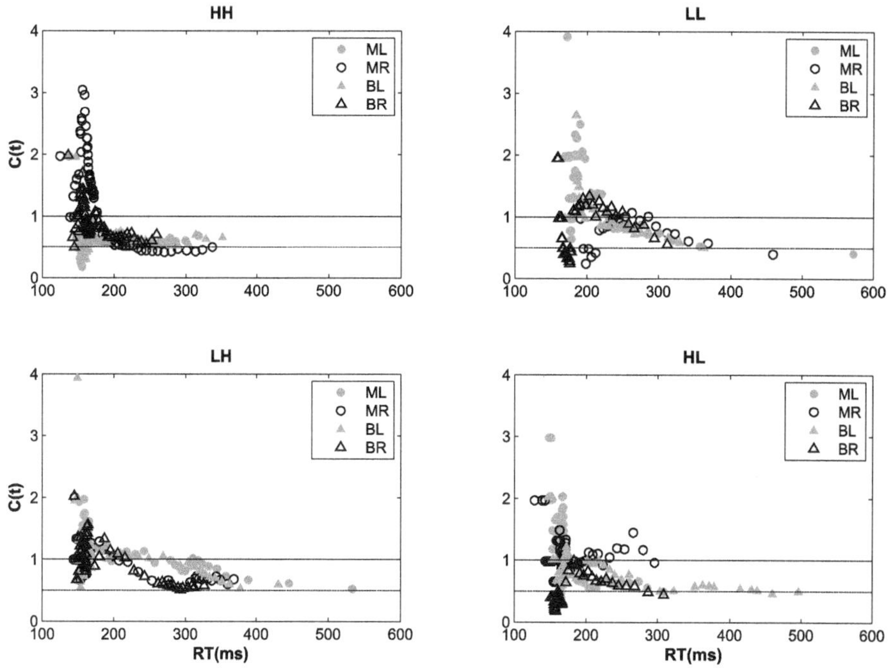

Figure 11.9 Capacity functions for four salience levels. Data are from Obs. 1.

Capacity Functions

Again, due to the large size of the data set and the similarity of capacity functions across observers and conditions, capacity data for one subject (Obs. 1) are plotted in Fig. 11.9. This subject shows representative capacity functions that were observed across the data set. As can be seen in this figure, $C(t)$ ranges from a fairly high value (anywhere from 2 to 4) at the fastest *RT*s to somewhere near $1/2$ for the slowest *RT*s. Across the majority of *RT*s, the results consistently demonstrate $1 \geq C(t) \geq 1/2$. As shown for Obs. 1 in Fig. 11.9, many of the $C(t)$ functions had small *RT* ranges (for the short *RT*s only) in which capacity values tend to exceed 1.0. We observed a similar pattern in other three subjects. However, the reliability of those portions of the functions is poor, and we do not make strong conclusions of supercapacity for any of the subjects tested here.

Generally speaking, the trend is for capacity values to range from unlimited capacity $[C(t) = 1]$ to limited/fixed capacity, with a dominance of limited capacity $[0.5 < C(t) < 1]$. For most *RT*s, capacity tends to be at or slightly better than $1/2$. The statistical analysis of Houpt and Townsend (2012) demonstrated that 53 of 64 comparisons on all subjects and conditions were statistically significant limited capacity. For the other 11 cases, we had strong support for unlimited capacity.

Among the cases demonstrated to be unlimited capacity, three of these cases were for the data from Obs. 1 that are plotted in Fig. 11.9, and occurred in for the HL

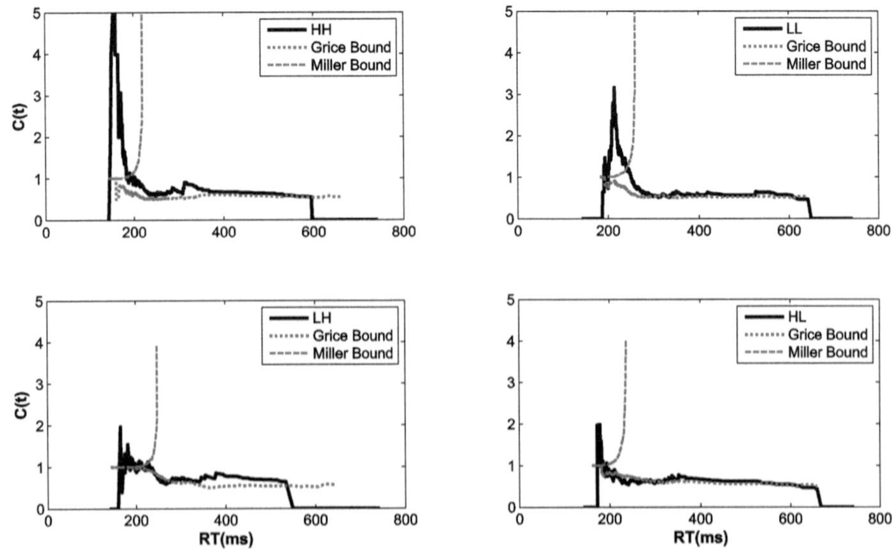

Figure 11.10 Capacity functions with Grice and Miller bounds for four salience levels. Data are from Obs. 2 in condition MR.

salience level in the ML and BL conditions and for the LH salience level in the MR condition. As one can observe from Fig. 11.9, these functions do tend to hover around $C(t)$ values of 1.0. It is worth noting that 10 of the 11 conditions to test as unlimited capacity were in the HL or LH conditions, hinting at a capacity difference for these asymmetric level conditions. Nine of the 11 conditions were associated with parallel processing, consistent with the prediction of a standard unlimited-capacity independent parallel model.

For cases of limited capacity, however, a number of these limited capacity functions are indeed near the Grice bound, a lower boundary for processing (Grice, Canham, & Gwynne, 1984). Values at this boundary, which is determined by the faster of the two channels, indicate no redundancy gain. For illustrative purposes, Figs. 11.10 and 11.11 show capacity functions plotted with the Grice bounds for condition MR for Obs. 2 and Obs. 4, respectively. These capacity functions were selected as the architecture for Obs. 2 appeared to be serial and that for Obs. 4 appeared to be parallel. For illustrative purposes, an upper bound (Miller, 1982 boundary, which when exceeded provides some support for supercapacity) is also plotted: In both figures, capacity coefficients at short *RT*s tend to exceed the Miller bound, but the longer *RT*s are associated with capacity values that are near (but no not typically fall below) the Grice bound.

At the bound performance level, there is no redundancy gain, and subjects are performing as fast as if there were only one target. This type of behavior is consistent with a *fixed capacity* system, or a system in which the system shares a fixed amount of capacity between the two channels. It is also consistent with a standard serial ar-

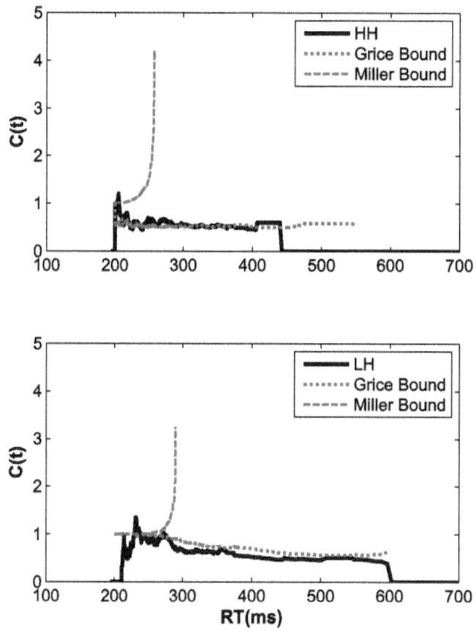

Figure 11.11 Capacity functions with Grice and Miller bounds for four salience levels. Data are from Obs. 4 in condition MR.

chitecture. Of course, one must be careful drawing conclusions on architecture from the capacity functions due to the notorious challenge of model mimicking. In fact, it is exactly serial-like performance that can be perfectly mimicked by fixed capacity parallel systems (Townsend, 1971, 1990).

As Fig. 11.9 shows, capacity functions are very similar for the various conditions, and because of the complexity of the data set, it is difficult to observe any systematic trends within the data set plotted this way. To illustrate general trends, the mean capacity data are plotted in Fig. 11.12, which essentially demonstrates two major findings. First, the mean of the capacity function is much greater than a fixed capacity system ($C(t) = 0.5$). On average, mean capacity values always exceed 0.75. Some mean capacity values even approach 1.0 (unlimited capacity). Second, there are no observable differences in mean capacity for the different conditions tested or the different salience levels. None of the parameter manipulations in this study had a profound effect on capacity. A repeated-measures ANOVA conducted on the mean capacities confirm this interpretation, as there were no significant effects of level or condition.

On the whole, global processing appears to be either serial, or parallel-limited or unlimited capacity. We see only limited evidence of supercapacity in this data set and only at the shortest *RT*s. The question of why observers show capacity over 1.0 ($C(t) > 1$) with faster *RT*s remains unclear. One possibility is that a self-terminating stopping rule is associated with faster responses and the regular and slower responses are results of exhaustive processing.

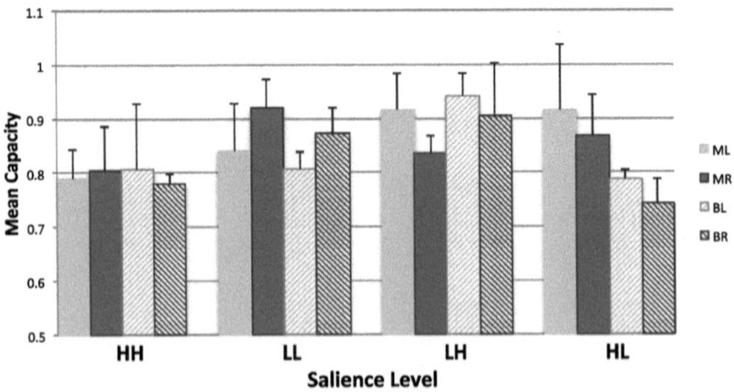

Figure 11.12 Mean capacity values are plotted for the various conditions. Error bars represent standard errors of the mean.

General Discussion

To date, we are aware of only accuracy experiments that have investigated the ability to detect multiple stimuli within a single ear and compared that ability to detection of stimuli presented across the ears. This study presents the first study in which *RT* tools have been used to evaluate the architecture of both monaural and binaural spectral integration using *SIC* functions and capacity measures.

We aimed to achieve two primary goals with this study: (i) to establish the architecture for monaural and binaural spectral integration and (ii) to evaluate the relative efficiency of monaural and binaural spectral integration. As Lentz et al. (2016) previously reported data on monaural spectral integration, it was of considerable interest to evaluate the differences between the binaural and monaural auditory systems.

Architecture

A primary goal of this study was to establish whether binaural and monaural auditory processing follows a parallel architecture. As intimated in the introduction, a serial architecture for a task like the one proposed here (detecting two simultaneously presented tones) is almost implausible. Yet, this concept has not been rigorously tested, and the tools of SFT allow a strong test of parallel vs. serial architecture. We argue that we have evidence for a parallel architecture in both monaural and binaural processing of two tones, as defined within the confines of the SFT theory. Although we believe that we have support for parallel architecture, the failure to find strong support for selective influence in the dual-target data indeed tempers our ability to make a robust rejection of serial processing.

The failure to find strong evidence of selective influence for the dual targets is somewhat perplexing, especially as the single target data show such a strong ordering of distributions obtained at different intensity levels. Lentz et al. (2016) suggested that more stimulus trials could resolve this issue but that there is a possibility added trials may not garner greater statistical power. Their argument was rooted in the idea that pure tones (even those widely spaced in frequency) may indeed interact at a peripheral level (see Egan & Hake, 1950). Notably, this idea can only explain a failure to find selective influence for the monaural conditions as peripheral interactions between the tones would not be present in the binaural conditions. Based on the data presented here, we can reject this notion, as the failure of selective influence was fairly evenly distributed across monaural and binaural conditions. If the cause is interactions within the auditory system, these interactions are more central in nature.

We must also consider the possibility that we have encountered ceiling effects: If HL and LH are already associated with the fastest possible *RT* achievable by the subject, HH could not possibly have been faster. It is noteworthy that the mean reaction times reported here are no faster than those that have been observed in the past for pure tones. Kohfeld (1971) and Simon (1967) observed mean *RT*s around 200 ms for single targets whereas our mean *RT*s for the dual HH targets are around 215 ms. Yet, it is possible that subjects may not receive additional benefits from increasing stimulus intensity, and we must address this in future studies.

The tools of SFT would allow us to make much stronger conclusions if we could demonstrate selective influence at the distributional level for all subjects and all salience levels. However, it is worth mentioning that the one subject who showed the strongest evidence for distributional ordering is the subject who showed the weakest evidence for a parallel architecture.

As mentioned in the results, despite failure to demonstrate strong evidence of selective influence, we feel that we can conclude that architectures are parallel for both monaural and binaural processing. Examination of Fig. 11.8 allows one to confidently believe that a parallel architecture is present. Perhaps this parallel structure is present in conjunction with a serial structure, yielding a serial–parallel hybrid.

Integration Efficiency

We posited two potential hypotheses regarding the ability of the binaural system to integrate information across frequency. One hypothesis was that the binaural system has similarly efficient spectral integration compared to monaural integration, and is able to fuse sounds presented across the ears into unified percepts. A second hypothesis was that binaural spectral integration operates more poorly than monaural spectral integration. Both hypotheses have some support in the accuracy literature, and evaluating this question using *RT* provides a new perspective.

Generally speaking, we observe that spectral integration (either monaural or binaural) is a relatively inefficient process as tested here. Efficient integration would, at a minimum, yield capacity functions consistent with the UCIP model, or $C(t) = 1$. 53 of 64 assessments of the capacity function were significantly limited capacity, and the mean capacities were always less than 1. This result is similar to Schröter et al. (2007)'s result, who also found that there was little redundancy gain for two tones (500 and 700 Hz) presented to opposing ears. Interestingly, Schröter et al. (2007) argued that fusion across the ears prevented the redundancy gain, and they suggested that the two tones in their studies were integrated into a unified percept.

As mentioned in the introduction. Schröter et al. (2007)'s tools, unlike the capacity function, did not allow for a quantitative assessment of the degree of integration. They simply compared the *RT*s to a benchmark. We suggest that the absence of spectral fusion would appear as a *limited* capacity result ($C(t)$ between 0.5 and 1), or a result in which detection is determined by the tone (or ear) with the fastest reaction time. Complete fusion across the ears would be reflected in capacity values that are greater than 1. That the capacity functions are generally limited suggests very inefficient spectral integration, and, in some cases, we observed that capacity functions approached the fixed capacity boundary. Although we did not measure whether listeners truly experienced spectral fusion, the informal reports of listeners suggested that they were typically able to identify which ear contained the high and low frequency tones and they were able to "hear out" the individual tones when presented to the same ear. Our results appear consistent with a failure of spectral fusion, but gradations of this perception likely exist.

We also aimed to determine whether integration efficiency was similar between the monaural and binaural presentation models, and we can address this question by evaluating the distributional data from the dual targets as well as the capacity functions. The single target data also provide a baseline reference so that we can use the dual target survivor functions to address this question. Notably, we observed no differences in *RT* of the single targets for the various contexts. Thus, even though subjects were required to divide their attention across the ears in the binaural contexts, this dividing of attention did not influence the *RT*s measured. Thus, we have a firm baseline within which to evaluate the differences between binaural and monaural processing. Should the results have demonstrated that one context led to faster reaction times than the other for the single targets, we would not be able to directly compare the survivor functions for the dual target conditions (as the baseline *RT*s would have been different for the two contexts). Capacity functions would have been our only level of analysis.

Two main findings from this study support that the binaural and monaural systems follow *similar* patterns of spectral fusion. First, as Fig. 11.5 demonstrates, there is overall a general lack of differences between the *RT* distributions of the dual targets for the different contexts tested: *RT*s are no different for monaural or binaural contexts. Further, no matter the intensity level (HH, LH, or one of the intermediate conditions), the *RT* distributions for the different contexts overlap. Thus, in the *RT* distributions themselves, we see no advantage or disadvantage of the binaural system over the monaural system.

Second, the capacity functions for monaural vs. binaural conditions are also similar. Limited capacity is observed in both cases, and the capacity functions are not statistically different from each other. Further, the cases in which we observed unlimited capacity were split evenly between the monaural and binaural conditions, suggesting no advantage at the individual level of one condition over another. Consequently, we see no evidence that binaural spectral integration is impoverished compared to monaural spectral integration. Both systems are relatively inefficient for the accuracy levels tested here, but both systems demonstrate similar patterns of inefficiency.

At this point, we cannot pinpoint the source of the limited capacity. Potentially, it could be the result of simply limitations in attentional resources. Alternatively, it could be due to something like mutual inhibition across the parallel channels. However, it seems strange that mutual inhibition would follow the same pattern for monaural as for binaural conditions. Thus, it seems more likely that the limited capacity result is indeed limitations in attentional resources. The fact that even binocular dot experiments reveal limited capacity (e.g., Townsend & Nozawa, 1995) suggests that certain kinds of interaction or restricted sources of processing facility can intrude in incredibly simple and presumably independent, channels.

Next, how can we explain the seeming disconnect between accuracy findings which suggest efficient integration and ours, which imply inefficient integration? These results agree with a growing number of other investigations where performance is unlimited or even super capacity at low signal-to-noise ratios, but is limited to extremely limited at high levels of accuracy. In particular, the study of auditory–visual speech perception has found phenomenal benefits, both behavioral (e.g., see Sumby & Pollack, 1954; Summerfield, 1987; Altieri et al., 2014; Altieri, Pisoni & Townsend, 2011) and physiological (e.g., Stevenson & James, 2009), of the visual information at low signal-to-noise ratios, but lower capacity values at higher accuracy. Lentz et al. (2014) also demonstrated this trend for detection of binaural tones added to binaural noise. We speculate that the auditory system may deploy specific mechanisms to facilitate listening in high-noise environments. Nonlinearities present throughout the auditory pathway render this a strong possibility.

Summary and Conclusions

In sum, we find evidence for binaural and monaural spectral integration, and that both integration processes appear to follow a similar pattern of architecture and workload capacity. At these accuracy levels tested, we see little benefit of stimulating two ears over a single ear, as the reaction times and subsequent analyses are strikingly similar for the two modes of presentation. Further assessment should be completed to determine whether efficiency improves for low accuracy levels, and we suggest that using the $A(t)$ function, which is a capacity measure that takes accuracy into account (Townsend and Altieri, 2012), would be a strong tool to address these questions further.

Acknowledgements

We would like to thank Rutendo Chikuku and Matthew Walker for assistance with data collection and analysis. Work was supported, in part, by grant No. R21DC013171 from NIH to the first author.

References

Akeroyd, M. A., & Summerfield, Q. (2000). Integration of monaural and binaural evidence of vowel formants. *The Journal of the Acoustical Society of America*, *107*(6), 3394–3406.

Altieri, N., Fifić, M., Little, D. R., & Yang, C-T. (2017). A tutorial and historical introduction to systems factorial technology. In D. R. Little, N. Altieri, M. Fifić, & C-T. Yang (Eds.), *Systems factorial technology: A theory driven methodology for the identification of perceptual and cognitive mechanisms*. Elsevier (in this book).

Altieri, N., Pisoni, D. B., & Townsend, J. T. (2011). Some behavioral and neurobiological constraints on theories of audiovisual speech integration: A review and suggestions for new directions. *Seeing and Perceiving*, *24*(6), 513–539.

Altieri, N., Townsend, J. T., & Wenger, M. J. (2014). A measure for assessing the effects of audiovisual speech integration. *Behavior Research Methods*, *46*, 406–415.

Broadbent, D. E. (1955). A note on binaural fusion. *Quarterly Journal of Experimental Psychology*, *7*, 46–47.

Buus, S., Schorer, E., & Zwicker, E. (1986). Decision rules in detection of simple and complex tones. *The Journal of the Acoustical Society of America*, *80*(6), 1646–1657.

Cutting, J. E. (1976). Auditory and linguistic processes in speech perception: Inferences from six fusions in dichotic listening. *Psychological Review*, *83*(2), 114–140.

Durlach, N. I., Braida, L. D., & Ito, Y. (1986). Towards a model for discrimination of broadband signals. *The Journal of the Acoustical Society of America*, *80*(1), 63–72.

Egan, J. P., & Hake, H. W. (1950). On the masking pattern of a simple auditory stimulus. *The Journal of the Acoustical Society of America*, *22*, 622–630.

Egeth, H. E. (1966). Parallel vs. serial processes in multidimensional stimulus discrimination. *Perception & Psychophysics*, *1*(4), 245–252.

Green, D. M. (1958). Detection of multiple component signals in noise. *The Journal of the Acoustical Society of America*, *30*(10), 904–911.

Green, D. M., & Kidd Jr, G. (1983). Further studies of auditory profile analysis. *The Journal of the Acoustical Society of America*, *73*(4), 1260–1265.

Green, D. M., McKey, M. J., & Licklider, J. C. R. (1959). Detection of a pulsed sinusoid in noise as a function of frequency. *The Journal of the Acoustical Society of America*, *31*(11), 1446–1452.

Grice, G. R., Canham, L., & Gwynne, J. W. (1984). Absence of a redundant-signals effect in a RT task with divided attention. *Perception & Psychophysics*, *36*(6), 565–570.

Hicks, M. L., & Buus, S. (2000). Efficient across-frequency integration: Evidence from psychometric functions. *The Journal of the Acoustical Society of America*, *107*(6), 3333–3342.

Houpt, J. W., & Townsend, J. T. (2011). An extension of SIC predictions to the Wiener coactive model. *Journal of Mathematical Psychology*, *55*, 267–270.

Houpt, J. W., & Townsend, J. T. (2012). Statistical measures for workload capacity analysis. *Journal of Mathematical Psychology*, *56*(5), 341–355.

Kohfeld, D. L. (1971). Simple RT as a function of stimulus intensity in decibels of light and sound. *Journal of Experimental Psychology*, *88*(2), 251–257.

Lentz, J. J., He, Y., Houpt, J. W., Delong, J. M., & Townsend, J. T. (2016). Processing characteristics of monaural tone detection: A reaction-time perspective on a classic psychoacoustic problem. In J. W. Houpt, & L. M. Blaha (Eds.), *Mathematical models of perception and cognition Volume II: A Festschrift for James T. Townsend*. Taylor and Francis.

Lentz, J. J., He, Y., & Townsend, J. T. (2014). A new perspective on binaural integration using response time methodology: Super capacity revealed in conditions of binaural masking release. *Frontiers in Human Neuroscience*, *8*.

Marill, T. (1956). *Detection theory and psychophysics* (Doctoral dissertation). Massachusetts Institute of Technology, Dept. of Economics and Social Science.

Miller, J. (1982). Divided attention: Evidence for coactivation with redundant signals. *Cognitive Psychology*, *14*(2), 247–279.

Rand, T. C. (1974). Dichotic release from masking for speech. *The Journal of the Acoustical Society of America*, *55*(3), 678–680.

Schafer, T. H., & Gales, R. S. (1949). Auditory masking of multiple tones by random noise. *The Journal of the Acoustical Society of America*, *21*(4), 392–397.

Schlittenlacher, J., Ellermeier, W., & Arseneau, J. (2014). Binaural loudness gain measured by simple RT. *Attention, Perception, & Psychophysics*, *76*(5), 1465–1472.

Schröter, H., Ulrich, R., & Miller, J. (2007). Effects of redundant auditory stimuli on RT. *Psychonomic Bulletin & Review*, *14*(1), 39–44.

Schweickert, R. (1978). A critical path generalization of the additive factor method: Analysis of a Stroop task. *Journal of Mathematical Psychology*, *18*(2), 105–139.

Schweickert, R., & Townsend, J. T. (1989). A trichotomy: Interactions of factors prolonging sequential and concurrent mental processes in stochastic discrete mental (PERT) networks. *Journal of Mathematical Psychology*, *33*(3), 328–347.

Silbert, N. H., Townsend, J. T., & Lentz, J. J. (2009). Independence and separability in the perception of complex nonspeech sounds. *Attention, Perception, & Psychophysics*, *71*(8), 1900–1915.

Simon, J. R. (1967). Ear preference in a simple reaction-time task. *Journal of Experimental Psychology*, *75*(1), 49–55.

Sternberg, S. (1966). High-speed scanning in human memory. *Science*, *153*(3736), 652–654.

Stevenson, R. A., & James, T. W. (2009). Neuronal convergence and inverse effectiveness with audiovisual integration of speech and tools in human superior temporal sulcus: Evidence from BOLD fMRI. *NeuroImage*, *44*, 1210–1223.

Sumby, W. H., & Pollack, I. (1954). Visual contribution to speech intelligibility in noise. *The Journal of the Acoustical Society of America*, *26*(2), 212–215.

Summerfield, Q. (1987). Some preliminaries to a comprehensive account of audio-visual speech perception. In B. Dodd, & R. Campbell (Eds.), *Hearing by eye: The psychology of lip-reading*. London: Lawrence Erlbaum Associates.

Tanner Jr, W. P. (1956). Theory of recognition. *The Journal of the Acoustical Society of America*, *28*(5), 882–888.

Townsend, J. T. (1971). A note on the identifiability of parallel and serial processes. *Perception & Psychophysics*, *10*(3), 161–163.

Townsend, J. T. (1984). Uncovering mental processes with factorial experiments. *Journal of Mathematical Psychology*, *28*, 363–400.

Townsend, J. T. (1990). Truth and consequences of ordinal differences in statistical distributions: Toward a theory of hierarchical inference. *Psychological Bulletin*, *108*(3), 551–567.

Townsend, J. T., & Altieri, N. (2012). An accuracy-response time capacity assessment function that measures performance against standard parallel predictions. *Psychological Review*, *199*(3), 500–516.

Townsend, J. T., & Ashby, F. G. (1983). *The stochastic modeling of elementary psychological processes*. Cambridge, England: Cambridge University Press.

Townsend, J. T., & Nozawa, G. (1995). Spatio-temporal properties of elementary perception: An investigation of parallel, serial, and coactive theories. *Journal of Mathematical Psychology*, *39*(4), 321–359.

Townsend, J. T., & Schweickert, R. (1989). Toward the trichotomy method: Laying the foundation of stochastic mental networks. *Journal of Mathematical Psychology*, *33*, 309–327.

Townsend, J. T., & Wenger, M. J. (2004). A theory of interactive parallel processing: New capacity measures and predictions for a response time inequality series. *Psychological Review*, *111*(4), 1003.

Van den Brink, W. A., & Houtgast, T. (1990a). Efficient across-frequency integration in short-signal detection. *The Journal of the Acoustical Society of America*, *87*(1), 284–291.

Van den Brink, W. A., & Houtgast, T. (1990b). Spectro-temporal integration in signal detection. *The Journal of the Acoustical Society of America*, *88*(4), 1703–1711.

Wagner, E., Florentine, M., Buus, S., & McCormack, J. (2004). Spectral loudness summation and simple RT. *The Journal of the Acoustical Society of America*, *116*(3), 1681–1686.

Logical-Rule Based Models of Categorization: Using Systems Factorial Technology to Understand Feature and Dimensional Processing

12

David W. Griffiths, Anthea G. Blunden, Daniel R. Little
The University of Melbourne, Melbourne, VIC, Australia

Categorization is of primary importance to cognition. The mechanisms underlying categorization have been termed the "pulsating heartbeat of thought" (Hofstadter & Sander, 2013, p. 17). A foundational question for understanding categorization is how information from multiple stimulus dimensions or attributes is combined when making categorization decisions. Of course, this question is important for a much broader class of decisions (e.g., buy or sell? innocent or guilty? friend or foe?) and has been addressed using a variety of paradigms. The application of Systems Factorial Technology (SFT) to categorization decisions has allowed for novel insights as to whether features are processed and combined serially, in parallel, or pooled together into a single object.

This question is novel in the study of categorization since the most successful alternative theories of categorization (especially those developed to address categorization response time, RT) assume that information is pooled across dimensions into a single object representation. For instance, consider Nosofsky and Palmeri's (1997) Exemplar-based Random Walk model (EBRW). In this model, categorization decisions are made by comparing a to-be-categorized item with a set of previously stored exemplars that are stored as multidimensional instances, represented in a psychological space, along with a category label. The model assumes that a similarity value, based on a negative exponential function of the distance in the psychological space between the to-be-categorized item and each stored exemplar, is computed for each category by summing the similarity scores over all items within a category. The summed similarity value for each category is converted to a sampling probability by dividing it by the total summed similarity to all exemplars and is then used to drive a random-walk decision model (Laming, 1968; Link & Heath, 1975; Nosofsky & Palmeri, 1997; Ratcliff, 1978; Thornton & Gilden, 2007). A key feature of the EBRW is that the random walk is driven by a pooled, summed-similarity signal; that is, the dimensions of a stimulus do not exert an independent influence on the RT after they are weighted and used to compute the summed similarity signal.

By contrast, Ashby's (2000) stochastic general recognition theory model (GRT; see also Ashby, 1989; Ashby & Townsend, 1986) assumes that each stimulus is represented by a multidimensional perceptual distribution. Observers establish a decision

Systems Factorial Technology, DOI: 10.1016/B978-0-12-804315-8.00015-X boundary separating two (or more) category regions. On each time step of the categorization process, a sample is taken from the perceptual distribution; if the sample falls into, for instance, that region representing the target category, then a sequential sampling model (e.g., a random walk) takes a step toward the target category criterion. Samples are accumulated in this way until the criterion for the target or contrast category is reached. Despite the differences in stimulus representation, like the EBRW, stochastic GRT also assumes that all of the evidence from a stimulus is "collected" in a single processing channel. Such a model is consistent with a coactive processing architecture (Fifić, Little, & Nosofsky, 2010). It is evident that SFT allows for exploration of other types of processing including serial and parallel processing architectures.

In this chapter, we describe the progress of a research program that has utilized SFT to address the question of how multidimensional stimulus information is combined when making categorization decisions. This research has focused on the development of a parametric modeling framework, the logical rule models (Fifić et al., 2010), to complement the nonparametric SFT tools (Townsend & Nozawa, 1995). Although this framework has much in common with Ashby's (2000) stochastic GRT model, the logical rule models extend that approach to allow for different processing architectures. For instance, the logical-rule models allow separate boundaries to be established along each dimension. Separate unidimensional decisions can then be combined either in a serial or parallel architecture. Hence, one of the key developments of this program has been the focus on using SFT to differentiate the processing of different types of separable and integral stimulus dimensions. We first review this work and then introduce the logical rule models. Finally, we will discuss the connection between these models and new formal extensions of the General Recognition Theory framework to response times (Townsend, Houpt, & Silbert, 2012) with specific regard for the theoretical concepts of decisional separability, perceptual separability, and perceptual independence.

SFT Applied to Perceptual Categorization

SFT was first applied to the question of multidimensional perceptual categorization in Fifić, Nosofsky, and Townsend (2008) and Fifić and Townsend (2010). In these experiments, on each trial the observer had to make a speeded decision as to whether the presented stimulus belonged to the target or the contrast category. Fig. 12.1 shows the categorization design used in their experiment. (Note that the redundant, R, stimulus – explained below – was not presented in their experiment.) In this design, the stimuli comprised two dimensions (dimension x and dimension y). As in the double factorial detection task (see tutorial chapter, this book, Altieri, Fifić, Little, & Yang, 2017; Townsend & Nozawa, 1995), the discriminability of each dimension is systematically manipulated. That is, each dimension varies on three discriminability levels which combine orthogonally. In contrast to the double factorial detection task, the discriminability is determined by the distance of a stimulus from the category boundary (cf. Ashby & Gott, 1988).

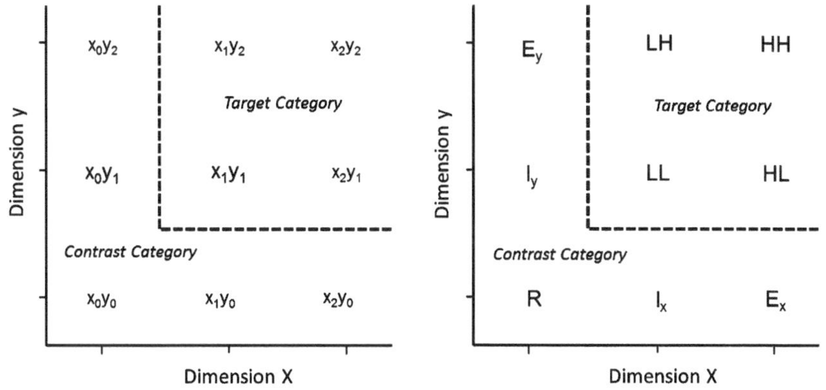

Figure 12.1 (Left panel) The category structure used in experiments testing the logical-rule models of classification. The stimuli in the upper right (x_1y_1, x_1y_2, x_2y_1, and x_2y_2) are the members of the target category, whereas the remaining stimuli are the members of the contrast category. The dotted boundaries illustrate the category boundaries. (Right panel) Main stimulus types. H and L refer to high- and low-discriminability dimension values, respectively; *R* redundant stimulus; *I* interior stimulus; *E* exterior stimulus.

The stimulus space is divided into two categories: the target category and the contrast category (see the dotted line in Fig. 12.1). In order to correctly classify an item as belonging to the target category, the values on each stimulus dimension must exceed a criterion value on both dimension x AND dimension y. Conversely, items from contrast category need only satisfy one of the decision rules in order for a correct classification to be made (i.e., an OR decision rule).

In accordance with decision bound theory (Ashby & Gott, 1988), items which lie closer to the boundary should be more difficult to discriminate from the other category, whereas items which lie further away should yield an easier (and therefore faster) decision. The items in the upper right quadrant (target category) have dimensions which require either a high discriminability (H) decision or a low discriminability (L) decision. Hence, these dimensions factorially combine to form the HH, HL, LH, and LL stimuli necessary to utilize SFT's nonparametric Mean Interaction Contrast (MIC) and Survivor Interaction Contrast (SIC) measures. In addition, the remaining contrast category items also provide a qualitative distinction between several models of interest; however, in the initial investigations only the target category predictions were examined. We first review these initial tests and then turn to the contrast category predictions.

The Processing of Separable and Integral Dimensions

Fifić et al. (2008) used this task to compare the processing of separable and integral stimulus dimensions. The separable dimensions were the saturation of a red color square and the horizontal position of an inset vertical bar. These were presented either as separate objects (i.e., the saturated square on the left and the inset vertical bar on the right) or as a single object (i.e., spatially overlapped). The integral stimulus dimensions were the saturation and brightness of a red color square. Given the factorial design of the target category, contrasts between the target category items can be used to adjudicate between serial, parallel, and coactive processing architectures. The patterns of RTs across the LL, LH, HL, and HH items can be usefully summarized using the mean interaction contrast (MIC) and the survivor interaction contrast (SIC) (see Altieri et al., 2017).

For the separable dimensioned stimuli, the MIC and SIC analyses revealed no evidence of overadditivity as expected from a coactive processing model. For the separable dimensions in separate locations, four of their five participants show strong evidence of serial exhaustive processing. The remaining participant and both of the participants who categorized the overlapped separable dimensions showed significant underadditivity indicating parallel exhaustive processing. Of course, the conjunctive rule design necessitates exhaustive processing; early termination of the decision would result in inaccurate performance. For the integral dimensioned stimuli, the MIC and SIC results pointed clearly to overadditivity, and, hence, coactive processing, for seven of their eight observers. (The eighth observer had a substantially higher error rate on the LL stimulus which might have obscured the signature coactive stimulus pattern.)

Mental Architecture and the Concept of Holism

Fifić and Townsend (2010) used a similar design to test how different mental architectures and stopping rules mapped on to the concept of holism when processing faces based on their second-order spatial features (e.g., eye distance). Holistic processing is generally thought to encompass the notion of processing the entire object rather than the individual features of an object and consequently bears some resemblance to the notion of stimulus integrality (Amishav & Kimchi, 2010). Holistic processing is often identified on that basis of a failure to selectively attend to parts of a face in the context of the whole face (i.e., in the composite face task; Richler & Gauthier, 2013). Fifić and Townsend (2010) suggest, however, that failure of selective attention is insufficient to differentiate between different processing architectures. In particular, although coactive processing would seem to be the architecture most aligned with theoretical definitions of holistic processing (Richler, Palmeri, & Gauthier, 2012), an independent parallel process would also be able to predict a failure of selective attention. Hence, in order to identify the underlying processing architecture, Fifić and Townsend (2010) utilized the categorization design shown in Fig. 12.1.

In their experiment, eye separation and lip height of a schematic face served as the two dimensions. Further, Fifić and Townsend (2010) varied whether these two facial features were presented in the old facial context (i.e., the same general head shape, nose, and ears as was used during the early training sessions), a new facial context, or just the features alone. Coactive processing was only found for half of the observers and only in the old face context. The remaining observers in the old face context demonstrated serial processing. By contrast, most of the participants in the new face context exhibited serial processing, and most of the participants in the features alone condition exhibited parallel processing (i.e., two-thirds of the observers had underadditive SICs). Hence, strong holistic (i.e., coactive) processing was only found in the old face context condition for a subset of the participants.

As an alternative hypothesis, Fifić and Townsend (2010) suggested that there might be a shift from independent parallel processing to coactive processing over the course of experience with the stimuli. In support, an analysis of one subject's data across sessions showed a marked shift from parallel processing early in the experiment to coactive processing late in the experiment in the old face context condition. Intriguingly, in the intermediate stages between the underadditive parallel SIC and the overadditive coactive SIC, the SIC appeared to have the characteristic S-shape of serial processing. Consequently, the different processing architectures inferred for each of their observers in different conditions might represent an intermediate stage in the development of holistic processing.

In sum, differences in the MIC and SIC appear to empirically distinguish the categorization of separable stimulus dimensions, integral stimulus dimensions, and, to some extent, holistic processing. The categorization of separable stimulus dimensions was most consistent with serial or parallel processing whereas the categorization of integral color stimulus dimensions was most consistent with coactivity. On the other hand, the processing of facial features was only coactive in some contexts (or, alternatively, may have not yet developed the properties commensurate with stimulus integrality). Nonetheless, it is worth considering how the independent architecture vs coactive architecture distinction accords with other converging operations that point to a difference between separable and integral stimulus dimensions.

Empirical Distinctions Between Separable and Integral Dimensions

There is a long tradition in the study of perception and cognition of identifying key empirical distinctions between the processing of separable- and integral-dimensioned stimuli. These results cover findings from a number of different domains but all converge on the idea that separable dimensions, unlike integral dimensions, are broken down into their component parts which are processed independently of one another. For instance, consider the following:

1. When modeling distances between pairs of stimuli derived from some proximity estimate (e.g., identification confusions, similarity ratings), the metric assumed in a multidimensional scaling (MDS; Borg, 2011; Borg & Groenen, 2005) solution is typically thought to be city-block for separable dimensioned stimuli but Euclidean for integral dimensioned stimuli (Attneave, 1950; Nosofsky, 1992; Shepard, 1987; Shepard & Chang, 1963; Torgerson, 1958).

2. Stimuli with separable dimensions are sorted on the basis of those individual dimensions. By contrast, stimuli with integral dimensions are sorted on the basis of overall similarity (Garner, 1974; Handel & Imai, 1972; Imai & Garner, 1968).
3. With separable-dimensioned stimuli, there is a distinct failure of the mapping hypothesis, which states that one should be able to predict categorization accuracy from identification confusions. For separable-dimensioned stimuli, this is not possible without additional assumptions about changes in selective attention between tasks (Nosofsky, 1986; Shepard, Hovland, & Jenkins, 1961). By contrast, the mapping hypothesis works well for integral-dimensioned stimuli (Shepard & Chang, 1963).
4. Learning to selectively attend to valid dimensions occurs rapidly and efficiently for separable stimulus dimensions (Nosofsky, 1986; Posner, 1964; Shepard et al., 1961) but not for integral dimensions (Nosofsky, 1987; Nosofsky & Palmeri, 1996). The aforementioned results concerning failures of selective attention in holistic processing are also relevant to this point.
5. Integral stimulus dimensions tend to interfere with one another if one dimension must be ignored, but integral dimensions facilitate each other if the dimensions are presented in a correlated fashion (Biederman & Checkosky, 1970; Egeth, 1967; Garner, 1969; 1974, Garner & Felfoldy, 1970; Lockhead, 1966). This effect arises both at the level of accuracy and RT (Garner, 1974; Nosofsky & Palmeri, 1997). By contrast, no interference or facilitation effects are observed for separable dimensions.
6. Using rules to evaluate dimensions proceeds in a serial and self-terminating fashion for separable dimensions but not for integral dimensions (Trabasso, Rollins, & Shaughnessy, 1971; see also Bourne, Dominowski, Loftus, & Healy, 1979; Ketchum & Bourne, 1980). This result is noteworthy in the present context; however, as we will argue below, this result applies strongly only to certain types of separable dimensions (specifically, dimensions which are located in separate spatial locations as in Fifić et al., 2008; Trabasso et al., 1971).

We add to the above list the results of Fifić et al. (2008) and Fifić and Townsend (2010).

7. Separable dimensions are best characterized by additivity (MIC $= 0$) or underadditivity (MIC < 0) in the mean RTs and RT distributions for factorially combined stimulus dimensions. By contrast, integral dimensions are best characterized by overadditivity (MIC > 0) in the mean RTs and RT distributions for factorially combined stimulus dimensions. Of course, these RT patterns allow us to infer that the processing of separable dimensions is best thought of as occurring in independent processing channels arrayed either serially or in parallel. The processing of integral dimensions is best characterized by coactivity.

Taken together, these converging operations point to the underlying fact that the information conveyed by separable dimensions can be thought of as being represented by distinct information sources (e.g., organized by independent dimensional axes), whereas integral dimensions do not appear to have a coherent representation and instead appear to form a single source of information. Despite this compelling notion,

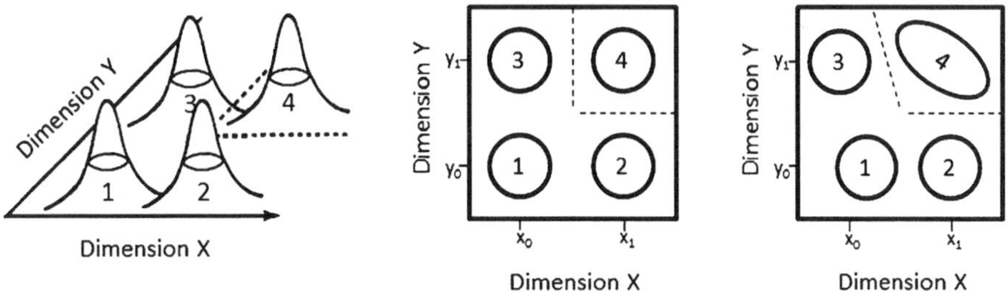

Figure 12.2 Example illustration of major General Recognition Theory (GRT) concepts. (Left) Each stimulus is represented as a bivariate normal distribution. Stimulus 4 belongs to one category, the remaining stimuli belong to the other category. (Middle) Isoprobability contours for the four stimuli. The four stimuli in this panel exhibit perceptual independence, perceptual separability, and decisional separability. (Right) Isoprobability contours for the four stimuli illustrating violations of perceptual independence (stimulus 4), violations of perceptual separability (compare stimuli 1 and 3 and stimuli 2 and 4), and violations of decisional separability (see the diagonal boundary between stimuli 3 and 4).

a difficulty with pursuing this line of reasoning (as foreshadowed above) is that several of the theoretical ideas invoked to explain the above list of empirical results at times conflate several important information processing concepts. Specifically, the above results do not allow for distinctions to be made between the concepts of independence and separability or between perceptual and decisional factors that could affect information processing. This muddling of concepts was the impetus behind the development of Ashby and Townsend's (1986) General Recognition Theory (GRT). Since GRT forms a key component of the logical-rule based models that we describe below, we will briefly provide an overview of several concepts using GRT, keeping with the example of perceptual categorization.

General Recognition Theory

GRT is a multidimensional extension of signal detection theory (Green & Swets, 1966). In GRT, like its stochastic extension (Ashby, 2000), each stimulus is represented by a multivariate distribution which captures the mean location of the stimulus (i.e., in relation to other stimuli), and the variable perceptions of that stimulus along each stimulus dimension. This distribution is often assumed to be Gaussian but GRT applies generally to any multivariate distribution (Ashby, 1992; Ashby & Townsend, 1986; Kadlec & Townsend, 1992; Thomas, 1995). As described above, when an individual makes a decision about, for instance, category, a decision boundary is established to separate regions of the stimulus space associated with each stimulus or category. Consider the categorization example shown in Fig. 12.2 (a somewhat simplified version of the design shown in Fig. 12.1). The left-hand panel shows four two-dimensional stimuli represented by their perceptual distributions. In the illustrated task, the stimulus in the upper left-hand corner is assigned to a different category than the remaining stimuli. The dotted line indicates the decision boundary established by the observer. The middle panel illustrates the same four stimuli as viewed "from above", where each circle represents an isoprobability contour for each stimulus.

GRT provides a framework for formally defining several concepts important for distinguishing separability from integrality: namely, perceptual independence, perceptual separability, and decisional separability. Each of these concepts can be illustrated by comparing the middle and right-hand panels of Fig. 12.2.

Perceptual Independence

In GRT, perceptual independence is defined as stochastic independence. That is, in the multivariate perceptual stimulus representation, two dimensions are perceptually independent if the correlation between the dimensions equals 0. For instance, all of the stimuli in the middle panel and the three stimuli numbered 1 to 3 in the right-hand panel are represented by perceptual distributions characterized by the absence of a correlation between dimensions. By contrast, stimulus 4 in the right-hand panel exhibits a strong negative correlation between dimensions x and y and would therefore be classed as having violated perceptual independence.

Perceptual Separability

Perceptual separability holds when the perceptual effects of one dimension do not depend on the level of the other dimension. In practice, the implication is that a dimension can be represented by the marginal perceptual distributions along that dimension. For instance, in the middle panel of Fig. 12.2, it is evident that each of the stimuli could be represented by the marginal distributions on dimension x and on dimension y. By contrast, for the stimuli shown in the right-hand panel, perceptual separability only holds for dimension y. That is, despite the violation of perceptual independence for stimulus 4, the marginal distributions for the values of the y dimensions are equivalent across levels of dimension x. On the other hand, perceptual separability is violated for dimension x for stimuli 1 and 3. These two stimuli have different marginal distributions on dimension x indicating that the perception of value x_0 depends on the value of dimension y. Perceptual separability can be violated in a number of ways but primarily through shifts in the mean stimulus locations (termed mean shift integrality) or through changes in the stimulus variances (termed variance shift integrality).

Decisional Separability

Finally, if decisional separability holds on dimension x, then the decisions on x are invariant across levels of dimension y. In practice, this corresponds to a decision boundary which is orthogonal to the x axis (see, for instance, the middle panel of Fig. 12.2). By contrast, in the right-hand panel, decisional separability is violated by the diagonal boundary separating stimuli 3 and 4. In general, decisional separability can be readily violated if perceptual separability is violated and people also respond in an optimal fashion.

In the following section, we describe the development of a set of models, termed logical-rule models, which synthesize GRT and mental architecture approaches by using sequential sampling models to represent the accumulation of evidence for each dimension. We review a series of studies in which these models have been applied to the questions of dimensional processing with a focus on questions of separability and integrality. To add further foreshadowing, it is useful to note here that Townsend et al. (2012) have recently introduced a dynamic extension of GRT (GRT-RT) which provides formal definitions of perceptual independence, perceptual separability, and decisional separability which act the level of response time distributions. These definitions, which we review below, are developed within the framework of stochastic differential equations (SDE; see, e.g., Smith, 2000). Since the logical rule models reviewed here are a special class of SDEs, there is a direct interpretation of the parametric assumptions of the logical-rule models within the GRT-RT framework. Hence, the empirical results modeled using the logical rule models provide a strong theoretical verification of the theoretical definitions specified in the standard, static GRT and in the dynamic GRT-RT.

Logical Rule-Models: Combining Mental Architectures with Perceptual Representations

The logical rule-based models synthesized developments in decision-bound approaches to categorization (Ashby & Lee, 1991) with evidence accumulation models (Brown & Heathcote, 2008; Busemeyer, 1985; Luce, 1986; Ratcliff, 1978) and the mental architecture approaches to response time (Schweickert, 1992; Schweickert & Dzhafarov, 2000; Sternberg, 1969; Townsend, 1984; 1990). In the logical rule models, GRT (Ashby & Townsend, 1986) and some assumptions from decision boundary theory (Ashby & Lee, 1991) form a model "front-end" that is used to compute the probability that a random walk takes a step toward either the target or contrast category decision thresholds (see Fig. 12.3). The "front-end" works analogously to the stochastic GRT model (Ashby, 2000) described above. The total time taken to reach a decision on a particular dimension is determined by the number of steps taken by the random walk to reach the criterion.

To capture different architectures, decisions from dimension x and dimension y are driven by two independent random-walk processes (see Fig. 12.3). These random walks, coupled with different decision rules (i.e., AND or OR rules), form the "back-end" used to predict decision times for each process. The final decision is determined by combining the outcomes of both random walk processes under each of the candidate mental architectures plus additional time capturing non-decision time processes (Luce, 1986). For example, a target category decision can only be reached by satisfying the conjunctive rule (i.e., both the random-walk from dimension x and the random-walk from dimension y must reach a target category decision), whereas a contrast category decision can be made by satisfying the disjunctive rule (i.e., only one random-walk need reach a contrast category decision). In a serial process, each random walk takes place one at a time, whereas in a parallel process, both random walks take place simultaneously. In combination with the self-terminating and exhaustive stopping rules, the logical rule models implement four possible architectures:

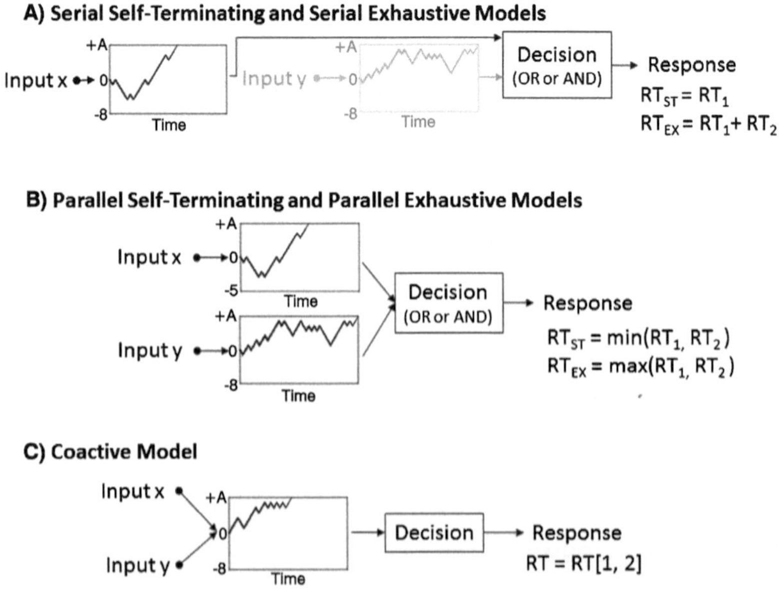

Figure 12.3 Illustration of the "back-end" logical rule models. The top row illustrates (A) a serial self-terminating (ST) model which terminates processing after the first dimension and a serial exhaustive (EX) model which exhaustively processes both dimensions. Note that in serial self-terminating model, the second input is only processed if necessary (i.e., if the first input fails to satisfy the OR rule or if an AND rule is used; hence, this process is greyed out). By contrast, in the serial exhaustive model, the second input is always processed. The middle row illustrates (B) a parallel self-terminating (ST) and a parallel exhaustive (EX) model. The bottom row illustrates (C) a coactive processing model in which both inputs are pooled into a single processing channel.

serial self-terminating, serial exhaustive, parallel self-terminating, and parallel exhaustive.

The logical rule models also include a fifth coactive architecture in which information from both dimensions is pooled into a single random walk process. This model is commensurate with many of successful categorization models such as EBRW (Nosofsky & Palmeri, 1997) and stochastic GRT (Ashby, 2000); importantly, the coactive model makes the same qualitative predictions as these models in the categorization task shown in Fig. 12.2.

For the target category, the serial, parallel, and coactive logical rule models make MIC and SIC predictions consistent with the theoretical predictions outlined by SFT (see the tutorial chapter). In Fifić et al. (2008) and Fifić and Townsend (2010), only the target category predictions were considered in the differentiation of serial, parallel, and coactive processing; however, Fifić et al. (2010) demonstrated that the contrast category predictions also allowed for diagnostic distinctions to be made between each of the models (see Fig. 12.4).

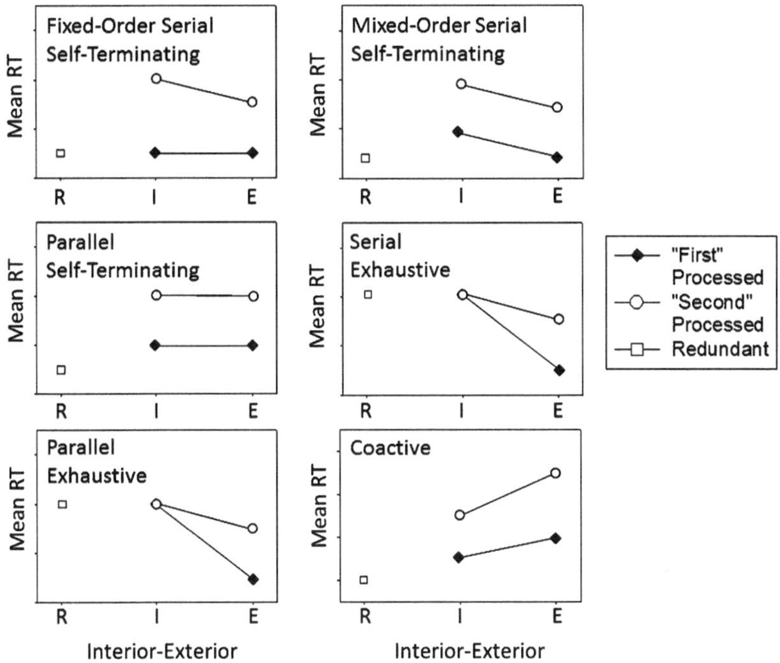

Figure 12.4 Mean RT predictions for the contrast category stimuli.

Diagnostic Contrast Category Predictions

Because the contrast category permits self-termination of the decision process, the contrast category predictions are useful not only in differentiating processing architectures but also in differentiating stopping rules. To explain, the items in the contrast category can be identified by their position in the stimulus space. The redundant stimulus, R, satisfies both of the boundary decisions necessary to classify a stimulus as belonging to the contrast category (i.e., it is both to the left and below the decision boundary). The stimuli adjacent to R are termed the interior stimuli, I_x and I_y, and the stimuli at the far edges are termed the exterior stimuli, E_x and E_y.[1]

If the stimulus dimensions shown in Fig. 12.1 are processed in a fixed-order serial and self-terminating fashion, then we would expect that all of the contrast category stimuli with the same value on the first-processed dimension (e.g., x_0y_0, x_0y_1, and x_0y_2 assuming that dimension x is processed first) to have the same processing time. Hence, the fixed-order serial self-terminating model predicts equally fast RTs for all stimuli on the first processed dimension with RTs on the second processed dimension being slower overall. The exterior stimulus on the second processed dimension should be faster than the interior stimulus under serial self-terminating processing. To explain, after processing the first processed dimension (and determining that the decision cannot yet terminate due to a value greater than 0 on that dimension), processing switches to the second dimension. The time to this switch will be shorter for the exterior than the interior stimulus because the exterior stimulus is further away from the decision boundary on that dimension – and consequently, easier to process.

The contrast category predictions allow a distinction to be made between a fixed-order serial model, which always processes the same dimension first, and mixed-order serial processing, which assumes that the dimension which is processed first varies from trial to trial. A mixed-order serial self-terminating model makes similar predictions to the fixed order model but additionally predicts that the exterior stimulus should be faster than the interior stimulus on both dimensions. Averaged across trials where a participant switches from, for instance, dimension x to dimension y and trials where a participant switches from dimension y to dimension x, the time up to that switch will be shorter for exterior stimulus.

In a serial exhaustive model, the contrast category predictions reflect that fact that both of the dimensions are processed even if one or both of those dimensions satisfy the contrast category decision. The serial exhaustive model predicts that the processing time for each stimulus is simply the sum of processing time for both dimensions. Hence, the redundant and interior stimuli (i.e., I_x and I_y), which are approximately equidistant from the decision bounds, should have approximately equivalent RTs. The exterior stimuli, by contrast, should be faster than the interior stimuli due to fact that one dimension should be faster than the other.

Since in a parallel self-terminating model, the processing time for the contrast category is the minimum processing time across both dimensions, the predictions for the interior and exterior stimuli should be equivalent. We note, however, that one dimension might be processed faster than the other. The redundant stimulus should be faster than the interior and exterior stimuli due to statistical facilitation. That is, when there are two chances for the stimulus to terminate, the minimum time will be faster than the processing time when there is only one chance to terminate (Raab, 1962). By contrast, the parallel exhaustive model predicts that the processing time will be the maximum processing time across both dimensions regardless of whether or not a dimension satisfies one of the contrast category decisions rules. Hence, like the serial exhaustive model, a parallel exhaustive model predicts that the redundant and interior stimuli will have similar RTs and that the exterior stimuli will be faster than the interior stimuli.

In the coactive model, the interior stimuli are predicted to be faster than the exterior stimuli. This prediction is unique to the coactive model and can be motivated by considering the fact that in the coactive logical rule model, each stimulus is represented by a bivariate normal distribution. As one moves from the exterior to the interior to the redundant stimulus, an increasing proportion of the volume of the bivariate distribution will be located in the contrast category region. Hence, the probability of sampling a percept from the contrast category increases for the redundant and interior stimuli compared to the exterior stimuli. This, in turn, results in a faster predicted RT. In the next section, we (a) review how these predictions, in concert with the predictions for the factorial target category stimuli, have been used to differentiate the parametric logical rule models and (b) provide further converging evidence about the nature of information processing for separable and integral dimension.

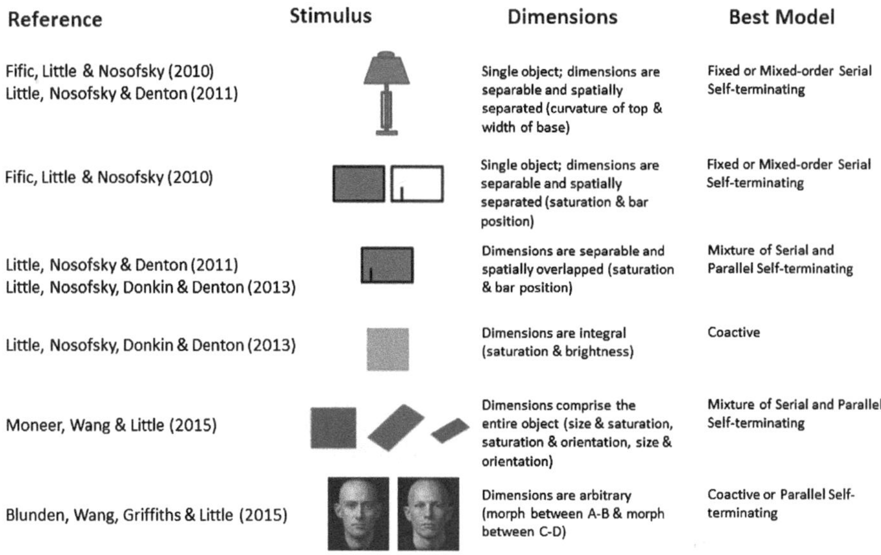

Figure 12.5 Stimuli and dimensions which have been used to evaluate the logical rule models.

Architecture, Integrality, and Separability

Separable Dimensions

Fifić et al. (2010) replicated Fifić et al.'s (2008) experiment using saturation and bar position dimensions (located in different spatial locations) but also included tests of the contrast category predictions. In the initial tests, participants were explicitly instructed to process the dimensions in a fixed-order serial, self-terminating manner. These results confirmed the fixed-order serial, self-terminating predictions for all nine of the stimuli in the categorization design. A further test of the model predictions utilized schematic drawings of lamps which varied on the width of the base and the curvature of the lamp's top piece (or finial; see Fig. 12.5).

The lamp condition results generalized the serial self-terminating model results to stimuli which had a number of additional properties beyond the saturation and bar position stimuli. First, the dimensions of the lamps, although located in different spatial locations, were part of a single object. This stimulus provides an important contrast to the separate objects in separate locations stimuli, particularly with regard to questions of whether whole objects are selected for processing (cf. object-based attentional theories; Chen, 2012). Second, on each trial, there was additional irrelevant dimensional variation; that is, although not relevant for the categorization task, the body of the lamp and angle of the lamp shade also varied from trial to trial. Evidently, participants were able to effectively ignore these irrelevant dimensions as the results conformed to the predictions of the serial, self-terminating process.

One advantage of the parametric modeling approach taken by the logical rule models over the nonparametric measures is that additional mechanisms can be tested and compared quantitatively, even when these additional mechanisms do not change the qualitative (e.g., MIC or SIC) predictions. To explain, in the logical rule models, like many RT models, the final RT is assumed to be the sum of the decision time and the time taken for non-decision processes (Luce, 1986; Ratcliff, 1978). To account for the RTs observed for the lamp stimuli, Fifić et al. (2010) added an additional attention switch cost. This attention switch cost is a plausible reflection of the time it takes to disengage and reallocate attention to a different location (Sperling & Weichselgartner, 1995), and its inclusion improved the quantitative fit of the serial self-terminating model (even accounting for the additional parameter). This is a clear instantiation of what Townsend and Wenger (2004) term the "methodological sieve" approach whereby the strong qualitative tests of SFT can be followed by principled tests of specific mechanisms allowing the development of "increasingly precise and successful predictive theories" (p. 392).

Two further contributions of Fifić et al. (2010) were: (i) testing subjects under conditions where the rule was provided but not specific processing instructions; these subjects also showed RTs consistent with serial self-terminating processing, and Little, Nosofsky, and Denton (2011) confirmed that serial ST processing was adopted for the lamp stimuli even when the task was learned through trial-by-trial feedback. (ii) An additional set of participants was tested under speeded-response instructions. This manipulation is important because the SFT measures depend on accurate responding and do not provide diagnostic predictions when error rates are high. Nonetheless, the error RT distributions could be modeled parametrically allowing Fifić et al. (2010) to determine that the serial self-terminating model made accurate predictions for both the correct and error RT distributions.

The benefit of parametric modeling was also apparent in Little et al. (2011), who investigated the target and contrast category predictions of the overlapped saturation and bar position stimuli (see Fig. 12.5). For these stimuli, the data were best captured by a model which assumed a trial-by-trial mixture of serial and parallel self-terminating processing. Moneer, Wang, and Little (2016) extended this result to the important case of stimuli composed of dimensions which comprised the entire object, such as size and shape or size and saturation (see Fig. 12.5). These dimensions, while nominally separable, have been previously found to show facilitation and interference effects which have been taken to indicate some level of, at least, partial integrality (Biederman & Checkosky, 1970; Smith & Kilroy, 1979). For instance, Keele and Neill (1978) defined integrality as "those [dimensions] that belong to the same object. Thus, size and color of the same object are integral but size and color of different objects are separable." (p. 14). Moneer et al. (2016) showed that across all combinations of size, orientation, and saturation, processing was best accounted for by a mixture of serial and parallel self-terminating processing. Using only the nonparametric analyses, this type of mixture model would not be wholly identifiable.

Integral Dimensions

Unlike for separable dimensions, Fifić et al. (2008) found that integral dimensions (i.e., Munsell colors varying in brightness and saturation) were processed coactively.

Little, Nosofsky, Donkin, and Denton (2013) confirmed that the performance with these stimuli confirmed the target and contrast category predictions (i.e., that the interior stimulus would be faster than the exterior stimulus). The faster interior than exterior RT is highly diagnostic of coactivity. Consequently, we further add to the list of converging operations:

8. Separable dimensions are best characterized by assuming either equal or greater mean RTs for the interior than exterior stimuli. Integral dimensions are best characterized by smaller mean RTs for the interior than exterior stimuli. These results are, of course, consistent with serial or parallel processing in the case of separable dimensions and with coactive processing in the case of integral dimensions.

Assumptions and Generalizations

When fitting the logical rule models to data, several simplifying assumptions have been made to constrain the parameters in certain ways. For instance, for the serial and parallel logical rule models, only a single set of random walk criteria has been assumed even though these models have two random walk processes. With regard to the GRT "front-end" model, most of the applications of the logical rule models have assumed that the mean locations of each of the stimuli on dimensions x and y can be fixed to a grid. (In our research, this assumption is typically verified using techniques such as MDS; see, e.g., Little et al., 2011.) Although separate perceptual variances have been estimated for both dimensions, the correlation between dimensions has been assumed to be zero. Likewise, the decision boundaries have been assumed to be orthogonal to the dimensional axes constraining the model to assume decisional separability. This set of constraints implies that perceptual independence, perceptual separability, and decisional separability hold for the stimulus representation (see the middle panel of Fig. 12.2).

An important exception is recent work by Blunden, Wang, Griffiths, and Little (2015) who used the categorization design to examine processing of a set of face morphs for which the dimensions are arbitrarily defined (see Fig. 12.5). Rather than being mapped to a single perceptual features, each of these arbitrary dimensions are comprised of changes to a number of features. The stimuli were created using a field morphing technique to proportionally mix the pixel values of four base faces. Goldstone and Steyvers (2001) provided preliminary evidence that these faces exhibited interference when one of the dimensions was to be ignored – one of the hallmarks of integral dimensions (Garner, 1974). Blunden et al. (2015) tested participants with either upright or inverted face morphs and fitted the resulting RT data using each of the logical rule models. In addition, Blunden et al. (2015) also conducted a systematic examination of the interaction between violations of perceptual separability, decisional separability, and processing architecture. Three classes of models were fit: (i) perceptual separability (PS) and decisional separability (DS) were held constant as in the other applications of the logical-rule models. (ii) A second class of models was fit that allowed violations of perceptual separability by assuming that the stimulus representation could allow mean shift integrality (as revealed through multidimensional scaling applied to the separate similarity rating data on the same stimuli). Decisional separability was assumed to hold for this set of models. (iii) Finally, perceptual separability and decisional separability were assumed to be violated by allowing optimal responding (i.e., diagonal decision boundaries).

Blunden et al. (2015) found that the overall best fitting models were either a parallel self-terminating model or a coactive model. There was, however, substantial between-participant variation in the "front-end" representation assumed by these models. Four of the participants were best fit by models that assumed both perceptual and decisional separability, but two were best fit by assuming a violation of perceptual separability (but not decisional separability), and two were best fit by models that assumed violations of both perceptual and decisional separability.

Allowing the logical rules models to test both representation and decision architecture allowed us to rule out serial and parallel exhaustive processing architectures. Nonetheless, different representational assumptions were necessary in order accurately model the RTs. Hence, although these stimuli show some characteristics of integrality and are processed coactively by some participants, this is not always the case. There was a good deal of individual variation in the representation and architecture.

Summary

The logical rule model have been applied to a large array of different stimulus types providing a comprehensive picture of the processing strategies employed during multidimensional categorization (see Fig. 12.5). Nevertheless, there remain several questions about how to simultaneously account for both the perceptual representations and the processing architecture, and further, to determine what these empirical observations mean for an underlying theory of integrality and separability. Blunden et al. (2015) provided initial investigations into what certain violations of the perceptual and decisional separability have on inferences of processing architectures. An alternative approach, taken by Townsend et al. (2012), was to develop dynamic concepts of perceptual and decisional separability. In the next section, we review their formal theory and discuss how these concepts are implemented by the logical rule models.

Link Between Logical Rule Models and GRT-RT

Townsend et al. (2012) introduced a dynamic version of GRT which extended definitions of decisional separability, perceptual separability, and perceptual independence to the temporal domain. Comparing the logical rule model predictions to the formal dynamic GRT definitions provides a way of interpreting the empirical results reviewed above. That is, from certain assumptions about the representation and the process, we expect certain invariances to hold in the data. These invariances, which arise at the level of accuracy and identification choice probabilities in the static GRT and at the level of RT distributions in GRT-RT, are called perceptual independence, perceptual separability, and decisional separability in order to differentiate important concepts. The logical rule models make a number of representation and processing assumptions when fit to data and by doing so predict RT invariances in certain situations which correspond to the GRT-RT concepts. Thus, finding that a given data set (e.g., saturation and bar position in different locations, Fifić et al., 2010) is better fit by a serial model than a coactive model, the logical rule models are also asserting a theoretical claim about separability and integrality. The link to dynamic GRT then provides a theoretically rigorous foundation for each of the assumptions in the logical rule models.

To demonstrate that evaluating the logical rule model assumptions using GRT-RT is possible, note that GRT-RT implements concepts at the level of RT distributions which can be evaluated using the class of stochastic differential equations, which take the following form:

$$d\mathbf{x}(t) = \mathbf{A}\mathbf{x}(t)dt + \mathbf{B}\mathbf{u}(t)dt + \sigma(t)dW(t). \tag{12.1}$$

Eq. (12.1) describes the change of the state of a process, $\mathbf{x}$, at time t. The length of the vector $\mathbf{x}$ represents the number of processing channels in the system. The vector $\mathbf{u}(t)$ represents the input to the system at time t. The matrices $\mathbf{A}$ and $\mathbf{B}$ govern interactions between the channels and between the inputs, respectively. A diagonal matrix indicates that the channels are independent; the variety and amount of cross-channel interaction is governed by the off-diagonal elements. $dW(t)$ is a Brownian motion process which is added to the inputs, and σ is diffusion coefficient (Smith, 2000).[2]

The well-studied drift diffusion model (Ratcliff, 1978) is a special case of Eq. (12.1) in which $\mathbf{A}$ is a zero matrix, $\mathbf{B}$ is a diagonal matrix (which simply rescales the drift rate vector, $\mathbf{u}(t)$, for each channel), and $\sigma(t) = \sigma$ (i.e., $d\mathbf{x}(t) = \mathbf{u}(t)dt + \sigma W(t)$; Smith, 2000). The random walk process used in the logical rule models is a discrete approximation to this continuous time model (Diederich & Busemeyer, 2003; Little, 2012; Luce, 1986; Ratcliff, 1978); hence, the logical rule models can be described using this same framework. For instance, in the coactive model, the SDE generalization would be identical to the standard diffusion model but with the values of the input vector $\mathbf{u}(t)$ determined using static GRT and decision bound theory. That is, although the applications of the logical rule models have assumed a discrete time random walk process to model RTs, by considering how the different mental architectures would be implemented using Eq. (12.1), we can directly relate the logical rule models to GRT-RT.

For the serial and parallel models, the logical rule models assume that each dimension is processed by a single random walk process. Further, the channels were always assumed to be independent (i.e., the off-diagonals in $\mathbf{A}$ and $\mathbf{B}$ equal 0). Assuming that $\mathbf{x} = \left[\begin{smallmatrix} x \\ y \end{smallmatrix}\right]$, the parallel model is represented exactly by Eq. (12.1). To implement the serial model, one could assume that the time varying input vector, $\mathbf{u}(t)$, represents the sequential processing of different stimulus dimensions. The difference between self-terminating and exhaustive processing is implemented by assuming different decision rules for the state of the process (see, e.g., Eidels, Houpt, Altieri, Pei, & Townsend, 2011, Appendix).

In the following, we will use the example of processing the spatially separated saturation and bar position stimuli. The full generality of Eq. (12.1) can be appreciated by noting that the parallel channels model used by Townsend et al. (2012) used separate parallel accrual channels for each value of two dimensions (e.g., low vs high saturation and left vs right bar position), namely $\mathbf{x} = \begin{bmatrix} x_1 \\ x_2 \\ y_1 \\ y_2 \end{bmatrix}$. By contrast, in the logical rule models, the random walk models have a perfect negative correlation between the values within a channel (analogous to continuous diffusion channels). That is, positive evidence that the saturation is low is negative evidence that the saturation is high, for example.

The temporal definitions of separability and independence are formulated within this framework in terms of interactions either between inputs, $\mathbf{u}$, or between channels, $\mathbf{x}$. Consequently, the definitions can be empirically evaluated by examining changes in the RT distributions for different stimulus combinations (e.g., examining timed marginal response invariance, which implies dynamic decisional and perceptual separability, can be evaluated by looking for equality of RT distributions for a given value of saturation across levels of bar position). The logical rule models make predictions which are commensurate with the dynamic definitions of separability and independence. Hence, in the following, we compare these definitions with the assumptions needed in the logical rule models for those definitions to hold.

Decisional Separability

The logical rule models instantiate the static GRT definition of decisional separability by assuming an orthogonal decision boundary in the GRT "front-end" model. In the dynamic GRT-RT framework, decisional separability is defined as an invariance of the response criteria on the processing of one dimension as the processing of another dimension (or as a function of the state of the other channel or dependent on the specific stimulus).

In the logical rule models, for dynamic decisional separability to hold the response criteria in the random walk "back-end" processes on each channel must be assumed to be independent. Applications of the logical rule models have estimated a single set of criteria for both random walk models (see, e.g., Fifić et al., 2010). This implies that the value of the criterion on, say, the saturation channel is not affected by the value of the stimulus on the bar position channel; hence, dynamic decisional separability holds in previous applications of the logical rule models. One must note, however, that the parallel systems model used by Townsend et al. (2012) has considerably more generality. For instance, violations of decisional separability in the dynamic framework can be caused by many things (e.g., direct interaction between decision criteria of two channels or the interaction between inputs which might indirectly affect the setting of decisional criterion).

Perceptual Independence

In static GRT, perceptual independence is defined as stochastic independence and is modeled in the logical rule model front-end by assuming zero correlation between the perceptual dimensions. In dynamic GRT, the concept of perceptual independence is invariance in the state of one channel given the state of another channel. That is, the off-diagonals of the **A** matrix representing the between-dimension interactions are 0. All of the logical rule models, except for the coactive model, have assumed channel independence. The coactive model, by contrast, can be implemented by assuming a perfect correlation between a set of parallel channels. That is, although one can model the coactive model as a single channel diffusion model, the same predictions result if one assumes (a) that equivalent inputs enter in to both channels (i.e., the entries in the $\mathbf{u}(t)$ are equivalent), (b) the off-diagonals in the **A** matrix equal 1 (Eidels et al., 2011), and (c) a single signed noise term is added to each channel (i.e., if a positive value, w, is added to channel 1, then a negative value, $-w$, is added to channel 2). Hence, the coactive logical rule model violates dynamic perceptual independence even if static perceptual independence is maintained.

Direct Separability

In dynamic GRT, a new concept termed direct separability is introduced. Unlike perceptual independence (i.e., channel independence), direct separability refers to invariance of the input to one dimension across values of the other dimension. For direct separability to hold, it is the off-diagonal elements of the **B** matrix representing the between-dimension interactions which equal 0. It should be clear that by assuming that each of the random walk channels is driven by the marginal perceptual distributions, the logical rule models instantiate direct separability for the serial and parallel processing models. This assumption also satisfies the static GRT assumption of perceptual separability and, when combined with the assumption of perceptual independence, is an important determinant of dynamic perceptual separability. The coactive logical rule model, by assuming that each channel is driven by the joint distribution, violates direct separability.

Perceptual Separability

In dynamic GRT-RT, perceptual separability is invariance in the distribution of evidence collected at or before time t on one dimension across levels of the other dimension. A violation of perceptual separability could occur through the dependence of the channel x on the input of stimulus dimension y or through an influence of the state of channel y on channel x. Townsend et al. (2012) refer to these as direct and indirect interaction, respectively. These concepts are comparable to the assumptions underlying the pre- and postaccumulator interactive models in Eidels et al. (2011) and the concepts of feed-forward and lateral inhibition (Usher & McClelland, 2001).

In the dynamic GRT-RT theory, the definition of perceptual separability applies at the level of the RT distributions. Dynamic perceptual separability holds if the cumulative distribution function arising from the presentation of dimension x_1 is invariant across levels of dimension y (e.g., y_1 and y_2). The assumptions of direct separability and dynamic perceptual independence imply dynamic perceptual separability. Hence, in the logical rule models, the assumption of static perceptual separability ensures that the random walk accumulation rates for a value on one dimension are equal across levels of the other dimension. Coupled with the assumption of channel independence, the serial and parallel logical rule models, thus, assume perceptual separability. In the logical rule models, only the coactive models allow for any violation of perceptual separability; hence, in the logical rule framework, integrality is solely defined as coactivity.

Summary

By combining GRT with different mental architectures, the logical rule models provide one method for making inferences about the different representations and processes that give rise to data. Importantly, this approach allows for inferences not only within the domain of SFT but also about particular invariances which arise in GRT-RT. Within SFT, the logical rule models only vary architecture to explain the difference between separable and integral dimensions, but in terms of GRT, the assumptions might be quite restrictive. In short, the logical rule models account for separable dimensions by assuming perceptual separability, perceptual independence, channel independence, decisional separability, and serial or parallel processing. Integral dimension processing is accounted for by violating perceptual separability, perceptual independence, channel independence, and assuming static decisional separability (but not dynamic decisional separability) and coactivity.

Perhaps by adopting a more general SDE approach, one could specifically test which of the different assumptions were fundamental for distinguishing separable from integral dimensions. For instance, one could consider violating each of the above assumptions independently of the other assumptions. The SDE approach also allows channel interactions to be incorporated in a straightforward manner. We note that a similar model has been proposed by Eidels et al. (2011) who extended the SFT predictions to a class of parallel models with interactive channels revealing that this important class of models can potentially be differentiated using the full suite of SFT tools.

Conclusion and Future

This chapter has focused on how SFT has helped elucidate the processing strategy used for a number of different stimuli, containing different psychological properties, using a categorization design which implements and extends the SFT methodology. There are, of course, a number of remaining questions for which SFT provides tools to begin investigating; we conclude our chapter by posing the following two questions:

1. How does selective attention (see, e.g., Nosofsky, 1986) interact with the dimensional processing strategy? Experiments using a deadline procedure have demonstrated that under time pressure decisions are made based solely on salient, attention-grabbing information (Cohen & Nosofsky, 2003; Lamberts, 1995, 1998,

2000). More valid, task relevant (but less salient) information is only available at longer response deadlines. One idea is that initial processing of salient information could arise due to preferential serial processing of that information. This idea is attractive because it coheres with eye-tracking studies which show that fixation is correlated with attention weights in categorization models (Rehder & Hoffman, 2005) and explains why attention to one stimulus attribute can result in an inability to predict values of an alternative stimulus attribute (Little & Lewandowsky, 2009). The interaction of attention with processing is considered in the chapter in this book by Yang (2017).

2. How does the categorization strategy change with learning? Theories of perceptual learning assume that a stimulus which is initially processed as a whole object might be broken down into its component parts (termed differentiation; Goldstone, Lippa, & Shiffrin, 2001) or, alternatively, that a stimulus which is initially processed as a set of component parts might come to be processed as a whole object (termed unitization; Goldstone, 2000). The former could reflect a change from an initially coactive processing strategy to a serial or parallel strategy. The latter could reflect a change from an initial parallel processing strategy to a coactive processing strategy. Indeed, there is some initial evidence supporting the idea of unitization as a change in processing architecture (Blaha, Busey, & Townsend, 2009; Fifić et al., 2010).

References

Altieri, N., Fifić, M., Little, D. R., & Yang, C.-T. (2017). A tutorial introduction and historical background to systems factorial technology. In D. R. Little, N. Altieri, M. Fifić, & C.-T. Yang (Eds.), *Systems factorial technology: A theory driven methodology for the identification of perceptual and cognitive mechanisms*. Elsevier (in this book).

Amishav, R., & Kimchi, R. (2010). Perceptual integrality of componential and configural information in faces. *Psychonomic Bulletin & Review*, *17*, 743–748.

Ashby, F. G. (1989). Stochastic general recognition theory. *Human information processing: Measures, mechanisms, and models*, 435–457.

Ashby, F. G. (1992). Multidimensional models of categorization. In F. G. Ashby (Ed.), *Multidimensional models of perception and cognition* (pp. 449–483). Hillsdale, NJ, US: Lawrence Erlbaum Associates, Inc.

Ashby, F. G. (2000). A stochastic version of general recognition theory. *Journal of Mathematical Psychology*, *44*, 210–329.

Ashby, F. G., & Gott, R. E. (1988). Decision rules in the perception and categorization of multidimensional stimuli. *Journal of Experimental Psychology: Learning, Memory and Cognition*, *14*, 33–53.

Ashby, F. G., & Lee, W. W. (1991). Predicting similarity and categorization from identification. *Journal of Experimental Psychology. General*, *120*(2), 150.

Ashby, F. G., & Townsend, J. T. (1986). Varieties of perceptual independence. *Psychological Review*, *93*(2), 154–179.

Attneave, F. (1950). Dimensions of similarity. *The American Journal of Psychology*, 516–556.

Biederman, I., & Checkosky, S. F. (1970). Processing redundant information. *Journal of Experimental Psychology*, *83*, 486–490.

Blaha, L. M., Busey, T., & Townsend, J. T. (2009). An LDA approach to the neural correlates of configural learning. In *Proceedings of the 31st annual conference of the cognitive science society*. Springer.

Blunden, A., Wang, T., Griffiths, D., & Little, D. (2015). Logical-rules and the classification of integral dimensions: Individual differences in the processing of arbitrary dimensions. *Frontiers in Psychology*, *5*(1531).

Borg, I. (2011). Multidimensional scaling. In *International encyclopedia of statistical science* (pp. 875–878). Springer.

Borg, I., & Groenen, P. J. F. (2005). *Modern multidimensional scaling: Theory and applications*. Springer Science & Business Media.

Bourne, L. E., Dominowski, R. L., Loftus, E. F., & Healy, A. (1979). *Cognitive processes*. Englewood Cliffs, NJ: Prentice-Hall.

Brown, S. D., & Heathcote, A. (2008). The simplest complete model of choice response time: Linear ballistic accumulation. *Cognitive Psychology*, *57*(3), 153–178.

Busemeyer, J. R. (1985). Decision making under uncertainty: A comparison of simple scalability, fixed-sample, and sequential-sampling models. *Journal of Experimental Psychology: Learning, Memory and Cognition*, *11*, 538–564.

Chen, Z. (2012). Object-based attention: A tutorial review. *Attention, Perception, & Psychophysics*, *74*, 784–802.

Cheng, X. J., Moneer, S., Christie, N., & Little, D. R. (2017). Capacity, categorization, conflict, and resilience. In D. R. Little, N. Altieri, M. Fifić, & C.-T. Yang (Eds.), *Systems factorial technology: A theory driven methodology for the identification of perceptual and cognitive mechanisms*. Elsevier (in this book).

Cohen, A., & Nosofsky, R. M. (2003). An extension of the exemplar-based random-walk model to separable-dimension stimuli. *Journal of Mathematical Psychology*, *47*, 150–165.

Diederich, A., & Busemeyer, J. R. (2003). Simple matrix methods for analyzing diffusion models of choice probability, choice response time, and simple response time. *Journal of Mathematical Psychology*, *47*, 304–322.

Egeth, H. (1967). Selective attention. *Psychological Bulletin*, *67*(1), 41.

Eidels, A., Houpt, J. W., Altieri, N., Pei, L., & Townsend, J. T. (2011). Nice guys finish fast and bad guys finish last: Facilitatory vs. inhibitory interaction in parallel systems. *Journal of Mathematical Psychology*, *55*, 176–190.

Fifić, M., Little, D. R., & Nosofsky, R. (2010). Logical-rule models of classification response times: A synthesis of mental-architecture, random-walk, and decision-bound approaches. *Psychological Review*, *117*, 309–348.

Fifić, M., Nosofsky, R. M., & Townsend, J. (2008). Information-processing architectures in multidimensional classification: A validation of test of the systems factorial technology. *Journal of Experimental Psychology: Human Perception & Performance*, *34*, 356–375.

Fifić, M., & Townsend, J. T. (2010). Information-processing alternatives to holistic perception: Identifying the mechanisms of secondary-level holism within a categorization paradigm. *Journal of Experimental Psychology: Learning, Memory, and Cognition*, *36*(5), 1290.

Garner, W. R. (1969). Speed of discrimination with redundant stimulus attributes. *Perception and Psychophysics*, *6*(4), 221–224.

Garner, W. R. (1974). *The processing of information and structure*. Psychology Press.

Garner, W. R., & Felfoldy, G. L. (1970). Integrality of stimulus dimensions in various types of information processing. *Cognitive Psychology*, *1*(3), 225–241.

Goldstone, R. L. (2000). Unitization during category learning. *Journal of Experimental Psychology: Human Perception and Performance*, *26*(1), 86.

Goldstone, R. L., Lippa, Y., & Shiffrin, R. M. (2001). Altering object representations through category learning. *Cognition, 78*, 27–43.

Goldstone, R. L., & Steyvers, M. (2001). The sensitization and differentiation of dimensions during category learning. *Journal of Experimental Psychology. General, 130*(1), 116.

Green, D., & Swets, J. (1966). *Signal detection theory and psychophysics*. New York: Wiley.

Handel, S., & Imai, S. (1972). The free classification of analyzable and unanalyzable stimuli. *Perception & Psychophysics, 12*, 108–116. http://dx.doi.org/10.3758/BF03212854.

Hofstadter, D., & Sander, E. (2013). *Surfaces and essences – analogy as the fuel and fire of thinking*. Basic Books.

Imai, S., & Garner, W. R. (1968). Structure in perceptual classification. *Psychonomic Monograph Supplements, 2*, 153–172.

Kadlec, H., & Townsend, J. T. (1992). Implications of marginal and conditional detection parameters for the separabilities and independence of perceptual dimensions. *Journal of Mathematical Psychology, 36*, 325–374.

Keele, S. W., & Neill, W. G. (1978). Mechanisms of attention. In *Handbook of perception. Perceptual processing* (pp. 1–47).

Ketchum, R. D., & Bourne Jr, L. (1980). Stimulus-rule interactions in concept verification. *The American Journal of Psychology*, 5–23.

Lamberts, K. (1995). Categorization under time pressure. *Journal of Experimental Psychology. General, 124*, 161–180.

Lamberts, K. (1998). The time course of categorization. *Journal of Experimental Psychology: Learning, Memory & Cognition, 24*, 695–711.

Lamberts, K. (2000). Information–accumulation theory of speeded classification. *Psychological Review, 107*, 227–260.

Laming, D. R. J. (1968). *Information theory of choice reaction times*. New York: Wiley.

Link, S. W., & Heath, R. A. (1975). A sequential theory of psychological discrimination. *Pscyhometrika, 40*, 77–105.

Little, D. R. (2012). Numerical predictions for serial, parallel and coactive logical rule-based models of response times. *Behavior Research Methods, 44*, 1148–1156.

Little, D. R., & Lewandowsky, S. (2009). Better learning with more error: Probabilistic feedback increases sensitivity to correlated cues. *Journal of Experimental Psychology: Learning, Memory, and Cognition, 35*, 1041–1061.

Little, D. R., Nosofsky, R., & Denton, S. E. (2011). Response time tests of logical rule-based models of categorization. *Journal of Experimental Psychology: Learning, Memory and Cognition, 37*, 1–27.

Little, D. R., Nosofsky, R. M., Donkin, C., & Denton, S. E. (2013). Logical-rules and the classification of integral dimensioned stimuli. *Journal of Experimental Psychology: Learning, Memory and Cognition, 39*, 801–820.

Lockhead, G. R. (1966). Effects of dimensional redundancy on visual discrimination. *Journal of Experimental Psychology, 72*(1), 95.

Luce, R. D. (1986). *Response times: Their role in inferring elementary mental organization*. New York: Oxford University Press.

Moneer, S., Wang, T., & Little, D. R. (2016). The processing architectures of whole-object features: A logical rules approach. *Journal of Experimental Psychology: Human Perception & Performance, 42*, 1443–1465.

Nosofsky, R. M. (1986). Attention, similarity, and the identification–categorization relationship. *Journal of Experimental Psychology. General, 115*, 39–61.

Nosofsky, R. M. (1987). Attention and learning processes in the identification and categorization of integral stimuli. *Journal of Experimental Psychology: Learning, Memory & Cognition*, *13*, 87–108.

Nosofsky, R. M. (1992). Similarity scaling and cognitive process models. *Annual Review of Psychology*, *43*, 25–53.

Nosofsky, R. M., & Palmeri, T. J. (1996). Learning to classify integral-dimension stimuli. *Psychonomic Bulletin & Review*, *3*(2), 222–226.

Nosofsky, R. M., & Palmeri, T. (1997). An exemplar-based random walk model of speeded classification. *Psychological Review*, *104*, 266–300.

Posner, M. I. (1964). Information reduction in the analysis of sequential tasks. *Psychological Review*, *71*(6), 491.

Raab, D. (1962). Statistical facilitation of simple reaction time. *Transactions of the New York Academy of Sciences*, *43*, 574–590.

Ratcliff, R. (1978). A theory of memory retrieval. *Psychological Review*, *85*, 59–108.

Rehder, B., & Hoffman, A. B. (2005). Thirty-something categorization results explained: Selective attention, eye-tracking, and model of category learning. *Journal of Experimental Psychology: Learning, Memory & Cognition*, *31*, 811–829.

Richler, J., & Gauthier, I. (2013). When intuition fails to align with data: A reply to Rossion (2013). *Visual Cognition*, *21*, 254–276.

Richler, J., Palmeri, T., & Gauthier, I. (2012). Meanings, mechanisms, and measures of holistic processing. *Frontiers in Psychology*, *3*, 553.

Schweickert, R. (1992). Attention and performance. In *Synergies in experimental psychology, artificial intelligence, and cognitive neuroscience – a silver jubilee: Vol. 14* (pp. 535–566). MIT Press.

Schweickert, R., & Dzhafarov, E. (2000). Selective influence and response time cumulative distribution functions in serial-parallel task networks. *Journal of Mathematical Psychology*, *44*(4), 504–535.

Shepard, R. N. (1987). Toward a universal law of generalization for psychological science. *Science*, *237*, 1317–1323.

Shepard, R. N., & Chang, J.-J. (1963). Stimulus generalization in the learning of classifications. *Journal of Experimental Psychology*, *65*(1), 94.

Shepard, R. N., Hovland, C. I., & Jenkins, H. M. (1961). Learning and memorization of classifications. *Psychological Monographs: General and Applied*, *75*(13), 1–42.

Smith, P. L. (2000). Stochastic dynamic models of response time and accuracy: A foundational primer. *Journal of Mathematical Psychology*, *44*(3), 408–463.

Smith, L. B., & Kilroy, M. C. (1979). A continuum of dimensional separability. *Perception & Psychophysics*, *25*, 285–291.

Sperling, G., & Weichselgartner, E. (1995). Episodic theory of the dynamics of spatial attention. *Psychological Review*, *102*, 503–532.

Sternberg, S. (1969). Memory scanning: Memory processes revealed by reaction-time experiments. *American Scientist*, *4*, 421–457.

Thomas, R. D. (1995). Gaussian general recognition theory and perceptual independence. *Psychological Review*, *102*, 192–200.

Thornton, T. L., & Gilden, D. L. (2007). Parallel and serial processes in visual search. *Psychological Review*, *114*, 71–103.

Torgerson, W. S. (1958). *Theory and methods of scaling*. Wiley.

Townsend, J. T. (1984). Uncovering mental processes with factorial experiments. *Journal of Mathematical Psychology*, *28*, 363–400.

Townsend, J. T. (1990). Serial vs. parallel processing: Sometimes they look like Tweedledum and Tweedledee but they can (and should) be distinguished. *Psychological Science, 1*, 46–54.

Townsend, J. T., Houpt, J. W., & Silbert, N. H. (2012). General recognition theory extended to include response times: Predictions for a class of parallel systems. *Journal of Mathematical Psychology*, *56*(6), 476–494.

Townsend, J. T., & Nozawa, G. (1995). Spatio-temporal properties of elementary perception: An investigation of parallel, serial and coactive theories. *Journal of Mathematical Psychology*, *39*, 321–340.

Townsend, J. T., & Wenger, M. J. (2004). The serial-parallel dilemma: A case study in a linkage of theory and method. *Psychonomic Bulletin & Review*, *11*, 391–418.

Trabasso, T., Rollins, H., & Shaughnessy, E. (1971). Storage and verification stages in processing concepts. *Cognitive Psychology*, *2*(3), 239–289.

Usher, M., & McClelland, J. L. (2001). The time course of perceptual choice: The leaky, competing accumulator model. *Psychological Review*, *108*(3), 550.

Yang, C.-T. (2017). Attention and perceptual decision making. In D. R. Little, N. Altieri, M. Fifić, & C.-T. Yang (Eds.), *Systems factorial technology: A theory driven methodology for the identification of perceptual and cognitive mechanisms*. Elsevier (in this book).

Endnotes

1. The contrast category stimuli, I and E, provide conflicting information regarding category membership. An interior stimulus, for example, has one dimension which provides positive evidence that the item belongs to the contrast, but the other dimension provides evidence that the item belongs to the target category. That is, one dimension satisfies one of part of the conjunctive rule. By varying the discriminability of this conflicting dimension (i.e., from low to high in the interior and exterior stimuli, respectively), one can generate novel distributional contrasts. These are discussed in the following chapter on conflict in categorization (Cheng, Moneer, Christie, & Little, 2017); for now, we focus on the mean RT predictions that were introduced in Fifić et al. (2010), which are shown in Fig. 12.5.
2. Various generalizations of this equation are possible. For instance, both **A** and **B** can be time dependent. Likewise, the noise process $W(t)$ can be state dependent. We direct the reader to Smith's (2000) excellent primer on stochastic dynamic models.

Applying Systems Factorial Technology to Accumulators with Varying Thresholds

13

Bradley Harding, Vincent LeBlanc, Marc-André Goulet, Denis Cousineau
University of Ottawa, Ottawa, ON, Canada

Before the inception of Systems Factorial Technology (SFT; Townsend & Nozawa, 1995), methods that inferred the information processing architecture present in a cognitive system were based on changes in mean response times (RT), with notable examples being Sternberg's additive method (1969, 1998) and Donders's subtractive method (1969). However, while these methods are monumental additions to experimental psychology, they offered little discrimination power, as various architectures can make similar predictions (also known as mimicking; Snodgrass & Townsend, 1980; Townsend, 1972, 1990). SFT aims to eliminate this uncertainty by using a nonparametric approach that focuses on the entire distribution of RT rather than only the mean RT.

SFT is based on the core assumption that a process is composed of subprocesses that can be *selectively influenced*, i.e., that a subprocess can be significantly impacted without affecting any other subprocesses present. Thus, the most frequent SFT experimental design involves a *Double Factorial Paradigm* where two levels of salience (High – H, or Low – L) are possible for two subprocesses (1 and 2). A complete SFT design requires six conditions: four where both subprocesses are receiving information together at various levels of salience (H_1H_2, H_1L_2, L_1H_2, and L_1L_2), and two conditions where only one subprocess is operating (for example, H_1 and H_2). For a discussion on how to apply this experimental design, consult Houpt, Blaha, McIntire, Havig, and Townsend (2014, pp. 320–326) or the tutorial chapter of this book (Altieri, Fifić, Little, & Yang, 2017).

When data from these six experimental conditions is available, SFT provides an analysis "toolbox" that is used to identify the process's underlying organization. This organization can be characterized by its *architecture*, its *stopping rule*, and its *workload capacity*, assuming *stochastic independence* is met. The *Mean Interaction Contrast* (MIC) and *Survival Interaction Contrast* (SIC) obtained from the first four conditions (H_1H_2, H_1L_2, L_1H_2, L_1L_2) identify the architecture and stopping rule that link both subprocesses. Additionally, *workload capacity* gives information on the process's overall processing capability by comparing its throughput when each subprocess works alone (H_1, H_2) versus when they work simultaneously (H_1H_2). The capacity indicators C_{OR} (for self-terminating and coactive processes) and C_{AND} (for exhaustive processes) describe how combining the subprocesses affects the process's overall performance, be it negatively (limited capacity), positively (supercapacity), or neutrally (unlimited capacity; Townsend & Wenger, 2004). Finally, *stochastic (in)dependence* provides information on the level of correlation between subprocesses, or the extent to

Systems Factorial Technology, DOI: 10.1016/B978-0-12-804315-8.00016-1

which one subprocess affects the other's capabilities. A way to verify subprocesses' independence is to assess *stochastic dominance* between the four conditions' cumulative distribution functions (Heathcote, Brown, Wagenmakers, & Eidels, 2010) and to confirm that the ordering of RT distributions meets the theoretical expectations. More thoroughly, stochastic dominance is met when the H_1H_2 condition's cumulative RT distribution is always above those of the H_1L_2 and L_1H_2 conditions, which in turn must always be above the L_1L_2 condition. This can also be verified by making sure that the survivor functions of all four conditions never intersect. If any experimental condition falls out of order, stochastic independence does not hold, leading to uninterpretable SFT results; the salience factors manipulated in the factorial design must be re-evaluated to ensure that they are sufficiently different. A main strength behind SFT is that it is nonparametric, giving interpretable results regardless of the RT distribution as long as all assumptions are met and respected. For an entry-level tutorial to the SFT methodology and its analyses, see Harding, Goulet, Jolin, Tremblay, Villeneuve, and Durand (2016).

In Fig. 13.1, we summarize the typical MIC, SIC, and capacity results for each of the five types of organization detected by SFT when both subprocesses are stochastically independent, when selective influence is achieved, and, in the case of capacity, when context invariance holds when expected (Townsend & Wenger, 2004). The first column of Fig. 13.1 helps visualizing the architectures and how they differ from one another.

While SFT was successful in diagnosing processes involved in many cognitive paradigms (such as visual search, Fifić, Townsend, & Eidels, 2008; local–global information processing for people affected by autism, Johnson, Blaha, Houpt, & Townsend, 2010, etc.), one cannot expect it to be accurate if its assumptions are not met. As noted by Eidels, Houpt, Altieri, Pei, and Townsend (2011), models may mimic others' results if selective influence is not respected, leading to uninterpretable results. Additionally, SFT diagnoses must fit what is theoretically expected from the tested data. For example, Townsend and Nozawa (1995) have noted that:

> *Architectures other than serial or parallel can, in some cases, mimic the factorial predictions of these. For instance, a bare Wheatstone bridge predicts underadditivity in an exhaustive processing situation.*
>
> **(Townsend & Nozawa, 1995, p. 330)**

Both cases above had either a violation of SFT's core assumption or were not simulating a processes' organization that is expected nor can be identified by SFT. In what follows, we present cases of models that do not violate SFT's assumption, are expected and diagnosable by SFT, yet lead to possible misdiagnoses.

Accumulator Models and Threshold Variability

Accumulator models of decision making assume that perceptual mechanisms send activations (often referred to as *evidence*) to a decision process. This process ac-

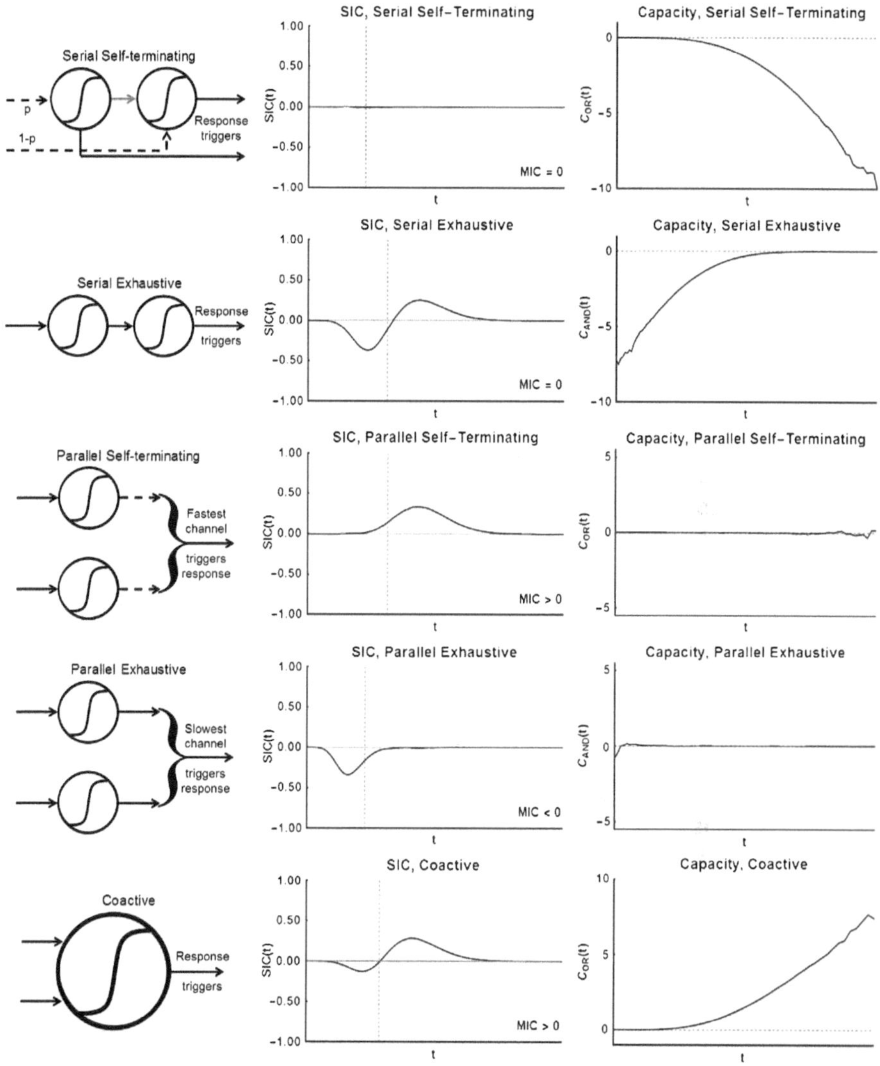

Figure 13.1 Summary of typical SFT results for each of the five information processing architectures assuming stochastic independence between processes (adapted from Townsend & Nozawa, 1995). Column 1 shows schematics of the architectures, column 2 shows the SIC curve along with a typical MIC, and column 3 shows the capacity curves of all five architectures (using the appropriate measure C_{OR} or C_{AND}). In column 1, the circles represent the decision process; the sigmoid curves represent an accumulation-to-threshold implementation of that process; the arrows show the process's input and output (or in the case of serial exhaustive, the shift from one subprocess to another); the dashed arrows denote the fact that only a single subprocess's threshold breach is needed; p is a probability. In columns 2 and 3, the vertical dashed line shows the SIC centerline (see text) and the horizontal dashed line shows the unlimited capacity level.

Table 13.1 LBA threshold parameters values for lower and upper bounds (B and $B + A$ respectively) fitted to four participants (A1, A2, S1, S2) in a lexical decision task. Only the first and last blocks (1 and 25) were estimated using Fig. 4 from Heathcote and Hayes (2012; located on p. 132 in their article)

Participants	Block	A	B	$b = B + A$	Ratio $B : (A + B)$	Proportion $A/(B + A)$
A1	1	1.3	0.1	$0.1 + 1.3$	1: 14.0	93%
	25	0.4	0.1	$0.1 + 0.4$	1: 5.0	80%
A2	1	0.6	0.6	$0.6 + 0.6$	1: 2.0	50%
	25	0.6	0.1	$0.1 + 0.6$	1: 7.0	86%
S1	1	0.6	0.5	$0.5 + 0.6$	1: 2.2	54%
	25	0.6	1.1	$1.1 + 0.6$	1: 1.6	35%
S2	1	2.3	0.6	$0.6 + 2.3$	1: 4.8	80%
	25	0.0	1.4	$1.4 + 0.0$	1: 1.0	0%
Min					1: 1.0	0%
Max					1: 14.0	93%
Geometric mean					1: 3.4	n/a
Mean					1: 4.7	52%

cumulates evidence until a critical amount (a *threshold*) is reached, at which time a decision is made. Accumulator models have a long history in cognitive psychology (e.g., Townsend & Ashby, 1978; Luce, 1986), and their ability to model human RT and response accuracy has been extensively studied (for a recent and complete review of accumulator models, see Forstmann, Ratcliff, & Wagenmakers, 2016; Teodorescu & Usher, 2013). Their flexibility allows the implementation of many factors to model RT distributions; *inter alia*, these models can evolve in discrete or continuous time steps, accumulate discrete or continuous evidence or have either constant or variable thresholds between trials. *Threshold variability* was first introduced in Ratcliff's Drift Diffusion Model (DDM; Ratcliff, 1978) and is a main component in Brown and Heathcote's Linear Ballistic Accumulator (LBA; 2008). It is now commonly used to explain performance variability and the occurrence of fast-errors in RT distributions. This model component will be the focus of our simulations.

In Heathcote and Hayes (2012), the LBA model was fitted to data from a large experiment conducted by Dutilh, Vandekerckhove, Tuerlinckx, and Wagenmakers (2009). In order to grasp the magnitude of their four participants' thresholds variability, we synthesized Heathcote and Hayes (2012) results in Table 13.1, focusing more specifically on the first and last training blocks found in their Fig. 4 on p. 132. In this model, B represents the minimum amount of evidence that must be accumulated to reach the threshold from a starting point that varies uniformly between 0 and A, and b (or $A + B$) represents the maximum amount of evidence that must be accumulated to reach the threshold. We visually estimated B and b, equivalent to the lower and upper threshold bounds.

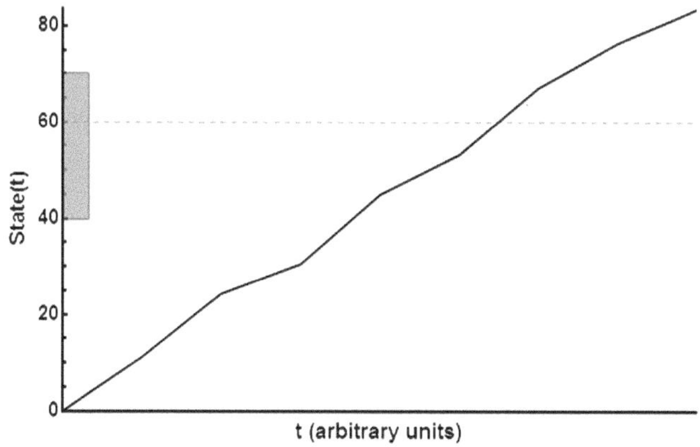

Figure 13.2 Schematic of the DAVT, a discrete accumulator model with varying threshold. In this schematic, the distribution of evidence arrival times is normal with a mean of 4 and standard deviation of 1 (truncated at zero). Threshold variation follows a uniform distribution with bounds at 40 and 70. In this specific trial, the threshold was randomly selected to be 60.

Across trials, the starting point is variable, whereas the threshold (b) is a fixed value. A mathematical equivalent would be to fix the starting point at B and vary the threshold between 0 and A above B. Hence, as few as B evidence may be required on some trials (if the threshold is at 0, its minimal value) to cross the threshold, or as much as $A + B$ (if the threshold is at its maximum value). Therefore, the $B : (A + B)$ ratio is an astute indicator of variability. In this ratio, B represents the minimal threshold value (noted as k_{MIN} in the first model variant presented next) and $A + B$ represents the maximal threshold value (noted as k_{MAX} in the first model variant presented next). A ratio close to 1:1 indicates a negligibly variable threshold whereas a ratio of 1:5, for example, suggests considerable threshold variability (k_{MAX} is five times larger than k_{MIN}). Another way to quantify threshold variability would be to measure the proportion of possible threshold values on the total accumulator's size. This can be done by calculating $A/(A + B)$ where a proportion of 1 indicates that the threshold can vary on the totality of the accumulation's size.

As seen from Table 13.1, the threshold ratio varies greatly between participants and between sessions, going from as low as 1:1 and as high as 1:14, being roughly 1:4 across participants (1:3.4 using the geometric mean or 1:4.7 using the arithmetic mean). Given the magnitude of the threshold variability observed in these empirical results, it is reasonable to explore its impact on SFT diagnostic capabilities.

In this chapter, we investigate SFT's capabilities when analyzing models implementing variable thresholds. For all simulations, we demonstrate that SFT's assumptions are met and the simulated processes' architectures are part of SFT's domain. We do this by simulating the five architectures presented in Fig. 13.1 within two variants of the independent race model class that differ with respect to the locus of the noise (i.e., the stochastic component). The first model variant is a convenient model for demonstration purposes: a stochastically independent discrete accumulator with varying thresholds (hereafter abbreviated to DAVT for readability purposes). DAVT is

Table 13.2 Implementation and parameters of the simulations presented herein. In the top panel we give the parameters of the DAVT. In the bottom panel, we give the implementation equations for all five architectures detected by SFT

List of parameters

Parameters	Description	Value
k_{MIN}	Lower bound of the uniform distribution where threshold values are randomly selected on every trial	(4, 16, 64, 256)
k_{MAX}	Upper bound of the uniform distribution where threshold values are randomly selected on every trial	$(1.25,\ 2,\ 4) \times k_{MIN}$
β_1	Scale parameter of the Weibull distribution for subprocess 1's evidence arrival times	High = 8 Low = 12
β_2	Scale parameter of the Weibull distribution for subprocess 2's evidence arrival times	High = 10 Low = 20
γ	Shape Parameter of the Weibull distribution for both subprocesses' evidence arrival times	1.8
T_0	Motor time	0

Implementation equations

Architecture	Equation
General equations	$t_i \sim Weibull(\gamma; \beta_i)$ $k \sim Uniform(k_{MIN}, k_{MAX})$ $RT_X = T_0 + \sum_{i=1}^{k} t_i$ where t_i is a random sample of an arrival time distribution and k is randomly selected on every trial for each individual subprocess
Serial Self-Terminating	RT_1 or RT_2 (50% Probability)
Serial Exhaustive	$RT_1 + RT_2$
Parallel Self-Terminating	$\min(RT_1, RT_2)$
Parallel Exhaustive	$\max(RT_1, RT_2)$
Coactive	Identical to the general equations. However, t_i is sampled from two sources of evidence consulted in parallel

schematized in Fig. 13.2 and its implementation is summarized in Table 13.2. The second model is the well-known and documented LBA model (see Table 13.3 for an implementation summary).

Although these models share many similarities, as they are both from the same class of independent race models, they differ in the way they implement their variability. The LBA uses between-trial variability, sampling a different starting point and accumulation rate for each subprocess at each trial. On the other hand, DAVT uses within-trial variability, sampling random arrival times for each individual accumulator.

Table 13.3 Implementation and parameters of the simulations presented herein. In the top panel we give the parameters of the LBA. In the bottom panel, we give the implementation equations for all five architectures detected by SFT

List of parameters

Parameters	**Description**	**Value**
A_1	Starting point range of subprocess 1	(1000, 4600, 2300)
A_2	Starting point range of subprocess 2	(1000, 4600, 6900)
b	Threshold	10,000
ν_1	Mean accumulation rate of subprocess 1	High = 27 Low = 18
ν_2	Mean accumulation rate of subprocess 2	High = 33 Low = 20
s	Standard deviation of the accumulation rate	3
T_0	Motor time	100

Implementation equations

Architecture	**Equation**
General equations	$v_1 \sim N(\nu_i; s)$ $a_i \sim Uniform(0; A_i)$ $\mathrm{RT}_X = \frac{b-a_x}{v_x} + T_0$
Serial Self-Terminating	RT_1 or RT_2 (50% Probability)
Serial Exhaustive	$\mathrm{RT}_1 + \mathrm{RT}_2$
Parallel Self-Terminating	$\min(\mathrm{RT}_1, \mathrm{RT}_2)$
Parallel Exhaustive	$\max(\mathrm{RT}_1, \mathrm{RT}_2)$
Coactive	$\mathrm{RT} = \frac{b-a_1-a_2}{v_1+v_2} + T_0$

DAVT is a flexible accumulator and its implementation allows more intuitive controllability over thresholds variation which only necessitates changing the amount of required, summed, arrival times. Hence, it is intuitive when simulating specific threshold ratios (e.g., $k_{\mathrm{MIN}} = 4$, $k_{\mathrm{MAX}} = 8$ means that threshold values can only be 4, 5, 6, 7, or 8 with equal probability). While DAVT is apt at demonstrating proof of concepts, it is not designed to be an applied data-fitting model, i.e., it cannot predict as many facets of human RT as the LBA such as the occurrences of fast errors. Nonetheless, due to its intuitive, discrete accumulation, our simulations will first focus on the DAVT in order to grasp the full effect of threshold variability on SFT diagnoses. Subsequently, we will simulate the five architectures using the LBA to show that DAVT results are generalizable to the stochastically independent race models class.

In the simulations below, we incrementally increased the threshold variability of the race models for all five architectures, and observed whether SFT could still return appropriate results. We used empirically plausible threshold ratios taken from Heathcote and Hayes' (2012) recent model fit of the LBA (1:1.25, 1:2, and 1:4 for the DAVT;

1:1.25 and 1:12.5 for the LBA). Additionally, we verified that the absolute number of evidence required was not responsible for our results. For the DAVT, we did this by varying the lower threshold bound, k_{MIN}, for each threshold ratios ($k_{\text{MIN}} = 4, 16, 64$ and 256). For the LBA, we ran one 1:12.5 simulation where both subprocesses had the same value of A (4600), and another with different values of A for each subprocess (2300 and 6900). For all simulations, we assured that the stochastic independence and selective influence requirements of SFT were respected. We expect both model simulations to show similar results as they are from the same class of independent race models. If it is indeed the case, changes in threshold variability, the common source of variability between models, is the component which necessarily affects diagnostic accuracy.

Preliminary Simulations and the Literature on Coactive Architectures

All five architectures in SFT's domain can be implemented within DAVT and LBA. However, the four combinations of serial and parallel architectures with self-terminating and exhaustive stopping rules do not challenge SFT's diagnostic capabilities. While threshold variability increases the processes' decision time variability, diagnostics do not falter as SFT is not sensitive to the amount of variance in the individual processing times.

By contrast, in coactive architectures, threshold variability affects the system as a whole as arrival times from both subprocesses are pooled. For this reason, we will focus solely on threshold variability in the coactive architecture.

Coactive models are much more diverse, and their implementation requires more assumptions compared to serial and parallel models. The original proof describing the SIC curve of a coactive architecture found in Townsend and Nozawa (1995, Theorem 5) is based on a specific implementation of a coactive model, the *Poisson Channel Summation Model* (Schwarz, 1989; Townsend & Ashby, 1983). The same conclusions regarding the shape of the SIC curve were extended to a more general implementation, the *Wiener Coactive Model* (Houpt & Townsend, 2011). However, in both cases, demonstrations were made using sampled accumulation rates (u in Townsend and Nozawa's Theorem, ν_1 and ν_2 in Houpt and Townsend's article). These accumulation rates, within the context of these demonstrations, implied constant thresholds. In Fifić, Little, and Nosofsky (2010), a coactive architecture was implemented within a random walk accumulator model; again, thresholds were set at a fixed value.

These choices were made for simplicity's sake. In the absence of evidence that threshold variability had any impact on coactive diagnoses, there was no point in assuming this parameter could vary. However, the results presented next highlight the importance of this factor.

Results

Simulations were performed with 50,000 trials for each condition (H_1H_2, H_1L_2, L_1H_2, L_1L_2, H_1 and H_2). The survivor functions are shown in the first columns of Figs. 13.3–13.6, the SIC and MIC results (including the 95% confidence interval for MIC) are shown in the second columns, and capacity curves are shown in the third columns. We used the alternative "difference" version of C_{OR} and C_{AND} found in Houpt et al. (2014; for more details, see Houpt & Townsend, 2012). Also presented on all SIC plots are the p-values from a modified Kolmogorov–Smirnov test (Houpt & Townsend, 2010), which detects if the SIC's negative (D^-) and positive (D^+) deviations are significantly different from 0.

The arrival times in DAVT are sampled from a Weibull distribution for implementation purposes. The results presented hereafter are also extendable to other arrival time distributions such as the normal distribution (see Appendix for a demonstration).

DAVT

As seen in the first column of Fig. 13.3, H_1H_2 conditions are the first ordered survivor functions across all k_{MIN} values and the L_1L_2 conditions are always the last ordered. Additional stochastic dominance tests (Heathcote et al., 2010) also indicate that the H_1L_2 and L_1H_2 survivor functions always fall between both extreme conditions ($\Pr(H_1H_2 > H_1L_2) \approx 1$, $\Pr(H_1H_2 > L_1H_2) \approx 1$, $\Pr(H_1L_2 > L_1L_2) \approx 1$, and $\Pr(L_1H_2 > L_1L_2) \approx 1$). Finally, no survivor function crosses any of the other survivor function. When taking the large number of simulations into account, these results indicate that stochastic dominance is present. As seen in the second column of Fig. 13.3, small threshold variability has little to no influence on the interpretation of the SIC nor of the MIC. Our results reproduce what is typically expected of coactive architectures in a SFT analysis. Moreover, the Kolmogorov–Smirnov tests show that the positive and negative portions of all curves are significantly different than 0. Finally, the capacity curves (the third column of Fig. 13.3) indicate supercapacity for all conditions, evidence of the presence of a coactive model. Here, one would make an appropriate diagnosis of the underlying architecture.

In the second set of simulations, where threshold ratio was increased to 1:2, we observe similar results to the ones presented above. In the first column of Fig. 13.4, again, we show that stochastic dominance is met for all four values of k_{MIN}. Moreover, in the second column of Fig. 13.4, the general trend of the coactive SIC curve is still present (an S shape, decreasing below zero, increasing above zero, then returning to zero). However, the entirety of the SIC's amplitude is decreased, with the reduction of the negative portion of the curves being more important. Still, the Kolmogorov–Smirnov tests indicate that all deviations are significantly different than 0.

As threshold variability increases (translated by an increase in the value of the threshold's higher bound, k_{MAX}), so does the possible total duration of the process.

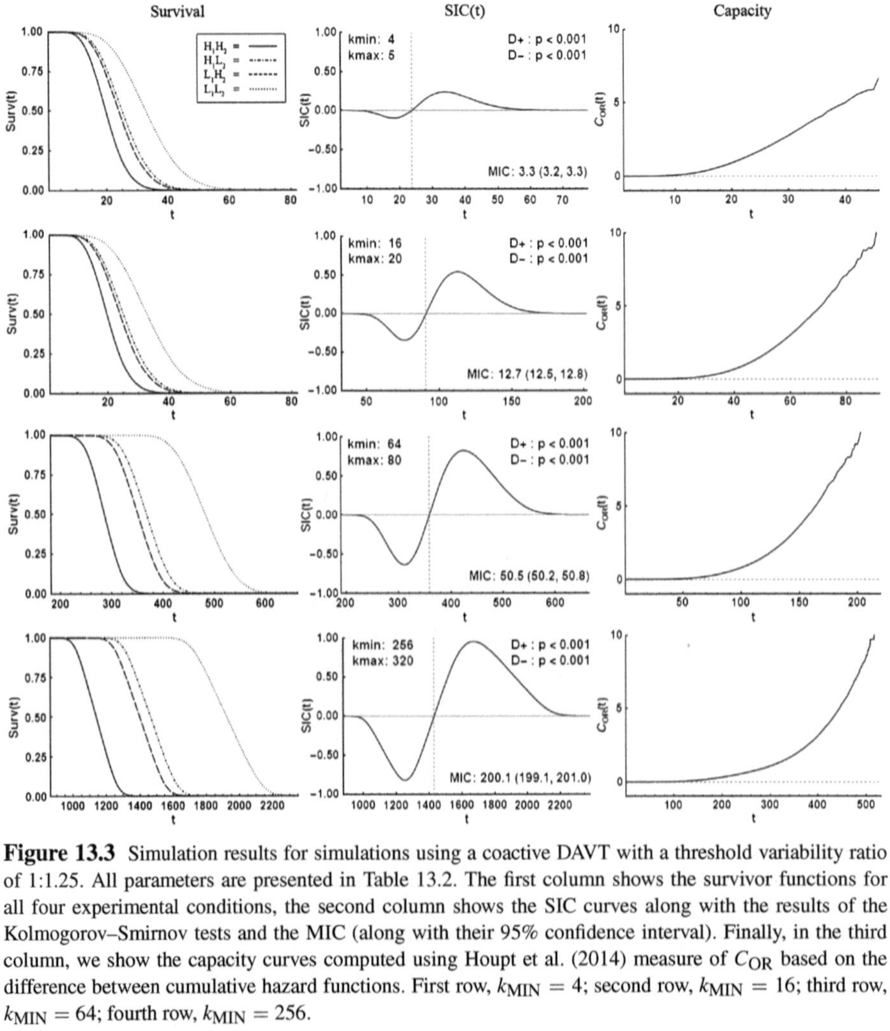

Figure 13.3 Simulation results for simulations using a coactive DAVT with a threshold variability ratio of 1:1.25. All parameters are presented in Table 13.2. The first column shows the survivor functions for all four experimental conditions, the second column shows the SIC curves along with the results of the Kolmogorov–Smirnov tests and the MIC (along with their 95% confidence interval). Finally, in the third column, we show the capacity curves computed using Houpt et al. (2014) measure of C_{OR} based on the difference between cumulative hazard functions. First row, $k_{MIN} = 4$; second row, $k_{MIN} = 16$; third row, $k_{MIN} = 64$; fourth row, $k_{MIN} = 256$.

This results in more variable and platykurtic RT distributions. The survivor functions are therefore less pronounced and drop to 0 much more slowly. As seen, this leads to smaller differences between the survivor functions of H_1H_2, H_1L_2, and L_1H_2, which explains the reduction in SIC amplitude. Additionally, the slower drop of the H_1H_2 survivor functions indicates that the condition benefits less from being organized in a coactive architecture; the overall process's decision time may be extended if the distance between both threshold bounds is at its maximum value. This increase in variability also leads to more overlap between the H_1H_2 and the L_1L_2 survivor function, explaining the later onset of the positive area and the diminishing of the negative area. Finally, the later onset of the positive area combined with the diminishing of the

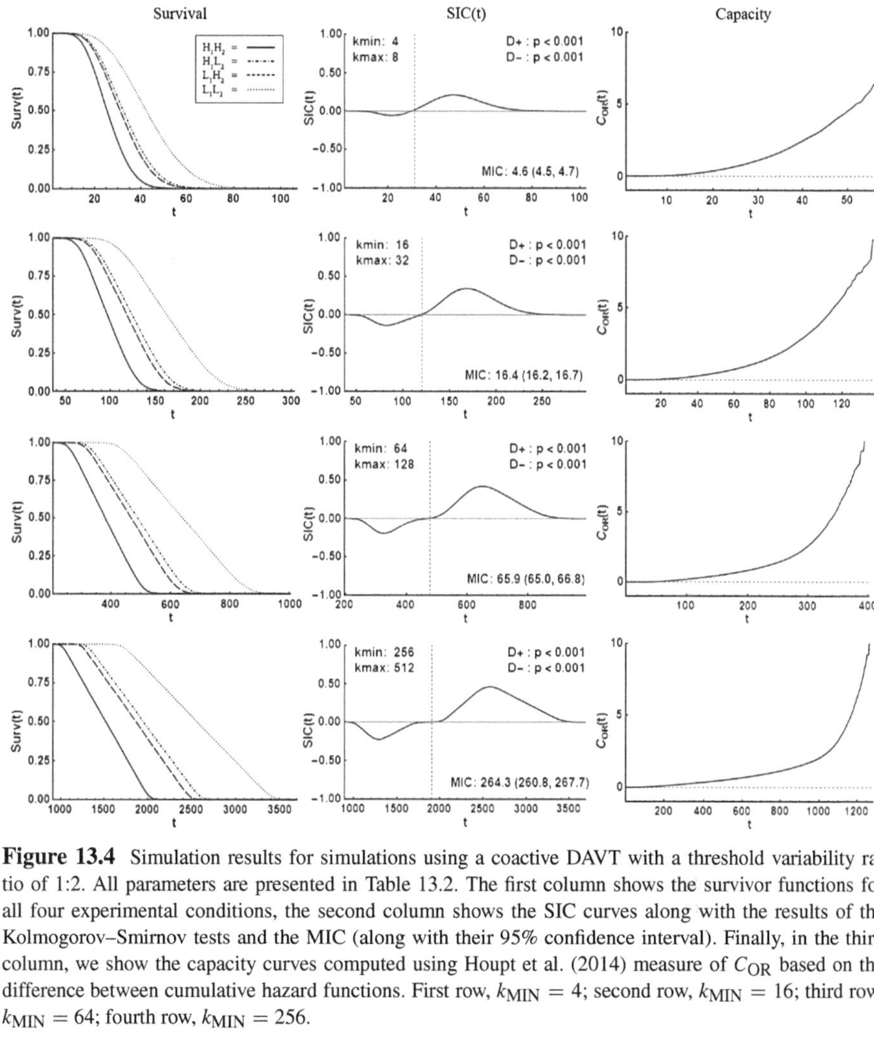

Figure 13.4 Simulation results for simulations using a coactive DAVT with a threshold variability ratio of 1:2. All parameters are presented in Table 13.2. The first column shows the survivor functions for all four experimental conditions, the second column shows the SIC curves along with the results of the Kolmogorov–Smirnov tests and the MIC (along with their 95% confidence interval). Finally, in the third column, we show the capacity curves computed using Houpt et al. (2014) measure of C_{OR} based on the difference between cumulative hazard functions. First row, $k_{MIN} = 4$; second row, $k_{MIN} = 16$; third row, $k_{MIN} = 64$; fourth row, $k_{MIN} = 256$.

negative area creates an atypical "plateau" between the underadditive and the overadditive portions of the curves. This SIC trend depends only on the size of threshold's variability ratio, as it is present across all values of k_{MIN}. Nevertheless, the capacity curves (shown in the third column of Fig. 13.4) still indicate supercapacity. Looking at the SIC and MIC results, the correct coactive diagnosis can be made.

For a threshold variability ratio of 1:4, stochastic dominance remains present (survivor functions are presented in the first column of Fig. 13.5). However, as the increase in ratio increases the amount of possible RT scores, the slopes of all survival functions are further attenuated from both previous simulations. As shown in the second column of Fig. 13.5, the SIC's amplitude is diminished with the negative portion of all SIC

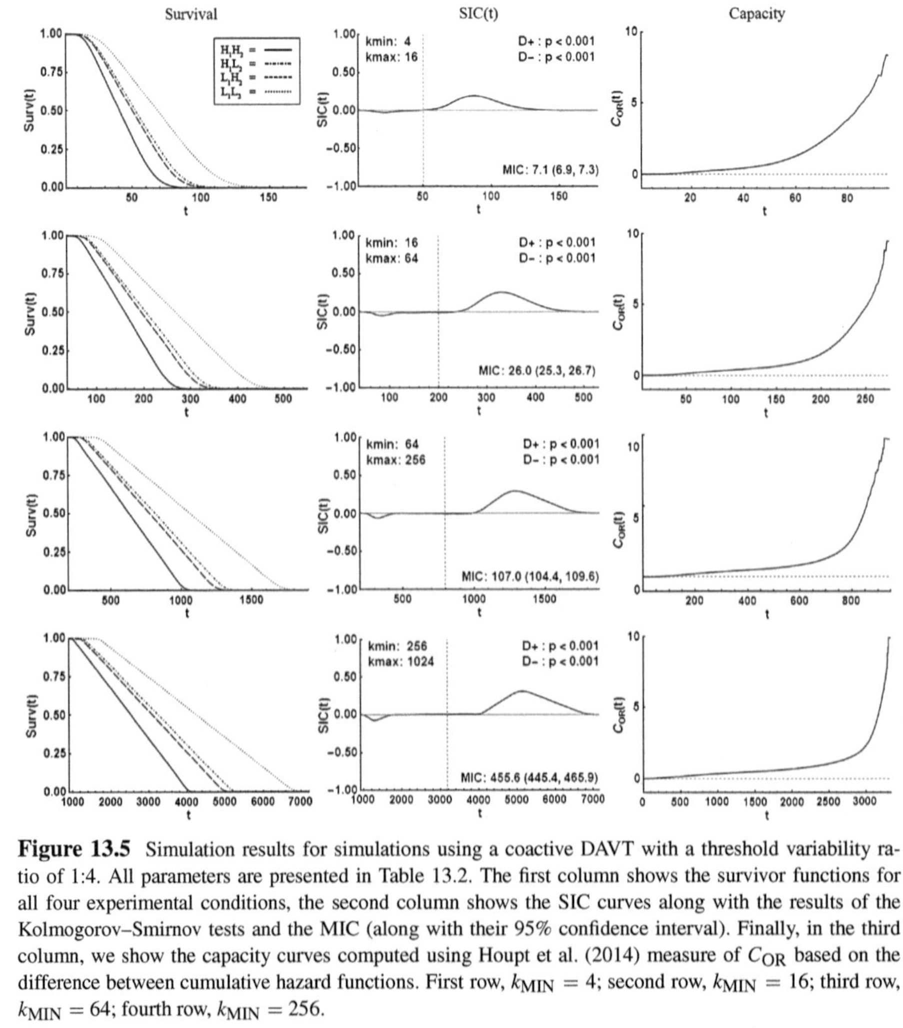

Figure 13.5 Simulation results for simulations using a coactive DAVT with a threshold variability ratio of 1:4. All parameters are presented in Table 13.2. The first column shows the survivor functions for all four experimental conditions, the second column shows the SIC curves along with the results of the Kolmogorov–Smirnov tests and the MIC (along with their 95% confidence interval). Finally, in the third column, we show the capacity curves computed using Houpt et al. (2014) measure of C_{OR} based on the difference between cumulative hazard functions. First row, $k_{\text{MIN}} = 4$; second row, $k_{\text{MIN}} = 16$; third row, $k_{\text{MIN}} = 64$; fourth row, $k_{\text{MIN}} = 256$.

curves being almost completely absent from the plot. Results from the Kolmogorov–Smirnov tests still indicate that both negative and positive portions of the SIC curves are significantly different than 0. However, this is only caused by the very large sample size ($n = 50{,}000$, atypical of empirical research) where any small deviation is considered significant. Nonetheless, we believe that if consulted alone, the SIC shape and positive MIC could possibly result in a false parallel self-terminating diagnosis. This possible misdiagnosis is impactful as all of SFT assumptions have been met. Despite these atypical results, as shown in the third column of Fig. 13.5, the capacity curves still indicate supercapacity, which is impossible for a parallel self-terminating process with stochastically independent channels. This highlights the importance of using the entire SFT toolbox to characterize processes.

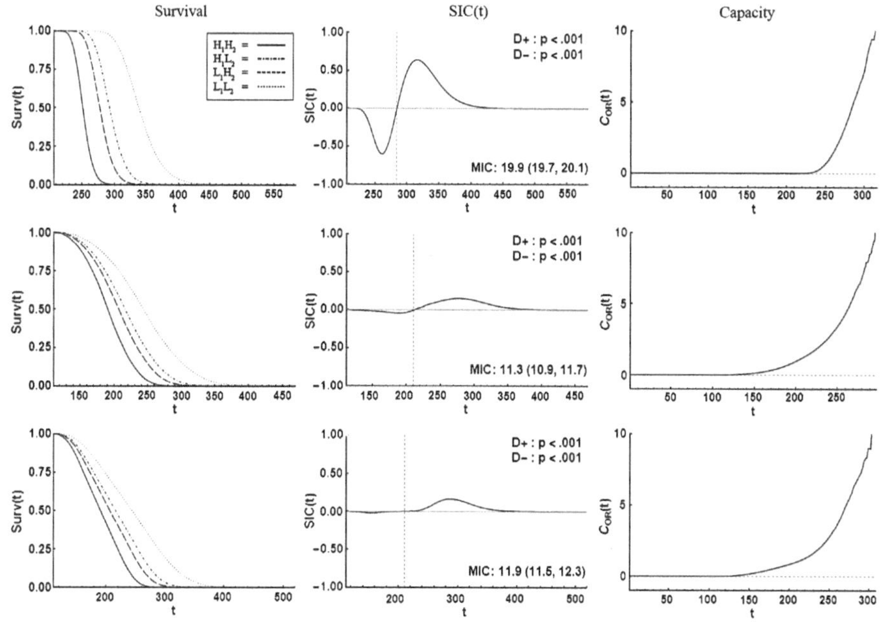

Figure 13.6 Simulation results for simulations using a coactive LBA. All parameters are presented in Table 13.3. The first column shows the survivor functions for all four experimental conditions, the second column shows the SIC curves along with the results of the Kolmogorov–Smirnov tests and the MIC (along with their 95% confidence interval). Finally, in the third column, we show the capacity curves computed using Houpt et al. (2014) measure of C_{OR} based on the difference between cumulative hazard functions. First row, 1:1.25 threshold ratio; second row, 1:12.5 threshold ratio (with even starting points); third row, 1:12.5 threshold ratio (with uneven starting points).

LBA

In order to test whether the presence of threshold variability affects other more complete processing models of RT, we have conducted an SFT analysis on an LBA model (Brown and Heathcote, 2008). In these simulations, shown in Fig. 13.6, we have simulated three LBAs: one with little starting point variability (1:1.25 variability ratio), one with large starting point variability (1:12.5 variability ratio), and one with a large starting point variability and unequal starting point boundaries for each subprocess.

As seen, there is no issue whatsoever with SFTs interpretation of the LBA with little threshold variability. All survivor functions (shown in the first column of Fig. 13.6) follow the expected theoretical order and do not cross at any point. As shown in the second column of Fig. 13.6, the MIC is positive and the SIC follows the expected coactive pattern where the positive and negative portion of the curve are significantly different from 0. Finally, the capacity curve (shown in the third column of Fig. 13.6) correctly indicates supercapacity. From here, we can conclude that a LBA, with little starting point variability, will be correctly diagnosed.

When the starting point variability is large, results are drastically different than the ones presented above and mirror the SIC trend identified using a DAVT. In this simulation, we can see that the survivor functions are correctly ordered and do not cross at any point. The highlight of this simulation is that the negative area of the SIC curve is greatly diminished. Much like what was found with DAVT, Kolmogorov–Smirnov tests return significant results for both negative and positive portions of the curve, which is due to the very large sample size.

In the third simulation, we observe the same results as with the high threshold variability DAVT simulations. The negative area of the SIC curve is seemingly not present. Once again, Kolmogorov–Smirnov tests show a significant negative and positive portion of the curve. Furthermore, just like it is the case with DAVT, the model is correctly deemed to operate in supercapacity.

These findings highlight the impact of threshold variability on SFT's SIC interpretation of coactive architectures. These atypical SIC findings seem to be generalizable to stochastically independent race models.

SIC Centerline

During the analysis of the simulations presented above, we also developed the *SIC centerline*, a complementary SFT diagnostic tool that helps to visually discriminate between architecture alternatives. The centerline is calculated by pooling all four conditions' RT (assuming that all four conditions have roughly the same amount of trials) and measuring the median of the pooled data. Afterwards, the centerline, representing an RT value, is directly plotted on the SIC curve. Depending on the underlying architecture, the SIC centerline falls in specific areas of the SIC curve. In Fig. 13.1, we see where the SIC centerline should typically be in the SIC plots of all five architectures. In parallel processes, the SIC centerline passes through an area of over/underadditivity, whereas in serial exhaustive architectures and coactive architectures with no threshold variability, the SIC centerline should fall very near (and sometimes directly on) the negative and positive's area of intersection.

When threshold variability increases, as in the 1:2 and 1:4 simulations, the SIC centerline systematically falls in the atypical plateau. Thus, the SIC centerline can also be used to distinguish coactive from parallel self-terminating processes in models using variable thresholds. We observe the same results using both DAVT and LBA, showing the tool's usefulness and generalizability across accumulator models. As shown in Appendix, the SIC centerline is also informative when other distributions of interarrival times are assumed.

Although this measure may not be as reliable as an analysis of capacity, it is worth examining when using SFT. We suggest that if the SIC centerline does not pass near the onset of the over/under-additive portions of the SIC curve nor their point of intersection (if the curve has both negative and positive sections), the possibility of an atypical architecture should be investigated further. There are many ways of calculating the SIC centerline such as the mean of pooled conditions or the median (or mean) of only the H_1H_2 and L_1L_2 conditions. However, we found that the median of pooled RT from all four conditions gave us the most consistent results across simulations and models.

Discussion

Although we only illustrated simulations up to a thresholds ratio of 1:4 using DAVT, and 1:12.5 using the LBA, threshold ratios up to 1:14 (representing a threshold that can cover 93% of the accumulator's total size) have been empirically observed (Heathcote & Hayes, 2012; synthesized in Table 13.1). These results, in tandem, show that when threshold variability increases, regardless of model implementation, the amplitude of the negative area becomes increasingly hard to detect in coactive SIC curves. Thus, the fact that such large ratios are empirically possible (based on model fits) highlights the relevance of this chapter. Additionally, supplementary simulations using DAVT show that, by increasing the threshold ratio to 1:8, the negative portion of the curve visually disappears, and with a threshold ratio of 1:25, the Kolmogorov–Smirnov tests return consistently insignificant results.

This diminishing underadditivity is problematic because the standard coactive SIC signature increasingly resembles the standard parallel self-terminating SIC curve as threshold variability increases. Researchers could possibly make a wrongful diagnosis if their decision is based on MIC and the SIC curve alone. Additionally, as both parallel self-terminating and coactive architectures are somewhat similar in theory (both include two subprocesses working in "parallel" with a decision being made as soon as a sufficient amount of information is accumulated), falsification of one architecture over the other is increasingly difficult. To eliminate this possibility, it is primordial that all possible tools be exhausted.

Moreover, as we wished to provide a proof of concept, our samples sizes were very large to ensure a smooth SIC curve. For a realistic sample size (in the hundreds rather than in the tens of thousands), it may be even more difficult to differentiate models with large threshold variability as the SIC curve will be much noisier. As an example, we simulated a coactive and a parallel self-terminating DAVT, both with a ratio of 1:4 and a $k_{\mathrm{MIN}} = 64$ using 500 simulations rather than 50,000. The results are presented in Fig. 13.7.

As seen in the second column of Fig. 13.7, the model's SICs are easier to confound with one another when the SIC curves are not as smooth. The already attenuated negative portion of the coactive SIC curve, combined with the positive MIC, could be attributed to noise leading to a possible parallel self-terminating misdiagnosis. In fact, a Kolmogorov–Smirnov test indicates that the negative portion of the curve is not significantly different from 0 in both cases, evidence towards a possible erroneous parallel self-terminating diagnosis for the coactive architecture. However, as the capacity curves of both simulated architectures (shown in the third column of Fig. 13.7) are quite different, we can correctly diagnose both architectures assuming that SFTs assumptions are met and respected (which they are in both cases). Furthermore, the SIC centerline falls in a flat portion of the SIC for the coactive architecture rather than in the overadditive area as it is the case in the parallel self-terminating architecture. This observation helps the discrimination between architecture alternatives.

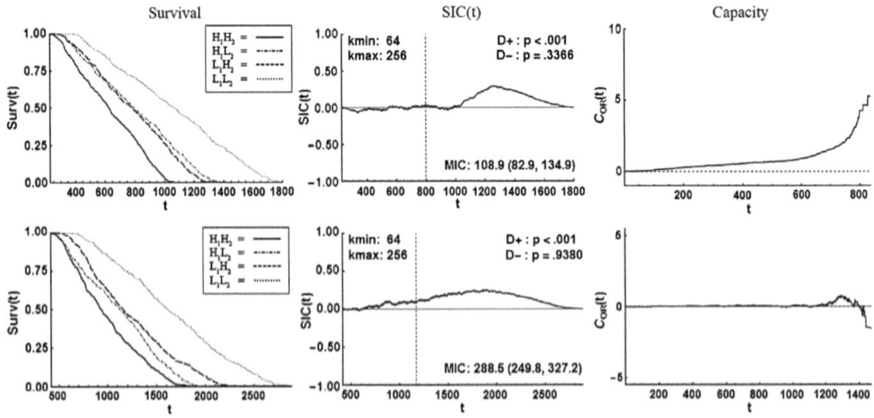

Figure 13.7 DAVT simulation results using $k_{\mathrm{MIN}} = 64$, $k_{\mathrm{MAX}} = 256$ (1:4 ratio) and $n = 500$ rather than $n = 50{,}000$ (as used throughout this chapter). The first column shows the survivor functions for all four experimental conditions, the second column shows the SIC curves along with the results of the Kolmogorov–Smirnov tests and the MIC (along with their 95% confidence interval). Finally, in the third column, we show the capacity curves computed using Houpt et al. (2014) measure of C_{OR} based on the difference between cumulative hazard functions. First row, a coactive process; second row, a parallel self-terminating process.

Conclusion

As noted by Houpt and Townsend (2011), coactive models are not as broadly defined as the other architectures, limiting the predictions of SIC to the specific cases that have been studied. The present chapter adds to this research and shows that a standard coactive model, with the sole addition of varying thresholds, may make SFT diagnoses on SIC and MIC alone increasingly difficult. These findings were performed with two stochastically independent race model variants of which the only shared feature was threshold variability (or the mathematically equivalent randomly varying starting point) in an environment where selective influence is respected, underlining the impact of our results. This is of importance as very variable thresholds have been used to explain certain participants' RT (Heathcote & Hayes, 2012). Fortunately, we show that the capacity curve eliminates the possibility of user misdiagnosis, a strong argument in favor of using the entire range of the SFT toolbox. We also introduced the SIC centerline, an easy to compute qualitative measure that we developed to assist in diagnosing architectures.

As SFT is fast entering more researchers' repertoires of analyses, it is important to know how varying thresholds, an accepted component to explain human performances (Brown & Heathcote, 2008), affects diagnoses. We believe that with the simulations presented here, one should increase diagnostic prudency and ensure that all tools have been exhausted before making a diagnosis.

Future research should expand on this work and focus on whether SFT can make correct diagnoses of other types of accumulator models with added threshold variability, such as the DDM (Ratcliff, 1978), or the Leaky Competing Accumulator model (LCA; Usher & McClelland, 2001).

Acknowledgement

This research project was supported in part by the National Science and Engineering Council of Canada (NSERC).

Appendix: DAVT Simulations Using a Normal Distribution for Evidence Arrival Times

When using normally distributed arrival times of evidence using a normal distribution, it is possible to sample negative arrival times, especially when using small means and reasonable standard deviations. As noted in Donkin, Averell, Brown and Heathcote's (2009), *makedata.r* program, this forces simulated datasets to resample negative arrival times or to truncate them at zero. We avoided this difficulty in our independent race model by using two-parameter Weibull distributions of arrival times. Because it does not require truncation as all the variates are positive or null and because simulation results were identical to the ones with the normal distribution, we opted to keep these distributions. However, to show that the theoretical distribution of the evidence arrival time distributions does not affect SFT results, we replicate in this appendix the simulation with a ratio of 1:4 and a $k_{\text{MIN}} = 64$ using a normal distribution rather than a Weibull as was used throughout DAVT simulations. Implementation is identical to the one presented in Table 13.2 with the sole exception that subprocess arrival times are sampled from the following distributions:

$$\mathrm{H}_1 \sim N(20; 5), \qquad \mathrm{H}_2 \sim N(23; 5),$$
$$\mathrm{L}_1 \sim N(36; 5), \qquad \mathrm{L}_2 \sim N(40; 5)$$

where $N(\mu; \sigma)$ is a normal distribution with mean parameter μ and standard deviation parameter σ.

The survivor functions, the SIC (along with the modified Kolmogorov–Smirnov test), the MIC, as well as the capacity curve are presented in Fig. 13.A.

As seen, the results of the simulation are almost indistinguishable from the ones presented using the Weibull distribution. All survivor functions are ordered correctly with no crossing between conditions. Moreover, the negative portion of the curve is attenuated which could lead to a possible parallel self-terminating misdiagnosis. With 50,000 simulated RT, the Kolmogorov–Smirnov tests return significant results meaning that both negative and positive areas of the curve are different from 0. Finally, once again, the capacity curve returns a supercapacity signature. Any evidence inter-arrival time distribution could be used to replicate the trends stated in the body of this chapter.

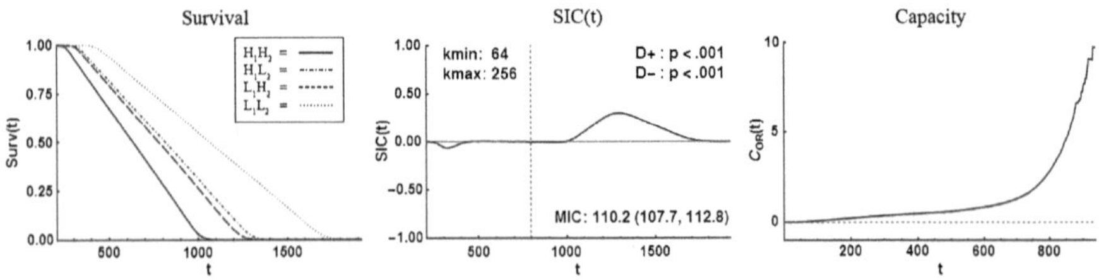

Figure 13.A Results from simulations using a normal distribution rather than a Weibull distribution for evidence arrival times. All DAVT parameters were otherwise identical to the third DAVT simulation (1:4 threshold ratio, $k_{\text{MIN}} = 64$) of which the results are shown in Fig. 13.5. The first column shows the survivor functions for all four experimental conditions, the second column shows the SIC curves along with the results of the Kolmogorov–Smirnov tests and the MIC (along with their 95% confidence interval). Finally, in the third column, we show the capacity curves computed using Houpt et al. (2014) measure of C_{OR} based on the difference between cumulative hazard functions.

References

Altieri, N., Fifić, M., Little, D. R., & Yang, C-T. (2017). A tutorial and historical introduction to systems factorial technology. In D. R. Little, N. Altieri, M. Fifić, & C-T. Yang (Eds.), *Systems factorial technology: a theory driven methodology for the identification of perceptual and cognitive mechanisms*. San Diego, CA: Elsevier Publishing (in this book).

Brown, S. D., & Heathcote, A. (2008). The simplest complete model of choice response time: Linear ballistic accumulation. *Cognitive Psychology*, *57*(3), 153–178. http://dx.doi.org/10.1016/j.cogpsych.2007.12.002.

Donders, F. C. (1969). On the speed of mental processes. *Acta Psychologica*, *30*, 412–431. http://dx.doi.org/10.1016/0001-6918(69)90065-1.

Donkin, C., Averell, L., Brown, S., & Heathcote, A. (2009). Getting more from accuracy and response time data: Methods for fitting the linear ballistic accumulator. *Behavior Research Methods*, *41*(4), 1095–1110. http://dx.doi.org/10.3758/BRM.41.4.1095.

Dutilh, G., Vandekerckhove, J., Tuerlinckx, F., & Wagenmakers, E.-J. (2009). A diffusion model decomposition of the practice effect. *Psychonomic Bulletin & Review*, *16*(6), 1026–1036. http://dx.doi.org/10.3758/16.6.1026.

Eidels, A., Houpt, J. W., Altieri, N., Pei, L., & Townsend, J. T. (2011). Nice guys finish fast and bad guys finish last: Facilitatory vs. inhibitory interaction in parallel systems. *Journal of Mathematical Psychology*, *55*(2), 176–190. http://dx.doi.org/10.1016/j.jmp.2010.11.003.

Fifić, M., Little, D. R., & Nosofsky, R. M. (2010). Logical-rule models of classification response times: A synthesis of mental-architecture, random-walk, and decision-bound approaches. *Psychological Review*, *117*(2), 309–348. http://dx.doi.org/10.1037/a0018526.

Fifić, M., Townsend, J. T., & Eidels, A. (2008). Studying visual search using systems factorial methodology with target–distractor similarity as the factor. *Perception & Psychophysics*, *70*(4), 583–603. http://dx.doi.org/10.3758/PP.70.4.583.

Forstmann, B. U., Ratcliff, R., & Wagenmakers, E. J. (2016). Sequential sampling models in cognitive neuroscience: Advantages, applications, and extensions. *Annual Reviews in Psychology*, *67*, 641–666. http://dx.doi.org/10.1146/annurev-psych-122414-033645.

Harding, B., Goulet, M. A., Jolin, S., Tremblay, C., Villeneuve, S.-P., & Durand, G. (2016). Systems factorial technology explained to humans. *The Quantitative Methods for Psychology*, *12*(1), 39–59. http://dx.doi.org/10.20982/tqmp.12.1.p039.

Heathcote, A., Brown, S., Wagenmakers, E. J., & Eidels, A. (2010). Distribution-free tests of stochastic dominance for small samples. *Journal of Mathematical Psychology*, *54*(5), 454–463. http://dx.doi.org/10.1016/j.jmp.2010.06.005.

Heathcote, A., & Hayes, B. (2012). Diffusion versus linear ballistic accumulation: Different models for response time with different conclusions about psychological mechanisms? *Canadian Journal of Experimental Psychology/Revue Canadienne de Psychologie Expérimentale*, *66*(2), 125–136. http://dx.doi.org/10.1037/a0028189.

Houpt, J. W., Blaha, L. M., McIntire, J. P., Havig, P. R., & Townsend, J. T. (2014). Systems factorial technology with R. *Behavior Research Methods*, *46*(2), 307–330. http://dx.doi.org/10.3758/s13428-013-0377-3.

Houpt, J. W., & Townsend, J. T. (2010). The statistical properties of the survivor interaction contrast. *Journal of Mathematical Psychology*, *54*, 446–453. http://dx.doi.org/10.1016/j.jmp.2010.06.006.

Houpt, J. W., & Townsend, J. T. (2011). An extension of SIC predictions to the Wiener coactive model. *Journal of Mathematical Psychology*, *55*(3), 267–270. http://dx.doi.org/10.1016/j.jmp.2011.02.002.

Houpt, J. W., & Townsend, J. T. (2012). Statistical measures for workload capacity analysis. *Journal of Mathematical Psychology*, *56*(5), 341–355. http://dx.doi.org/10.1016/j.jmp.2012.05.004.

Johnson, S. A., Blaha, L. M., Houpt, J. W., & Townsend, J. T. (2010). Systems factorial technology provides new insights on global–local information processing in autism spectrum disorders. *Journal of Mathematical Psychology*, *54*(1), 53–72. http://dx.doi.org/10.1016/j.jmp.2009.06.006.

Luce, R. D. (1986). *Response times: Their role in inferring elementary mental organization*. New York, NY: Oxford University Press.

Ratcliff, R. (1978). A theory of memory retrieval. *Psychological Review*, *85*(2), 59–108. http://dx.doi.org/10.1037/0033-295X.85.2.59.

Schwarz, W. (1989). A new model to explain the redundant-signals effect. *Perception & Psychophysics*, *46*(5), 498–500. http://dx.doi.org/10.3758/BF03210867.

Snodgrass, J. G., & Townsend, J. T. (1980). Comparing parallel and serial models: Theory and implementation. *Journal of Experimental Psychology: Human Perception and Performance*, *6*(2), 330–354. http://dx.doi.org/10.1037/0096-1523.6.2.330.

Sternberg, S. (1969). Memory-scanning: Mental processes revealed by reaction-time experiments. *American Scientist*, *57*(4), 421–457.

Sternberg, S. (1998). Inferring mental operations from reaction-time: How we compare objects. In D. Scarborough, & S. Sternberg (Eds.), In *Methods, models, and conceptual issues: Vol. 4. An invitation to cognitive science* (2nd ed.) (pp. 365–454). Cambridge, MA: MIT Press.

Teodorescu, A. R., & Usher, M. (2013). Disentangling decision models: from independence to competition. *Psychological Review*, *120*(1), 1–38. http://dx.doi.org/10.1037/a0030776.

Townsend, J. T. (1972). Some results concerning the identifiability of parallel and serial processes. *British Journal of Mathematical and Statistical Psychology*, *25*(2), 168–199. http://dx.doi.org/10.1111/j.2044-8317.1972.tb00490.x.

Townsend, J. T. (1990). Serial vs. parallel processing: Sometimes they look like Tweedledum and Tweedledee but they can (and should) be distinguished. *Psychological Science*, *1*(1), 46–54. http://dx.doi.org/10.1111/j.1467-9280.1990.tb00067.x.

Townsend, J. T., & Ashby, F. G. (1978). Methods of modeling capacity in simple processing systems. In N. J. Castellan Jr., & F. Restle (Eds.), *Cognitive theory, Vol. 3* (pp. 199–239). Hillsdale, NJ: Erlbaum.

Townsend, J. T., & Ashby, F. G. (1983). *Stochastic modeling of elementary psychological processes*. New York, NY: Cambridge University Press.

Townsend, J. T., & Nozawa, G. (1995). Spatio-temporal properties of elementation perception: An investigation of parallel, serial, and coactive theories. *Journal of Mathematical Psychology*, *39*(4), 321–359. http://dx.doi.org/10.1006/jmps.1995.1033.

Townsend, J. T., & Wenger, M. J. (2004). A theory of interactive parallel processing: New capacity measures and predictions for a response time inequality series. *Psychological Review*, *111*(4), 1003–1035. http://dx.doi.org/10.1037/0033-295X.111.4.1003.

Usher, M., & McClelland, J. L. (2001). On the time course of perceptual choice: The leaky competing accumulator model. *Psychological Review*, *108*, 550–592. http://dx.doi.org/10.1037//0033-295X.108.3.550.

Can Confusion-Data Inform SFT-Like Inference? A Comparison of SFT and Accuracy-Based Measures in Comparable Experiments

14

Zachary L. Howard, Ami Eidels*, Noah H. Silbert*[†], *Daniel R. Little*[‡]
*University of Newcastle, Callaghan, NSW, Australia, [†]University of Cincinnati, Cincinnati, OH, United States, [‡]University of Melbourne, Melbourne, VIC, Australia

Many psychological tasks, as well as most everyday-life decisions, require us to evaluate multiple pieces or aspects of information. For example, both cost and performance might be important factors to consider when buying a new car. Likewise, most people consider both personality and appearance important aspects when choosing a romantic partner. In the laboratory, experimental tasks may approximate these decisions by requiring participants to consider stimuli that vary along several dimensions, such as size, shape, or color. In all these cases it is necessary to *integrate* information from several sources in order to make a decision. Investigating the mechanisms through which we integrate information from different sources is thus an endeavor worthy of scientific investigation.

An important consideration in these investigations is whether people need to simply detect the presence of a signal, or determine its identity. *Detection* of signals, such as the detection of warning signals in case of an emergency, is one important role the cognitive system must accomplish in real life. To probe how human observers detect multiple information sources in the lab we could ask participants to decide whether there is an auditory signal or a visual signal, or both modalities presented on a given trial (or whether there was no signal presented). Often, however, we need to not only detect the mere presence of a stimulus but also determine its identity out of a set of alternatives. For example, a warning signal could be presented in an emergency and we may need to identify whether it is a lockdown signal, or an evacuation signal. Simply detecting the presence of a signal is not enough in this case; *identification* is needed to drive the most appropriate behavior. In the current chapter we discuss properties of the cognitive system for both detection and identification of stimuli.

Townsend and colleagues (e.g., Ashby & Townsend, 1983; Townsend, 1974) identified four important properties that are basic for understanding how the cognitive processing system integrates information from various sources (for an overview see the tutorial chapter of this book, Altieri, Fifić, Little, & Yang, 2017). The four basic properties of multiple-information processing they defined are *processing architecture* (e.g., serial vs parallel vs coactive processing), *capacity* (i.e., how processing

Systems Factorial Technology, DOI: 10.1016/B978-0-12-804315-8.00017-3

efficiency changes with workload; Townsend & Wenger, 2004; Townsend & Eidels, 2011), *stopping rule* (self-terminating or exhaustive), and (*in*) *dependence* (to what extent do two or more channels communicate with one another). Almost any combination of these properties is possible (Townsend & Wenger, 2004). Certain tasks may lend themselves to certain kinds of processing (for example, task instructions may require participants to consider all attributes of a stimulus – exhaustive processing); however, there is evidence that participants sometimes adopt a nonoptimal strategy or decision rule (i.e., they might respond based on partial information when this is not task-appropriate, as demonstrated by Bushmakin, Eidels, & Heathcote, 2015). There is hence great merit in a principled method of identifying each of these properties from empirical data, as we cannot be sure participants actually perform a given task as instructed. Townsend and Nozawa (1995) developed Systems Factorial Technology (SFT), a theoretical framework and associated experimental methodology, which allows the identification of these basic properties based on response time (*RT*) distributions. In the next section of this chapter we briefly outline SFT (for more details see Townsend & Nozawa, 1995; Townsend & Wenger, 2004; Altieri et al., 2017). We discuss how SFT is most useful in tasks that require *detection* of signals, but needs to be augmented for tasks that require *identification* of stimuli out of several response-options.

The contribution of this chapter is twofold: First, it extends SFT-like system inference to the identification paradigm, by considering data from three new identification experiments (4, 5, 6). These experiments were modeled after previous SFT studies (Experiments 1, 2, 3; Eidels, Townsend, Hughes, & Perry, 2015, Experiment 1; Fifić, Nosofsky, & Townsend, 2008, Experiment's 1 & 2), and use similar kinds of stimuli. The main dependent variable in the new identification experiments is response accuracy, not *RT*. Thus, the second contribution is a demonstration of the potential utility as well as possible shortcomings of accuracy-based inferences in identifying basic properties of information processing. For this purpose, we report a set of simulation-based results that complement the empirical results.

Systems Factorial Technology

Several approaches have been proposed to investigate one or more of the basic properties of cognitive processing systems identified above, but arguably the method that has found most traction is SFT (Townsend & Nozawa, 1995). SFT provides a framework for identifying these properties of models through unique signatures of *RT* distributions. SFT has been applied in areas as broad as memory search (Townsend & Fifić, 2004), visual search (Fifić et al., 2008), simple detection (Townsend & Nozawa, 1995; Eidels et al., 2015), Stroop color–word stimuli (Eidels, Townsend, & Algom, 2010), word processing (Houpt, Townsend, & Donkin, 2014), and even questions concerning the perception of self vs other (Sui, Yankouskaya, & Humphreys, 2015).

SFT is a powerful framework equipped to investigate cognitive processing under certain conditions. However, the diagnostic ability of SFT stems from mathematical derivations that make strict assumptions about the experimental set up; specifically, the framework is best suited for the redundant target detection design (see Fifić & Little, 2017). Furthermore, SFT analysis relies on response times, which are not always available, especially in psychophysical experimentation or studies that focus on other measures (such as accuracy). In this sense, the strengths of SFT also limit its applicability to other domains. SFT cannot currently operate within an identification paradigm where each stimulus is assigned a unique response.

To extend SFT-like inference to another domain, a useful first step would be to adapt existing studies into a new paradigm. This would require non-SFT analysis to be performed, but the new analyses can be performed in light of the known processing strategies identified in the original studies. The study outlined in this chapter aims to achieve this goal by comparing SFT-based inference from published studies (Fifić et al., 2008, Experiments 1 & 2; Eidels et al., 2015, Experiment 1) with other analysis tools in order to extend the model-diagnostic capabilities of SFT to a broader range of experimental paradigms. In the section Three *RT* Experiments Using SFT, we summarize findings from three published SFT experiments (Experiments 1, 2, 3) that used SFT to uncover parallel, serial, and coactive architectures, respectively. In the section Three New Accuracy Experiments Using GRT, we present results from three new *identification* experiments (Experiments 4, 5, 6), using stimuli similar in nature to those used in the SFT studies. We employ a general yet powerful accuracy-based framework, General Recognition Theory (GRT; Ashby & Townsend, 1986), to investigate these data. We highlight in the section Three New Accuracy Experiments Using GRT the difficulty in interpreting GRT solutions in terms of the basic properties of processing systems, particularly those that reflect "dynamic" properties (architecture and stopping rule, see, e.g., Eidels et al., 2015). Consequently, in the section Simulations we report a new simulation study aimed at systematically investigating how these properties manifest themselves in the GRT analyses. In the final part of this chapter, we discuss the *RT* and accuracy measures and results, and how they relate to each other.

Three RT Experiments Using SFT

We briefly outline the methodology and results of three published SFT studies (which we later replicated with some changes in the accuracy domain, see section Three New Accuracy Experiments Using GRT). For a full description we direct readers to the original papers. These studies were chosen as each found clear evidence for a different processing architecture. Experiment 1 provided evidence that dots in two locations are processed in parallel. Experiment 2 provided evidence that colored rectangles and vertical lines are processed serially when presented in nonoverlapping spatial locations. Experiment 3 provided evidence that the brightness and saturation of a colored rectangle are coactively processed. The stimuli are illustrated in Fig. 14.1 and the results are summarized in Fig. 14.2 and Table 14.1.

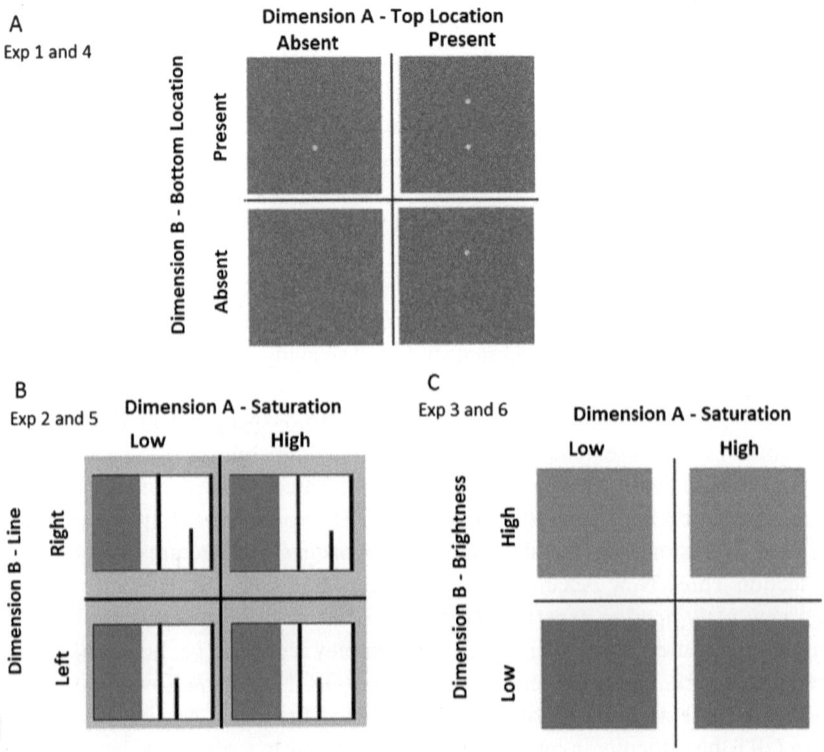

Figure 14.1 Stimulus sets used in Experiments 4, 5 and 6, respectively. Images are for illustration only, and actual stimulus size and other attributes were different. Stimuli details are discussed in section Three New Accuracy Experiments Using GRT. Readers should note that some versions of this chapter are not printed in color; therefore, the stimulus dimensions in panels B and C may not be discriminable in this figure. All stimulus sets result from a 2 × 2 factorial combination of their respective dimensions.

Experiment 1 – Dot Detection

Eidels et al. (2015) asked participants to judge whether or not a dot was presented in one or both of two locations. Thus, the "dimensions" of interest were target location (top, bottom) and target presence (present, absent). The salience (contrast of the dot target) was also manipulated as either high or low contrast, resulting in a total of nine conditions: four with both targets present (HH – both targets in high contrast, HL – one high and one low, LH, and LL), four where one target was present (top-only target high or low, bottom-only target high or low), and a no-target display. The target was a small dot of a lighter shade than the background. Both OR (respond affirmatively if there is a target in the top *or* bottom location) and AND (respond affirmatively if there is a target in the top *and* bottom location) paradigms were tested, on separate days. Thus, self-terminating or exhaustive processing, respectively, were required to properly complete the task.

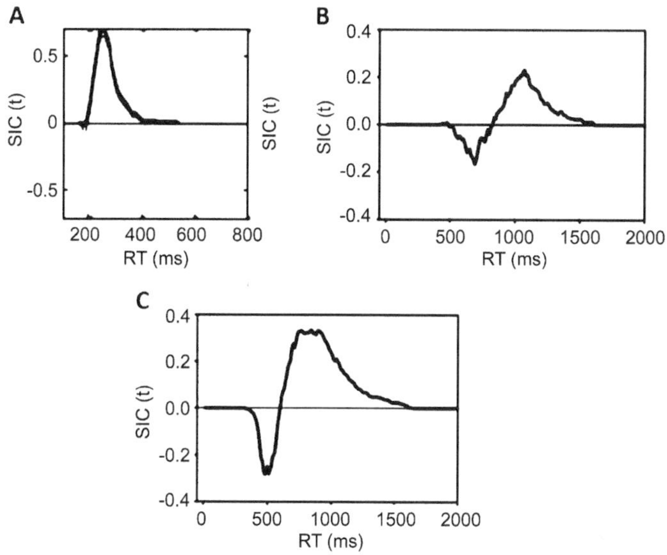

Figure 14.2 Prototypical *SIC* results from the three SFT studies summarized in the section Three *RT* Experiments Using SFT. Panel A shows a typical participant from Eidels et al.'s OR task (2015; Exp. 1). The all-positive *SIC* curve suggests parallel self-terminating processing (appropriate for the OR task). Panel B shows a typical participant from Fifić et al.'s (2008, Exp. 1) separable AND condition, and suggests serial-exhaustive processing. Panel C shows a typical participant from Fifić et al.'s integral task (2008, Exp. 2), and suggests a co-active processing strategy.

In both the OR and the AND paradigms the SFT measures (*MIC* and *SIC*) converged to suggest parallel processing with the appropriate stopping rule for the given task. Capacity in the OR task was predominantly (moderately) limited, whereas in the AND task capacity varied considerably between participants. Channel dependence is not directly tested by the SFT analyses; however, the *SIC* signatures were typical of independent processing (see Eidels, Houpt, Altieri, Pei, & Townsend, 2011, for further discussion on the impact of channel dependence on *SIC* signatures). The overall error-rate for these studies was low (3.6% across all tasks) and only correct responses were analyzed. Data from a typical participant in the OR task is presented in Fig. 14.2A.

Experiment 2 – Saturation and Line Position

Fifić et al. (2008, Experiment 1; see also Fifić, Little, & Nosofsky, 2010) employed saturation of a colored rectangle and the position of a vertical line in a spatially separated rectangle (see Fig. 14.1B), stimulus dimensions typically classified as separable (Garner, 1974). Fifić et al.'s study implemented a novel variation of the SFT paradigm involving categorizing stimuli based on the values of each dimension. Overall, evidence from Fifić and colleagues suggested that processing of the color and line position of the stimuli occurs in a serial fashion, with a task-appropriate stopping rule (processing was self-terminating where possible, but exhaustive when necessary).

Table 14.1 Summary of findings from *RT* and accuracy based measures using comparable stimuli

	SFT (*RT*-based) measures	GRT (accuracy-based) measures
Exp. 1 & 4: Dot in two spatial locations	Exp. 1: Parallel, task appropriate stopping rule, slightly limited capacity	Exp. 4: PS_A and PS_B hold. PI holds for all response regions but A_1B_1. Response bias toward "no target" (A_1B_1). *Consistent with independent processing.*
Exp. 2 & 5: Saturation and line position	Exp. 2: Serial, task-appropriate stopping rule	Exp 5: PS_A and PS_B hold. Minor violations of PI. No response bias, little overlap between perceptual distributions. *Consistent with independent processing.*
Exp. 3 & 6: Saturation and brightness	Exp. 3: Coactive processing	Exp. 6: PS_B fails, PS_A holds. PI slightly violated for all regions, but strongly violated when both dimensions are high A_2B_2. *NOT consistent with independent processing, but not consistent with postaccumulator coactivity.*

PS_A and PS_B denote Perceptual Separability of dimension A and B, respectively. PI denotes Perceptual Independence. See text in section Three New Accuracy Experiments Using GRT for more details. GRT summaries only include group-level trends.

Fifić et al. (2008) found that two participants used parallel processing; in another similar study (Fifić et al., 2010, Experiment 1) serial processing was explicit in the instructions, and all participants whose data allowed clear inference exhibited serial processing. Using related stimuli composed of separable dimensions, Little, Nosofsky, and Denton (2011; see also Fifić et al., 2010, Experiment 2) found that people naturally adopt a serial processing strategy when learning from trial and error. Capacity estimates are not available for these data. *SIC* data of a typical participant is presented in Fig. 14.2B.

Experiment 3 – Saturation and Brightness

Fifić et al. (2008, Experiment 2; see also Little, Nosofsky, Donkin, & Denton, 2013) repeated the categorization task reported in Study 2 with stimuli defined by a combination of two *integral* dimensions (Garner, 1974) – the saturation and brightness of a colored rectangle. Both Fifić et al. and Little et al. studies found strong evidence for coactive processing, with all participants exhibiting an over-additive *MIC* and an *SIC* with an initial, small negative blip, followed by a larger period of positive *SIC* (*SIC* curve from a typical participant is shown in Fig. 14.2C). Coactive processes are a special case of highly interactive systems in which the evidence from each dimension is completely pooled into a common, global conduit. This finding conforms to the theoretical prediction that integral dimensions cannot be "teased-apart" and examined individually (Garner, 1974), as coactive processes lose individual-channel identity by pooling all evidence into a single accumulator.

Three New Accuracy Experiments Using GRT

To address our aim of extending SFT-like inference to a new paradigm we conducted three new experiments (4, 5, and 6), using stimuli similar to those explored under the SFT framework. Using stimuli for which the processing architectures and other properties are known (at least in the context of target detection) allows a more focused and informed examination of processing attributes. The *RT*-based SFT approach is particularly useful in assessing architecture, stopping rule, and capacity, but inference about channel (in)dependence is less direct. GRT and its confusion-based measures, on the other hand, are particularly useful for assessing independence, but have typically not been used for assessing dynamic properties of processing (although see Townsend, Houpt, & Silbert, 2012, for a recent extension of GRT to *RT*). The current chapter thus provides a new direction for comprehensive examination of cognitive processing by combining two powerful theory-driven approaches, utilizing information from both accuracy and response-times to inform conclusions.

Each new experiment consisted of four stimuli, defined by the factorial combinations of two dimensions, and in each experiment the processing architecture was known from previous *RT* studies. The stimuli are presented in Fig. 14.1. In Experiment 4, we adapted a canonical dot-detection task following Eidels et al. (2015). The task was to detect a dot of light that could appear in either or both of two locations. Thus the "dimensions" are the top and bottom locations, which can each take present or absent values. Eidels et al. found these dimensions were processed in parallel. In Experiment 5 we combined two levels of saturation of a colored rectangle with two positions of a vertical line. These dimensions have been shown to be processed serially (Fifić et al., 2008). In Experiment 6 we combined the two levels of saturation of a colored rectangle with two levels of brightness of the same colored rectangle. These dimensions, when presented within the same spatial location, are considered *integral* (Garner, 1974), which implies they cannot be processed separately from each other. Indeed, Fifić et al. (2008) found the processing of saturation and brightness is best characterized by a coactive mode of processing, which is the antipode of separate or independent channels.

The new experiments were designed to use stimuli as similar as possible to those used in the SFT studies, but modified slightly to yield enough errors for confusion analysis in an identification paradigm. Slight modifications to the original methods were necessary to adjust to identification under threshold conditions, in both instructions and quality of stimuli (degraded, to allow sufficient confusions for analysis). The same participants performed in all three experiments. All three experiments shared a common design and procedure, so we provide the full method for Experiment 4, and a summary of methodological changes and description of stimuli for Experiments 5 and 6.

Experiment 4 – Dots

Ten students from the University of Newcastle, eight females ($M = 23.1$ years, $SD = 2.9$ years) and two males ($M = 24.5$ years, $SD = 3.5$ years), completed three experiments in separate sessions, and were remunerated with $25 shopping vouchers for each session. All participants had normal or corrected-to-normal vision.

For each experiment, stimuli were the factorial combinations of two dimensions with two levels each. Each of the four resulting conditions required a unique identification response. Experiments 4–6 maintained the 2×2 factorial design but the specifics of the stimuli were different as we report below.

We recorded the accuracy of identification, as well as the entire confusion patterns (what responses were made on incorrect trials), which are essential to the GRT analysis. *RT*s were also recorded for future use, but were not used in the current analysis and will not be reported.

Apparatus and Stimuli

The experiment was conducted in a dimly lit room in the Newcastle Cognition Lab. We used Dell OptiPlex 990 computers attached to 25.5 inch screens, with 1920×1080 pixel displays at 60 Hz. Brightness and Contrast were each set to 75. The experiments ran in SuperLab 4.5 and MATLAB R2013b was used for stimulus preparation and data analysis.

The stimuli were equivalent to the dot stimuli in Eidels et al. (2015) study: two dots, dot on top only, dot on bottom only, and no dots. However, our stimuli were embedded in Gaussian noise in order to impair performance, as illustrated in Fig. 14.1A.

Each stimulus comprised a 250×250 square pixels (6.5 cm^2) display, subtending a $6.2° \times 6.2°$ visual angle at a viewing distance of 60 cm. The area outside this display was grey (RGB, 127–127–127 in MS Paint). The dots were bright disks with a diameter of 5 mm each; each dot subtending a visual angle of 0.48°. Brightness was scaled between 0 (black) and 1 (white); the background was set to 0.5, and dots were sampled with equal probability from a range of brightness values from 0.535 to 0.584 in increments of 0.007, making them lighter than the background.

Dots were located ± 1 cm vertically from the center of the display, and the two dots together subtended a total visual angle of 0.48° (horizontal) $\times$ 2.39° (vertical). The dots were embedded in Gaussian noise with a mean of 0 and a standard deviation of 1, with the noise serving to impair perception and induce confusions.

A poststimulus mask of Gaussian noise ($M = 0$, $SD = 1$), was presented after each stimulus presentation. The masks were matched for size to the stimulus display. To create a distinction between the stimulus display and the mask, the mask was generated at a lower resolution (50 × 50 pixels instead of 250 × 250).

Procedure

Brief demographic information (age, gender, and handedness) was collected. Before commencing Experiment 4 participants performed in a 10-minute calibration session to adjust the level of difficulty. Following the calibration session the stimuli contrast range was adjusted individually for each observer, to ensure that each of the individual participants' accuracy level was around 65–75%; better than chance performance but allowing enough errors to fill the entries of the confusion matrix. The calibration phase also served as practice. Participants completed equivalent practice in Experiments 5 and 6, but calibration was not required for these experiments.

Practice (and, if necessary, calibration) was followed by five experimental blocks. In each block there were 24 instances of each of the four stimuli, for a total of 96 trials per block, and a total of 480 trials in each experiment.

Fig. 14.3 illustrates the timeline of a single trial. The stimulus was presented for 150 ms, and then replaced by a static-noise mask for 500 ms. The screen then remained blank until a response was recorded, or the trial timed out after 5 seconds from stimulus onset. Responses could be entered from stimulus presentation onwards. Each stimulus was assigned a unique response key, from the set {"*z*", "*x*", "." and "/"}, with mapping counterbalanced across participants. Procedure of Experiment 5 and 6 was identical to Experiment 4, without calibration.

Experiment 5 – Line and Saturation

The stimuli for Experiment 5 were a subset of Fifić et al.'s "separable" stimuli (2008; Experiment 1). They comprised the factorial combinations of two saturation values (low, high) and two vertical line locations (left, right). Each stimulus consisted of a left rectangle of a red hue that varied in saturation, and a right rectangle containing a short vertical line that varied in its left–right location (see Fig. 14.1B).

The colors of the left rectangle were defined in the Munsell color system by a constant red hue (5R) and brightness (value 5), with saturation values of 10 and 8, respectively (see Fifić et al. for more details). The area outside of the stimulus display was white. High Saturation was defined in the RGB color space as 194–90–87, and low Saturation was defined as 181–98–94. The line closest to the left was presented 30 pixels from the left edge of the right rectangle, with the line closer to the right presented 40 pixels from the left edge of the right rectangle.

Each stimulus frame measured 220 pixels × 80 pixels (6 cm × 2 cm), subtending a total visual angle of 5.72° (horizontal) × 1.91° (vertical). Each rectangle measured 88 pixels × 80 pixels, with 30 pixels separating the two, plus 14 pixels for the black borders (Fig. 14.1B).

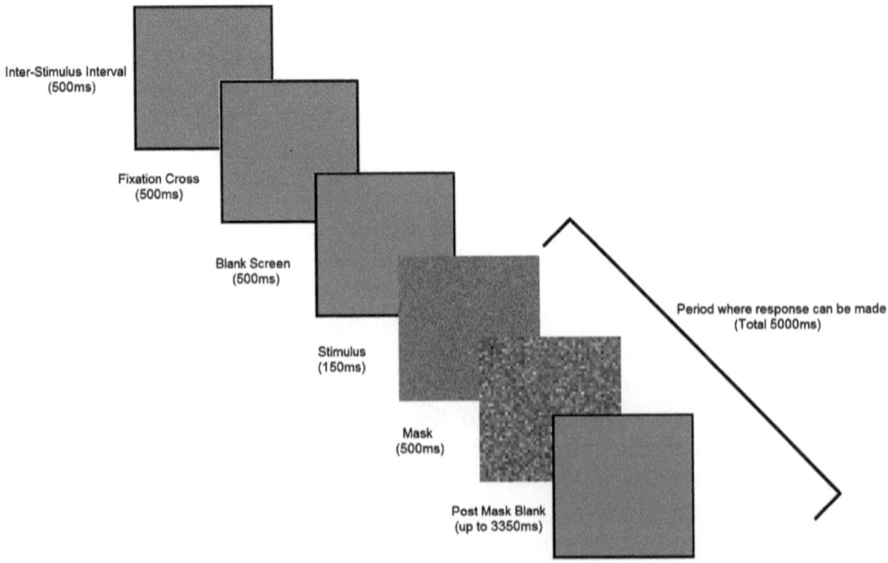

Figure 14.3 Timeline of a typical trial from Experiment 4. Experiments 5 and 6 used a similar trial timeline but different stimuli, and the background color was white rather than grey.

The poststimulus mask consisted of Gaussian noise, with mean 0.5 and standard deviation 0.15, defined in 3 dimensions (RGB values), such that the noise was "colored". The masks were matched for size to the stimulus display.

Experiment 6 – Saturation and Brightness

The stimuli for Experiment 6 were the factorial combinations of two saturation values (low, high) and two brightness values (low, high). These stimuli were a subset of Fifić et al.'s "integral" stimuli (2008; Experiment 2). Each stimulus comprised a single rectangle measuring 88 pixels × 80 pixels (2.5 cm × 2 cm), subtending a visual angle of 2.39° (horizontal) × 1.91° (vertical). The colors were defined in the Munsell color system by a constant red hue (5R), with saturation values of 10 and 8, and Brightness values of 5 and 6. The RGB values for the four stimuli were 222–117–112, 194–90–87, 208–125–119, and 181–98–94, for the High–High (high saturation, high brightness), High–Low, Low–High, and Low–Low, respectively. The stimuli are illustrated in Fig. 14.1C. The area outside of the stimulus display was a constant white. The poststimulus mask was identical to Experiment 5, but matched for the size of the stimuli in Experiment 6.

GRT Analysis

The SFT studies we reported earlier make use of *RT* distributions to estimate the mean and survivor interaction contrasts (*MIC* and *SIC*), as well as the capacity coefficient.

These measures inform researchers about the way information from multiple sources is processed, but cannot be estimated from accuracy rates and confusion data. Instead, we fit a multilevel 2×2 Gaussian General Recognition Theory model (GRT; Silbert, 2012, 2014) to the confusion matrices of each participant in each identification experiment. It is beyond the scope of this chapter to describe GRT in detail, but we direct readers to a number of informative papers (Kadlec & Townsend, 1992; Ashby, 2000; Silbert & Hawkins, 2016; Thomas, 2001a, 2001b), and also chapters by Townsend and Liu (2017) and Griffiths, Blunden, and Little (2017) in this volume for a more comprehensive overview. For the novice reader it is sufficient to know that GRT is a model-based approach for exploring accuracy data in the form of confusion matrices, and can be considered a multidimensional extension of the well-known Signal Detection Theory (Green & Swets, 1966).

GRT is typically used to explore the relationships between dimensions in cognitive processing (Silbert & Hawkins, 2016); for example, how do brightness and saturation of a colored rectangle interact to influence perception? In this sense, the "dimensions" explored in GRT can be considered equivalent to those in SFT. Three key concepts in GRT are *Perceptual Separability* (PS), *Decisional Separability* (DS) and *Perceptual Independence* (PI). Fig. 14.4 illustrates PS, DS, and PI using a bird's-eye view of the 2×2 Gaussian GRT model. A convenient way to think about this figure is as four bivariate normal distributions arranged as a 2×2 grid and sliced across their horizontal plane (thereby generating the "equal likelihood contours" in the form of circles or ellipses). PS holds if the marginal distribution of perceptual effects on one dimension (e.g., brightness) is equal across levels of the other dimension (e.g., saturation). PS is evident in Fig. 14.4 by virtue of aligned means of perceptual distribution along one or both dimensions. If perceptual separability holds on both dimensions in the 2×2 model, the means of the perceptual distributions will fall at the vertices of a square or a rectangle (see Fig. 14.4A). If perceptual separability fails, the means will describe a nonrectangular quadrilateral, such as Fig. 14.4C, where dimension A is not perceptually separable from dimension B, as the marginal perceptual distributions (not shown) of perceptual effects are closer together at the level of B_1 than B_2. In that figure, the marginal perceptual distributions of dimension B are equidistant at level A_1 and A_2, therefore Perceptual Separability for dimension B (PS_B) holds. DS holds on a given dimension if the decision bound on that dimension is parallel to the coordinate axis. Because failures of decisional separability are not, in general, identifiable in GRT models (Silbert & Thomas, 2013), we assume that decisional separability holds in the GRT models fit to data in the present work. Finally, PI holds within a given perceptual distribution if the perceptual effects of the two dimensions (e.g., brightness and saturation) are stochastically independent. In Gaussian GRT, perceptual independence is equivalent to zero correlation. In the top-down view of a 2×2 Gaussian GRT model, perceptual independence is indicated by circular equal likelihood contours (Fig. 14.4A and C), and failures of perceptual independence are evident in tilted ellipses (Fig. 14.4B and D).

The multilevel version of GRT used in this chapter is detailed in Silbert (2012; 2014). Broadly speaking, this multilevel model estimates group-level parameters in each experiment to constrain the individual subject-level GRT parameters. We fo-

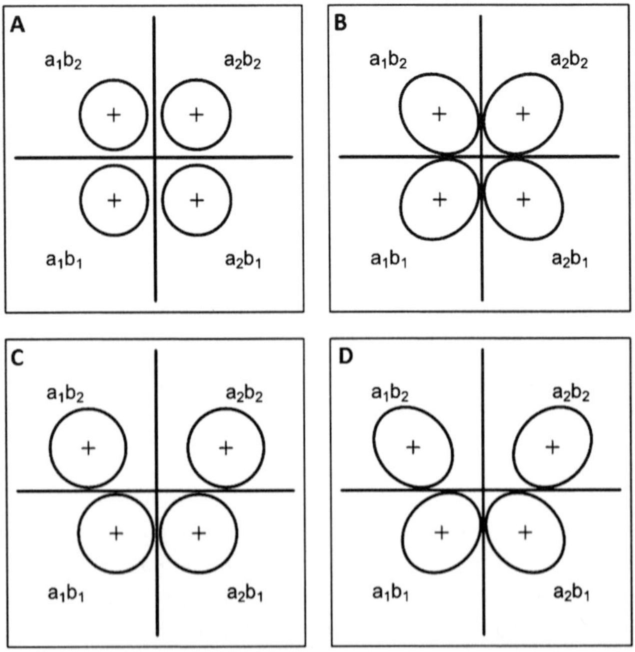

Figure 14.4 Illustrations of violations in GRT parameters. Panel A shows both PS and PI hold, evidenced by the square formed by the means of the equal likelihood contours, and the circular equal likelihood contours. Panel B shows a violation of PI for all distributions, as evidenced by the elliptical equal likelihood contours. Panel C shows a violation of PS for dimension A (PS_A), as the distance between the marginal perceptual distributions of A are different at level B_1 and B_2, but PS_B holds, as the distance between the perceptual distributions of B at A_1 and A_2 are equal. Panel D shows a violation of PI and PS_A.

cus on these multilevel results (over the traditional, individual-subject GRT) in this chapter, as the multilevel model allows simultaneous examination of individual and group-level processing, which is not possible in the traditional approach. For completeness, we also fit traditional, individual GRT models for each participant, and report the trends of these results.

The individual GRT results were obtained by fitting increasingly restricted GRT models (allowing PI, PS for dimension A (PS_A), and PS for dimension B (PS_B) to all hold [least complex], all violate [most complex], or any combination) and the best fit was selected by the Bayesian Information Criterion (BIC; Schwartz, 1978). The multilevel GRT model was fit using the Python and the PyMC package (Patil, Huard, & Fonnesbeck, 2010). Within each experiment, each individual subject is modeled with a full 2×2 Gaussian GRT model. Across subjects, the individual-level parameters are governed by group-level parameters. The decision-bound intercepts and perceptual-distribution means are modeled as normal random variables, and the perceptual correlations are modeled as truncated normal random variables to constrain the correlation estimates to fall between -1 and $+1$. The location and scale of the model must be set to make the model identifiable. The location of the model was set by fixing the mean for the A_1B_1 perceptual distribution at the origin (i.e., [0, 0]) for each subject and at the group-level. The scale of the model was set by fixing all marginal variances to 1. The hyperprior distributions governing the group-level mean vectors described a square with sides of length 1.25, with hyper-prior standard deviations of 2. The hyper-priors on the decision bound intercepts had means and standard deviations both equal to 1. The hyperpriors on the correlation parameters were centered at 0 with standard deviation 2. All individual- and group-level parameters are estimated simultaneously.

All GRT figures presented in this chapter represent equal likelihood contours of each of the bivariate perceptual distributions, representing a top-down view of the 2×2 Gaussian GRT model. Each response region (A_1B_1, A_1B_2, etc.) in the plots of experimental data corresponds to the perceptual distribution for the equivalently-located stimulus display in Fig. 14.1. For example, in Experiment 4, the perceptual distribution labeled A_2B_2 (top-right) corresponds to the two-dot stimulus in Fig. 14.1A. In the multilevel GRT model, the large middle panel corresponds to the group-level estimates, and the smaller panels around it correspond to the labeled participant. In all GRT plots the circles, or in some cases ellipses, represent equal likelihood contours of perceptual distributions, the crosses represent the mean of those perceptual distributions (with the square being the mean fixed at the origin), and the vertical and horizontal lines represent the decision bounds.

Results

Experiment 4

The dimensions that comprised the stimuli in Experiment 4 were top target (present, absent) $\times$ bottom target (present, absent), as illustrated in Fig. 14.1A. SFT studies using comparable stimuli identified a parallel, limited-capacity process model with a task-appropriate stopping rule (e.g., Eidels et al., 2015). In the case of the AND task, which is a closer relative to the present study due to its exhaustive nature, these findings are typically supported by a negative *MIC* and a fully negative *SIC*, suggesting parallel exhaustive processing. We performed both multilevel and traditional GRT analyses on the individual confusion matrices of each participant.

In Experiment 4, mean accuracy across all participants was $M = 0.62$ ($SD = 0.08$). The plot of group-level parameters from the multilevel GRT model shows the means of the perceptual distributions form a shape very close to a square, suggesting that overall PS_A and PS_B hold (Fig. 14.5, middle panel). Within individuals, this same trend holds for Participants 1, 2, 3, and 9. At the individual level of the multilevel fit, Participant 5 shows violation of PS_A, Participants 6, 8 and 10 show violation of PS_B, and Participants 4 and 7 show violations of PS on both dimensions. At the group-level, PI is strongly violated for A_1B_1 (No-dots), and shows weak violations in A_1B_2 and A_2B_2. Within individuals, PI is consistently violated for A_1B_1, and varies considerably between individuals for the other perceptual distributions. The location of the decision boundaries relative to the perceptual distributions suggests a response bias toward responding “no dot” on a given location. In the group-level plot, for example, the distributions fall further below the horizontal line (no-dot response for bottom lo-

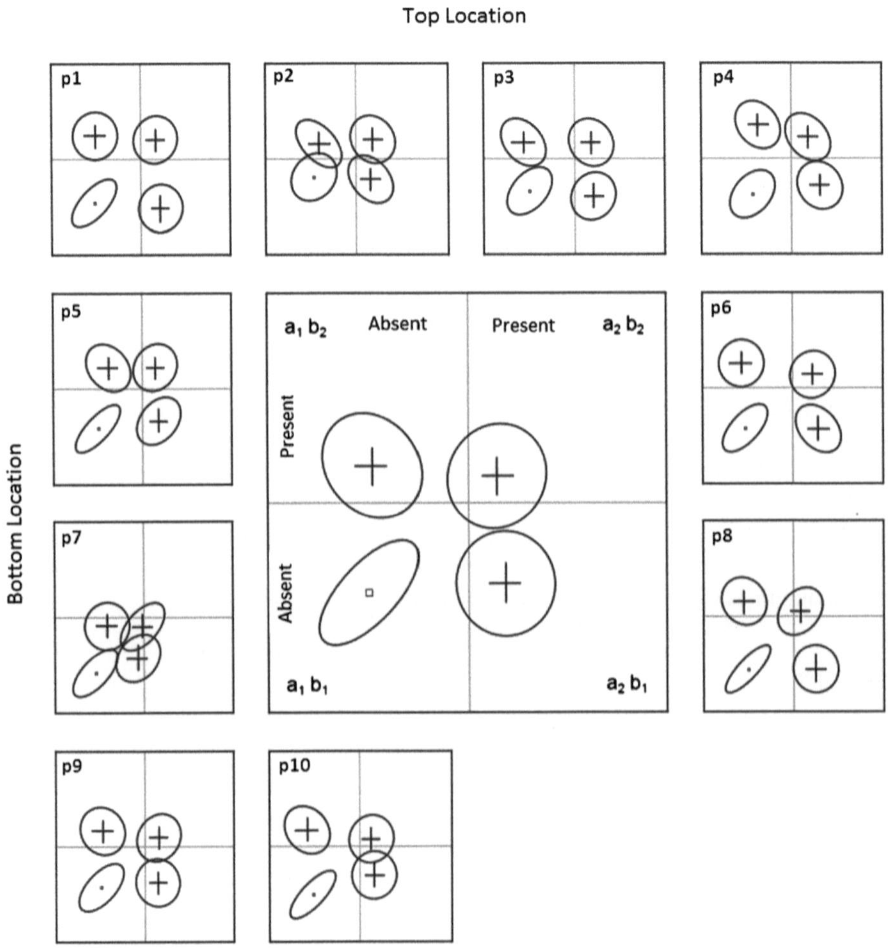

Figure 14.5 Multilevel GRT solution for Experiment 4. Large middle panel reflects the "group-level" estimates, and labeled smaller panels around the center reflect the estimate for each participant, constrained by the group parameters.

cation) and further to the left of the vertical line (no-dot response for top location) than would be expected if there was no bias.

For traditional GRT, using BIC (Schwartz, 1978) to select the best fitting model, PS_A and PS_B held for all participants, except for Participant 10 for whom PS_B was violated. This is consistent with the group-level estimates of the multilevel GRT model. PI also held for six of the ten participants [1, 3, 4, 6, 9, and 10]. For the remaining four, PI failed with a single failure parameter (i.e., all perceptual distributions "tilted" to the same degree) for Participants 2, 7, and 8, and failed independently for all perceptual distributions for Participant 5. The traditional GRT measure reflected the same bias toward "no-dot" response in a given location that was identified in the multilevel fits. Taken together, the multilevel and traditional fits suggest that PS holds for both dimensions, and that there is a bias toward "no-dot" response in a given location. The multilevel fit is more likely to exhibit violations as it is not penalized for complexity and violations require more parameters (our traditional GRT fits are penalized using BIC).

Experiment 5

The dimensions that comprised the stimuli in Experiment 5 were the factorial combinations of saturation (low, high) × line location (left, right) in two spatially separated rectangles, as illustrated in Fig. 14.1B. SFT studies using comparable stimuli found these stimulus dimension were processed serially with a task-appropriate stopping rule (see, e.g., Fifić et al., 2008, 2010). As with the results of Experiment 4, our analyses focused on confusion patterns.

Mean accuracy across participants was $M = 0.70$ ($SD = 0.20$). We excluded Participant 9 from the multilevel model due to poor performance ($M = 0.19$), and excluding this participant increased mean accuracy to 0.75 ($SD = 0.10$). In the multilevel GRT fit (Fig. 14.6), the group-level shows PS_A and PS_B both hold. This trend is also reflected in the individual-level plots for all participants, apart from Participant 10 who shows a slight violation for PS_A (Saturation). PI is slightly violated for each perceptual distribution in the group level, and is slightly-to-moderately violated for all perceptual distributions for each individual. Unlike Experiment 4, the decision bounds for Experiment 5 do not suggest biased responding.

In the traditional GRT fits, PS_A and PS_B held for all participants. PI also held for all participants in the traditional analysis. Taken together, the analyses suggest that PS holds for both dimensions, and that PI is, if at all, only slightly violated. This implies that the dimensions of color-saturation and line location were processed independently, as expected (recall these dimensions are considered separable, and were identified as such in the SFT studies reported in section Three *RT* Experiments Using SFT, above), and that processing was, except for the weaker violation of PI for A_1B_1, almost identical to Experiment 4.

Experiment 6

In Experiment 6 stimuli were the factorial combinations of Brightness (high, low) × Saturation (high, low) of a single colored rectangle, as illustrated in Fig. 14.1C. In contrast to Experiments 4 and 5, these dimensions were found in previous SFT studies to be processed in a coactive or holistic fashion (e.g., Little et al., 2013). Although serial and parallel architectures may be difficult to uncover using accuracy patterns alone due to the dynamic nature of processing architecture (as we show in section Simulations below), coactive systems are defined by complete channel interaction (Eidels et al., 2011; Townsend & Eidels, 2011). It is thus plausible that coactivity could be identified based on confusion data, as GRT is able to identify dependence relationships between processing channels (Ashby & Townsend, 1986).

In Experiment 6, mean accuracy across participants was $M = 0.65$ ($SD = 0.21$). We excluded Participant 5 due to poor performance ($M = 0.16$), and a complete

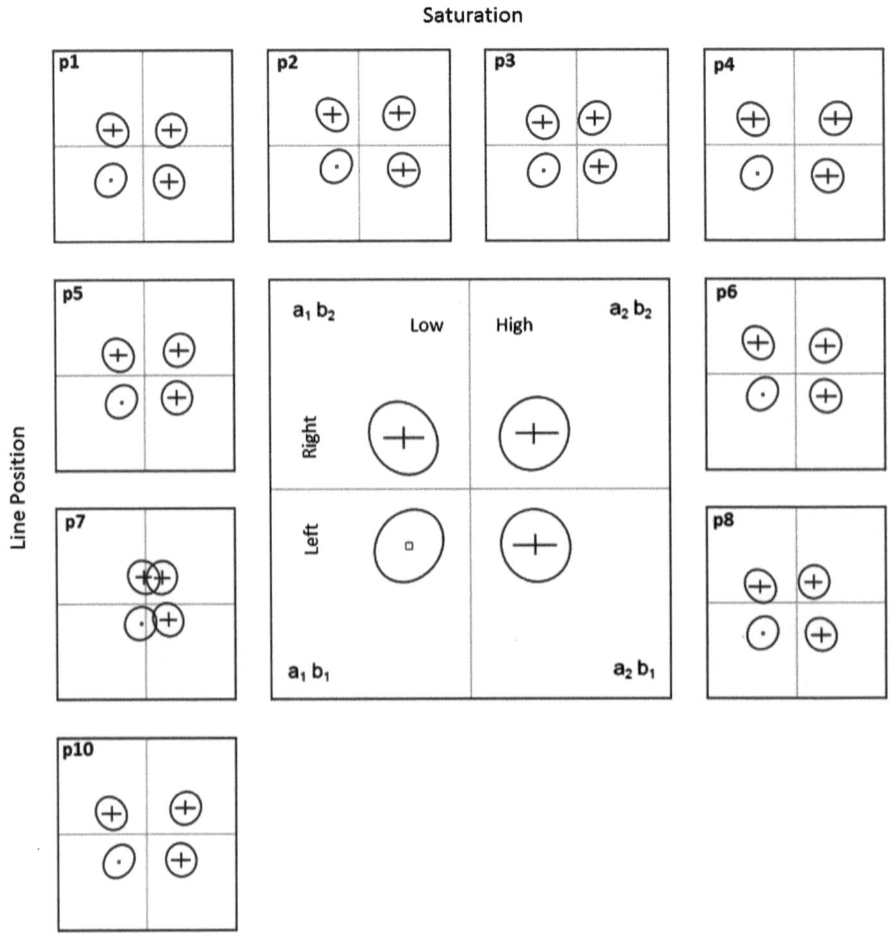

Figure 14.6 Multilevel GRT solution for Experiment 5. The large middle panel reflects the "group-level" estimates, and labeled smaller panels reflect the estimate for each participant, constrained by the group parameters. Participant 9 was excluded due to below-chance accuracy ($M = 0.19$).

inability to discriminate between the two levels of brightness. Excluding this participant, mean accuracy rose to $M = 0.69$ ($SD = 0.12$). In the multilevel GRT model (Fig. 14.7), the group-level shows a violation of PS_B (saturation), but PS_A (brightness) appears to hold. PI is slightly violated for each perceptual response region, but strongly violated when both brightness and saturation are high (A_2B_2). These general trends hold for Participants 3, 4, 6, 7, 8, 9, and 10. PS fails on both dimensions for Participant 1, and holds on both dimensions for Participant 2, but PI is violated at least slightly for all perceptual distributions for all participants.

The specific patterns of results for the group-level, as well as Participants 3, 6, 8, 9 and 10, whereby the means of the equal likelihood contours form a diamond shape rather than a rectangle, is known as mean shift integrality and is discussed in de-

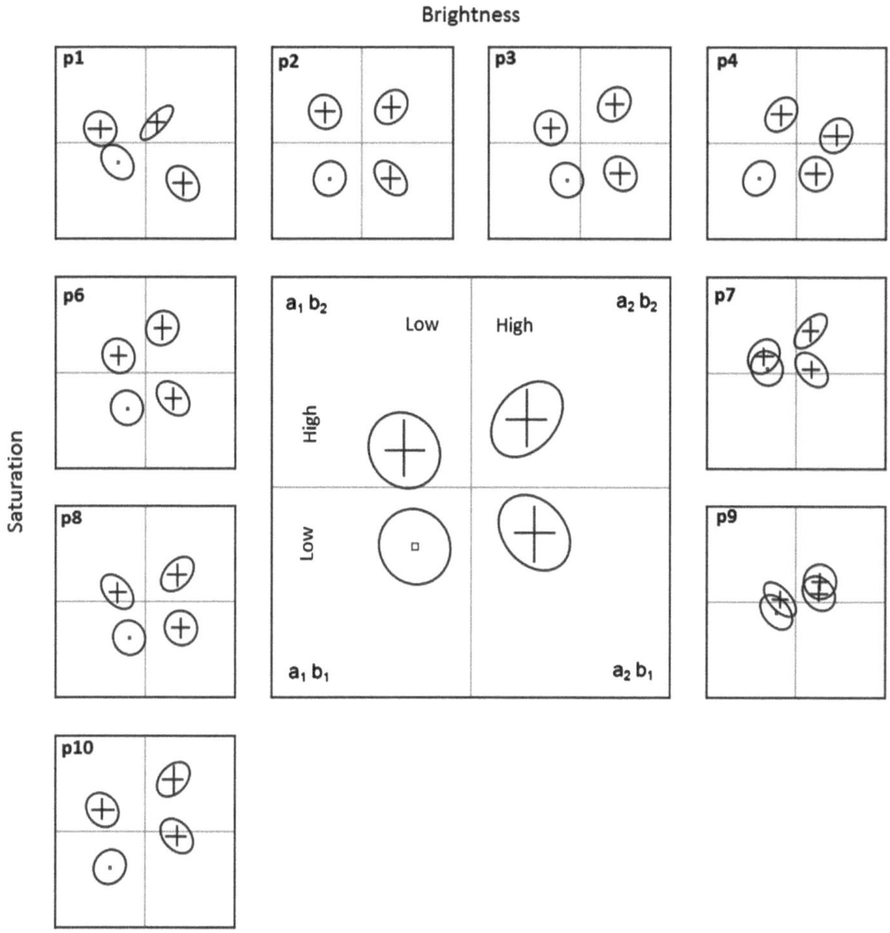

Figure 14.7 Multilevel GRT solution for Experiment 6. The large middle panel reflects the "group-level" estimates, and labeled smaller panels reflect the estimate for each participant, constrained by the group parameters. Participant 5 was excluded due to below-chance accuracy ($M = 0.16$).

tail elsewhere (see, e.g., Ashby & Maddox, 1994, p. 444). Mean shift integrality is a specific violation of PS where the variances of the perceptual regions on a given dimension are equal, but the means differ. Mean shift integrality may indicate positively dependent channels.

In the traditional GRT analysis, Perceptual Separability fails on at least one dimension for all participants, except for Participant 2, for whom both PS_A and PS_B hold. PS_B (saturation) fails for Participants 5, 6, 7, 8, 9 and 10, and both PS_A and PS_B fail for Participants 1, 3 and 4. In addition, PI fails for Participants 1, 4, 5, 7, and 9. Taken together, the results of the two GRT analyses strongly suggest that most participants were unable to separately attend to each of the two dimensions. Although the results of this experiment suggest a lack of independence between the channels processing brightness and saturation of a single rectangle, they are not consistent with our simulations of complete coactivity, based on complete pooling of perceptual information, presented in section Simulations. Coactivity was expected based on the SFT results of Fifić et al. (2010), and Little et al. (2013). The discrepancy is addressed in the conclusion of this chapter.

Simulations

Although GRT is an excellent technique for uncovering dependencies between processing channels, our analyses of the experimental data did not uncover obvious trends that can identify dynamic processing properties. For example, for the dimensions investigated in Experiments 4 and 5, SFT uncovers parallel processing and serial processing, respectively. However, the GRT results are almost identical across the two, with PS holding across both dimensions, and slight-to-moderate violations of PI within certain perceptual distributions. To allow a more comprehensive understanding of the relationship between the basic properties of cognitive processing and GRT, we undertook a systematic simulation study, whereby we constructed models that could vary on processing architecture, stopping rule, and interchannel dependencies. We simulated identification data from all relevant combinations of these different properties in order to investigate which properties, if any, were evident in GRT solutions.

Method

We simulated five standard SFT models, serial and parallel processing with either exhaustive or "nonexhaustive" stopping rules (details below), as well as a coactive model. Within the parallel models we allowed 5 levels of channel dependence, ranging from 0 to 100% chance for information from one channel to be communicated to the other channel on each time-step of a random-walk accumulation process (Link & Heath, 1975). The interaction, when it existed, was facilitatory, in that the accumulation of evidence in one channel (a step towards a response criterion) could be transferred with some probability to another channel to assist its completion. This is commensurate with a postaccumulator interaction in that the facilitation occurs between the evidence states of each of the channels (i.e., rather than in the input to the channels; Eidels et al., 2011). The extreme cases of the interaction levels we considered were equivalent to the independent–parallel model on one end (0% interaction) and a coactive model on the other (100% interaction). Overall we simulated 11 models (2 serial models, 1 coactive model, plus 2 parallel models with 4 levels of interaction each).

We use the term "nonexhaustive" here to contrast with the SFT terminology "self-terminating." A self-terminating model under the SFT-framework processes one channel to completion. If this channel carries sufficient information then a decision can be made (e.g., the channel contains a target in an OR task), even if other channel(s) have not completed processing. If not, the system continues to process the other channel.

However, in our design exhaustive processing is always "necessary" to complete the task, as all stimuli are defined by the unique combination of two attributes (e.g., high saturation, low brightness). Therefore, to allow investigation of the stopping rule we constructed task-inappropriate "nonexhaustive" models. In a serial model, the nonexhaustive stopping rule means that only one channel is processed (the other being subject to a "guess"). In a parallel model, one channel is processed to completion, and the other makes the decision of the boundary it is closest to at the time the first channel completes.

The models were instantiated as two random walk processes (Link & Heath, 1975). These random-walk processes corresponded to the two stimulus dimensions, with each random walk determining the response to its pertinent dimension. For example, in relation to Experiment 4, there could be one random walk for the top dot-signal, with response options "target present" or "target absent." There would be another, equivalent random walk for the bottom signal. Or, in the context of Experiment 6, the two random-walk processes would be for the "Brightness" and "Saturation" dimensions. We term these two random walk processes "channel A" and "channel B", corresponding to the dimensions in the GRT plots. We set the parameters of the random walk (drift rate, boundary separation) to yield an overall accuracy level of 65–75%, to match our empirical data.

We manipulated architecture and stopping rule by changing the rules by which the model combined the two random walk outcomes. For example, in a serial exhaustive model the random-walk processes occurred in a strictly serial fashion, and both processes were allowed to complete. Alternatively, in a serial nonexhaustive model, the second channel (order randomly selected on each "trial") did not receive processing, but instead selected a random outcome. For parallel nonexhaustive models, the slower channel did not complete; however, the outcome selected was the "closest" bound to the state of activation at that point.

Results

First, we consider whether architecture alone influences the GRT solution. Note that for all the following models, except the coactive model, "best fit" is determined by BIC (the coactive model was fit by AIC, since it was not possible to fit it with BIC in the R package we used). All subsequent GRT analyses are "traditional", not multilevel, as these are simulated data (thus there are not different individuals), and we use the generic labels A and B to denote the two dimensions. There was no difference in the GRT parameter fits across different architectures (we kept channels independent and stopping rule exhaustive for this comparison). This result is illustrated in the GRT fits in Fig. 14.8A and B, where the solutions for parallel and serial models look identical. That is, the visual outcomes of parallel and serial processing on the GRT space "mimic" each other (cf. Townsend, 1990), with PS_A, PS_B and PI all holding. For an intuition, consider how the simulation treated architecture: two random walk processes decide the outcome on channels A and B. In the serial model, the processes occur in a strictly serial fashion, in the parallel model they accumulate evidence at the same time.

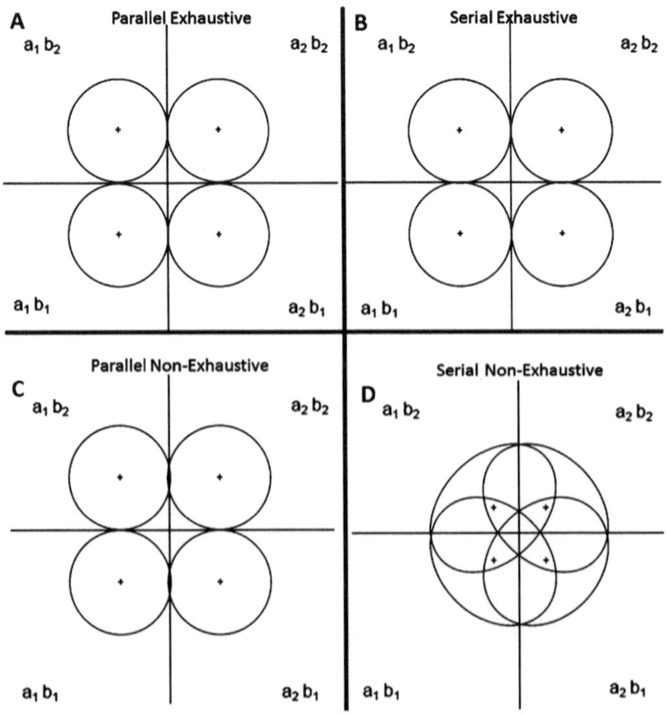

Figure 14.8 GRT solutions of serial and parallel architectures combined with exhaustive and nonexhaustive stopping rules.

However, in a noninteractive system these processes do not communicate or influence one another at all. Therefore, there is little reason to expect the *decision* to be different. This differs when considering *RT*, as in a serial system there is, effectively, additional processing time compared to a parallel system, which allows the models to make differing *RT* predictions. This explains why *RT*-based techniques such as SFT are able to detect differences in processing architecture between the experimental tasks and simulations we have considered, whereas the accuracy based GRT analyses were not. Townsend et al. (2012) extended GRT to consider how violations of independence impact *RT*, and their approach has been discussed in relation to the categorization SFT task by Griffiths et al. (2017).

Focusing on parallel models, we were unable to detect GRT-related differences across various stopping rules. Fig. 14.8A and C illustrate how two different stopping rules produce nearly identical GRT solutions, with PS_A, PS_B and PI again holding. The implications of the mimicry findings are that in our data we might neither be able to detect architecture differences between Experiment 4 (expected parallel, Eidels et al., 2015) and Experiment 5 (expected serial, Fifić et al., 2008) nor confirm that a task-appropriate stopping rule (exhaustive) was used by our participants.

Turning to serial models, the results are pleasantly different. There was a dramatic difference between the GRT solutions of the two stopping rules, with the serial nonexhaustive perceptual distributions largely overlapping (Fig. 14.8D), and showing violations of PI. However, recall that the model makes a decision with inadequate and partial information, as it is task-inappropriate. Therefore, the dramatic performance degradation of this model is quite predictable.

The most encouraging results for accuracy-based measures come from our manipulation of channel interactions. As we increase the likelihood that a channel will communicate with the other channel we observe a marked change in the GRT solution (Fig. 14.9). Inducing any level of interaction causes violations to both PS and PI. As the level of interaction increases, the equal likelihood contours stretch along the main diagonal, and the contours for items A_1B_2 and A_2B_1 approach the origin, as they become increasingly difficult to distinguish.

The apparent changes in the GRT signature with increasing interaction (Fig. 14.9) are trivial to explain. As interaction in our simulations was facilitory, if the random-walk process for channel A steps toward the top boundary, and communicates this to the random walk process for channel B, the latter then also steps toward the top boundary, and vice versa. As the likelihood for interaction increases, the random walks necessarily converge to the same boundary ("top" or "bottom"), which corresponds to *either* value 1 or 2 for the corresponding dimension. At the extreme, where all steps between random walks are communicated, the two processes *cannot reach opposing bounds*, as there is, in effect, only a single accumulator which makes the same decision for both channels. This model is equivalent to the coactive model (Townsend & Eidels, 2011). Fig. 14.9E illustrates how the coactive model produces a completely degenerate, unidimensional GRT solution (recall our application of GRT is generally two-dimensional). The same outcome was apparent in a different disguise in the simulated confusion patterns, where response options A_1B_2 and A_2B_1 were never selected. As the model is equally likely to choose either of the two *remaining* responses when A_1B_2 or A_2B_1 stimuli are presented, the response regions completely overlap in the middle of the unidimensional equal likelihood contour.

Discussion

We conducted three identification studies using stimuli that have previously been examined within the SFT *RT*-based framework. The SFT results, and our GRT findings, were summarized in Table 14.1. In Experiment 4 we found that dots of light in two spatial locations were processed independently. In Experiment 5 the processing of saturation and a vertical line is also best described as independent. In Experiment 6 we found the dimensions of saturation and brightness were not processed independently, as both Perceptual Independence and Perceptual Separability failed for most participants. These results reinforce results from SFT studies using response times, which revealed that stimuli akin to those used in Experiment 6 were processed in a coactive fashion whereas stimuli comparable to those used in Experiments 4 and 5 were processed in an independent manner, either parallel or serial, respectively. Simulations of random-walk processes revealed that confusion data alone cannot tell apart serial and parallel processes, but can help identify the stopping rule (at least in a serial model),

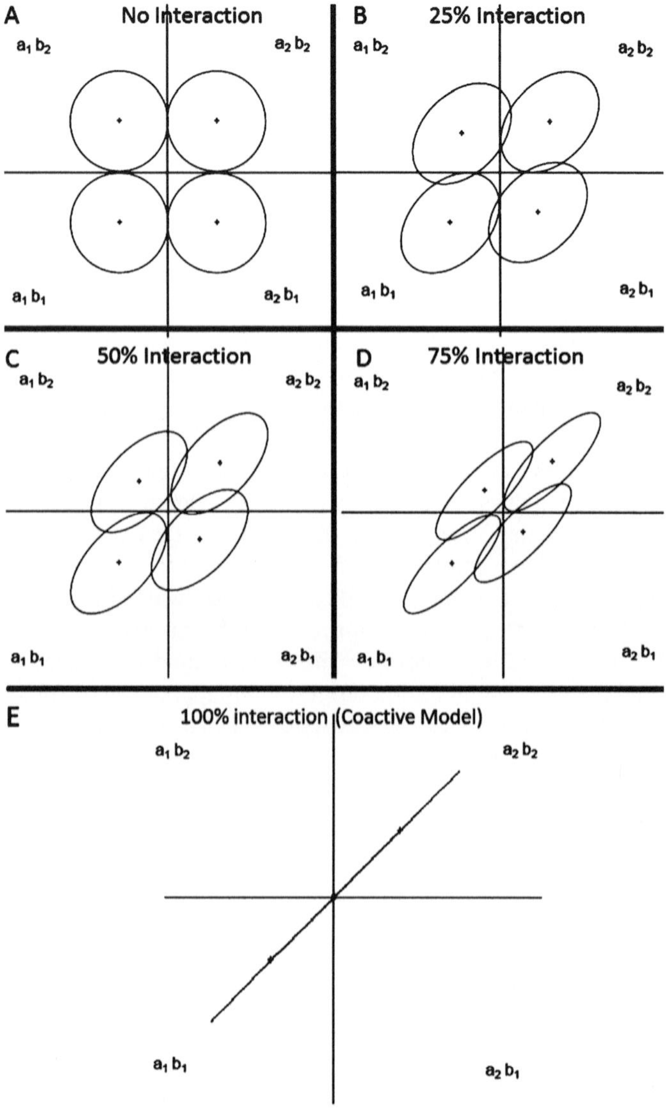

Figure 14.9 GRT solutions as cross-channel interaction increases from 0% (panel A, the standard noninteractive model) to 100% (panel E, a completely interactive coactive model).

and whether multiple processing channels operate independently or not. The latter point deserves further discussion.

Pre- vs. Post-Accumulator Interactions

In the simulation section of the present chapter (section Simulations) we constructed and tested models that varied in the degree of cross-channel interaction, from nil to coactive. We defined coactivity as a complete pooling (or facilitation) of the evidence for each response across the channels for each dimension. That is, coactivity is assumed to result from a complete loss of channel identity. Hence, stimuli with nonmatching components (e.g., the two single dot displays in Fig. 14.1A, which each have a target, but in opposite locations) are indistinguishable to the coactive model, as shown by our simulations. This coactivity prediction, however, was not observed in our Experiment 6. How do we reconcile the lack of complete coactivity here with previous results identifying coactive processing using the same stimuli (e.g., using *SIC*s, Fifić et al., 2008; Little et al., 2013)? One solution may simply be that the task is different, and therefore a different type of processing is used. In a detection task, perceptual information can be pooled without undesired consequence (thus coactivity is a viable strategy). In the identification task, individual channel information is required to completely identify the stimulus, and a completely coactive model performs poorly as it loses such channel identity. Nevertheless, it is possible that processing in both tasks was coactive despite our simulated results.

Consider the stochastic differential equation specifying the change in the state of a process, x, at time t as a function of the current state and the current input to the system:

$$d\mathbf{x}(t) = \mathbf{Ax}(t)\,dt + \mathbf{Bu}(t)\,dt + \sigma dW(t).$$

This equation describes the evolution of the process in continuous time where $\mathbf{u}(t)$ is a vector of inputs to the system representing the level of activation on each dimension, $\mathbf{x}(t)$ is the current state of each processing channel. $dW(t)$ represents Brownian noise process, the level of which is determined by the diffusion coefficient, σ (Smith, 2000). For present purposes, specific understanding of the model is not necessary; simply note that the random walk models that we used to simulate the model predictions for each channel are an approximation of this continuous time process (see, e.g., Diederich & Busemeyer, 2003; Luce, 1986; Ratcliff, 1978). In the current chapter, the interaction between channels is modeled by increasing the values of the off-diagonals entries of the **A** matrix. This matrix controls the interaction between channels representing the state of accumulation of each dimension. By allowing the off-diagonals to equal 1, we instantiate a complete facilitatory interaction between channels, resulting in the coactive predictions (Fig. 14.9E).

Note, however, that the interaction can also be controlled at the level of the stimulus *input*, specified by the vector $\mathbf{u}(t)$. The matrix **B** controls the interaction in the input to the system analogously to the **A** matrix. However, this interaction only affects the level of input to the system and not the state of the system itself. This means that coactivity can result from two different sources of interaction: input to the system, and current state of the system. Eidels et al. (2011) refer to the former type of interaction as a preaccumulator interaction and the latter type of interaction as a postaccumulator interaction. Both types have been used extensively in the literature to model cross-channel interaction. For instance, a postaccumulator interaction was proposed as an explanation for *RT* results observed in a visual-search experiment (Fifić et al., 2008; see also Mordkoff & Yantis, 1991). Preaccumulator interactions have been assumed in coactive models proposed to explain the *SIC*s for color categorization observed by Little et al. (2013). While postaccumulator interaction predicts a complete confusion of stimuli with nonmatching components (as evidenced by our simulations in Fig. 14.9E), the preaccumulator interaction model does not. Thus, the results observed in our current Experiment 6 (Fig. 14.7) do not preclude a preaccumulator coactive model.

Combining Accuracy and *RT* Measures

A complete account of human behavior should take into consideration both the accuracy and the speed of responses. Parametric models of information processing, such as the diffusion model and other evidence accumulation models (e.g., Ratcliff, 1978; Usher & McClelland, 2001; Brown & Heathcote, 2008), successfully account for both accuracy and *RT*, but make strong assumptions about the nature of the internal processes. The appeal of SFT, celebrated in this volume, lies in its nonparametric nature, which makes it very general, beyond any specific model. Several recent papers have made progress toward a unified nonparametric approach that takes into account both accuracy and *RT*. Townsend and Altieri (2012) proposed a nonparametric measure for workload capacity that simultaneously takes into account both accuracy and *RT*. Their statistic – the Assessment Function, $A(t)$ – thus represent an improvement of the original, *RT*-based capacity coefficient developed by Townsend and Nozawa in their seminal 1995 paper.

Eidels et al. (2015) similarly offered a unified *RT*-accuracy approach, but focused on other statistics. They calculated a contrast of response probabilities (the *no response probability contrast*, NRPC; see also Mulligan & Shaw, 1980) and compared it to *RT*-based measures from SFT (namely, the capacity coefficient and the survivor interaction contrast). They found general agreement in the models identified by the *RT* and accuracy measures, but showed the accuracy measure cannot discriminate between parallel and serial processes. The findings from our accuracy-based GRT analysis, section Three New Accuracy Experiments Using GRT (empirical data) and section Simulations (simulation results), corroborate Eidels et al. conclusion. GRT measures were not sensitive to dynamic properties such as serial vs parallel processing (although other versions of GRT exist, see Ashby, 1989, 2000; Townsend et al., 2012). However, the hallmark of GRT has been evident in identifying channel dependencies and separating response bias from perceptual effects. The merit of the current chapter is the potential combination of accuracy-based (confusion) measures, in GRT, with *RT*-based measures from SFT, to inform about the entire gamut of attributes: channel (in)dependence, capacity, architecture, and stopping rule. Future research should strive to integrate both dependent variables in a way that further extends SFT to deal with accuracy, and extends GRT to *RT*, with applicability in a shared design.

Acknowledgement

The preparation of this chapter was supported by ARC Discovery Project grants to AE and DRL.

References

Altieri, N., Fifić, M., Little, D. R., & Yang, C-T. (2017). Historical foundations and a tutorial introduction to systems factorial technology. In D. R. Little, N. Altieri, M. Fifić, & C-T. Yang (Eds.), *Systems factorial technology: A theory driven methodology for the identification of perceptual and cognitive mechanisms*. Elsevier (in this book).

Ashby, F. G. (1989). Stochastic general recognition theory. In D. Vickers, & P. L. Smith (Eds.), *Human information processing: measures, mechanisms, and models* (pp. 435–457). Amsterdam: Elsevier.

Ashby, F. G. (2000). A stochastic version of general recognition theory. *Journal of Mathematical Psychology*, *44*(2), 310–329.

Ashby, F. G., & Maddox, W. T. (1994). A response time theory of separability and integrality in speeded classification. *Journal of Mathematical Psychology*, *38*(4), 423–466.

Ashby, F. G., & Townsend, J. T. (1986). Varieties of perceptual independence. *Psychological Review*, *93*(2), 154–179.

Brown, S. D., & Heathcote, A. (2008). The simplest complete model of choice response time: Linear ballistic accumulation. *Cognitive Psychology*, *57*(3), 153–178.

Bushmakin, M., Eidels, A., & Heathcote, A. (2015). *Breaking the rules in perceptual information integration*. Presented at the meeting of the Mathematical Psychology Society in Chicago, November 2015.

Diederich, A., & Busemeyer, J. R. (2003). Simple matrix methods for analyzing diffusion models of choice probability, choice response time, and simple response time. *Journal of Mathematical Psychology*, *47*(3), 304–322.

Eidels, A., Houpt, J. W., Altieri, N., Pei, L., & Townsend, J. T. (2011). Nice guys finish fast and bad guys finish last: Facilitatory vs. inhibitory interaction in parallel systems. *Journal of Mathematical Psychology*, *55*(2), 176–190.

Eidels, A., Townsend, J. T., & Algom, D. (2010). Comparing perception of Stroop divided attention: evidence for dramatic processing differences. *Cognition*, *114*, 129–150.

Eidels, A., Townsend, J. T., Hughes, H. C., & Perry, L. A. (2015). Evaluating perceptual integration: Uniting response-time- and accuracy-based methodologies. *Attention, Perception, & Psychophysics*, *77*(2), 659–680.

Fifić, M., & Little, D. R. (2017). Stretching mental processes: An overview of and guide for SFT applications. In D. R. Little, N. Altieri, M. Fifić, & C-T. Yang (Eds.), *Systems factorial technology: A theory driven methodology for the identification of perceptual and cognitive mechanisms*. Elsevier (in this book).

Fifić, M., Little, D. R., & Nosofsky, R. (2010). Logical-rule models of classification response times: A synthesis of mental-architecture, random-walk, and decision-bound approaches. *Psychological Review*, *117*, 309–348.

Fifić, M., Nosofsky, R. M., & Townsend, J. T. (2008). Information-processing architectures in multidimensional classification: A validation test for systems factorial technology. *Journal of Experimental Psychology*, *34*, 356–375.

Garner, W. R. (1974). *The processing of information and structure*. New York: Wiley.

Green, D. M., & Swets, J. A. (1966). *Signal detection theory and psychophysics*. New York: Wiley.

Griffiths, D. W., Blunden, A. G., & Little, D. R. (2017). Logical-rule based models of categorization: Using systems factorial technology to understand feature and dimensional processing. In D. R. Little, N. Altieri, M. Fifić, & C-T. Yang (Eds.), *Systems factorial technology: A theory driven methodology for the identification of perceptual and cognitive mechanisms*. Elsevier (in this book).

Houpt, J. W., Townsend, J. T., & Donkin, C. (2014). A new perspective on visual word processing efficiency. *Acta Psychologica*, *145*, 118–127.

Kadlec, H., & Townsend, J. T. (1992). Signal detection analysis of multidimensional interactions. In F. G. Ashby (Ed.), *Probabilistic multidimensional models of perception and cognition*. Hillsdale, NJ: Lawrence Erlbaum Associates.

Link, S. W., & Heath, R. A. (1975). A sequential theory of psychological discrimination. *Psychometrika*, *40*, 77–105.

Little, D. R., Nosofsky, R. M., & Denton, S. E. (2011). Response-time tests of logical-rule models of categorization. *Journal of Experimental Psychology: Learning, Memory, and Cognition*, *37*, 1–27.

Little, D. R., Nosofsky, R. M., Donkin, C., & Denton, S. E. (2013). Logical rules and the classification of integral-dimension stimuli. *Journal of Experimental Psychology: Learning, Memory, and Cognition*, *39*, 801–820.

Luce, R. D. (1986). *Response times* (No. 8). Oxford University Press.

Mordkoff, J. T., & Yantis, S. (1991). An interactive race model of divided attention. *Journal of Experimental Psychology: Human Perception and Performance*, *17*(2), 520.

Mulligan, R. M., & Shaw, M. L. (1980). Multimodal signal detection: Independent decisions vs. integration. *Perception & Psychophysics*, *28*(5), 471–478.

Patil, A., Huard, D., & Fonnesbeck, C. J. (2010). PyMC: Bayesian stochastic modelling in python. *Journal of Statistical Software*, *35*(4), 1–81.

Ratcliff, R. (1978). A theory of memory retrieval. *Psychological Review*, *85*(2), 59.

Schwarz, G. (1978). Estimating the dimension of a model. *The Annals of Statistics*, *6*(2), 461–464.

Silbert, N. H. (2012). Syllable structure and integration of voicing and manner of articulation information in labial consonant identification. *The Journal of the Acoustical Society of America*, *131*(5), 4076–4086.

Silbert, N. H. (2014). Perception of voicing and place of articulation in labial and alveolar English stop consonants. *Laboratory Phonology*, *5*(2), 289–335.

Silbert, N. H., & Hawkins, R. X. (2016). A tutorial on general recognition theory. *Journal of Mathematical Psychology*, *73*, 94–109.

Silbert, N. H., & Thomas, R. D. (2013). Decisional separability, model identification, and statistical inference in the general recognition theory framework. *Psychonomic Bulletin & Review*, *20*(1), 1–20.

Smith, P. L. (2000). Stochastic dynamic models of response time and accuracy: A foundational primer. *Journal of Mathematical Psychology*, *44*(3), 408–463.

Sui, J., Yankouskaya, A., & Humphreys, G. W. (2015). Super-capacity me! Super-capacity and violations of race independence for self-but not for reward-associated stimuli. *Journal of Experimental Psychology: Human Perception and Performance*, *41*(2), 441–452.

Thomas, R. D. (2001a). Perceptual interactions of facial dimensions in speeded classification and identification. *Perception & Psychophysics*, *63*(4), 625–650.

Thomas, R. D. (2001b). Characterizing perceptual interactions in face identification using multidimensional signal detection theory. In M. G. Wenger, & J. T. Townsend (Eds.), *Compu-*

tational, geometric, and process perspectives on facial cognition: Contexts and challenges (pp. 193–227). Hillsdale, NJ: Erlbaum Press.

Townsend, J. T. (1974). Issues and models concerning the processing of a finite number of inputs. In B. H. Kantowitz (Ed.), *Human information processing: Tutorials in performance and cognition* (pp. 133–168). Hillsdale, NJ: Erlbaum Press.

Townsend, J. T. (1990). Serial vs. parallel processing: Sometimes they look like Tweedledum and Tweedledee but they can (and should) be distinguished. *Psychological Science, 1*, 46–54.

Townsend, J. T., & Altieri, N. (2012). An accuracy–response time capacity assessment function that measures performance against standard parallel predictions. *Psychological Review, 119*(3), 500–516.

Townsend, J. T., & Ashby, F. G. (1983). *The stochastic modelling of elementary psychological processes*. Cambridge, UK: Cambridge University Press.

Townsend, J. T., & Eidels, A. (2011). Workload capacity spaces: A unified methodology for response time measures of efficiency as workload is varied. *Psychonomic Bulletin & Review, 18*, 659–681.

Townsend, J. T., & Fifić, M. (2004). Parallel & serial processing and individual differences in high-speed scanning in human memory. *Perception & Psychophysics, 66*, 953–962.

Townsend, J. T., Houpt, J. W., & Silbert, N. H. (2012). General recognition theory extended to include response times: Predictions for a class of parallel systems. *Journal of Mathematical Psychology, 56*(6), 476–494.

Townsend, J. T., & Liu, Y. (2017). Selective influence and classificatory separability (perceptual separability) in perception and cognition: Similarities, distinctions, and synthesis. In D. R. Little, N. Altieri, M. Fifić, & C-T. Yang (Eds.), *Systems factorial technology: A theory driven methodology for the identification of perceptual and cognitive mechanisms*. Elsevier (in this book).

Townsend, J. T., & Nozawa, G. (1995). Spatio-temporal properties of elementary perception: An investigation of parallel, serial, and coactive theories. *Journal of Mathematical Psychology, 39*, 321–359.

Townsend, J. T., & Wenger, M. J. (2004). The serial-parallel dilemma: A case study in a linkage of theory and method. *Psychonomic Bulletin & Review, 11*, 391–418.

Usher, M., & McClelland, J. L. (2001). The time course of perceptual choice: The leaky, competing accumulator model. *Psychological Review, 108*(3), 550.

The Advantages of Combining the Simultaneous–Sequential Paradigm with Systems Factorial Technology

15

Piers D.L. Howe, Adam Ferguson
University of Melbourne, Melbourne, VIC, Australia

Both the simultaneous–sequential paradigm (Eriksen & Spencer, 1969; Shiffrin & Gardner, 1972) and systems factorial technology (Townsend, 1992; Townsend & Nozawa, 1995) attempt to identify the type of processing underlying a particular mental act. However, these competing methods attempt to do this utilizing different behavior measures and by making different assumptions. In this sense, the two methods are complementary with the strengths of one being able to compensate for the weaknesses of the other and vice versa. We argue that this sometimes makes it advantageous to utilize both methods because then if they both arrive at the same conclusion this would amount to very strong evidence in favor of that conclusion.

Systems factorial technology typically measures the reaction time of an observer to two events that occur simultaneously. This allows direct inferences about the processing of the two events to be made (Townsend, 1992; Townsend & Nozawa, 1995). Conversely, the simultaneous–sequential paradigm typically divides a given task into two halves and compares the observers' performance (usually quantified by percentage correct on the task) when the two halves are performed sequentially as opposed to when they are performed simultaneously. In effect it measures the observer's processing capacity. From this the practitioners attempt to infer the underlying mental processing, specifically whether the processing is likely to be serial or parallel (Eriksen & Spencer, 1969; Shiffrin & Gardner, 1972). The advantage of the simultaneous–sequential paradigm is that it is usually relatively easy to adapt it to a given experimental paradigm. Its disadvantage is that it is more susceptible to parallel–serial mimicry since different mental architectures can in principle have the same capacity (Townsend, 1990). While a finding of unlimited capacity is indicative, though by no means proof, of parallel processing (Townsend, 1990), a finding of limited capacity is much harder to interpret as it is readily predicted by both parallel and serial models. Conversely, systems factorial technology suffers less from model mimicry but it can be harder to apply it in practice. For both methods it is easiest to describe them with reference to a particular task. In this chapter we will illustrate their use by using them to determine whether identity–location bindings are maintained and updated by a serial, parallel or coactive process.

The binding problem is central to visual perception. It is the problem of distinguishing the properties of an object from the other objects in a visual scene and associating together only those properties that correspond to the same object (Milner, 1974;

Systems Factorial Technology, DOI: 10.1016/B978-0-12-804315-8.00018-5

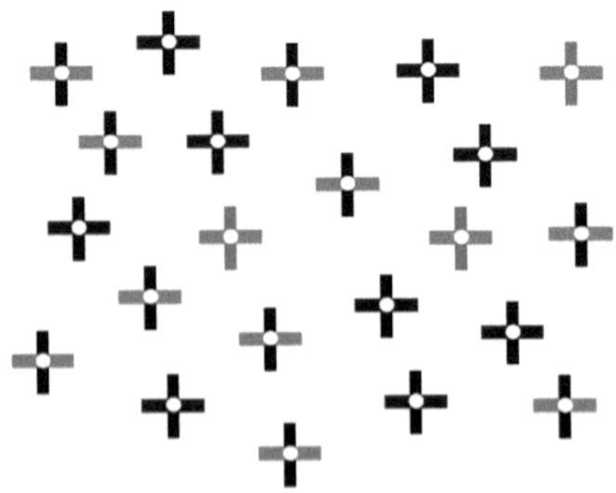

Figure 15.1 Before you attend to the display you are probably aware that it contains a large number of plus signs, some of them black or with black parts and others gray or with gray parts. However, if you were asked to search for a particular plus sign, say one with a gray vertical and a black horizontal bar, you would need to attend to the items, probably in a sequential fashion.

von der Malsburg, 1981; von der Malsburg & Schneider, 1986; Treisman, 1996). For example, in Fig. 15.1 you are probably aware of a number of plus signs and that some of these plus signs are black or have black parts and others are gray or have gray parts. However, before you attend to any of the objects, you are probably not aware whether any of the plus signs comprise a gray vertical bar and a black horizontal bar. If you search for this particular target, you will probably find yourself doing so by attending to each item in turn (Treisman & Gelade, 1980; Wolfe, Cave, & Franzel, 1989). In this display, only by attending to an item can you determine whether it is the target of your search. Attention is needed to bind item's features together so as to allow you to determine what it is (Treisman & Gelade, 1980). Without binding you can be aware of the individual features present in the scene (Treisman & Gelade, 1980; Wolfe et al., 1989) but not whether a particular combination of these features is present (Milner, 1974; von der Malsburg, 1981; von der Malsburg & Schneider, 1986; Treisman, 1996). For this reason, the binding problem strongly constrains visual awareness (Crick & Koch, 1990; Howe et al., 2009; Wolfe, 2012).

Although often not recognized, the binding problem takes a number of different forms (Treisman, 1996; Di Lollo, 2012). The one most commonly considered is the feature binding problem, which is the problem of determining which features belong to which object (Treisman, 1996). The above illustration is an example of the feature binding problem. Conversely, the identity–location binding problem is the problem of associating the correct object identity with the correct location. In other words, it refers to knowing what is where in the visual scene (Treisman, 1996). This binding problem is typically studied using objects whose identities are known but whose locations are continuously changing. In this chapter we will consider only this type of binding problem.

In our experiments, we studied the identity–location binding problem using the multiple identity tracking (MIT) task (Oksama & Hyona, 2004; Horowitz et al., 2007). In the MIT task, the observers are shown a display containing a number of moving objects. In our case, these objects were differently colored disks. A typical trial starts

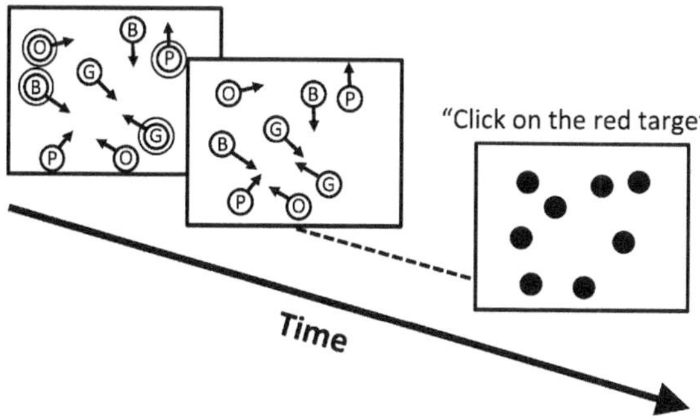

Figure 15.2 At the start of the trial the observer is shown a display containing a number of colored disks (blue, green, purple and orange denoted by the letters "B", "G", "P" and "O", respectively) a subset of which are briefly ringed to indicate that these are the targets to be tracked. The rings then disappear and the disks move around. At a random point in time, all the disks stop moving, turn black and the observer is asked to indicate the location of a particular target, for example, the red one.

with a subset of these disks being briefly ringed to indicate that these are the targets to be tracked during the trial. The rings then disappear and all the objects move around the screen in a pseudo-random fashion. At the end of the trial the objects all stop moving and become the same color. The observer is then asked to indicate the location of a particular target, for example, the red one (Fig. 15.2).

It is important to emphasize that the duration of the trial is random so the observer does not know in advance when the trial is likely to end. This forces the observer to continuously keep track of where each target is located. This ensures that the observer must continuously solve the identity–location binding problem for each target.

A potential concern with this task is that the observers may be tempted to make eye movements. Eye movements are commonly observed when observers freely view a tracking display (Fehd & Seiffert, 2008; Zelinsky & Neider, 2008; Fehd & Seiffert, 2010; Huff, Papenmeier, Jahn, & Hess, 2010). These eye movements necessarily introduce a serial component into the task. Thus, even if the mental processing underlying tracking was itself parallel, it might appear to be serial because of the serial component introduced by the eye movements. To avoid this potential confound, in all our experiments observers were required to maintain fixation on a fixation cross. We know that they were successful in doing this because we did not observe any seriality in their tracking.

Simultaneous–Sequential Paradigm

In our first two experiments we utilized the simultaneous–sequential paradigm. To do this, in each experiment we introduced two conditions. In both conditions, the disks did not move continuously. Instead each disk moved and paused for half the trial. Thus the motion discontinuities were exactly the same in the two conditions and in each condition each disk traveled exactly the same distance. The difference between the two conditions was whether the disks moved and paused synchronously. In the *simultaneous* condition, all the disks moved and paused together. Conversely, in the *sequential* condition, half the disks moved while the other half paused and then the

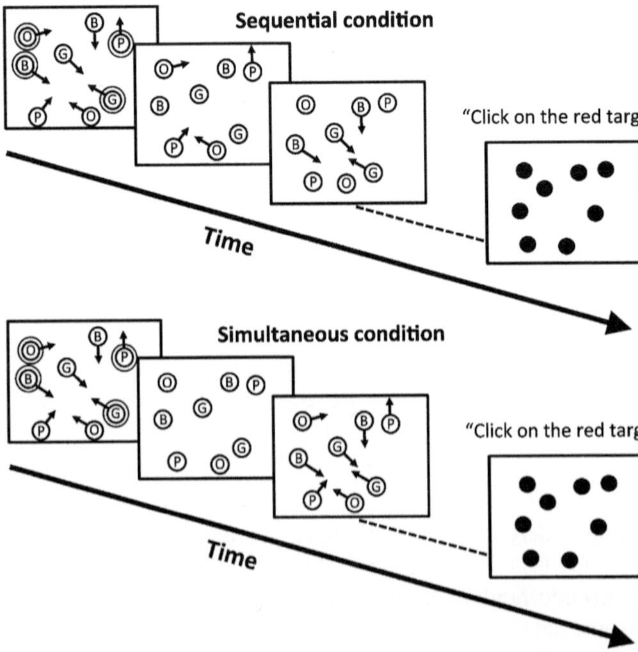

Figure 15.3 In both conditions, each disk moves and pauses for exactly half the trial. In the sequential condition, at any one time half the disks are moving. In the simultaneous condition, all the disks move and pause together.

first half paused while the second half moved. This sequence repeated throughout the trial so that at any one time only half the disks were moving (Fig. 15.3).

To understand the utility of this paradigm, it worth considering what predictions a parallel model with independent channels and a serial model with independent stages would make. Because the channels are independent, the parallel model by definition has unlimited capacity. Conversely, the capacity of the serial model is assumed to be limited. In the literature these are often referred to as a standard parallel model and a standard serial model (Townsend & Asby, 1983). A standard parallel model assumes that all targets are tracked continuously and independently, regardless of their state of motion. Thus it predicts that the maximum speed at which the targets can be tracked at should be the same in both the simultaneous and sequential conditions. Conversely, a standard serial model makes a very different prediction, as discussed below.

The model of multiple identity tracking (MOMIT) is currently the only model of MIT and is an example of a standard serial model in that it assumes that the targets are attended independently, one at a time in a sequential fashion (Oksama & Hyona, 2008). Every time a target is attended, the observer notes the target's location. When it is time to reattend a given target (i.e., after attending to all the other targets in turn), the model assumes that whichever object is closest to the last remembered position for that target is assumed by the observer to be that target. If this assumption turns out not to be true, for example, if the observer has taken too long to reattend a particular target or if the targets are moving too quickly, then a tracking error will be made. Crucially, the model assumes that the observer will attend preferentially to the targets whose locations are least certain, which in this case would be the moving targets. Assuming that there are four targets in total, it follows that in the simultaneous condition the effective tracking load, i.e., the number of disks to which the observer needs to attend at any given time, will sometimes be four disks because sometimes all four disks will be moving at the same time so will need to be attended. Conversely, in the sequential condition only two of the disks will be moving at any one time. Thus the effective tracking load will be approximately two disks in the sequential condition. According to the serial model, halving the effective tracking load should halve the time it takes the observer to reattend any given target and so halve the distance traveled by each target during the time it takes the observer to reattend it. This model predicts that the probability of losing a target is determined by the distance the target travels in the time it takes the observer to reattend it. It follows that, to hold the probability of making a tracking error constant, when the effective tracking load is halved the speed at which the targets move needs to be doubled so that the total distance traveled by each target in the time it takes for the target to be reattended is held constant. Consequently, the maximum speed at which the targets can be tracked is predicted to be approximately double in the sequential condition than in the simultaneous condition.

The serial and parallel models therefore make different predictions with regards the maximum speed at which the targets can be tracked in the two conditions. Thus, by measuring this maximum speed we can determine which model is more likely to be correct. However, this analysis rests on the assumption that if tracking occurs serially then the tracking mechanism would prioritize the moving targets. This assumption is reasonable for at least three reasons. First, it is known that motion onsets preferentially attract attention to moving targets, thereby presumably facilitating their tracking (Abrams & Christ, 2003). Second, there is both fMRI (Howe, Horowitz, Morocz, Wolfe, & Livingstone, 2009) and EEG (Drew, Horowitz, Wolfe, & Vogel, 2011) evidence that in tracking attention is indeed directed preferentially to the moving targets as opposed to the stationary ones. Finally, it has been shown that during tracking observers attend preferentially to the targets that are most in danger of being lost, which in the case of Experiments 1 and 2 would be the moving ones (Iordanescu, Grabowecky, & Suzuki, 2009). The above supporting evidence notwithstanding, we could come to a stronger conclusion if we did not have to make this assumption. For this reason we also investigated the same issue using systems factorial technology since we were able to do this in a way that avoided making the above assumption. Specifically, when we used systems factorial technology, all disks moved continuously, with the consequence that we did not have to make any assumptions regarding the difference in processing of moving versus stationary disks. Given that the two techniques make different assumptions, if they both arrive at the same conclusion then this would be strong evidence in favor of the veracity of that conclusion.

Systems Factorial Technology

As systems factorial technology has been discussed extensively elsewhere (see the tutorial in this book, Altieri, Fifić, Little, & Yang, 2017) in this chapter we will provide only a brief overview of how this method applies to our particular paradigm, referring the reader to the original sources for the mathematical proofs (Townsend & Nozawa, 1995; Townsend & Wenger, 2004). In our study, observers were presented with an MIT stimulus similar to the experiment outlined above except that all the disks moved continuously, during the tracking phase all the disks were the same gray color and there were only two targets. At a random point during the movement phase the two targets darkened by a small amount (S), by a large amount (L) or not at all (N). If they both darkened, they always did so simultaneously. For the situation where both targets did darken, there were three possible conditions. They could both darken by a large amount (the LL condition), one could darken by a large amount and the other by a small amount (the mixed condition) or both might darken only by a small amount (the SS condition). Note that because both targets were free to move, we do not distinguish between the SL and the LS condition. Instead, we refer to both conditions jointly as the mixed condition. The observer was requested to push a response button as quickly as possible if either target darkened. The greater the darkening, the faster it is likely to be detected, so the shorter the reaction time is likely to be. By measuring the distributions of the reaction times it is possible to determine the type of processing, for example, whether the targets are processed in series, in parallel or coactively (Townsend & Nozawa, 1995). The most straightforward way to do this is to measure the mean reaction time for the three conditions and use this to calculate the mean interaction contrast (*MIC*) given by the following formula (Townsend & Wenger, 2004):

$$MIC = RT_{\mathrm{LL}}(t) + RT_{\mathrm{SS}}(t) - 2 \times RT_{mixed}(t) \tag{15.1}$$

and analogously for the *SIC*:

$$SIC = S_{\mathrm{LL}}(t) + S_{\mathrm{SS}}(t) - 2 \times S_{mixed}(t) \tag{15.2}$$

where the survivor function is the probability that on a trial where the observer will respond, he has not yet done so by time t.

In our experiment, the observers were instructed to respond when either target darkened. Thus, if the observers notice that one of the targets has darkened they do not need to check whether the other target has darkened before responding. In other words, the observers can perform the task by applying a self-terminating stopping rule (Townsend & Nozawa, 1995). However, despite this, the observers may in practice always check both targets, even though this is not always necessary, in which case the observers would be said to be applying an exhaustive stopping rule (Townsend & Nozawa, 1995). By calculating the *SIC*, we can determine which stopping rule the observers employ.

It is also useful to quantify the capacity of the system to process multiple items simultaneously. In the present MIT task, this can be done by measuring the change in processing speed when the observers are asked to process two stimuli as opposed to just one stimulus. Detailed capacity predictions are presented in the tutorial chapter.

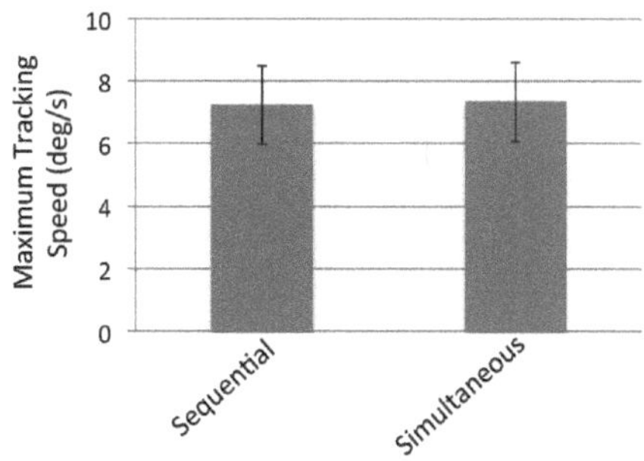

Figure 15.4 The results from the first experiment. There is no difference in the maximum tracking speed in the sequential and simultaneous conditions. Error bars represent within-subject standard error of the means (Cousineau, 2005; Morey, 2008).

Experiments

Below we will briefly summarize three experiments that show how the simultaneous–sequential paradigm can be profitably combined with systems factorial technology to mitigate the potentially limiting assumptions of either method. For further details on these experiments, the reader is referred to the original article (Howe & Ferguson, 2015).

Experiment 1: Simultaneous–Sequential Paradigm with Targets Whose Unique Identities Were Continuously Visible

This experiment utilized the paradigm outline above and illustrated in Figs. 15.2 and 15.3. Fifteen observers were asked to keep track of four targets among eight disks while maintaining fixation on a fixation cross. To prevent the observers from verbally reciting the color names of the targets, the observers were required to repeatedly say the word "animal" during the tracking phase of each trial. At the end of each trial two disks were highlighted one at a time, and the observers were asked whether each disk in turn was a target. In simultaneous and sequential conditions, during the movement phase, each disk moved only half the time. In the simultaneous condition all the disks moved and paused simultaneously. Conversely, in the sequential condition, only half the disks moved at any one time. The QUEST staircase routine (Watson & Pelli, 1983) was used to find the maximum tracking speed at which the observers could track the disks at 75% tracking accuracy. In other words, the speed at which on 75% of the trials the observer was able to correctly answer whether the two disks sequentially highlighted at the end of the trial were targets or distractors. Observers were not provided feedback on their performance.

As explained previously, the standard serial model predicts that the maximum tracking speed in the sequential condition should be double that of the simultaneous condition. Conversely, the standard parallel model predicts that the maximum tracking speed should be the same in the two conditions. The results are shown in Fig. 15.4. Consistent with the prediction of the parallel model, a within-subjects *t* test found no

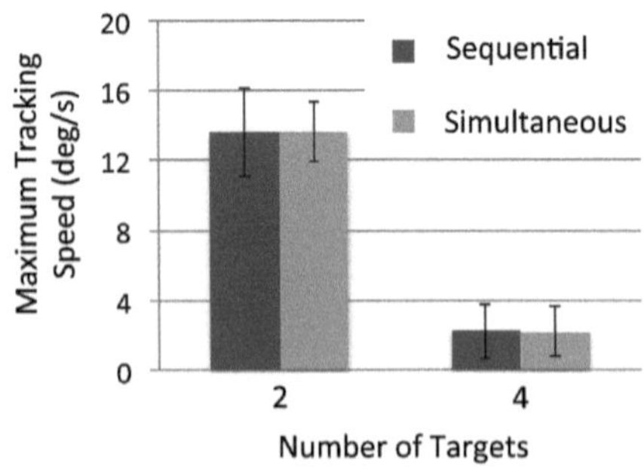

Figure 15.5 The results from the second experiment. As before, there is no difference in the maximum tracking speed in the sequential and simultaneous conditions. Error bars represent within-subject standard error of the means (Cousineau, 2005; Morey, 2008).

difference between the maximum tracking speeds of the two conditions, $t(14) = 0.71$, $p = 0.49$, *Cohen's d* $= 0.22$.

Experiment 2: Simultaneous–Sequential Paradigm with Targets Whose Unique Identities Are not Continuously Visible

In most previous studies of MIT, the identities of the objects were continuously visible during the tracking phase (Horowitz et al., 2007; Oksama & Hyona, 2008; Pinto, Howe, Cohen, & Horowitz, 2010; Cohen, Pinto, Howe, & Horowitz 2011). The advantage of this procedure is that it mimics real life where the identities of objects are also typically visible during tracking. However, a potential disadvantage is that having the identities of the object continuously visible makes it possible for observers to sometimes recover from tracking errors. Thus, the performance of the observers on the tracking task reflects not just their tracking proficiency but also their ability to recover from errors. Because we wished to have a pure measure of the ability to track objects and their distinct identities, in Experiment 2, objects were initially presented in different colors but became identical during the tracking phase (Pylyshyn, 2004; Hudson, Howe, & Little, 2012), thereby making target recovery impossible. This ensured that the performance of observers on this task reflected only their tracking ability. It is important to emphasize that this experiment still required observers to continuously refresh the identity–location bindings of the targets since if they failed to do that they would not know where the targets were located at the end of the trial. Thus, their tracking performance was a true measure of their ability to solve the identity–location binding problem.

After running the previous experiment it occurred to us that observers may employ different strategies when tracking different numbers of targets. For example, they might have the capacity to track two targets in a parallel fashion but are forced to track four targets in a serial fashion. To investigate this possibility, in Experiment 2 we sometimes had observers track two targets and sometimes four targets. Other than these differences, the experiment was conducted the same as previously.

The results are shown in Fig. 15.5. A two-way ANOVA found a significant main effect for the number of targets, with the maximum tracking speed being significantly greater in the two target condition than in the four target condition, $F(1, 14) = 75.1$, $p < 0.001$, *partial* $\eta^2 = 0.86$. However, no main effect was found for type of motion with the maximum tracking speed not being significantly different between the sequential and simultaneous conditions, $F(1, 14) = 0.01$, $p = 0.93$. No significant interaction was observed, $F(1, 14) = 0.02$, $p = 0.90$. This experiment therefore supports our previous finding that performance is equivalent in the simultaneous and sequential conditions. This result is consistent with the standard parallel model but not with the standard serial model.

Experiment 3: Using Systems Factorial Technology

While the previous two experiments provide strong evidence against serial accounts of tracking, they both rely on the assumption that if tracking is serial then the tracking mechanism would prioritize the tracking of the moving targets thereby reducing the effective tracking load in the sequential condition. While this assumption is clearly plausible, we could be more confident in our conclusions if we could reach them without making this assumption. That is why in Experiment 3 we used systems factorial technology as this method does not make this assumption.

Systems factorial technology requires one to measure the reaction time to a discrete event, such as the appearance of two stimuli (Townsend & Nozawa, 1995). However, tracking is a temporally extended process, so it is not obvious how one can directly measure tracking performance in terms of a reaction time. Instead, in Experiment 3, we assumed that tracking is mediated by attention and used systems factorial technology to measure whether the two targets were attended simultaneously or sequentially by measuring the response time to the darkening of the two targets. This in turn allowed us to infer whether tracking occurs in a serial or in a parallel fashion.

This assumption that tracking is mediated by attention is widespread (Scholl, 2001, 2009; Cavanagh & Alvarez, 2005) and is supported by experimental evidence. For example, performing an attentionally demanding task concurrently with tracking is known to reduce tracking performance (Kunar, Carter, Cohen, & Horowitz, 2008). Furthermore, probes that are briefly flashed on targets are detected more readily than probes that are briefly flashed on distractors, indicating that targets are preferentially attended (Pylyshyn, 2006; Flombaum, Scholl, & Pylyshyn, 2008; Pylyshyn, Haroutioun, King, & Reilly, 2008). Despite this evidence, the issue is still debated and at least one theory of tracking claims that tracking is preattentive (Pylyshyn & Storm, 1988).

Previously it has been suggested that tracking may occur independently in the left and right visual hemifields (Alvarez & Cavanagh, 2005). If so, serial tracking might occur only when there was more than one target in a given visual hemifield. Consequently, for Experiment 3 there were two sets of four disks, with one set of disks confined to the left hemifield and the other to the right hemifield. Both targets were confined to same hemifield thereby ensuring that seriality could be observed regardless of any hemifield independence.

At the start of each trial, each disk within a hemifield was colored differently and the two targets were indicated by being briefly ringed. The disks all then became the same color and moved around their hemifield. During this movement phase the

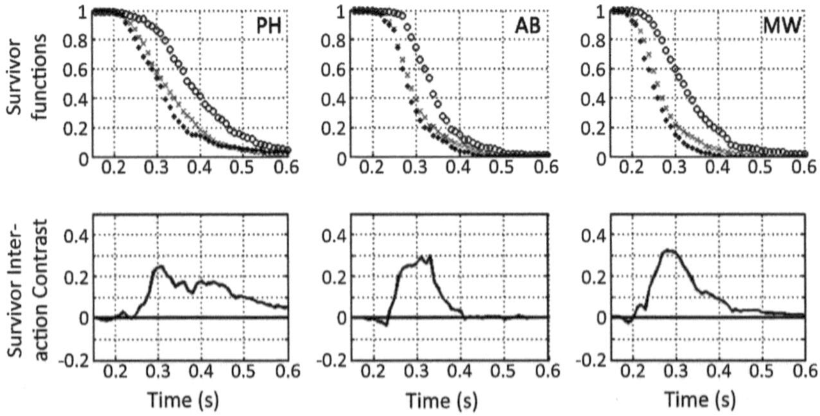

Figure 15.6 Results of the third experiment for each of the three observers. The top row represents the survivor functions (circles represent the SS condition, the gray crosses the mixed condition and the black diamonds the LL condition). The bottom row represents the survivor interaction contrasts (*SIC*s).

disks would suddenly and unpredictably darken. Each disk would darken by either a small amount (S), a large amount (L) or not at all (N). If both disks darkened they would do so at the same time. The observer was instructed to push a button on a response box a quickly as possible whenever he noticed either target darkening. At the end of the trial all the disks would stop moving and the observers were asked to indicate the location of each target. On average observers were able to correctly indicate the individual locations of both targets on 95% of the trials. In calculating reactions times, we discarded any trial were observers were not able to do this. This ensured that we analyzed only those trials where observers had been able to maintain accurate identity–location bindings.

As it is not possible to directly test for selective influence, a key assumption of systems factorial technology (Townsend & Nozawa, 1995), we instead tested for the implied ordering of the survivor functions (Houpt, Blaha, McIntire, Havig, & Townsend, 2013). The survivor functions for the three observers are shown in the top row of Fig. 15.6. By performing a series of Kolmogorov–Smirnov tests we were able to show the expected ordering.

For all observers the *MIC* was found to be significantly greater than zero (adjusted rank transform test, average $MIC = 0.046$), allowing us to reject serial processing but not to distinguish between parallel and coactive processing. To make this distinction we need to consider the *SIC* of each observer, shown in the bottom row of Fig. 15.6. The Houpt–Townsend KS–SIC test showed that for each observer the *SIC* was at some point significantly greater than zero but never significantly less than zero. This allowed us to rule out coactive processing and conclude that processing must be parallel. Furthermore, by looking at the shape of the *SIC*'s we could conclude that each observer employed a self-terminating stopping rule (please see the tutorial chapter in this volume for further details). For each observer, the capacity coefficient was found to be significantly less than one under the Houpt–Townsend UCIP test leading us to conclude that our data is compatible with both a limited capacity independent parallel model (Townsend & Asby, 1983) and a inhibitory, interactive parallel model (Eidels, Houpt, Altieri, Pei, & Townsend, 2011).

Discussion

Both the simultaneous–sequential paradigm and systems factorial technology have arrived at the same conclusion, that in MIT the targets can be tracked in parallel implying that their identity–locations bindings must also be capable of being updated in parallel. The main difference between these two methods is the assumptions that they make.

The simultaneous–sequential paradigm assumes that any serial model would preferentially track the moving targets. While, this assumption is certainly plausible, we could reach a stronger conclusion if we did not have to make it. It was for this reason that we decided to also use systems factorial technology.

Systems factorial technology does not make this assumption; however, to use it we need to make a number of different assumptions, two of which are particularly important. One is the assumption of selective influence (Townsend & Nozawa, 1995). This assumption cannot be proven but does imply a particular ordering of the survivor functions. As this ordering of survivor functions was observed for all our observers in Experiment 3, we can be fairly confident that this assumption holds for that experiment.

The other assumption that we need to make to is that tracking is mediated by attention. Systems factorial technology requires one to measure the reaction time to a discrete event (Townsend & Nozawa, 1995) so it cannot be used to directly study tracking because tracking is a temporally extended process. Instead, we assumed that tracking is mediated by attention and used systems factorial technology to study the deployment of attention in tracking. We found that during tracking the targets were attended simultaneously and from this we concluded that if tracking is mediated by attention it follows that tracking must occur in parallel.

In summary, both our techniques arrived at the same conclusion but both required us to make significant assumptions. However, the assumptions made by the two techniques were different. We argue that while neither technique on its own can be considered to be conclusive, combined they provide strong converging evidence that tracking occurs in parallel. This is therefore a good example of when it is beneficial to utilize both methods so as to come to a stronger conclusion than would be possible if either method was used on its own.

References

Abrams, R. A., & Christ, S. E. (2003). Motion onset captures attention. *Psychological Science: A Journal of the American Psychological Society*, *14*, 427–432.

Altieri, N., Fifić, M., Little, D. R., & Yang, C.-T. (2017). Historical foundations and a tutorial introduction to systems factorial technology. In D. R. Little, N. Altieri, M. Fifić, & C.-T. Yang (Eds.), *Systems factorial technology: A theory driven methodology for the identification of perceptual and cognitive mechanisms*. Elsevier (in this book).

Alvarez, G. A., & Cavanagh, P. (2005). Independent resources for attentional tracking in the left and right visual hemifields. *Psychological Science*, *16*(8), 637–643.

Cavanagh, P., & Alvarez, G. A. (2005). Tracking multiple targets with multifocal attention. *Trends in Cognitive Sciences*, *9*(7), 349–354.

Cohen, M. A., Pinto, Y., Howe, P. D., & Horowitz, T. S. (2011). The what–where tradeoff in multiple identity tracking. *Attention, Perception, & Psychophysics*, *73*, 1422–1434.

Cousineau, D. (2005). Confidence intervals in within-subject designs: A simpler solution to Loftus and Masson's method. *Tutorial in Quantitative Methods for Psychology*, *1*(1), 42–45.

Crick, F., & Koch, C. (1990). Towards a neurobiological theory of consciousness. *Seminars in the Neurosciences*, *2*, 263–275.

Di Lollo, V. (2012). The feature-binding problem is an ill-posed problem. *Trends in Cognitive Sciences*, *16*(6), 317–321.

Drew, T., Horowitz, T. S., Wolfe, J. M., & Vogel, E. K. (2011). Delineating the neural signatures of tracking spatial position and working memory during attentive tracking. *Journal of Neuroscience*, *31*(2), 659–668.

Eidels, A., Houpt, J. W., Altieri, N., Pei, L., & Townsend, J. T. (2011). Nice guys finish fast and bad guys finish last: Facilitatory vs. inhibitory interaction in parallel systems. *Journal of Mathematical Psychology*, *55*(2), 176–190.

Eriksen, C. W., & Spencer, T. (1969). Rate of information processing in visual perception: Some results and methodological considerations. *Journal of Experimental Psychology*, *79*(2), 1–16.

Fehd, H. M., & Seiffert, A. E. (2008). Eye movements during multiple object tracking: Where do participants look? *Cognition*, *108*(1), 201–209.

Fehd, H. M., & Seiffert, A. E. (2010). Looking at the center of the targets helps multiple object tracking. *Journal of Vision*, *10*(4), 19.1–19.13.

Flombaum, J. I., Scholl, B. J., & Pylyshyn, Z. W. (2008). Attentional resources in visual tracking through occlusion: The high-beams effect. *Cognition*, *107*(3), 904–931.

Horowitz, T. S., Klieger, S. B., Fencsik, D. E., Yang, K. K., Alvarez, G. A., & Wolfe, J. M. (2007). Tracking unique objects. *Perception & Psychophysics*, *69*(2), 172–184.

Houpt, J. W., Blaha, L. M., McIntire, J. P., Havig, P. R., & Townsend, J. T. (2013). Systems factorial technology with R. *Behavior Research Methods*, *46*(2), 307–330.

Howe, P., Evans, K., Pedersini, R., Cohen, M., Horowitz, T., & Wolfe, J. (2009). Attention: Selectice attention and consciousness. In W. P. Banks (Ed.), *Encyclopedia for consciousness, Vol. 1* (pp. 61–75). Amsterdam: Elsevier.

Howe, P. D., Horowitz, T. S., Morocz, I. A., Wolfe, J., & Livingstone, M. S. (2009). Using fMRI to distinguish components of the multiple object tracking task. *Journal of Vision*, *9*, 10.1–10.11.

Howe, P. D. L., & Ferguson, A. (2015). The identity–location binding problem. *Cognitive Science*, *39*, 1622–1645.

Hudson, C., Howe, P. D., & Little, D. R. (2012). Hemifield effects in multiple identity tracking. *PLoS ONE*, *7*(8), e43796.

Huff, M., Papenmeier, F., Jahn, G., & Hess, R. F. (2010). Eye movements across viewpoint changes in mulitple object tracking. *Visual Cognition*, *18*(9), 1368–1391.

Iordanescu, L., Grabowecky, M., & Suzuki, S. (2009). Demand-based dynamic distribution of attention and monitoring of velocities during multiple-object tracking. *Journal of Vision, 9*(4), 1–12.

Kunar, M. A., Carter, R., Cohen, M., & Horowitz, T. S. (2008). Telephone conversation impairs sustained visual attention via a central bottleneck. *Psychonomic Bulletin & Review, 15*(6), 1135–1140.

Milner, P. M. (1974). A model for visual shape recognition. *Psychological Review, 81*(6), 521–535.

Morey, R. D. (2008). Confidence intervals from normalized data: A correction to Cousineau (2005). *Tutorial in Quantitative Methods for Psychology, 4*(2), 61–64.

Oksama, L., & Hyona, J. (2004). Is multiple object tracking carried out automatically by an early vision mechanisms independent of higher-order cognition? An individual difference approach. *Visual Cognition, 11*, 631–671.

Oksama, L., & Hyona, J. (2008). Dynamic binding of identity and location information: A serial model of multiple identity tracking. *Cognitive Psychology, 56*(4), 237–283.

Pinto, Y., Howe, P. D., Cohen, M. A., & Horowitz, T. S. (2010). The more often you see an object, the easier it becomes to track it. *Journal of Vision, 10*(10), 4.

Pylyshyn, Z. W. (2004). Some puzzling findings in multiple object tracking (MOT): I. Tracking without keeping track of object identities. *Visual Cognition, 11*(7), 801–822.

Pylyshyn, Z. W. (2006). Some puzzling findings in multiple object tracking (MOT): II. Inhibition of moving nontargets. *Visual Cognition, 14*(2), 175–198.

Pylyshyn, Z. W., Haroutioun, H. H., King, C. E., & Reilly, J. E. (2008). Selective nontarget inhibition in multiple object tracking. *Visual Cognition, 16*(8), 1011–1021.

Pylyshyn, Z. W., & Storm, R. W. (1988). Tracking multiple independent targets: Evidence for a parallel tracking mechanism. *Spatial Vision, 3*(3), 179–197.

Scholl, B. J. (2001). Objects and attention: The state of the art. *Cognition, 80*(1–2), 1–46.

Scholl, B. J. (2009). What have we learned about attention from multiple object tracking (and vice versa)? In D. Dedrick, & L. Trick (Eds.), *Computation, cognition, and Pylyshyn* (pp. 49–78). Cambridge, MA: MIT Press.

Shiffrin, R. M., & Gardner, F. T. (1972). Visual processing capacity and attentional control. *Journal of Experimental Psychology, 93*(1), 72–83.

Townsend, J. T. (1990). Serial vs. parallel processing: Sometimes they look like Tweedledum and Tweedledee but they can (and should) be distinguished. *Psychological Science, 1*(1), 46–54.

Townsend, J.T. (1992). On the proper scales for reaction time. In S. L. H. Geissler, & J. T. Townsend (Eds.), *Cognition, information processing and psychophysics: Basic issues, Vol. 3* (pp. 105–120). Hillsdale, NJ: Erlbaum.

Townsend, J. T., & Asby, F. G. (1983). Methods of modeling capacity in simple processing systems. In J. C. F. Restle (Ed.), *Cognitive theory, Vol. 3* (pp. 200–239). Hillsdale, NJ: Erlbaum.

Townsend, J. T., & Nozawa, G. (1995). On the spatio-temporal properties of elementary perception: An investigation of parallel, serial, and coactive theories. *Journal of Mathematical Psychology, 39*, 321–359.

Townsend, J. T., & Wenger, M. J. (2004). A theory of interactive parallel processing: New capacity measures and predictions for a response time inequality series. *Psychological Review, 111*(4), 1003–1035.

Treisman, A. (1996). The binding problem. *Current Opinion in Neurobiology, 6*(2), 171–178.

Treisman, A. M., & Gelade, G. (1980). A feature-integration theory of attention. *Cognitive Psychology, 12*(1), 97–136.

von der Malsburg, C. (1981). *The correlation theory of brain function*. MPI biophysical chemistry, Internal Report 81-2. (Reprinted in J. L. Van Hemmen, E. Domany, & K. Schulten (Eds.), *Models of neural networks II (1994)*, Berlin: Springer.)

von der Malsburg, C., & Schneider, W. (1986). A neural cocktail-party processor. *Biological Cybernetics*, *54*(1), 29–40.

Watson, A. B., & Pelli, D. G. (1983). QUEST: A Bayesian adaptive psychometric method. *Perception & Psychophysics*, *33*(113–120), 113–120.

Wolfe, J. M. (2012). The binding problem lives on: Comment on Di Lollo. *Trends in Cognitive Sciences*, *16*(6), 307–308; author reply pp. 308–309.

Wolfe, J. M., Cave, K. R., & Franzel, S. L. (1989). Guided search: An alternative to the feature integration model for visual search. *Journal of Experimental Psychology: Human Perception and Performance*, *15*(3), 419–433.

Zelinsky, G. J., & Neider, M. B. (2008). An eye movement analysis of multiple object tracking in a realistic environment. *Visual Cognition*, *16*(5), 553–566.

Part Four

Bridging Levels of Explanation

The Continuing Evolution of Systems Factorial Theory: Connecting Theory with Behavioral and Neural Data

16

Michael J. Wenger, Erin M. Ingvalson†, Stephanie E. Rhoten**
*The University of Oklahoma, Norman, OK, United States, †Florida State University, Tallahassee, FL, United States

Effects, tasks, and models – we have many of all three in the behavioral sciences. Generally, it has been the case that an effect (the generation effect, the inversion effect, the composite face effect, etc., the list could be extended well past the page limits for this chapter) emerges from the use of a task (Townsend, 2008). A model typically follows, and serves as a representation of the theory of the effect, as it is specifically expressed in the task. The work with systems factorial theory and the double-factorial paradigm (SFT/DFP, as we refer to it here), as evidenced in the literature and the essays in this volume, turns this general set of relationships on its head. A general theory is used to inform and frame specific hypotheses, and the task design then follows.

There are numerous strengths to this approach. Two central strengths of the conjoined metatheory/methodology that we wish to focus on are its generality and its emphasis on strong-inference hypothesis testing. These two characteristics need to be understood as the most-recent expression of a dedication to generality and strong-inference hypothesis testing that has been a hallmark of the preceding work. In the initial section of this chapter, we briefly review two intellectual predecessors to the SFT/DFP: the parallel–serial testing paradigm (PST) and the trichotomy method. In both, one can find the ideas that have evolved to become the present-day approach. In the second section, we survey a set of studies that have applied the conjoined metatheory and methodology, illustrating the range of questions that have been addressed to date. We close with a preview of a new application of the approach, illustrating the potential for the impact of this work in cognitive neuroscience, further highlighting the generality, comprehensiveness, and elegance of the SFT/DFP.

Two Predecessors

A fact that should be powerfully evident in the present collection of essays is that the foundational issues addressed by SFT have an intellectual history that is exceptionally deep and rich.[1] Central to that history is an ongoing commitment to comprehensiveness, generality, and a link between theory and experimentation that makes systematic use of converging sources of evidence (Bridgman, 1945; Garner, Hake, & Eriksen, 1956) and supports strong-inference hypothesis testing (Platt, 1964). In this section,

Systems Factorial Technology, DOI: 10.1016/B978-0-12-804315-8.00020-3

we briefly review two intellectual predecessors to the SFT/DFP: the parallel–serial testing paradigm and the trichotomy method. The strengths of these two approaches have carried forward to the current theoretical and empirical methods, and the limitations of these two approaches have and continue to inform the evolution of current methods.

The concern for model mimicry and identifiability, most prominently with respect to the distinctions between parallel and serial processing (see reviews in Townsend & Wenger, 2004a, 2004b), is the issue most-frequently associated with SFT/DFP and its predecessors. However, as Townsend began demonstrating in the late 1960s and early 1970s (e.g., Townsend, 1969, 1971, 1972, 1974), there are a range of other issues that, if not taken into both theoretical and empirical consideration, can lead to experiments that support inferences that are, at best, ambiguous. These include but are not limited to assumptions regarding capacity, how it may be distributed, order of computations and comparisons, independence and dependence in processing rates, and the particulars of any given perceptual or cognitive task.

The Parallel–Serial Testing Paradigm

A first attempt at comprehensively addressing these issues appeared in the late 1970s, in part as a collaboration between Townsend and Snodgrass (Townsend, 1976; Townsend & Snodgrass, 1977; Snodgrass & Townsend, 1980). Its initial instantiation took the form of a set of theoretical characterizations joined to an experimental methodology designed specifically to address the set of conditions and comparisons identified as critical by the theory. The approach was known as the *parallel–serial testing* (PST) paradigm. A basic version of the PST, as applied by Snodgrass and Townsend (1980), began with two simplifying assumptions, both of which allowed them to derive closed-form prediction equations for mean reaction time (RT). The first of these was that the distributions of item intercompletion times—the time between the completion of processing for any two stimulus items—were exponential, and the second was that capacity was divided by the number of potential comparisons or computations.

The PST paradigm was intended to address the question of processing architecture, and was thus designed to allow for comparisons across rather than within particular cognitive tasks. For simplicity, it limited consideration to situations in which only one or two items needed to be held in memory and when only one or two items were present in the stimulus display. Based on the literature at the time, Snodgrass and Townsend identified a set of experimental conditions, all involving simple visual matrixes or sets of letters, that included a simple same-different task, variants of a match location task, a visual search task with two items in the display, a memory search task with two items held in memory, and both a conjunctive and disjunctive same–different task. Closed-form expressions for the predicted mean RT in each of the 18 display conditions were derived for a serial and a parallel self-terminating model, and the models were separately fit to the means of each individual subject. The results were most consistent with serial processing (see Townsend & Ashby, 1983, Chapter 13, for a discussion of these results).

Townsend and Ashby (1983, Chapter 13) further refined and generalized the PST, and reviewed results of another application of the PST (Townsend & Snodgrass, 1974).[2] In this work, a total of 10 experimental conditions were dictated as necessary by the theoretical analyses. As in Snodgrass and Townsend (1980), predictions were generated for each of the conditions and the models were fit separately to the data of each of the subjects. In this case, the best account of the data was given by the parallel models.

In the presentation of the PST in Townsend and Ashby (1983), one can find the authors considering the costs and benefits of the commitment to comprehensiveness and breadth: "... we face a dilemma associated with virtually all scientific theory testing: The broader the class of models tested, the more complex the set of experimental conditions must be to permit testability, but the more complex the experimental conditions, the less likely it is that models of the same subsystems operating with the same parameter values are applicable across all experimental conditions" (Townsend & Ashby, 1983, pp. 417–418). An alternative approach is to generalize: to find classes of models that can encompass the specific variations. A step in this direction, and towards what has become the general approach of the SFT/DFP, can be found in a collaboration between Townsend and Schweickert.

The Trichotomy Method

This second approach, known as the trichotomy method, was summarized in two critical papers from 1989 (Schweickert & Townsend, 1989; Townsend & Schweickert, 1989). The two papers advanced a general goal of the PST—the ability to test among as broad a set of potential models as possible by framing them all in the same theoretical "language"—by building on Schweickert and Fisher's work with acyclic directed networks and models based on critical path methods (e.g., Fisher & Goldstein, 1983; Schweickert, 1978, 1982, 1983). A notable aspect of this work was the synthesis and generalization of a set of efforts on parallel–serial testing based on factorial methods (Schweickert, Townsend, & Fisher, 1987; Townsend & Schweickert, 1985). In addition, it extended the class of architectures that could be identified by factorial experiments, assuming selective influence.

The first of the two papers (Townsend & Schweickert, 1989) established a set of foundational definitions, including a detailed treatment of selective influence, factor interactions, and marginal selectivity, issues which continue to be the focus of both theoretical and empirical investigation (e.g., Dzhafarov, 2003; Dzhfarov, Schweickert, & Sung, 2004; Kujala & Dzhafarov, 2008; Schweickert, Giorgini, & Dzhafarov, 2000). The second paper (Schweickert & Townsend, 1989) applied the theoretical foundations to a broad class of directed acyclic networks, including processes in sequential and concurrent arrangements. Directed acyclic networks are composed of sets of processes arranged with respect their temporal relations. An example of a directed acyclic network is presented in Fig. 16.1; this particular form is known as an embellished Wheatstone bridge, and was the focus of the analysis in the second of the two trichotomy papers. As the basis for modeling cognitive processes, they are typically

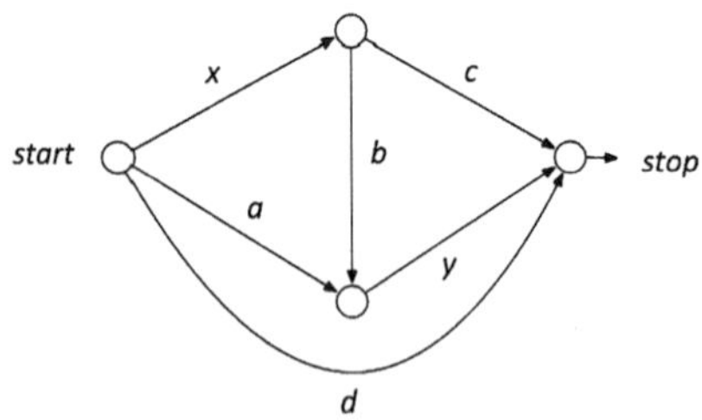

Figure 16.1 A directed acyclic network known as an embellished Wheatstone bridge. In this network, two processes of interest—x and y—are components of a larger hypothesized process that takes inputs at its start and produces an output at its completion. Modified from Fig. 1 in Schweickert and Townsend (1989).

constructed as sets of processes that represent the hypothesized components of a mental act, such as visual or memory search. The overall process unfolds by way of the completion of the various sequences of the component processes, and these various sequences can be understood visually as the set of paths that go from the initiation to the completion of the process.

In this example, there are two component processes of interest, x and y. This particular example provided an ideal target for application of the theoretical analysis, as the two processes are arranged so as to contain four fundamental classes of paths (see Schweickert & Townsend, 1989, p. 342): paths containing both x and y, paths containing x and not y, paths containing y and not x, and paths containing neither x or y. The trichotomy analysis focused on the effects of selectively manipulating the process durations of the two processes of interest at the level of the presence, absence, and sign of the factorial interaction. The three possible outcomes—subadditivity, additivity, and superadditivity—allowed Schweickert and Townsend to draw very strong and general conclusions about the arrangement of the two processes. Specifically, the three outcomes pointed to three nonoverlapping sets of process architectures, establishing the basis for strong-inference hypothesis testing (i.e., hypotheses that can be unambiguously falsified; Platt, 1964).

The limitation of the trichotomy approach, as acknowledged in the two papers, was the fact that models framed in terms of directed acyclic require that a component process cannot begin until all of its predecessors have been completed. This, of course, prevented the approach from being applied to cases in which the hypothesized stopping rule was not exhaustive. However, the approach has continued to evolve (see in particular Schweickert, Fisher, & Sung, 2012) and has been applied to a range of questions, including the role of memory retrieval in the expression of a cognitive skill (e.g., Wenger, 1999).

A Survey of Applications

With the history underlying the SFT/DFP in place, we can begin to assess its current impact. Perhaps the simplest way to gauge impact is through a review of applications: a citation search on Web of Science reveals that Townsend and Nozawa (1995) has been referenced in 182 publications, including disciplines such as cognitive psychology and vision science to neuroscience and auditory perception. Perhaps more impressively, the number of citations continues to grow, with more citations in recent years (2014 and 2015) than in the years immediately following the original publication.

The impact of SFT/DFP may be best appreciated in the variety of its applications. A quick count of the Web of Science citations shows application of the concepts and measures of SFT/DFP to approximately 25 unique problem areas. These applications range from studies of serial and parallel processing (e.g., Blaha, Johnson, & Townsend, 2007; Schweickert et al., 2000; Sung, 2008; Ulrich, Miller, & Schröter, 2007; Williams, Eidels, & Townsend, 2014; Yamani, McCarley, Mounts, & Kramer, 2013), visual search (e.g., Ben-David & Algom, 2009; Schweickert, Fortin, & Sung, 2007), and response times (e.g., Diederich & Colonius, 2004; Rouder, Lu, Speckman, Sun, & Jiang, 2005; Schweickert & Giorgini, 1999; Wenger, Negash, Petersen, & Petersen, 2010), to applications to autism spectrum disorders (e.g., Johnson, Blaha, Houpt, & Townsend, 2010), healthy aging (e.g., Gottlob, 2007), and mild cognitive impairment (Wenger et al., 2010). The first applications of the constructs of SFT/DFP were to the modal issue of serial and parallel processing (e.g., Townsend and Fifić, 2004; Wenger and Townsend, 2001), psychological modeling and assessment (e.g., Carter, Neufeld, & Benn, 1998; Neufeld, Vollick, Carter, Boksman, & Jetté, 2002), visual search (e.g., Fifić, Townsend, & Eidels, 2008), and processing of facial stimuli (e.g., Donnelly, Cornes, & Menneer, 2012; Fitousi & Wenger, 2013; Ingvalson & Wenger, 2005; Mestry, Menneer, Wenger, & Donnelly, 2012). More recently, we see applications to audiovisual integration (e.g., Altieri, 2013; Altieri & Hudock, 2014; Altieri, Townsend, & Wenger, 2014; Altieri & Townsend, 2011; Altieri & Wenger, 2013), olfactory–visual integration (e.g., Höchenberger, Busch, & Ohla, 2015), visual word processing and reading (e.g., Houpt, Townsend, & Donkin, 2014; Staub, 2011), including dyslexia (e.g., Houpt, Sussman, Townsend, & Newman, 2015), working memory capacity (e.g., Endres, Houpt, Donkin, & Finn, 2015; Heathcote et al., 2015; Yu, Chang, & Yang, 2014), and threat detection (e.g., Richards, Hadwin, Benson, Wenger, & Donnelly, 2011).

Having demonstrated the breadth of SFT's influence, we will delve a little deeper into applications of the theory by describing the question, approach, and findings from specific applications. Wenger and Townsend (2001) was one of the earliest applications, using SFT/DFP to test the gestalt nature of facial stimuli. As they described, the hypothesis that a face may be perceived as a gestalt has direct implications for information processing, particularly the architecture, process independence, stopping rule, and capacity processes outlined by Townsend and Nozawa (1995). Using an experimental task typical to face-perception studies (i.e., asking the participant to indicate if a given feature, say a nose, was present), they outlined four potential outcomes that would be consistent with gestalt processing: a parallel exhaustive system that preserves independence and exhibits at a minimum unlimited capacity processing; a parallel exhaustive system that violates independence and exhibits supercapacity processing; a coactive architecture that preserves independence and exhibits supercapacity processing; and a coactive architecture that violates independence and exhibits supercapacity processing (O'Toole, Wenger, & Townsend, 2001; Townsend & Wenger, 2014).[3]

Having outlined the information processing characteristics that would be consistent with gestalt processing, they then examined the extent to which these characteristics were evidenced in human learners using the double factorial paradigm (DFP). Observers were asked, on each trial, to indicate if they detected the presence of at least one (of two) targets; if no targets were present, they were to respond in the negative. The two targets were the eyes and mouth, and each target could be clear or blurry, resulting in a 2 (target: eyes, mouth) × 2 (clarity level: clear, blurry) × 2 (target presence: present, absent) factorial design. Targets were presented in standard faces, inverted faces, scrambled faces, or in their standard positions with the facial context removed. Survivor functions for the latency data were consistent with a parallel architecture utilizing a self-termination stopping rule that exhibits limited capacity processing. Architecture did not appear to change across presentation contexts, only the efficiency of the target search, with canonical faces being faster in some instances but slower than others. For example, all observers were found to be faster in scrambled than canonical faces but faster for canonical faces than inverted faces. Additionally, there was some evidence of coactivation across conditions and no evidence of exhaustive processing. Wenger and Townsend concluded that though more work was clearly needed—particularly regarding the evidence of coactivation in the scrambled-face condition—as these data did not appear to support gestalt processing of faces.

Ingvalson and Wenger (2005) followed up on Wenger and Townsend's (2001) study into the gestalt nature of faces by investigating the extent to which individuals utilize configural and featural information in face perception as characterized in the dual mode hypothesis. The dual mode hypothesis suggests that featural and configural information are simultaneously available, independent of orientation, both sources of information are processed independently, and orientation determines which source dominates processing (Leder & Bruce, 2000; Searcy & Bartlett, 1996). Ingvalson and Wenger noted that the three assumptions of the dual-mode hypothesis could be described using the terminology of SFT, and thereby tested utilizing the DFP. They predicted that the dual mode hypothesis would be best supported by evidence of a parallel architecture that preserves independence and exhibits unlimited-to-supercapacity with a self-terminating stopping rule.[4]

Observers were asked to indicate whether the second of a pair of images was different from the first based on the configuration or on the features; detection of any change was sufficient for a positive response and a failure to detect any change was to receive a negative response. Configural and featural changes could be ambiguous or unambiguous, for a 2 (change type: configural, featural) × 2 (clarity: ambiguous, unambiguous) × 2 (change presence: present, absent) factorial design. Further, to test the dual mode hypothesis' claim that this pattern of information processing was unique to human faces, facelike schematics were used along with faces. Across stimulus types and orientations, RTs were consistent with a parallel architecture that evidenced supercapacity processing with a self-terminating stopping rule, and suggested a violation of independence. To determine the effects of inversion, those trials on which there was only one ambiguous change were compared in their upright and inverted orientations with the expectation that there should be a processing cost to configural information in the inverted condition, but no change in the processing of featural information and that this effect should hold only for faces. While a processing cost was seen for configural information in the inverted condition, it was seen in both the face and the schematic stimuli. Ingvalson and Wenger concluded that while the dual mode hypothesis' claims regarding the separation of featural and configural information and the impact of inversion were supported, these effects were not limited to the processing of human faces.

Similar to configural and featural information is global and local processing. Specifically, information can be processed at the level of the global stimulus information or at the local stimulus details.The global-precedence hypothesis states that people process global stimulus information without interference from local stimuli (Kimchi, 1992; Navon, 1977). However, the global-precedence hypothesis is thought to be disrupted in individuals who have autism spectrum disorders (ASD), and instead show a bias for identifying detail information (Frith, 1989; Frith & Happé, 1994; Happé & Frith, 2006). This bias toward detail-level information is referred to as the weak central coherence theory of ASD, and refers to a poor ability to integrate information into a whole. Support for this hypothesis is mixed, with some researchers suggesting that the ability to integrate information remains intact in ASD, but individuals also have an enhanced ability to process local information relative to controls (Mottron & Belleville, 1993).

Like gestalt processing of faces and the dual mode hypothesis, the weak central coherence theory lends itself to the use of SFT/DFP. Previous work indicated that typically developing individuals process hierarchical stimuli via a parallel architecture exhibiting a self-terminating stopping rule and unlimited capacity (including some individual variations, such as some individuals who show supercapacity exhaustive processing Blaha et al., 2007). To determine if this information processing pattern would be violated in individuals with ASD, consistent with the weak central coherence theory, Johnson et al. (2010) recruited 10 high functioning adolescents and young adults diagnosed with ASD and 11 age- and cognitive-ability matched typically developing controls. Participants engaged in a divided-attention task, in which the presence of a stimulus at either the global or local level was sufficient for a "yes" response and the presence of a stimulus at neither level should receive a "no" response. Stimuli at both levels were right-facing arrows; the absence of stimuli at both levels was marked with dashes. Stimuli could be either high or low salience for a 2 (level: global, local) × 2 (salience: high, low) × 2 (target presence: present, absent) design.

Johnson et al.'s results showed that all participants were faster and more accurate at the global than the local level. As in Blaha et al.'s (2007) study of typically developing adults, the control observers in Johnson et al.'s study showed evidence of a parallel architecture and most showed evidence of a self-terminating stopping rule. All control observers showed evidence of limited capacity and of inhibitory interaction between the channels. In contrast, the observers with ASD also showed evidence of a parallel architecture, but with facilitatory interaction and an exhaustive stopping rule. Though individuals with ASD and typically developing controls were found to process the stimuli differently, these data were taken as a refutation of the weak central coherence theory because individuals with ASD were found to process global and local information in parallel. Thus, not only has the SFT allowed for careful assessment of theory of information processing, recent applications to populations other than typically developing controls allows for greater understanding of the information processing system as a whole.

A New Application

In this final section of the chapter we describe a new application of SFT/DFP, one in which the timing of a feature of the electroencephalogram (EEG), recorded during the performance of a perceptual learning task, is used along with RTs to draw inferences regarding processing characteristics. Our presentation here is, of necessity, brief. A full description of the study can be found in Wenger and Rhoten (in preparation).

The central question for this work is the extent to which improvements in perceptual performance as a function of practice with multielement stimuli may lead to organization of the stimulus information into a meaningful perceptual object. This has been referred to as "unitization" (e.g., Goldstone, 2000) or the learning of a Gestalt (e.g., Blaha & Townsend, 2004; Blaha et al., 2007), and is coherent with the SFT characterization of a gestalt, as reviewed earlier (see also O'Toole et al., 2001; Townsend & Wenger, 2014; Wenger & Townsend, 2001). Evidence consistent with this hypothesis can be found in Blaha et al. (2007), who observed dramatic improvements in capacity as a function of perceptual practice. One goal of the present effort was to determine whether timings on a feature of the EEG—specifically, the lateralized readiness potential (LRP)—could be analyzed using the SFT/DFP measures that are applied to RTs in order to provide neural evidence consistent with the behavioral evidence.

The LRP is a negative-going waveform, measured in central electrodes contralateral to the motor response that it precedes (Coles, 1989; Hackley & Miller, 1995; Miller & Hackley, 1992; Mordkoff & Grosjean, 2001; Ray, Slobounov, Mordkoff, Johnston, & Simon, 2000). The LRP is estimated by subtracting the ipsilateral from the contralateral potential for each hand. This is done so as to have a measure that reflects only movement-related parameters, and the LRP is generally interpreted as reflecting motor preparation for an intended response. Our concern was with the start time for the LRP, here operationalized as the earliest time at which the LRP became reliably less than 0 (following the approach in Kuefner, Jacques, Prieto, & Rossion, 2010).

Four undergraduate students (three females, 19–21 year old) from the University of Oklahoma were paid to participate in 12–15 sessions of the study. The participants were all right-handed and reported having normal to corrected-normal vision.

Stimuli consisted of either 0, 1, or 2 contrast-defined target pattern features at varying contrast levels. These features were taken from the original line-drawing of the Cheshire cat in Lewis Carroll's *Alice in Wonderland* (1865). Stimuli (see Fig. 16.2)

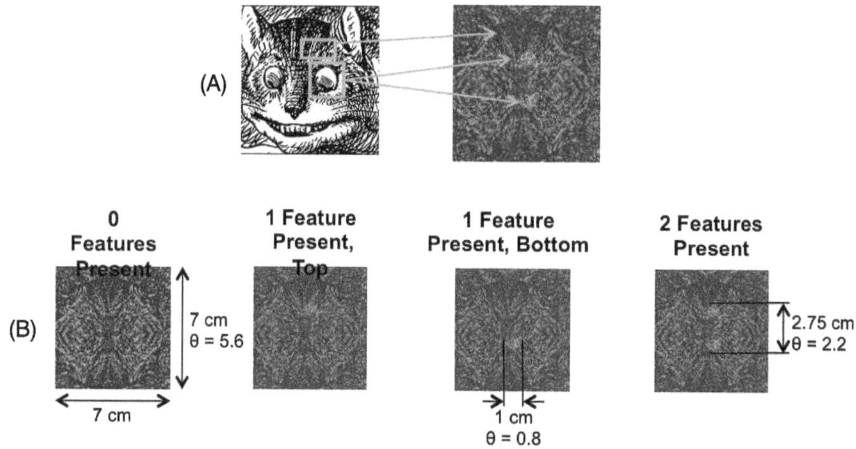

Figure 16.2 (A) Construction of the stimuli; (B) example of the four types of stimuli with dimensions (θ = size in degrees of visual angle).

were constructed using the left eye as the target feature and the region above the eye for the background pattern, to which Gaussian noise was added. Features were sized such that both could be foveated simultaneously. Stimuli were constructed at levels of contrast (Michaelson ratio) running from 1% to 60%, in steps of 0.1%.

Participants began by performing a DFP detection task with stimuli at two suprathreshold levels of contrast (30%, 60%). This was followed by an extended period of perceptual practice using a modified three-down one-up adaptive staircase procedure, which included target–absent trials (see Wenger & Rasche, 2006; Wenger, Copeland, Bittner, & Thomas, 2008). Following this, participants repeated the DFP detection task at three levels of contrast (final threshold, 30%, 60%). All analyses were conducted at the level of the individual participant, and the analyses of the distributional contrasts and the capacity coefficients were performed according to the algorithms in Houpt and Townsend (2010, 2012), Houpt, Blaha, McIntire, Havig, and Townsend (2014). We report here results for one representative participant.

This participant showed substantial and reliable reductions in detection thresholds along with substantial and reliable increases in false alarm rates (Fig. 16.3A), consistent with our previous work (Wenger & Rasche, 2006; Wenger et al., 2008). Examination of the RTs and the start times for the LRPs revealed a modest but reliable correlation (Fig. 16.3B). For this and the analyses to follow, we restricted consideration to those LRPs that (a) preceded RTs by at least 100 ms and (b) were obtained on trials on which the participants response was correct. Mean interaction contrasts on the start times for the LRPs as a function of contrast and training are presented in Table 16.1. Both of the contrasts before training and the stimulus contrast at threshold after training were not reliably different from 0, suggesting some form of serial processing. Mean interaction contrasts at both 30% and 60% levels of stimulus contrast after practice were reliably positive, suggesting some form of parallel processing. Survivor function interaction contrasts are presented in Fig. 16.3C, and were analyzed

Table 16.1 Mean interaction contrasts calculated on the start times for the LRPs, as a function of contrast and test time

Contrast	Test relative to practice	
	Before	After
Threshold	–	2
30%	10	109*
60%	11	88*

* Indicates $p < 0.001$.

using the methods of Houpt and Townsend (2010). The contrasts before training and the contrast at threshold after training are negative early and go positive later, though fail to deviate reliably from 0 at any time. However, the interaction contrast functions for stimuli at 30% and 60% contrast after training were reliably positive across the majority of their range. Taken together, the interaction contrasts at the levels of the mean and the survivor function, estimated using the start times for the LRPs, suggest that this observer processed the features in a serial exhaustive manner before training, and in a parallel self-terminating manner after training.

Capacity coefficients estimated on the start times for the LRPs as a function of training and contrast are presented in Fig. 16.3D. The capacity coefficients for the two contrast levels before training were reliably less than 1 (per Houpt & Townsend, 2012), and the capacity coefficient for 60% contrast after training was reliably greater than 1, indicating a shift from limited to supercapacity processing as a function of practice. In sum, it appears that perceptual practice with these two contrast-defined features produced a shift from serial exhaustive, limited-capacity processing to parallel-self-terminating, unlimited to supercapacity processing. Not reported here (see Wenger and Rhoten, in preparation, for details) are the analyses of the RTs for this observer. Critically, the results of those analyses are completely consistent with those of using the start times of the LRPs and suggest that perceptual learning may produce significant qualitative changes in perceptual processing, rather than simply an increase in the efficiency of otherwise unchanged aspects perceptual function.

Conclusions

The SFT/DFP in its current form is an expression of a commitment to generality and strong-inference hypothesis testing. It represents a refinement of ideas and pretheoretical commitments that can be appreciated in at least two of its intellectual predecessors, the parallel–serial testing paradigm and the trichotomy method. These two significant and substantive strengths have allowed this approach to be the source of insights in an impressive range of topics. And its generality with respect to the timing of measurable

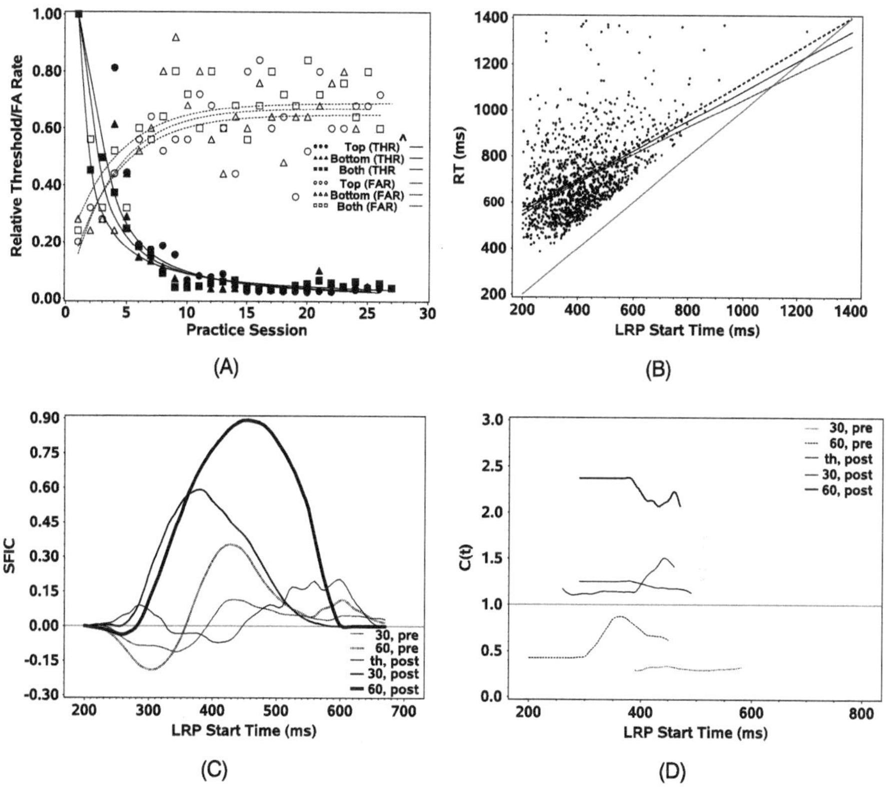

Figure 16.3 (A) Relative thresholds and false alarm rates from the practice trials; (B) correlation between the start times for the LRPs and the observed RTs; (C) survivor function interaction contrasts on the start times for the LRPs as a function of training level and contrast; (D) capacity coefficients calculated on the start times for the LRPs as a function of training level and contrast.

events suggests its potent utility in new applications, including the timing of neural events such as those associated with EEG. All of this suggests that, at 20 years on from its original publication, the SFT/DFP approach is one whose continuing evolution promises to be the basis for substantial theoretical and empirical advances.

References

Altieri, N. (2013). Audiovisual integration: An introduction to behavioral and neuro-cognitive methods. *Frontiers in Psychology, 4*.

Altieri, N., & Hudock, D. (2014). Hearing impairment and audiovisual speech integration ability: A case study report. *Frontiers in Psychology, 5*.

Altieri, N., & Townsend, J. T. (2011). An assessment of behavioral dynamic information processing measures in audiovisual speech perception. *Frontiers in Psychology, 2*.

Altieri, N., Townsend, J. T., & Wenger, M. J. (2014). A measure for assessing the effects of audiovisual speech integration. *Behavior Research Methods*, *46*(2), 406–415.

Altieri, N., & Wenger, M. J. (2013). Neural dynamics of audiovisual speech integration under variable listening conditions: An individual participant analysis. *Frontiers in Psychology*, *4*.

Ben-David, B. M., & Algom, D. (2009). Species of redundancy in visual target detection. *Journal of Experimental Psychology: Human Perception and Performance*, *35*(4), 958.

Blaha, L. M., Johnson, S. A., & Townsend, J. T. (2007). An information processing investigation of hierarchical form perception: Evidence for parallel processing. *Visual Cognition*, *15*, 73–77.

Blaha, L. M., & Townsend, J. T. (2004). *From nonsense to Gestalt: The influence of configural learning on processing capacity*. Paper presented at the 2004 Meeting of the Society for mathematical psychology. Ann Arbor, MI. July.

Bridgman, P. W. (1945). Some general principles of operational analysis. *Psychological Review*, *52*(5), 246.

Carroll, L. (1865). *Alice in wonderland*. London: Macmillan.

Carter, J. R., Neufeld, R. W., & Benn, K. (1998). Application of process models in assessment psychology: Potential assets and challenges. *Psychological Assessment*, *10*(4), 379.

Coles, M. G. (1989). Modern mind-brain reading: Psychophysiology, physiology, and cognition. *Psychophysiology*, *26*(3), 251–269.

Diederich, A., & Colonius, H. (2004). Bimodal and trimodal multisensory enhancement: Effects of stimulus onset and intensity on reaction time. *Perception & Psychophysics*, *66*(8), 1388–1404.

Donnelly, N., Cornes, K., & Menneer, T. (2012). An examination of the processing capacity of features in the Thatcher illusion. *Attention, Perception, & Psychophysics*, *74*(7), 1475–1487.

Dzhafarov, E. N. (2003). Selective influence through conditional independence. *Psychometrika*, *68*, 7–26.

Dzhfarov, E. N., Schweickert, R., & Sung, K. (2004). Mental architectures with selectively influenced but stochastically interdependent components. *Journal of Mathematical Psychology*, *48*, 51–64.

Endres, M. J., Houpt, J. W., Donkin, C., & Finn, P. R. (2015). Working memory capacity and redundant information processing efficiency. *Frontiers in Psychology*, *6*, 594.

Fifić, M., Townsend, J. T., & Eidels, A. (2008). Studying visual search using systems factorial methodology with target—distractor similarity as the factor. *Perception & Psychophysics*, *70*(4), 583–603.

Fisher, D. L., & Goldstein, W. M. (1983). Stochastic PERT networks as models of cognition: Derivation of the mean, variance, and distribution of reaction time using order-of-processing diagrams. *Journal of Mathematical Psychology*, *27*, 121–151.

Fitousi, D., & Wenger, M. J. (2013). Variants of independence in the perception of facial identity and expression. *Journal of Experimental Psychology: Human Perception and Performance*, *39*(1), 133.

Frith, U. (1989). *Autism: Explaining the enigma*. Wiley Online Library.

Frith, U., & Happé, F. (1994). Autism: Beyond "theory of mind". *Cognition*, *50*(1), 115–132.

Garner, W. R., Hake, H. W., & Eriksen, C. W. (1956). Operationism and the concept of perception. *Psychological Review*, *63*(3), 149.

Goldstone, R. L. (2000). Unitization during category learning. *Journal of Experimental Psychology: Human Perception and Performance*, *26*, 86–112.

Gottlob, L. R. (2007). Aging and capacity in the same-different judgment. *Aging, Neuropsychology, and Cognition, 14*(1), 55–69.

Hackley, S. A., & Miller, J. (1995). Response complexity and precue interval effects on the lateralized readiness potential. *Psychophysiology, 32*(3), 230–241.

Happé, F., & Frith, U. (2006). The weak coherence account: detail-focused cognitive style in autism spectrum disorders. *Journal of Autism and Developmental Disorders, 36*(1), 5–25.

Heathcote, A., Coleman, J. R., Eidels, A., Watson, J. M., Houpt, J., & Strayer, D. L. (2015). Working memory's workload capacity. *Memory & Cognition*, 1–17.

Höchenberger, R., Busch, N. A., & Ohla, K. (2015). Nonlinear response speedup in bimodal visual-olfactory object identification. *Frontiers in Psychology, 6*.

Houpt, J. W., Blaha, L. M., McIntire, J. P., Havig, P. R., & Townsend, J. T. (2014). Systems factorial technology with R. *Behavior Research Methods, 46*(2), 307–330.

Houpt, J. W., Sussman, B. L., Townsend, J. T., & Newman, S. D. (2015). Dyslexia and configural perception of character sequences. *Frontiers in Psychology, 6*.

Houpt, J. W., & Townsend, J. T. (2010). The statistical properties of the survivor interaction contrast. *Journal of Mathematical Psychology, 54*(5), 446–453.

Houpt, J. W., & Townsend, J. T. (2012). Statistical measures for workload capacity analysis. *Journal of Mathematical Psychology, 56*(5), 341–355.

Houpt, J. W., Townsend, J. T., & Donkin, C. (2014). A new perspective on visual word processing efficiency. *Acta Psychologica, 145*, 118–127.

Ingvalson, E. M., & Wenger, M. J. (2005). A strong test of the dual mode hypothesis. *Perception & Psychophysics, 67*, 14–35.

Johnson, S. A., Blaha, L. M., Houpt, J. W., & Townsend, J. T. (2010). Systems factorial technology provides new insights on global–local information processing in autism spectrum disorders. *Journal of Mathematical Psychology, 54*(1), 53–72.

Kimchi, R. (1992). Primacy of wholistic processing and the global/local paradigm: A critical review. *Psychological Bulletin, 112*, 24–38.

Kuefner, D., Jacques, C., Prieto, E., & Rossion, B. (2010). Electrophysiological correlates of the composite face illusion: Disentangling perceptual and decisional components of holistic face processing in the human brain. *Brain and Cognition, 74*, 225–238.

Kujala, J. V., & Dzhafarov, E. N. (2008). Testing for selectivity in the dependence of random variables on external factors. *Journal of Mathematical Psychology, 52*(2), 128–144.

Leder, H., & Bruce, V. (2000). When inverted faces are recognized: The role of configural information in face recognition. *Quarterly Journal of Experimental Psychology: Human Experimental Psychology, 53A*, 513–536.

Mestry, N., Menneer, T., Wenger, M. J., & Donnelly, N. (2012). Identifying sources of configurality in three face processing tasks. *Frontiers in Psychology, 3*.

Miller, J., & Hackley, S. A. (1992). Electrophysiological evidence for temporal overlap among contingent mental processes. *Journal of Experimental Psychology. General, 121*(2), 195.

Mordkoff, J. T., & Grosjean, M. (2001). The lateralized readiness potential and response kinetics in response-time tasks. *Psychophysiology, 38*(5), 777–786.

Mottron, L., & Belleville, S. (1993). A study of perceptual analysis in a high-level autistic subject with exceptional graphic abilities. *Brain and Cognition, 23*(2), 279–309.

Navon, D. (1977). Forest behind trees: The precedence of global features in visual perception. *Cognitive Psychology, 9*, 353–383.

Neufeld, R. W. J., & McCarty, T. (1994). A formal analysis of stressor and stress-proneness effects on basic information processing. *British Journal of Mathematical and Statistical Psychology, 47*, 193–226.

Neufeld, R. W., Vollick, D., Carter, J. R., Boksman, K., & Jetté, J. (2002). Application of stochastic modeling to the assessment of group and individual differences in cognitive functioning. *Psychological Assessment*, *14*(3), 279.

O'Toole, A. J., Wenger, M. J., & Townsend, J. T. (2001). Quantitative models of perceiving and remembering faces: Precedents and possibilities. In M. J. Wenger, & J. T. Townsend (Eds.), *Computational, geometric and process perspectives on facial cognition: Contexts and challenges* (pp. 1–38). Mahwah, NJ: Erlbaum.

Platt, J. R. (1964). Strong inference. *Science*, *146*, 347–353.

Ray, W., Slobounov, S., Mordkoff, J., Johnston, J., & Simon, R. (2000). Rate of force development and the lateralized readiness potential. *Psychophysiology*, *37*(6), 757–765.

Richards, H. J., Hadwin, J. A., Benson, V., Wenger, M. J., & Donnelly, N. (2011). The influence of anxiety on processing capacity for threat detection. *Psychonomic Bulletin & Review*, *18*(5), 883–889.

Rouder, J. N., Lu, J., Speckman, P., Sun, D., & Jiang, Y. (2005). A hierarchical model for estimating response time distributions. *Psychonomic Bulletin & Review*, *12*(2), 195–223.

Schweickert, R. (1978). A critical path generalization of the additive factor method: Analysis of a Stroop task. *Journal of Mathematical Psychology*, *18*, 105–139.

Schweickert, R. (1982). The bias of an estimate of coupled slack in stochastic PERT networks. *Journal of Mathematical Psychology*, *26*, 1–12.

Schweickert, R. (1983). Latent network theory: Scheduling of processes in sentence verification and the Stroop effect. *Journal of Experimental Psychology: Learning, Memory, and Cognition*, *9*, 353–383.

Schweickert, R., Fisher, D. L., & Sung, K. (2012). *Discovering cognitive architecture by selectively influencing mental processes, Vol. 4*. World Scientific.

Schweickert, R., Fortin, C., & Sung, K. (2007). Concurrent visual search and time reproduction with cross-talk. *Journal of Mathematical Psychology*, *51*(2), 99–121.

Schweickert, R., & Giorgini, M. (1999). Response time distributions: Some simple effects of factors selectively influencing mental processes. *Psychonomic Bulletin and Review*, *6*, 269–288.

Schweickert, R., Giorgini, M., & Dzhafarov, E. (2000). Selective influence and response time cumulative distribution functions in serial-parallel task networks. *Journal of Mathematical Psychology*, *44*, 504–535.

Schweickert, R., & Townsend, J. T. (1989). A trichotomy method: Interactions of factors prolonging sequential and concurrent mental processes in stochastic PERT networks. *Journal of Mathematical Psychology*, *33*, 328–347.

Schweickert, R., Townsend, J.T., & Fisher, D.L. (1987). Simple tests distinguishing sequential and concurrent processes in task networks. Paper presented at *the meeting of the Psychonomic Society*, Seattle, WA.

Searcy, J. H., & Bartlett, J. C. (1996). Inversion and processing of component and spatial-relational information in faces. *Journal of Experimental Psychology: Human Perception and Performance*, *22*, 904–915.

Snodgrass, J. G., & Townsend, J. T. (1980). Comparing parallel and serial models: Theory and implementation. *Journal of Experimental Psychology: Human Perception and Performance*, *6*(2), 330.

Staub, A. (2011). Word recognition and syntactic attachment in reading: Evidence for a staged architecture. *Journal of Experimental Psychology. General*, *140*(3), 407.

Sung, K. (2008). Serial and parallel attentive visual searches: Evidence from cumulative distribution functions of response times. *Journal of Experimental Psychology: Human Perception and Performance*, *34*(6), 1372.

Townsend, J. T. (1969, April). *Mock parallel and serial models and experimental detection of these*. Paper presented at the *Purdue Centennial Symposium on Information Processing*, Purdue University, West Lafayette, Indiana.

Townsend, J. T. (1971). A note on the identifiability of parallel and serial processes. *Perception & Psychophysics*, *10*, 161–163.

Townsend, J. T. (1972). Some results concerning the identifiability of parallel and serial processes. *British Journal of Mathematical and Statistical Psychology*, *25*, 168–199.

Townsend, J. T. (1974). Issues and models concerning the processing of a finite number of inputs. In B. H. Kantowitz (Ed.), *Human information processing: Tutorials in performance and cognition* (pp. 133–168). Hillsdale, NJ: Erlbaum.

Townsend, J. T. (1976). A stochastic theory of matching processes. *Journal of Mathematical Psychology*, *14*, 1–52.

Townsend, J. T. (2008). Mathematical psychology: Prospects for the 21st century. *Journal of Mathematical Psychology*, *52*(5), 269–280.

Townsend, J. T., & Ashby, F. G. (1983). *Stochastic modeling of elementary psychological processes*. Cambridge: Cambridge University Press.

Townsend, J. T., & Fifić, M. (2004). Parallel versus serial processing and individual differences in high-speed search in human memory. *Perception & Psychophysics*, *66*, 953–962.

Townsend, J. T., & Nozawa, G. (1995). On the spatio-temporal properties of elementary perception: An investigation of parallel, serial, and coactive theories. *Journal of Mathematical Psychology*, *39*, 321–359.

Townsend, J., & Schweickert, R. (1985). Interactive effects of factors prolonging processes in latent mental networks. In G. d'Ydewalle (Ed.), *Cognition, information processing, and motivation* (3rd ed.). Amsterdam: North Holland.

Townsend, J. T., & Schweickert, R. (1989). Toward the trichotomy method: Laying the foundation of stochastic mental networks. *Journal of Mathematical Psychology*, *33*, 309–327.

Townsend, J.T., & Snodgrass, J.G. (1974, November). A serial vs. parallel testing paradigm when "same" and "different" comparison rates differ. Paper presented at *the meeting of the Psychonomic Society*, Boston MA.

Townsend, J. T., & Snodgrass, J. G. (1977). Masking effects of similar and dissimilar letters: A test of the interactive channels model. *Perceptual and Motor Skills*, *44*, 1212–1228.

Townsend, J. T., & Wenger, M. J. (2004a). The serial-parallel dilemma: A case study in a linkage of theory and method. *Psychonomic Bulletin & Review*, *11*, 391–418.

Townsend, J. T., & Wenger, M. J. (2004b). A theory of interactive parallel processing: New capacity measures and predictions for a response time inequality series. *Psychological Review*, *111*, 1003–1035.

Townsend, J., & Wenger, M. (2014). On the dynamic perceptual characteristics of Gestalten: Theory-based methods. In *Oxford handbook of perceptual organization*. Oxford University Press.

Townsend, J. T., Wenger, M. J., & Houpt, J. W. (in press). Uncovering mental architecture and related mechanisms in elementary human perception, cognition and action. In E. J. Wagenmaker (Ed.), *The Stevens handbook of experimental psychology and cognitive neuroscience*.

Ulrich, R., Miller, J., & Schröter, H. (2007). Testing the race model inequality: An algorithm and computer programs. *Behavior Research Methods*, *39*(2), 291–302.

Wenger, M. J. (1999). On the whats and hows of retrieval in the acquisition of a simple skill. *Journal of Experimental Psychology: Learning, Memory and Cognition*, *25*, 1137–1160.

Wenger, M. J., Copeland, A. M., Bittner, J. L., & Thomas, R. D. (2008). Evidence for criterion shifts in visual perceptual learning: Data and implications. *Perception & Psychophysics, 70*, 1248–1273.

Wenger, M. J., Negash, S., Petersen, R. C., & Petersen, L. (2010). Modeling and estimating recall processing capacity: Sensitivity and diagnostic utility in application to mild cognitive impairment. *Journal of Mathematical Psychology, 54*, 73–89.

Wenger, M. J., & Rasche, C. (2006). Perceptual learning in contrast detection: Presence and costs of shifts in response criteria. *Psychonomic Bulletin & Review, 13*, 656–661.

Wenger, M.J., & Rhoten, S.E. (in preparation). *Changes in process architecture and capacity as a function of perceptual learning: Evidence from EEG.*

Wenger, M. J., & Townsend, J. T. (2001). Faces as Gestalt stimuli: Process characteristics. In M. J. Wenger, & J. T. Townsend (Eds.), *Computational, geometric and process perspectives on facial cognition* (pp. 229–284). Mahwah, NJ: Erlbaum.

Williams, P., Eidels, A., & Townsend, J. T. (2014). The resurrection of Tweedledum and Tweedledee: Bimodality cannot distinguish serial and parallel processes. *Psychonomic Bulletin & Review, 21*(5), 1165–1173.

Yamani, Y., McCarley, J. S., Mounts, J. R., & Kramer, A. F. (2013). Spatial interference between attended items engenders serial visual processing. *Attention, Perception, & Psychophysics, 75*(2), 229–243.

Yu, J-C., Chang, T-Y., & Yang, C-T. (2014). Individual differences in working memory capacity and workload capacity. *Frontiers in Psychology, 5*.

Endnotes

1. A more comprehensive review of the intellectual history can be found in Townsend, Wenger, and Houpt (in press).
2. Although the PST has not been applied as widely as the SFT/DFP, it has seen rather diverse application, including application to questions in clinical science (e.g., Neufeld & McCarty, 1994).
3. The notion of a nonindependent coactive system may at first consideration seem odd, given that such systems intermingle channel activations prior to a decisional operator. However, if the two processing channels have any source of correlation prior to the combination of their activations, such as might occur in early perceptual processing, then the channels prior to combination would be dependent in their rates.
4. It is interesting to note that the dual-mode hypothesis actually does not predict that faces will be processed as gestalts, as that would require an exhaustive stopping rule (O'Toole et al., 2001; Townsend & Wenger, 2014).

Systems-Factorial-Technology-Disclosed Stochastic Dynamics of Stroop Processing in the Cognitive Neuroscience of Schizophrenia

17

Reggie Taylor, Jean Théberge, Peter Williamson, Maria Densmore, Richard W.J. Neufeld
The University of Western Ontario, London, ON, Canada

Introduction

Schizophrenia (Sz) has long been considered to be among the most challenging syndromes in clinical science (e.g., Maher, 1966). Because of the prominence of thought disorder in Sz symptomatology, performance on cognitive tasks has been a focus of study. Mathematical modeling of cognitive performance has revealed several functions that are spared by the disorder (e.g., short-term or working memory; response registration) and functions that are adversely affected (stimulus encoding, preparation and transformation of stimulation for collateral processes; Neufeld, 2007a; Neufeld, Boksman, Vollick, George, & Carter, 2010; Boksman et al., 2005).

Here we address Stroop performance in conjunction with the monitoring of glutamatergic activity [levels of glutamine (Gln) and glutamate (Glu)] in the anterior cingulate cortex (ACC; Taylor, Schaefer et al., 2015; Taylor, Neufeld et al., 2015). Abnormal ACC functioning coupled with cognitive encoding demands has been one of the more reliable findings in the cognitive neuroscience of Sz (Neufeld, 2007a; Taylor, Neufeld et al., 2015). Likewise, glutamatergic abnormalities have been reliably documented in Sz (for reviews, see Williamson & Allman, 2011, 2012). The present developments illustrate the potential value of formal modeling of cognitive performance in maximizing the functional significance of glutamatergic abnormalities, studied here via functional magnetic resonance spectroscopy (fMRS) at 7.0 T. Potential contributions go beyond the present application, and extend more broadly, to functional neuroimaging generally.

The Stroop task is defensibly the most prominent selective-attention task in cognitive science (Eidels, Townsend, & Algom, 2010). Its wide usage extends to clinical cognitive science (Macleod, 2010), including the study of cognitive performance in Sz (Minzenberg, Laird, Thelen, Carter, & Glahn, 2009). In clinical science, the Stroop task typically requires the naming of the ink color in which a word is written, the naming of the color of a color patch (color-only) or the reading of a color-neutral word (word only). Speed, and possibly accu-

Systems Factorial Technology, DOI: 10.1016/B978-0-12-804315-8.00021-5

racy, suffer on trials where the color name is different from the color of its letters (color–word incongruent condition) relative to trials where the two agree (color–word congruent condition) or where color-only is presented. The mathematical signatures of the cognitive structure and workings of task transaction, authorized by explicitly analytical proofs (Townsend & Nozawa, 1995), implemented in the Stroop task (Eidels et al., 2010), invites a similar analysis of Stroop performance in Sz.

Overview of fMRS Technique and Results

Magnetic resonance spectroscopy (MRS) is often used to monitor concentrations of metabolites that have considerable contributions from their protons to the MRS spectrum in a small (typically 1–10 cm^3), localized area of the brain. Examples of such measurable metabolites include glutamate, glutamine, N-acetylaspartate, creatine, choline, and myo-inositol, to name a few (Govindaraju, Young, & Maudsley, 2000). fMRS is an extension of its parent technique, MRS, with the added dimension of time. It is possible to measure dynamic metabolic correlates of cognitive-functional activity if an fMRS dataset is acquired.

Taylor, Schaefer et al. (2015) showed that the Stroop task generates increases in ACC glutamate among Healthy Control (HC) participants. Following this, Taylor, Neufeld et al. (2015) examined ACC levels of Glu and Gln among Sz, major depressive disorder (MDD), and HC participants during Stroop performance. Using results from this, as well as findings from previous Stroop-task fMRI studies, our study targeted a location centered medially and bilaterally in the Anterior Cingulate Cortex (ACC). Our own fMRI follow-up study, which participants completed 1 to 1.5 hours after their fMRS session[1] (Taylor, Neufeld et al. 2015; Taylor, Théberge, Williamson, Densmore, & Neufeld, 2016) ascertained activation in the selected site.

The essential glutamatergic results were as follows: Unlike either control group, the Sz group evinced increased Gln during the first block of Stroop trials, which receded back to the baseline level during the first recovery period. The same pattern occurred for the HC group, except for Glu rather than Gln. The MDD group showed only a second-block reduction in Glu from the preceding recovery period. Also, during trial-block 1, for both clinical groups, there was a negative correlation between incremental Gln occurring to the more demanding, incongruent trials, and individuals' mean incongruent-trial response latencies.

Disruption of the Gln–Glu replenishment cycle and possible indirect involvement of Gln in task performance were theoretically integrated with the obtained pattern of fMRS findings. Tentative mechanisms of disruption in Gln–Glu neurochemical dynamics are stipulated in the original article (Taylor, Neufeld et al., 2015). The present developments, then, focus on identifying cognitive-model properties that defensibly supervene on the observed Gln and Glu deviations and their proposed mechanisms.

Assets of Current Modeling Context

Mathematically Modeled Cognitive Deviation in Schizophrenia

Experimental paradigms from mainstream cognitive psychology, such as those directed to visual and memory search (Townsend & Ashby, 1983), have been used to separate out spared and affected processes in Sz.[2] Empirical evidence, including mathematical modeling of cognitive-performance data, has pointed to stimulus encoding as an Sz-affected process. Stimulus encoding entails the cognitive preparation and transformation of presenting stimuli into a format undergirding other processes (e.g., extracting physical features of an alphanumeric probe so as to ascertain its presence in a memorized list of items through template matching). Experimental isolation of this process, and its prolongation in Sz, has capitalized upon divergent experimental paradigms (reviewed in Neufeld, 2007a; Neufeld et al., 2010). Clinical significance, such as potential involvement of protracted completion of encoding in thought-content symptomatology (delusions and thematic hallucinations; cf. Yates, 1966), has also been formally explored (e.g., Neufeld, 2007a; Neufeld, Vollick, & Highgate, 1993).

Formal modeling of the encoding process has indicated that the speed of completing constituent encoding operations (encoding subprocesses, such as implementing individual alphanumeric features) is preserved in Sz. In SFT terms, cognitive-workload capacity within the subprocess level appears *not* to have suffered. Efficiency of its deployment, however, has failed to survive intact. Reduced efficiency here takes the form of additional subprocesses evidently being required to complete the encoding process. Importing a race-horse analogy, the actual pace of running is preserved, but the route taken lies closer to the outside rail, requiring more strides to complete the consequently expanded circuit.

Possible sources of the added subprocesses include, for example, preliminary activity, required to marshal the encoding apparatus. Bluhm et al. (2007) have reported abnormal resting-state, default-network neural circuitry in Sz, consonant with potential delay in assembling resources to the service of presented cognitive-encoding demands (see also Penner et al., 2016). Drawing on a military analogy, staging of combat units is less facilitative of scrambling to an external challenge. Moreover, Williamson and Allman (2012) have cited evidence of reduced suppression of the default network, potentially exacerbating task-network recruitment. In addition to the possible nature of added subprocesses, there may be a failure to tag those already completed, producing repetition ("novelty excess" Hemsley, 1993, 1994). As well, encoding of extra stimulus features, not essential to correct responding, may be undertaken (stopping-rule impairment; "disengagement deficit" Cromwell & Dokecki, 1968).

Empirical support for the present account emanates from various experimental paradigms. This support has involved the synthesis of trace-susceptibility theory (Chechile, 1987) with multidimensional scaling of interstimulus similarity judgments (Carter & Neufeld, 1999) and their neuro-connectionist model extensions (Carter & Neufeld, 2007); the analysis of eye-movement dysfunction in visually tracking a continuously moving target (Neufeld, Mather, Merskey, & Russell, 1995); selected clinical measures, including card-sort tasks (Neufeld & Williamson, 1996); and relevant cognitive-performance findings from other settings (Neufeld, 2007a).

The modeling of Sz encoding performance in terms of an increase in the number of subprocesses and intact speed of subprocess execution is expected to extend to Stroop performance. The Stroop task is considered to be encoding intensive in that it requires the extraction of specified properties from a stimulus complex. These requirements increase in the color–word incongruent condition, where steps must be taken to filter out color–name impingements. In the results, we introduce a modeling framework based on Erlang distributions which includes parameters representing the rate of processing within a subprocess and the number of subprocesses. As an encoding-rich task, releasing the subprocess parameter, but fixing the subprocess-rate parameter, across groups, should accommodate Sz deviations in empirical performance data. Also, additivity of changes in performance latency should be observed with increased encoding load (specifically, word–color incongruency) and the entry of Sz diagnostic status, in compliance with model predictions.

Altogether, we report the modeling of Sz performance deviations on the Stroop task comprising, first, an additional number of constituent stimulus-encoding operations (subprocesses), and second, an intact rate of completing individual subprocesses themselves. The basic model is extended to accommodate an MDD psychiatric control group but with a smaller increase in the number of encoding subprocesses. Such modeling exploits parametric precursors of SFT (e.g., Townsend, 1984; Townsend & Ashby, 1983). We then illustrate the use of distribution-general measures emanating from SFT—the Capacity-OR-Coefficient, and the Capacity Ratio (described below)—to estimate within-trial dynamics of Stroop performance, in relation to the parametrically modeled clinical deviations. Other distribution-general measures of intratrial dynamics, nevertheless embodied by SFT developments (Townsend & Nozawa, 1995)—Race-Model and Grice Inequalities—also are brought to bear.

Latent Assets of Mathematical Cognitive Modeling in Clinical Cognitive Neuroscience

Analytical modeling of cognitive-task performance stands as a behavioral touchstone bridging fMRS and fMRI findings, potentially brokering their symptom and ecological significance. When it comes to fMRI measurement, a welcome by-product of stochastic dynamical modeling comprises estimation of cognitive-process time trajectories. Charting these temporal properties in principle can inform navigation of times of measurement interest, complementing regions of interest, in calibrating space-time coordinates of MRI signal selection. Methods of MRI-signal analysis, in turn, can be determined according to their congruity with cognitive-process dynamics (Neufeld, 2012; Taylor et al., 2016).

Another modeling asset is that results from diverse experimental paradigms can be integrated through a common formally modeled mechanism. For example, as described above, several sets of results can be understood as consequences of Sz-related additional encoding subprocesses.

By quantitatively stipulating the functional component of functional neuroimaging, cognitive modeling also can provide an antidote to the problem of "reverse logic" (Poldrack, 2011). Here, neuroimaging data itself is consulted to infer cognitive functions at work in undertaking an imaging-monitored cognitive task. Firmly anchoring functional inferences in an analytically detailed formal infrastructure (e.g., Ahn, Krawitz, Kim, Busemeyer, & Brown, 2011; White, Mumford, & Poldrack, 2012) can avoid appealing to patterns of neuro-activation for information as to the very functions whose neuro-circuitry is being studied.[3]

Mathematical cognitive modeling stands to broker clinical-symptom significance to abnormalities in monitored neurophysiological events. For example, a formal-theoretical analysis of potential consequences of prolonged encoding (Neufeld, 2007a; Neufeld et al., 2010) has indicated that intake of contextual cues anchoring other stimulus intake in its objective significance, can be disproportionately jeopardized ("context deficit"; e.g., Dobson & Neufeld, 1982; George & Neufeld, 1985). The remaining "reality dislodged information" stands to be fodder for "thought-content disorder" (delusions and thematic hallucinations).

To elaborate, degraded portions of the attentional field nevertheless may play an important role as objectifying anchors, thereby reality-grounding an episode of information intake. In the workplace setting, for instance, a pair of fellow employees quietly planning a hunting expedition, may have ready to hand an equipment catalogue and topographical map. If these items are attentionally peripheral, they may be missed during a limited encoding interval—more so with impaired completion of the encoding process. That which does get encoded, such as the occurrence of a quiet conversation, may be construed as personally significant, even conspiratorial (cf. Maher, 1988).

Note that certain prominent formal developments, specifically SFT (Townsend & Nozawa, 1995; Townsend & Wenger, 2004), allow for the evaluation of diverse forms of cognitive deficit (e.g., compromised cognitive architecture; diminished rate of dispatching cognitive subprocesses; suboptimal deployment of processing resources; e.g., Neufeld, Townsend et al., 2007; Shanahan, Townsend, & Neufeld, 2015; Townsend, Fifić, & Neufeld, 2007), with respect to their ecological criticality (Neufeld & Broga, 1981) or "functional significance." For example, alternate forms and amounts of deficit can be quantitatively transduced to the SFT Capacity Index and its related coefficients (Wenger & Townsend, 2000). Doing so allows for the expression within a common-metric framework, of the degree to which global cognitive-workload capacity has been affected, regardless of the source(s).

Mediating Different Levels of Imaging Analysis

Analytical modeling can act as a functional linchpin between different levels of functional neuro-imaging (e.g., fMRI, fMRS, functional magnetoencephalography). Each level in principle unveils a unique aspect of neuro-physiological workings on which cognitive functions, and their clinical deviations supervene (cf. Marr, 1982). Linking functional neuroimaging findings from alternate measurement methods, applied during different experimental sessions, and possibly in different settings, hinges on comparability of associated cognitive undertakings. For example, if fMRS-measured deviations in glutamatergic mechanisms are to be understood as a candidate source of Sz neuro-connectivity—shown by fMRI to be less concentrated at encoding-intensive sites and less adaptive to change in task demands (Taylor et al., 2016)—cognitive processing of Stroop trials must remain more or less constant between the two imaging sessions. Establishing cognitive-function invariance arguably requires the formal dissection of raw cognitive-performance data into its latent cognitive-processes, with an eye to their intersession stability.

Modeling fMRS-Monitored Stroop Performance

Current Stroop Paradigm

Performance on the Stroop task was undertaken during 7.0 T fMRS neuro-imaging, among Sz, major depressive disorder (MDD), and healthy control (HC) participant groups (fMRS methodology detailed in Taylor, Neufeld et al., 2015). In the present study, we included the following conditions: Participants were required to state the color of the ink in which a color–word was written with four possible color combinations (e.g., all combinations of the words red, green, blue, yellow in those colors). In the congruent condition, the word and ink-color matched, and in the incongruent condition, they mismatched, as above. In a third condition, a color of a "color-patch", consisting of a row of 5 "*X*"s, was to be named (color only). A fourth condition (word only) required the reading of a word (a color name) printed in white against a black background and now in lower case letters. Therefore, in every trial the correct response was the color of the ink, with the exception of the word-only condition in which the response was the word itself.

In SFT terms, the present incongruent condition is analogous to a single target condition as employed by Eidels et al. (2010; e.g., the word "red" presented in green). The color-only and word-only conditions also are analogous to single-target conditions, but the target is not embedded in a context of incongruity. The color–word congruent trials, in turn, represented the condition closest to that of a double target. These trials, however, were not strictly double target, in that color remained the only feature of the stimulus combination to be reported rather than "redness" per se.

The color-only, word-only and congruent trials together represented potential single- and double-target conditions – providing a provisional platform for evaluating SFT-based cognitive-workload-capacity properties of the processing system, such as "redundancy gain" (i.e., reduced latencies) occurring to the congruent condition (see tutorial chapter by Altieri, Fifić, Little, & Yang, 2017).

Note further that the formats of the present word-only and color-only conditions differed from those of the congruent condition (e.g., color "*x*" vs. word-print in color), which inadvertently may have introduced display features that became incidental distractors with the switch in format (Little, Eidels, Fifić, & Wang, 2015).

Table 17.1 **Participant demographics**

Group	Controls	MDD	SZ	*p*
n	14	17	15	
Age	23.9±5.0	22.5 ± 4.8	22.7 ± 3.0	0.526
M/F	10/4	6/11	12/3	**0.025**
R/L	12/2	15/2	15/0	0.773
Educ	2.9 ± 0.8	2.6 ± 0.6	2.2 ± 0.9	0.059
PEduc	3.1 ± 0.9	2.9 ± 0.8	3.2 ± 0.8	0.497
HAM-A		12.8 ± 10.5		
HAM-D		12.8 ± 8.9		
Mania		5.1 ± 6.7		
Montg		18.0 ± 10.4		
CPZ (mg)			368.8 ± 314.7	
SANS			9.6 ± 8.0	
SAPS			7.8 ± 10.7	
Illness Duration (months)		28.6 ± 14.5	30.4 ± 15.9	

M/F – male/female.
R/L – right/left.
Educ – education rating of the participant (1, gr. 10 or lower; 2, completed high school; 3, 1–3 years of college/university; 4, >3 years of college/university).
PEduc – education rating of the participant's parent (1, gr. 10 or lower; 2, completed high school; 3, 1–3 years of college/university; 4, >3 years of college/university).
H Anx – Hamilton Anxiety Scale (Hamilton, 1959).
H Dep – Hamilton Depression Scale (Hamilton, 1960).
Mania – mania rating from the Young Mania Rating Scale (Young, Biggs, Ziegler, & Meyer, 2011).
Montg – result of the Montgomery Asperg Depression Scale (Montgomery and Asberg, 1979).
CPZ – chloraprornazine equivalent.
SANS – Scale for Assessment of Negative Symptoms (Andreasen, 1984a).
SAPS – Scale for Assessment of Positive Symptoms (Andreasen, 1984b).
p-ANOVA test for significance (alpha = 0.05, two-tailed), bold values indicate significance.

Method

Participants

Stroop performance data was obtained from 15 Sz, 17 MDD, and 14 HC participants.

Demographic information including age, handedness, education, parental education, clinical rating scores, and length of illness were collected in accordance with methods described in our previous study (Aoyama et al., 2011) and are shown in Table 17.1.

Procedure

Stroop Administration

Each stimulus was presented for two seconds and participants were asked to respond as quickly and accurately as possible within this time frame. A trial began with 1 second of cross fixation ("+") in the center of the screen on a black background.

Participants first practiced outside the scanner until they could achieve at least 80% accuracy in all conditions. Participants then underwent a 20-minute fMRS protocol to examine glutamatergic activity in the anterior cingulate cortex. fMRS consisted of five, four-minute blocks (Rest, Stroop, Recovery, Stroop, Recovery) of which there was a total of eight minutes of Stroop Task activity (two four-minute blocks; Taylor, Neufeld et al., 2015). One hundred and sixty Stroop stimuli were presented in total during the fMRS acquisition (40 from each condition) presented pseudo-randomly throughout the session (i.e., conditions appeared in a random order to the participants, yet with a consistent order between participants). The paradigm was written and presented using PsychoPy (Peirce, 2007).

Cognitive-Behavioral Data Organization and Analytical Methods

Means and intertrial variances for responses within the 2 s trial-time window were computed and adjusted for movement time. A value of 0.160 s was subtracted from the means, and $(0.036\ \text{s})^2$ was subtracted from intertrial variances (Townsend, 1984; Woodworth & Schlossberg, 1954; cf. endnote 4 of Townsend & Wenger, 2004).

Because trial numbers had to accommodate reasonable demands on clinical participants performing in an MRI environment, it was necessary to aggregate data across participants, while avoiding the conflation of systematic individual differences (Estes, 1956; Neufeld, 2007b; Neufeld & Gardner, 1990). As previously done in clinical cognitive science, significant heterogeneity could be accommodated through mixture-model structures, allowing for interparticipant differences in model properties (e.g., Batchelder, 1998, 2007; Batchelder & Riefer, 2007). With relative homogeneity of performance, on the other hand, a group could be represented as a homogeneous participant according to the data centroid (e.g., Carter & Neufeld, 1999; Neufeld, Townsend et al., 2007; Townsend, 1984). Tacks to modeling comprised a combination of nonparametric and parametric methods (described in Neufeld, Townsend et al., 2007).

Results

Participant Characteristics

The proportion of males in the Sz and MDD group did not differ from the HC group, $p > 0.10$, the two patient groups differed significantly from each other ($p \approx 0.025$). Overall, males responded significantly faster than females, $p < 0.05$. Any effect of sex differences on response latency therefore would be expected to be in the direction of increased speed in the Sz group. Note, as well, that Sz individuals, especially those with paranoid symptomatology (all but 3 of the present sample) tend more often to be male. The ratio of female to male prevalence rates for MDD, in turn, is approximately 1.64 (Romans, Tyas, Cohen, & Silverstone, 2007). Eliminating such (intrinsic) group differences risks the introduction of other, more intractable issues of interpretation (e.g., Cochran, 1957; Evans & Anastasio, 1968; Meehl, 1971). There were no significant correlations between Chlorpromazine (CPZ) daily-dosage equivalencies (mg per day) and any of the performance variables (e.g., $r_{CPZ,all\ response\ latencies} = -0.014$, $p \approx 0.960$).

Data Overview

Results from analyses of all latency responses, and those from analyses of correct-only responses, were highly similar throughout. Analyses of correct-only responses yielded no additional information (proportion correct generally exceeded 0.90, and in no case were there significant group differences on proportion correct). Therefore, only results based on all responses are reported (cf. Link, 1982). Table 17.2 presents adjusted latency means and intertrial variances, in each case along with corresponding interparticipant standard deviations – taking into account all responses occurring inside the 2-s trial intervals. Also listed are the percent of correct trials and their interparticipant standard deviations. Table 17.3 presents latency means and intertrial variances, along with interparticipant standard deviations, but for correct responses only.

Note that mean latencies reported in Tables 17.2 and 17.3 were computed directly from all values rather than as the average of participant-wise means. Data ensembles from individual participants therefore de facto were weighted according to their numbers of valid observations. Likewise, intertrial variances were computed as the sum of squared deviations from the grand mean, above, of all observations in the group–condition combination, divided by the total number in that combination (maximum-likelihood estimate; e.g., Evans, Hastings, & Peacock, 2000). Like mean latency values, data ensembles from individual participants consequently were weighted according to their numbers of valid observations.

Although such variance estimates included between-participant variance in mean latencies, they were logically coherent with a homogeneous-participant approach to data treatment, including relative homogeneity of mean latencies. Interparticipant standard deviations appearing in Tables 17.2 and 17.3, in turn, were obtained as standard deviations in participant-wise latency means, and in participant-wise intertrial latency variances. Preliminary analyses indicated that group centroids were not unrepresentative of data configurations for the separate participants.

Data Properties Narrowing Model Selection

We now turn our attention to the stochastic cognitive modeling of performance and its account of differences across groups. Examination of the pattern of latencies in Table 17.2 discloses marked similarities and differences in values across groups and conditions. Mean latencies for the color-only and congruent conditions were highly similar for all groups (2-tailed p's ≥ 0.773). This result suggests that in the color–word congruent condition, each group attended to the property of color, as they did under the color-only condition (cf. Wenger, Negash, Petersen, & Petersen, 2010; returned to below).

The main effect of condition was highly significant, $F_{(Huynh\text{–}Feldt\ df=2.459,105.741)} = 137.32$, $p \to 0$, partial $\eta^2 = 0.762$, with the incongruent exceeding the congruent condition for each group, p's <0.001. As expected, the latency of the Sz group exceeded that of the HC group, $p < 0.01$.

Also apparent was the similarity in profiles of intercondition mean latencies across all groups, $F_{(Huynh\text{–}Feldt\ df=4.918,105.741)} = 0.730$, $p = 0.600$. The effects of encoding load, and diagnostic status, therefore were highly additive. Such additivity narrows

Table 17.2 Response time latencies to each of the Stroop conditions with inter-participant standard deviations using all responses

Group	Condition	Means (s)	Variances (s)[a]	% Correct[b]	% Correct[c]
HC	*Congruent*	0.671 ± 0.108	0.067 ± 0.038	0.916 ± 0.110	0.944 ± 0.034
	Incongruent	0.880 ± 0.142	0.089 ± 0.019	0.884 ± 0.141	0.915 ± 0.080
	Word-Only	0.753 ± 0.089	0.063 ± 0.027	0.925 ± 0.131	0.958 ± 0.048
	Color-Only	0.667 ± 0.104	0.063 ± 0.029	0.911 ± 0.137	0.946 ± 0.037
MDD	*Congruent*	0.714 ± 0.094	0.068 ± 0.030	0.947 ± 0.032	
	Incongruent	0.925 ± 0.120	0.081 ± 0.032	0.912 ± 0.069	
	Word-Only	0.766 ± 0.091	0.063 ± 0.021	0.959 ± 0.040	
	Color-Only	0.716 ± 0.088	0.061 ± 0.024	0.966 ± 0.032	
SZ	*Congruent*	0.755 ± 0.093	0.083 ± 0.035	0.918 ± 0.082	
	Incongruent	0.978 ± 0.089	0.081 ± 0.032	0.830 ± 0.145	
	Word-Only	0.793 ± 0.098	0.075 ± 0.035	0.960 ± 0.047	
	Color-Only	0.756 ± 0.092	0.070 ± 0.028	0.912 ± 0.093	

HC – healthy controls; MDD – Major Depressive Disorder; SZ – schizophrenia.

[a] Variances, intertrial latencies.

[b] Nonresponses are considered incorrect.

[c] Excluding responses from one healthy control subject who confused green and yellow buttons during the fMRI task. Latencies were retained for analysis.

Table 17.3 Response time latencies to each of the Stroop conditions with interparticipant standard deviations using correct responses only

Group	Condition	Means (s)	Variances (s)[a]
HC	*Congruent*	0.654 ± 0.098	0.059 ± 0.028
	Incongruent	0.861 ± 0.138	0.082 ± 0.018
	Word-Only	0.742 ± 0.083	0.059 ± 0.026
	Color-Only	0.656 ± 0.100	0.058 ± 0.028
MDD	*Congruent*	0.712 ± 0.096	0.067 ± 0.030
	Incongruent	0.926 ± 0.120	0.079 ± 0.032
	Word-Only	0.765 ± 0.092	0.062 ± 0.020
	Color-Only	0.713 ± 0.091	0.060 ± 0.024
SZ	*Congruent*	0.743 ± 0.091	0.081 ± 0.034
	Incongruent	0.963 ± 0.092	0.080 ± 0.037
	Word-Only	0.787 ± 0.099	0.072 ± 0.039
	Color-Only	0.747 ± 0.094	0.068 ± 0.027

HC—healthy controls; MDD—Major Depressive Disorder; SZ—schizophrenia.
[a] Variances, intertrial latencies.

down candidate model structures to a family whose expected latencies potentially assume such a pattern across experimental factors.

Candidate Model Structures

The combination of spared and disorder-affected parameters of the encoding process takes its meaning from stochastic latency distributions in which the combination participates. One such distribution is the Erlang distribution (e.g., Evans et al., 2000). Its density function is $(vt)^{k'-1}/(k'-1)!\, v\exp(-vt)$, with mean k'/v, and variance k'/v^2, where k' (distribution-shape parameter) represents the number of subprocesses, and v (distribution-scale parameter) represents their rate of completion.

The additional-subprocess account also has been implemented in a mixture-model architecture, accommodating individual differences in values of the above parameters (e.g., Neufeld, Carter, Boksman, Jetté, & Vollick, 2002). Mixing the parameter k' using a Poisson mixing distribution, with hyperparameter m, and mixing the rate parameter v using a gamma mixing distribution, with scale and shape parameters r and k, produces a density function, $\sum_{k'=1}^{\infty} \frac{m^{k'}}{k'} \exp(-m) \frac{r^k \Gamma(k'+k) t^{k'-1}}{\Gamma(k)(k'-1)!(r+t)^{k+k'}}$, the mixture-distribution mean now being $\frac{mr}{k-1}$, the expected variance given k' and v – $E[\mathrm{Var}(T|k', v)]$–being $\frac{mr^2}{(k-1)(k-2)}$, and total variance (i.e., $E[\mathrm{Var}(T|k', v)] + \mathrm{Var}[E(T|k', v)]$) being $\frac{mr^2(2(k-1)+m)}{(k-1)^2(k-2)}$. For this mixture distribution, the sole parameter to change with the occurrence of Sz diagnostic status is that of the hyperparameter m of k''s mixing distribution; the estimated increase in m with Sz diagnostic status moves the mixing distribution of k' upward.

A further mixture – this time of m via $\Gamma_{R,K}$, thus allowing for individual differences in a Poisson process that randomly distributes k' over trials of individual performance (e.g., Neufeld, Vollick et al., 2007; see also Busemeyer & Diederich, 2010, pp. 169–170) – also accommodates an account of increased subprocesses with intact subprocess-level processing rate. It too accords with empirical-performance patterns of task encoding demands, and diagnostic status.[4]

Mean Diagnostics

Focusing initially on the Sz and HC groups, the Erlang distribution is a model generating mean additivity with increased encoding load and Sz clinical diagnosis; increasing k' across encoding load and Sz diagnosis produces the requisite mean additivity. Other structures (reviewed in Neufeld et al., 2010) also produce the requisite configuration of latency means. One such structure is the Independent Parallel Moderately Limited Capacity structure (IPMLC; Townsend & Ashby, 1983), whose $E(T)$ is $\sum_{i=1}^{k'} \frac{1}{(k'-i+1)(\frac{v}{k'}\sum_{i=1}^{k'}\frac{1}{i})}$. Another is a parallel structure with unlimited capacity during completion of the first subprocess, followed by a decline and then partial recovery – known as the First-Stage Unlimited Capacity Parallel model (FSUCP; Neufeld et al., 2010; originating with Townsend, 1984). For this model, $E(T)$ is $\sum_{i=1}^{k'} \frac{1}{(k'-i+1)(\frac{k'v}{2(i-\frac{1}{2})(k'-i+1)})}$. Each of the above candidates is considered further in the next section.

Intertrial Variance Considerations

Like latency means, intertrial variances in principle can contribute to the selection of eligible model structures and their parameter changes across experimental factors. For example, intertrial variance of the Erlang distribution is k'/v^2, which again increases linearly with an increase in k'. The variance of the FSUCP model is $\sum_{i=1}^{k'} \frac{1}{\lfloor (k'-i+1)(\frac{k'v}{2(i-\frac{1}{2})(k'-i+1)})\rfloor^2} = \frac{1}{3}\frac{(4k'^2-1)}{k'v^2}$, which to all intents and purposes also is linear on k'. That for the IPMLC model is $\sum_{i=1}^{k'} \frac{1}{\lfloor (k'-i+1)\frac{v}{k'}(\sum_{i=1}^{k'}\frac{1}{i})\rfloor^2}$, which accelerates on k'.

A difficulty with the diagnostic significance of intertrial variances, and those of higher-order moments, is the instability of their empirical estimates (e.g., Ratcliff, 1979). Supposing a progressive increase in k' with greater encoding load and Sz group membership, sample variances somewhat decelerated, opposite to theoretical variances of the IPMLC model. The linear increases in variances of the Erlang and FSUCP structures at minimum were not opposite to the sample values' second-order difference for encoding condition and diagnostic groups.

The relative instability of empirical variances presents a challenge to models in which variances figure into parameter estimation and tests of empirical fit. On balance, conjecturing random departure of sample variances from model linearity on k', and considering its simplicity of expressions, the Erlang distribution was selected as the structure to be tested for empirical fit. Although this selection was spawned by performance data of the Sz and HC groups, in the interests of parsimony, it was also tested against data of the MDD group.

Hazard-Function Considerations

Note that the Erlang distribution's hazard function increases monotonically over t. Empirical estimates of $h(t)$, however, have been nonmonotonic among latency distributions, first increasing, and then decreasing over t (Bloxom, 1984, 1985; Luce, 1986). Note that latency aggregates, such as those emphasized in the current work, nevertheless, can be functions of $h(t)$, with values of these functions themselves being similar for monotonic and nonmonotonic shapes. For example, the survivor function $S(t)$ can be expressed for any continuous distribution. Simulation of $S(t)$'s from monotonic and nonmonotonic $h(t)$'s—the latter created via probability mixtures (Barlow & Proschan, 1975)—shows that their trajectories across t can essentially converge. Observe, as well, that the nth distribution moment $E(T^n)$ is equal to $n \int_0^\infty S(t)t^{n-1}\,dt$. Inferences from $S(t)$ and $E(T^n)$ generated by monotonic $h(t)$'s, as opposed to certain nonmonotonic extensions, therefore arguably are not imperilled, given acceptable model fit at this level of analysis.

Parameter Estimation and Tests of Empirical Fit

The values of v were estimated through moment-matching and moment-fitting procedures, using the means and intertrial variances from all 3 groups and both encoding load combinations (12 observations in all). Estimated k' was obtained from the HC group's low encoding load condition; estimates of g and g' were acquired from the Sz and MDD data, respectively, addressing both low and high encoding load conditions. Finally, h was estimated from all three groups' data produced under the high encoding load condition. The six low encoding load observations (mean and intertrial variance for each of the three groups) therefore were involved in four parameter estimates, v, k', g, g'; and the six high encoding load observations also were involved in 4 parameter estimates, v, g, g', and h. Taken together, 5 parameters, v, k', g, g', and h, were estimated from a total of 12 observations.

Sz and HC Groups

The Sz and HC groups first were considered separately, because previous modeling of Sz cognition has emphasized its departure from an HC benchmark. In this way, designs have comprised a 2 (high vs. low encoding load) by 2 (Sz vs. HC) factorial layout (e.g., Neufeld et al., 1993). Higher encoding load was represented by the incongruent condition, and the color-only and congruent conditions were amalgamated for the low encoding load. A relatively strong test of whether Sz performance deviations within this design extended to the present paradigm, took the following form. Parameters v, k', and h were estimated from the HC data, and fixed at those values for both groups. The Sz additional-subprocess parameter g then was estimated from the Sz data.

First, a provisional estimate of the rate parameter v was obtained via moment matching (mean/variance) using the HC low encoding data. This value was set, and separate subprocess-number estimates were obtained, first for k', which then was allowed to increase by h under higher encoding – using the corresponding HC means and variances (i.e., moment fitting, by setting the model predictions equal to the empirical values, and solving for subprocess-number in each case). The subprocess-numbers then were set according to averages of their moment-fitting estimates, and v in turn was re-estimated using the HC means and variances and averaged. Estimation values essentially stabilized at this point. Importing these parameter values, estimates of g then were obtained separately from the Sz group's low and high encoding load data and averaged. In compliance, then, with the proposed profile of spared and Sz-affected encoding parameters, all values were set at HC levels, except for the Sz additional-subprocess parameter g which alone was released with Sz diagnostic status.

The estimate of v was 10.42, and that of k' for the HC group under the low encoding condition was 7. This value was incremented by a value of $h = 2$, and/or $g = 1$, accompanying the occurrence of higher encoding load, and/or Sz diagnostic status. Estimated subprocess numbers thus ranged from $k' = 7$ to $k' + h + g = 10$. Resulting model fit was quite excellent. We tested this fit using two chi-square tests. The first used a standard chi-square test to compare empirical mean latency, or intertrial latency variance, to the corresponding model prediction, $\chi^2_{(df=4)} = 0.87$, $p \approx 0.88$. The second computed a chi-square value which compared the average latency to the model predictions and the variance in trial-wise latencies to the model-predicted inter-trial variance (Carter & Neufeld, 1999; Neufeld et al., 2010; Snodgrass & Townsend, 1980; see, Kirk, 2013), $\chi^2_{(df=234)} = 239.60$, $p \approx 0.39$. Empirical latencies and their model predictions are presented in Fig. 17.1; those for inter-trial variances are presented in Fig. 17.2.

In agreement, segregating the 2-s trial interval into 5 0.4-s bins, Pearson $\chi^2_{(df=12)} = 8.79$, $p = 0.72$, and G^2 $(\approx\chi^2)_{(df=12)} = 9.84$, $p = 0.63$.

Sz, MDD, and HC Groups

An increase in Sz subprocess number is coherent with the pattern of processing latencies across encoding load and diagnostic status. It is conjectured that a change in the same parameter will extend to group differences when MDD participants are included. If so, this account parsimoniously applies to the psychiatric control group's deviation from HC performance.

Parameter estimation commenced with moment-matching solutions for the subprocess-rate parameter v, separately at each combination of group–encoding load condition. For all 3 groups, higher encoding load was represented by the incongruent condition, and the color-only and congruent conditions were amalgamated for the low encoding load. These estimates of v were then simply averaged with the resulting value provisionally fixed for all groups. The subprocess-number parameters then were estimated using the mean and intertrial variance for each combination of group and encoding load. The pairs of estimates rendered by the mean and intertrial variance in turn were averaged at each group/encoding-level combination. Values of g and g'

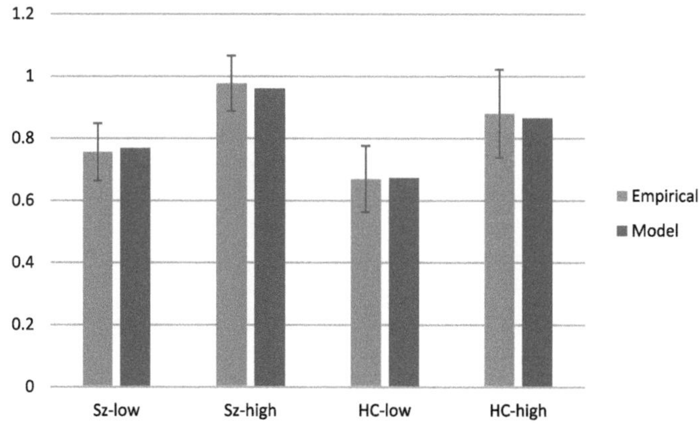

Figure 17.1 Empirical latencies and model predictions across High and Low Encoding Loads and Schizophrenia (Sz) and Healthy Control (HC) diagnostic groups. Low Encoding Load, Mean of color-only and congruent Stroop conditions; High Encoding Load, Incongruent color–word condition. Error bars are standard deviations (pooled for low encoding conditions) across participants within groups and Encoding Load.

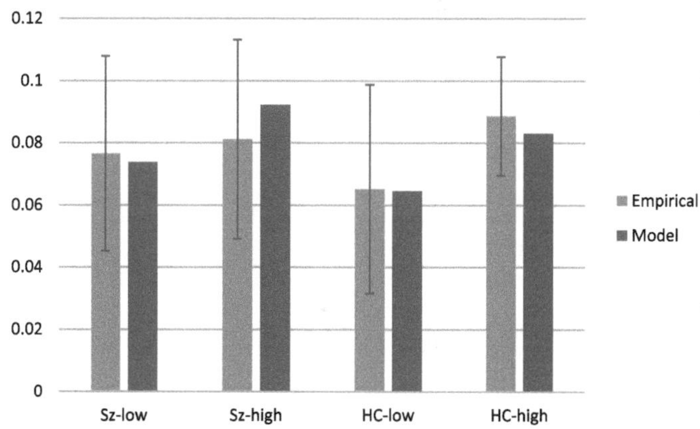

Figure 17.2 Empirical intertrial variances in latencies and model predictions, across High and Low Encoding Loads and Schizophrenia (Sz) and Healthy Control (HC) diagnostic groups. High and Low Encoding Loads, and error bars are as those for mean latencies (Fig. 17.1).

were based on average incrementation in estimated number of subprocesses attending the respective clinical groups, and h was based on average incrementation in estimated subprocess number attending the higher encoding load across all three groups. Subprocess numbers then were set according to group–encoding load combinations, and the parameter v subsequently was re-estimated from the mean and intertrial variance at each of these combinations, with its overall mean in turn being fixed throughout. As estimates essentially converged at this point, they were retained for subsequent tests of empirical fit.

The parameter estimate for v was 10.92; that of k', for the HC group, was 7. This value was incremented for all 3 groups under the incongruent condition by an esti-

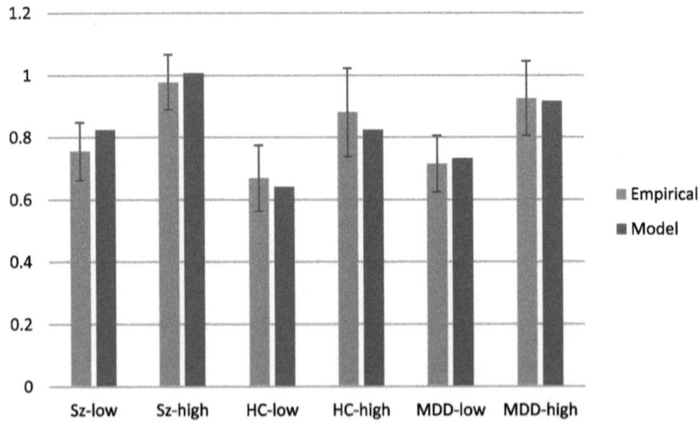

Figure 17.3 Empirical latencies and model predictions across High and Low Encoding Loads and Schizophrenia (Sz), Major Depressive Disorder (MDD), and Healthy Control (HC) diagnostic groups. High and Low Encoding Loads, and error bars are as those for mean latencies (Fig. 17.1).

mated constant $h = 2$. The added subprocess-number for the Sz group was $g = 2$, and that for the MDD group was $g' = 1$. Estimated subprocesses thus ranged from $k' = 7$ to $k' + h + g = 11$. Using these parameter values led to model fit of $\chi^2_{(7)}$ of 9.90, $p \approx 0.19$ using the first test and $\chi^2_{(df=352)} = 372.92$, $p \approx 0.21$ using the second.

Again dividing the 2-s trial intervals into 5 equally spaced bins of 0.4-s each, Pearson $\chi^2_{(df=19)} = 17.21$, $p \approx 0.58$, and $G^2_{(df=19)} = 18.21$, $p \approx 0.51$. Note that a small-simulation sensitivity analysis indicated considerable shift of model fit to change in parameter values in the vicinity of those adopted here. Empirical latencies and their model predictions are presented in Fig. 17.3. Those for intertrial variances are displayed in Fig. 17.4.

Observe that the theoretical model was empirically tenable according to tests of empirical fit, all 3 groups and encoding loads considered. Model fit, however, was not uniform throughout. Specifically, it faltered under the low encoding conditions (e.g., first $\chi^2_{(df=2)} = 6.91$, $p \approx 0.03$). Addition of the result obtained from the high load condition, $\chi^2_{(df=2)} = 2.99$, $p \approx 0.22$, nevertheless, produced the overall value of 9.90, $p \approx 0.19$. Overall, empirical tests of model predictions were supportive, although less so under low encoding conditions.

Intratrial System Dynamics: Distribution-General Indexes

Capacity-OR-Coefficient

We next applied an analysis of the capacity coefficient (see tutorial chapter, this book). In the present implementation, the color/word congruent stimuli were used as the double target and compared to the color-only and word-only stimuli as the single targets. Values of $C_{OR}(t)$, across successive 0.1-s time bins of the 2-s trials, are presented for each group in Fig. 17.5.

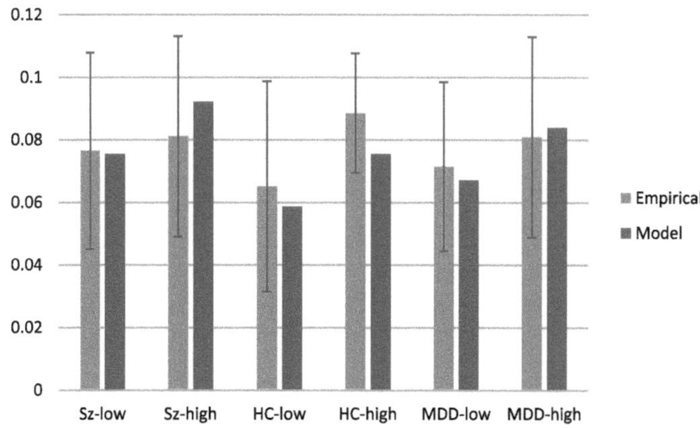

Figure 17.4 Empirical intertrial variances in latencies and model predictions, across High and Low Encoding Loads and Schizophrenia (Sz), Major Depressive Disorder (MDD), and Healthy Control (HC) diagnostic groups. High and Low Encoding Loads, and error bars are as those for mean latencies (Fig. 17.1).

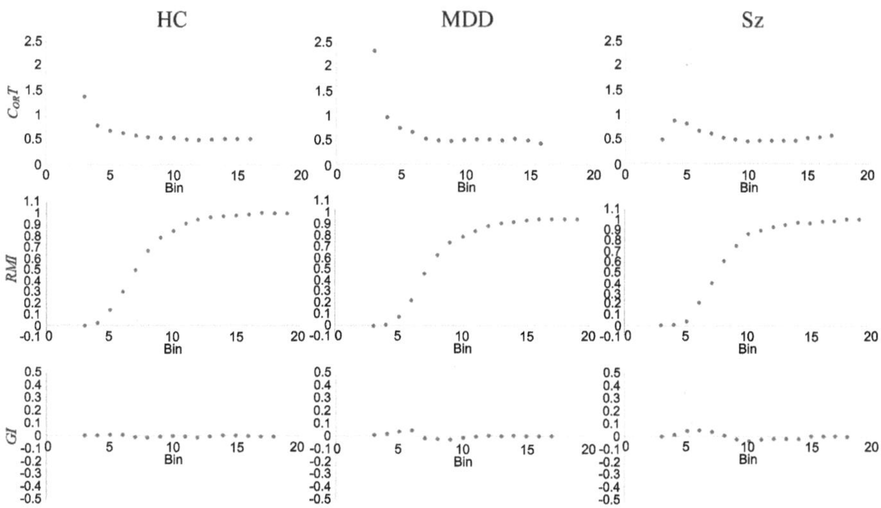

Figure 17.5 Capacity-OR-Coefficient ($C_{OR}T$), Race-Model Inequality (*RMI*) and Grice Inequality (*GI*), for Healthy Control (HC), Major Depressive Disorder (MDD), and Schizophrenia (Sz) Groups. Plotted are time-interval bins with sufficient data points for meaningful computations.

Average $C_{OR}(t)$ values for the Sz, MDD, and HC groups were 0.57, 0.70, and 0.63. By the structure of $C_{OR}(t)$, these values, moderately exceeding the fixed-capacity benchmark of 0.5, are in agreement with a net dominance in the color–word congruent condition, of color processing, whose overall completion was faster than that of word processing (Table 17.2; also Grice Inequality, below). The last half of the graph for the Sz group shows a modest upturn, relative to the other groups; separate inspection of comparative $S(t)$ values across the time demarcations indicates that this trend is associated with a decrease in the denominator of $C_{OR}(t)$, owing to a slight, disproportionately higher $S_{word}(t)$ for the Sz group in the corresponding bin intervals.

It can be said that the CI's, and their combination in $C_{OR}(t)$, penetrate raw response frequencies to educe the processing influences at play over a trial. Their mathematically-authorized verdict in this instance is that interchannel dynamics remain essentially intact within the present clinical disorders.

Race-Model and Grice Inequalities

The Race-Model Inequality (*RMI*) consists of $S_{congruent}(t) - S_{color}(t) - S_{word}(t) + 1.0 \geq 0$. Inequality violations (negative values) indicate supercapacity. The Grice Inequality (*GI*) is $\text{MIN}[S_{color}(t), S_{word}(t)] - S_{congruent}(t) \geq 0$. Violations indicate highly limited capacity. Values for these indexes for all three groups are presented in Fig. 17.5. There is no evidence of supercapacity throughout.

Turning to estimates of *GI*, each group exhibits a special case, with values hovering near 0. A value of 0 would be expected where color processing, as revealed in the color-only condition, also governed the color–word congruent condition. With respect to the structure of *GI*, $S_{color}(t)$ was less than $S_{word}(t)$ for each time demarcation, regardless of group. Once again, there is little to choose from when it comes to differences among these groups in the organization of processing.

Capacity Ratio and Efficiency in Implementing a Common Processing System

The capacity and inequality analyses indicated generally a similar alignment of encoding strategies across diagnostic groups. The Erlang distributional analyses nevertheless supported an interpretation of additional constituent operations, or subprocesses in strategy execution, notably in the Sz group. It would be expected, therefore, that such added subprocesses would take a toll on the system's cognitive-workload capacity for encoding process completion. The cost of these additional subprocesses on capacity, and its variation across intratrial epochs, is expressed as the capacity ratio (*CR*) at each time demarcation, between the Sz and control groups, CI_{Sz}/CI_{HC}, CI_{Sz}/CI_{MDD}. Estimates of these *CR*'s are presented in Fig. 17.6. Also presented are values of CI_{MDD}/CI_{HC}.

Average *CR*'s for the above pairings, under the lower encoding conditions, were 0.70, 0.75, and 0.92, respectively. Under the high encoding condition, they were 0.65, 0.73, and 0.84. Processing dynamics unfolded similarly across all groups, as assessed by the within-trial progression of the capacity and inequality measures. Capacity-Ratio values revealed that the incremental number of subprocesses with Sz, and to a lesser extent MDD status, took their toll on process completions earlier in the trial, with process-completion capacity subsequently evening out across groups. A corollary of this observation is that encoding completions are more imperilled in the event of shorter time windows for their finalization (see also Neufeld et al., 2002, Fig. 10; Neufeld et al., 2010, Fig. 5).

Performance Accuracy

Tests on group differences in performance accuracy were negative throughout. A more pronounced accuracy reduction under incongruent conditions among Sz participants

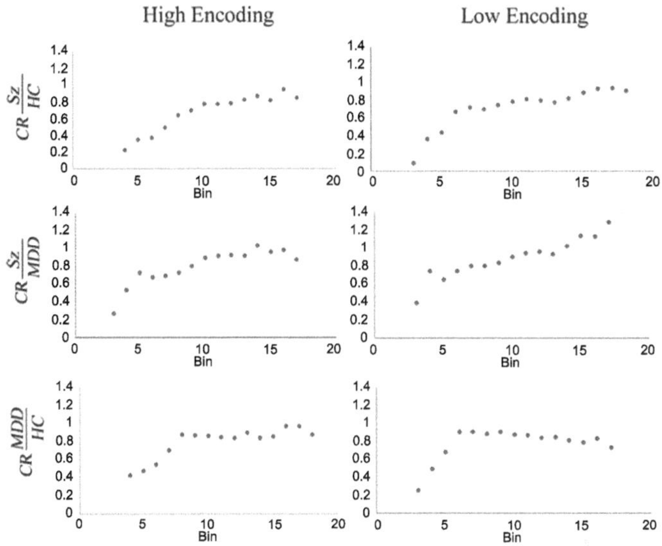

Figure 17.6 Capacity Ratios (Ratios of Capacity Indexes, CI) Between Groups, Within Low (Color-Only, Congruent combination) and High (Color–Word Incongruent) Encoding Load Conditions. Plotted are values from time-interval bins with sufficient data points for meaningful computations.

(Sz impairment), however, has been obtained in selected studies (e.g., Perlstein, Carter, Barch, & Baird, 1998). Such accuracy differences, where found, are interpretable within the present theoretical formulation of additional subprocesses. This account is presented in Appendix (section 'Performance accuracy').

Where significant accuracy differences have not been obtained, as in the present case, some investigators (e.g., Barch, Carter, & Cohen, 2004) have opted for so-called Process-Dissociation analysis of response proportions at various times t following trial onset (Lindsay & Jacoby, 1994). Using this analysis, group differences signifying Sz deficit purportedly have been revealed with respect to probabilities of color and word completions by a time t. Question is raised, however, as to coherence of this analysis with the present developments, and indeed with analytical validity of the Process-Dissociation measurement model altogether. Taken up in Appendix (section 'Evaluation of Process-Dissociation Analysis'), these issues contraindicate the use of this analysis in clinical cognitive science (or anywhere else).

Discussion

Main Results of Formal Performance Modeling

Formal modeling indicates an absence of differences in system architecture across Sz, MDD, and HC groups. Each group evidently processed the color feature of the color–word congruent condition. Equivalently, a single-target, self-terminating system was operative in the Stroop congruent condition. Processing in the word–color incongruent condition parsimoniously was considered to be an extension of that in the congruent condition. In this case, however, color–feature encoding required additional subprocesses to disentangle it from the distracting word feature.

For all groups, $C_{OR}(t)$ was less than 1, a result inconsistent with the baseline race model predictions (see tutorial chapter by Altieri et al., 2017). The distributions of response latencies for the color-only and word-only single targets for all groups and conditions were deemed to follow an Erlang distribution. Its structure corresponds with a serial undertaking of the respective encoding subprocesses – or its parallel mimicker, the fixed capacity parallel model, and capacity reallocation with subprocess completions (processing stages; Townsend & Ashby, 1983).

The model parameter setting apart the Sz group, and to a lesser degree the MDD group, under each Stroop condition was one signifying increased constituent encoding operations or number of encoding subprocesses (the Erlang shape parameter). In this way, model architecture itself was common, but was accompanied by more "noise", in the case of Sz and somewhat so in that of MDD (Neufeld & Broga, 1981). The difference in cognitive performance occurring with clinical disorder could be expressed in terms of a specific stochastic model parameter. Such a configuration is not unlike tracing chaotic behavior of a nonlinear dynamical system to a specific, organized set of coupled differential equations (see, e.g., Levy et al., 2012).

The above account is considered alongside the fine-grained analyses of stochastic processing dynamics available from SFT. Epistemically, SFT's capacity indexes, and their combination, educe the processing influences at play throughout a task trial, as revealed in the relative frequencies of responses during various trial-wise time intervals. These indexes show that stochastic dynamics of task execution are spared with the present clinical disorders. What is affected with Sz is the efficiency of the implementation of processing.

Model Stability Across fMRI and fMRS Recording Sessions

Formal analysis indicated that cognitive processing—the functional side of fMRS and fMRI—by and large was stable between sessions devoted to the alternate forms of neuroimaging. The ACC-centered, spectroscopy-monitored glutamatergic activity, and BOLD-estimated neurocircuitry stood to be mutually informative, because it was ascertained that essentially the same model-monitored cognitive functioning, including its clinical deviations, attended each level of neuroimaging analysis.

The present performance configurations did not indicate systematic individual differences in model properties that would call for stochastic model-property mixing distributions (cf. Neufeld et al., 2010). Certain between-session differences, nevertheless, should be noted. Processing latencies were uniformly higher across groups and conditions in the initial fMRS session. Relative subprocess-number parameters were the same, except for that of h (expressing a group-general increase under the high encoding, incongruent condition), which went from the present value of 2 to 3 in the second session. In line with faster responding in the second session, the rate (Erlang scale parameter) increased from 10.92 to 12.07. There was no significant interaction of any factor with that of performance halves of the present session.

Also, in the second, fMRI session, a unique finding for the Sz group was that response latencies for the word-only and color-only conditions were nearly identical. This amalgamation was thought to be an expression of default network infiltration among this group during the second session (Williamson & Allman, 2011, 2012; cf. Ongur et al., 2010).

Finally, contrary to goodness of fit throughout for the fMRI session, when incorporating all 3 groups, the present fit of the Erlang structure faltered under the low encoding condition. In light of the substantial transfer of essential model findings from one session to the next, however, this does not prevent the functional bridging of the two MRI studies.

Cognitive Work Done and Quantification of Entropic Processing

A consequence of lower encoding efficiency, and its associated neurocircuitry, is an increase in work-output for completing a given encoding task. The number of discrete events (subprocesses) completed by time t for an Erlang distribution is $\int_0^t v\,dt' = vt$ (e.g., Townsend & Ashby, 1978). The across-trial expected value is $\int_{t=0}^{\infty} f(t) \int_{t'=0}^{t} v\,dt'\,dt = vE(t)$. From this perspective, elevated $E(T)$ through increased k' is tantamount to additional outlay of cognitive work done in Sz, to achieve a normal encoding result.

Recalling that variance in processing latency according to the Erlang distribution is k'/v^2. The added noise to the system with increased k' observed in Sz suggests the possibility of more entropy, or less predictability, in these participants' modeled encoding latency distribution. Computation of Shannon–Weaver entropy was carried out using the probability values for the five bin intervals described above. Shannon–Weaver bits of uncertainty for the HC, MDD and Sz groups, under the low encoding load were 1.45, 1.51 and 1.57. Those under the high encoding load condition were 1.57, 1.64, and 1.70. These values were slightly higher, but otherwise resembled those computed for performance during the subsequent fMRI session.

In this way, the impaired efficiency in deploying cognitive-workload capacity produces less ordered responding to stimulus onset, as judged by this classic information-theoretic quantification of response uncertainty. The elevated entropy at the cognitive function level of analysis parallels the more diffuse, less ACC-concentrated neuroconnectivity (Taylor et al., 2016), along with abnormalities in glutamatergic mechanisms Taylor, Neufeld et al. (2015), observed at neuroimaging levels of analysis.

Integrating Other Findings on Schizophrenia Cognition

The present results encourage the continued integration of observations from other paradigms and settings, according to a picture of Sz deviations comprising extra stimulus-encoding subprocesses, combined with a spared rate of subprocess completion (Neufeld, 2007a). This finding agrees with recent reports from Heathcote et al. (2015) showing that the drift rate parameter in a Linear Ballistic Accumulator model (Brown & Heathcote, 2005) was not lower for Sz than controls, but there was an elevated threshold for accumulation activity prior to a response for Sz. This pair of observations appears to map onto the current spared rate of encoding-subprocess transactions, conjoint with an added number of subprocesses to which the rate is applied. In a similar vein, using a neuroconnectionist model of facial processing, Carter and Neufeld (2007) reported a common time constant among the Sz participants, for network-unit adjustments, but an additional number of adjustment iterations pending process completion. Generalizing a step further, it is possible that neurophysiological observations accompanying the present processing composition, including Sz deviations, may extend to cognitive performance studies whose findings can be understood in terms of that specific composition.

Concluding Comments

The concept of efficiency has had a longstanding role in clinical science (Wishner, 1955). Psychopathology has been characterized in part as an unfavorable ratio of focused to diffuse behavior, analogous to a reduced amount of work accomplished by a machine, relative to its energy consumption. In the current work, this concept has been tied to cognitive neuroscience specifics, including cognitive work transacted, cognitive system entropy, neurocircuitry diffuseness, and reduced matching of network connectivity to processing conditions (Taylor et al., 2016). SFT has potentiated progress in clinical cognitive neuroscience. Included has been the ability to disclose otherwise invisible nuances of schizophrenia deviation in cognition, so as to enrich the functional significance of neuroimaging results; embellish these results with symptom and ecological significance; and ascertain stability of the functional apparatus at play across alternate sessions of neuroimaging analyses. Measure-theoretic advances arising from SFT moreover have unveiled poststimulus times of processing strengths and weaknesses, thereby informing dynamical aspects of potential clinical intervention and assessment. SFT arguably epitomizes Kurt Lewin's edict, that "There is nothing as practical as a good theory."

Appendix

Performance Accuracy

Additivity of performance latency does not imply additivity of performance accuracy. Let correct responding occur by time t whenever the necessary processing for an informed answer has taken place, as defined by the distribution function $F(t)$. In the absence of such information, $1 - F(t)$, a correct response may happen through guessing, with probability g. The probability of an accurate response at t thus becomes

$F(t) + (1 - F(t))g = F(t)(1 - g) + g$, and the probability of an error is

$$1 - F(t)(1 - g) - g. \tag{A.1}$$

With g being a constant, (A.1) obviously is linear in $F(t)$.

For an $Erlang_{v,k'}$ structure, $F(t)$, in turn, is nonlinear in k' (Neufeld & Williamson, 1996). Specifically,

$$F(t) = 1 - \frac{\Gamma(k', vt)}{\Gamma(k')}, \tag{A.2}$$

where $\Gamma(k', vt)$ is the incomplete gamma function $\int_{vt}^{\infty} x^{k'-1}e^{-x}\,dx$. Its second-order difference, $\Delta^2_{k'}F(t)$, is seen to be negative in regions of k' and v representative of the present parameter estimates (e.g., $k' = 9$, $v = 11$), and notably in the vicinity of the current trial deadlines (e.g., $t = 1.9$ s). Incrementation in subprocesses therefore implies nonadditive (potentially, disproportionately greater) error rates alongside additive latencies.

Evaluation of Process-Dissociation Analysis

In the Process-Dissociation model (PD), the probability of a correct response (indicating the presented color) in a Stroop color–word congruent condition, at a designated time from trial commencement, is defined as

$$\Pr(\mathit{correct}|\mathit{congruent}) = \Pr(\mathit{color}) + \Pr(\mathit{word}) - \Pr(\mathit{word})\Pr(\mathit{color}). \tag{A.3}$$

Eq. (A.3) obviously is tantamount to an independent race model for a correct response in an OR experimental paradigm (encoding of either the color or the word produces a correct response, the contribution of guessing set aside; see, e.g., Townsend & Wenger, 2004).

Using notation of a dynamical stochastic process, for a designated time of trial progression t, Eq. (A.3) can be written as

$$F(t)_{color} + F(t)_{word} - F(t)_{color}F(t)_{word}, \tag{A.4}$$

where $F(t)$ is a stochastic process distribution function.

The PD stated probability of a correct response in a color–word incongruent condition, at a designated time from trial commencement, is

$$\Pr(\mathit{color})(1 - \Pr(\mathit{word})). \tag{A.5}$$

Restated in terms of stochastic process distribution and survivor $[S(t) = 1.0 - F(t)]$ functions, (A.5) becomes

$$F(t)_{color}S(t)_{word}. \tag{A.6}$$

Eq. (A.5), hence (A.6), putatively provide for the necessity of only color completion by time t, whereby responding is said exclusively to be controlled by the color-naming process.

Coherent with a race-model structure implied by (A.3), however, dominance of the color-naming process requires only that the color process be completed before the word process. Remaining with stochastic process notation, its race-model probability is

$$\int_0^t f(t')_{color} S(t')_{word}\, dt', \tag{A.7}$$

where the integrand is the density function for color first-completion (i.e., color–feature first-passage time; Eq. (5) of Khodadadi & Townsend, 2015). Note in passing that instead of the density function that appears in (A.7), the density function resulting from (A.6), obtained as its time derivative, is

$$f(t)_{color} S(t)_{word} - f(t)_{word} F(t)_{color}.$$

Eq. (A.5) therefore is mis-specified. Arranging empirical observations according to the PD measurement model results in the following consequences for estimation of $F(t)_{word}$ and of $F(t)_{color}$.

Unlike the distribution function (A.7), and to be sure, that of the Erlang structure (text Section Modeling fMRS-Monitored Stroop Performance; Candidate Model Structures), each of which monotonically increase on t, the expression (A.6) first increases and then recedes back to 0 as $S(t)_{word}$ decreases to 0. As with continuous stochastic distribution functions generally, the empirical $\Pr(correct|incongruent, @t)$ itself is monotone increasing (e.g., Lindsay and Jacoby's Fig. 17.2).

The mis-specification in (A.5) ramifies to other expressions in which it participates. Included are estimates of $F(t)_{word}$ and $F(t)_{color}$. By the structures of PD equations (A.3) and (A.5), $F(t)_{word}$ becomes (A.3)–(A.5), estimated as the corresponding difference in empirical congruent and incongruent condition values. A result of this subtraction is a *reduction* in PD-based estimation of $F(t)_{word}$ across t (as seen in Lindsay and Jacoby's Fig. 17.3). Again, this direction of change is contrary to an inevitable stochastic distribution increase for any continuous distribution function $F(t)$. More specifically, with equation (A.3) modeling $\Pr(correct|congruent, @t)$, and Eq. (A.5) modeling $\Pr(correct|incongruent, @t)$, positive values of the PD-estimated $F(t)_{word}$ (evident in Lindsay and Jacoby's Fig. 17.3), require only that empirical $\Pr(correct|congruent, @t) > \Pr(correct|incongruent, @t)$, as indeed is seen in their Fig. 17.2. For PD-estimated $F(t)_{word}$ then to actually *decrease* over time, the empirical $\Pr(correct|incongruent, @t)$ must increase with t more than does the empirical $\Pr(correct|congruent, @t)$, again as is seen in Fig. 17.2. The implausible decrease in estimated $F(t)_{word}$ once more presents itself as a product of a mis-specified measurement model.

Turning to higher estimated $F(t)_{word}$, and lower estimated $F(t)_{color}$ among Sz participants (Barch et al., 2004), such a result is compatible with model mis-specification combined with lower empirical $\Pr(correct|incongruent, @t)$. The PD expression of $F(t)_{word}$ as (A.3)–(A.5), obviously is a decreasing function of (A.5). The same combination is sufficient to generate a reduction in estimated $F(t)_{color}$. The PD equations are combined to estimate $F(t)_{color}$ as

$$\frac{\Pr(correct|incongruent, @t)}{1 - \lfloor \Pr(correct|congruent, @t) - \Pr(correct|incongruent, @t) \rfloor}$$
$$= \frac{1}{\frac{1-\Pr(correct|congruent, @t)}{\Pr(correct|incongruent, @t)} + 1},$$

which is seen to be an increasing function of $\Pr(correct|incongruent, @t)$.

References

Ahn, W., Krawitz, A., Kim, W., Busemeyer, J. R., & Brown, J. (2011). A model-based fMRI analysis with hierarchical Bayesian parameter estimation. *Journal of Neuroscience, Psychology and Economics*, *4*, 95–110.

Altieri, N., Fifić, M., Little, D. R., & Yang, C-T. (2017). Historical foundations and a tutorial introduction to systems factorial technology. In D. R. Little, N. Altieri, M. Fifić, & C.-T. Yang (Eds.), *Systems factorial technology: A theory driven methodology for the identification of perceptual and cognitive mechanisms*. Elsevier (in this book).

Andreasen, N. C. (1984a). *Scale for the assessment of negative symptoms (SANS)*. Iowa City: The University of Iowa.

Andreasen, N. C. (1984b). *Scale for the assessment of positive symptoms (SAPS)*. Iowa City: The University of Iowa.

Aoyama, N., Théberge, J., Drost, D. J., Manchanda, R., Northcott, S., Neufeld, R. W. J., et al. (2011). Grey matter and social functioning correlates of glutamatergic metabolite loss in schizophrenia. *British Journal of Psychiatry*, *198*(6), 448–456. http://doi.org/10.1192/bjp.bp.110.079608.

Ashby, F. G., & Helie, S. (2011). A tutorial on computational cognitive neuroscience: Modeling the neurodynamics of cognition. *Journal of Mathematical Psychology*, *55*, 273–289.

Barch, D. M., Carter, C. S., & Cohen, J. D. (2004). Factors influencing Stroop performance in schizophrenia. *Neuropsychology*, *18*, 477–484.

Barlow, R. E., & Proschan, F. (1975). *Statistical theory of reliability and life testing*. New York: Holt, Rinehart & Winston Inc.

Batchelder, W. H. (1998). Multinomial processing tree models and psychological assessment. *Psychological Assessment*, *10*, 331–344.

Batchelder, W. H. (2007). Cognitive psychometrics: Combining two psychological traditions. In *CSCA lecture*. The Netherlands.

Batchelder, W. H., & Riefer, D. M. (2007). Using multinomial processing tree models to measure cognitive deficits in clinical populations. In R. W. J. Neufeld (Ed.), *Advances in clinical cognitive science: Formal modeling of processes and symptoms* (pp. 19–50). Washington, D.C.: American Psychological.

Bloxom, B. (1984). Estimating response time hazard functions: An exposition and extension. *Journal of Mathematical Psychology*, *28*, 401–420.

Bloxom, B. (1985). A constrained spline estimator of a hazard function. *Psychometrika*, *50*, 301–321.

Bluhm, R. L., Miller, J., Lanius, R. A., Osuch, E. A., Boksman, K., Neufeld, R. W. J., et al. (2007). Spontaneous low frequency fluctuations in the BOLD signal in schizophrenic patients: Anomalies in the default network. *Schizophrenia Bulletin*, *33*, 1004–1012.

Boksman, K., Théberge, J., Williamson, P., Drost, D., Malla, A., Densmore, M., et al. (2005). A 4.0 Tesla fMRI study of brain connectivity during word fluency in first episode schizophrenia. *Schizophrenia Research*, *75*, 247–263.

Brown, S. D., & Heathcote, A. (2005). A ballistic model of choice response time. *Psychological Review*, *112*, 117–128.

Busemeyer, J. R., & Diederich, A. (2010). *Cognitive modeling*. Thousand Oaks, CA: Sage.

Carter, J. R., & Neufeld, R. W. J. (1999). Cognitive processing of multidimensional stimuli in schizophrenia: Formal modeling of judgment speed and content. *Journal of Abnormal Psychology*, *108*, 633–654.

Carter, J. R., & Neufeld, R. W. J. (2007). Cognitive processing of facial affect: Neuro-connectionist modeling of deviations in schizophrenia. *Journal of Abnormal Psychology*, *166*, 290–305.

Chechile, R. A. (1987). Trace susceptibility theory. *Journal of Experimental Psychology*, *116*, 203–222.

Cochran, W. G. (1957). Analysis of covariance: Its nature and uses. *Biometrics*, *13*, 261–281.

Cromwell, R. L., & Dokecki, P. R. (1968). Schizophrenic language: A disattention interpretation. In S. Rosenberg, & J. H. Koplin (Eds.), *Developments in applied psycholinguistic research* (pp. 209–260). New Jersey: Macmillan.

Cutler, C. (2015). *Addressing very short stimulus encoding times in modeling schizophrenia cognitive deficits*. Unpublished Master's thesis. London, ON: Faculty of Graduate Studies, University of Western Ontario.

Cutler, C., & Neufeld, R.W.J. (2015). *Addressing very short stimulus encoding times in modeling schizophrenia cognitive deficits*. Paper presented at annual meetings of the Society for Mathematical Psychology, Newport Beach, CA, July, 2015.

Dobson, D., & Neufeld, R. W. J. (1982). Paranoid–nonparanoid schizophrenic distinctions in the implementation of external conceptual constraints. *The Journal of Nervous and Mental Disease*, *170*, 614–621.

Eidels, A., Townsend, J. T., & Algom, D. (2010). Comparing perception of Stroop stimuli in focused versus divided attention paradigms: Evidence for dramatic processing differences. *Cognition*, *114*, 129–150.

Estes, W. K. (1956). The problem of inference from curves based on group data. *Psychological Bulletin*, *53*, 134–140.

Evans, S. H., & Anastasio, E. (1968). Misuse of analysis of covariance when treatment effect and covariate are confounded. *Psychological Bulletin*, *69*, 225–234.

Evans, M., Hastings, N., & Peacock, B. (2000). *Statistical distributions* (3rd ed). New York: Wiley & Sons.

George, L., & Neufeld, R. W. J. (1985). Cognition and symptomatology in schizophrenia. *Schizophrenia Bulletin*, *11*, 264–285.

Govindaraju, V., Young, K., & Maudsley, A. A. (2000). Proton NMR chemical shifts and coupling constants for brain metabolites. *NMR in Biomedicine*, *13*, 129–153.

Hamilton, M. (1959). The assessment of anxiety states by rating. *British Journal of Medical Psychology*, *32*, 50–55.

Hamilton, M. A. (1960). A rating scale for depression. *Journal of Neurology, Neurosurgery and Psychiatry*, *23*, 56–62.

Heathcote, A., Suraev, A., Curley, S., Gong, Q., Love, J., & Michie, P. T. (2015). Decision processes and the slowing of simple choices in schizophrenia. *Journal of Abnormal Psychology, 124*, 961–974.

Hemsley, D. R. (1993). Cognition in schizophrenia. In R. L. Cromwell, & C. R. Snyder (Eds.), *Schizophrenia: Origins, processes, treatment and outcome* (pp. 135–150). New York: Oxford University Press.

Hemsley, D. R. (1994). Perceptual and cognitive normality as the basis for schizophrenic symptoms. In A. S. David, & J. Cutting (Eds.), *The neuropsychology of schizophrenia*. Hillsdale, NJ: Erlbaum.

Khodadadi, A., & Townsend, J. T. (2015). On mimicry among sequential sampling models. *Journal of Mathematical Psychology, 68–69*, 37–48.

Kirk, R. E. (2013). *Experimental design: Procedures for the behavioural sciences* (4th ed.). New York: Sage.

Levy, L. R., Yao, W., McGuire, G., Vollick, D. N., Jetté, J., Shanahan, M. J., et al. (2012). Nonlinear bifurcations of psychological stress negotiation: New properties of a formal dynamical model. *Nonlinear Dynamics, Psychology and Life Sciences, 16*, 429–456.

Lindsay, D. S., & Jacoby, L. L. (1994). Stroop process dissociations: The relationship between facilitation and interference. *Journal of Experimental Psychology: Human Perception and Performance, 20*, 219–234.

Link, S. W. (1982). Correcting response measures for guessing and partial information. *Psychological Bulletin, 92*, 469–486.

Little, D. R., Eidels, A., Fifić, M., & Wang, T. (2015). Understanding the influence of distractors on workload capacity. *Journal of Mathematical Psychology, 68–69*, 25–36.

Luce, R. D. (1986). *Response times: Their role in inferring elementary mental organization*. New York: Oxford University Press.

Macleod, C. (2010). Current directions at the juncture of clinical cognitive science: A commentary on the special issue. *Applied Cognitive Psychology, 24*, 450–463.

Maher, B. (1966). *Principles of psychopathology: An experimental approach*. New York: McGraw-Hill.

Maher, B. A. (1988). Delusions as the product of normal cognitions. In T. F. Oltmanns, & B. A. Maher (Eds.), *Delusional beliefs* (pp. 333–336). New York: Wiley.

Marr, D. (1982). *Vision*. San Francisco: Freeman.

Meehl, P. E. (1971). High school yearbooks: A reply to Schwartz. *Journal of Abnormal Psychology, 77*, 143–148.

Minzenberg, M. J., Laird, A. R., Thelen, S., Carter, C. S., & Glahn, D. C. (2009). Meta-analysis of 41 functional neuroimaging studies of executive function in schizophrenia. *Archives of General Psychiatry, 66*, 811–822. http://dx.doi.org/10.1002/mrm.20094.

Montgomery, S. A., & Asberg, M. (1979). Scale designed to be sensitive to change. *British Journal of Psychiatry, 134*, 382–389.

Neufeld, R. W. J. (2007a). On the centrality and significance of encoding deficit in schizophrenia. *Schizophrenia Bulletin, 33*, 982–993.

Neufeld, R. W. J. (2007b). Introduction. In R. W. J. Neufeld (Ed.), *Advances in clinical cognitive science: Formal modeling of processes and symptoms* (pp. 3–18). Washington: American Psychological Association.

Neufeld, R. W. J. (2012). *Quantitative clinical cognitive science, cognitive neuroimaging, and tacks to fMRI signal analysis: The case of encoding deficit in schizophrenia*. Paper presented at the 45th Annual meeting of the society for mathematical psychology. Columbus, Ohio, July 21–24.

Neufeld, R. W. J. (2015). Mathematical modeling applications in clinical psychology. In J. R. Busemeyer, J. T. Townsend, Z. Wang, & A. Eidels (Eds.), *Oxford handbook of computational and mathematical psychology* (pp. 341–368). Oxford, UK: Oxford University Press.

Neufeld, R. W. J., Boksman, K., Vollick, D., George, L., & Carter, J. (2010). Stochastic dynamics of stimulus encoding in schizophrenia: Theory, testing, and application. *Journal of Mathematical Psychology, 54*, 90–108.

Neufeld, R. W. J., & Broga, M. I. (1981). Evaluation of information sequential aspects of schizophrenic performance, II: Research strategies and methodological issues. *Journal of Nervous and Mental Disease, 169*, 569–579.

Neufeld, R. W. J., Carter, J. R., Boksman, K., Jetté, J., & Vollick, D. (2002). Application of stochastic modelling to group and individual differences in cognitive functioning. *Psychological Assessment, 14*, 279–298.

Neufeld, R. W. J., & Gardner, R. C. (1990). Data aggregation in evaluating psychological constructs: Multivariate and logical deductive considerations. *Journal of Mathematical Psychology, 24*, 276–296.

Neufeld, R. W. J., Mather, J. A., Merskey, H., & Russell, N. C. (1995). Multivariate structure of eye-movement dysfunction in schizophrenia. *Multivariate Experimental Clinical Research, 11*, 1–21.

Neufeld, R. W. J., Townsend, J. T., & Jetté, J. (2007). Quantitative response time technology for measuring cognitive-processing capacity in clinical studies. In R. W. J. Neufeld (Ed.), *Advances in clinical cognitive science: Formal modeling and assessment of processes and symptoms* (pp. 207–238). Washington, D.C.: American Psychological Association.

Neufeld, R. W. J., Vollick, D., Carter, J. R., Boksman, K., Levy, L., George, L., et al. (2007). A mathematical process account of group and individual differences in memory-search facilitative stimulus encoding, with application to schizophrenia. In R. W. J. Neufeld (Ed.), *Advances in clinical cognitive science: Formal modeling and assessment of processes and symptoms* (pp. 147–177). Washington, D.C.: American Psychological Association.

Neufeld, R. W. J., Vollick, D., & Highgate, S. (1993). Stochastic modelling of stimulus encoding and memory search in paranoid schizophrenia: Clinical and theoretical implications. In R. L. Cromwell, & R. C. Snyder (Eds.), *Schizophrenia: Origins, processes, treatment, and outcome: The second Kansas series in clinical psychology* (pp. 176–196). Oxford: Oxford University Press.

Neufeld, R. W. J., & Williamson, P. (1996). Neuropsychological correlates of positive symptoms: Delusions and hallucinations. In C. Pantelis, H. E. Nelson, & T. R. E. Barnes (Eds.), *Schizophrenia: A neuropsychological perspective* (pp. 205–235). London: John Wiley & Sons.

Ongur, D., Lundy, M., Greenhouse, I., Shinn, A. K., Menon, P. E., Cohen, B. M., et al. (2010). Default mode network abnormalities in bipolar disorder and schizophrenia. *Psychiatry Research, 183*, 59–68.

Peirce, J. W. (2007). PsychoPy-Psychophysics software in Python. *Journal of Neuroscience Methods, 162*(1–2), 8–13. http://doi.org/10.1016/j.jneumeth.2006.11.017.

Penner, J., Ford, K. A., Taylor, R., Schaefer, B., Théberge, J., Neufeld, R. W. J., et al. (2016). Medial prefrontal and anterior insular connectivity in early schizophrenia and major depressive disorder: A resting functional MRI evaluation of large-scale brain network models. *Frontiers in Human Neuroscience, 10*, 132. http://dx.doi.org/10.3389/fnhum.2016.00132.

Perlstein, W. M., Carter, C. S., Barch, D. M., & Baird, J. W. (1998). The Stroop task and attention deficits in schizophrenia: A critical evaluation of card and single-trial Stroop methodologies. *Neuropsychology, 12*(3), 414–425.

Poldrack, R. A. (2011). Inferring mental states from neuroimaging data: From reverse inference to large scale decoding. *Neuron, 72*, 692–697. http://dx.doi.org/10.1016/j.neuron.2011.11.001.

Ratcliff, R. (1979). Group reaction time distributions and an analysis of distribution statistics. *Psychological Bulletin, 86*, 446–461.

Romans, S. E., Tyas, J., Cohen, M. M., & Silverstone, T. (2007). Gender differences in the symptoms of major depressive disorder. *Journal of Nervous and Mental Disease, 195*, 905–911.

Shanahan, M. J., Townsend, J. T., & Neufeld, R. W. J. (2015). Mathematical models in clinical psychology. In R. Cautin, & S. Lilienfield (Eds.), *Encyclopedia of clinical psychology* (1st ed.) (pp. 594–603). London: John Wiley & Sons.

Snodgrass, J. G., & Townsend, J. T. (1980). Comparing parallel and serial models: Theory and implementation. *Journal of Experimental Psychology: Human Perception and Performance, 6*, 330–354.

Taylor, R., Neufeld, R. W. J., Schaefer, B., Densmore, M., Osuch, E. A., Rajakumar, N., et al. (2015). Functional magnetic resonance spectroscopy of glutamate in schizophrenia and major depressive disorder: Anterior cingulate activity during a color-word Stroop task. *Nature Partner Journals Schizophrenia, 15028*, 1–8.

Taylor, R., Schaefer, B., Densmore, M., Neufeld, R., Rajakumar, N., Williamson, P., et al. (2015). Increased glutamate observed upon functional activation in the Anterior Cingulate Cortex using the Stroop task and functional spectroscopy. *NeuroReport, 26*(3), 107–112.

Taylor, R., Théberge, J., Williamson, P., Densmore, M., & Neufeld, R. W. J. (2016). ACC neuro-over-connectivity is associated with mathematically modeled additional encoding operations of Schizophrenia Stroop-Task performance. *Frontiers in Quantitative Psychology and Measurement*, 1–23. http://dx.doi.org/10.3389/fpsyg.2016.01295.

Townsend, J. T. (1984). Uncovering mental processes with factorial experiments. *Journal of Mathematical Psychology, 28*, 363–400.

Townsend, J. T., & Ashby, F. G. (1978). Methods of modeling capacity in simple processing systems. In J. Castellan, & F. Restle (Eds.), *Cognitive theory: Vol. 3* (pp. 200–239). Hillsdale, NJ: Erlbaum.

Townsend, J. T., & Ashby, F. G. (1983). *Stochastic modelling of elementary psychological processes*. Cambridge University Press.

Townsend, J. T., & Nozawa, G. (1995). Spatio-temporal properties of elementary perception: An investigation of parallel, serial, and coactive theories. *Journal of Mathematical Psychology, 39*, 321–359.

Townsend, J. T., Fifić, M., & Neufeld, R. W. J. (2007). Assessment of mental architecture in clinical/cognitive research. In T. A. Treat, R. R. Bootzin, & T. B. Baker (Eds.), *Psychological clinical science: Papers in honor of Richard M. McFall* (pp. 223–258). Hillsdale, NJ: Erlbaum.

Townsend, J. T., & Wenger, M. J. (2004). The serial–parallel dilemma: A case study in a linkage of theory and method. *Psychonomic Bulletin & Review, 11*, 391–418.

Wenger, M. J., Negash, S., Petersen, R. C., & Petersen, L. (2010). Modeling and estimating recall processing capacity: sensitivity and diagnostic utility in application to mild cognitive impairment. *Journal of Mathematical Psychology, 54*, 73–89.

Wenger, M. J., & Townsend, J. T. (2000). Basic tools for attention and general processing capacity in perception and cognition. *Journal of General Psychology: Visual Attention, 127*, 67–99. Invited article in special issue.

White, C. N., Mumford, J. A., & Poldrack, R. A. (2012). Perceptual criteria in the human brain. *The Journal of Neuroscience, 32*, 16716–16724.

White, C. N., & Poldrack, R. A. (2013). Using fMRI to constrain theories of cognition. *Perspectives in Psychological Science*, *8*, 79–83.

Williamson, P. C., & Allman, J. M. (2011). *The human illnesses: Neuropsychiatric disorders and the nature of the human brain*. New York, NY: Oxford University Press.

Williamson, P. C., & Allman, J. M. (2012). Framework for interpreting functional networks in schizophrenia. *Frontiers in Human Neuroscience*, *6*, 184. http://dx.doi.org/10.3389/fnins.2012.00184.

Wishner, J. (1955). The concept of efficiency in psychological health and psychopathology. *Psychological Review*, *62*, 69–80.

Woodworth, R. S., & Schlossberg, H. (1954). *Experimental psychology*. New York: Holt, Rinehart & Winston.

Yates, A. (1966). Psychological deficit. *Annual Review of Psychology*, *17*, 111–144.

Young, R. C., Biggs, J. T., Ziegler, V. E., & Meyer, D. A. (2011). A rating scale for mania: Reliability, validity and sensitivity. *British Journal of Psychiatry*, *133*, 429–435. http://doi.org/10.1192/bjp.133.

Endnotes

1. The fMRS study was consistently scheduled first, in an effort to maximize cognitive challenge for what was considered to be the functionally less sensitive measure. Indeed, latencies were uniformly lower across groups and Stroop conditions during the fMRI session.
2. A review of mathematical modeling of schizophrenia cognition, along with distinctions among analytical (mathematical), computational (with an emphasis on computer simulation), and statistical modeling in clinical science, are presented in Neufeld (2015).
3. Neuroimaging and neurodynamic data, nevertheless, can aid in discerning the validity of formal cognitive models, some of which may be empirically equivalent at the cognitive-behavioral level of analysis (e.g., Ashby & Helie, 2011; White & Poldrack, 2013).
4. An additional mixture model, incorporating geometric and gamma distributions, with similar accommodation of performance patterns tied to incremental subprocesses, has been developed by Cutler (2015), Cutler and Neufeld (2015).

Applications of Capacity Analysis into Social Cognition Domain

18

Alla Yankouskaya, Jie Sui*, Zargol Moradi*, Pia Rotshtein†, Glyn W. Humphreys**

*University of Oxford, Oxford, United Kingdom, †University of Birmingham, Birmingham, United Kingdom

From the early days of experimental psychology, researchers have been interested in how social information modulates perceptual and cognitive processes. A major problem in methodology reflects a difficulty in quantifying the interaction between social factors and perceptual information. Recent advancement in mathematical psychology offers a powerful way to assess this by examining the properties of the processing system in terms of its efficiency. This method provides a way of investigating whether and how social factors modulate perceptual processing. In three separate experiments, we show that individual experience with stimuli, in-group preference and social salience changes the way processing streams interact. Higher integration across processing streams, resulting in increased processing efficiency and system capacity, is observed for stimuli that we have high experience with and that are associated with greater reward and are more socially relevant.

The idea of processing efficiency (Townsend & Ashby, 1983) is conceptualized in a framework of capacity measurements that models reaction time (RT) distributions in a finer grained manner permitting quantitative prediction of behavioral changes by varying the number of available sources of information. The capacity measurements have been used in a wide variety of applications such as anxiety and emotional processing (Neufeld, Townsend, & Jetté, 2007; Wenger & Townsend, 2000), perceptual illusion (Donnelly, Cornes, & Menneer, 2012), multisensory integration (Hugenschmidt, Hayasaka, Peiffer, & Laurienti, 2010; Altieri & Wenger, 2013; Altieri & Townsend, 2011), visual selective attention (Gottlob, 2007), age-related differences in visual processing (McCarley, Yamani, Kramer, & Mounts, 2012), face processing (Yankouskaya, Humphreys, & Rotshtein, 2014; Yankouskaya, Rotshtein, & Humphreys, 2014), and social-self-processing (Sui & Humphreys, 2015; Sui, Rotshtein, & Humphreys, 2013; Sui, Yankouskaya, & Humphreys, 2015). In this chapter, we show how capacity analysis can be used as a finer grained evaluation method in social cognition domain. Specifically, we demonstrate how the utility of processing efficiency can be used to quantify the effects of social and motivational biases (i.e., race bias, in-group bias, self-bias, and monetary reward bias) on visual perception. We illustrate this by reviewing three studies: (i) own-race biases in faces; (ii) in-group and out-group biases; (iii) self- and reward-biases. Contrasting to previous studies where the capacity measures were employed with double factorial experimental design, these three studies in social biases provide a new application of the capacity framework by combining the divided attention task with recently developed associative learning task. We begin with a short introduction to the divided

Systems Factorial Technology, DOI: 10.1016/B978-0-12-804315-8.00022-7

attention task and the capacity framework emphasizing the key methodological points that are crucial for computation and interpretation of the capacity measures. Then, we illustrate the three studies focusing on how efficiency processing can be defined and interpreted in a context of social biases. Finally, we discuss implications of the capacity framework within the social cognition domain.

The Divided Attention Task and Capacity Measurements

In a divided attention task, participants are required to monitor two or more sources of information simultaneously for a target to decide if the target is present or absent. For example, observers may be asked to detect a target shape and a target color that can be presented separately or together by responding “target present”, or “target absent” if none of the targets appeared in the display. There are two main advantages in employing the divided attention task. First, the task requires people to attend to facial identity and emotional expression simultaneously – a situation that closely resembles daily life. Second, in contrast to the selective attention task, the divided attention task controls for performance in the single target conditions by including the double target display. There is considerable evidence that, when a visual display contains two targets that require the same response, reaction times (RTs) are faster compared to when only one target appears (Miller, 1982; Miller, Ulrich, & Lamarre, 2001; Mordkoff & Miller, 1993; Wenger & Townsend, 2006). For example, in Mordkoff and Miller’s (1993) study participants were required to divide their attention between the separable dimensions of color and shape, with all stimulus features being attributes of a single object. Participants were asked to press a button if the target color (green), the target shape (X), or both target features (green X) were displayed, or to withhold their response. The mean RT on redundant target trials was significantly less than the mean RT on single target trials (Mordkoff & Miller, 1993).

Quantitatively, the RT advantage for two-target trials, known as redundancy gain (RG), is defined by testing whether the two-target displays are responded to more quickly than any single target trial using the “favored dimension” test (Biederman & Checkosky, 1970). It has been shown that, when some observers favor one dimension over another there is an overestimation of the mean RT redundancy gain relative to the fastest single dimension condition for each observer (Biederman & Checkosky, 1970; Mordkoff & Miller, 1993). The fixed favored dimension test involves comparing the two single target conditions for each observer against each other. When the two single-target conditions differ, the faster mean RT is retained as the conservative estimate of single-target mean RT; when the two conditions do not differ, the overall mean from both single target conditions is used. The more conservative measure RT across the two single-targets (e.g., color only, or shape only) is substracted from the mean RT for redundant targets for each participant. A positive value following this subtraction is considered a redundancy gain.

The RG can be explained in terms of efficiency of processing (the capacity-producing ability of the system) that is characterized by assessing a probability distribution on work done at a given time. The methodology of capacity measurement allowing the capture of dynamic changes over time provides robust and useful estimates of information processing (Altieri & Hudock, 2014; Eidels, Houpt, Altieri, Pei, & Townsend, 2011; Houpt, Blaha, McIntire, Havig, & Townsend, 2014; Townsend & Eidels, 2011).

Conceptually, capacity measurements reflect changes in processing efficiency of an information processing system that occurs as the workload (the number of to-be-processed signals) increases. For example, in a simple target detection task where participants have to monitor two sources of information and make a fast and accurate decision based on whether either or both sources are present, capacity is calculated by comparing dynamic changes in the system when either single or double (two) targets appear. If the processing speed of an individual target is not affected by an increase in workload, the information processing system is defined as being unlimited in capacity (i.e., either single target is processed simultaneously in a stochastically independent way). This model of processing is referred as unlimited capacity, independent, parallel (UCIP) and considered as a baseline for capacity measures (Townsend & Ashby, 1983; Townsend & Eidels, 2011; Townsend & Wenger, 2004b). If the processing speed increases, the system is considered to have supercapacity relative to the unlimited capacity system. The supercapacity processing indicates that the two single targets interact, producing qualitative changes to the system. If the processing speed slows down, the system is considered to have limited capacity relative to the unlimited capacity processing. In this case the system can be described as limited resources (Townsend & Wenger, 2004b) or serial processing (Townsend & Wenger, 2004a).

It has been demonstrated that in order to access the efficiency of processing, it is critical to take into account the stopping rule used by participants to perform the task (Townsend & Eidels, 2011). In the OR-task either stimulus containing a target can produce a correct response. In AND-task the system must complete information from two sources (the decision is made only when two targets are detected) (Townsend & Altieri, 2012; Townsend & Eidels, 2011). Here we focus on OR-task only (see the implication of AND-task in the further direction section).

Mathematically, processing efficiency is conceptualized in the capacity index ($C(t)$) which can[1] be represented as the ratio of integrated hazard function (Townsend & Ashby, 1983; Townsend & Eidels, 2011) that represents the cumulative amount of work done up to the time[2] (t) (Altieri & Townsend, 2011). The ratio of integrated hazard expresses the likelihood of completing the task in the next instant when the task is still in process. In other words, at each time point the ratio of integrated hazard function captures the conditional probability of the system for completing the task.[3] Therefore, a system with a high capacity coefficient can be interpreted as being able to perform more work, because it has higher conditional probability of finishing the task before time (t). In this case the capacity coefficient is expected to be greater than 1. If capacity coefficient <1, conditional probability of finishing the task before time (t) is low and this indicates that the system has limited capacity to perform this work. If the integrated hazard function for two targets is identical to the sum of the integrated hazards for processing each target separately, then the ratio will be equal to zero ($C(t) = 1$). Cumulating capacity coefficients across entire RT distribution provide us with information about dynamic changes in capacity processing and precise estimates of processing efficiency at or before time (t).

It has to be noted that the capacity coefficient does not depend on particular probability distributions or the parametric characteristics of the single target RT distributions (Miller, Beutinger, & Ulrich, 2009) that makes it useful at the group level analysis where individual mean responses varies substantially across subjects.

Own-Race Biases in Face Perception

It is well established that there are advantages in both perception and memory when we process faces belonging to our own race compared to faces belonging to another race (Ackerman et al., 2006; Anthony, Cooper, & Mullen, 1992; Elfenbein & Ambady, 2003). However, despite over 20 years of research, it remains unclear exactly how the processing of own- and other-race faces differ. Here, we used a modification of a redundant target task (Miller, 1982) to assess whether there are qualitative differences in the processing of identity and emotion in faces belonging to own versus other races.

We report three experiments with participants from three different ethnic groups: European, African, and Asian, and compared the effects of own race face processing (Elfenbein & Ambady, 2003; Elfenbein, Mandal, Ambady, Harizuka, & Kumar, 2002; Marsh, Elfenbein, & Ambady, 2003; Yankouskaya, Humphreys et al., 2014) to the processing of other race faces. Three different sets of faces, one set for each ethnic group (European, African, Asian) were selected (Yankouskaya, Humphreys et al., 2014). In each set, three of the photographs depicted targets: (i) the *redundant stimulus* had both the target identity and the target emotion; (ii) the *identity alone* face depicted the target identity and a nontarget emotional expression; and (iii) the *expression alone* face depicted the target emotional expression and a nontarget identity. There were also three nontarget faces – these were photographs of three different people that expressed emotions different from those in the target faces (Fig. 18.1).

Participants were required to respond quickly and accurately if they see any of the targets and withhold a response if a nontarget was displayed. Each participant performed the task separately for the three sets of face images (European, African and Asian) (see details about experimental set up in Yankouskaya, Humphreys et al., 2014). After completing the task, subjects performed two self-reported questionnaires (Walker, Silvert, Hewstone, & Nobre, 2008) for each of the other races. One questionnaire measured the quantity of the social contact with other races (Cronbach's $\alpha = 0.87$). This questionnaire included questions such as "I often see other-race people at social events I attend." The second measured the degree of interaction between the participant and individuals from the other races. It included questions like "How often have you had other-race persons on your team during sports or your group during other activities?"

Using capacity analysis, we compared the amount of work completed by the system while processing a face with redundant targets (when both the target identity and expression are present) to when only a single target is present (either the facial iden-

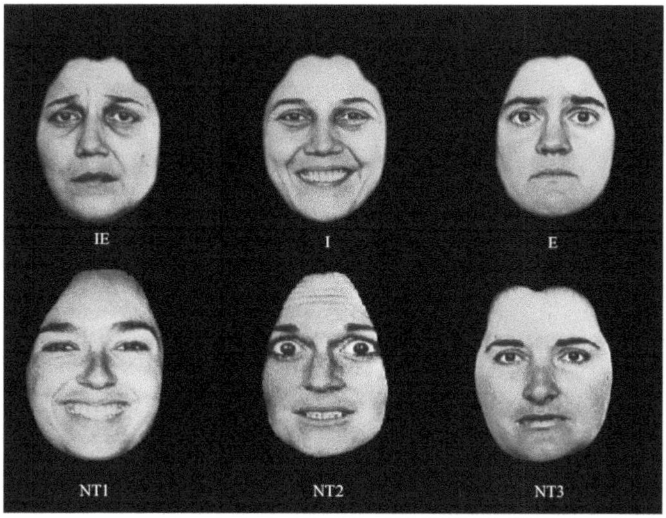

Figure 18.1 An example of stimuli set. IE – a face containing both target identity and target emotional expression; I – a face containing target identity; E – a face containing target emotional expression; NT1–NT3 faces containing neither target identity nor target emotion. In this study we used faces from the NimStim database (Tottenham et al., 2009), but because of publication restriction on faces from that database, we presenting other faces here (Ekman, 1992) as examples only.

tity or expression). By doing this we aimed to test whether the processing of same- and other-race faces not only differs quantitatively (e.g., due to overall better processing of own-race faces), but also qualitatively (e.g., in terms of whether identity and expression interact and are processed with supercapacity). We predicted that, if the interaction between facial identity and expression (see, for example, Yankouskaya, Booth, & Humphreys, 2012; Yankouskaya, Humphreys et al., 2014) depends on experience (or motivation), then the reduced expertise with other-race faces should be associated with diminished coactive processing of identity and expression for other-race faces manifested as reduced workload capacity as compared to own-race faces.

We first examined the redundancy gain effects: the amount of benefit from the presence of two targets in the stimulus. This was computed by subtracting response times of the redundant target trials from the slowest of the single target trials. The average redundancy effects for each condition are displayed in Fig. 18.2.

The degree of benefit from the presence of both the expression and identity targets depended on the ethnicity of the face and the participant (race by face interaction: $F(4, 66) = 3.74$, $p = 0.008$). Specifically, European participants (Fig. 18.2) showed larger redundancy gain when processing European faces compared to both African and Asian faces. African participants showed larger gain when processing African faces and to a lesser degree European faces but very weak gain when processing Asian faces. Asian participants showed similar benefit for Asian and European faces when processing both targets but very limited benefit when processing African faces. Taken together, the results indicate reliable redundancy gains for own race faces in all three

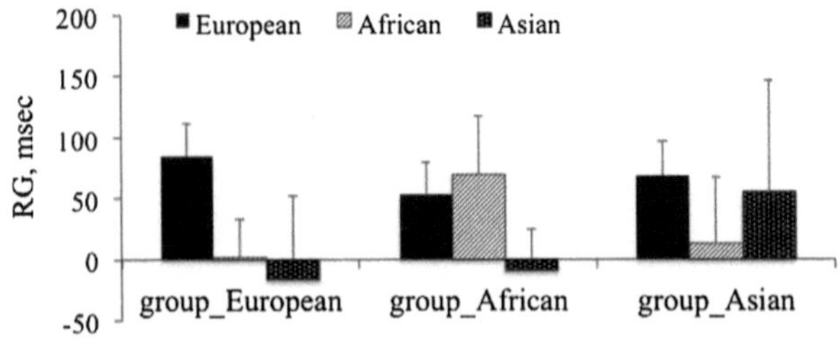

Figure 18.2 Size of the redundancy gains (ms) for groups of European, African, and Asian participants across the three stimulus sets. The negative value means that the RT for the single target was shorter than RTs for redundant targets image (no redundancy gain). Error bars represent +/−1 SEM.

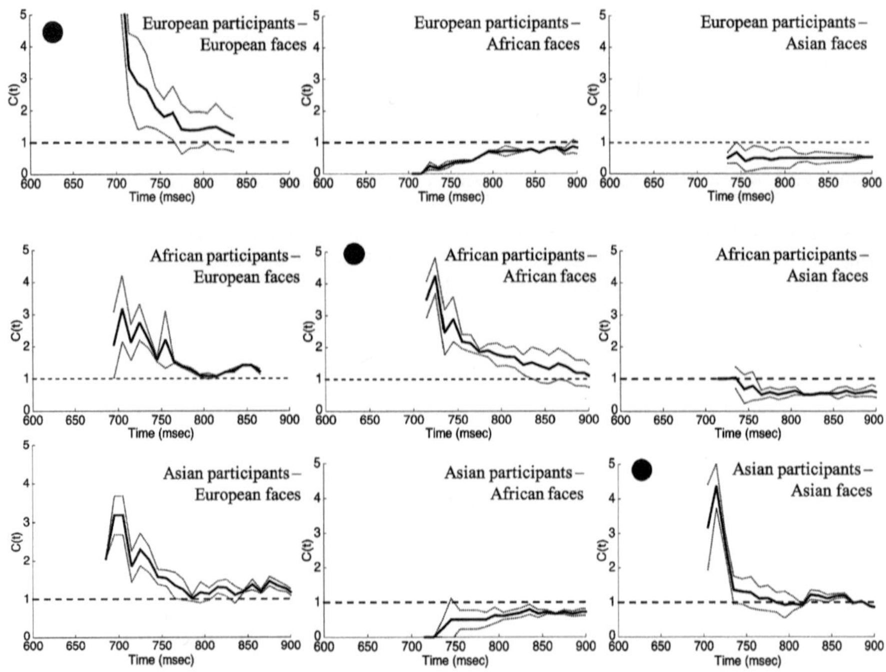

Figure 18.3 Capacity coefficients for the three groups of participants (for own-race faces are marked by a black dot). The horizontal line at $C(t) = 1$ indicates the reference value for unlimited capacity. The capacity coefficients are depicted as a solid line; the confident interval for capacity coefficient as a dashed–dotted line.

groups, with African and Asian (living in the UK) also showing relative higher RG for European faces.

We next investigated efficiency of processing in own and other-race faces by plotting group capacity coefficients for each face set across time (Fig. 18.3). Capacity coefficients that are reliably higher than 1, at any time provide evidence for supercapacity. In other words, processing is facilitated through the integration of identity and expression information prior to the decision point.

Fig. 18.3 demonstrated supercapacity processing of identity and emotional expression within own-race faces (diagonal line plots, Fig. 18.3), indicating that the observed responses for the redundant target face were greater than predicted by the combined single targets. This means that for own race faces there is a higher conditional probability that responses for stimuli will be completed before the time it takes to complete a single target; this is true when both identity and emotional targets are presented. It indicates positive dependency (co-activation) between the targets that facilitated performance. African (6 out of 12) and Asian (seven out of 12) participants also showed evidence for supercapacity when processing European faces (left column, Fig. 18.3). Interestingly, when European processed African and Asian faces, and when Asian and African processed each other faces, the evidence suggests limited capacity.

The reduced other race effects for European faces in both African and Asian raises the intriguing possibility that experience can change the way information from faces is integrated and processed. To test this possibility, we performed correlation analysis between individual processing efficiency (capacity coefficients averaged across time bins) and experience with other-race people for each group of participants. The scores of experience with faces were calculated as averaged scores for the amount of social contact and individual experience with other-race people from questionnaires ("Quantity of social contact" and "Individual experience"). For the European group there was a significant positive relationship between individual processing efficiency and experience for African ($r = 0.65$, $p < 0.016$[4]) and Asian faces ($r = 0.73$, $p < 0.016$) (Fig. 18.4A). The African group showed significant correlation between individual experience and capacity coefficients for European faces ($r = 0.69$, $p < 0.016$), and strong correlation for Asian faces ($r = 0.92$, $p < 0.016$) (Fig. 18.4B). For the Asian group the correlation between experience with European and African faces and processing efficiency showed a significant relationship ($r = 0.79$, $p < 0.016$ and $r = 0.82$, $p < 0.016$, respectively) (Fig. 18.4C). Correlations between capacity processing and experience with own-race faces were significant in European and African groups ($r = 0.82$, $p < 0.016$; $r = 0.69$, $p = 0.014$; $r = 0.78$, $p < 0.016$ for European, African, respectively), but not in the Asian group ($r = 0.37$, $p > 0.016$).

The results of the correlation analyses suggest that individual experience with other-race faces has a strong link to processing efficiency: the greater experience the higher processing efficiency. Taken together, we propose that some degree of familiarity with the properties of the faces within particular racial groups is needed before information about identity and expression can be processed in a more efficient manner (i.e., supercapacity). In the absence of this experience, however, facial identity and emotional expressions may be processed independently, because unfamiliar faces demand more resources and increasing workload leads to slower responses for faces containing two targets. An alternative interpretation is that capacity maybe driven by motivation, assuming higher experience with other races, make these other race individuals also socially more relevant which can change the way identity and expressions are processed, making it more likely to integrate these two processing stream than executing them in parallel.

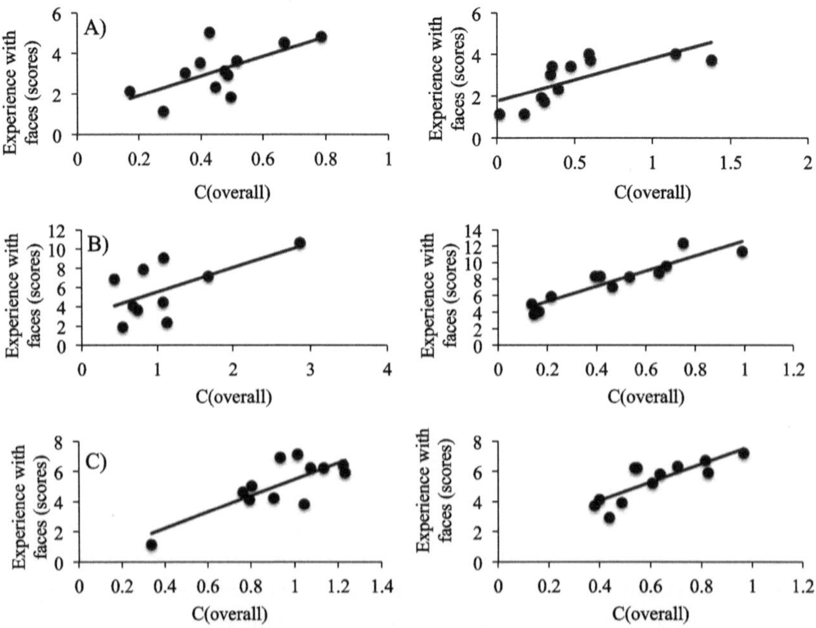

Figure 18.4 Correlation between individual overall capacity coefficients *C*(overall) and Scores of Experience with other-race faces in European (A), African (B), and Asian (C) groups. The Scores of Experience with faces were calculated as averaged scores for the amount of social contact and individual experience with other-race people from questionnaires ("Quantity of social contact" and "Individual experience").

In-Group Biases

Previous studies showed that social associations, no matter if long-term or newly established, modulate integrative processing in perception (Stolte, Humphreys, Yankouskaya, & Sui, 2015; Sui et al., 2015; Yankouskaya, Rotshtein et al., 2014). There remains a question, though, whether newly learned group-based associations can modulate processing efficiency, and whether the effects of social grouping on visual processing can be rapidly established and increase processing efficiency. Here we used combined associative learning and divided attention tasks. In the associative learning stage, participants learnt to associate an arbitrary shape as well as an arbitrary color with a label relating to their in-group (Oxford University, for participants who were members of Oxford University) and similarly another arbitrary shape and color with a label relating to an out-group (Cambridge University, for Oxford University participants) (Fig. 18.5A). In the divided attention task participants viewed either single or redundant targets and were instructed to decide if the stimuli were associated with Oxford University or Cambridge University (Fig. 18.5B). Participants were required to press a response key if the color (we used four color patches), the shape (a diamond, a square, a hexagon, and a circle), or both target features were present for each of the categories (Oxford or Cambridge), and to make no response if neither of the target features was present. On redundant target trials (Color–Shape), both features always

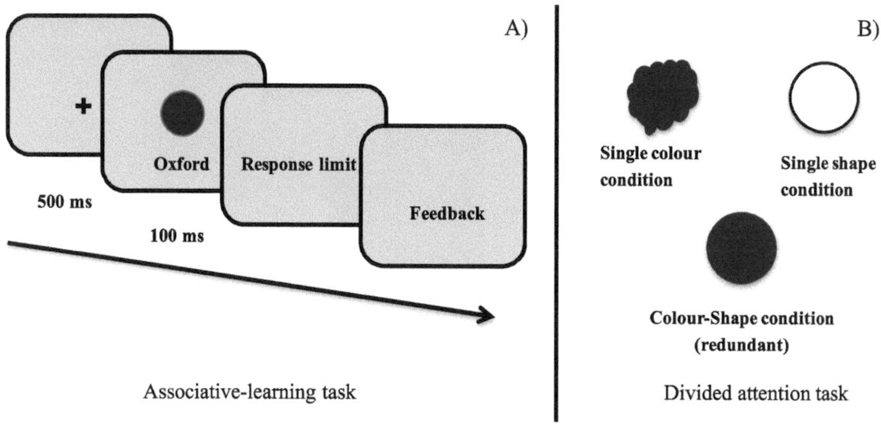

Figure 18.5 An example of stimuli in (A) associative learning task; (B) divided attention task.

belonged to the same category (either Oxford or Cambridge) (see details for stimuli and procedure in Moradi, Yankouskaya, Duta, Hewstone, & Humphreys, in press).[5]

Importantly, in this study there were no prior experiences related to the visual features associated to in- and out-group. Moreover, prior to the experiment, we asked participants to rate how much they "like" each visual feature (colors, shapes) to ensure that any potential findings are not driven by participants' preference for a certain visual stimulus. This design allowed us to assure that any possible differences in processing efficiency cannot be attributed to differential familiarity or preferences related to the visual features of the in-group compared with the out-group.

To examine the magnitude of the enhancement for redundant targets (redundancy gain) we tested whether redundant targets trials were responded to more quickly than any single target trial using the "favored dimension" test (Biederman & Checkosky, 1970). The more conservative RTs across the two single targets (e.g., color or shape) were substracted from the mean RT for redundant targets (color–shape) for each participant for in-group and out-group associations. We found that RG for in-group was significantly greater compared to the out-group (Fig. 18.6).

Facilitation of performance when more work has to be done may imply that association with in-group membership increases processing efficiency. If it is the case, we should observe changes in capacity for in-group attributes compared to out-group. To test this we analyzed response distributions for target stimuli on process completion times in context of in-group and out-group membership. To assess the dynamic characteristics of capacity processing (i.e., changes in processing efficiency with increasing workload), we computed capacity coefficients for each time bin and plotted it as a function of time for in-group (Fig. 18.7A) and out-group (Fig. 18.7B).

The dynamics of capacity processing (Fig. 18.7) indicated that both in-group and out-group membership associations increased efficiency of processing. However, the time window where capacity increases (compared to the UCIP model) for in-group was wider compared to out-group. The difference between predicted UCIP performance and true performance were tested for each individual data by using the standard

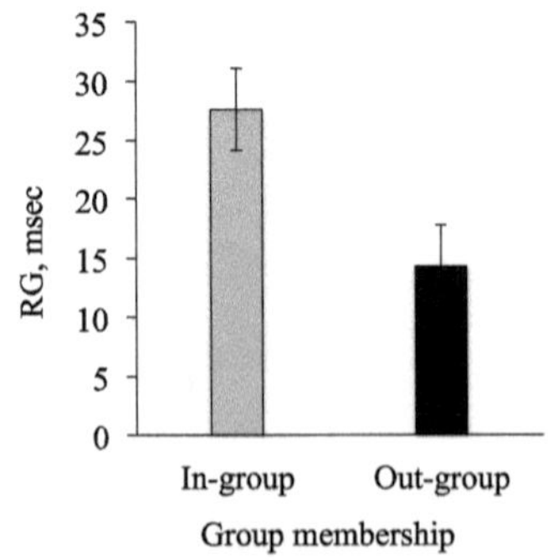

Figure 18.6 RT advantage for Color–Shape stimulus compared to the fastest of the single targets for in-group and out-group membership. Error bars represent +/−1 SEM.

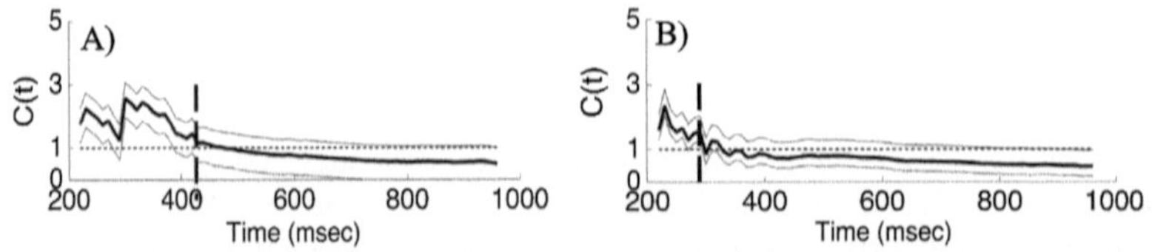

Figure 18.7 The capacity coefficient across the group of participants for in-group (A) and out-group (B) membership associations. The horizontal line at $C(t) = 1$ indicates the reference value for unlimited capacity. The capacity coefficients are depicted with the solid line; the confidence interval for the capacity coefficient is illustrated in the dashed–dotted line. The vertical dashed line indicates the window of supercapacity (determined by UCIP-OR test Houpt & Townsend, 2012).

normal distribution for null-hypothesis-significance tests for UCIP-OR model (Houpt & Townsend, 2012). The test showed significant violations of the UCIP model for 37 out of 42 participants for in-group in the time window between 220 and 430 msec. For out-group only 3 out of 42 participants showed violation of the UCIP model in the time window between 220–430 ms, but 35 out of 42 participants showed performance above UCIP in the time window between 220 and 300 ms.

Taken together, the data suggest enhanced perception of visual stimuli associated with in-group attributes. Previously the effect of in-group biases was found in perception of faces (Amodio, 2010), ethnic group (Correll, Park, Judd, & Wittenbrink, 2002), and gender (Wolff, Kemter, Schweinberger, & Wiese, 2014). Here, we demonstrated the effect of group membership on simple visual features such as a color and a shape. In particular, participants responded faster when two visual features associated with group membership were present compared to single features. Although this effect was found for both in-group and out-group associations, the extent of this effect was different. Specifically, the magnitude of the facilitation for two versus single features and overall capacity were greater for in-group compared to out-group. Importantly, the time window where processing efficiency showed super-capacity was also wider (110 ms) for the in-group. This indicates that features associated with in-group attributes have a greater chance to be detected and processed compared to out-group attributes.

Self- and Reward-Biases

The potential impact of motivation and social relevance on processing capacity was assessed in the following study. Here we describe a study which assesses the relations between self and reward biases in perceptual matching. Understanding the nature of self-representations has been a core issue since the inception of experimental psychology, but it is still far from developing a full account. It is well established that people showed enhanced performance (e.g., faster RT, higher accuracy, better memory recall) for stimuli associated with self-compared to stimuli associated with other. Similar effects were found for items associated with high reward compared to low reward. For example, Sui and colleagues (Sui, He, & Humphreys, 2012) have shown that the reduction of luminance of stimuli less affected the self and high-reward related processing compared with other and low-reward related processing. The data indicate that self and reward processing modulates perception. This similarity in performance pattern between self and high reward raise a question whether self-biases are driven by the potential inherent reward value of the self (Northoff & Hayes, 2011). To further assess whether advantages of self and rewarded stimuli are mediated by the same or different mechanism we designed a study assessing effects of processing capacity in these two contexts.

We carried out two separate experiments (self-experiment and reward-experiment) which had identical procedure. Each experiment had two stages: association learning stage and redundant task stage. In the associative learning stage, participants learned to associate two simple geometrical shapes (e.g., circle and square) with themselves, and two shapes with one of their best friends (e.g., triangle and diamond) (Fig. 18.8A). After the learning stage we conducted a redundant target experiment. In the redundant experiment participants made a personal discrimination task, indicating whether the geometrical shape(s) represents the self or the friend (Fig. 18.8B). There were two types of trials: single and redundant trials. In the single-target trials a single geometrical shape (associated with the self or the friend) was presented on the left or the right of the screen. In the redundant-target trials, two flanker geometrical shapes were presented, both associated with either the self or the friend. To control for perceptual confounds on redundancy gains, the two-item trials could either present the same shape or the two different shapes (e.g., in a self-trial, two circles or a circle and a square). The design was a 2 (friend, other) by 2 (single, redundant), and the redundant condition had (same, different) a nested factor. The reward experiment had an identical procedure, but geometrical shapes were now associated with high (£8) or low (£0.5) reward. In the redundant task, participants had to indicate whether the geometrical shape is associated with high or low reward.

We focus here on the results of the redundant-target task. First, we examined the magnitude of the redundancy gains in the self-experiment with two factors – the association (friend vs. self) and the shape (2 different vs. 2 same shapes). There was a significant main effect of association ($F(1, 19) = 51.71$, $p = 0.001$), indicating a larger redundancy gain in the self- than friend-association condition. Neither significant main effect of shape ($p = 0.10$) nor interaction association x shape ($p = 0.78$) was found here (Fig. 18.9A). In the reward-experiment, there was a significant main effect of

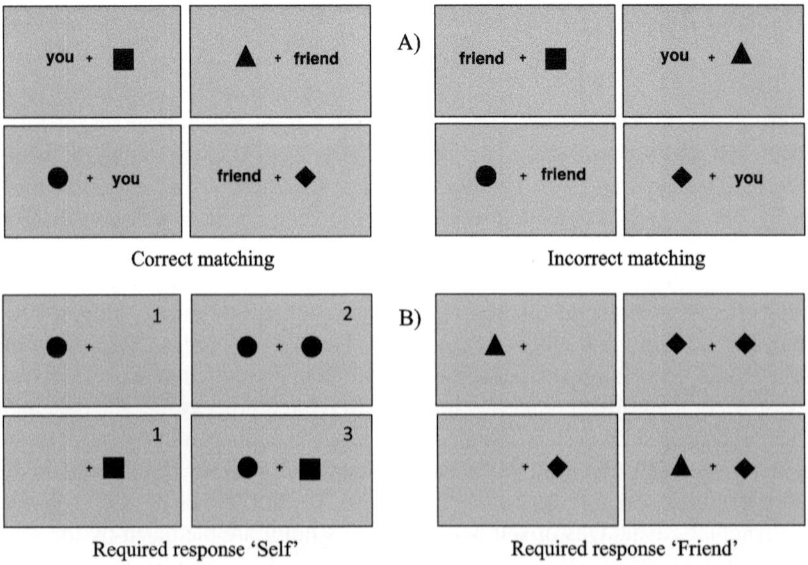

Figure 18.8 An example of stimuli in self-experiment: (A) associative learning task; (B) redundant target task (1, single shape conditions; 2, redundant same condition; 3, redundant different condition).

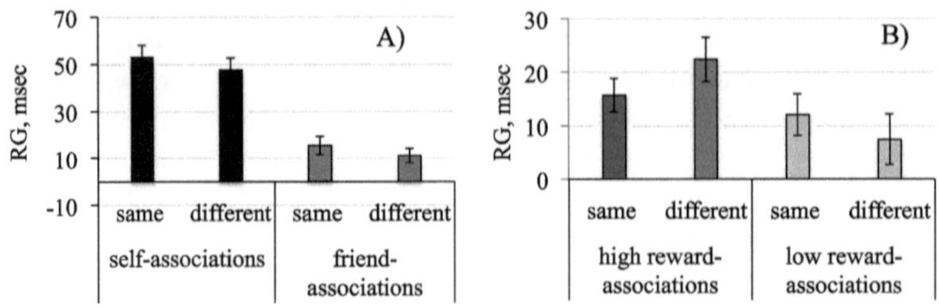

Figure 18.9 Redundancy gains (A) in self-association experiment: the redundancy gains (2 stimuli vs. single stimulus baselines) as a function of the association (friend vs. self) and shape (2 different vs. 2 same shapes); (B) in reward association experiment: the redundancy gains (2 stimuli vs. single stimulus baselines) as a function of the association (low- vs. high-reward) and shape (2 different vs. 2 same shapes). Error bars represent +/−1 SEM.

association (high reward vs. low reward) ($F(1, 18) = 6.16$, $p = 0.03$), indicating a greater redundancy gain for the high- than the low-reward stimuli. There was also a marginally significant interaction ($F(1, 18) = 3.86$, $p = 0.07$) (Fig. 18.9B). The interaction arose because the redundancy gain for high-reward stimuli was higher than for low-reward stimuli when the shapes were different ($t(18) = 3.21$, $p = 0.005$), but not when they were the same ($p = 0.46$).

The RG data indicate a differential effect for self and high reward for both redundant target conditions. However, knowing the magnitude of the facilitation effects does not imply that self-relevant information is processed in a more efficient way than high reward information. For example, the difference may exist across specific subsets of RT distribution (e.g., at shortest RT) (see discussion on this issue in Townsend & Ashby, 1983). On the other hand, if a particular condition (e.g., one single shape in reward experiment) shows capacity advantage in one portion of the RT distribution and a deficit in another, then the data will not show a difference in terms of mean RT. The solution here would be to assess the dynamic characteristics of RT distributions by indexing the cumulative amount of work that the system can perform to process self-relevant information across time and compare it with the work that the system does for reward information.

To explore the dynamics of processing redundant-target stimuli we first, computed capacity coefficients for self and high reward associations for each redundant target condition across time. Individual capacity coefficients and averaged capacity coefficients across the group of participants for self and reward experiments are presented in Fig. 18.10.

Fig. 18.10 demonstrated that in the self-experiment, there was supercapacity for both the same-shape and different-shape trials with self-associated redundant stimuli. This was observed through time bins from 380 to 480 ms. In contrast, for both types of trials with friend-associated stimuli, there was no evidence for supercapacity with some trends toward a limited capacity. In the reward experiment, supercapacity across time bins from 350 to 400 ms was observed for high- and low-reward redundant stimuli, both when the shapes were the same and when they were different. Confirmatory analyses on the peak of the capacity coefficient (Altieri & Hudock, 2014; Altieri & Wenger, 2013), showed a greater peak capacity coefficient in the self than the friend association condition, but there was no significant difference between high- and low-reward associations (for details see Sui et al., 2015).

Finally, we compared performance in the self- and reward-association experiments using log-linear analyses on the numbers of participants showing supercapacity with redundant-target stimuli (individual plots of capacity coefficients are displayed in Fig. 18.11). There were three factors: experiment (self vs. reward), association (self or high reward value vs. friend or low reward value), and effect (number of participants showing supercapacity vs. the number who did not). The analysis showed significant three-way interactions both when the shapes were the same and when they differed, $\chi^2 = 11.38$ and $\chi^2 = 11.31$, $ps = 0.001$; more participants showed supercapacity for redundant self-relative to redundant friend trials, when compared with the numbers – showing supercapacity for the high- and low-reward redundant conditions. The direct comparison between the self- and high-reward trials revealed that, for both same- and different-shape trials, more participants demonstrated supercapacity for self- than for high-reward associated shapes, $\chi^2 = 10.92$ and $\chi^2 = 10.92$, $ps = 0.001$. In contrast, there were no differences between the friend- and the low-reward stimuli, irrespective of whether the shapes were the same or different, $p = 0.27$ and $p = 0.26$. The cross-experimental analyses confirmed the differences between the self-associated stimuli and both friend-associated and high-reward associated items, when supercapacity was observed. The results indicated that supercapacity was more prevalent for self-associated stimuli than for the other conditions.

Taken together, we found that self-associated stimuli were consistently processed with supercapacity, both in the same- and in the different-shape condition. With high-

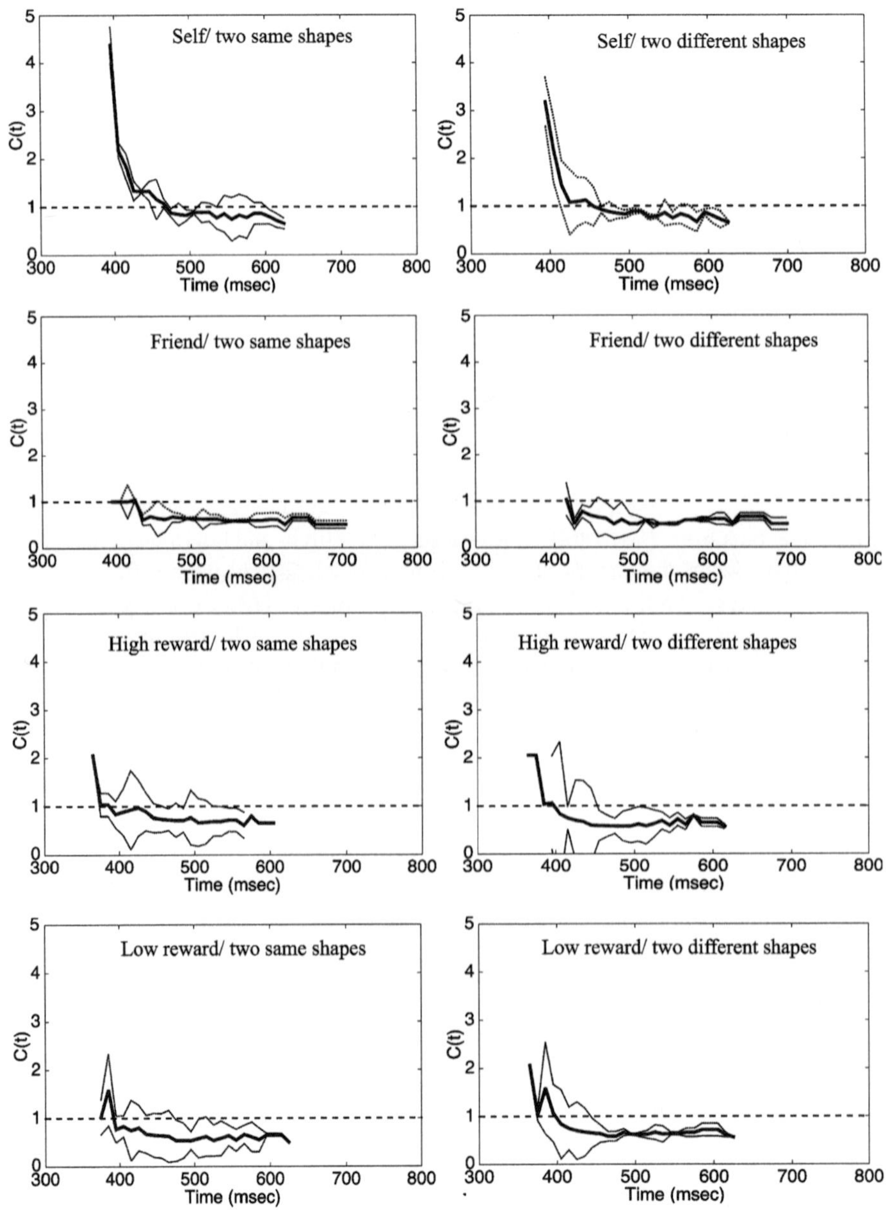

Figure 18.10 Capacity coefficients across the group of participants for the person- and reward-associations. The horizontal line at $C(t) = 1$ indicates the reference value for unlimited capacity. The capacity coefficients are depicted with the solid line; the confidence interval for the capacity coefficient is illustrated in the dashed–dotted line.

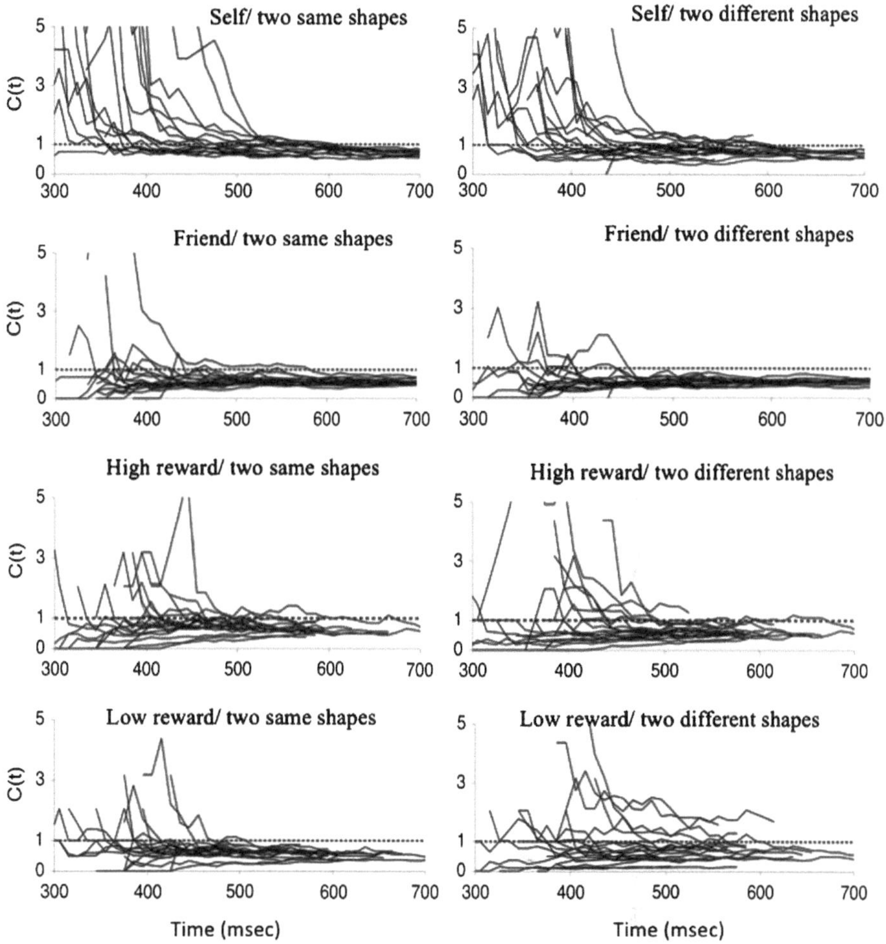

Figure 18.11 Capacity coefficients for individual participants in the self and reward association conditions. The horizontal line at $C(t) = 1$ indicates the reference value for unlimited capacity. The capacity coefficients are depicted using a solid line; the confidence interval for capacity coefficient is shown using the dashed line.

reward stimuli there was not strong evidence for supercapacity, although performance on average fell at a level close to that expected if there were fully independent processing of the shapes associated with high reward. With friend-associated shapes and low-reward stimuli the capacity analyses suggested that the shapes were each processed with limited capacity, so there was interference when both were present. Alternatively, limited resources may be distributed across the two channels represented by each reward-associated shape as the processing work load increased from one to two items (Eidels et al., 2011). Thus, the limited capacity may stem from constraints on parallel processing, from possible serial processing of each shape (Eidels et al., 2011).

A key theoretical contribution was the demonstration that the effects of self-association can differ from those of reward. For example, self-association but not high-reward generated larger redundancy gains with redundant shapes and only self-associations consistently violated the independent processing model (UCIP) and produced evidence of supercapacity. In contrast, there was an apparent qualitative shift in the processing of reward-related items, where limited capacity was evident. These results are consistent with the idea that self-associations uniquely enhance the binding of information at both perceptual (two identical shapes) and conceptual levels (two different shapes). In contrast, high-reward may lead to gains at a conceptual level but these stimuli do not escape capacity limitations.

Conclusion

Here, we reported three studies where we investigated the effects of social factors (race, in-group and self-biases) on perceptual processes using capacity analysis. We conclude that capacity framework offers a new perspective for understanding the modulatory effects of social biases on information processing. In summary, we found that social biases enhance integration of information by modulating perceptual processing. The modulatory effect of social biases on perception reflects quantitative and qualitative changes in the system. Quantitative changes are expressed in terms of RT advantage that does not preclude changes in processing efficiency/capacity. Qualitative changes reflect increases in processing efficiency during information processing and are defined as supercapacity. Own-race biases in faces, self- and in-group biases consistently showed strong quantitative and qualitative changes in the system. We verified this by testing RT advantage for responding to stimuli associated with own-race, self, high reward and in-group membership using integrative hazard function. The magnitude of the changes in processing efficiency/capacity is also related to individual differences (e.g., individual social experience with own versus other race faces, a strength of in-group identification, subjective value of reward amount, etc.).

Depending on the nature of the biases, increasing processing efficiency can be sourced: (i) from learned configural properties of perceptual objects (such as facial configuration), (ii) stronger perceptual and conceptual representations for objects associated with self or high reward, and (iii) currently salient social categorization (e.g., team membership). It is to be mentioned that the manner in which we applied capacity measurements here provides information about processing efficiency at the level of system functioning, but formally does not provide strong support for a particular source of enhanced performance.

Further Directions

Finer-grained mathematical modeling and parameters can be applied to issues in social cognition by providing details of the dynamic processing of information. For example, the above studies assessed how social factors modulate perception by using tasks a minimum-time decisional rule (the process can be terminated as soon as one target is detected in a display containing two targets, OR-operator). Our data suggest that people take advantage of the opportunity when the targets are associated with social biases. For example, there was larger redundancy gain and greater processing efficiency for two shapes associated with self-compared to two shapes associated with friend. However, to make more precise conclusions, it would be interesting to assess changes in processing efficiency in a situation when people do not have the opportunity to take an advantage of one of two targets (i.e., when the features of both targets in a display have to be processed, and participants' decision would be based on AND-decision stopping rule). Comparing the processing efficiency under different decisional components is important for making inference about the effect of social biases on perceptual processes.

One approach for exploring mechanisms underlying social biases is to focus on each bias separately, and assess the effect of the bias on perceptual processes. This approach is widely used in the literature. Another approach is to examine changes in processing efficiency by comparing the effects of different biases (e.g., comparing processing efficiency between self, reward and in-group biases using a within-subject design). The latter approach has a potential for establishing the relationship and predictive inferences between different biases. The capacity framework provides a means to use either approach separately or combine them. Furthermore, recently developed functional principal component analysis (fPCA) in capacity framework (Burns, Houpt, Townsend, & Endres, 2013) provides a mathematically rigorous way of representing the differences between participants and conditions, and can be useful in selecting those parts of the capacity function which are most useful in distinguishing among observers or conditions.

References

Ackerman, J. M., Shapiro, J. R., Neuberg, S. L., Kenrick, D. T., Becker, D. V., Griskevicius, V., et al. (2006). They all look the same to me (unless they're angry): from out-group homogeneity to out-group heterogeneity. *Psychological Science*, *17*(10), 836–840. 10.1111/j.1467-9280.2006.01790.x. Retrieved from http://www.ncbi.nlm.nih.gov/pubmed/17100781.

Altieri, N., & Hudock, D. (2014). Variability in audiovisual speech integration skills assessed by combined capacity and accuracy measures. *International Journal of Audiology*, *55*(4), 206–214. http://dx.doi.org/10.3109/14992027.2015.1120895.

Altieri, N., & Townsend, J. T. (2011). An assessment of behavioral dynamic information processing measures in audiovisual speech perception. *Frontiers in Psychology*, *2*(238), 1–15. http://dx.doi.org/10.3389/fpsyg.2011.00238.

Altieri, N., & Wenger, M. J. (2013). Neural dynamics of audiovisual integration efficiency under variable listening conditions: An individual participant analysis. *Frontiers in Psychology*, *4*(615), 1–15. http://dx.doi.org/10.3389/fpsyg.2013.00615.

Amodio, D. M. (2010). Coordinated roles of motivation and perception in the regulation of intergroup responses: Frontal cortical asymmetry effects on the P2 event-related potential and behavior. *Journal of Cognitive Neuroscience*, *22*(11), 2609–2617. http://dx.doi.org/10.1162/jocn.2009.21395.

Anthony, T., Cooper, C., & Mullen, B. (1992). Cross-racial facial identification: a social cognitive integration. *Personality and Social Psychology Bulletin*, *18*, 296–301. Retrieved from http://psp.sagepub.com/content/18/3/296.refs.

Biederman, I., & Checkosky, S. F. (1970). Processing redundant information. *Journal of Experimental Psychology*, *83*, 486–490.

Burns, D. M., Houpt, J. W., Townsend, J. T., & Endres, M. J. (2013). Functional principal components analysis of workload capacity functions. *Behavior Research Methods*, *45*(4), 1048–1057. http://dx.doi.org/10.3758/s13428-013-0333-2.

Correll, J., Park, B., Judd, C. M., & Wittenbrink, B. (2002). The police officer's dilemma: Using ethnicity to disambiguate potentially threatening individuals. *Journal of Personality and Social Psychology*, *83*(6), 1314–1329. Retrieved from http://www.ncbi.nlm.nih.gov/pubmed/12500813.

Donnelly, N., Cornes, K., & Menneer, T. (2012). An examination of the processing capacity of features in the Thatcher illusion. *Attention, Perception & Psychophysics*, *74*(7), 1475–1487. http://dx.doi.org/10.3758/s13414-012-0330-z.

Eidels, A., Houpt, J. W., Altieri, N., Pei, L., & Townsend, J. T. (2011). Nice guys finish fast and bad guys finish last: Facilitatory vs. inhibitory interaction in parallel systems. *Journal of Mathematical Psychology*, *55*(2), 176–190. http://dx.doi.org/10.1016/j.jmp.2010.11.003.

Ekman, P. (1992). Facial expressions of emotion: An old controversy and new findings. *Philosophical Transactions of the Royal Society of London*, *335*(1273), 63–69. http://dx.doi.org/10.1098/rstb.1992.0008.

Elfenbein, H. A., & Ambady, N. (2003). When familiarity breeds accuracy: cultural exposure and facial emotion recognition. *Journal of Personality and Social Psychology*, *85*(2), 276–290. Retrieved from http://www.ncbi.nlm.nih.gov/pubmed/12916570.

Elfenbein, H. A., Mandal, M. K., Ambady, N., Harizuka, S., & Kumar, S. (2002). Cross-cultural patterns in emotion recognition: Highlighting design and analytical techniques. *Emotion*, *2*(1), 75–84. Retrieved from http://www.ncbi.nlm.nih.gov/pubmed/12899367.

Gottlob, L. R. (2007). Aging and capacity in the same-different judgment. *Neuropsychology, Development, and Cognition. Section B, Aging, Neuropsychology and Cognition*, *14*(1), 55–69. http://dx.doi.org/10.1080/138255890969528.

Houpt, J. W., Blaha, L. M., McIntire, J. P., Havig, P. R., & Townsend, J. T. (2014). Systems factorial technology with R. *Behavior Research Methods*, *46*(2), 307–330. http://dx.doi.org/10.3758/s13428-013-0377-3.

Houpt, J. W., & Townsend, J. T. (2012). Statistical measures for workload capacity analysis. *Journal of Mathematical Psychology*, *56*, 341–355. http://www.indiana.edu/~psymodel/papers/acta14.pdf.

Hugenschmidt, C. E., Hayasaka, S., Peiffer, A. M., & Laurienti, P. J. (2010). Applying capacity analyses to psychophysical evaluation of multisensory interactions. *Information Fusion*, *11*(1), 12–20. http://dx.doi.org/10.1016/j.inffus.2009.04.004.

Marsh, A. A., Elfenbein, H. A., & Ambady, N. (2003). Nonverbal "accents": Cultural differences in facial expressions of emotion. *Psychological Science*, *14*(4), 373–376. Retrieved from http://www.ncbi.nlm.nih.gov/pubmed/12807413.

McCarley, J. S., Yamani, Y., Kramer, A. F., & Mounts, J. R. (2012). Age, clutter, and competitive selection. *Psychology and Aging*, *27*(3), 616–626. http://dx.doi.org/10.1037/a0026705.

Miller, J. (1982). Divided attention: Evidence for coactivation with redundant signals. *Cognitive Psychology*, *14*(2), 247–279. Retrieved from http://www.ncbi.nlm.nih.gov/pubmed/7083803.

Miller, J., Beutinger, D., & Ulrich, R. (2009). Visuospatial attention and redundancy gain. *Psychological Research, 73*(2), 254–262. http://dx.doi.org/10.1007/s00426-008-0212-0.

Miller, J., Ulrich, R., & Lamarre, Y. (2001). Locus of the redundant-signals effect in bimodal divided attention: a neurophysiological analysis. *Perception & Psychophysics, 63*(3), 555–562. Retrieved from http://www.ncbi.nlm.nih.gov/pubmed/11414141.

Moradi, Z., Yankouskaya, A., Duta, M., Hewstone, M., & Humphreys, G. W. (in press). Coactive processing of sensory signals for in-group but not out-group stimuli. *Visual Cognition*, 1–26. http://dx.doi.org/10.1080/13506285.2016.1147512.

Mordkoff, J. T., & Miller, J. (1993). Redundancy gains and coactivation with two different targets: The problem of target preferences and the effects of display frequency. *Perception & Psychophysics, 53*(5), 527–535. Retrieved from http://www.ncbi.nlm.nih.gov/pubmed/8332422.

Neufeld, R. W. J., Townsend, J. T., & Jetté, J. (2007). Quantitative response time technology for measuring cognitive-processing capacity in clinical studies. In R. W. J. Neufeld (Ed.), *Advances in clinical cognitive science: Formal modeling of processes and symptoms* (pp. 207–238). Washington, DC, USA: American Psychological Association.

Northoff, G., & Hayes, D. J. (2011). Is our self nothing but reward? *Biological Psychiatry, 69*(11), 1019–1025. http://dx.doi.org/10.1016/j.biopsych.2010.12.014.

Stolte, M., Humphreys, G., Yankouskaya, A., & Sui, J. (2015). Dissociating biases towards the self and positive emotion. *Quaterly Journal of Experimental Psychology (Hove)*, 1–34. http://dx.doi.org/10.1080/17470218.2015.1101477.

Sui, J., He, X., & Humphreys, G. W. (2012). Perceptual effects of social salience: Evidence from self-prioritization effects on perceptual matching. *Journal of Experimental Psychology. Human Perception and Performance, 38*(5), 1105–1117. http://dx.doi.org/10.1037/a0029792.

Sui, J., & Humphreys, G. W. (2015). More of me! Distinguishing self and reward bias using redundancy gains. *Attention, Perception, & Psychophysics, 77*(8), 2549–2561. http://dx.doi.org/10.3758/s13414-015-0970-x.

Sui, J., Rotshtein, P., & Humphreys, G. W. (2013). Coupling social attention to the self forms a network for personal significance. *Proceedings of the National Academy of Sciences USA, 110*(19), 7607–7612. http://dx.doi.org/10.1073/pnas.1221862110.

Sui, J., Yankouskaya, A., & Humphreys, G. W. (2015). Super-capacity me! Super-capacity and violations of race independence for self- but not for reward-associated stimuli. *Journal of Experimental Psychology. Human Perception and Performance, 41*(2), 441–452. http://dx.doi.org/10.1037/a0038288.

Tottenham, N., Tanaka, J. W., Leon, A. C., McCarry, T., Nurse, M., Hare, T. A., et al. (2009). The NimStim set of facial expressions: Judgments from untrained research participants. *Psychiatry Research, 168*(3), 242–249. http://dx.doi.org/10.1016/j.psychres.2008.05.006.

Townsend, J. T., & Altieri, N. (2012). An accuracy-response time capacity assessment function that measures performance against standard parallel predictions. *Psychological Review, 119*(3), 500–516. http://dx.doi.org/10.1037/a0028448.

Townsend, J. T., & Ashby, F. G. (1983). *The stochastic modeling of elementary psychological processes*. Cambridge: Cambridge University Press.

Townsend, J. T., & Eidels, A. (2011). Workload capacity spaces: A unified methodology for response time measures of efficiency as workload is varied. *Psychonomic Bulletin & Review, 18*(4), 659–681. http://dx.doi.org/10.3758/s13423-011-0106-9.

Townsend, J. T., & Wenger, M. J. (2004a). The serial-parallel dilemma: A case study in a linkage of theory and method. *Psychonomic Bulletin & Review, 11*(3), 391–418. Retrieved from http://www.ncbi.nlm.nih.gov/pubmed/15376788.

Townsend, J. T., & Wenger, M. J. (2004b). A theory of interactive parallel processing: New capacity measures and predictions for a response time inequality series. *Psychological Review*, *111*(4), 1003–1035. http://dx.doi.org/10.1037/0033-295X.111.4.1003.

Walker, P. M., Silvert, L., Hewstone, M., & Nobre, A. C. (2008). Social contact and other-race face processing in the human brain. *Social Cognitive & Affective Neuroscience*, *3*(1), 16–25. http://dx.doi.org/10.1093/scan/nsm035.

Wenger, M. J., & Gibson, B. S. (2004). Using hazard functions to assess changes in processing capacity in an attentional cuing paradigm. *Journal of Experimental Psychology. Human Perception and Performance*, *30*(4), 708–719. http://dx.doi.org/10.1037/0096-1523.30.4.708.

Wenger, M. J., & Townsend, J. T. (2000). Basic response time tools for studying general processing capacity in attention, perception, and cognition. *The Journal of General Psychology*, *127*(1), 67–99. http://dx.doi.org/10.1080/00221300009598571.

Wenger, M. J., & Townsend, J. T. (2006). On the costs and benefits of faces and words: Process characteristics of feature search in highly meaningful stimuli. *Journal of Experimental Psychology. Human, Perception and Performance*, *32*(3), 755–779. http://dx.doi.org/10.1037/0096-1523.32.3.755.

Wolff, N., Kemter, K., Schweinberger, S. R., & Wiese, H. (2014). What drives social in-group biases in face recognition memory? ERP evidence from the own-gender bias. *Social Cognitive & Affective Neuroscience*, *9*(5), 580–590. http://dx.doi.org/10.1093/scan/nst024.

Yankouskaya, A., Booth, D. A., & Humphreys, G. (2012). Interactions between facial emotion and identity in face processing: Evidence based on redundancy gains. *Attention, Perception & Psychophysics*, *74*(8), 1692–1711. http://dx.doi.org/10.3758/s13414-012-0345-5. http://www.ncbi.nlm.nih.gov/pubmed/22814949.

Yankouskaya, A., Humphreys, G. W., & Rotshtein, P. (2014). Differential interactions between identity and emotional expression in own and other-race faces: Effects of familiarity revealed through redundancy gains. *Journal of Experimental Psychology: Learning, Memory, Cognition*, *40*(4), 1025–1038. http://dx.doi.org/10.1037/a0036259.

Yankouskaya, A., Rotshtein, P., & Humphreys, G. W. (2014). Interactions between identity and emotional expression in face processing across the lifespan: Evidence from redundancy gains. *Journal of Aging Research*, *2014*, 136073. http://dx.doi.org/10.1155/2014/136073.

Endnotes

1. Capacity coefficient can be also defined by RT or CDF of the RT distribution (e.g., Townsend & Ashby, 1983) and survivor function (Townsend & Eidels, 2011).
2. Here we focus on capacity analysis based on correct response time. A nonparametric statistic that accommodates accuracy as well as RTs is available in Townsend and Altieri (2012).
3. The integrated hazard function is specified in terms of task-completion times, and acts, therefore, as measures of capacity at the level of the entire processing system (Wenger & Gibson, 2004).
4. *p* values are adjusted for multiple correlations.
5. Original study by Moradi et al. presented data from their pilot (19 participants) and replication experiment (23). Here we presented results from pooled data (42 participants in total).

Index

T